Insights Into International Higher Education Leadership and the Skills Gap

Mustafa Kayyali
HE Higher Education Ranking, Syria

Bryan Christiansen
Soluvex, LLC, USA

Published in the United States of America by
    IGI Global
    701 E. Chocolate Avenue
    Hershey PA, USA 17033
    Tel: 717-533-8845
    Fax: 717-533-8661
    E-mail: cust@igi-global.com
    Web site: https://www.igi-global.com

Library of Congress Cataloging-in-Publication Data

CIP Data Pending
ISBN: 979-8-3693-3443-0
eISBN: 979-8-3693-3444-7

Vice President of Editorial: Melissa Wagner
Managing Editor of Acquisitions: Mikaela Felty
Managing Editor of Book Development: Jocelynn Hessler
Production Manager: Mike Brehm
Cover Design: Phillip Shickler

British Cataloguing in Publication Data
A Cataloguing in Publication record for this book is available from the British Library.

Table of Contents

Detailed Table of Contents

Chapter 1

    Mandla Sibanda, National University of Science and Technology,
        Zimbabwe
    Doris Chasokela, National Uiversity of Science and Technoogy,
        Zimbabwe

The impact of globalization on higher education has been both profound and complex. Globalization has opened up opportunities for higher education institutions to collaborate and exchange knowledge across borders. On the other hand, it has brought new challenges, such as increased competition, greater efficiency, and balancing internationalization with national identity. This chapter explores the challenges and opportunities of globalization focusing on how to best navigate these complexities and maximize the benefits of globalization. Focusing on international partnerships, sustainability, adaptive learning models, and equity and access can help institutions position themselves for success in an increasingly interconnected and globalized world. Universities must adapt to changing demands and expectations and prioritize equity and access to remain relevant and effective in the globalized world. Also discussions on how universities can use digital technologies and international partnerships to fostering lifelong learning and global citizenship will be done on this chapter.

Olabode Gbobaniyi, Global Banking School, UK
Shalini Srivastava, Global Banking School, UK

This chapter explores the influence of inclusive leadership in higher education institutions (HEIs), from an inclusive approach, on academic loyalty based on the purview of its antecedents and consequence on perceived institutional support (PIS). The future of leadership in higher education depends on how academics, as members of collectives, communicate and negotiate with their institutions, through their leaders and managers, to be recognised and supported for their multiple understandings and practices. Inclusive leadership provides academics a feel of a sense of belonging thus contributing to the vision and goals of the HEI. To move leadership towards a more inclusive manner, there is a need for HEIs to ensure equality, diversity, and inclusion as the right conditions to ensure open manager-subordinate communication for academics to be able to perceive and understand the institutional support available to them towards achieving and fulfilling their professional goals and ambitions.

Edythe Weeks, Washington University, USA

Higher education faces a pivotal moment. While historical exploration often fueled inequality, the emerging frontiers of outer space and the Polar Regions demand a different approach. This chapter argues for the inclusion of dedicated studies in these regions within the curriculum. A diverse range of experts, from astrophysicists to climate scientists, will be essential for ensuring the sustainable development of these new frontiers. Currently, a significant knowledge gap exists regarding three regions. Most people lack awareness of the critical issues and exciting developments taking place. This chapter explores how the core values of education, alongside existing international law, present a unique opportunity. We can reimagine exploration and development to prioritize equality, environmental sustainability, and conflict reduction. By bridging the knowledge gap, higher education can equip all of humanity to navigate the future of our expanding world responsibly.

Chapter 4

Case pedagogy remains one of the vital strategies to promote critical thinking and problem-solving abilities in nursing and midwifery education globally. In Namibia little research exists on the perspectives of nursing students on the use of a case pedagogy as a strategy to promote critical thinking in nursing and midwifery education. The purpose of this chapter is to explore the experiences of students on the use of case pedagogy as a strategy to promote critical thinking among nursing students. The study found that most students developed critical thinking skills and that they were equipped with problem solving skills which they can use for analysis and evaluations of their patients' conditions. Findings from this chapter may help identify strengths and weaknesses in the use of case pedagogy for assessment purposes in nursing and midwifery education.

Chapter 5

In recent decades the world has found itself in an era of rapid globalisation and migration. In many contexts and cultures, citizens are still coming to terms with the implications of globalisation. The vital role that higher education (HE) institutions can play must not only be emphasised, but strategies, new approaches and initiatives also need to be embraced and adopted to ensure diversity is an advantage and not a source of conflict. It is further noted that notions of 'interculturalism' are still not understood in many contexts and are still confused with 'multiculturalism'. This chapter demonstrates that interculturalism goes beyond multiculturalism, and further locates its place and usefulness within Higher Education, particularly through co-creation efforts. The chapter posits a need for higher educational institutions to embed intercultural competencies, advance understanding of one's own culture and promote intercultural dialogue in multicultural contexts, especially in Higher education as part of bridging the skills gap and enhancing employability.

Nabil El Kadhi, Applied Science University, Bahrain
Minerva Mabborang Bunagan, Higher Colleges of Technology, UAE

This chapter aims to provide comprehensive guidelines for the successful integration of technology and the adoption of innovative teaching methodologies to enhance students' skills acquisition and effectiveness. Drawing upon experiences and implementations in the Mena region, specifically the GCC region, this chapter addresses key questions surrounding the selection and implementation of innovative teaching methods. The structure of the chapter encompasses an introduction to innovative teaching methodologies, identification of skills and appropriate methodologies, monitoring of implementation, the impact of technology, and a concluding summary of findings and future research directions.

Doris Chasokela, National University of Science and Technology,
Zimbabwe

This book chapter proposes a framework for implementing STEM learning technologies to help students develop the 21st-century skills they need to succeed in the modern world. The framework focuses on four key elements: curriculum, instruction, assessment, and professional development. It also emphasizes the importance of partnerships with the community to provide students with opportunities to apply their skills and knowledge in real-world settings. This framework provides lecturers with a roadmap for integrating STEM learning technologies into the classroom in a way that is effective, engaging, and relevant to the needs of 21st-century students. The framework focuses on addressing the challenges that students face in developing these skills. The chapter outlines a step-by-step approach to implementing STEM technologies, from identifying the specific needs of students to evaluating the effectiveness of the technologies. It also discusses the importance of a collaborative approach, involving students, lecturers, and other stakeholders in the implementation process.

Hartini Mashod, Universiti Teknologi Brunei, Brunei
Kabiru Maitama Kura, Bahrain Polytechnic, Bahrain

The chapter "Innovative Teaching Methods for Skill Development" explores groundbreaking educational approaches surpassing traditional pedagogy to enhance skill acquisition in learners amidst rapid technological advancements and evolving workplace demands. It evaluates the effectiveness of methods like experiential learning, project-based approaches, and technology integration in fostering critical thinking, creativity, and collaboration. Embracing online and hybrid learning environments, it caters to diverse learner needs. Additionally, it examines adaptive learning technologies, gamification, and interdisciplinary collaboration's role in shaping modern education, emphasizing their contribution to cognitive and emotional development. As educators aim to connect theory with practice, this chapter serves as a valuable resource for transforming teaching methods, emphasizing student-centered learning to prepare individuals for success in today's dynamic professional world.

Chapter 10

Against the background of insights into international higher education leadership and the skills gap, the purpose of this chapter will be to especially focus on cultivating creativity and innovation in higher education. Drivers of Individual Innovative Behavior (IIB) obtained from Structural Equation Modelling (SEM) of the mediating effect of Knowledge Sharing Behavior (KSB) on technology students' individual and contextual antecedents, including those related to Course Design Characteristics (CDC) and Self-Regulated Learning (SRL), are explained.

This chapter proposes an in-depth study of higher education leaders (HELs) in Saudi Arabia, with a particular focus on the challenges, obstacles and success factors of talent management (TM) in Saudi universities. A mixed methods study design was adopted in which a general literature review was conducted to uncover the skills gap in the higher education sector and its impact on university leadership, taking into account both the external and internal environments. In addition, a survey would be conducted among a wide range of university leaders, including rectors, vice-rectors, deans, vice-deans and department heads, on the existing TM practices in their respective universities. Through this approach, the authors have uncovered how HELs perceive and deal with the skills gap phenomenon, including the barriers and success factors in TM in their universities, with due consideration of the influence of both external market forces and internal institutional dynamics.

Chapter 12

The role of technical education in the progress and growth of a nation is well acknowledged all over the world. In India the number of people entering into the technical education system has never been a problem. But the relevant problem has been the relative skills and employability of the people. The widening of skill gap and increase in the unemployability of engineering graduates has become a tremendous pain point for government as well as other stake holders. There is an urgent need to improve the technical education system and reducing the skill gap to convert youth into educated employable citizens for both their own development as well as the development of the Nation. The skills demanded by the industries are often not found in the engineering graduates and the skills that they possess are often termed as obsolete or are presently not needed by the employers. Hence, there is a need to identify the factors responsible for the widening gap. Therefore, paper focuses on detail analysis of various responsible factors for creating disparity between demand and supply.

Chapter 13

Doris Chasokela, National University of Science and Technology, Zimbabwe

Funa Moyo, National University of Science and Technology, Zimbabwe

The book chapter explores the integration of learning management systems and course/module software in science, technology, engineering, and mathematics learning and 21st-century skills in Zimbabwe's higher education. The chapter introduces the concepts of STEM and their importance for developing the skills needed for success in the 21st century. It presents an overview of the implementation of learning management systems and course/module software in the Zimbabwean higher education system. The potential benefits of these technologies for STEM are highlighted. In this chapter, it is argued that the integration of information and communication technology in the teaching of science, technology, engineering, and mathematics plays a crucial role in addressing quality-related issues. Finally, the chapter presents case studies of higher education institutions in Zimbabwe that have successfully implemented learning management systems and course/module software and describes the positive effects on student learning.

Chapter 14

The Disparities of Higher-Educated Men and Women in Leadership Positions

Hennigusnia Hennigusnia, National Research and Innovation Agency of Indonesia, Indonesia

Ardhian Kurniawati, National Research and Innovation Agency of Indonesia, Indonesia

Devi Asiati, National Research and Innovation Agency of Indonesia, Indonesia

Ngadi Ngadi, National Research and Innovation Agency of Indonesia, Indonesia

Zantermans Rajagukguk, National Research and Innovation Agency of Indonesia, Indonesia

This paper analyzes gender disparities in leadership among highly educated workers in Indonesia. The data for the analysis is the August NLFS 2023. The research data shows variations in gender inequality according to generation, marital status, and main industry. The younger the generation, the greater the proportion of highly educated women as managers. The proportion of women in leadership positions in the service sector is greater than in the agricultural and manufacturing sectors. Based on marital status, the proportion of married women as managers is lower than that of single women. The results of the inferential analysis show that the average income of men is 44.6 percentage points greater than the average income of women. Furthermore, of the 44.6 percentage points of the wage gap, only 7.9 percentage points (17.646%) can be explained by differences in the characteristics of men and women. The unobserved and unexplained factors for wage differences that can be perceived as discrimination were 36.7 percentage points (82.354%).

Chapter 15

Anatoly Zhuplev, Loyola Marymount University, USA
Francisco J. Valle, Loyola Marymount University, USA
José J. Rincón, Loyola Marymount University, USA
Max Plithides, University of California, Los Angeles, USA

This chapter examines the evolution of American higher education (HE) and business schools (B-schools) in the historical and contemporary strategic context. It explores the influence of the Humboldtian model on the contemporary HE industry in America. The chapter analyzes the current HE landscape, revenue sources, and global reach. The chapter investigates strategic disruptors like demographic shifts, skyrocketing costs of college and student loan burden, technological impacts, including proliferation of IT and AI, eroding public confidence in HE, and political and regulatory trends. The chapter explores solutions like accreditation reform and diversified credentials. It examines pressures on B-schools, including slow technology adoption and competition. It emphasizes the need for B-schools to embrace innovation, technology, and industry partnerships. The chapter concludes with a collaborative educational project focused on regional socio-economic development grounded in comparative analysis of best global practices, highlighting the potential of HE to address real-world issues.

This chapter explores the significance of emotional Intelligence in educational leadership. Emotional Intelligence is a critical trait for effective educational leaders as it facilitates the development of positive learning environments. Leaders with high emotional possess the ability to understand and manage their own emotions, as well as emotions and empathize with others. This enables them to build strong relationships with students, teachers, and staff, fostering open communication and collaboration. Additionally, emotional equips leaders with the skills to handle conflicts and make informed decisions in a composed manner. By modeling emotional Intelligence, leaders encourage the development of these skills among students and staff, promoting emotional well-being and growth. Overall, emotional Intelligence plays a pivotal role in educational leadership, enhancing the Leader's capacity to create an inclusive and supportive academic environment that nurtures the holistic development of students and the entire school community.

Lister Siphathisiwe Tshuma, National University of Science and
Technology, Zimbabwe
Doris Chasokela, National University of Science and Technology,
Zimbabwe

The rise of online learning and the technological revolution in higher education are
having a profound impact on the way learning and teaching are done. The rise of
online learning has revolutionized the way students learn, with many institutions
now offering a range of online courses. This shift has been driven by the increasing
adoption of digital technologies, such as learning management systems, virtual
and augmented reality, and artificial intelligence. The technological revolution
in higher education has also enabled new models of education, such as massive
open online courses (MOOCs), online degree programs, and competency-based
education. Moreover, the rise of online learning has also created new opportunities
for institutions to collaborate with industry partners, foster innovation, and develop
new revenue streams. However, the technological revolution in higher education
also poses challenges. This chapter explores the rise of online learning and the
technological revolution in higher education, examining the key drivers, trends, and
implications of this transformation.

The new education 5.0 model vision 2030 in Zimbabwe is anchored on heritage-based philosophy in tertiary education institutions aimed at the production of goods and services. The education model aspires to industrialise and modernise the Zimbabwean economy to attain a middle economic position by the year 2030. Industrialization and innovation can be realised in contribution towards the attainment of Vision 2030. It is prudent to adopt learning that is congruent with the prevailing digital age. The future of learning in the digital age therefore proposes a new framework for education that integrates digital technologies to improve student learning outcomes. The model takes into account specific challenges, including inadequate infrastructure, curriculum issues, a lack of digital literacy among instructors, and a lack of synergy between the education sector and industry. Recommendations include improving infrastructure, providing instructor training in digital literacy and curriculum design, and building partnerships with industry and government.

Preface

The evolving landscape of higher education demands adaptive and forward-thinking leadership that can respond to the rapid changes in global economies, technologies, and societal needs. As editors of *Insights Into International Higher Education Leadership and the Skills Gap*, we find ourselves at the intersection of two critical areas: leadership within academic institutions and the growing gap between the skills imparted by these institutions and the demands of the global workforce.

This book seeks to address these issues with a comprehensive, research-driven approach. Our aim is to provide readers with an in-depth exploration of how leadership in higher education can shape the future of learning and, by extension, the global labor market. From leadership strategies to policy recommendations, this collection highlights both the challenges and opportunities that education leaders face in navigating the pressures of preparing students for an increasingly competitive world.

We believe that effective leadership in higher education is not only about administrative capabilities but also about visionary thinking—understanding that the classroom is no longer confined to the traditional four walls and that the workforce requires more than technical skills. Higher education institutions must be engines of innovation, fostering creativity, critical thinking, and adaptability to bridge the skills gap that exists between academic curricula and employer expectations.

The contributions explore a wide range of themes, from the impact of globalization and inclusive leadership to innovative teaching methods and the role of emotional intelligence in educational leadership. Through these diverse topics, the chapters provide in-depth analyses and practical insights aimed at addressing the critical challenges and opportunities facing higher education institutions worldwide. Below is a summary of each chapter, highlighting key concepts and takeaways.

The opening chapter delves into the profound and multifaceted impact of globalization on higher education. It examines both the opportunities for international collaboration and the challenges that come with increased competition and the need to balance global integration with national identity. The chapter emphasizes the importance of equity, access, and sustainability, encouraging institutions to adapt through international partnerships and digital technologies. Additionally, it highlights the role of universities in fostering lifelong learning and promoting global citizenship in an interconnected world.

Chapter 2 explores the role of inclusive leadership in higher education institutions (HEIs) and its influence on academic loyalty through the lens of perceived institutional support (PIS). It emphasizes the importance of fostering an inclusive environment where academics feel a sense of belonging, leading to greater commitment to the institution's goals. Through a focus on equality, diversity, and open communication, the chapter highlights how inclusive leadership can enhance professional growth and institutional cohesion.

Focusing on emerging frontiers, chapter 3 calls for the integration of studies on outer space and the Polar Regions into higher education curricula. It argues for the inclusion of diverse experts such as astrophysicists and climate scientists in developing sustainable practices for these regions. By addressing the existing knowledge gap, the chapter emphasizes the role of higher education in promoting equality, environmental sustainability, and conflict reduction in global exploration.

Chapter 4 investigates the use of case pedagogy as a strategy to promote critical thinking in nursing and midwifery education in Namibia. Through a detailed examination of student experiences, the study reveals the positive impact of case-based learning on problem-solving and analysis. The findings contribute to understanding how this teaching method can be optimized for better educational outcomes in health-related fields.

Chapter 5 explores the impact of globalization and migration on higher education, particularly in the context of fostering interculturalism. It differentiates between multiculturalism and interculturalism, advocating for the latter as a more dynamic and co-creative approach to diversity. The chapter stresses the need for higher education institutions to embed intercultural competencies, enhancing employability and preparing students for a globalized workforce.

Chapter 6 offers a comprehensive guide to integrating technology and innovative teaching methodologies in higher education, with a specific focus on the MENA and GCC regions. It explores the selection and implementation of new teaching strategies, monitoring their impact, and suggests future directions for research. The goal is to enhance skills acquisition through a combination of technology and creative pedagogy, making education more relevant and effective in modern contexts.

A framework for implementing STEM learning technologies to foster 21st-century skills is the focus of chapter 7. It outlines key elements such as curriculum development, instructional strategies, and assessment, with an emphasis on real-world applications. The chapter stresses the importance of community partnerships and a collaborative approach in ensuring that students acquire the necessary skills to thrive in the modern world.

Chapter 8 examines the relationship between education, gender, age, and employability in Brunei Darussalam. Using data from JobCentre Brunei, the study reveals a significant correlation between education and employability but finds no substantial link between gender or age and employment outcomes. The findings provide insights into how education can enhance job prospects and address skills gaps among graduates.

Chapter 9 explores innovative teaching methods that go beyond traditional pedagogy to promote critical thinking, creativity, and collaboration. It evaluates the role of experiential learning, project-based approaches, and technology integration in shaping modern education. The chapter also addresses the challenges of connecting theory with practice, offering practical strategies for educators to enhance skill development in an ever-changing professional environment.

Focusing on creativity and innovation, chapter 10 examines the drivers of Individual Innovative Behavior (IIB) in higher education. Through an analysis of knowledge-sharing behavior, course design characteristics, and self-regulated learning, the chapter presents a framework for cultivating innovation in students. It offers insights into how educational institutions can foster a culture of creativity and innovation, aligning with the needs of technology-driven industries.

Chapter 11 presents a study on higher education leadership (HEL) in Saudi Arabia, focusing on talent management (TM) practices. Through surveys and literature reviews, the authors identify the challenges and success factors of TM in Saudi universities. The study highlights the influence of external market forces and internal dynamics on leadership strategies, offering valuable insights for addressing the skills gap in higher education.

The widening skills gap in India's technical education system is the subject of chapter 12. It explores the challenges faced by engineering graduates in meeting industry demands, with a particular focus on the disparity between the skills taught in universities and those required in the workforce. The chapter calls for systemic reforms to align technical education with industry needs, thus improving employability and national development.

Chapter 13 explores the integration of learning management systems (LMS) and course software in STEM education in Zimbabwe. It highlights the role of technology in addressing quality-related issues in education and presents case studies of successful implementations. The chapter underscores the importance of technology in modern education, offering practical examples of how it can enhance learning outcomes and address the skills gap.

Gender disparities in leadership roles among highly educated workers in Indonesia are analyzed in chapter 14. Using data from the 2023 NLFS, the chapter examines the wage gap between men and women and highlights the unobserved factors contributing to this inequality. The findings offer insights into the challenges women face in leadership and propose strategies for promoting gender equality in the workforce.

Chapter 15 explores the evolution of American higher education and business schools, focusing on strategic disruptors such as technological advancements, demographic shifts, and rising costs. It calls for innovation and collaboration in addressing these challenges, with a particular emphasis on the role of business schools in fostering regional socio-economic development. The chapter provides a roadmap for reforming higher education to better align with real-world needs.

The significance of emotional intelligence in educational leadership is the focus of chapter 16. It argues that emotionally intelligent leaders can create positive learning environments by fostering open communication and collaboration. The chapter highlights the role of emotional intelligence in conflict resolution and decision-making, making it a critical trait for effective leadership in education.

The rise of online learning and its impact on higher education are examined in chapter 17. It explores the role of digital technologies such as LMS, virtual reality, and AI in transforming education. The chapter also discusses the challenges and opportunities presented by online learning, including new models of education like MOOCs and competency-based learning, and the implications for higher education institutions.

Chapter 18 focuses on Zimbabwe's Education 5.0 model, which is designed to industrialize and modernize the economy by 2030. It explores the integration of digital technologies into tertiary education and addresses the challenges posed by inadequate infrastructure and a lack of digital literacy among instructors. The chapter offers recommendations for improving infrastructure, curriculum design, and industry partnerships to ensure the success of this educational model.

The contributors to this volume come from diverse backgrounds, representing a wide range of experiences, perspectives, and regions. They examine leadership models, skills development programs, and institutional reforms that have the potential to revolutionize higher education worldwide. By bringing together these global insights, we hope to inspire leaders in academia to critically reflect on their practices and adapt them to the needs of both the learners they serve and the industries that await them.

We would like to extend our gratitude to all the authors who have contributed their time, expertise, and insights to this publication. It is our hope that *Insights Into International Higher Education Leadership and the Skills Gap* will serve as a vital resource for academics, policymakers, and education leaders alike, offering practical solutions to close the skills gap and pave the way for a more informed and agile workforce.

Editors

Mustafa Kayyali

HE Higher Education Ranking, Syrian Arab Republic

Bryan Christiansen

Soluvex, LLC, United States

Chapter 1
The Challenges and Opportunities of Globalization for Higher Education

Mandla Sibanda

National University of Science and Technology, Zimbabwe

Doris Chasokela

https://orcid.org/0009-0001-5983-8508

National Uiversity of Science and Technoogy, Zimbabwe

ABSTRACT

The impact of globalization on higher education has been both profound and complex. Globalization has opened up opportunities for higher education institutions to collaborate and exchange knowledge across borders. On the other hand, it has brought new challenges, such as increased competition, greater efficiency, and balancing internationalization with national identity. This chapter explores the challenges and opportunities of globalization focusing on how to best navigate these complexities and maximize the benefits of globalization. Focusing on international partnerships, sustainability, adaptive learning models, and equity and access can help institutions position themselves for success in an increasingly interconnected and globalized world. Universities must adapt to changing demands and expectations and prioritize equity and access to remain relevant and effective in the globalized world. Also discussions on how universities can use digital technologies and international partnerships to fostering lifelong learning and global citizenship will be done on this chapter.

DOI: 10.4018/979-8-3693-3443-0.ch001

INTRODUCTION

Globalization is a complex phenomenon that has had far-reaching effects. It is not surprising, therefore, that the term "globalization" has acquired many emotive connotations. At one extreme, globalization is seen as an irresistible and being force for delivering economic prosperity to people throughout the world. On the other, it is blamed as a source of all contemporary ills. Higher education institutions around the world are facing new challenges and opportunities in the age of globalization. As the world becomes more interconnected, higher education institutions are finding new ways to collaborate and share knowledge across borders. At the same time, the increasing globalization of higher education has created new competition, as well as challenges related to balancing internationalization with national identity.

Globalization, the increasing interconnectedness of people, ideas, and economies across the world, has had a significant impact on higher education. This transformation has been fuelled by the rise of technology and the growing demand for international education. While globalization has opened up new opportunities for higher education institutions, it has also presented a range of challenges. This chapter therefore explores these challenges and opportunities, considering how they influence the management, teaching, and research functions of higher education institutions. Globalization has brought about several changes to higher education. These include, but are not limited to:

- Increased Competition: With the emergence of global markets for higher education, institutions now face increased competition from both local and international players. This competition has led to a greater focus on ranking and reputation as well as a need to differentiate offerings.
- Growing Demand for International Education: Globalization has led to a growing demand for international education, with students seeking a more globalized education that includes diverse perspectives, cultural experiences, and opportunities for mobility.
- Changes in Funding Models: Globalization has led to a shift in funding models for higher education, with a growing reliance on private sources of funding such as tuition fees and philanthropic donations. This has put pressure on institutions to adapt and diversify their revenue streams.
- Shifting Priorities: Globalization has also impacted the priorities of higher education institutions, with a greater focus on research impact, international partnerships, and transnational education. Institutions must balance these priorities with traditional functions such as teaching and community engagement.

The effects of globalization on higher education are far-reaching and multifaceted. On the one hand, globalization has created new opportunities for collaboration, research, and exchange, enabling institutions to expand their reach and impact beyond national borders. On the other hand, it has introduced challenges such as increased competition, changing funding models, and shifting priorities. To navigate these challenges and capitalize on the opportunities presented by globalization, higher education institutions must be adaptable and innovative.

This chapter explores the impact of globalization on higher education, with a focus on the challenges and opportunities it presents. The chapter also examines how globalization has shaped higher education policy, and how institutions have responded to these changes. The growing importance of international collaboration, as well as the challenges of balancing internationalization with national identity, are discussed. Finally, the chapter considers the implications of globalization for the future of higher education.

THE GLOBAL CONTEXT OF HIGHER EDUCATION

The global context of higher education refers to the broader landscape and trends that shape and influence higher education systems and institutions worldwide (Altbach et al., 2019). It encompasses various factors, including educational policies, economic conditions, technological advancements, demographic changes, and global collaborations. Zaleniene and Pereira (2021) assert that higher education can be seen as the primary vehicle for nations to improve the economic conditions for citizens in this new economy. Concurrently, technology has impacted the ability of higher education to respond to the multiple difficulties of virtual learning, increased communication efficiency, and how to respond to the anytime, anywhere learning demands. Global higher education continues to develop and evolve and global leaders should recognize the essential mission of global higher education to the creation, exchange, and implementation of knowledge in a global marketplace (Lemoine et al., 2017). Guardia et al. (2021) state that technology has transformed higher education, impacting teaching, learning, and research. Online learning, digital resources, virtual classrooms, and educational technologies are increasingly integrated into educational practices. Massive Open Online Courses (MOOCs) and blended learning models are gaining popularity, enabling flexible and accessible education (Syahid et al., 202; Yadav, 2024).

Higher education is increasingly globalized, with the growing mobility of students, faculty, and knowledge across borders. Institutions are engaging in international collaborations, offering joint degree programs, and attracting students from diverse countries (Gao & Liu, 2020). There is a focus on fostering global competence and preparing graduates for a globalized workforce. Expanding access to higher education and promoting equity are significant goals globally. Efforts must be made to increase enrolment rates, reduce barriers to entry, and provide support for underrepresented groups, including women, individuals from marginalized communities, and students with disabilities.

Ensuring quality and maintaining standards in higher education is a global concern. Aburizaizah (2022) states that accreditation agencies and quality assurance mechanisms exist in many countries to assess and monitor institutions, programs, and educational outcomes. International frameworks, such as the Bologna Process, contribute to the harmonization of quality standards across different countries. Higher education financing models vary globally, with a mix of public funding, private investments, and tuition fees. Affordability and student financial aid are key issues, and debates surround the balance between public investment, cost-sharing, and the impact on access and quality. Higher education institutions play a crucial role in research and innovation. Research collaborations, knowledge transfer, and commercialization of research outcomes contribute to societal development and economic growth. Universities are increasingly focused on producing impactful research and fostering innovation ecosystems. Higher education is responding to global challenges such as climate change, public health crises, and social inequalities. Interdisciplinary approaches, cross-sector collaborations, and community engagement are promoted to address complex problems and promote sustainable solutions. It is important to note that the global context of higher education is diverse, with significant variations across countries and regions. Each country has its own unique higher education system and priorities shaped by historical, cultural, and socio-economic factors.

THE IMPACT OF GLOBALIZATION ON HIGHER EDUCATION POLICY

The impact of globalization on culture and the educational system is a major concern. Some people saw it as a threat to traditional institutions such as the family and the school, another argument saw benefits in overturning traditional and developing modern attitudes. Kasimbara et al. (2024) noted that effective education systems are the foundation of opportunities to lead a decent life. Ensuring that all children have adequate access to education is an essential public sector function for countries at all income levels. The large difference in opportunities in education between countries is one of the basic causes of global inequality. Mganda, in the 6th Applied Research Conference (p. 556) noted that people can only contribute and benefit from globalization if they are endowed with knowledge, skills, and values and with the capabilities and rights needed to pursue their basic likelihoods.

Zekos (2021) describes globalization as a force that encompasses the virtual economy and how knowledge and information are shared and used. It has a profound impact on higher education policy, shaping how institutions, governments, and stakeholders approach and adapt to the changing landscape of education. Globalization has led to a growing emphasis on internationalization in higher education policy (De Wit & Altbach, 2021). Governments and institutions have recognized the importance of preparing students for a globalized world and promoting cross-cultural understanding. Policies now often include initiatives to attract international students, facilitate student and faculty exchanges, and foster international research collaborations. Globalization has spurred efforts to ensure quality assurance and accreditation systems align with international standards.

Governments and institutions seek to enhance the credibility and comparability of their programs and degrees, often through participation in international accreditation processes and adherence to global quality benchmarks (Gray et al., 2022; Muhammad, 2024). This facilitates the recognition and transferability of qualifications across borders. According to Mlambo (2020), globalization has prompted policies aimed at facilitating student and academic mobility. Ratanawaraha et al. (2024) further state that efforts are made to streamline visa processes, simplify credit transfer mechanisms, and promote the recognition of qualifications obtained abroad. These policies aim to encourage the free flow of students, scholars, and knowledge, helping students gain a diverse education.

Globalization has had significant impacts on higher education policy. The impacts therefore include:

- Internationalization: Higher education institutions have become more focused on internationalization, establishing partnerships with institutions abroad, recruiting international students, and offering study abroad programs.
- Cross-border Education: Globalization has also led to the growth of cross-border education, as universities offer online courses and establish branch campuses in other countries.
- Quality Assurance: Globalization has created a need for international quality assurance, as governments and accrediting agencies seek to establish common standards and procedures for assessing the quality of higher education institutions.
- Funding: Globalization has led to changes in higher education funding, as governments and institutions explore alternative revenue sources, such as philanthropy, corporate sponsorship, and international student fees.

- Rankings and Reputation: Global university rankings have become increasingly influential, driving institutional behavior and policymaking as institutions compete for higher rankings.
- Mobility and Immigration: Globalization has increased the demand for skilled workers, leading to changes in immigration policies and the creation of new visa categories for international students and researchers.
- English Language Proficiency: Globalization has resulted in a global shift towards the use of English as the lingua franca in higher education, leading to changes in language policies and teaching practices.
- Academic Freedom: Globalization has also raised questions about academic freedom, as universities balance the need for open dialogue and inquiry with the need to maintain relationships with international partners and governments.

POSITIVE AND NEGATIVE IMPACTS OF GLOBALIZATION

Bakhtiari and Shajar (2006) proclaimed that globalization seems to be unavoidable to many countries, and numerous initiatives and efforts have been made to adapt to it to take the opportunities created from it to develop societies and people. The impact of globalization is far-reaching and has had a profound effect on the world economy, politics, and society. On the economic front, globalization has led to the increasing integration of national economies into a single global market, resulting in increased trade and investment, and economic growth. However, it has also led to income inequality, job displacement, and the widening of the gap between the rich and the poor. In terms of politics, globalization has led to a shift towards more liberal and democratic forms of governance, as well as the rise of international organizations such as the United Nations, the World Trade Organization, and the International Monetary Fund. At the same time, globalization has also led to increased tensions and conflicts between nations, as well as a growing sense of disillusionment and disconnection among citizens. In terms of society, globalization has led to the increasing interconnectedness of cultures, ideas, and values, resulting in a more diverse and complex global culture. However, it has also led to the erosion of traditional ways of life, cultural homogenization, and the loss of national identity. Overall, the impact of globalization is complex and multifaceted, with both positive and negative effects on different aspects of our lives.

Globalization has had a profound impact on Africa, with both positive and negative consequences. On the positive side, globalization has increased economic growth and investment in the continent, with many countries experiencing rapid growth and development. It has also brought about improved access to technology, international markets, and human rights. However, globalization has also had negative consequences, including job displacement, income inequality, and environmental degradation. Many African countries have been forced to adapt to the demands of the global market, which has led to a loss of cultural identity and a widening of the gap between the rich and the poor. Additionally, globalization has led to a dependence on foreign aid and has eroded the sovereignty of African countries. Despite these challenges, many African countries are working to leverage the benefits of globalization to drive economic growth and development, while also addressing the social and environmental impacts of globalization.

In Sub-Saharan Africa, globalization has had a mixed impact. While it has brought increased economic growth, investment, and access to technology, it has also exacerbated poverty, income inequality, and environmental degradation. The region's natural resource-rich economies have made it vulnerable to the "resource curse," where foreign investment and exploitation of natural resources have led to corruption, conflict, and environmental degradation. Additionally, the region's limited institutional capacity and infrastructure have made it difficult to benefit fully from globalization. However, some countries such as Ghana, South Africa, and Ethiopia have managed to leverage globalization to drive economic growth and development. The region's youth population is also driving entrepreneurship and innovation, with many starting small businesses and creating new opportunities in the digital economy. Overall, while globalization has presented challenges for Sub-Saharan Africa, it has also created opportunities for growth and development if managed effectively.

However, globalization has also brought opportunities for higher education in Zimbabwe, such as:

- Access to new technologies and knowledge.
- Globalization has expanded opportunities for Zimbabwean higher education institutions to engage in international collaboration. Institutions can form partnerships with universities and research institutions from around the world, leading to joint research projects, faculty exchanges, and student mobility programs. These collaborations enhance the quality of education and research by exposing students and faculty to diverse perspectives and resources.
- Globalization has opened doors for international student exchange programs and the recruitment of foreign students. Zimbabwean universities can attract students from different countries, contributing to a diverse campus environment and promoting cultural exchange. This not only enhances the educational experience for local students but also generates revenue for institutions.

- Globalization allows for the transfer of knowledge, expertise, and technologies to Zimbabwean higher education institutions (McGrath et al., 2021). Through partnerships and collaborations with international institutions, Zimbabwean universities can gain access to cutting-edge research (Mpofu et al., 2024), best practices, and innovative teaching methods. This facilitates the improvement of academic programs, research capabilities, and the overall quality of education.
- Globalization enables Zimbabwean higher education institutions to stay informed about global trends, developments, and best practices in various disciplines. This exposure helps institutions align their programs and curricula with international standards and emerging fields, ensuring that graduates are globally competitive and relevant to the evolving job market.
- According to Shava (2015), globalization brings opportunities for professional development and capacity building for faculty and staff in Zimbabwean universities. They can attend international conferences, workshops, and training programs, which will expose them to new teaching methodologies, research techniques, and advancements in their respective fields. This strengthens the expertise and skills of faculty, ultimately benefitting students and the institution as a whole.
- Globalization has expanded funding and resource opportunities for Zimbabwean higher education institutions. They can access international grants, scholarships, and partnerships that provide financial support for research, infrastructure development, and academic programs. This helps institutions overcome financial constraints and invest in improving the quality of education and research facilities.
- Increased Economic Growth: Globalization has led to increased economic growth, as countries open their markets to foreign investment and trade, leading to the creation of jobs, the transfer of knowledge, and the development of new industries.
- Improved Standards of Living: Globalization has also contributed to improved standards of living, particularly in developing countries, as increased trade, investment, and remittances have helped to reduce poverty and improve health and education.
- Technological Advancements: Globalization has facilitated technological advancements, as countries share knowledge, skills, and resources, leading to faster innovation and the spread of new technologies.
- Cultural Exchange: Globalization has also led to a greater exchange of cultures, as people travel, study, and work abroad, leading to the diffusion of ideas, traditions, and customs.

- Strengthened International Relations: Globalization has helped to strengthen international relations, as countries become more interconnected and dependent on each other for economic, political, and security reasons.

In recent years, there have been increasing international concerns about the dangerous impacts of globalization on indigenous and national developments. Various social movements have been initiated against the threats of globalization particularly in developing countries. The potential negative impacts of globalization are various types of political, economic, and cultural colonization. In particular, the potential negative impacts include the following:

- Brain drain, as skilled professionals seek opportunities abroad. Globalization can result in the migration of skilled workers from developing countries to developed countries, depriving their home countries of valuable human capital.
- Increased competition from international universities.
- Limited access to funding and research opportunities.
- Uncertainty due to global political and economic instability.
- Barriers to international mobility and collaboration.
- Inadequate infrastructure and technology.
- Lack of international recognition of Zimbabwean qualifications.
- Increased Inequality: Globalization can exacerbate existing inequalities, as low-skilled workers in developed countries may face job losses due to competition from low-wage labor in developing countries.
- Loss of Local Culture and Identity: Globalization can lead to the spread of Western culture and values, potentially resulting in the erosion of local traditions and identities.
- Environmental Degradation: Globalization has also contributed to environmental degradation, as industrialization and resource exploitation in developing countries can result in air and water pollution, deforestation, and climate change.
- Increased Vulnerability to Economic Shocks: Globalization can increase the interconnectedness of economies, making them more vulnerable to external shocks such as financial crises or economic downturns.
- Rise of Protectionism and Nationalism: In response to the negative impacts of globalization, some countries have turned to protectionism and nationalism, erecting trade barriers and isolating themselves from the global economy.
- Spread of Disease: Globalization has also facilitated the spread of diseases, as increased travel and trade can accelerate the transmission of infectious diseases across borders.

- Digital Divide: While technology has facilitated globalization, there is a digital divide between those who have access to information and communication technologies and those who do not, perpetuating existing inequalities.
- Cultural Homogenization: Globalization can lead to the homogenization of culture, as local traditions, languages, and customs are replaced by global trends and fashions.
- Corporate Dominance: Globalization has led to the rise of multinational corporations, which can exert significant political and economic influence, sometimes at the expense of local businesses and communities.
- Diminished Labor Rights: Globalization has also contributed to the erosion of labor rights, as companies shift production to countries with weaker labor laws and lower wages.
- Loss of Sovereignty: Globalization has challenged traditional notions of national sovereignty, as multinational corporations and international organizations increasingly wield power on a global scale.
- Capital Flight: Globalization can lead to capital flight, as wealthy individuals and corporations move their assets offshore to avoid taxes and regulations.
- Trafficking and Exploitation: Globalization has also facilitated trafficking in persons, as vulnerable individuals, particularly women and children, are lured into forced labor or sexual exploitation.
- Cybercrime: The rise of digital technologies has also created new opportunities for cybercrime, as criminals can operate across borders and evade detection by law enforcement.

INTERNATIONAL COLLABORATION AND KNOWLEDGE SHARING

De Wit and Altbach (2021) stated, "Internationalization is a process in constant evolution, which changes in response to local, national, regional, and global environments. Current global trends appear to be more radical than in the past and require stronger attention and international cooperation than ever; nationalist-populist movements, the need for climatic change, and the impact of the COVID-19 pandemic are particularly vital"(pp.17-18). International collaboration and knowledge sharing play a vital role in advancing research, innovation, and education in today's interconnected world (Oyewole et al., 2024). International collaboration allows researchers, scholars, and educators to access a diverse pool of expertise and perspectives from around the world. By working together across borders, individuals can tap into a broader range of knowledge, methodologies, and approaches, leading to more comprehensive and impactful outcomes. Collaborating internationally enables the pooling of resources, infrastructure, and intellectual capital to tackle complex global challenges. It facilitates the sharing of data, research findings, and best practices, thereby fostering innovation and accelerating the pace of scientific discovery.

According to Vahed and Rodriguez (2021), international collaboration promotes cross-cultural learning and understanding. Through interactions with colleagues from different cultural backgrounds, individuals gain insights into diverse perspectives, practices, and ways of thinking. This exposure enhances intercultural competence, fosters empathy, and promotes a broader worldview. Portilla (2023) further affirms that collaborating internationally increases the visibility and impact of research and scholarly work. Joint publications and collaborations with researchers from different countries can lead to broader dissemination of research findings, wider readership, and increased citations. This, in turn, strengthens the reputation and recognition of researchers and institutions.

International collaboration builds strong networks and partnerships across institutions, disciplines, and regions. These networks provide opportunities for future collaborations, joint funding applications, and exchange programs. Amey and Eddy (2023) proclaim that collaborative partnerships also contribute to institutional development, promote knowledge transfer, and facilitate access to funding and resources as cited also by Eddy (2010). Many of today's complex challenges, such as climate change, public health, and inequality, require global cooperation and interdisciplinary approaches. International collaboration brings together experts from various fields and regions to collectively address these challenges, share insights, and develop innovative solutions. International collaboration enriches the educational experience for students thereby providing opportunities for international research projects, study abroad programs, and cross-cultural exchange. Through collaborations with international peers, students gain exposure to different educational systems, perspectives, and research methodologies, fostering their personal and academic growth.

BALANCING INTERNATIONALIZATION AND NATIONAL IDENTITY

Woldegiorgis (2024) proclaims that internationalization through communication, mobility, and partnerships within and outside Africa, makes it possible for the knowledge, skills, products, and services so produced to be shared for mutual and global benefit. This respect for each other's contributions, cultures, and value systems is key to promoting an increased awareness and appreciation of everyone's values. Balancing internationalization and national identity in higher education is a complex task that requires careful consideration and strategic decision-making (Knight, 2008). Higher education institutions should start by clarifying their core values and mission, which includes defining their commitment to both internationalization and the preservation of national identity. This clarity will help guide decision-making and ensure that internationalization efforts align with the institution's identity and goals. Internationalization does not necessarily mean diluting national identity. Institutions can embrace cultural diversity while still preserving their national or regional heritage (Labadi et al., 202; Tahiri et al., 2022; Meskell, 2002). Encouraging the celebration of different cultures, traditions, and perspectives can enrich the educational experience and foster an inclusive environment that respects and values diverse identities.

According to Beribe (2023), institutions can balance international perspectives in the curriculum without compromising national identity. This can be achieved by incorporating global perspectives and examples alongside national or regional case studies. Providing opportunities for students to engage critically with both local and global issues can help them develop a well-rounded understanding of the world. Morton, et al. (2022) assert that institutions can prioritize research and innovation that addresses local or national challenges while still engaging in international collaborations (Togo & Gandidzanwa, 2021). By focusing on local needs and leveraging national strengths, institutions can contribute to the development of solutions that reflect their national identity while benefiting from global knowledge and expertise. According to Liu (2021), internationalization can be an opportunity to develop global competencies while maintaining a strong national identity. Institutions can provide students with the skills and knowledge needed to navigate the globalized world, including intercultural communication, adaptability, and global citizenship, while also nurturing a sense of pride and connection to their own culture and heritage. Higher education institutions can actively engage with local communities to contribute to their development and address their unique needs. This can include partnerships with local businesses, community organizations, and government agencies to foster social and economic growth while maintaining a connection to the institution's national or regional identity.

Balancing internationalization and national identity requires the involvement of various stakeholders, including students, faculty staff, alumni, and community members. (Jeffery, 2021; lhamad, 2023). Engaging in open dialogue, seeking diverse perspectives, and incorporating feedback can help ensure that decisions reflect the interests and values of the broader community. Institutions according to Amey and Eddy (2023) can establish strategic partnerships with international counterparts that align with their values and goals. These partnerships can facilitate meaningful exchanges while maintaining a focus on the preservation of national identity. By carefully selecting partners that share similar values and objectives, institutions can ensure that international collaborations are mutually beneficial and supportive of their national identity. Liu (2021) further proclaims that balancing internationalization and national identity in higher education is an ongoing process that requires continuous reflection, adaptation, and dialogue. By embracing cultural diversity, promoting global competencies, and staying true to their core values, institutions can create an environment that successfully integrates internationalization while preserving their national or regional identity.

THE IMPLICATIONS OF GLOBALIZATION FOR THE FUTURE OF HIGHER EDUCATION

Globalization has significant implications for the future of higher education and it facilitates increased collaboration and partnerships between higher education institutions worldwide. Institutions are likely to engage in more joint research projects, international conferences, faculty and student exchanges, and collaborative programs (Nurdiana et al., 2023; Abazov, 2021). This collaboration enhances the exchange of knowledge, fosters innovation, and promotes the global advancement of education and research. Yildiri et al. (2021) and Sharipov (2020) proclaim that globalization has led to increased student mobility and a diverse student body in higher education institutions. Institutions are likely to see a greater influx of international students, creating a more multicultural and inclusive learning environment. This diversity enriches the educational experience, promotes cross-cultural understanding, and prepares students for a globalized workforce (Zalli, 2024).

According to Clarke and Kirby (2022), globalization necessitates the internationalization of curricula to equip students with global perspectives and intercultural competencies. Institutions are likely to incorporate more courses on global issues, offer language and cultural studies programs, and integrate international case studies and perspectives into various disciplines. This prepares students to navigate and contribute to a globalized world. Globalization is accompanied by rapid advancements in technology, which significantly impact higher education (Matyushok et al., 2021). Online learning platforms, digital resources, and virtual collaboration tools enable institutions to reach learners globally, offer online courses and degree programs, and support remote collaboration between students and researchers across borders.

Haleem et al. (2022) assert that technological advancements enhance access to education and expand educational opportunities. Globalization has transformed the job market, emphasizing the need for graduates with global competencies and a broad skill set. Higher education institutions must prepare students for a globalized workforce by equipping them with skills such as intercultural communication, adaptability, critical thinking, and problem-solving (Aithal & Aithal, 2023). Institutions may need to offer co-curricular activities, internships, and study abroad programs to develop these skills. Abu-Rumman and Qawasmeh (2022) believe that globalization can necessitate robust quality assurance mechanisms in higher education. Institutions are likely to participate in international accreditation and quality assessment processes to ensure their programs meet global standards. International rankings and evaluation systems may play a more significant role in assessing institutional performance and attracting students and faculty from around the world.

According to Uy et al. (2024), globalization requires individuals to engage in lifelong learning and continuous professional development to adapt to changing global trends and demands. Higher education institutions may offer more flexible and modular learning opportunities, including online micro-credentials, short-term courses, and professional development programs to cater to the needs of learners throughout their careers. Globalization encourages the formation of research networks and collaboration across borders. Institutions are likely to foster international research partnerships, participate in global research initiatives, and leverage digital platforms to facilitate interdisciplinary and cross-national research collaborations (Gonzalez-Pinero et al., 2021; Olatunji et al., 2023). This collaboration accelerates scientific discovery, knowledge dissemination, and the development of innovative solutions to global challenges.

Direction for Future Research

Future research on the challenges and opportunities of globalization for higher education should focus on exploring the implications of globalization on the curriculum, pedagogy, and assessment of higher education institutions. Specifically, research should investigate the impact of globalization on the development of soft skills, such as cultural competence, adaptability, and critical thinking, which are essential for students to navigate the global workforce. Additionally, research should examine the role of internationalization in promoting diversity and inclusion on campus, and how higher education institutions can create a more inclusive and welcoming environment for international students. Furthermore, research should explore the potential of online learning platforms in facilitating global connectivity and collaboration among students, faculty, and institutions. Future research should also investigate the impact of globalization on the workforce and economy, and how higher education institutions can prepare students for the changing job market. Finally, research should examine the role of government policies and regulations in promoting or hindering globalization in higher education, and how institutions can navigate these complexities to achieve their goals. By exploring these areas, future research can provide valuable insights for higher education institutions to adapt to the changing global landscape and provide students with a world-class education that prepares them for a rapidly changing global economy. Implications and future directions for higher education relate to:

- Increased Interconnectivity: With the continued growth of globalization, higher education institutions must prepare for increased levels of interconnectivity and collaboration across borders. This will require a focus on developing strong partnerships, leveraging digital tools, and fostering a culture of internationalization.
- Focus on Sustainability: Globalization has also brought about an increased awareness of environmental and social issues. As such, higher education institutions will need to focus on developing sustainable practices and addressing these issues through research, teaching, and community engagement.
- Adaptive Learning Models: The traditional model of higher education is being challenged by globalization. With the rise of online learning, microcredentials, and hybrid learning models, institutions will need to adapt their teaching and learning practices to meet the changing needs of students.
- Lifelong Learning: With longer life spans and rapid technological advancements, lifelong learning is becoming increasingly important. Higher education institutions will need to develop more flexible and adaptable learning models that cater to the needs of both traditional and non-traditional learners.
- Role of Universities: Globalization has also raised questions about the role of universities in society. Institutions will need to reexamine their mission and values, focusing on how they can contribute to social and economic development while also upholding academic freedom and intellectual rigor.
- Equity and Access: Globalization has widened disparities between institutions and countries. As such, higher education institutions will need to prioritize equity and access, ensuring that opportunities are available to all students regardless of background or location.

CONCLUSION

Globalization has brought both challenges and opportunities to higher education. While institutions face increased competition and funding constraints, they also have the opportunity to expand their reach, collaborate internationally, and foster cultural diversity. Embracing globalization can lead to enhanced educational quality, research advancements, and a more globally connected and inclusive higher education sector. Implications highlight the need for higher education institutions to adapt and embrace globalization. Institutions must prioritize international collaboration, curriculum internationalization, technology integration, and the development of global competencies to prepare students for a globalized world and contribute to the advancement of knowledge and society. Globalization has fostered the global university rankings "game", in which research-intensive universities jockey for global stature and prestige (Yudkevich et al., 2016). With a world of opportunities to choose from and a variety of incentives to entice them, talented students, researchers, and academics circulate internationally and on highly competitive terms. By way of these dynamics and others, there is clear evidence that globalization has introduced a range of new priorities and considerations for higher education institutions around the world. In many ways, these are exciting developments that place universities, in particular, at a cutting edge of new knowledge development and global engagement. Globalization has had a profound impact on higher education, creating both opportunities and challenges. While institutions must adapt and innovate to remain competitive, there are also opportunities to strengthen their role as global actors in knowledge creation and dissemination. To maximize the benefits of globalization while mitigating its challenges, higher education institutions should focus on building strong international partnerships, diversifying revenue streams, and ensuring that their offerings are globally relevant and attractive to students and faculty alike. By doing so, they can position themselves as leaders in the global higher education landscape.

Recommendations

Recommendations on the challenges and opportunities of globalization for higher education include developing a global strategy: universities should develop a comprehensive strategy to address the challenges and opportunities of globalization; internationalized curricula: universities should incorporate international perspectives and topics into their curricula to prepare students for a globalized world; foster partnerships: universities should establish partnerships with international institutions and organizations to facilitate research collaborations, student exchanges, and staff development; invest in technology: universities should invest in technology to enhance online learning experiences, facilitate communication with international students and faculty, and promote global connectivity; develop language support programs: universities should develop language support programs to assist international students and faculty in adapting to their new academic environment; provide cultural support services: universities should provide cultural support services, such as counselling and mentoring, to help international students and faculty navigate the challenges of academic life in a new country and monitor accreditation and recognition: universities should monitor accreditation and recognition processes to ensure that their international qualifications are recognized globally. By addressing challenges and opportunities, universities can position themselves as leaders in the global higher education landscape, attract top talent from around the world, and provide students with a world-class education that prepares them for a rapidly changing global economy.

REFERENCES

Abazov, R. (2021). Engaging in the internationalization of education and SDGs: A case study on the global hub of UNAI on sustainability. In *E3S Web of Conferences* (Vol. 307, p. 06001). EDP Sciences. DOI: 10.1051/e3sconf/202130706001

Abu-Rumman, A., & Qawasmeh, R. (2022). Assessing international students' satisfaction with a Jordanian university using the service quality model. *Journal of Applied Research in Higher Education*, 14(4), 1742–1760. DOI: 10.1108/JARHE-05-2021-0166

Aburizaizah, S. J. (2022). The role of quality assurance in Saudi higher education institutions. *International Journal of Educational Research Open*, 3, 100127. DOI: 10.1016/j.ijedro.2022.100127

Aigboje, J., & Abhulimen, J. & Asika, M. (2022). Global trends in technology and its impact on adult education as a catalyst for national growth. *Innovative Journal of Science (ISSN: 2714-3309), 4*(4), 42-52.

Aithal, P. S., & Aithal, S. (2023). Super Innovation in Higher Education by Nurturing Business Leaders through Incubationship. [IJAEML]. *International Journal of Applied Engineering and Management Letters*, 7(3), 142–167. DOI: 10.47992/IJAEML.2581.7000.0192

Altbach, P. G., Reisberg, L., & Rumbley, L. E. (2019). *Trends in global higher education: Tracking an academic revolution*. Brill.

Amey, M. J., & Eddy, P. L. (2023). *Creating strategic partnerships: A guide for educational institutions and their partners*. Taylor & Francis.

Bakhtiari, S., & Shajar, H. (2006). Globalization and education: Challenges and opportunities. [IBER]. *The International Business & Economics Research Journal*, 5(2). Advance online publication. DOI: 10.19030/iber.v5i2.3461

Beribe, M. F. B. (2023). The Impact of Globalization on Content and Subjects in the Curriculum in Madrasah Ibtidaiyah: Challenges and Opportunities. *At-Tasyrih: jurnal pendidikan dan hukum. Der Islam*, 9(1), 54–68.

Clarke, L., & Kirby, D. (2022). Internationalizing higher education curricula: Strategies and approaches. *Universal Journal of Educational Research*, 10(6), 408–417. DOI: 10.13189/ujer.2022.100605

Dagen, T., & Kovacevic, M. (2023). The Impact of Globalization on the Internationalization of Higher Education Policies: A Southeast European Perspective. In *Reimagining Border in Cross-border Education* (pp. 74–97). Routledge. DOI: 10.4324/9781003427827-4

Dai, K., Mok, K. H., & Li, X. (2023). Mapping the historical development and landscape of research about transnational higher education: A scientometric analysis from comparative and international perspectives. *Compare: A Journal of Comparative Education*, ●●●, 1–19. DOI: 10.1080/03057925.2023.2292517

De Wit, H., & Altbach, P. G. (2021). Internationalization in higher education: global trends and recommendations for its future. In *Higher education in the next decade* (pp. 303–325). Brill. DOI: 10.1163/9789004462717_016

Deardorff, D. K., De Wit, H., Leask, B., & Charles, H. (Eds.). (2023). *The handbook of international higher education*. Taylor & Francis.

Gao, Y., & Liu, J. (2020). International student recruitment campaign: Experiences of selected flagship universities in China. *Higher Education*, 80(4), 663–678. DOI: 10.1007/s10734-020-00503-8

Gonzalez-Pinero, M., Paez-Avilés, C., Juanola-Feliu, E., & Samitier, J. (2021). Cross-fertilization of knowledge and technologies in collaborative research projects. *Journal of Knowledge Management*, 25(11), 34–59. DOI: 10.1108/JKM-04-2020-0270

Gray, J., Ross, J., & Badrick, T. (2022). The path to continual improvement and business excellence: Compliance to ISO standards versus a business excellence approach. *Accreditation and Quality Assurance*, 27(4), 195–203. DOI: 10.1007/s00769-022-01503-0

Guardia, L., Clougher, D., Anderson, T., & Maina, M. (2021). IDEAS for transforming higher education: An overview of ongoing trends and challenges. *International Review of Research in Open and Distance Learning*, 22(2), 166–184. DOI: 10.19173/irrodl.v22i2.5206

Haleem, A., Javaid, M., Qadri, M. A., & Suman, R. (2022). Understanding the role of digital technologies in education: A review. *Sustainable Operations and Computers*, 3, 275–285. DOI: 10.1016/j.susoc.2022.05.004

Ion, S., & Ilie-Prica, M. (2020). Higher Education and Globalization in the Context of the COVID-19 Crisis. *European Journal of Education*, 3(2), 34–48. DOI: 10.26417/812dro50g

Jeffery, J. S. (2021). *Navigating internationalization at a public flagship university: The balancing act of senior leadership* (Doctoral dissertation, University of Georgia).

Juusola, K., Wilkins, S., & Jamous, S. (2023). Branding discourses in transnational higher education in the era of hyper-competition: Leveraging secondary brand associations. *Compare: A Journal of Comparative Education*, ●●●, 1–18. DOI: 10.1080/03057925.2023.2292533

Kalandarovna, A. G., & Qizi, A. M. A. (2023). Development and increase of competitiveness of the organization. *ASEAN Journal of Educational Research and Technology*, 2(3), 265–274.

Kasimbara, R. P., Imron, A., & Supriyanto, A. (2024). Strategic Marketing of Higher Education in a Developing World: A Multiple Cases Study of Localized Marketing Of Indonesia's Private Higher Education. *Educational Administration: Theory and Practice*, 30(5), 702–719.

Knight, J. (2008). *Higher education in turmoil: The changing world of internationalization* (Vol. 13). Brill. DOI: 10.1163/9789087905224

Labadi, S., Giliberto, F., Rosetti, I., Shetabi, L., & Yildirim, E. (2021). Heritage and the sustainable development goals: Policy guidance for heritage and development actors. *International Journal of Heritage Studies*.

Lemoine, P. A., Jenkins, W. M., & Richardson, M. D. (2017). Global higher education: Development and implications. *Journal of Education and Development*, 1(1), 58. DOI: 10.20849/jed.v1i1.253

lhamad, B. (2023). Quality Assurance Breaking Down Barriers with External Stakeholders: An Investigation of Current and Potential Roles of Stakeholders. In *Quality Assurance in Higher Education in the Middle East: Practices and Perspectives* (pp. 19-48). Emerald Publishing Limited.

Liu, W. (2021). The Chinese definition of internationalization in higher education. *Journal of Higher Education Policy and Management*, 43(2), 230–245. DOI: 10.1080/1360080X.2020.1777500

Matyushok, V., Vera Krasavina, V., Berezin, A., & Sendra García, J. (2021). The global economy in technological transformation conditions: A review of modern trends. *Ekonomska Istrazivanja*, 34(1), 1471–1497. DOI: 10.1080/1331677X.2020.1844030

McGrath, S., Thondhlana, J., & Garwe, E. (2021). Internationalization of higher education and national development: The case of Zimbabwe. *Compare: A Journal of Comparative Education*, 51(6), 881–900. DOI: 10.1080/03057925.2019.1684241

Meskell, L. (2002). Negative heritage and past masters in archaeology. *Anthropological Quarterly*, 75(3), 557–574. DOI: 10.1353/anq.2002.0050

Mganda, V. O. The role of corporate multilateral agencies in enhancing quality education in Tanzania in the era of globalization: challenges and opportunities. In *6th applied research conference in Africa* (p. 556).

Mlambo, D. N. (2020). Student Mobility, Brain Drain and the Internationalisation of Higher Education in Southern Africa. *African Journal of Development Studies (formerly AFFRIKA Journal of Politics, Economics and Society), 10*(2), 59-82.

Morton, B., Vercueil, A., Masekela, R., Heinz, E., Reimer, L., Saleh, S., & Oriyo, N. (2022). Consensus statement on measures to promote equitable authorship in the publication of research from international partnerships. *Anaesthesia, 77*(3), 264–276. DOI: 10.1111/anae.15597 PMID: 34647323

Moshtari, M., & Safarpour, A. (2024). Challenges and strategies for the internationalization of higher education in low-income East African countries. *Higher Education, 87*(1), 89–109. DOI: 10.1007/s10734-023-00994-1 PMID: 36713135

Mpofu, F. Y., Mpofu, A., Mantula, F., & Shava, G. N. (2024). Towards the Attainment of SDGs: The Contribution of Higher Education Institutions in Zimbabwe. *International Journal of Social Science Research and Review, 7*(1), 474–493.

Muhammad, N. I. (2024). Obstacles to the application of quality and reliability indicators in education colleges and the requirements for their achievement. *International Development Planning Review, 23*(1), 588–614.

Nurdiana, R., Effendi, M. N., Ningsih, K. P., Abda, M. I., & Aslan, A. (2023). Collaborative partnerships for digital education to improve students' learning achievement at the Institute of Islamic Religion of Sultan Muhammad Syafiuddin Sambas, Indonesia. *International Journal of Teaching and Learning, 1*(1), 1–15.

Olatunji, G., Emmanuel, K., Osaghae, O. W., Timilehin, I., Aderinto, N., & Abdulbasit, M. O. (2023). Enhancing clinical and translational research in Africa: A comprehensive exploration of challenges and opportunities for advancement. *Journal of Clinical and Translational Research, 9*(5), 357–368.

Oyewole, A. T., Adeoye, O. B., Addy, W. A., Okoye, C. C., & Ofodile, O. C. (2024). Enhancing global competitiveness of US SMES through sustainable finance: A review and future directions. *International Journal of Management & Entrepreneurship Research, 6*(3), 634–647.

Portilla, L. U. (2023, December). Scientific fraud: attack on the credibility of science. In *Seminars in Medical Writing and Education* (Vol. 2, pp. 34-34).

Ratanawaraha, A., Torquato Cruz, R., & Perez Cuso, M. (2024). Policies to promote private sector engagement in Science, Technology, and Innovation: Workbook.

Rudhumbu, N. (2020). Unlocking the Cultural Diversity Black Box: Application of Culturally Responsive Pedagogies in University Classrooms in Zimbabwe. *International Journal of Learning. Teaching and Educational Research*, 19(12), 146–162.

Sharipov, F. (2020). Internationalization of higher education: definition and description. *Mental Enlightenment Scientific-Methodological Journal*, 127-138.

Shava, G. N. (2015). Professional development, a major strategy for higher education student success, experiences from a university in Zimbabwe. *Zambia Journal of Science and Technology*, 10(1), 11–25.

Shen, W., Xu, X., & Wang, X. (2022). Reconceptualising international academic mobility in the global knowledge system: Towards a new research agenda. *Higher Education*, 84(6), 1317–1342. DOI: 10.1007/s10734-022-00931-8 PMID: 36211225

Syahid, A., Kamri, K. A., & Azizan, S. N. (2021). Usability of Massive Open Online Courses (MOOCs): Malaysian Undergraduates' Perspective. *The Journal of Educators Online*, 18(3), n3. DOI: 10.9743/JEO.2021.18.3.11

Tahiri, A., Kovaçi, I., & Trajkovska Petkoska, A. (2022). Sustainable tourism as a potential for promotion of regional heritage, local food, traditions, and diversity—Case of Kosovo. *Sustainability (Basel)*, 14(19), 12326. DOI: 10.3390/su141912326

Togo, M., & Gandidzanwa, C. P. (2021). The role of Education 5.0 in accelerating the implementation of SDGs and challenges encountered at the University of Zimbabwe. *International Journal of Sustainability in Higher Education*, 22(7), 1520–1535. DOI: 10.1108/IJSHE-05-2020-0158

Uy, F., Abendan, C. F., Andrin, G., Vestal, P., Suson, M., & Kilag, O. K. (2024). Exploring Strategies for Fostering a Culture of Continuous Professional Development and Learning: A Systematic Literature Review. [IMJRISE]. *International Multidisciplinary Journal of Research for Innovation, Sustainability, and Excellence*, 1(3), 191–198.

Uzhegova, D., & Baik, C. (2022). Internationalization of higher education in an uneven world: An integrated approach to internationalization of universities in the academic periphery. *Studies in Higher Education*, 47(4), 847–859. DOI: 10.1080/03075079.2020.1811220

Vahed, A., & Rodriguez, K. (2021). Enriching students' engaged learning experiences through the collaborative online international learning project. *Innovations in Education and Teaching International*, 58(5), 596–605. DOI: 10.1080/14703297.2020.1792331

Woldegiorgis, E. T. (2024). Internationalization of Higher Education under Neoliberal Imperatives: The Political Economy of Student Mobility in Africa. In *Critical Reflections on the Internationalisation of Higher Education in the Global South* (pp. 13–31). Emerald Publishing Limited. DOI: 10.1108/978-1-80455-778-520241002

Yadav, N. (2024). The Impact of Digital Learning on Education. *International Journal of Multidisciplinary Research in Arts. Science and Technology*, 2(1), 24–34.

Yildirim, S., Bostanci, S. H., Yildırim, D. Ç., & Erdogan, F. (2021). Rethinking mobility of international university students during COVID-19 pandemic. *Higher Education Evaluation and Development*, 15(2), 98–113. DOI: 10.1108/HEED-01-2021-0014

Zaleniene, I., & Pereira, P. (2021). Higher education for sustainability: A global perspective. *Geography and Sustainability*, 2(2), 99–106. DOI: 10.1016/j.geosus.2021.05.001

Zalli, E. (2024). Globalization and Education: Exploring the Exchange of Ideas, Values, and Traditions in Promoting Cultural Understanding and Global Citizenship. *Interdisciplinary Journal of Research and Development, 11*(1 S1), 55-55.

Zekos, G. I., & Zekos, G. I. (2021). E-Globalization and Digital Economy. *Economics and Law of Artificial Intelligence: Finance, Economic Impacts, Risk Management and Governance*, 13-66.

KEY TERMS AND DEFINITIONS

Internationalization: in higher education is a steerable process of greater cooperation and cross-border formal relations between states, institutions, and organizations (Dagen and Kovacevic, 2023). Uzhegova and Baik, (2022) define internationalization in higher education as a process of integrating international perspectives, experiences, and activities into the core functions of institutions. Internationalization in higher education involves fostering global awareness, promoting intercultural understanding, and creating opportunities for international learning, research, and collaboration (Deardorff et al., 2023). In the context of higher education, internationalization refers to the purpose and integration of the global dimension into the main activities and events of universities and colleges and it involves expanding international cooperation, promoting social understanding, and encouraging cooperation and exchange within organisations and individuals in different countries.

Higher Education Policy: is an international, peer-reviewed journal that focuses on issues of significance in higher education policy (Jeroen, 2024), Higher education policy refers to the set of principles, regulations, and actions implemented by governments and educational institutions to shape and guide the development, provision, and governance of higher education. It encompasses a wide range of areas, including access and equity, quality assurance, funding and financing, curriculum and pedagogy, research and innovation, internationalization, and governance.

International collaboration: in higher education involves partnerships, agreements, or cooperative activities between institutions or researchers from different countries (Moshtari and Safarpour, 2024). International collaboration in higher education includes joint research projects, exchange programs, faculty mobility, curriculum development, and other forms of collaboration aimed at advancing knowledge, sharing resources, and promoting mutual understanding (Deardorff et al., 2023). Thus international collaboration refers to the cooperation between different countries, individuals, or organizations from different countries working together to achieve a common goal. It involves the exchange of knowledge, skills, resources, and best practices across national borders to solve different problems, stimulate innovation, and achieve good results. International collaboration can take many different forms, including education, and research.

Globalisation: in higher education involves the flow of students, faculty, knowledge, ideas, and practices across borders, influenced by economic, social, and technological factors (Ion & Ilie-Prica, 2020). According to Algboje et al., 2022), globalization may refer to the transfer, adaptation, and development of values, knowledge, technology, and behavioral norms across countries and societies in different parts of the world. Therefore globalisation in the context of higher education, refers to the integration of educational systems, institutions, and stakeholders on a global scale.

Global mobility: is defined as the movement of individuals, such as students, faculty, researchers, and professionals, across national borders for educational, work, or research purposes (Shen & Wang, 2022). It reflects the increased opportunities and accessibility for individuals to study, work, or collaborate in different countries, contributing to the exchange of knowledge, skills, and cultural experiences.

Transnational education (TNE): refers to educational programs and activities provided by an institution in one country to students located in another country and it involves the delivery of educational services across national borders, allowing students to access international education without physically relocating (Juusola et al., 2023). TNHE is used as an umbrella concept that refers to types of international higher education provision in which the program is offered for learners in a different country than the one where the awarding institution is located (Juusola et al., 2023). TNE is also often referred to as cross-border, offshore, or borderless higher education (Dai, Mok & Li, 2023), which may take various forms, such as distance/virtual education; franchised programs, or programs offered in partnership with another institution; joint or double degree programs; and international branch campuses (IBCs)

Global competition: In the context of higher education, global competition refers to competition between institutions, countries, or regions to attract students, teachers, research funds, and international recognition. It involves efforts to enhance reputation, quality, and distinctiveness to stand out in the global higher education market. Global competition drives institutions to improve performance and offer unique educational experiences to remain competitive (Kalandarovna & Qizi, 2023).

Chapter 2
Ensuring Inclusivity in Higher Education Leadership

Olabode Gbobaniyi
https://orcid.org/0000-0002-0722-0335
Global Banking School, UK

Shalini Srivastava
Global Banking School, UK

ABSTRACT

This chapter explores the influence of inclusive leadership in higher education institutions (HEIs), from an inclusive approach, on academic loyalty based on the purview of its antecedents and consequence on perceived institutional support (PIS). The future of leadership in higher education depends on how academics, as members of collectives, communicate and negotiate with their institutions, through their leaders and managers, to be recognised and supported for their multiple understandings and practices. Inclusive leadership provides academics a feel of a sense of belonging thus contributing to the vision and goals of the HEI. To move leadership towards a more inclusive manner, there is a need for HEIs to ensure equality, diversity, and inclusion as the right conditions to ensure open manager-subordinate communication for academics to be able to perceive and understand the institutional support available to them towards achieving and fulfilling their professional goals and ambitions.

DOI: 10.4018/979-8-3693-3443-0.ch002

1.0 INTRODUCTION

Higher education institutions (HEIs) are environments that comprise interprofessional teams that are highly intelligent, focused, and, innovative in collaborating on service delivery and decision-making that is shifting our world forward in many ways (Aboramadan, et al., 2022). These interprofessional teams also consist of diverse people with different areas of specialisation, culture, demography and many more (Montani, et al., 2014). As a result, HEIs benefit greatly based on their level of diversity at the staff, organisation, and community levels (Najmaei & Sadeghinejad, 2019). It has also been identified that the level of diversity in HEIs is an important contributor to the effectiveness of their knowledge-related advantages which is associated with the institution's professional expertise (Mitchell, et al., 2015). However, it has been argued that the leadership in most HEIs have not taken the fullest advantage of the opportunity of their level of diversity because of the high level of internal friction, hostility, and underperformance across faculty or departmental levels (Stefani & Blessinger, 2018; Temple & Ylitalo, 2009). This has been identified to be a reason for the increased call for inclusivity and inclusive leadership, particularly, in the management of academics in HEIs (Handforth, 2018). What may seem to be a response from leaders and managers in HEIs, indicates that they agree towards the need for increased inclusivity and inclusive leadership across faculties and departments (Bolden, et al., 2009; Macfarlane, et al., 2024). Still, they claim their expanding array of institutional demands has made them shift from a collegial decision-making approach that emboldens inclusivity to more managerial, corporate, or entrepreneurial leadership/management models (Currie, et al., 2008; Handforth, 2018; Macfarlane, et al., 2024).

Additionally, it is argued that the increasing ever-present need for HEI management to 'do more with less' (i.e., enhancing teaching and research quality) is driving the increased competition many HEIs are experiencing from other related institutions such as Colleges and Further Education institutions that are now offering degree-level programmes. This has also been acknowledged to impact HEI leadership which has always been identified as multifaceted to become even more complicated as they need to ensure they are not only relevant in their communities but also meet the goal of ensuring they deliver quality teaching and satisfactory student experiences (Aung & Hallinger, 2023). Despite the challenges HEIs and their leadership may face, the question, however, is, should institutional demands affect the leadership in engaging and practising inclusive leadership, or should they not encourage the need for it? We hope to be able to use this literature to provide a broad-based answer to the question and in doing so, we will start by providing a solid foundation in this introduction starting with a well-grounded definition of leadership. Gerard A. Cole, in his article, *Management: Theory and Practice*, published in 1990, defined leadership as "a dynamic process within a group, in which an individual influence others to voluntarily contribute to the fulfilment of the group's task, in a given situation" (Drugus & Landoy, 2014). Based on the definition, subsequent authors and scholars have further dissected the definition and provided more elaborate meaning and understanding that leadership refers to the promotion of behaviour, nurturing the achievement of the institution's objectives, motivating academics by using various leadership styles, a quality interpersonal relationship 'based on how communication and cooperation are favoured within the organisation and the academics are engaged in the decision-making process' (Hellman, 2023; Kuknor & Bhattacharya, 2022). Furthermore, knowledge from relevant literature indicates that leadership and management represent separate dimensions of the people in charge (Fagan, et al., 2020; Kogan & Hanney, 2000). While leadership is indicated to be about the capacity to determine the actions of people; the manager, is the person who makes sure that the organisational objectives are achieved, by planning, organising, and directing the work towards its conclusion (Charalampous & Papademetriou, 2019). Additionally, while management is more of a formal, institutionalised type of leading; leadership is perceived as leading at an informal group level, and the leader is the one who leads this group; it represents the ability to influence others towards the fulfilment of the tasks (Kezar, 2023). As a result for this chapter, we use leader, manager, or line manager interchangeably in the context of a line manager or management, be it at a departmental or faculty level as a person who is formally institutionalised to lead and use that position to informally influence members of the group towards the fulfilment of given tasks and achieving set objectives and goals.

The core objective of this chapter is to advance knowledge of inclusivity and inclusive leadership in HEIs to advance our understanding of the importance of inclusive leadership and its adoption in the management of faculties and academics in HEIs. This is because the inclusive leadership framework is being found robust and relevant when tested in the context of leadership in similar organisations and institutions like HEIs. Moreover, the current approach of managerial, corporate, and entrepreneurial management and leadership being used in many HEIs has been found not to sit well in academic administration and management in many HEIs (Aboramadan, et al., 2022). This has been argued to be because they are not enacted within the ideological concept and context of collegiality, collaboration, and participative decision-making (Gronn, 2009; Kogan & Hanney, 2000). Additionally, studies have continued to urge HEIs to develop their leadership and management approach that is based on the theme of inclusivity rather than mimicking those of the corporate sector for academic management (McFarlane, 2014; Sastry & Bekandria, 2007; Quayson, 2019). This is because inclusion is said to be about making insiders of those who are or believe they are outsiders (Stamper & Masterson, 2002). More so, the core components of inclusive leadership practice in HEIs are equality, diversity, and inclusion (EDI) which ensures the collection of safe and sound judgment to evaluate the institution's value and growth (Najmaei & Sadeghinejad, 2019). EDI must be woven into all aspects of HEIs' operations with a strong vision and intent from the leadership. Additionally, EDI leads to better outcomes, and increased revenue, and attracts talents from a wider pool, thereby improving the satisfaction and culture of the academics and the value and growth of the institution (Charalampous & Papademetriou, 2019). The value and growth of HEIs depend on their creativity and renewable resources, as a result, faculty/departmental managers should ensure they do not marginalise the capabilities of their academic team and ensure they put in place collaborative approaches that foster innovative work behaviour, retention, and loyalty to the institution (Aboramadan, et al., 2022; Cissna, 2020).

Lastly, the field of leadership has continued to seek to explain how a leader can facilitate inclusion in an HE environment. However, leadership literature continues to struggle to adequately conceptualise the social dynamics typically encountered in contexts of social diversity, despite the discipline of leadership has experienced rapid growth and boasts an impressive scope of research and theoretical advancement (Fitzsimmons & Callan, 2020). In their study, Dinh et al. (2014) provided 23 themes of leadership theory and 66 different leadership theory domains that illustrate the increasing reach and complexity of contemporary leadership studies. Gardner, et al. (2010) indicated that the field of leadership research has become more diverse, robust, multifaceted, and multi-focused. As a result, this chapter's contribution to the literature on inclusive leadership in HEIs will be based on its relationships with equality, diversity, and inclusion (EDI) and their impact on fostering academic loyalty and innovative work behaviour. This is because most of the literature on inclusive leadership focused mainly on its impact on either the organisational or employee performance, employee satisfaction and involvement with little or no emphasis on the influence of the components (Fagan, et al., 2022; Kuknor & Bhattacharya, 2022). In their study, Nembhard and Edmondson indicated that leaders' inclusiveness reflects behaviour that encourages an appreciation for the disparate and diverse contributions of all members, particularly, in situations in which their input might not be attended to (2006). Moreso, studies have shown that the top-down leadership approach in HEIs is counterproductive and misaligned with a myriad of issues because leaders in the sector seemingly forget they are to provide both managerial and intellectual leadership (Gbobaniyi, et al., 2023). This affirms that the paramount role of academic leaders/managers in HEIs is to use inclusivity as a tool to inspire academics to produce the highest standard of teaching and innovative research, thus ensuring their commitment to innovative work behaviour and staying (i.e., loyalty) at the institution (Aboramadan, et al., 2022; Gbobaniyi, et al., 2023). As a result, this chapter integrates our extant knowledge of EDI and leaders' inclusiveness on their influence on academic loyalty.

2.0 EQUALITY, DIVERSITY, AND INCLUSION

Promoting and delivering EDI in HE leadership is an essential aspect of good people management (Klarsfield, et al., 2016). EDI is acknowledged to be important for HEIs based on two core reasons, first, based on the business case "that it has a positive financial and reputational impact" and second, based on the moral case "that it creates a better society within and outside of the HEI" (Brammer, et al., 2009; Bhopal, 2018). However, it has been argued that EDI policies in HEIs have mostly been used to obscure structural inequalities and as a smokescreen to address or challenge real inequalities (Bhopal, 2023). Additionally, relevant literature has suggested that the reporting and bureaucracy associated with doing EDI have not resulted in real change in HEIs but rather a "lip service" endeavour of leadership engaging in a tick-box exercise or at most only address the related issues for their benefit (Bhopal & Pitkin, 2020).

2.1 Equality

In HEIs, equality is about ensuring that academics have equal opportunities to make the most of their talents and professional lives (Wolbring & Nguyen, 2023). The moral case for building fairer and more inclusive academic teams in HEIs is indisputable: recognising and valuing identity, background, or circumstance. Academics like all other employees have a right to the opportunity to develop their skills and talents to their full potential, work in a safe, supportive, and inclusive environment, be rewarded and recognised for their work and have a meaningful voice (Mullin, 2021). Equality recognises that historically this has not been possible for some groups but now it is being pushed towards social justice and changing the systems for not seeing the deficit in the individual or group. From a leadership/management viewpoint, the achievement of equality of outcomes requires leadership to identify barriers and biases and take targeted action to overcome specific inequalities, discrimination, disadvantages, and marginalisation experienced by certain groups and individuals (Pilkington, 2013). Leadership must be aware that inequality can be manifested through prejudice, oppression, and discrimination, can be direct and indirect, and can also be systemic through behaviour, policies, and cultures (Tatli, et al., 2015).

2.2 Diversity

In the context of HEIs, diversity is defined as the variety of diverse people and ideas within an institution, and the creation of an environment in which people feel involved, respected, valued, connected, and able to bring their 'authentic' selves (e.g., their ideas, backgrounds, values, perspectives) to the team and the HEI (Essandoh & Suflas, 2016). Based on this definition, the diversity of academics in HEIs can be argued as the extent of variety or degree to which the academic team in a faculty or department differs in their ideas, backgrounds, values, and perspectives (Harrison & Klein, 2007). A review of relevant literature identified two main perspectives on its relevance in interprofessional teams. First, the information/decision-making perspective, which suggests that diversity is a proxy for knowledge differences and holds that it provides teams with knowledge assets to enable more comprehensive analysis and informed and innovative solutions (DeDreu & West, 2001). Second, the social identity perspective suggests that the perception of similarities and dissimilarities between members provides a basis for social categorisation. Hornsey (2008) described social categorisation as "the process of dividing different individuals into distinct groups that are represented as a prototypical set of attributes, which are held to characterise one group and differentiate it from another". However, diversity should be viewed from a holistic approach that highlights it is not limited to race, ethnicity, gender, or sexual orientation but the willingness of HEIs to reshape their power structure and leadership/management approach (Wolbring & Nguyen, 2023). This chapter does not underplay the importance of these identities but acknowledges that diversity must not stop there. In the HE, the importance of these identities in the leadership and management team must be seen as this will bring some sense of belonging to the academics who aim to reach such positions in their career at the institution.

Gardenswartz et al. (2010) highlight diversity in four dimensions *personality*, *internal* (age, race, gender, etc.), *external* (religion, educational background, work experience, etc.), and *organisational* (department unit, seniority, management status, etc.). As a result, while a leader can promote individual uniqueness by encouraging diverse contributions to a team, s/he should also promote inclusivity by potentially enhancing positive team outcomes by influencing the social identification processes to promote collaboration and minimise circumstances that arouse intergroup hostility (Mitchell, et al., 2015; Randel et al., 2018). Relevant HEI studies have shown that diversity is beneficial for leadership in decision-making, innovation, and problem-solving as academics bring a diverse range of backgrounds and experiences with them. However, the literature also indicates that the tolerance of difference and having a diverse workforce is not enough, employees need to feel empowered, have a sense of belonging, and feel safe to contribute their ideas and viewpoints and to achieve their full potential (Conner, 2015).

2.3 Inclusion

Inclusion has been argued by scholars that it should come first within the context of EDI because it is that which makes equality and diversity possible (Bossu, et al., 2023; Kornau, et al., 2023). While Shore et al. (2011) defined inclusion "as the degree to which an employee perceives that s/he is an esteemed member of the work group through experiencing treatments that satisfy his or her need for belongingness and uniqueness, Stefani & Blessinger (2017) defined inclusive leadership as the critical capability to leverage diverse thinking in a workforce with increasing diverse knowledge, skills, and talent. These definitions are based on Brewer's (1991) optimal distinctiveness theory and the inclusion framework used to identify how inclusive leaders create an environment of inclusion for followers based on the elements of uniqueness and belongingness. A leader's inclusiveness is argued to be the use of influence-based relationships to enhance team identity (Carmeli, et al., 2010), by enhancing collaboration through the perception of shared goals (Mitchell, et al., 2015). Thus, it enables a balance between an employee's feeling of being like others (belongingness) and being appreciated for their differences (uniqueness) resulting in positive impacts in the workplace (Fagan, et al., 2022). Simply, inclusion within a leadership context requires the removal of barriers, whether attitudinal, structural, or societal, to allow the full and equal participation of all individuals. In a HEI leadership context, removing barriers could require adjustment to policies, environments, habits, and cultures, as well as fostering open communication and trust.

Additionally, this form of leadership has been identified to decrease members' perception of status differences, differences in terms of the respect and influence accorded based on profession, (Anderson, et al., 2001), by convincing subordinates that their varied perspectives and ideas are respected and appreciated (Hirak, et al., 2012). This leadership approach requires the removal of barriers, whether attitudinal, structural, or societal, to allow the full and equal participation of all individuals (Temple & Ylitalo, 2009). The analysis of an inclusive leadership approach based on its engagement and development in HEIs is identified to exist in different forms and levels, including organizational or managerial leadership (executed through formal leadership positions), professional leadership (executed through upholding professional standards and performing in functional roles), intellectual and disciplinary leadership (expanding the boundaries of knowledge and conceptual understanding), personal leadership (based on credibility, charisma, expertise, and other qualities), team leadership (developed through collaborative agendas and working practices) and political leadership (building coalitions, networks, and social capital) (Bolden, et al., 2009). Therefore, the author argues that with an inclusive leadership approach in HEIs, academics are more likely to have increased job satisfaction levels and loyalty because they are the primary and most-valued asset that brings about overall achievement and improvement to the institution (Veli Korkmaz, et al., 2022).

3.0 INCLUSIVE LEADERSHIP AND ACADEMIC LOYALTY

Initially seen as a managerial oversight role, leadership emerges when someone helps others accomplish goals and assumes a pivotal role when faced with a novel challenge (Matzler & Renzl, 2006). The leader provides superior solutions and fosters a safe environment that guides followers toward a new shape. Relationships are the foundation of leadership, and it is an ongoing process of mutual learning and information sharing between superiors and subordinates (Booker & Williams, 2022). The undervaluation of the dynamics of power and politics in forming perception and exercising leadership, however, is revealed by a study of pertinent literature on management and leadership research in HE that is based on psychological and behavioural approaches (Bolden, et al., 2009). An effective leader must be flexible enough to adjust to changing circumstances and make sure that the requirements of their subordinates are fully met to maximise their effectiveness in achieving both personal and group objectives (Juntrasook, et al., 2013). As a result, HE leaders and managers need to be able to enliven and motivate their staff members in both managerial and intellectual domains to engage them in group processes, activities, and decisions that will guarantee appropriate output and standards of quality within the organisation. Research on leader-subordinate interactions in organisational behaviour has shown that trust fostered by a leader affects employee commitment, performance, and satisfaction (Dirks & Ferrin, 2002; Matzler & Renzl, 2006).

In HEIs, although not widely found to be used, studies have shown that compared to ethical, servant, and transformational leadership, inclusive leadership is the most effective style for managing diversity because it is built upon influenced-based relationships (Aboramadan, et al., 2022; Zeng & Xu, 2020). According to the literature, inclusive leadership in HEIs increases performance, by promoting knowledge sharing and open discussion of different perspectives (Kuknor & Bhattacharya, 2022; Michell, et al., 2015). Still, research indicates that only one in three HEI leaders accurately perceive their capacity for inclusive leadership (Stefani & Blessinger, 2018). A third of people think they are more inclusive than people around them think they are, while the other third do not think they can be an inclusive leader because they do not mentor others and challenge the status quo as much as they can to let their subordinates perceive they can support them towards achieving their developmental goals (Bourke, et al., 2020; Michell, et al., 2015). The literature suggests that academic leaders/managers (i.e., Deans, Head of Departments) are faced with challenges towards their inclusive approach which is a critical reason for the disparities in their views. Nevertheless, the research advises managers and leaders to foster followers' psychological safety "through trust" so that they feel free to express their thoughts and participate in group initiatives or organisational change rather than undervaluing their colleagues' talents (Bilimoria & Singer, 2019). Cooperative behaviour, a network-based strategy, improved work outputs, and problem-solving are all made possible by trust (Aguinis, 2011). Furthermore, trust reduces the probability of disagreements, minimizes transaction costs, facilitates the swift formation of ad hoc groups, and promotes the creation of effective crisis management plans. Since there is no single definition of inclusive leadership that is accepted by all, this chapter focuses on expanding on a previous definition that indicates that inclusive leadership is a style of leadership that ensures team members are treated fairly and with respect, are motivated to be creative in their work, and are free to voice their opinions even when they conflict with those of the organization or other people (Bourke, et al., 2020). Thus, the authors go on to say that inclusive leadership is that which encourages academics to be distinctive, fortifies their sense of belonging to the HEI, and persuades academics to endorse the HEI's endeavours and contributions to their advancement (Veli Korkmaz, et al., 2020).

In their study, Allen and Grisaffe made the case that academic loyalty is the psychological state that underlies the interaction between academics and HEIs and influences their choice to stay on staff (Allen & Grisaffe, 2001). Previous research suggests that academics considered their positions as permanent positions after they were hired, and administrators demanded unwavering devotion to the institution (Mehta, et al., 2010). However, as HEIs started to experience globalisation, the concept of academic loyalty changed. Restructuring brought about internationalisation, which resulted in partnerships both locally and internationally, and relocations, which led to the reduction of academic staff due to a variety of needs (Mehta, et al., 2010). Since lifetime employment and devotion are no longer required, the difficulties' manifestation has caused a divergence in the obligations that HEIs have to their academics (Putra, et al., 2019).

The loyalty of an employee to an organisation has been argued to be a manifestation of several dimensions. The internal dimension of employee loyalty, according to Metha et al., is focused on the emotional component (i.e., the sense of caring, affiliation, and commitment), which is said to be the dimension that managers and employers need to foster and appeal to (Mehta, et al., 2010). The research also suggested that loyalty's exterior manifestation—that is, its emotional component—comes in the form of behaviours (Mehta, et al, 2010; Wulandari, et al., 2021). Studies have identified and differentiated multiple dimensions and indicators of employee loyalty (Boussalem, 2014; Wulandari, et al., 2021). For instance, emotional loyalty is indicated to be derived when an employee is aware of the distinctive characteristics of their work, in terms of the degree of independence, urgency, skills needed, availability of supervision and guidance; while, moral loyalty is indicated to be an employee's commitment to remain with an organisation, and, continuous loyalty is the investment value that can be achieved if the employee remains with an organisation (Boussalem, 2014). Furthermore, pertinent research on the relationship between organisational leadership and job satisfaction showed that supportive, non-authoritarian leadership is positively correlated with workplace atmosphere, job happiness, productivity, and loyalty to the organisation (Kim, et al., 2021). In essence, leadership enhances performance by creating an environment in the workplace where workers feel encouraged to grow and achieve their objectives. Therefore, it can be argued that there is a higher chance of increased productivity in settings where academics view leadership as non-authoritative, participatory, inclusion-based, and open to supporting teaching and research activities within that institution. This effect can also extend to the retention of academics and their loyalty to the institution. This is founded on studies showing that a ten per cent rise in the feeling of inclusion raises employees' levels of loyalty, value orientation, and job attendance (Castro, et al., 2018). Therefore, it can be argued that academics become less loyal to the institution and are more likely to look for full- or part-time employment on contractual bases with other HEIs when they feel undervalued, and the leadership is closed off to and unsupportive of their growth goals and objectives.

Four primary factors are utilised to measure the ratings, according to a review of the literature on global HEI rankings: academic performance, research output, faculty quality, and educational quality (Liu & Cheng, 2005). Research has also shown that HEIs may not be able to meet these four primary requirements for good evaluations and high rankings if they do not foster an academic culture that encourages faculty loyalty (McCormack, et al., 2014; Rauhvargers, 2013). Likewise, according to Marconi and Ritze, there is a favourable correlation between a HEI's rankings and several variables that could affect academics' work satisfaction and loyalty, such as the HEI's size, mission, cost per student, and productivity (Gbobaniyi, et al., 2023). The study further emphasised the need for academics to have high levels of loyalty and job satisfaction for a HEI to attain productive efficiency (Marconi & Ritzen, 2015).

4.0 INCLUSIVE LEADERSHIP AND PERCEIVED INSTITUTIONAL SUPPORT (PIS)

Inclusive leadership helps to eliminate negative attitudes and views about race, ethnicity, sex, gender, sexual orientation, lifestyle, socioeconomic class, age, language, religion, disability, and their intersections (Kuknor & Bhattacharya, 2022). Available knowledge indicates that inclusive leaders foster an open and approachable environment for the workforce, ensuring that workers feel psychologically comfortable voicing views that frequently do not align with the organisation's established norms (Carmeli, et al., 2010). In essence, employees who are emotionally committed to their organisation show heightened performance, reduced absenteeism, and a reduced likelihood of quitting their jobs because they feel included, heard, and valued (Musenze & Mayende, 2023). Being valued by the organisation can yield benefits such as approval and respect, pay and promotion, access to information and other forms of aid needed to support an employee to carry out their job properly. The norm of reciprocity allows employees and employers to reconcile these distinctive orientations (Greco, et al., 2019).

Organisational support (OS) theorists suppose that to determine the organisation's readiness to reward increased work effort and to meet socioemotional needs, employees develop beliefs concerning the extent to which the organisation values their contributions and cares about their well-being (Musenze & Mayende, 2023). This theory addresses the psychological processes underlying perceived organisational support (POS) by employees. Eisenberger et al. (1986) discussed that the development of the POS is encouraged by employees' tendency to assign the organisation humanlike characteristics. Furthermore, Levinson (1965) noted that actions taken by agents of the organisation are often viewed as indications of the organisation's intent rather than being attributed to the agents. This personification of the organisation is mostly supported by the organisation's legal, moral, and financial responsibility for the actions of its agents; by its policies, norms, and culture that provide continuity and prescribe role behaviour; and the power the agents exert over individual employees. For this literature, we adapt the perceived organisational support to the perceived institutional support (PIS) to enhance understanding as we focus on HEIs. The authors adopt Gbobaniyi et al. (2023) on the adaptation of the POS to PIS because HEIs are considered differentiated forms of organisations acknowledged globally as part of an overall national innovation system where numerous theoretical, empirical, and normative questions emerge as knowledge (Musenze & Mayende, 2023). Additionally, HEIs, like most organisations, rely on diverse and multidisciplinary individuals with various degrees of knowledge-based assets, though they are more involved in developing, producing, and disseminating knowledge (Middlehurst, et al., 2009). This adaptation of the POS to PIS is used to set the basis for the differentiation and grounded explanation of academics from employees. Though academics are employees of HEIs, their engagements in the learning, teaching, and research activities identify primarily with their individuality and not the HEI (Musselin, 2007).

Likewise, social exchange (SE) theorists have alluded to employment as the trade of effort and loyalty for tangible benefits and social rewards (Ahmad, et al., 2023). When an employer is seen and perceived to treat employees well, the reciprocity norm obliges the return of favourable treatment from the employees to the employer (Riggle, et al., 2009). To the extent that both the employee and the employer apply the reciprocity norm to their relationship, as both parties reciprocate favourable treatment leading to beneficial outcomes for them. Additionally, social exchange theorists argue that resources received from others are more highly valued if they are based on discretionary choice rather than circumstances beyond the donor's control (Ahmad, et al., 2023). As a result, voluntary aid from an HEI to an academic is welcomed as an indication that the HEI and its leadership genuinely value and respect them which can influence their job satisfaction, retention, and loyalty. Institutional rewards and favourable job conditions such as pay, promotions, job enrichment (i.e., research grants and funding; conferences, workshops, and training attendance) and influence over institutional policies contribute more to PIS if academics believe it is a result of the HEI's voluntary actions, as opposed to external constraints such as union negotiations or governmental health and safety regulations (Rhoades & Eisenberger, 2002). As faculty or departmental managers act as HEI agents, the academic's receipt of favourable treatment from a line manager contributes to PIS. However, the receipt of favourable treatment from a direct line leadership depends on the leadership style or approach and strength of the relationship between the manager and subordinate, as opposed to viewing the line manager's actions as idiosyncratic. The literature has shown that for HEIs' leadership/management to manifest such a relationship with their academics they must look towards ensuring inclusivity which will allow them to understand the needs of their academics and provide for them.

4.1 Inclusive Leadership and PIS Antecedents.

In line with the OS theory (Eisenberger et al., 1986), to increase PIS and loyalty, academics through leadership should receive from their HEIs three general forms of favourable treatment. However, for leaders/managers to be able to bring about these treatments to their subordinates, they must have an inclusive approach that will endow these three treatments.

(i). Fairness – This is based on how procedural justice is used in determining the distribution of resources among academics at the departmental or faculty level (Greenberg, 1990). Relevant literature suggested that repeated instances of fairness in decisions concerning resource distribution should have a strong cumulative effect on PIS by indicating a concern for academic welfare, workload and distribution, and conference and research grants (Ahmad, et al., 2023). Relevant literature distinguished between structural and social aspects of procedural justice (Mitchell, et al., 2012). The structural aspect involves the HEI's formal rules and policies concerning decisions that affect employees, including an acceptable notification period before decisions are implemented, receipt of accurate information, and voice (i.e., employee input in the decision process) (Cropanzano, et al., 2017). The social aspects otherwise called interactional justice, involve the quality of interpersonal treatment in resource allocation. Social aspects include treating employees with dignity and respect and providing them with information concerning how outcomes are determined (Cropanzano, et al., 2017).

Related to fairness and based on procedural justice, is the concept of perceived organisational politics. Organisational politics refers to attempts by a group or individual to influence others in ways that promote self-interest, often at the expense of rewards for group or individual merit or the betterment of the organisation (Mehmood, et al., 2023). Workplace politics is a fact of organisational life, as a result, scholars have argued that political behaviour can have both positive and negative outcomes for leadership and followership (Landells & Albrecht, 2017, 2019). Research indicates that workplace or organisational politics in most cases is detrimental to employees' engagement, performance, trust, and loyalty. Academics in faculties or departments that are engrained in politics have been found to have a negative approach to PIS and a low perception of fair procedures and outcomes thus lowering their loyalty, job satisfaction and performance (Hossen, et al., 2020; Landells & Albrecht, 2017, 2019).

(ii). Line manager support – Academics have been found to form perceptions concerning their valuation by their department or faculty and they develop an overview concerning the degree to which their line management values their contributions and cares about their well-being (Gbobaniyi, et al., 2023). This is because line managers act as agents of the institution, having responsibility for directing and evaluating subordinates' performance, thus making employees view their line manager's favourable or unfavourable actions and behaviours toward them as indicative of the institution's support (Levinson, 1965). In the context of HEIs, academics understand that line managers' (i.e., programme leaders, departmental heads) evaluations of subordinates are often conveyed to upper management, further contributing to associating line management support with PIS. As a result, based on the literature, support from line management becomes assessed with related measures involving leader-member exchange (Conner, 2015).

(iii). Institutional rewards and job conditions – Relevant literature has shown that human resources practices showing recognition of employee contributions are positively related to POS (Riggle, et al., 2009). Related studies on HEIs concerning POS or PIS have indicated its effect on a variety of rewards and job conditions, e.g., awards, recognition, promotions, autonomy, job security, job-related stressors, and access to professional development and training i.e., research funding and grants and funds for conferences (Bilimoria & Singer, 2019; Musenze & Mayende, 2023).

Based on the OS theory, favourable opportunities for rewards contribute to PIS and serve to convey a positive valuation of an academic's contributions to their department, faculty, and the institution (Rhoades & Eisenberger, 2002). Unlike other forms of employees in workplaces, academics are one of those that reward based on pay is their least motivator, this is because of their mindset that they are top achievers. Academics have been found to favour being recognized and valued for their performance and contribution to their HEI through awards, promotions, and autonomy (Eisenberger, et al., 1999; Putra, et al., 2019). By autonomy, we mean an academic's perceived control over their job, including scheduling, work procedures, and task variety. Autonomy indicates HEIs' trust in their academics to decide how they will carry out their job, thereby increasing PIS (Eisenberger, et al., 1999). Furthermore, when an academic perceives that the HEI recognizes excellence and provides necessary support towards achieving their goals, the likelihood of loyalty to the institution increases. This will further influence their decision to remain in the HEI longer and be willing to claim the HEI as part of their societal identity to keep up with the demands in their professional or social circle (Gbobaniyi, et al., 2023; Wulandari, et al., 2021).

On *job security*, the literature indicates that HEIs tend to assure job security which tends to provide a strong indication of PIS for academics, particularly in recent years when downsizing has become prevalent in many other sectors (Anwar, et al., 2021). On *job-related stressors* are work-related demands with which employees feel unable to cope and they feel are controllable by the organisation (Brief & George, 2020). In HEIs, studies identified three main types of work-related stressors on academics that tend to have negative effects on PIS, including work overload, involving demands that exceed what an academic can reasonably accomplish at a given time, role ambiguity, involving the absence of clear information about one's job responsibilities; and role conflict, involving mutually incompatible job responsibilities (Rhoades & Eisenberger, 2002). The higher the job-related stressors on an employee the lower the PIS. Lastly, on *access to professional development and training*, Wayne et al. (1997) suggested that access to professional development and training is a discretionary practice communicating an investment in the academic by the HEI, thus leading to increased PIS.

4.2 Inclusive Leadership and PIS Consequences.

(i) *Institutional Commitment* - Based on the reciprocity norm, as academics perceive and receive the institutional support they need through the HEI and leaders, PIS in return creates a felt obligation to also care about the HEI's welfare (Eisenberger, et al., 2001; Greco, et al., 2019). The obligation to exchange caring for caring should enhance employees' affective commitment and trust to the personified organisation

(Ahmad, et al., 2023). PIS should also increase affective commitment by fulfilling an academic's socioemotional needs (i.e., affiliation and emotional support) that will strengthen their loyalty to the organisation (Eisenberger et al., 1986). Additionally, it is suggested that while PIS might increase trust and loyalty towards the institution, it might reduce feelings of entrapment (i.e., continuance commitment) which occur when employees are forced to stay with an organisation because of the high costs of leaving (Salah El-Din, et al., 2021).

(ii) *Job-related Affection* – While the relevant literature has shown that inclusive leadership in HEIs allow academics to develop PIS, trust, and loyalty (Gbobaniyi, et al., 2023), studies have also hypothesised that the PIS influences academics' general affective reactions to their jobs, including job satisfaction and positive mood (Riggle, et al., 2009). According to Witt (1992), job satisfaction is an employee's overall affect-laden attitude toward their job. As a result, it can be argued that as inclusive leadership influences PIS, PIS will be able to contribute to an employee's overall job satisfaction by meeting socioemotional needs, increasing performance-reward expectancies, and signalling the availability of aid when needed (Nembhard & Edmondson, 2006; Salah El-Din, et al., 2021).

(iii) *Job Involvement* – This refers to the identification with an interest in the

specific work one performs (Cropanzano, et al., 2017). HEIs that promote and ensure inclusivity in their leadership are more likely to enhance PIS which can transcend to increasing not only the academic's loyalty to the institution but also advance their interest in their work (Fagan, et al., 2022).

(iv) *Performance* – As discussed in previous sections, inclusive leadership enhances academics' PIS which in turn should increase the performance of standard job activities and actions favourable to the HEI that go beyond assigned responsibilities (Hirak, et al., 2012). In HE, such extra-role activities include aiding fellow academics in the community of practice, offering constructive suggestions, taking actions that not only protect the HEI from risk but bolster its recognition nationally and internationally, and gaining knowledge and skills that are beneficial to the HEI (George & Brief, 1992).

(v) *Strains* – Knowledge from the relevant literature suggests that inclusive leadership and PIS in HEIs may reduce aversive psychological and psychosomatic reactions (i.e., strains) to stressors by indicating the availability of material aid and emotional support when needed (Brief & George, 2020; Conner, 2015; Nembhard & Edmondson, 2006).

(vi) *Academic loyalty "Desire to remain"* – Studies that have examined the relationship between POS/PIS, inclusive leadership, and the employees' loyalty or desire to remain with the organisation or HEI have indicated positive effects (e.g., Gbobaniyi, et al., 2023; Hellman, 2023; Matzler & Renzl, 2006).

5.0 BARRIERS TO INCLUSIVE LEADERSHIP IN HEIs

(i). Biases – everyone has biases, with most being unconscious and impossible to remove completely. Biases influence how people work with others, especially in pressured situations and environments such as in HEIs. Examples of some biases academics in HE have identified to face include - the Halo Effect (i.e., the tendency to place another person in higher regard after learning something impressive about them); ageism (i.e., the tendency to have negative feelings about another person based in their age which often occurs with academics that are much older or younger than the average age in faculty or department); looks bias (i.e., the tendency to place someone who's more physically attractive than average, according to cultural standards, as more competent or favourable than people of average or below average perceived physical attractiveness) (Bourke, et al., 2020; Whitfield, 2024).

(ii). Diversity of thought – this means recognising that people are diverse from one another, in terms of their, thinking styles and perspectives; experiences and backgrounds; work styles (decision-making, communication, leading); and personality types (Eurich, 2018).

(iii). The self-perception trap – many leaders/managers perceive themselves to have more inclusive behaviour than they do, making them do less than they could to promote, encourage, and develop an inclusive environment (Bourke, et al., 2020). The study by Bourke et al. (2020) showed that a third of leaders believe they are more inclusive than they are perceived by those around them. It is assumed that part of the problem with inclusive leadership is that organisational leaders/managers do not have the tools or training on inclusive behaviours (Bardhan & Gower, 2022; Hellman, 2023). This is the reason HEIs are being encouraged and urged to cultivate, use, and further develop an inclusive leadership approach based on their inherent diversity, because being an educational environment, they can be able to research, design, and train leaders and managers on inclusive behaviours (Bolden, et al., 2009; Handforth, 2018).

(iv). Organisations are not designed to support inclusion – the systems, processes, and cultures of most organisations do not support inclusive behaviours. The relevant literature argued that corporations have historically placed a high value on efficiency, which is usually achieved through a decision-making process that involves fewer people and challenges, which is the opposite of diversity (Booker & Williams, 2022; Mitchell, et al., 2015; Özbilgin, 2023).

(v). Inclusive skills and behaviours have not been acquired – Inclusive leadership is a sought-after skill set that is increasingly becoming a critical capability in some industries and sectors (Booker & Williams, 2022). Unfortunately, not every leader/ manager has this skill set, this is because only 1 in 3 organisations have a strategy for training leaders to be inclusive which has been argued to be the reason that 33% of leaders lack confidence in inclusion (Kuknor & Bhattacharya, 2022).

6.0 PRACTICAL IMPLICATION AND RECOMMENDATION FOR INCLUSIVE LEADERSHIP ON ACADEMIC LOYALTY

This chapter contributes to practice through recommendations to HEIs and their leaders. To start with, this literature has gained insights into the perception of academics and HEI leadership regarding inclusive leadership and academic loyalty. Although there are studies on the perception of organisational support towards organisational loyalty (Mehmood, et al., 2023), the literature on perceived institutional support (PIS) on the loyalty of academics to their HEIs is scarce. This chapter shines a light on PIS, which is important because academic managers or leaders are change agents in working towards inclusivity Providing more insights into not only what leaders and managers see but also what academics observe as obstructing and enabling inclusivity advances available knowledge and fills a gap in the existing literature. Advancing discussions on these insights helps toward enhancing the facilitators for inclusivity and inclusive leadership in HEIs. For instance, Aboramadan et al. indicated that inclusive leadership creates opportunities for academics to engage in the decision-making process, which implies that they will act in a collaborative and participatory manner and will go beyond their required work in terms of extra-role behaviours thus having positive implication on their loyalty and extension of stay in the HEI (2020).

Additionally, this chapter is of value because it brings together a variety of studies on inclusive leadership and further contributes to the existing literature on equality, diversity, and inclusion. Based on this, this literature provides further insight that inclusive leadership not only provides avenues but also ensures continuous dialogue and collaboration which empowers academic colleagues, thus significantly affecting loyalty (Al Wali, et al., 2023; Javed, et al., 2019; Wulandari, et al., 2021).

Finally, this chapter contributes to the theory of the PIS and that it plays a significant role in mediating the connection between inclusive leadership and academic loyalty (Gbobaniyi, et al., 2023). While findings in research indicate that leaders who possess a higher level of inclusive leadership can influence greater loyalty from academics, HEIs that provide institutional support for their academics towards achieving their developmental growth goals have also been found to have a great influence on their academics (Gbobaniyi, et al., 2023). Therefore, while leaders in HEIs should motivate themselves to engage in further self and leadership developments to attain a higher level of inclusivity in their leadership approach, HEIs should encourage their leaders towards this personal development objective. This will have an increased effect on academics' psychological level of the institution's perceived support and their loyalty and retention in the institution.

7.0 CONCLUSION AND SUGGESTIONS FOR FUTURE RESEARCH

This chapter focused on the relationship between inclusivity, from a leadership perspective in HEIs, perceived institutional support (PIS), and academic loyalty. This is because, despite the impressive development within the discipline of leadership, there remained gaps to be explored, particularly the perceived impasse regarding how research on inclusion concepts has been conducted in HE environments. As a result, this chapter suggests some future research directions towards a mixed methodology that would enable an in-depth analysis of the influence of PIS on the impact of inclusive leadership. Additionally, with the growing context of the use of PIS in HEI related studies, future research should explore the influence of PIS on the empowerment of academics. This is because empowerment has been identified to have a positive and significant effect on loyalty.

Based on the OS theory the chapter recontextualised knowledge on the POS focused on organisation to the PIS to focus on HEIs. As a result, the PIS supposes that academics personify the HEI, infer the extent to which the HEI values their contributions and cares about their well-being, and reciprocate such perceived support with increased commitment, loyalty, and performance. Like studies that examined the role of POS in the relationship between various types of favourable treatment and outcomes that are beneficial to employees and the organisation, the authors contribute to the literature on the PIS and its relationship with inclusive leadership towards academic loyalty. However, to provide the needed grounded understanding of the effect of inclusive leadership in HEI, we provided background knowledge on EDI through the review of relevant literature (Wulandari, et al., 2021).

Considering that leaders are one of the most important sources who significantly build norms and rules in a HEI, the leader's characteristics, such as inclusivity, would critically influence employees' perceptions of institutional support. This chapter, therefore, will help HEIs leaders and managers recognise the influence of inclusive leadership on PIS and its corresponding effect on the loyalty of academics. HEIs want loyalty from their academics towards achieving the vision, mission, and objectives of the institution. To achieve this, HEIs' leadership must ensure they apply inclusive strategies to increase PIS which in turn will impact academic loyalty. We provide some understanding towards PIS based on its antecedents (i.e., fairness, line manager support, institutional rewards and job conditions, and job security) and consequences (i.e., institutional commitment; job-related affection, job involvement, performance, strains, and academic loyalty). If the level of inclusive leadership is low, the positive influence of equality and diversity practices on the academics' perceptions would be eroded. In other words, academics are likely to regard the level of inclusive leadership as a practical gauge to evaluate whether the inclusion values of their institution are authentic. Therefore, top management in departments and faculties in HEIs must not only understand the need to increase the loyalty of their academics based on the effect of PIS but it should be grounded on the degree of inclusive leadership.

REFERENCES

Aboramadan, M., Dahleez, K. A., & Farao, C. (2022). Inclusive leadership and extra-role behaviours in higher education: Does organizational learning mediate the relationship? *International Journal of Educational Management*, 36(4), 397–418.

Aguinis, H. (2011). Organizational responsibility: Doing good and doing well. In Zedeck, S. (Ed.), *Handbook of Industrial and Organisational Psychology*. APA. DOI: 10.1037/12171-024

Ahmad, R., Nawaz, M. R., Ishaq, M. I., Khan, M. M., & Ashraf, H. A. (2023). Social exchange theory: Systematic review and future directions. *Frontiers in Psychology*, 13, 1015921. DOI: 10.3389/fpsyg.2022.1015921 PMID: 36710813

Al Wali, J., Muthuveloo, R., Teoh, A. P., & Al Wali, W. (2023). Disentangling the relationship between employees' dynamic capabilities, innovative work behavior and job performance in public hospitals. *International Journal of Innovation Science*, 15(2), 368–384. DOI: 10.1108/IJIS-01-2022-0012

Allen, N. J., & Grisaffe, D. B. (2001). Employee commitment to the organization and customer reactions: Mapping the linkages. *Human Resource Management Review*, 11(3), 209–236. DOI: 10.1016/S1053-4822(00)00049-8

Anderson, C. O. P. J., Keltner, D., & Kring, A. M. (2001). Who attains social status? Effects of personality and physical attractiveness in social groups. *Journal of Personality and Social Psychology*, 81(1), 116–132. DOI: 10.1037/0022-3514.81.1.116 PMID: 11474718

Anwar, S., Chandio, J. A., Ashraf, M., Bhutto, S. A., Anwar, S., Chandio, J. A., & Bhutto, S. A. (2021). Does transformational leadership affect employees' commitment? A mediation analysis of perceived organizational support using VB-SEM. *International Journal of Disaster Recovery and Business Continuity*, 12, 734–746.

Aung, P. N., & Hallinger, P. (2023). Research on sustainability leadership in higher education: A scoping review. *International Journal of Sustainability in Higher Education*, 24(3), 517–534. DOI: 10.1108/IJSHE-09-2021-0367

Bardhan, N., & Gower, K. (2022). *The role of leadership in building inclusive diversity in public relations*. Taylor & Francis. DOI: 10.4324/9781003170020

Bhopal, K. (2018). *White privilege: The myth of a post-racial society*. Policy Press.

Bhopal, K. (2023). 'We can talk the talk, but we're not allowed to walk the walk': The role of equality and diversity staff in higher education institutions in England. *Higher Education*, 85(2), 325–339. DOI: 10.1007/s10734-022-00835-7

Bhopal, K., & Pitkin, C. (2020). 'Same old story, just a different policy': Race and policy making in higher education in the UK. *Race, Ethnicity and Education*, 23(4), 530–547. DOI: 10.1080/13613324.2020.1718082

Bilimoria, D., & Singer, L. T. (2019). Institutions developing excellence in academic leadership (IDEAL): A partnership to advance gender equity, diversity, and inclusion in academic STEM. *Equality, Diversity and Inclusion*, 38(3), 362–381. DOI: 10.1108/EDI-10-2017-0209

Bolden, R., Petrov, G., Gosling, J., & Bryman, A. (2009). Leadership in higher education: Facts, fictions, and futures — Introduction to the special issue. *Leadership*, 5(3), 291–298. DOI: 10.1177/1742715009337761

Booker, D. L., & Williams, M. R. (2022). An inclusive leadership model insights from the tech industry. *Advances in Developing Human Resources*, 24(4), 263–274. DOI: 10.1177/15234223221118955

Bossu, C., Iniesto, F., Vladimirschi, V., Jordan, K., & Pete, J. (2023). GO-GN Guidelines for Equity Diversity and Inclusion in Open Education with a focus on Africa and Latin America.

Bourke, J., Titus, A., & Espedido, A. (2020). The key to inclusive leadership. *Harvard Business Review*, ●●●, 6.

Brammer, S., Millington, A., & Pavelin, S. (2009). Corporate reputation and women on the board. *British Journal of Management*, 20(1), 17–29. DOI: 10.1111/j.1467-8551.2008.00600.x

Brief, A. P., & George, J. M. (2020). Psychological stress and the workplace: A brief comment on Lazarus' outlook. In *Occupational stress* (pp. 15–19). CRC Press. DOI: 10.1201/9781003072430-3

Bryman, A., & Lilley, S. (2009). Leadership researchers on leadership in higher education. *Leadership*, 5(3), 331–346. DOI: 10.1177/1742715009337764

Carmeli, A., Reiter-Palmon, R., & Ziv, E. (2010). Inclusive leadership and employee involvement in creative tasks in the workplace: The mediating role of psychological safety. *Creativity Research Journal*, 22(3), 250–260. DOI: 10.1080/10400419.2010.504654

Castro, D. R., Anseel, F., Kluger, A. N., Lloyd, K. J., & Turjeman-Levi, Y. (2018). Mere listening effect on creativity and the mediating role of psychological safety. *Psychology of Aesthetics, Creativity, and the Arts*, 12(4), 489–502. DOI: 10.1037/aca0000177

Charalampous, C. A., & Papademetriou, C. D. (2019). Intermediate inverted leadership: The inclusive leader's model. *International Journal of Leadership in Education*.

Cissna, K. (2020). *Self-actualized leadership: Exploring the intersection of inclusive leadership and workplace spirituality at a faith-based institution of higher education* (Publication No.27831823) [Doctoral dissertation, Pepperdine University]. ProQuest Dissertations Publishing.

Conner, T. (2015). Relationships and Authentic Collaboration: Perceptions of a Building Leadership Team. *Leadership and Research in Education*, 2(1), 12–24.

Cropanzano, R., Anthony, E. L., Daniels, S. R., & Hall, A. V. (2017). Social exchange theory: A critical review with theoretical remedies. *The Academy of Management Annals*, 11(1), 479–516. DOI: 10.5465/annals.2015.0099

Currie, G., Humphreys, M., Ucbasaran, D., & McManus, S. (2008). Entrepreneurial leadership in the English public sector: Paradox or possibility. *Public Administration*, 86(4), 987–1008. DOI: 10.1111/j.1467-9299.2008.00736.x

De Dreu, C. K., & West, M. A. (2001). Minority dissent and team innovation: The importance of participation in decision making. *The Journal of Applied Psychology*, 86(6), 1191–1201. DOI: 10.1037/0021-9010.86.6.1191 PMID: 11768061

Dinh, J. E., Lord, R. G., Gardner, W. L., Meuser, J. D., Liden, R. C., & Hu, J. (2014). Leadership theory and research in the new millennium: Current theoretical trends and changing perspectives. *The Leadership Quarterly*, 25(1), 36–62. DOI: 10.1016/j.leaqua.2013.11.005

Dirks, K. T., & Ferrin, D. L. (2002). Trust in leadership: Meta-analytic findings and implications for research and practice. *The Journal of Applied Psychology*, 87(4), 611–628. DOI: 10.1037/0021-9010.87.4.611 PMID: 12184567

Drugus, D., & Landøy, A. (2014). Leadership in higher education.

Eisenberger, R., Armeli, S., Rexwinkel, B., Lynch, P. D., & Rhoades, L. (2001). Reciprocation of perceived organizational support. *The Journal of Applied Psychology*, 86(1), 42–51. DOI: 10.1037/0021-9010.86.1.42 PMID: 11302232

Eisenberger, R., Huntington, R., Hutchison, S., & Sowa, D. (1986). Perceived organizational support. *The Journal of Applied Psychology*, 71(3), 500–507. DOI: 10.1037/0021-9010.71.3.500

Eisenberger, R., Rhoades, L., & Cameron, J. (1999). Does pay for performance increase or decrease perceived self-determination and intrinsic motivation? *Journal of Personality and Social Psychology*, 77(5), 1026–1040. DOI: 10.1037/0022-3514.77.5.1026

Essandoh, V., & Suflas, S. (2016). The leader's role in diversity and inclusion: Transformational leadership. Law Week Colorado., Retrieved December 20, 2023, from.

Eurich, T. (2018). What self-awareness really is (and how to cultivate it). *Harvard Business Review*, ●●●, 4.

Fagan, H. A. S., Wells, B., Guenther, S., & Matkin, G. S. (2022). THE PATH TO INCLUSION: A Literature Review of Attributes and Impacts of Inclusive Leaders. *Journal of Leadership Education*, 21(1), 88–113. DOI: 10.12806/V21/I1/R7

Fitzsimmons, T. W., & Callan, V. J. (2020). The diversity gap in leadership: What are we missing in current theorizing? *The Leadership Quarterly*, 31(4), 101347. DOI: 10.1016/j.leaqua.2019.101347

Gardenswartz, L., Cherbosque, J., & Rowe, A. (2010). Emotional intelligence and diversity: A model for differences in the workplace. *Journal of Psychological Issues in Organizational Culture*, 1(1), 74–84. DOI: 10.1002/jpoc.20002

Gardner, W. L., Lowe, K. B., Moss, T. W., Mahoney, K. T., & Cogliser, C. C. (2010). Scholarly leadership of the study of leadership: A review of The Leadership Quarterly's second decade, 2000–2009. *The Leadership Quarterly*, 21(6), 922–958. DOI: 10.1016/j.leaqua.2010.10.003

Gbobaniyi, O., Srivastava, S., Oyetunji, A. K., Amaechi, C. V., Beddu, S. B., & Ankita, B. (2023). The Mediating Effect of Perceived Institutional Support on Inclusive Leadership and Academic Loyalty in Higher Education. *Sustainability (Basel)*, 15(17), 13195. DOI: 10.3390/su151713195

George, J. M., & Brief, A. P. (1992). Feeling good–doing good: A conceptual analysis of the mood at work–organizational spontaneity relationship. *Psychological Bulletin*, 112(2), 310–329. DOI: 10.1037/0033-2909.112.2.310 PMID: 1454897

Greco, L. M., Whitson, J. A., O'Boyle, E. H., Wang, C. S., & Kim, J. (2019). An eye for an eye? A meta-analysis of negative reciprocity in organizations. *The Journal of Applied Psychology*, 104(9), 1117–1143. DOI: 10.1037/apl0000396 PMID: 30762379

Gronn, P. (2009). Leadership configurations. *Leadership*, 5(3), 381–394. DOI: 10.1177/1742715009337770

Handforth, R. (2018). Considering the 'leaky pipeline' – are we missing the point on leadership diversity? WONKHE. Available: https://wonkhe.com/blogs/considering-the-leaky-pipeline-are-we-missing-the-point-on-leadership-diversity/ Accessed: 22/01/2024.

Hellman, Y. (2023). Inclusive Leadership: Guide and Tools. In *Inclusive Leadership: Equity and Belonging in Our Communities* (pp. 133-143). Emerald Publishing Limited.

Hirak, R., Peng, A. C., Carmeli, A., & Schaubroeck, J. M. (2012). Linking leader inclusiveness to work unit performance: The importance of psychological safety and learning from failures. *The Leadership Quarterly*, 23(1), 107–117. DOI: 10.1016/j.leaqua.2011.11.009

Hollander, E. (2012). *Inclusive leadership: The essential leader-follower relationship*. Routledge. DOI: 10.4324/9780203809914

Hornsey, M. J. (2008). Social identity theory and self-categorization theory: A historical review. *Social and Personality Psychology Compass*, 2(1), 204–222. DOI: 10.1111/j.1751-9004.2007.00066.x

Javed, B., Naqvi, S. M. M. R., Khan, A. K., Arjoon, S., & Tayyeb, H. H. (2019). Impact of inclusive leadership on innovative work behavior: The role of psychological safety. *Journal of Management & Organization*, 25(1), 117–136. DOI: 10.1017/jmo.2017.3

Juntrasook, A., Nairn, K., Bond, C., & Spronken-Smith, R. (2013). Unpacking the narrative of non-positional leadership in academia: Hero and/or victim? *Higher Education Research & Development*, 32(2), 201–213. DOI: 10.1080/07294360.2011.643858

Kezar, A. J. (Ed.). (2023). *Rethinking leadership in a complex, multicultural, and global environment: New concepts and models for higher education*. Taylor & Francis. DOI: 10.4324/9781003446842

Kim, B. J., Kim, M. J., & Kim, T. H. (2021). "The power of ethical leadership": The influence of corporate social responsibility on creativity, the mediating function of psychological safety, and the moderating role of ethical leadership. *International Journal of Environmental Research and Public Health*, 18(6), 2968. DOI: 10.3390/ijerph18062968 PMID: 33799360

Klarsfeld, A., Ng, E. S., Booysen, L., Christiansen, L. C., & Kuvaas, B. (2016). Comparative equality and diversity: Main findings and research gaps. *Cross Cultural & Strategic Management*, 23(3), 394–412. DOI: 10.1108/CCSM-03-2016-0083

Kogan, M., & Hanney, S. (2000). *Reforming higher education* (Vol. 50). Jessica Kingsley Publishers.

Kornau, A., Knappert, L., Tatli, A., & Sieben, B. (2023). Contested fields of equality, diversity, and inclusion at work: An institutional work lens on power relations and actors' strategies in Germany and Turkey. *International Journal of Human Resource Management*, 34(12), 2481–2515. DOI: 10.1080/09585192.2022.2086014

Kuknor, S. C., & Bhattacharya, S. (2022). Inclusive leadership: New age leadership to foster organizational inclusion. *European Journal of Training and Development*, 46(9), 771–797. DOI: 10.1108/EJTD-07-2019-0132

Landells, E. M., & Albrecht, S. L. (2017). The positives and negatives of organizational politics: A qualitative study. *Journal of Business and Psychology*, 32(1), 41–58. DOI: 10.1007/s10869-015-9434-5

Landells, E. M., & Albrecht, S. L. (2019). Perceived organizational politics, engagement, and stress: The mediating influence of meaningful work. *Frontiers in Psychology*, 10, 1612. DOI: 10.3389/fpsyg.2019.01612 PMID: 31354596

Levinson, H. (1965). Reciprocation: The relationship between man and organization. *Administrative Science Quarterly*, 9(4), 370–390. DOI: 10.2307/2391032

Liu, N. C., & Cheng, Y. (2005). The academic ranking of world universities. *Higher Education in Europe*, 30(2), 127–136. DOI: 10.1080/03797720500260116

Macfarlane, B., Bolden, R., & Watermeyer, R. (2024). Three perspectives on leadership in higher education: Traditionalist, reformist, pragmatist. *Higher Education*, •••, 1–22. DOI: 10.1007/s10734-023-01174-x

Marconi, G., & Ritzen, J. (2015). Determinants of international university rankings scores. *Applied Economics*, 47(57), 6211–6227. DOI: 10.1080/00036846.2015.1068921

Matzler, K., & Renzl, B. (2006). The relationship between interpersonal trust, employee satisfaction, and employee loyalty. *Total Quality Management & Business Excellence*, 17(10), 1261–1271. DOI: 10.1080/14783360600753653

McCormack, J., Propper, C., & Smith, S. (2014). Herding cats? Management and university performance. *Economic Journal (London)*, 124(578), F534–F564. DOI: 10.1111/ecoj.12105

McFarlane, B. (2014). Challenging leaderism. *Higher Education Research & Development*, 33(1), 1–4. DOI: 10.1080/07294360.2014.864590

Mehmood, I., Macky, K., & Le Fevre, M. (2023). High-involvement work practices, employee trust and engagement: The mediating role of perceived organisational politics. *Personnel Review*, 52(4), 1321–1344. DOI: 10.1108/PR-03-2021-0151

Mehta, S., Singh, T., Bhakar, S. S., & Sinha, B. (2010). Employee loyalty towards organization—A study of academician. *International Journal of Business Management and Economic Research*, 1(1), 98–108.

Mitchell, M. S., Cropanzano, R. S., & Quisenberry, D. M. (2012). Social exchange theory, exchange resources, and interpersonal relationships: A modest resolution of theoretical difficulties. *Handbook of social resource theory: Theoretical extensions, empirical insights, and social applications*, 99-118.

Mitchell, R., Boyle, B., Parker, V., Giles, M., Chiang, V., & Joyce, P. (2015). Managing inclusiveness and diversity in teams: How leader inclusiveness affects performance through status and team identity. *Human Resource Management*, 54(2), 217–239. DOI: 10.1002/hrm.21658

Montani, F., Odoardi, C., & Battistelli, A. (2014). Individual and contextual determinants of innovative work behaviour: Proactive goal generation matters. *Journal of Occupational and Organizational Psychology*, 87(4), 645–670. DOI: 10.1111/joop.12066

Mullin, A. E., Coe, I. R., Gooden, E. A., Tunde-Byass, M., & Wiley, R. E. (2021, November). Inclusion, diversity, equity, and accessibility: From organizational responsibility to leadership competency. [). Sage CA: Los Angeles, CA: SAGE Publications.]. *Healthcare Management Forum*, 34(6), 311–315. DOI: 10.1177/08404704211038232 PMID: 34535064

Musenze, I. A., & Mayende, T. S. (2023). Ethical leadership (EL) and innovative work behavior (IWB) in public universities: Examining the moderating role of perceived organizational support (POS). *Management Research Review*, 46(5), 682–701. DOI: 10.1108/MRR-12-2021-0858

Musselin, C. (2007). Are universities specific organisations? In *Towards a multiversity*, Universities between Global Trends and National Traditions; Krücken, G., Kosmützky, A., Torka, M., Eds.; Transcript Verlag: Bielefeld, Germany, 2007; pp. 63–84. Available online: https://library.oapen.org/bitstream/handle/20.500.12657/ 22777 /1007- 385.pdf? sequence=1#page=64 (accessed on 20 January 2024).

Najmaei, A., & Sadeghinejad, Z. (2019). Inclusive leadership: a scientometric assessment of an emerging field. In *Diversity within Diversity Management: Types of Diversity in Organizations* (pp. 221–245). Emerald Publishing Limited.

Nembhard, I. M., & Edmondson, A. C. (2006). Making it safe: The effects of leader inclusiveness and professional status on psychological safety and improvement efforts in health care teams. *Journal of Organizational Behavior: The International Journal of Industrial. Journal of Organizational Behavior*, 27(7), 941–966. DOI: 10.1002/job.413

Özbilgin, M. F. (2023). *Diversity: A key idea for business and society*. Taylor & Francis. DOI: 10.4324/9780367824044

Pilkington, A. (2013). The interacting dynamics of institutional racism in higher education. *Race, Ethnicity and Education*, 16(2), 225–245. DOI: 10.1080/13613324.2011.646255

Putra, B. N. K., Jodi, I. W. G. A. S., & Prayoga, I. M. S. (2019). Compensation, Organizational Culture and Job Satisfaction In Affecting Employee Loyalty. *Journal of International Conference Proceedings*, 2(3), 11–15. DOI: 10.32535/jicp.v2i3.638

Quayson, F. (2019). The importance of inclusive leadership practice in higher education administration. *Interdisciplinary Journal of Advances in Research in Education, 1*(1).

Randel, A., Galvin, B., Shore, L., Holcombe Ehrhart, K., Chung, B., Dean, M., & Kedharnath, U. (2018). Inclusive leadership: Realizing positive outcomes through belonging and being valued for uniqueness. *Human Resource Management Review*, 28(2), 190–203. DOI: 10.1016/j.hrmr.2017.07.002

Rauhvargers, A. (2013). *Global university rankings and their impact: Report II*. European University Association.

Rhoades, L., & Eisenberger, R. (2002). Perceived organizational support: A review of the literature. *The Journal of Applied Psychology*, 87(4), 698–714. DOI: 10.1037/0021-9010.87.4.698 PMID: 12184574

Riggle, R. J., Edmondson, D. R., & Hansen, J. D. (2009). A meta-analysis of the relationship between perceived organizational support and job outcomes: 20 years of research. *Journal of Business Research*, 62(10), 1027–1030. DOI: 10.1016/j.jbusres.2008.05.003

Salah El-Din, D. N. S. M., & Al-kiyumi, D. A. R. A. (2021). Perceived organizational support for faculty members at Sultan Qaboos University: A field study. *Faculty of Education Journal Alexandria University*, 31(4), 109–145.

Sastry, T., & Bekhradnia, B. (2007). *Higher Education, Skills, and Employer Engagement*. HEPI.

Srivastava, S. (2011). Job burnout and managerial effectiveness relationship: Moderating effects of locus of control and perceived organisational support: An empirical study on Indian managers. *Asian Journal of Management Research*, 2(1), 329–347.

Stamper, C. L., & Masterson, S. S. (2002). Insider or outsider? How employee perceptions of insider status affect their work behavior. *Journal of Organizational Behavior: The International Journal of Industrial. Journal of Organizational Behavior*, 23(8), 875–894. DOI: 10.1002/job.175

Stefani, L., & Blessinger, P. (2018). Inclusive Leadership in Higher Education. *Journal of International Management*, 7(1).

Tatli, A., Nicolopoulou, K., Özbilgin, M., Karatas-Ozkan, M., & Öztürk, M. B. (2015). Questioning impact: Interconnection between extra-organizational resources and agency of equality and diversity officers. *International Journal of Human Resource Management*, 26(9), 1243–1258. DOI: 10.1080/09585192.2014.934893

Temple, J. B., & Ylitalo, J. (2009). Promoting inclusive (and dialogic) leadership in higher education institutions. *Tertiary Education and Management*, 15(3), 277–289. DOI: 10.1080/13583880903073024

Veli Korkmaz, A., van Engen, M., Schalk, R., Bauwens, R., & Knappert, L. (2022). INCLEAD: Development of an inclusive leadership measurement tool.

Whitfield, B. (2024). Unconscious Bias: 16 Examples and How to Avoid Them. Available at https://builtin.com/diversity-inclusion/unconscious-bias-examples. Accessed 25/01/2024.

Witt, L. A. (1992). Exchange ideology as a moderator of the relationships between the importance of participation in decision-making and job attitudes. *Human Relations*, 45(1), 73–85. DOI: 10.1177/001872679204500104

Wolbring, G., & Nguyen, A. (2023). Equity/Equality, Diversity and Inclusion, and Other EDI Phrases and EDI Policy Frameworks: A Scoping Review. *Trends in Higher Education*, 2(1), 168–237. DOI: 10.3390/higheredu2010011

Wulandari, N., Arifin, A., Khoiriyah, M., Pujiningtiyas, R. I., & Arifin, M. (2021). Effect of Empowerment and Compensation on Employee Loyalty.

Zeng, J., & Xu, G. (2020). Ethical leadership and young university teachers' work engagement: A moderated mediation model. *International Journal of Environmental Research and Public Health*, 17(1), 21. DOI: 10.3390/ijerph17010021 PMID: 31861414

Chapter 3
Bridging the Knowledge– Expertise Gap for Outer Space and the Polar Regions, for All Humanity, and Beyond:
A New Vision for Education

Edythe Weeks
https://orcid.org/0009-0008-5559-4711
Washington University, USA

ABSTRACT

Higher education faces a pivotal moment. While historical exploration often fueled inequality, the emerging frontiers of outer space and the Polar Regions demand a different approach. This chapter argues for the inclusion of dedicated studies in these regions within the curriculum. A diverse range of experts, from astrophysicists to climate scientists, will be essential for ensuring the sustainable development of these new frontiers. Currently, a significant knowledge gap exists regarding three regions. Most people lack awareness of the critical issues and exciting developments taking place. This chapter explores how the core values of education, alongside existing international law, present a unique opportunity. We can reimagine exploration and development to prioritize equality, environmental sustainability, and conflict reduction. By bridging the knowledge gap, higher education can equip all of humanity to navigate the future of our expanding world responsibly.

DOI: 10.4018/979-8-3693-3443-0.ch003

THE IMPORTANCE OF HIGHER EDUCATION LEADERSHIP IN ADDRESSING THE GLOBAL SKILLS GAP FOR NEWLY EMERGENT FRONTIERS

Significant space and Polar Regions development is on the horizon driven by potential resources extraction and technological advancements. However, most people are unaware of this impending shift, which could lead to unequal distribution of benefits and potential instability. Thus, the chapter aligns with the core values of education by empowering individuals through knowledge, fostering global citizenship, promoting critical thinking, and equipping them to address complex challenges. It also contributes to the advancement of international law by advocating for its application, promoting peaceful and equitable development, and preventing harm to the environment and human rights. By equipping individuals with the knowledge and skills to become responsible global citizens, the chapter helps to shape a future that is more just, sustainable, and equitable.

The Emerging Frontiers: The Arctic, Antarctic, and Outer Space

While integrating these subjects may seem unconventional, it may prove to be a short-term investment with long-term gains in a variety of ways. First, taking this suggestion, may help universities to future-proofing graduates by providing them with knowledge on the focus areas (Arctic, Antarctica, and outer space) which might seem irrelevant for most people now, investing in these programs positions graduates for the high-demand jobs of tomorrow. A curriculum that goes beyond traditional subjects to address the emerging realities of space and polar development, can ensure students have the knowledge and skills necessary to participate in shaping the future of these regions. This highlights the limitations of the current education system in meeting the needs of a changing world. By integrating space and polar studies, the leaders can provide a more relevant education in critical areas.

These regions are on the precipice of significant development, and skilled professionals will be crucial for responsible resource management, legal and environmental issues, and technological advancements. Second, universities that take the lead in these emerging fields will attract top students and research talent and can provide them with a competitive advantage. This fosters a reputation for innovation and attracts grants and partnerships with industry leaders in these sectors, creating a virtuous cycle of prestige and resources. Third, the ability to adapt curriculum and programs to meet changing needs is a hallmark of a strong institution. Focusing on emerging frontiers demonstrates a proactive approach to preparing graduates for the evolving realities of the world. Fourth, this initiative can encourage more people to identify new problems, create creative solutions, discover possibilities for further research and expand new questions for tomorrow´s world. Fifthly, the ideas expressed in this chapter align with the spirit of Article 26 of the UN Declaration of Human Rights by providing a relevant education that prepares individuals for the complexities of the coming age of space and polar development.

The Need for Educational Reform and Article 26 of the UN Declaration of Human Rights

Article 26 of the United Nations´ Universal Declaration of Human Rights guarantees everyone the right to education. This right extends beyond basic literacy and numeracy to encompass relevant education that equips individuals to function effectively in a changing world. Currently, there is a significant knowledge gap. The exploration and development of space and the Polar Regions are on the horizon. These regions hold the potential for vast resources, new scientific discoveries, and geopolitical shifts. Currently, there's a significant knowledge gap regarding these emerging frontiers. Most people lack awareness of the pressing issues and ongoing developments. Unequal access to education could exacerbate this gap, leaving some nations and individuals unprepared for the coming changes. By educating everyone about space and polar development, we create a more informed citizenry. This fosters global understanding of resource distribution, legal frameworks, and sustainability challenges in these new frontiers. A population equipped with this knowledge can advocate for responsible development practices, ensuring benefits are shared equitably. This could prevent future conflicts and encourage international collaboration. Educating everyone about these emerging frontiers is an investment in the future. It empowers individuals to become active participants in shaping a more peaceful and prosperous world for all.

Most people lack awareness of the pressing issues and ongoing developments in the Polar Regions and outer space. To address this challenge, we need to integrate these areas of study into the standard curriculum. By equipping students with this knowledge, we can empower them to become leaders and change makers in the emerging economies of space and the Polar Regions. These leaders will shape the future of the 21st century and beyond. The link between higher education leadership and the global skills gap is a compelling and urgent subject for research. As we stand at the crossroads of innovation, technological advancement, and the changing nature of work, it becomes necessary to analyze the leadership methods within higher education institutions that can bridge the gap between academic pursuits and the skills expected by the modern workplace. This chapter will explore the emerging trends that highlight the urgent need for educational reform. It will examine how the fundamental purpose of education and existing international laws present a unique opportunity to reimagine the future. The exploration and development of these new frontiers will require a diverse range of experts. We can create a future where exploration and development prioritize equality, environmental sustainability, and reducing conflict and inequality. This future will learn from the mistakes of past colonization and ensure a more just and prosperous world. Providing an education that is relevant to the current and future challenges facing humanity ensures all individuals, not just a select few, have the opportunity to understand and participate in shaping the future of space and polar exploration.

Colonization, Development and Exploration Paradigms in the Past, Present and Future

Like past colonization efforts, the exploration and development of these regions possess the potential for significant power and wealth redistribution. However, unlike the past, we can anticipate the future need for a diverse range of experts across many disciplines. Experts will be crucial for the sustainable development of these new frontiers. Currently, a significant knowledge gap exists. Most people lack awareness of the pressing issues and ongoing developments in the Polar Regions and outer space. This is where education comes in. The solution is to integrate these study areas into each standard curriculum. By integrating knowledge about emerging scenarios in these regions into the standard curriculum, we can empower a wider range of people. This knowledge will equip people to become leaders and change makers in the emerging economies of space and the Polar Regions. Leadership roles in these areas will shape the future of the 21st century and beyond. This chapter will explore the emerging trends that highlight this urgent need for education. Furthermore, it will examine how the fundamental purpose of education and existing international laws present a unique opportunity. We can use this opportunity to reimagine the future. Imagine a future where exploration and development prioritize equality, environmental sustainability, and reducing conflict and inequality. Imagine a future that learns from the mistakes of past colonization.

A Role of the Dice: Who will be the Subaltern in the Next Millennium?

Throughout history, empires have risen and fallen, leaving behind a trail of magnificent ruins and cautionary tales. From the vast Roman Empire to the powerful British Empire, no empire has proven invincible. Even ancient civilizations like Persia, Egypt, and Ethiopia's Kingdom of Kush, all witnessed periods of great expansion followed by decline. Studying these cycles of rise and fall helps us understand the forces that shape history, reminding us that even the mightiest empires are not eternal. This legacy is reflected in terms like "First World," "Second World," and

"Third World," but who will be on top in the future millennia remains a mystery. The international relations critical theory literature highlights historical instances where similar dynamics triggered wars and fueled colonization across continents. Since we cannot predict future winners and losers in the unfolding development and social hierarchies, we all have a vested interest in ensuring equality and justice reign supreme – economically, environmentally, and socially.

Critical approaches, post development, postcolonial and others provide detailed reminders of the many things that went wrong during past colonization and development activities (Isbister, 2006; Escobar, 1995; Said, 1997; Shiva, 1997). They are informed by the principles of critical theory as outlined by Stephen D. Brookfield (2007), offer trenchant critiques of past colonization and development efforts, highlighting the numerous missteps and their lasting impacts. By understanding these historical failures, we can strive to prevent similar mistakes in the future, ensuring more equitable and sustainable development practices. Critical learning as an important tool for social and political awareness, empowering individuals to challenge dominant ideologies and work towards a just world (Brookfield, 2005).

Leadership must actively engage learners in understanding the ongoing dynamics shaping the future of the Arctic, Antarctica, and outer space through a critical analytical lens. These regions hold the potential for future colonization and development, and the scenarios are already unfolding. The potential colonization and development of outer space, the Arctic, and Antarctica could position people at the center of future geopolitics. Until education equips everyone with knowledge of these emerging activities, access to this knowledge will remain uneven. Visionary education leaders must bridge the gap between large-scale realities like space and polar development, and the current curriculum. History demonstrates the unequal outcomes of past colonization efforts, with some groups enriching themselves at the expense of others. Educating future generations is key to ensuring a more equitable and sustainable future for these regions.

Expanding educational access to these developments is crucial for two reasons. Firstly, it promotes equality by ensuring a wider range of people have the knowledge to participate as informed global citizens. Secondly, learning about these emerging frontiers can inspire a new generation to pursue Science, Technology, Engineering, and Math (STEM) fields. Integrating these topics into curriculums would allow students across disciplines, from arts and law to international affairs and filmmaking, to engage with cutting-edge paradigms at their nascent stages.

This New Vision in Higher Education

By incorporating these considerations into curriculum design and leadership practices, higher education can play a vital role in preparing future generations to build a sustainable and equitable future beyond Earth. The prospect of development and colonization in Polar Regions, outer space, and potentially other extraterrestrial locations presents a complex and multifaceted challenge. By fostering critical thinking skills, universities can prepare students to grapple with complex issues like resource management and legal frameworks in these new territories. Critical theory encourages questioning assumptions and dominant ideologies. The chapter highlights how past colonization often prioritized exploitation. Universities can use critical theory to encourage students to question these assumptions and envision alternative development models that prioritize sustainability and equity.

A core aspect of critical theory is understanding power dynamics. The chapter acknowledges the potential for new geopolitical struggles in these emerging frontiers. By encouraging students to understand these power dynamics, universities can prepare them to navigate complex international relations and advocate for ethical development practices. Incorporating these aspects of critical theory into curriculum design can empower students to become not just knowledgeable about these new frontiers, but also responsible and engaged participants in shaping their future.

Lifelong Learning and Adaptability in the Next New Worlds

The rapid pace of technological advancement, coupled with the lack of historical precedent for colonizing new worlds, demands graduates who are adaptable and committed to lifelong learning. Higher education leadership needs to equip students with strong critical thinking skills, the ability to learn new things quickly, a thirst for exploration, and a spirit of innovation. These skills can help prepare them for a future where the challenges and opportunities presented by these regions may evolve rapidly. This can also prepare people to navigate the uncertainties and challenges associated with building new societies in these nascent environments.

These ideas align perfectly with the focus of the book - *Insights into International Higher Education Leadership and the Skills Gap*, which is bridging the gap between academia and industry demands and ensuring students have the skills needed to thrive in a rapidly changing and interconnected world. To navigate these complexities, we need strong educational leadership. This means preparing future generations for global citizenship and responsible participation in international affairs. By integrating topics like international politics, law, and governance into standard curriculums, education can empower individuals to contribute to a more peaceful and sustainable future.

LITERATURE REVIEW

The world of work is rapidly transforming due to innovation, technology, and resource scarcity. Higher education must prepare graduates for this evolving landscape, particularly for the challenges and opportunities presented by new frontiers like the Arctic, Antarctica, and outer space. Critical thinking skills, as emphasized by Brookfield (2005), are crucial. Graduates need to question assumptions, navigate a rapidly changing world, and address issues of social justice. Learning from past mistakes, such as unsustainable colonization practices, will be vital for responsible development in these new frontiers. Traditional academic programs may not adequately prepare students for these new frontiers. The Arctic, Antarctica, and outer space hold immense potential for resources, scientific discovery, and economic development, but also present complex challenges in governance, resource management, and environmental protection. To thrive in this new era, graduates will need a broader skillset beyond resource management. Understanding international law, diplomacy, social sustainability, and advanced technological literacy will be essential for navigating these challenges. Higher education leadership needs to adapt and bridge the gap between traditional education and the skills and knowledge required for a future that extends beyond Earth.

The Arctic Landscape in Transition: A Melting Frontier on Top of Our World

The Arctic, once a frozen frontier, is rapidly transforming due to climate change. Melting ice caps reveal a landscape rich in resources and potential shipping routes. This newfound accessibility, however, sparks concern about resource ownership, environmental protection, and potential conflicts. Climate change is melting polar ice, revealing a landscape rich in resources and potential shipping routes.[1] History teaches us that this could trigger a scramble for resources and reshape global trade. Educational leaders should prepare future generations for these emerging challenges and opportunities. Access to land, fisheries, marine resources, transit routes, military navigation strategic advantage points, and other valued resources rare-earth items including diamonds, gold, silver, zinc, iron, lead, nickel, oil, gas, hydrocarbons, minerals could prompt and energize commercial and military geopolitical activities (Gross, 2020).

History of Cooperation and Geopolitical Future Significance

While the Arctic is currently seen as a zone of relative peace, the melting polar ice caps raise concerns about potential future conflicts over resources and territory. The Arctic region faces complex issues of governance, resource management, security, and jurisdictional disputes. The Arctic Council, the United Nations Convention on the Law of the Sea (UNCLOS), and the Northwest Passage are just some of the key considerations. Additionally, non-Arctic states and companies are increasingly interested in the region's economic potential, leading to competition for trade routes, fisheries, minerals, and energy resources. Geopolitical posturing, national security, military strategy and surveillance, access to Northwest Passage and other navigational passageways and sea routes are very real causes for concern.

In *Arctic Law in 1000 Words*, (Hossain & Roncero, 2023), inform that there is great potential for climate change to produce significant economic and political developments in the region as the ice melts. More specifically, Hossain (2023, pp 20-21) informs:

"This trend has been marked by catastrophic, extreme natural events both within the region and elsewhere, leading to environmental degradation, loss of biodiversity, imbalances in natural resource distribution, unsustainable demographic and political structures, peoples and communities losing their socio-cultural identity, and large-scale internal and external displacement"; and that "the melting of sea ice in the Arctic has created the prospect of access to its marine areas and thereby of opportunities to tap their rich resources, among other possibilities. Offshore hydrocarbons, significant deposits of rare-earth elements in Greenland and the other Arctic areas, and sizeable mineral deposits elsewhere in the Arctic make it an immensely resource-rich region. Evidence of the abundant resources available can be seen in a report of the United States Geological Survey in 2008 stating that the Arctic contains one-fourth of the world's yet-to-be-tapped hydrocarbon resources. The Arctic Ocean also includes a wide variety of living resources, such as fisheries, although the resource stock, particularly in the central Arctic Ocean, is currently unknown. The extraction of these resources and their transportation through the emerging Arctic Sea routes made possible by the ice-free Arctic Ocean has led to the intensification of human activities. The Northern Sea Route, for example, has become more operational in recent years because of the much shorter distance and higher cost-effectiveness it offers compared to traditional routes, such as the Suez Canal. A gradual increase in cargo volume through the Route has intensified human activity."

Who Owns the Arctic Territory?

The Arctic is home to eight nations and millions of Indigenous people who have thrived in the region for millennia. The Arctic includes the North Pole, Arctic Ocean, seas, surrounded by eight territorial nation states, and millions of Indigenous communities of people living in the region for millennia. The eight states the "Arctic States" include Canada, Denmark (there is often a parenthetical note to include Greenland and sometimes Faroe Islands as autonomous parts of Denmark), Finland, Iceland, Norway, Russia, Sweden, and the United States (via Alaska). The receding ice caps are exposing areas that were previously under permanent ice cover. As the ice recedes, questions arise about who controls the newly exposed areas. Mineral deposits, rare-earth elements, and potential hydrocarbon reserves make the Arctic an immensely valuable region. Additionally, the melting ice opens up shorter and more cost-effective shipping routes, like the Northern Sea Route, further intensifying human activity in the region. Arctic states, non-Arctic states and nonstate actors are interested in the region's economic potential and geopolitical importance (Menezes, Couser & Radkevitch, 2022).

To reiterate, Rainwater (2015) explains that non-Arctic states are "significantly disadvantaged by the legal regimes and norms administering the Arctic region. First, under the United Nations Convention on the Law of the Sea (UNCLOS), most of the Arctic's natural resources are divided among the sovereign jurisdictions of the five littoral Arctic states - Russia, Canada, Norway, Denmark (via Greenland and the Faroe Islands), and the United States (U.S.). Non-Arctic states are thus severely limited in their ability to exploit" (p. 116). It is important to note that non-Arctic states are seeking influence in the region and have continued to seek a greater role in Arctic diplomacy (Bloom, 2017; Rainwater, 2015). Additionally, Bloom (2017) explains non-Arctic states share similar interests in the region, but with some variations based on their unique histories and strengths. Several European nations, like the UK, France, and the Netherlands, boast a long history of exploration and interaction with the Arctic, despite lacking territorial claims. All non-Arctic states are drawn to the potential economic opportunities arising from an increasingly accessible Arctic, including shipping, tourism, energy, and future fisheries. Furthermore, these countries, along with their scientific communities, are eager to collaborate on cutting-edge Arctic research, especially concerning climate change. Finally, Bloom (2017) explains that non-Arctic states may also seek to influence environmental policies in the region to achieve greater protection or address the impacts of Arctic environmental changes on their own territories.

Who Governs? A Complex Legal Landscape

The legal framework governing the Arctic is a complex web of international agreements, national claims, and customary law. The United Nations Convention on the Law of the Sea (UNCLOS) establishes guidelines for ocean use and is a cornerstone of this framework. However, there's no single treaty governing the entire Arctic. The Arctic Council, an intergovernmental forum, serves as a platform for cooperation and coordination among Arctic states, Indigenous peoples, and other interested observers. It focuses on sustainable development and environmental protection but excludes military security issues. The Arctic's legal landscape is a complex mix of international agreements focused on regional concerns, national claims, and customary law. The United Nations Convention on the Law of the Sea (UNCLOS), which sets guidelines for ocean use, is a cornerstone of this framework. UNCLOS became effective in 1994 and it is generally accepted as a codification of customary international law of the sea. Although there's no single treaty specifically governing the entire Arctic region, there is an Arctic Council.

The Arctic Council, an intergovernmental forum that serves to address concerns regarding Arctic people and Arctic issues, began functioning in 1996 as the political intergovernmental organization established to help govern the region. It aims to serve as an international forum to promote cooperation, coordination, and interaction among Arctic states, Indigenous peoples and other interested observers. It focuses on sustainable development and environmental protection, but not issues related to military security. The eight Arctic States are members, along with Indigenous groups, known as the Permanent Participants. Decisions are taken by consensus of the states.[2]

Five countries - Canada, Denmark, Norway, Russia, and the United States - border the Arctic Ocean and have exclusive economic zones (EEZs) extending 200 nautical miles offshore. These are called "littoral" or "coastal" Arctic states. The remaining three Arctic states - Finland, Iceland, and Sweden - have territories in the region but do not have Arctic Ocean coastlines (Hossain and Roncero, 2023: 23). Adding to this complexity, portions of the region, for example, the Arctic Ocean, is governed by the Law of the Sea provisions. As an Ocean, the Arctic Ocean is considered beyond the reach of sovereign claims; it is a global commons entity. Russia, Finland, Canada, Iceland, Sweden, Norway and Denmark have all ratified the Law of the Sea Treaty, but the United States has not[3].

The Arctic's melting ice, fueled by climate change and economic prospects, has thrust the region into the international spotlight. Rapid development is anticipated (Zhiltsov & Zonn, 2021). This newfound attention lays bare a complex web of overlapping claims. Resources, maritime boundaries, and even the North Pole itself are contested (Breum, 2022). The legal status of waterways like the Northwest Passage, a vital link between the Atlantic and Pacific Oceans, further complicates the picture. Adding to this complexity is the growing international interest in the Arctic's untapped potential, alongside the longstanding concerns of Indigenous communities. Despite these challenges, a spirit of cooperation seems to be the prevailing trend. International institutions like the Arctic Council play a crucial role in mediating historical tensions, fostering dialogue between nations like Russia and NATO, and incorporating the concerns of Indigenous peoples. While some argue that cooperation has been the predominant political mood (Byers, 2013), underlying potential for competition for resources and land remains.

Climate change is melting the Arctic ice caps, revealing a treasure trove of resources and new shipping routes. This newfound accessibility sparks concerns about resource ownership, environmental protection, and potential conflicts. Resource-rich territories throughout history serve as a stark reminder that conflicts can erupt. Vigilance is necessary, but education is also key. By fostering international understanding of the Arctic's delicate balance, we can ensure a future of collaboration, not competition.

Relevance for Leaders in Higher Education

Visionary leaders in higher education should consider the Arctic's transformation for several reasons. First, the Arctic's Indigenous communities hold invaluable knowledge. Educational leaders must partner with them to document their traditions and ensure their voices shape the Arctic's future. Second, this situation presents a complex geopolitical situation and rising tensions, demanding training in international cooperation and diplomacy. A new legal landscape demands education in resource management and international law to navigate ownership disputes. Third, the region holds immense economic potential and environmental risk, requiring a skilled workforce that understands the delicate balance. Fourth, the urgency of climate change calls for programs in environmental science and sustainable development specific to the Arctic's fragile ecosystem. Fifth, technological advancements for resource extraction and new shipping routes require university programs in engineering, logistics, and polar science. Finally, this situation is a reminder of the ongoing battle against climate change, and the need to educate future generations on both the challenges and opportunities it presents. By addressing these complexities, visionary leaders in higher education can prepare future generations to manage a rapidly changing Arctic, fostering collaboration, sustainability, and respect for all stakeholders.

The Antarctic Region: A Future Frontier, as a Massive Continent

Unlike other continents with established countries, Antarctica is governed by a unique international treaty system known as the Antarctic Treaty System (ATS). Established in 1959, the ATS prioritizes peace and scientific collaboration on the continent. However, the melting polar ice cap raises concerns about access to potential resources and the possibility of future conflicts. As the Antarctic polar ice melts, it's revealing potential access to resources like oil, gas, minerals (including gold, silver, copper, platinum, iron ore, chromium, cobalt, molybdenum, zinc, manganese lead, titanium, nickel, uranium and even land and water. Melting ice also raises concerns about the environmental impact of increased human activity in Antarctica. Today, is considered the coldest place on Earth (Henry, 2022).[4] However, the Antarctic temperatures are warming (Clem et al., 2020).

Who Governs Antarctica?

The Antarctic Treaty System

The current governance system relies on a series of agreements within the ATS framework. Today, Antarctica is governed by an international treaty which put existing *terra nullus*-style claims provisionally on hold due to the Antarctic Treaty System (ATS), an international agreement signed in 1959. The Antarctic Treaty System (ATS) governs Antarctica through a series of agreements. The main treaty, established in 1961, suspended all territorial claims and promotes freedom of scientific investigation and exchange of information. A key addition came in 1998 with the Environmental Protocol. This protocol prohibits mineral and oil exploration for a minimum of 50 years and includes regulations for environmental protection. The protocol designates Antarctica as a "natural reserve, devoted to peace and science." However, this critical ban on mineral exploration is set for review in 2048, raising concerns about the future ability of the ATS to protect Antarctica. The ATS promotes scientific research and environmental protection efforts in Antarctica. Additionally, a growing number of countries participate in research activities and tourism ventures on the continent.

The future of Antarctica's governance faces uncertainties. As the ice melts, it could reveal resources that could become a source of conflict between nations vying for territory and riches. The ability of the ATS to handle these future challenges is unclear, especially considering the growing geopolitical competition and the effects of climate change. A significant point of concern is the expiry of the current ban on mineral exploitation in Antarctica, set for 2048. This will necessitate international discussion and a potential revision of the existing framework.

Who Owns Antarctica?

Notably, no single country holds ownership of Antarctica. Seven nations have laid territorial claims on overlapping territories, but these claims are currently put on hold by the treaty. This is distinct from the jurisdictional claims which exist in the Arctic region.

Historical Claims and Exploration

The seven countries mentioned include: New Zealand, Australia, France, Norway, the UK, Chile, and Argentina – who laid claim to different parts of Antarctica – with a few that are conflicting. Butler (1977: 35) provides:

The history of Antarctic discovery and use has been punctuated by territorial and other disputes between nations. New assessments of the economic value of Antarctic natural resources could exacerbate tensions between the Treaty Powers themselves and between those states and the world community. For example, seven nations have made terra nullius type claims to territories in Antarctica, prior to the Treaty.

Melting ice unlocks new possibilities for new shipping routes, military interests (navigation, surveillance) and commercial ventures, research and tourism. Commercial interests exist and are increasing. For example, the tourism industry is already thriving. Commercial Antarctica tourism is an important industry in the region.

Research Stations, Antarctic Gateway Cities, Commercial Tourism Industry and Other Expanding Activities

Antarctica has a diverse group of stakeholders with varying interests. Examples include about thirty-two countries that maintain research stations, the growing tourism industry with its tour operators and visitors, and the five southern hemisphere gateway cities that provide logistical support.

There are approximately 98 research stations (research bases or field stations) buildings in Antarctica maintained, owned and operated by countries including: Argentina, Australia, Belarus, Belgium, Brazil, Bulgaria, Chile, China, Czech Republic, Ecuador, Finland, France, Germany, India, Italy, Japan, Norway, Pakistan, Peru, Poland, the Netherlands, New Zealand, Romania, Russia, South Korea, Spain, Sweden, Turkey, Ukraine, United States, United Kingdom and Uruguay.

Other key activities involve the cities acting as gateways to Antarctica are Christchurch (New Zealand), Hobart (Australia), Ushuaia (Argentina), Punta Arenas (Chile), and Cape Town (South Africa). This role as Antarctic access points fosters cultural, economic, environmental, and political ties between these cities and the frozen continent.[5] Scientific organizations and environmental groups also have a stake in Antarctica, advocating for research and conservation efforts. All these stakeholders share an interest in the peaceful and sustainable future of the continent.

Another example of significant activities in the region is the International Association of Antarctica Tour Operators estimates that 106,000 visitors travelled to the region in the 2022-2023.[6] A variety of about thirty Antarctic cruise ships, which travel to Antarctica. Some commercial enterprises are restricted. For example, commercial fishing is strictly limited in Antarctica by the Commission for the Conservation of Antarctic Marine Living Resources (CCAMLR) which was established by international agreement in 1982. The reason for this is to protect the fragile marine ecosystems of the Southern Ocean.

The Potential for Geopolitical Competition

The success of the ATS in maintaining peace in Antarctica thus far is commendable. However, moving forward, proactive measures are needed to address the challenges on the horizon. Continued international collaboration, informed by a deep understanding of the legal and political landscape, is essential for a peaceful and sustainable future for Antarctica, benefiting all stakeholders.

Collis (2017) explains that Antarctica presents a unique legal challenge. It's a land with competing claims based on the idea of "terra nullius" (no one's land) alongside the concept of "terra communis omnium" (common heritage of humankind). The Antarctic Treaty System (ATS) has managed to forestall these tensions through a temporary ban on mining activities. The 1959 Antarctic Treaty effectively put a moratorium on territorial claims based on the "terra nullius" principle. This "freeze" on existing claims has helped to maintain peace in the region.

The Antarctica Treaty may have put conflict "on ice" by freezing existing *terra nullus* style claims temporarily on hold (Press, 2011). However, this situation could soon heat up as climate change continues to melt the polar ice. This is a real concern considering that prior to the enactment of the treaty, nations had been making territorial terra nullius-styled claims to regions in Antarctica. According to the U.S. Department of State:

By the 1950s, seven nations - Argentina, Australia, Chile, France, New Zealand, Norway, and the United Kingdom - had claimed territorial sovereignty over areas of Antarctica. Claims of Argentina, Chile, and the United Kingdom overlap. Eight other nations - the United States, the Soviet Union, Belgium, Germany, Poland, Sweden,

Japan, and South Africa - had engaged in exploration but had put forward no specific claims. The United States did not recognize the claims of other governments and reserved the right to assert claims. The Soviet Union took a similar position.[7]

The Antarctic Treaty System (ATS) faces growing challenges due to geopolitical competition, environmental change, and a shifting world order (McGee, Edmiston & Haward, 2022). Scenario planning, as proposed by these authors, can help explore potential futures beyond simple predictions. Abdel-Motaal (2016) raises concerns about the ATS's ability to manage future resource competition. She argues melting ice and climate change could make Antarctica more desirable, potentially leading to conflict. To avoid this, she suggests revisiting the ATS and emphasizes the need for international cooperation.

Relevance for Leaders in Higher Education

The melting ice caps in Antarctica are raising concerns about resource access and potential conflicts. The continent is currently governed by an international treaty system that prioritizes peace and science. Visionary leaders in higher education should consider this a significant development for several reasons. First, Antarctica presents a complex challenge in international cooperation and diplomacy. Second, the need for a skilled workforce to manage the environmental risks and potential economic opportunities requires focused education. Finally, Antarctica serves as a reminder of the ongoing battle against climate change, highlighting the need to educate future generations on how to address its challenges and opportunities.

OUTER SPACE: THE FINAL FRONTIER - LEGAL AND EDUCATIONAL CHALLENGES

Many of the technologies we take for granted, like cell phones, the internet, and even ATM machines, rely on advancements made in space. Space law, a legal framework governing activities beyond Earth, has played a crucial role in enabling these innovations. While space exploration and its legal underpinnings might seem unfamiliar, the groundwork has already been laid through the first and second waves of space development. International agreements have established processes and laws for space activities. My research focuses on raising awareness about space law, with the goal of empowering future generations to navigate the challenges and opportunities of space colonization and development.

This section of the chapter explores the exciting world of space exploration, highlighting the legal and educational challenges that lie ahead as we venture further into the cosmos. We will explore the existing legal framework for space activities and the need for future generations to be prepared for the opportunities and complexities of space development. This section delves deeper into outer space development and space law because these insights hold the key to unlocking a future filled with scientific breakthroughs and boundless potential for all people. By understanding the legal and educational challenges that lie ahead, we can prepare the next generation to explore the cosmos with both ambition and responsibility.

The New Space Race

Like the melting of polar ice, space activities are also accelerating. Earlier phases of space development are marked by advancements in satellite technology and missions to the Moon. Spaceport construction has drastically increased,[8] and national space agencies[9] and private space companies[10] have grown in recent years. In addition, the sheer number of government space agencies (with more than seventy globally) working on space programs underscores the international effort pushing space exploration forward.

This new space race involves countries like China, Japan, Luxembourg, Russia, and the U.S. - all vying for a stake in the final frontier and aiming to possibly exploit the potential wealth of space resources (Varadarajan, 2020; Goswami, 2019). The potential for asteroid mining has led to discussions about who owns space resources. The U.S. Space Resource Exploration and Utilization Act, the creation of the U.S. Space Force, and Russia claiming Venus as their own challenge the Outer Space Treaty's principles. The current legal framework may not address future challenges like resource extraction and potential militarization of space.

Asteroid mining operations being seriously discussed, and these types of ventures are anticipated to accrue quadrillions of dollars' worth of natural resources, including gold, iridium, osmium and other platinum group metals, which have been discovered on Near Earth asteroids.[11] In addition, plans and discussions are happening aimed at building up and expanding the outer space infrastructure, beyond the International Space Station. The ultimate goal might be permanent settlements beyond Earth, but for now, the focus is on unlocking the economic potential of space. This could lead to the establishment of permanent human outposts in the future, although that might still be a long way off. Also, military activities, with regard to outer space, are also accelerating.

A Thriving Space Industry Demands Educated Professionals

Koetsier (2021) highlights a space industry boom, with over 10,000 companies worldwide and the US leading the pack with over half that number. This surge in commercial activity suggests a future with more resources being dedicated to space exploration and utilization. Koetsier also details the diverse range of companies involved. This broad involvement indicates the development of a space infrastructure, a necessary precursor to any large-scale human presence in space.

Who Owns Outer Space? Tensions Rise over Country-Specific Asteroid Mining Legislation

There's a growing concern over national legislation involving countries claiming ownership of outer space, particularly regarding asteroid mining. National laws, like the 2015 U.S. Asteroid Mining Act, raise questions about whether domestic legislation such as this, contradict international space treaties. This has led to international tensions, with some questioning whether national laws on asteroid mining contradict existing space treaties. International space law operates under the principle of "res communis," meaning space resources are considered as belonging to the global commons. This principle has been instrumental in fostering international cooperation and peaceful development in space ventures. The United Nations Office for Outer Space Affairs, along with its Committee on Peaceful Uses of Outer Space and its legal arm, play a central role in shaping space law. A major point of contention is the U.S. Asteroid Mining Act of 2015.

This law appears to grant U.S. citizens the legal right to mine asteroids. However, legal experts are divided on whether this act clashes with international agreements like the Outer Space Treaty and the Moon Agreement. Proponents of the Act argue it aligns with existing space law, while others, including the International Institute of Space Law, express skepticism. The potential economic windfall from asteroid mining is significant, with estimates suggesting trillions of dollars' worth of resources like gold and platinum group metals up for grabs. This economic incentive, coupled with the legal ambiguity surrounding the U.S. Act, has further heightened international tensions. The history of international space law serves as a reminder. Established during the Cold War, it aimed to prevent celestial conflicts by fostering cooperation. Maintaining this collaborative spirit is crucial. By working together, nations can ensure that space exploration benefits all of humanity, ushering in an era of shared prosperity amidst the stars.

International Outer Space Law

These principles emerged during the Cold War to prevent superpowers from extending their rivalry into space. In exchange for giving up claims of national sovereignty over space, nations gained freedom of navigation and the potential to benefit from future space exploration. The basic foundation of international space law consists of five international space treaties, along with various written resolutions and declarations.[12] The main international treaty is the Outer Space Treaty of 1967; it is generally viewed as the "Constitution" for outer space. The Moon Agreement (1979-1984) is often treated as though it is not a part of the body of international space law, and there has been extensive debate on whether or not the Moon Agreement is a valid part of international law (Doyle, 2002, pg. 83). It entered into force in 1984, because of a five-state ratification consensus procedure, agreed upon by the members of the United Nations Committee on Peaceful Uses of Outer Space (COPUOS) (Jasentuliyana, 1992: 36). Still today very few nations have signed and/or ratified the Moon Agreement.

Challenges to Space Law

Despite the successful history of international space law being used to promote global commercialization of a variety of industries, discursive complaints exist accusing it of hindering enterprise development. However, since the 1990s, there have been ongoing efforts to weaken or remove these provisions. Some argue that the "province of mankind" concept and the commons principle hinder space exploration and development by restricting property rights. This perspective further contends that current space law hinders private space ventures by not allowing property rights (Nelson, 2011; Fountain, 2003; Buxton, 2004; Keefe, 1995; Reynolds, 1992; and Schwind, 1986). These proponents want to change, remove or overrun the commons principle in space law. Critics say this principle slows down space exploration and development. Since the early 1990s, steady discursive attempts have been made to challenge the commons principle regarding outer space (Whitfield-Jones, 2020; Blodger, 2016; Twibell, 1997). The outcome of nearly ten years of meetings and negotiations, the international community came together to negotiate and write the laws for outer space (Hager, 1970).

Jakhu & Buzdugan (2008: 201) explain that the path of gradual commercialization of current space applications, such as launch services, satellite communication services, direct broadcasting services, satellite remote sensing and navigation services, and satellite weather monitoring services, will most likely be followed by future activities of use of space resources – space mining ventures. They argue that "the perceived regulatory barriers, i.e., the licensing requirement, the "common heritage of mankind" principle of international space law, and protection of intellectual property rights, are not obstacles to economic development". Despite these successes, there have been discursive practices aimed at complaining and efforts asserted change the very nature of international space law´s commons sentiments (Weeks, 2023).

Who Governs Outer Space?

Outer space is not governed by any one country. International space law, established soon after the launch of Sputnik 1, prevents countries from claiming ownership. This law emerged during the Cold War to prevent a space arms race and promote peaceful exploration. The space law regime has declared that outer space and its resources are to be used to benefit all humanity. The Outer Space Treaty recognizes that the common interest of all mankind in the progress of the exploration and use of outer space should be carried on for the benefit of all peoples irrespective of the degree of their economic or scientific development to contribute to broad international cooperation in the scientific as well as the legal aspects of the exploration and use of outer space for peaceful purposes. It further indicates that such cooperation will contribute to the development of mutual understanding and to the strengthening of friendly relations between states and peoples. The main rationale behind all of this was to promote peace, international collaboration, scientific cooperation and global understanding. The nations of the world made it clear that they wished to avoid conquest, scrambles and winner-take-all conflicts in the future (Jasentuliyana & Lee, 1979-1981).

In a Bargained for Exchange: The Politics of International Law

To understand how to maintain world peace, more people need to understand the history of international space law. While the Cold War raged between roughly 1945 and 1989 or 1991, international space law negotiations were taking place from 1957 through 1967. The record of these negotiations shows that there was an understanding that in exchange for giving up this otherwise right of sovereignty, peace would prevail, and all nations would be able to benefit from this new venture into outer space.

The Cold War involved the ideological battle (between communism and free market ideology). After the fall of the Soviet Union, free market ideology gained salience. In this new environment, assertions that international space law's commons principles need to be updated to suit the new political mood.

Aiming for Peace in a Bipolar Superpower Era of World Politics

International space law, established shortly after the launch of Sputnik 1, prevents countries, companies or individuals from claiming ownership of outer space. Those who worked to create the laws to govern outer space wished to prevent a nuclear arms race or a World War 3 over claims to outer space territories and they hoped to use the opportunity to promote equality and economic opportunity for all people from all nations. This philosophy, with its historical and political context, is evident throughout the drafting process – reflected in working papers, proposals, and, the final treaties and resolutions. In exchange, they established outer space as a shared resource for all nations (the commons) and guaranteed freedom of navigation. This international space law was supposed to benefit all of humanity. Scholars like Von Bencke (1997) highlight the intricate relationship between political considerations and the drafting of these key treaties. The Outer Space Treaty, UN Resolution 1472, UN Resolution 1962, UN Resolution 963 and other the other parts of international space law promote space as a "commons" emphasized ideas such as broad international cooperation for the betterment of mankind and benefiting states irrespective of their level of development, but national interests or economic goals can create tension. These resolutions, the working papers, and other legal documents, demonstrate a clear desire to prevent Cold War rivalries from extending into the cosmos and ensure space exploration benefitted all of humanity (Jasentuliyana & Lee, 1979-1981).

The Outer Space Treaty deems that outer space, and its resources is the "province of mankind" a cornerstone of the Outer Space Treaty, emerged as a compromise (Jasentuliyana & Lee, 1979-1981). It avoided the more contentious term "common heritage of mankind," and had been perceived as likely to cause an impasse in treaty negotiations (Von Bencke, 1997: 43). The province of mankind principle was never specifically defined thus allowing the superpowers to pursue their interests (Jasentuliyana, 1992; Hager, 1970). Negotiators appear to have known to stay away from the legal term Common Heritage of Mankind as it had been a sticking point, causing an impasse during earlier negotiations. The Moon Treaty does contain the legal principle "Common Heritage of Mankind". This underlying political dance illustrates the inseparable connection between the development of international space law and the geopolitical realities of the era. The existing legal framework, based on the Outer Space Treaty, promotes peaceful exploration and prevents countries from claiming space or celestial bodies. However, the potential for resource extraction and militarization raises concerns about resource ownership and potential conflicts.

A NOVEL PEDAGOGICAL APPROACH: ALIGNING WITH CORE VALUES OF EDUCATION AND INTERNATIONAL

Universities face a crucial challenge: equipping students with the knowledge and skills to navigate the burgeoning fields of space and polar exploration. This section proposes a multi-pronged approach to integrate these areas into existing curricula, fostering a new generation of leaders prepared for the complexities of exploration and development. This proposes a novel pedagogical approach that utilizes the challenges of the Polar Regions and outer space development to illuminate existing social and political issues on Earth. By studying these regions, students can gain a deeper understanding of resource scarcity, competition, and the need for equitable development practices. Thus, by incorporating these considerations into curriculum design and leadership practices, higher education can play a vital role in preparing future generations to be successful contributors to the development and colonization of these exciting but complex new frontiers. Furthermore, higher education can enable future generations to build a sustainable and equitable future beyond Earth. By adapting their curriculum and taking a proactive stance, universities can prepare future generations to explore outer space and the Polar Regions responsibly and sustainably. This may ensure a future where these new frontiers benefit all of humanity.

Integration Strategies:

- **Curriculum Revamping:**
  - **Interdisciplinary Courses:** Design courses that combine knowledge from diverse disciplines relevant to space and polar development (e.g., international relations, environmental science, space law).
  - **Modular Integration:** Integrate modules on resource management, space law, and sustainability challenges into existing courses.
  - **Project-Based Learning:** Implement projects where students tackle real-world challenges related to these regions.
- **Faculty Development:**
  - **Training Programs:** Equip faculty with the necessary knowledge and expertise to teach these new subjects effectively.
  - **Curriculum Design Workshops:** Guide faculty in designing innovative curriculum materials.
- **Global Issues and Collaboration:**
  - **International Focus:** Integrate topics like international politics, law, and governance to develop critical thinking and an understanding of global challenges.
  - **Case Studies:** Utilize real-world challenges in space and polar regions as case studies to illuminate complex social and political issues. This fosters a global perspective and equips students to navigate these challenges.

Focus on Sustainability:

Throughout the curriculum, emphasize the importance of sustainable development to ensure responsible exploration and development of space and Polar Regions.

Accessibility and Equity:

- Technology and Resources:
  - o Online Learning Modules: Develop online modules to increase accessibility for students in remote locations.
  - o Open Educational Resources (OERs): Develop and share OERs to reduce costs and make educational materials more readily available.
  - o Research Partnerships: Collaborate with research institutions to offer guest lectures, internships, and research opportunities.
- Focus on Developing Countries:
  - o Capacity Building: Partner with universities in developing countries to build expertise in areas critical for sustainable development. This can be achieved through faculty exchange programs, online learning platforms, and joint research initiatives.
  - o Addressing Local Needs: Ground international relations theory in the specific needs and contexts of developing countries. Work with local communities to develop solutions for resource management and explore the potential of space resources for tackling issues like poverty and energy access.
  - o Advocacy and Leadership: Empower students to become advocates for a just and peaceful world order by encouraging their involvement in research projects focused on international cooperation and sustainable development.

Fostering Future-Ready Skills:

- Interdisciplinary Learning: Develop programs that bridge traditional disciplines to foster innovative problem-solving approaches.
- Cross-Cultural Competence: Encourage collaboration between universities in different countries to develop cross-cultural understanding and communication skills.
- Critical Thinking: Integrate critical thinking skills to analyze international relations issues through a lens of global justice and sustainability.

Engaging Learning Methods:

- Simulation-Based Learning: Develop simulations that allow students to experience real-world scenarios related to resource management, space law disputes, or sustainability challenges.

- Project-Based Learning: Implement projects that tackle real-world challenges in space and polar regions, considering the specific needs of Indigenous communities, developing countries, and small polities.
- Metaverse and Second Life: Explore the use of these virtual environments to create immersive simulations and foster collaboration with students from around the world.
- MOOCs (Massive Open Online Courses)
  - o Develop MOOCs: Create MOOCs specifically focused on space, Arctic, and Antarctic studies.
  - o Supplement Existing Courses: Offer MOOCs as supplementary resources for existing courses.
  - o Faculty Training MOOCs: Develop MOOCs specifically designed to train faculty on teaching these subjects.
  - o Technology and Resource Access: Utilize existing MOOC platforms and design MOOCs with accessibility in mind.
  - o Global Collaboration on MOOCs: Partner with universities and research institutions

The proposed pedagogical approach offers a compelling and innovative way to enhance educational leadership. By utilizing the challenges of the Polar Regions and outer space development as case studies, it provides a unique lens through which to examine existing social and political issues on Earth. This approach aligns with the core values of education, including critical thinking, problem-solving, and global citizenship. By studying these regions, students can develop a deeper understanding of complex issues and learn to apply their knowledge to real-world challenges. The approach emphasizes the importance of international cooperation and equitable development practices, which are fundamental principles of international law. By studying the challenges and opportunities presented by the Polar Regions and outer space, students can gain a better understanding of the need for global governance and cooperation. By incorporating these considerations into curriculum design and leadership practices, higher education can equip future generations with the skills necessary to navigate the complexities of developing and colonizing these new frontiers, while also promoting sustainable and equitable development.

To effectively implement this approach, higher education institutions should:

- **Integrate relevant topics into standard curriculums:** Incorporate international politics, law, and governance into existing courses to empower students with the knowledge and skills necessary for global citizenship.
- **Foster interdisciplinary collaboration:** Encourage collaboration among faculty from various disciplines to provide a comprehensive understanding

of the challenges and opportunities presented by the Polar Regions and outer space.

- **Develop partnerships with industry and research institutions:** Collaborate with organizations working in these fields to provide students with practical experience and exposure to real-world challenges.
- **Promote critical thinking and problem-solving skills:** Equip students with the ability to analyze complex issues, develop innovative solutions, and make informed decisions.

By adopting this novel pedagogical approach, higher education can play a vital role in preparing future generations to be successful contributors to the development and colonization of the Polar Regions and outer space, while also ensuring a sustainable and equitable future for all of humanity.

CONCLUSION: THE CALL TO ACTION FOR A NEW FRONTIER FOR EDUCATION

The Arctic, Antarctica, and outer space offer vast opportunities but also hold the potential for conflict. Educational institutions have a crucial role to play in preparing future generations to navigate these complexities. To prepare future generations for the challenges of space and polar exploration, universities must adapt their curriculum to equip graduates for these new frontiers. By regularly assessing industry trends and emerging technologies, universities can develop and update curricula to incorporate relevant courses and create a learning environment that fosters creativity, problem-solving, and critical thinking. By taking a proactive stance on these issues, universities can position themselves as global leaders in space and polar studies. Establishing partnerships with research institutions, government agencies, and private companies, as well as supporting faculty and student research projects, can contribute to advancing knowledge in these fields. Universities have a responsibility to contribute to solving global challenges by educating future leaders who understand the importance of international cooperation and responsible development. Encouraging student involvement in international exchange programs, integrating sustainability into curricula, and teaching students about ethical considerations can help prepare graduates to address these complex issues. Educating students about these critical global issues fosters a sense of global citizenship, fulfilling a core mission of universities. By providing opportunities for community service, promoting intercultural understanding, and facilitating global dialogue, universities can help students develop a global perspective and become engaged citizens.

REFERENCES

Abdel-Motaal, D. (2016). *Antarctica: The battle for the seventh continent.* Praeger. DOI: 10.5040/9798400613272

Blodger, I. (2016). Reclassifying geostationary earth orbit as private property: Why natural law and utilitarian theories of property demand privatization. *Minnesota Journal of Law, Science & Technology*, 17(1), 408–440.

Bloom, E. T. (Winter 2022). The rising importance of non-Arctic states in the Arctic. *The Wilson Quarterly.* https://www.wilsonquarterly.com/quarterly/the-new-north/the-rising-importance-of-non-arctic-states-in-the-arctic

Blount, P. J., & Robison, C. (2016, December). One small step: The impact of the U.S. commercial space launch competitiveness act of 2015 on the exploitation of resources in outer space. *North Carolina Journal of Law & Technology*, 8(2), 160–186.

Breum, M. (21 December 2022). Canada extends its Arctic Ocean seabed claim all the way to Russian waters. *Artic Today.* https://www.arctictoday.com/canada-extends-its-arctic-ocean-seabed-claim-all-the-the-way-to-russian-waters

Brookfield, S. D. (2005). *The Power of Critical Theory: Liberating Adult Learning and Teaching.* John Wiley & Sons, Inc.

Brown. https://www.mayerbrown.com/en/perspectives-events/publications/2020/05/one-small-step-for-property-rights-in-outer-space

Butler, S. O. (1977, Spring/Summer). Owning Antarctica: Cooperation and jurisdiction at the South Pole. *Journal of International Affairs*, 31(1), 35–51.

Buxton, C. (2004). Property in outer space: The common heritage of mankind principle vs. the 'First in time, first in right' rule of property law. *Journal of Air Law and Commerce*, 69(4), 689–707.

Byers, M. (2013). *International law and the Arctic.* Cambridge University Press. DOI: 10.1017/CBO9781107337442

Christol, C. Q. (1980, April 2). The Moon Treaty: Fact and fiction. *The Christian Science Monitor.* https://www.csmonitor.com/1980/0402/040234.html

Christol, C. Q. (1999). The 1979 Moon Agreement: Where it is today? *Journal of Space Law*, 27(1), 1–33.

Christy, C. (2017, April 20). Territories beyond possession? Antarctica and outer space. *The Polar Journal*, 7(2), 287–302. https://www.tandfonline.com/doi/abs/10.1080/2154896X.2017.1373912?journalCode=rpol20. DOI: 10.1080/2154896X.2017.1373912

Clem, K. R., Fogt, R. L., Turner, J., Lintner, B. R., Marshall, G. J., Miller, J. R., & Renwick, J. A. (2020, August). Record warming at the South Pole during the past three decades. *Nature Climate Change*, 10(8), 762–770. DOI: 10.1038/s41558-020-0815-z

Demac, D. A., & McKay, A. (1985). Competition and cooperation in space. *Telecommunications Policy*, 9(1), 74–76.

Doyle, S. E. (2002). *Origins of International Space Law and the International Institute of Space Law of the International Astronautical Federation*. Univelt, Incorporated.

Escobar, A. (1995). *Encountering development: the making and unmaking of the Third World*. Princeton University Press.

Fountain, L. M. (2003). Creating momentum in space: Ending the paralysis produced by the 'Common heritage of mankind' doctrine. *Connecticut Law Review*, 35, 1753–1787.

Goswami, N. (February 28, 2019). China's get-rich space program. *The Diplomat*. https://thediplomat.com/2019/02/chinas-get-rich-space-program/

Gross, M. (December 2, 2020). Geopolitical competition in the Arctic Circle. *Harvard International Review*. https://hir.harvard.edu/the-arctic-circle/

Hager, D. R. (1970). *Space Law: The United Nations, and the Superpowers: A Study of International legal Development and Codification, 1957-1969*. Ph.D. Doctoral dissertation. University of Virginia.

Haley, A. (1963). *Space Law and Government*. Appleton-Century-Crofts.

Henry, L. R. (2022). *The call of Antarctica: Exploring and protecting earth's coldest continent*. Twenty-First Century Books.

Hossain, K. (2023). The Arctic legal system. In Hossain, K., & Roncero, J. M. (Eds.), *Arctic law in 1000 words. Juridica Lapponia* (pp. 20–21). University of Lapland.

Hossain, K., & Roncero, J. M. (Eds.). (2023). *Arctic law in 1000 words*. Juridica Lapponia, University of Lapland.

Suffolk University. Law School. (2000). Suffolk Transnational Law Review (Vol. 24). Suffolk University Law School.

Isbister, J. (2006). *Promises not kept: poverty and the betrayal of Third World development* (7th ed.). Kumarian Press.

Jakhu, R., & Buzdugan, M. (2008, November 4). Development of the natural resources of the moon and other celestial bodies: Economic and legal aspects. *Astropolitics*, 6(3), 201–250. DOI: 10.1080/14777620802391778

Jasentuliyana, N. (1992). *Space law: Development and scope*. Praeger.

Jasentuliyana, N. & Lee, R. S. K. (1979-1981). *Manual on space law, Volumes I, II, III and IV*. Oceana Publications, Inc., 1979-1981.

Keefe, H. (1995, July). Making the final frontier feasible: A critical look at the current body of outer space law. *Computer & High Technology Law Journal*, 11(2), 345–371.

Koetsier, J. (2021, May 23). Space, Inc: 10,000 companies, $4T value ... and 52% American. *Forbes - Innovation Consumer Teach: Forbes.com*. https://www.forbes.com/sites/johnkoetsier/2021/05/22/space-inc-10000-companies-4t-value--and-52-american/?sh=3ca624a755ac

Kolirin, L. (2020, September 18). Venus is a Russian planet -- say the Russians. *CNN.com*. https://www.cnn.com/2020/09/18/world/venus-russian-planet-scn-scli-intl/index.html

Lee, K. E. (2017, Fall). Colonizing the final frontier: Why space exploration beyond low earth orbit is central to U.S. foreign policy, and the legal challenges it may pose. *Southern California Interdisciplinary Law Journal*, 27(1), 231–253.

Lewis, S. (2020, October 28). *CBS News*. Hubble telescope gives closer look at rare asteroid worth $10,000,000,000,000,000,000. *CBS News.com*. https://www.cbsnews.com/news/hubble-space-telescope-rare-asteroid-16-psyche-worth-10000-quadrillion/

McGee, J., Haward, M. G., & Edmiston, D. (2022). *The future of Antarctica: Scenarios from classical geopolitics*. Springer. DOI: 10.1007/978-981-16-7095-4

Menezes, D. R., Couser, G., & Radkevitch, M. (2022). Highlighting businesses as key non-state actors in the Arctic: Collaboration between Arctic economic council and polar research and policy initiative. In N. Sellheim & D.R. Menezes (Eds.), *Non-state actors in the Arctic region* Springer Polar Sciences. Springer, Cham. https://doi.org/DOI: 10.1007/978-3-031-12459-4_5

Nelson, T. (2011, Spring). ILSA Journal of International &. *Comparative Law*, 17(2), 393–416.

of non-Arctic states in the high North". *Emory Law Review, 30*(1), 115-153. https://scholarlycommons.law.emory.edu/eilr/vol30/iss1/6

Press, T. (July 17, 2011). Keeping conflict on ice with the Antarctic Treaty. *The Conversation.*

https://theconversation.com/explainer-keeping-conflict-on-ice-with-the-antarctic-treaty-2197

Rainwater, S. (2015). International law and the "globalization" of the Arctic: Assessing the rights

Reynolds, G. H. (1992). International space law: Into the Twenty-first Century. *Vanderbilt Journal of Transnational Law*, 25(2), 225–255.

Roberts, L. D. (2000). A lost connection: Geostationary satellite networks and the International Telecommunication Union. *Berkeley Technology Law Journal*, 15(3), 1095–1144.

Said, E. (1997). *Covering Islam: How the media and the experts determine how we see the rest of*

Schwind, M. (1986). Open Stars: An examination of the United States push to privatize

Shiva, V. (1997). *Biopiracy: The plunder of nature and knowledge.* South End Press.

Twibell, T. S. (Spring 1997) Space law: legal restraints on commercialization and development of

United States Commercial Space Launch Competitiveness Act (2015) Pub. L. No. 114-90, 129

Varadarajan, T. (2020, August 7). The new "gold rush in space". *Wall Street Journal: Opinion*

https://www.wsj.com/articles/the-new-gold-rush-in-space-11596826062

Von Bencke, M.J. (1997). *The Politics of Space: A History of U.S. - Soviet/Russian*

Weeks, E. (2023). The benefit of international relations critical theory to highlight lessons

Whitfield-Jones, P. (2020, May 21). A small step for private property rights in space. *Mayer*

Wiles, G. E. (1998). The man on the moon makes room for neighbors: An analysis of the

Wiles, G. E. (1998, October). existence of property rights on the moon under a condominium-type ownership theory. *International Review of Law Computers & Technology*, 12(3), 513–534. DOI: 10.1080/13600869855342

Zhiltsov, S. S., & Zonn, I. S. (2021). *The Arctic: A drifting future.* Nova Science Publishers.

ENDNOTES

[1] See the Testimony by Esther Brimmer to the U.S. House Homeland Security Subcommittee on Transportation and Maritime Security addressing changing geopolitics in the Arctic as part of a broader conversation on strategic competition in the Arctic (July 18, 2023), Prepared statement by Esther D. Brimmer James H. Binger Senior Fellow in Global Governance Council on Foreign Relations Before the Subcommittee on Transportation and Maritime Security, United States House of Representatives 1st Session, 118th Congress Hearing on "Strategic Competition in the Arctic" "Changing Geopolitics in the Arctic" at: https://www.cfr.org/report/changing-geopolitics-arctic-0; Also see "Changes in the Arctic: Background and Issues for Congress CRS Report", Prepared for Members and Committees of Congress, Congressional Research Service, United States; https://crsreports.congress.gov; R41153: https://crsreports.congress.gov/product/pdf/R/R41153; NASA's GRACE and GRACE Follow-On satellites show that the land ice sheets in both Antarctica and Greenland have been losing mass since 2002: https://climate.nasa.gov/vital-signs/ice-sheets/; and "New Study Suggests Climate Models May Underestimate Rate of Melting", National Centers for Environmental Information, National Oceanic and Atmospheric Administration (NOAA): https://www.ncei.noaa.gov/news/arctic-ice-study.

[2] See The Arctic Council website at: https://arctic-council.org/

[3] United Nations Oceans and Law of the Sea Chronological Listing of accessions and successions to the Convention and the related Agreements at: https://www.un.org/Depts/los/reference_files/chronological_lists_of_ratifications.htm.

[4] Natasha Vizcarra (9 December 2013). "Landsat 8 helps unveil the coldest place on Earth", National Snow and Ice Data Center.

[5] Juan Francisco Salazar, Paul James, Liam Magee & Elizabeth Leane (2021), *Antarctic Cities: From Gateways to Custodial Cities* (Sydney: University of Western Sydney). Also see "Custodians of Antarctica: how 5 gateway cities

are embracing the icy continent" (November 30, 2020) *The Conversation*. https://theconversation.com/custodians-of-antarctica-how-5-gateway-cities -are-embracing-the-icy-continent-148006.

[6] Hayley Skirka Jan 11, 2024 Will Antarctica be the next victim of overtourism as visitor numbers continue to climb?: https://www.thenationalnews.com/ travel/2024/01/11/antarctica-overtourism/#:~:text=While%20the%20pause %20in%20tourism,environment%20are%20wary%20of%20this

[7] US Department of State, Narrative for the Antarctic Treaty of 1959 https:// 2009-2017.state.gov/t/avc/trty/193967.htm#treaty.

[8] See *Spaceport – Wikipedia*: https://en.wikipedia.org/wiki/Spaceport. There is a growing trend to commercialize existing spaceports. There is a trend towards new spaceport construction for both government and commercial purposes. Imagining various reasons for increased construction of spaceports, helps us to realize the connection between this anticipated rising demand for space launches which can only be for uses of outer space, for various purposes.

[9] Today, a wide variety of countries have their own NASA-style national space agency. See *List of government space agencies – Wikipedia*: https://en.wikipedia .org/wiki/List_of_government_space_agencies.

[10] John Koetsier, "Space Inc: 10,000 Companies, $4T Value ... And 52% American", *Forbes - Innovation Consumer Tech*:https://www.forbes.com/ sites/johnkoetsier/2021/05/22/space-inc-10000-companies-4t-value--and-52 -american/?sh=3ca624a755ac.

[11] Sophie Lewis (October 28, 2020) *CBS News*, "Hubble telescope gives closer look at rare asteroid worth $10,000,000,000,000,000,000":https://www .cbsnews.com/news/hubble-space-telescope-rare-asteroid-16-psyche-worth -10000-quadrillion/.

[12] The United Nations Office for Outer Space Affairs (UNOOSA) provides information and advice to governmental bodies, nongovernmental organizations as well as the general public. This office also provides copies of the treaties, declarations, working papers, minutes and other documents related to the creation and development of space and it prepares legal studies and informative documents on space law and acts as the secretariat for the Legal Subcommittee of the United Nations committee on the Peaceful Uses of Outer Space – the primary international forum for the development of laws and principles governing outer space and its resources. Member states use this forum to come together, discuss, deliberate, and make decisions concerning

space law. The International Institute of Space Law (IISL) cooperates with international organizations and national institutions in the field of space law and helps to foster space law development. For more information see: https://www.unoosa.org.

Chapter 4
Case Pedagogy as a Strategy to Promote Critical Thinking Among Nursing Students:
A Cooperative Learning Approach

Daniel O. Ashipala
https://orcid.org/0000-0002-8913-056X
University of Namibia, Namibia

ABSTRACT

Case pedagogy remains one of the vital strategies to promote critical thinking and problem-solving abilities in nursing and midwifery education globally. In Namibia little research exists on the perspectives of nursing students on the use of a case pedagogy as a strategy to promote critical thinking in nursing and midwifery education. The purpose of this chapter is to explore the experiences of students on the use of case pedagogy as a strategy to promote critical thinking among nursing students. The study found that most students developed critical thinking skills and that they were equipped with problem solving skills which they can use for analysis and evaluations of their patients' conditions. Findings from this chapter may help identify strengths and weaknesses in the use of case pedagogy for assessment purposes in nursing and midwifery education.

DOI: 10.4018/979-8-3693-3443-0.ch004

INTRODUCTION

Globally, case pedagogy has been seen as a signpost to legitimate scientific research or as a way of studying extremely rare once-off phenomena (Mostert, 2007); (Klimová & Lovászová, 2019). Case pedagogy is defined as a display of life situations for teaching people (Popil, 2011). Mahdi et al (2020) further describe case pedagogy as a case study, case study strategy, case method or case study method. According to Penn et al. (2016), the term was introduced by Harvard school faculty of law and it has been used for many years in business, law and medical schools.

Critical thinking is a crucial tool for nursing education, and its acquisition is one of the peak desired results of higher education today (Oliveira et al., 2016). Case pedagogy is used in nursing education to instil critical thinking in nursing students (Pagnucci et al., 2015). It is ordinarily directed at a tangible or theoretical situation, a community group or institution or an individual, and requires thorough analysis of the area of concern followed by judgemental decision making to solve the problem (Mellish, Brink & Paton, 1998).

Kaddoura (2011) states that case pedagogy has certain pedagogical advantages, the mainly ones being that it aids an active learning strategy, it focuses on students as the epicentre of the learning environment, it develops problem-solving ability, and it integrates theory into practice. Kaddoura (2011) continues, affirming that case pedagogy engages students and teachers in analytic dialogue about nursing situations by helping learners analyse an authentic case with a view to identifying client problems, comparing and evaluating optional solutions and deciding how to deal with clinical situations. Kaddoura (2011) further proposes that it helps integrate multiple sources of data, solves clinical problems, provides logical scientific rationale for the decision-making process and describes complex situations that can be used in learning about professional practice.

A case may be classified according to the level of complexity, depending on the students' level of learning; according to its duration as a sole educational intervention, covering a specific learning issue; or as a longitudinal approach that spans over time, with the possibility of developing the case into stages that are appropriate according to the year level in a learning programme (Daniels et al., 2015). Kaddoura (2011) mentions in this regard that students receive immediate feedback and are better able to enquire more deeply and broadly about diagnosis, treatment and appropriate nursing interventions for the patient.

Case pedagogy is not as prevalent as other methods such as the lecture method. If correctly utilised, case pedagogy has the potential to be effective in promoting critical thinking in nursing students (Forsgren et al., 2014). Moreover, students do not have the knowledge and experience required to analyse the problems adequately (Daniels et al., 2015). This study seeks to explore the students' experiences in using case study as a strategy to promote critical thinking. By understanding the students' experiences, we can better understand the way in which case studies influence students' learning and ultimately development of critical thinking. Mostert (2007) argues that a class size of 12 to 15 people seems to provide adequate diverse opinions and opportunities for lively participation in case discussion. As the sum of students increases, the less likely it will be that everyone will have an equal chance to participate. Also, the greater the class size, the more likely it will be that other distracters will proliferate. Additionally, given the complexity of most cases and the diverse views likely to be held by the participants, keeping the discussion focused according to the objectives of the course and the course content can be difficult.

According to Toofany (2008), Von Colln-Appling and Giuliano (2016) nursing schools must offer learning experiences that support students to think critically about complex issues instead of just becoming receptacles for information. Nelson (2017), Von Colln-Appling and Giuliano (2016) (as cited in Boso, Van der Merwe & Gross, (2020) further urges that it is the duty of nurse educators to help students to acquire critical thinking skills. At the University of Namibia (UNAM), the School of Nursing has introduced case pedagogy as a strategy to promote critical thinking. However, since inception there has been no formal evaluation of this strategy. Literature shows that critical thinking is difficult to teach and develop in students, and several methods such as problem-solving exams and case study assessments have been used but the results have not been positive. It is important that strategies used to promote critical thinking are evaluated to judge whether they are effective, starting with creating good learning experiences for the development of critical-thinking skills.

REVIEW OF A RELATED LITERATURE

Concept Of Critical Thinking

Bezanilla, Nogueira, Poblete, and Dominguez, (as cited in Mahdi, Nassar & Almuslamani, 2020) urged that critical thinking is a competency which is required by students in their personal and professional life, therefore, universities must do the utmost to include it in their classes, programs, and syllabus. Ignatavicius (as cited in Popil, 2010) noted characteristics of critical thinkers as being: outcome-driven, flexible, willing to change, innovative, creative, analytical, communicators, assertive, persistent, caring, energetic, risk-takers, knowledgeable, resourceful, observant, intuitive, and 'out of the box' thinkers. Klimová and Lovaszova (2019) further described a critical thinking person as an open-minded person that is naturally curious, understands diverse aspects, seeks arguments to formulate final decisions, rejects shallowness, and always considers proof before taking conclusions, no matter who carries them. Moreover, they added that critical thinking allows one to interpret, analyze and evaluate the quality of information and thought processes, to formulate judgments and defend conclusions.

In today's technologically forward-thinking healthcare realm, nursing students should be active learners and think critically to provide safe patient care Kaddoura (2011). Cant and Cooper (as cited in Von Colln-Appling & Giuliano, 2016) urged that nurses should be able to think swiftly as well as anticipate outcomes within seconds as it may mean life or death to a patient. They further stated that the skill to critically think through complex situations is essential to the success of the student following graduation.

In the nursing setting, critical thinking is the thought manner that underlies effective clinical problem-solving and decision-making (Wu, Heng & Wang, 2015). In addition, (Wu et al.,2015) continued by affirming that critical thinking provides a focused approach to clinical reasoning, requiring a tolerance of multiple perspectives reinforced by reason and evidence. Furthermore, Critical thinking is a major component in nursing education and is integral to the nursing practice, predominantly as nurses need to function in today's complex nursing environments and deal with issues such as advanced technology, greater acuity of patients and complex disease processes. Scholars believe that critical thinking is both a process and a product that can be fostered with active learning (Wu et al., 2015).

The level of skills at which a graduate from nursing school must perform has been raised and escalation of the competency level for nurses has been attributed to the increase in the complexity of patient conditions and the increase in technological skill required to practice in a complex healthcare environment Dutra (2013). Dutra continued by alleging that the concern now is not that the old pedagogies once relied upon are no longer sound techniques, but that nurse educators have not adapted their pedagogies to include newer methods that are believed to improve their student's levels of thinking and reflect practices in the existing healthcare setting.

A concept pointed out by Bastable (as cited in Dutra 2013) is that students' critical-thinking abilities are enriched if they have a voice in the learning process, furthermore an increase in the learning process is reported to be one of the key factors in developing sound, critical-thinking skills, a voice in the learning process is the basis of a learner-centered educational environment. Dutra stresses that a pedagogy linked with a learner-centered classroom atmosphere is a case. Finally, Dutra concluded that the growing body of research has been devoted to the need for teaching nursing students how to be critical thinkers.

PEDAGOGICAL ADVANTAGES

Leenders et al., (as cited in Popil 2010) stated that a case study (also called a case, case method, or case study method) is usually a description of a tangible situation, usually involving a decision, a challenge, an opportunity, a problem or an issue faced by a person or persons in an organization. Strengths of the case study method are discussed in detail by Dowd and Davidhizar (as cited in Popil 2010) these include: providing experience of clinical dilemmas; illuminating human intentions, feelings, and misinterpretations; providing models of expert practitioners' thoughts on clinical dilemmas; increasing students' range of strategies for problem solving; helping students to identify problems and teaching them professional thinking; providing emotional preparation for the real world.

Kunselman and Johnson (as cited in Popil 2010) stated that case studies are also useful to teachers and instructors, aiding them to rethink their approach to teaching, reintroducing instructors' interest in course material, and creating a greater level of interest that can be projected from teachers to students. For example, teaching similar themes in a lecture set-up can become redundant and lose its sparkle. Popil stresses that developing case studies and discussing them with scholars brings freshness, innovation, and food for thought to the table. Popil continuous by stating features of case studies, ordinarily being they provide supporting data and documents to be analyzed, and an open-ended question or problem is presented for possible solution. Finally, Popil ends by affirming that case studies can be presented to individuals or groups; most commonly, however, they are worked on in groups that can brainstorm solutions.

Uys and Gwele (as cited in Daniels et.al., 2015) affirmed that case pedagogy has many benefits, such as facilitating the students' lively involvement whilst providing actual life situations to which theoretical knowledge is applied. Daniels et.al, (2015) continued by confirming that by using group effort, case pedagogy provides numerous opportunities for creativity, collaborative work, and integration of sociocultural aspects of health care to be included in teaching and learning interventions. Research has found that the use of case-based education benefited students, as they scored higher on assessment tasks that required analysis and evaluation and on patient assessment, diagnosis and treatment plans (Daniels et. al, 2015).

PEDAGOGICAL CHALLENGES

Although numerous beneficial results are observed in scholars learning when using the case method, there are also some limitations and difficulties that may be stumbled upon. As discussed in Grupe and Jay (as cited in Popil 2010) detriments of case studies include: embedded author biases, a narrow focus on a dilemma facing a single person or group, and limitations in scope. Popil continues by arguing that case studies are beneficial in difficult situations requiring problem solving, but they are not appropriate in teaching concrete facts. Moreover, Popil stated that they may become frustrating for less prepared students or students who are used to more traditional methods.

For numerous students, discussing and analyzing a case is an unaccustomed experience (Mostert, 2007). Mostert stressed that even if students are able to respond to case dilemmas with insight and articulated argument, they may still find it challenging to relate their opinions to the theoretical content of the course. Mostert continued by alleging that deeper levels of complexity are not immediately clear and may take an inordinate amount of time to discover; students who lack classroom experience may be incapable of recognizing the finer issues presented in the case and without sufficient preparation and reflection, deeper case issues might remain unknown.

Nurses' practice surroundings are regularly complex, chaotic and changing, which makes each day different and challenging (Dale & Dale, 2017). Furthermore, Dale and Dale continued by arguing that, to enhance nurses' preparedness for handling a difficult and demanding clinical reality after graduation, it is of utmost importance that educational institutions implement teaching and learning methods that aid students thinking and clinical reasoning. Finally, Dale and Dale end by mentioning that developing cases is time consuming and may be difficult. Moreover, they may become frustrating for less prepared students or students who are used to more traditional methods Popil (2010).

EXPERIENES OF NURSING STUDENTS

A study conducted by (GholamI et al., 2016) explored the experiences of undergraduate nursing students on the implementation of case pedagogy in an emergency nursing course. The outcomes of the present study displayed that case pedagogy is a stressful but pleasant and empowering experience for Iranian nursing students that develops critical thinking and stress management skills, reinforces peers' potentials, improves diagnostic abilities, and helps acquire professional competencies for use in future practices through the creation of a positive environment.

In a study carried out in Central South University in China, Qi, Yi, Mo, Huang and Yang (2018) investigated the efficiency of case pedagogy in the course of practical skills on nursing undergraduate students. A total of 147 nursing students' undergraduate interns from class 2016 of their college were recruited and were assigned into experimental (N=74) and control groups (N=73) by random number table. Experimental group received case-based pedagogy whilst control group were instructed by classical method. Total score and all dimension scores were significantly higher in experimental group then control group (p<0.05). A critical thinking scale showed higher scores in experimental group at all dimensions comparing to control group (p<0.01).

Studies such as those of Mangena, Chabeli, Shell (as cited in Boso, van der Merwe and Gross 2019) assessed factors that prevent CT acquisition of nursing students, the study was based on educators and students' perspectives. They found that educators' lack of knowledge of critical thinking teaching methods and evaluation, negative attitudes of educators, student selection and educational background, socialization, culture and language prevented the development of critical thinking skills of students.

A study by Dinc and Gorgulu (as cited in Popil 2010) examined the views of students in relation to the contents of a nursing ethics unit that was part of a "Nursing History and Ethics" course. Data was collected from 113 students using a questionnaire. Popil found that Case study analysis has been shown to be an effective method of teaching ethics. It aids easy comprehension of the theories of ethics and philosophical principles. Case study also aids students to analyze the nature of moral problems and to differentiate these from the non-moral problems involved in the case situation. Furthermore, Popil's study found that most students found that discussions of case study analysis were very advantageous in developing ethical decision-making skills.

In a study done at the School of Nursing, University of the Western Cape, South Africa by Daniels et., al (2015) stated that having recognized assessment as a challenge in the implementation of case pedagogy at the school of nursing, it was noted that to further improve the implementation of case pedagogy, further workshops were needed with a specific focus on assessment strategies.

Methods

The proposed study used a qualitative design, which was explorative, descriptive and contextual in nature. In qualitative research, one of the important tasks of the researcher is to describe what they obtain and observe during their research process (Holloway & Galvin, 2023). Descriptive research is concerned with describing the existing condition, which provides a useful initial overview of a problem (Maree,2016). According to Maree (2016), a qualitative research design is naturalistic, focusing on natural settings in which interactions occur.

Participants and sampling

The accessible population in this study consisted of 15 fourth-year nursing students who were enrolled for the Bachelor of Nursing Science (Clinical) degree at the UNAM Rundu campus. The reason for including fourth-year students was because they have gone through all the levels from years 1 to 4 and as a result are likely to share more detailed experiences than the other students. According to the Rundu campus records, 78 students were enrolled for the fourth year in the School of Nursing at the time of the study. In this study, a purposive sampling technique, also known as judgemental sampling, was applied and interviews were carried out until data saturation was reached. Purposive sampling was chosen because the study had one specific predefined group in terms of which it sought to describe the experiences of students when using case pedagogy as a strategy to promote critical thinking. Data saturation was reached after the 15th interview. Brink et al. (2018) define data saturation as the point at which new data no longer emerge during the data-collection process. The researchers relied on their own judgement when choosing participants; therefore, participants were selected based on their knowledge of the study and according to the purpose of the study.

Setting

This study was conducted at the UNAM satellite campus in the north-eastern region of Namibia, which offers student nurses training to enable them to become professional nurses. The campus offers courses in Education, Nursing Science and Management Sciences. The School of Nursing at this campus only offers a four-year undergraduate bachelor honours degree programme. At the School of Nursing, case pedagogy is often used in the form of problem-solving examinations, in solving ethical dilemmas and in case studies in the subject General Nursing Science.

Data collection

After ethical clearance was granted, the researcher met potential participants and solicited their participation in the study. The researcher provided the participants with an information sheet stating the aim of the study and what was required from them. Consent was obtained from the participants by signing a consent form. Data were collected at campus lecture halls, specifically from fourth-year nursing students, using face-to-face semi-structured interviews which were conducted in accordance with an interview guide. The interviews were conducted in English since all the interviewees could understand and speak English fluently. Each session took approximately 14 minutes. During the interview the researcher took notes and used follow-up questions to probe deeper for increased detailed exploration. Further, the in-depth interview was recorded with the permission of the participants. Additionally, in this study two participants were used in a pilot study for the purpose of providing an opportunity to make adjustments to the data collection tool before the main study was carried out and to assess the feasibility of the study design. Data obtained from the pilot study w used in the main study.

Data analysis

Interviews were transcribed verbatim. Data analysis was adapted from the stages recommended by Hycner and Colaizzi (1978). The interviews were listened to while reading and re-reading the transcriptions, and phrases that pertained directly to the phenomenon were captured. The essence of participants' experiences was extracted as units of general meaning, as described by (Hycner,1985). Categories or units of meaning that clustered together naturally Hycner (1985) were then identified, and redundant ones were eliminated. Three themes subsequently emerged.

Rigour

The trustworthiness of the entire study was assessed using the criteria proposed by Lincoln and Guba (1985), namely, criteria relating to the credibility, transferability, dependability and confirmability of the study. Credibility was achieved through prolonged engagement, with the researcher spending a month in the clinical setting in which the research was conducted. Both individual interviews and field notes were used as methods of data collection. In addition, member checking was done with the researcher constantly checking his findings with the participants and controlling them against the literature control. Transferability was achieved through dense description that included a comprehensive description of the methods, including illustrative direct quotes. Dependability was achieved in this study as an audit trail was kept and is available on enquiry. The transferability of this study was achieved by means of a confirmability audit done by an independent expert researcher.

Ethical considerations

Ethical approval and permission to conduct the study were obtained from the School of Nursing Research Committee (SoNREC) reference no. 11/2020. Prior to conducting the individual interviews, the researcher explained the purpose of the study and the principle of voluntary participation to the students, using an information sheet. Students subsequently signed a consent form indicating that they agreed to their interview being audio-visually recorded. All data and files were kept strictly confidential by means of encryption and access was restricted to the members of the research team.

Findings

The participants were all undergraduate students and all were under the age of 40. Seven participants were female and eight were male. The demographic data that are discussed here are age, gender and year of study. The characteristics of study participants are given in Table 1.

Table 1. Characteristics of the study participants

Age	Total
20–30	12
31–40	3
Gender	
Male	8
Female	7

The four themes that emerged from the data analysis (as indicated in Table 2) are as follows: case pedagogy as a strategy; advantages of the case method; impact on student experiences; and recommendations for improvements.

Table 2. Themes and subthemes from the data analysis

Themes	Subthemes
Case pedagogy as a strategy	Teaching tool for real-life situations Assessment tool for testing knowledge
Advantages of the case method	Learning tool for acquiring critical thinking Linking theory to practice Equipped for analysis and evaluation of conditions Enabling understanding of diagnostic tests, treatment and management Confidence boost in identifying and solving health problems Broaden knowledge of specific conditions Scoring better marks
Impact on student experiences	Insufficient time for required reading Complex cases challenging Insufficient clinical support from clinical instructor
Recommendations for improvements	Allow practice to master and manage treatments Drafting more case studies to exercise thinking skills Encouraging groups to share ideas

Theme one: Case Pedagogy as a Strategy

This theme described students' insight and understanding of case pedagogy as a strategy to promote critical thinking. Subthemes explicated by the participants include the following: teaching tool for real-life situations; and assessment tool for testing knowledge.

Teaching Tool for Real-Life Situations

Participants expressed their understanding of case pedagogy as being a teaching tool/learning tool that prepared them for real life situations.

> *Case pedagogy is the use of real-life case scenarios and case studies as a teaching guide to help better understand how certain illnesses/conditions present themselves* (P1).
>
> *It is also used in such a way that students are given real-life scenarios that prepare them for clinical setting* (P6).

Assessment Tool for Testing Knowledge

Here, participants mentioned that case pedagogy is also used as an assessment tool by teachers and clinical instructors.

> *I think it's also an assessment tool that the teachers use to evaluate students' knowledge about a particular condition* (P2).
>
> *Case studies are also used as an assessment tool by clinical instructors* (P6).

Theme two: Advantages of the Case Method

This theme describes how the case method benefited the participants. The subthemes under this theme are the following: learning tool for acquiring critical thinking; equipped for analysis and evaluation of conditions; enabling understanding of diagnostic tests, treatment and management; confidence boost in identifying health problems; broaden knowledge of specific conditions; and scoring better marks.

Learning Tool for Acquiring Critical Thinking

Participants viewed case pedagogy as a tool that they used to promote their critical thinking skills. This was elaborated as follows:

> *In time it also helped me develop my critical thinking skills whereby I could relate why certain medications where given for certain conditions* (P15).
> *It helped me improve my critical thinking skills in the sense that I developed a rapid response on dealing with patients with similar burn wounds* (P3).

Linking theory to practice

Participants mentioned that case pedagogy helped them link what they were taught in class to what they experienced in the hospital setting.

> *Case pedagogy helps link theory to practice in nursing, in such a way that you are able to apply what you have learned in theory* (P6).

Equipped for analysis and evaluation of conditions

Students mentioned that the use of case pedagogy propelled them to better analyse and evaluate the case studies.

> *In this sense, it pushed me to read widely, analyse the case study critically and evaluate* (P9).
> *I learned how to analyse the patient's condition in order to weigh what has to be done* (P2).

Enabling an understanding of diagnostic tests, treatment and management

Participants explained that case pedagogy enabled them to better manage and learn how to treat patients' conditions.

> *It helped me understand better the condition of malaria in terms of the diagnostic tests, the treatment and management of the condition* (P8).
> *I got to understand better how to manage a patient with burn wounds* (P11).

Broaden knowledge of specific conditions

Participants stated that the use of case pedagogy helped them broaden their knowledge as they were motivated to do more research about certain conditions.

It helped me have broader knowledge on specific conditions (P6).
I was increasing my knowledge because I had to do more research (P12).

Scoring better marks

Participants expressed that using case studies, they were able to score better marks than when they were assessed using other assessment methods.

Case studies also allowed me to score better marks as compared to other assessment methods (P1).

Confidence boost in identifying and solving health-related problems

Participants stated that the use of case pedagogy enabled them to gain confidence and identify their patients' problems.

This made me happy and confident because at least I knew what to do; I knew where to start, unlike it being a new case. So at least I had an idea on how to tackle it (P5).

Theme three: impact on student experiences

In this theme, participants expressed the challenges they experienced with the use of case pedagogy. This theme contains the following subthemes: insufficient time for required reading, the challenging nature of complex cases and insufficient clinical support from clinical instructors.

Insufficient time

Participants expressed that they were not given adequate time to prepare and present their case studies.

I was only given a limited amount of time to present my case study; therefore, the time was not enough (P13).

Case studies are different, and the way they are tackled is different, some require more time (P7).

Complex cases are challenging

Participants stated that some case studies contained more than one diagnosis, which made them difficult to handle.

Some cases are very complex, for example, one finds a patient who has diagnosis of HIV (positive), and then you find that the same patient has liver cirrhosis and meningitis – cases which are actually difficult to report and understand (P2). Also, sometimes you find cases that are really complex, e.g. a patient with different diagnosis makes handling the case studies difficult (P3).

Insufficient clinical support from clinical instructors

Participants stated that they did not have adequate support from clinical instructors to carry out the case studies.

Usually, you are alone with the patient and there's no clinical instructor to follow up on you so you can just ask for clear guidance (P6).

Theme four: recommendations for improvement

In this theme, students expressed their views on what could be done to improve their critical thinking with the aid of case studies. The subthemes under this theme are as follows: allow practice to master and manage treatments, draft more case studies to exercise critical thinking and encourage groups to share ideas.

Allow practice to master and manage treatments

Participants stated that practising with different case studies and doing background research would improve their critical thinking skills.

It's very important to keep practising, to keep doing more of the case studies at school, going through case studies so we know the management and treatments (P7).
I think I could read more vastly and widely on different cases, by doing this I could enhance my critical-thinking skills because I'm preparing for what is yet to come (P2).

Drafting more case studies to exercise critical thinking skills

Most participants stated that their teachers could give them more case studies for them to exercise their critical thinking skills.

More case study scenarios should be integrated within the learning of students by the teachers (P8).
I would recommend that teachers give us more case studies so that we exercise [practise] (P3).

Encouraging groups to share ideas

One participant stated that teachers should encourage group work as this would allow the sharing of ideas to better address the case study.

The teachers should encourage students to do case studies in groups so that students are better able to share ideas on how to solve the case studies (P4).

Discussion

The purpose of the study was to explore the experiences of students in the use of case pedagogy as a strategy to promote critical thinking among nursing students. This section presents a discussion of the findings under the following themes: case pedagogy as strategy, advantages of the case method, impact on student experiences and approach to improve critical thinking.

Case pedagogy as a strategy

Participants stated that they understood case pedagogy as a teaching tool that uses real-life case scenarios and case studies to prepare them for real-life situations. This finding is related to that of Popil (2011), who defines case pedagogy as a case, case study strategy, case method or case study method. This correlates with Bi et al. (2019), who define case pedagogy as a form of patient-oriented, student-centred and inquiry-based teaching and learning method that aims to prepare students for clinical practice through the use of authentic clinical case studies. Furthermore, Leenders et al. (2001) state that a case study (also called a case, case method, or case study method) is usually a description of a tangible situation, usually involving a decision, a challenge, an opportunity, a problem or an issue faced by a person or persons in an organisation. Lastly, Klimová and Lovászová (2019) define case pedagogy as a display of life situations for teaching people. Participants in this study stated that case pedagogy was also used by their teachers as an assessment tool for testing knowledge. This is in line with Mostert (2007), who affirms that over the past 20 years, teacher educators have increasingly turned to case-based instruction with pre-service, novice, and even experienced teachers.

Advantages of the case method

Pagnucci et al. (2015) states that case pedagogy is used in nursing education to instil critical thinking in nursing students. Participants expressed that the use of case pedagogy helped them acquire critical thinking skills. This is related to the findings by Forsgren et al. (2014) who state that case pedagogy is not as prevalent as other methods such as the lecture method. If correctly utilised, case pedagogy has been found to be effective in promoting critical thinking in nursing students. Bastable (2021) supports the current study by stating that students' critical thinking abilities are enriched if they have a voice in the learning process, furthermore an increase in the learning process is reported to be one of the key factors in developing sound

A study conducted by Gholami et al. (2017) relates to the current study, as it explored the experiences of undergraduate nursing students in terms of the implementation of case pedagogy in an emergency nursing course. The outcomes of this study indicated that, for Iranian nursing students, case pedagogy was a stressful but pleasant and empowering experience that develops critical thinking.

In a study carried out in Central South University in China, Qi et al. (2018) investigated the efficiency of case pedagogy in a course on practical skills for nursing undergraduate students. The outcome of their study, based on a critical thinking scale, showed higher scores in the experimental group on all dimensions compared to the control group (p < 0.01). Their study also disclosed how case-based pedagogy improves critical thinking.

Furthermore, the participants of the current study expressed that case pedagogy advantaged them in numerous ways, the main ones being that they were able to link theory to practice, analyse and evaluate conditions, identify and solve health-related problems and broaden their knowledge. This finding agrees with that of Dale and Dale (2017), who state that case pedagogy is ordinarily directed towards a tangible or theoretical situation, a community group or institution or an individual, and requires thorough analysis of the area of concern followed by judgemental decision-making to solve the problem. It also correlates with Kaddoura (2011), who states certain pedagogical advantages, including that it assists in an active learning strategy, it focuses on students as the epicentre of the learning environment, it develops problem-solving ability and it integrates theory into practice.

Kaddoura (2011) affirms that case pedagogy engages students and teachers in analytic dialogue about nursing situations by helping learners analyse an authentic case with a view to identifying client problems, comparing and evaluating optional solutions and deciding how to deal with clinical situations. Kaddoura (2011) further proposes that it helps integrate multiple sources of data, solves clinical problems, provides logical scientific rationale for decision-making processes and describes complex situations that can be used in learning about professional practice. Klimová and Lovászová (2019) add that critical thinking allows one to interpret, analyse and evaluate the quality of information and thought processes, to formulate judgements and defend conclusions.

Participants expressed that case pedagogy enabled them to understand diagnostic tests, treatment and how to manage their patients. This finding is in line with that of Kaddoura (2011), who affirms that using case studies, students receive immediate feedback and are better able to enquire more deeply and broadly about diagnosis, treatment and appropriate nursing interventions for the patient. This also correlates to a study conducted by Gholami et al. (2017) who explored the experiences of under-graduate nursing students in the implementation of case pedagogy in an emergency nursing course. The outcomes of the present study indicated that case pedagogy improved diagnostic abilities and helped acquire professional competencies for use in future practice through the creation of a positive environment.

Participants affirmed that case studies allowed them to score better marks compared to other assessment methods. This is in agreement with Daniels et al.'s (2015) study conducted at the School of Nursing, University of the Western Cape, South Africa, which found that the use of case-based education benefited students, as they scored higher on assessment tasks that required analysis and evaluation and on patient assessment, diagnosis and treatment plans. In contrast, Daniels et al.'s (2015) study recognised that assessment was a challenge in the implementation of case pedagogy, noting that to further improve the implementation of case pedagogy, further workshops were needed with a specific focus on assessment strategies.

Impact on students' experiences

The level of skills at which a graduate from nursing school must perform has been raised, and the escalation of the competency level for nurses has been attributed to the increase in the complexity of patient conditions and the increase in technological skill required to practise in a complex healthcare environment. Dutra (2013) participants expressed that they found some case studies complex and they did not have enough time to do their case studies. This finding relates to Mostert's (2007) findings that deeper levels of complexity are not immediately clear and may take an inordinate amount of time to discover, that students who lack classroom experience may be incapable of recognising the finer issues presented in the case and that without sufficient preparation and reflection, deeper case issues might remain unknown. The current study also relates to Dale and Dale's (2017) study, which states that developing cases is time consuming and may be difficult. Furthermore, Dale and Dale (2017) conclude by stating that nurses' practice surroundings are regularly complex, chaotic and changing, which makes each day different and challenging (Dale and Dale, 2017).

Nelson (2017) and Von Colln-Appling and Giuliano (2016) urge that it is the duty of nurse educators to help students to acquire critical thinking skills. Participants in the current study complained that there was not enough support and guidance from their preceptor's side to help them carry out their case studies. The findings of this study relate to those of Mangena and Chabeli 2005) who assessed the factors that prevent critical thinking skills acquisition among nursing students. Their study was based on educators' and students' perspectives. They found that educators' lack of knowledge of critical thinking teaching methods and evaluation, negative attitudes of educators, student selection and educational background, socialisation, culture and language prevented the development of students' critical thinking skills.

Limitations

The research was conducted at one university satellite campus. This limited generalisation of the study findings to other campuses.

CONCLUSIONS

The study also shows that most students were able to acquire critical thinking skills and that they were equipped to analyse and evaluate conditions. Furthermore, the findings of the current study also show that students acquired the necessary confidence to identify and solve health-related problems. However, the study also found that students were not given sufficient time to complete/present their case studies. Furthermore, most of the participants in this study reported that clinical instructors did not provide sufficient support when students had to address complex case studies. Findings from this chapter may help identify strengths and weaknesses in the use of case pedagogy for assessment purposes in nursing and midwifery education.

Recommendations

The following recommendations are offered in order to improve the use of case pedagogy as a strategy to promote critical thinking among nursing students:

The nursing school should allow students to do case studies in groups so the students can share ideas. By doing this, students will be able to tackle complex cases. Preceptors should allocate adequate time for students to complete their case studies. If more time is allocated, students will not feel rushed and will not hand in hastily prepared case studies. Participants in the current study suggested that preceptors should draft more case studies for them to exercise their critical thinking skills. In turn, preceptors should come up efficient strategies that promote critical thinking skills.

REFERENCES

Bastable, S. B. (2021). *Nurse as educator: Principles of teaching and learning for nursing practice*. Jones & Bartlett Learning.

Bi, M., Zhao, Z., Yang, J., & Wang, Y. (2019). Comparison of case-based learning and traditional method in teaching postgraduate students of medical oncology. *Medical Teacher*, 41(10), 1124–1128. DOI: 10.1080/0142159X.2019.1617414 PMID: 31215320

Boso, C. M., van der Merwe, A. S., & Gross, J. (2020). Critical thinking skills of nursing students: Observations of classroom instructional activities. *Nursing Open*, 7(2), 581–588. DOI: 10.1002/nop2.426 PMID: 32089855

Brink, H., & Van der Walt, C. (2018). *Fundamentals of research methodology for health care professionals*. Juta and Company Ltd.

Colaizzi, P. F. (1978). Psychological research as the phenomenologist views it.

Dale, J. G., & Dale, B. (2017). Implementing a new pedagogy in nursing curriculum: Bachelor student's evaluation. *Journal of Nursing Education and Practice*, 7(12), 98–104. DOI: 10.5430/jnep.v7n12p98

Daniels, F. M., Fakude, L. P., Linda, N. S., & Modeste, R. R. M. (2015). Nurse educators' experiences of case-based education in a South African nursing programme. *Curationis*, 38(2), 1–8. DOI: 10.4102/curationis.v38i2.1523 PMID: 26842092

Dutra, D. K. (2013). Implementation of case studies in undergraduate didactic nursing courses: A qualitative study. *BMC Nursing*, 12(1), 1–9. DOI: 10.1186/1472-6955-12-15 PMID: 23826925

Forsgren, S., Christensen, T., & Hedemalm, A. (2014). Evaluation of the case method in nursing education. *Nurse Education in Practice*, 14(2), 164–169. DOI: 10.1016/j.nepr.2013.08.003 PMID: 24041633

Gholami, M., Saki, M., Toulabi, T., Moghadam, P. K., Pour, A. H. H., & Dostizadeh, R. (2017). Iranian nursing students' experiences of case-based learning: A qualitative study. *Journal of Professional Nursing*, 33(3), 241–249. DOI: 10.1016/j.profnurs.2016.08.013 PMID: 28577817

Holloway, I., & Galvin, K. (2023). *Qualitative research in nursing and healthcare*. John Wiley & Sons.

Hycner, R. H. (1985). Some guidelines for the phenomenological analysis of interview data. *Human Studies*, 8(3), 279–303. DOI: 10.1007/BF00142995

Kaddoura, M. A. (2011). Critical thinking skills of nursing students in lecture-based teaching and case-based learning. *International Journal for the Scholarship of Teaching and Learning*, 5(2), n2. DOI: 10.20429/ijsotl.2011.050220

Klimová, N., & Lovászová, G. (2019). Development of Critical Thinking in Education: A Case Study on Hoax Messages. In *2019 17th International Conference on Emerging eLearning Technologies and Applications (ICETA)* (pp. 396-402). IEEE. DOI: 10.1109/ICETA48886.2019.9040087

Leenders, M. R., Mauffette-Leenders, L. A., & Erskine, J. A. (2001). Writing cases. 4th ed. Ivey Publishing, Richard Ivey School of Business Lincoln, Y. S., & Guba, E. G. (1985). Naturalistic Inquiry London Sage Publications.

Mahdi, O. R., Nassar, I. A., & Almuslamani, H. A. I. (2020). The Role of Using Case Studies Method in Improving Students' Critical Thinking Skills in Higher Education. *International Journal of Higher Education*, 9(2), 297–308. DOI: 10.5430/ijhe.v9n2p297

Mangena, A., & Chabeli, M. M. (2005). Strategies to overcome obstacles in the facilitation of critical thinking in nursing education. *Nurse Education Today*, 25(4), 291–298. DOI: 10.1016/j.nedt.2005.01.012 PMID: 15896414

Maree, K. (2016). *First steps in research*. Van Schaik Publishers.

Mellish, J. M., Brink, H., & Paton, F. (1998). *Teaching and learning the practice of nursing*. Heinemann.

Mostert, M. P. (2007). Challenges of case-based teaching. *The Behavior Analyst Today*, 8(4), 434–442. DOI: 10.1037/h0100632

Nelson, A. E. (2017). Methods faculty use to facilitate nursing students' critical thinking. *Teaching and Learning in Nursing*, 12(1), 62–66. DOI: 10.1016/j.teln.2016.09.007

Oliveira, L. B. D., Díaz, L. J. R., Carbogim, F. D. C., Rodrigues, A. R. B., & Püschel, V. A. D. A. (2016). Effectiveness of teaching strategies on the development of critical thinking in undergraduate nursing students: a meta-analysis. *Revista da Escola de Enfermagem da USP, 50*, 0355-0364.

Pagnucci, N., Carnevale, F. A., Bagnasco, A., Tolotti, A., Cadorin, L., & Sasso, L. (2015). A cross-sectional study of pedagogical strategies in nursing education: Opportunities and constraints toward using effective pedagogy. *BMC Medical Education*, 15(1), 1–12. DOI: 10.1186/s12909-015-0411-5 PMID: 26303930

Penn, M. L., Currie, C. S., Hoad, K. A., & O'Brien, F. A. (2016). The use of case studies in OR teaching. *Higher Education Pedagogies*, 1(1), 16–25. DOI: 10.1080/23752696.2015.1134201

Popil, I. (2011). Promotion of critical thinking by using case studies as teaching method. *Nurse Education Today*, 31(2), 204–207. DOI: 10.1016/j.nedt.2010.06.002 PMID: 20655632

Qi, M., Yi, Q., Mo, M., Huang, H., & Yang, Y. (2018). Application of case-based learning in instructing clinical skills on nursing undergraduates. *Biomedical Research (Aligarh)*, 29(2), 300–304. DOI: 10.4066/biomedicalresearch.29-17-2377

Toofany, S. (2008). Critical thinking among nurses. *Nursing Management*, 14(9), 28–31. DOI: 10.7748/nm2008.02.14.9.28.c6344 PMID: 18372840

Von Colln-Appling, C., & Giuliano, D. (2016). A concept analysis of critical thinking: A guide for nurse educators. *Nurse Education Today*, 49, 106–109. DOI: 10.1016/j.nedt.2016.11.007 PMID: 27902948

Wu, X., Heng, M., & Wang, W. (2015). Nursing students' experiences with the use of an authentic assessment rubric and a case approach in clinical laboratories. *Nurse Education Today*, 35(4), 549–555. DOI: 10.1016/j.nedt.2014.12.009 PMID: 25577674

KEY TERMS AND DEFINITIONS

Case pedagogy: A form of patient oriented, student centered, and inquiry-based teaching and learning method that aims to prepare students for clinical practice, through the use of authentic clinical case studies.

Critical thinking: A purposeful thinking in which individuals systematically and habitually impose criteria and intellectual standards upon their thought.

Cooperative learning approach: involves pupils working together on activities or learning tasks in a group small enough to ensure that everyone participates.

Problem solving: the act of defining a problem; determining the cause of the problem; identifying, prioritizing, and selecting alternatives for a solution; and implementing a solution.

Chapter 5
Enhancing Graduates' Intercultural Competences and Awareness Through Cocreation in Higher Education

Icarbord Tshabangu
https://orcid.org/0000-0003-4875-9369
Leeds Trinity University, UK

Paul Lancaster
https://orcid.org/0009-0006-9884-152X
Global Citizenship and Children's Rights Network, UK

ABSTRACT

In recent decades the world has found itself in an era of rapid globalisation and migration. In many contexts and cultures, citizens are still coming to terms with the implications of globalisation. The vital role that higher education (HE) institutions can play must not only be emphasised, but strategies, new approaches and initiatives also need to be embraced and adopted to ensure diversity is an advantage and not a source of conflict. It is further noted that notions of 'interculturalism' are still not understood in many contexts and are still confused with 'multiculturalism'. This chapter demonstrates that interculturalism goes beyond multiculturalism, and further locates its place and usefulness within Higher Education, particularly through co-creation efforts. The chapter posits a need for higher educational institutions

DOI: 10.4018/979-8-3693-3443-0.ch005

to embed intercultural competencies, advance understanding of one's own culture and promote intercultural dialogue in multicultural contexts, especially in Higher education as part of bridging the skills gap and enhancing employability.

INTRODUCTION

This chapter posits that if education is not intercultural it is probably not education, further noting that low priority is given to the acquisition of Intercultural competencies (ICC) in higher education (HE), which then impacts wider practices by graduates, particularly in healthcare settings and in schools, where significant challenges face newly qualified practitioners when working with those of other cultures and ethnicities (Coulby 2006; Dollinger, Lodge & Coates, 2020). Embedding intercultural education within higher education through co-creation develops students' leadership skills within the multicultural context and provides helpful, quality interactions with clients and service users. Findings from a study of higher education students indicated that intercultural challenges both within their universities and work placements occurred particularly in the areas of; communication, decision-making, task orientation, attitudes to conflict, knowledge uses; prejudice, cultural barriers and many more (Bovill. 2020; Knoth, et al 2023). This chapter highlights some of these findings; outlines the models that underpin intercultural competencies and awareness; and explores the value of embedding intercultural competencies in higher education through co-creation to bridge the skills gap and further demonstrate ways to advance intercultural competencies and employability.

It is increasingly apparent in multicultural and super-diverse societies that diversity and lack of intercultural competencies may bring about conflict (Sani, 2015). From young children starting in nurseries and going through education, there is often constant exposure to different cultures and ways of life. Within an educational context, multiculturalism as a policy has accepted this reality but in recent years there has been much discussion about the difference between multicultural and intercultural education. For some, the terms are often used as synonyms, but there is an increasing understanding of the difference between them, especially in Europe as promoted by the Council of Europe (Hill 2007). Interculturalism should include interaction, exchange, reciprocity, and solidarity within the educational context. The term intercultural tends to focus more on the process of interactive competencies. In contrast, multiculturalism is perceived as a descriptive and less dynamic concept, largely defining a situation that embodies a diversity of cultures. Multiculturalism often affirms separateness, isolation, and a desire not to impose a particular worldview to become contaminated. Whilst not negating cultural diversity, intercultural education is a response to classroom diversity, aiming to go beyond a passive coexistence of cultures, to achieve a developing and sustainable way of living together in multicultural societies through the creation of understanding, respect for productive dialogue between the different groups (Hill, 2006; Perry & Southwell, 2011; Levey, 2012). The role and objectives of intercultural education according to UNESCO (2007), identify four main areas:

> *Learning to know:* - a general education brings content and substance.
> *Learning to do:* - developing competence to deal with many diverse situations.
> *Learning to live together:* - developing an understanding of others and appreciation of interdependence, cooperating among diverse individuals and groups in society resolving conflict in a spirit of solidarity.
> *Learning to allow:* - to develop one's personality, intercultural engagement and to act with sound judgment.

These objectives entail enhancing the efficiency of intercultural relations, increasing tolerance and acceptance towards those who are different, and offering training to help in perceiving, accepting and respecting diversity, especially in mediating social relations (Chiriac and Panciuc (2015). Developing intercultural competencies in higher education, through co-creation generates a global perspective alongside other forms of education that cover peace, human rights, and sustainable development. Intercultural education is not static but a concept in continuous development. Openness to different values, adaptation, intentionality, and commitment are vital to the ongoing processes, particularly when graduates join the workplace and are called upon to be effective in practice. Embedding interculturalism within higher education may be seen as a complex undertaking yet the intercultural principles and practices are inherently relevant to the entire educational environment in almost all its multifaceted components including employability. This chapter illustratively ponders on some of those opportunities for implementation.

BACKGROUND

The emerging concept of interculturalism

During the last twelve years, a fresh understanding of interculturalism has emerged, largely as a response to the failure of multiculturalism. At the Munich Security Conference (5th April 2011), the then British Prime Minister David Cameron stated that government policies of multiculturalism had failed. "Under the doctrine of state multiculturalism, we have encouraged different cultures to live separate lives. We've failed to provide a vision of society to which they feel they belong..."

It became increasingly apparent that people of different ethnicities may live in the same community but not necessarily engage with one another. Other terms and methods such as 'community cohesion', 'assimilation' and 'integration' have been used to establish a more equal and just society but have also failed to gain traction.

Cantle (2012) not only recognised the need for a new way forward but proffered interculturalism distinguishing it from multiculturalism even though this has been contested. Cantle states (2016 p158) that "Interculturalism… is more about a culture of openness than multiculturalism… it challenges identity politics and entrenchment of separate communities based on otherness. It is a…dynamic process in which, there will be tension and conflict as a necessary part of societal change." He sees interculturalism as moving away from a static position to a "multidirectional process". It is noted that the equality and diversity agenda associated with multiculturalism is still important but has tended to focus on ensuring the rights and protection of different cultures, while interculturalism focuses on "…an innovative outcome from the interaction. Through interaction, something new is potentially generated which drives individual and social developments" (Zapata-Barrero 2016: 11). Interculturalism is therefore seen as emphasising creativity and innovation, with diversity as an asset and an opportunity. The implications of this in education are enormous and will be considered later.

Wood and Landry (2004) argue that interculturalism opens the way to value different visions of dealing with intractable problems, thus creating hybrid intercultural projects pointing to a positive way forward. When it comes to wider issues of identity, interculturalism whilst recognising the importance of cultural identity, points to the influences of globalisation in helping cultures not to be static, but to be constantly evolving, spawning hybridity. Fanshawe and Sriskandarajah (2010) in their Public Policy Research Report *"You Can't Put Me in A Box"* also assert that interculturalism cannot be defined as interaction between 'formal identities'. IC also includes hybridisation between cultural communities. Such thinking challenges traditional approaches in the British Census 2001 with defined categories such as White, Mixed, Asian British, Black British, Chinese, etc. However, this raises the issue of corporate identity as distinct from individual identity. As Parekh points out, some cultural groups wish to remain within distinct community identities and therefore interculturalism must consider this too. From the context of French-speaking Canadians, Bouchard (2011) offers another standpoint advocating that interculturalism should be just as concerned about the majority, as it is with migrant minorities. Sen (2016) however argues that it is important to emphasise freedom of choice in determining cultural identity. He acknowledges that too much individualism in an intercultural society is not conducive but strongly opposes an 'imposed' communal identity, which limits individual gifts and talents. Recognising this, especially when one is in leadership, is useful in maintaining balance.

Intercultural dialogue

The place for dialogue within the concept of intercultural education is seen to be a vital component, and this can be contrasted with a multicultural approach. It is noted that multiculturalism celebrates differences in culture. It does not necessarily encourage interactions. On the other hand, interculturalism positively promotes honest, open, and critical interactions so that obstacles can be overcome, and shared values recognised (Alfridi, 2012). It is advocated that no culture should occupy a superior position over any other and that there should be openness to questioning cultural boundaries, especially when causing mono-cultural ethnocentrism. It is further observed that an intercultural political community cannot expect its members to develop a sense of belonging unless it equally values and cherishes their diversity and reflects this in its structures and policies (Cantle, 2012). The concept of 'cherishing' is important as it points to a heart response, underlining intentionality, rather than ideological policies. It is important therefore, for educational leaders to be aware of developments in interculturalism and the varied nuances that have emerged.

Co-creation in Higher Education (HE)

Co-creation within the Higher Education context is ideal for enhancing students' and staff's intercultural competence and awareness. Similar values such as inclusiveness, equality, building relationships, addressing diversity and dialogic communication all fall within the remit of co-creation. "Co-creating with students is a process by which students collaborate with teachers in designing their own learning experiences. With an emphasis on student perspectives, it is based on constructivist theory, which posits that learners construct knowledge and meaning from lived experiences rather than passively taking in information" (Katz, 2021; p1). As higher education institutions are increasingly internationalised, co-creation provides opportunities for enriched intercultural experiences and increased employability prospects. There are several advantages that co-creation brings in its wake. Staff-student partnerships tend to improve the overall quality of education, e.g., in developing courses together,' bridging gaps 'between the formal structures of HE and students, giving students opportunities to increase leadership and communication skills and staff mentoring and coaching ability. Co-creation also provides an environment of greater inclusiveness, social justice and equity which is particularly important for international students and those from disadvantaged backgrounds (Ohara, 2023).

Co-creation may mean different things to different people, coupled with a fundamental shift from teacher-led methods to more 'active learning processes and to what some have referred to as a move from "sage on the stage to the guide on the side" or "the muddler in the middle", which points to work things out from a different position (Lubicz -Nawroka, 2020; King, 1993; McWilliams, 2009). Co-creation posits a 'deeper relationship' between staff and students where processing educational outcomes is shared. Some would distinguish between the co-creation of the curriculum and co-creation in the curriculum, which suggests that staff may have reservations about how far to go with the co-creation process (Bovill, 2020; Bovill and Woolmer, 2018).

Some of the identified co-creation challenges highlight the general vulnerability of staff thus encouraging them to "take off their academic armour", through opening up and being able to demonstrate they were at par with students during co-creation. Such may proactively deal with further challenges, such as the need to address power dynamics, setting out different expectations, appreciating differences in communication styles and appreciating staff and students' workload which can have a restrictive impact on a co-creation project (Ohara, 2023).

Overall, the positive impacts of co-creation are generally seen as providing a way forward even though understanding is still evolving. Namvaret, et al (2021) emphasise the need for 'bridging experiences' such as extra-curricular activities supported by staff, especially those from disadvantaged or diverse backgrounds. Good academic relationships are seen as a key to success. Creative, inclusive, and informal social opportunities, provide ways for students and staff to learn from one another and become a co-creative community. Students can be seen as colleagues in co-creative research and curriculum designs. It is noted that if students' freshness and brilliance are affirmed there is 'no limit' to what they can offer due to being inspired, empowered, and motivated. (Namvaret et al., 2021).

CULTURAL AWARENESS AND UNDERSTANDING

There has been much research on culture, its concept, its characteristics, and how an understanding of our own culture and our worldview influences our response to other cultures. The impact of globalisation, especially second and third-generation migrants is another key issue. Having raised these issues with varied students, there seemed to be little awareness of intercultural knowledge's significance in education. This suggests there must be a more intentional approach to cultivating greater understanding and bringing a new dimension within educational leadership.

What is culture?

Amongst the many definitions of culture, some have relevance when considering intercultural leadership e.g., Shwartz (1992- Oatey. H. S p3) outlines the scope of culture. Culture consists of derivatives of experience, organised, learned, and created by the individuals of a population. These include images or encodement and their interpretation, transmitted from past generations, from contemporaries, or formed by an individual (Hofstede, 1994; 2020. Culture is seen as a collective programming of the mind which distinguishes the members of one group or category of people from another. It can also be defined as a fuzzy set of basic assumptions and values, orientations to life, beliefs, policies, procedures, and behavioural conventions shared by groups of people that influence each member's behaviour… (Oatey, 2012). Equality and diversity policies do not address the deeper aspects of culture and much teaching and learning only considers surface differences rather than penetrating to the core of what determines such differences. Bunkowske's (2011) cultural onion model identifies several layers to a given culture. It starts with the outer layer of artefacts and behaviours, then values and beliefs, and finally the worldview and ultimate allegiance.

The influence of globalisation on culture and work

The impact of globalisation is another important factor when considering the intercultural implications for educational leaders. The multicultural workforce is constantly increasing in most sectors allowing employers and employees from diverse backgrounds to foster collaboration, promote cross-cultural understanding, enhance creativity, and encourage the exchange of ideas. The virtual workplace creates greater flexibility and the opportunity to connect with global talent and move beyond traditional working patterns. (Pradham, 2023). Watson (2024) refers to this as 'time-space compression' providing 'instant communication'. Although global-isation affords greater access to different cultures, it can give rise to stereotyping, misrepresentation, and the loss of cultural property. Different cultures often express a profound loss of group identity in multicultural settings. In particular, the present education, legal and power structures reflect Western ideas and philosophies, and it is often assumed that such values and ideologies of the Global North, should be adopted by the Global South (Ziyan, 2023). Looking through an intercultural lens at the current composition of Western societies, such factors cannot be ignored.

In contrast, a more positive view of globalisation allows cultures to represent themselves and their identities and acquire new knowledge and the means of sharing information, thus strengthening relationships. Instead of destroying cultures the globalisation effect of mass media can help revitalise them, preserving traditions and collective identities. Furthermore, globalisation can bring a sharp focus on gov-ernment policies, provide access to education, and communicate injustices. (Haloi 2021)All these factors resonate with the more rigorous nature of interculturalism as distinct from more diluted policies.

Knowing your own culture to know others

An often-overlooked human behaviour is recognising the influences on one's cultural outlook. When doing courses on cross-cultural studies, there is a lot of emphasis on learning about other cultures but not learning about one's own culture. Most people don't realise that we possess our own culture and tend to draw strength from it like a fish in a fishbowl (Renee, 2022). It is noted that the fish is unaware of how water and the glass distort its view of the world. Our own culture is like the glass and the water and our view of the world. It is through such a distorted screen that has resulted in unconsciously held beliefs and worldviews. Surbhi (2019) has identified how enculturation has shaped an individual's development, values, and worldview in forming identity. These include race, gender, ethnicity, religion and socio-economic status. It can be useful for educators to ask probing questions about early memories of their family life and how attitudes and worldviews were formed. Although this may seem obvious it has profound implications on education. Educators may need to examine whether such experiences have shaped their unconscious attitudes, including their interactions with students within the educational processes. This kind of exercise helps to apply another important component of interculturalism, adopting a deeper approach to one's own culture which, in turn, provides scope for a greater appreciation and sensitivity to those from different cultures, thus leading the way for equipping educational leaders in Intercultural competence. It is noted that self-awareness is an integral component of navigating the world more comfortably. By taking some time to think about and understand your own culture...you will be better able to address different questions from people who might see you and the world differently than you do (Verghese, P 2016; Renee, 2022).

INTERCULTURAL COMPETENCE MODELS

Various models for developing intercultural competence (ICC) have been proposed to help those in educational leadership apply a new level of understanding in their given contexts and these will now be considered.

Deardorff- Knowledge, Skills, and Attitudes Model

Although cultural self-awareness is an important starting point, intercultural competence (ICC) by its very nature has an outward focus. The term acculturation broadens the scope of IC where educators can play a crucial role. *Cultural Knowledge* can be acquired in learning through experience e.g., in games, activities, traditional and social media, face-to-face interaction and projects. *Skills* could be developed when learners compare what is unfamiliar with what is familiar. They begin to understand what is normal for them, and not for others (Deardorff, 2006, 2020; Barrett, 2012). This can lead to developing analytical skills for different practices, values, and beliefs. Skills can also be acquired through action and co-operative projects such as improvements in the social and physical environment. When considering *Attitudes Deardorff* highlights 'respect, openness (withholding judgement), curiosity, (viewing difference as a learning opportunity) and discovery (tolerance for ambiguity). Furthermore, she points out that internal outcomes lead to 'greater flexibility, adaptability, empathy, appropriate behaviour, and effectiveness (Coventry Domain (2018), George Mason University(2024), Huish et al (2203).

Although knowledge, skills and attitudes can manifest in any interaction among people, they particularly apply to intercultural exchanges. ICC does not come about with random interactions, but rather from being intentional. Students and staff must be exposed to different methods including programmes, courses, and organised cross-cultural experiences. Institutional commitment to ICC lasts for a lifetime and is not some qualification.

Assessing intercultural competence

Deardorff also raises the question "How will we know?" how effective ICC learning has been for students as future educators, so she has developed an assessment tool (Assessing Students' Intercultural Learning in Education Abroad Programmes 2013). The content raises many questions for educational leaders to consider. What does student success look like in your course/programme regarding IC learning? How will students know they've been successful in their IC learning? How would others know your students have been successful in their IC learning? How do you define ICC? What frameworks (literature) are you currently using to frame ICC in your programme? What are some of the challenges you face in assessing students' IC learning and how realistic and achievable are the learning objectives?

Deardorff also references some common intercultural learning outcomes generated in an ACE roundtable discussion (Olson, Evans and Schoenberg. American Council on Education 2007) which helps bring some definition to what students should be able to do because of ICC learning.

Knowledge/ Content Orientated e.g.

- Understand various cultures and how culture is created
- Develop a nuanced/complex understanding of culture as a concept and the deep/complex/dynamic nature of culture.
- Understand how language frames thinking and perspective

- Understand the interconnectedness and interdependence of global systems
- Understand the cultural, economic and political forces that shape society
- Recognise how stereotypes develop and where they come from

Attitudes/Mode of Being e.g.

- Overcome provincial/parochial thinking
- Reduce own prejudice
- Appreciate difference; value and acknowledge other cultures as legitimate
- Improve cultural self-awareness and of one's self in a global context
- Develop empathy, open-mindedness and an understanding of complexity

Skills e.g.

- Link theory and practice through own experience both as citizens and professionals
- Develop and use IC skills
- Develop and use skills in conflict resolution
- Internalise and apply cultural understandings and knowledge
- Seek out multiple perspectives

Approaches and activities that help to develop Intercultural Competence

Huber and Reynolds (2014) have suggested some specific activities in teaching and learning that have proven helpful in the development of ICC. Research has shown that teaching or lecturing delivered to passive listeners is effective when limited time is given to skills and actions.

Huber and Reynold (2014) suggest that *cooperative learning* is useful in promoting ICC. Cooperative learning encourages students, pupils, or participants to be "individually responsible for their learning and the work of the group as a whole." Activities emphasising multiple perspectives help develop skills of observation; interpretation, and de-centring, such as narrating stories, fictional or non-fictional especially those drawn from their biographies. Compiling such writings creates rich pedagogical material for discussion and analysis. Other creative activities could include role play, simulation, and drama activities, in which learners must act completely differently from their usual ways. Ethnographic tasks such as interviewing people in a diverse neighbourhood, to find out how they live day to day and what matters to them can be useful in developing ICC. Films and texts on diversity can be a key to self-reflection and openness to understanding different contextualised perspectives. The use of social media, e.g. ZOOM and TEAMS are powerful tools that can encourage engagement with "otherness", not only in a localised context but across national borders. In considering themes such as Global Citizenship, and conflict resolution in international conflicts, ICC plays a vital role.

Intercultural Sensitivity- Bennet's Developmental Model of Intercultural Sensitivity (DMIS)

Although much has been written about ICC since Bennett (2004), it is noted that a vital aspect of what Deardorff would categorise as *Attitudes* defines two broad categories of ethnocentrism and ethno-relativism within those defined six stages. These stages are helpful for those in leadership, in not only understanding their position but also identifying where others may be when creating a more meaningful basis for both dialogue and application. His essential argument is that as people become more interculturally competent they move from 'ethnocentrism' to "ethno-relativism. Ethnocentrism is defined as seeing one's own culture as central to reality, beliefs and behaviours that are determined in primary socialisation. Such a position is unquestioned and understood as 'just the way things are'. On the other hand, ethno-relativism is the opposite of ethno-relativism and is defined as seeing one's own beliefs and behaviours as just one organisation of reality amongst many.

Within the first band of ***ethnocentrism,*** Bennet identifies three stages.

Stage 1 is *Denial* when one's own culture is seen to be the only real one. Cultural difference has either not been experienced or is experienced with an 'undifferentiated other' such as a foreigner or immigrant. People with a denial worldview tend to be disinterested in cultural differences e.g. they would tend to categorise immigrants and asylum seekers in generalised and simplistic ways.

Stage 2 is *Defence* when one's own culture is experienced as the only viable one and most developed. There is a tendency to stereotype different cultures and usually a feeling of being threatened, e.g., when immigrants are readily accused of taking people's jobs.

Stage 3 is *Minimisation* when there is an attempt to minimise cultural differences and focus on commonality rather than a more sophisticated understanding of difference. A typical comment might be "We're all human beings" when issues of cultural differences are being raised but a good question to ask is on whose terms?

The second band is described as ***ethno-relativism*** and again three stages are identified.

Stage 4 is classified as *Acceptance* when the cultural difference is acknowledged and one's own culture is seen as just one of the equally complex worldviews. With acceptance, it becomes possible to construct general categories of culture and differentiate between them without overly stereotyping.

Bennet points out that it is possible to have knowledge and skill in relating to another culture but not experience another's worldview. Acceptance does not mean liking or agreeing with another cultural worldview.

Stage 5 is described as *Adaptation* when empathy is expressed with those from another culture. Again, this does not mean surrendering one's worldview or losing a particular cultural identity to relate to a different cultural context. It may be asked, however, whether it is possible to behave and respond to another culture and still be true to oneself. Bennett suggests that perhaps a way forward is to define oneself more broadly. Those who may have lived in different cultural settings, especially during formative years usually can operate flexibly in this area.

The final Stage 6 *Integration* is thought to be the most important stage in development, when it is possible to construct one's own identity at the margin of two or three identities and central to none.

"Here people can experience themselves as multicultural beings …constantly choosing the most appropriate cultural context for their behaviour. Living on the edge of cultures may be stressful and alienating, but usually exhilarating. Integrating in this way does not mean losing one's identity, nor does it make better or superior people, but it does demonstrate a greater adaptability in different cultural contexts.

Bennet's template is not a prescriptive methodology or a 'jumping through hoops' to become interculturally competent, but rather a descriptive model of how progress is often made in coming to terms with cultural differences. This can provide a useful reference point for educators and students in developing different approaches and understanding of cultural backgrounds.

SALTO - European Youth Work Model: Intercultural Research Report (2012)

As part of its work, SALTO (2012 Support Advanced Learning and Training Opportunities for Youth) started a long-term project on how to better support the development of Intercultural Competence in youth work. SALTO's particular emphasis within ICC was on the implications for social justice. They suggest ICC enables a young person to "take an active role in confronting social injustice and discrimination and promote and protect human rights." (Bortini, P Motamed-Ashari, B (2012) p4 Therefore ICC requires an understanding of culture as a dynamic, multifaceted approach. Furthermore, it requires an "increased sense of solidarity in which the individual fear of the other and insecurity are dealt with through critical thinking, empathy and tolerance of ambiguity."(ibid p5) Included in confronting social justice and discrimination is also being aware of the reasons behind possible situations that arise. In understanding culture as multi-faceted (Bortini p34) it is recognised that it is not fixed and that coming to terms with one's own culture is an important part of the process. A balance is suggested between fostering critical thinking and creating empathy, moving away from stagnant and stereotypical viewpoints towards critical dialogue but pursuing it with mutual curiosity.

Finally, the report was not about discussions of the correctness of these aspects of intercultural competence but aimed to look at the respondents' understanding by looking back at their training (ibid p31)

DIALLS (Dialogue and Argumentation for Cultural Literacy Learning in Schools) 2019

The DIALLS project seeks to advance intercultural dialogue through "…developing the concept and idea of cultural literacy… For DIALLS cultural literacy means a social practice that is inherently dialogic and based on learning and gaining knowledge with others, through empathetic, tolerant and inclusive interaction". Maine F (2019) Thus, cultural literacy is the process of engaging with cultures, the disposition to do so, and the co-creation and expression of cultural identities and values (Maine, Cook & Lahdesmaki (2019). Based on their analysis of European and national education policy they have recommended that policymakers pay attention to the meaning of culture as firstly not being static but taught and transmitted to young people based on 'constantly transforming and fluid collective action' and interaction between diverse groups; secondly that factual knowledge of culture and heritage should not be used as the main focus for cultural interaction as this may lead to cultural stereotyping and categorising that prevents people from being seen as individuals; thirdly individual and collective identities should be seen as multi-layered, processual and transforming. (ibid p6)

Amongst other recommendations, are more attention being given to the variety of meanings of citizenship; that dialogic interaction with others is vital to the learning process; a greater understanding of how power structures can be both inclusive and exclusive; that much European education policy tends to be 'problem-based' responding to a particular issue rather than a positive engagement with diversity advantage (ibid p7).

Other dialogic techniques

Several practitioners have identified several dialogic techniques which encourage people to engage in dialogue which seeks to avoid stoking up conflict e.g., Leeds Faiths Forum promotes the use of 'oops/ouch' which encourages young people to say 'ouch' when a question or statement hurts them or 'oops' when a statement comes out wrong. For example, Together for Peace (Leeds) uses 'Open Space' and 'World Café'. These have proved useful because they maximise interaction and decision-making among diverse groups. They create a 'non-judgemental' environment which enables people to 'get things off their chest'.

Worldly Leadership

Whilst what has been presented so far is relevant to educational leadership, it is important to emphasise that leadership perspectives of the global south be considered as part of bridging gaps and understanding. Western academics have almost exclusively developed leadership theory. Turnbull and Case, Khakwani (2012: 6) have coined the term 'Worldly leadership' in contrast to a globalised worldview. They suggest "this globe is made up of all kinds of worlds" (Mintzberg 2004 p304) Someone who is defined as being 'worldly' can carry negative connotations, especially from a religious perspective but they argue that a worldly leader has "not only be aware but be open to and inclusive of national and cultural differences and uniqueness of colleagues and subordinates."(Tunball et al 2012: 18). This includes learning from non-western aspects of leadership, especially within the educational context as this can determine how intercultural methodology, bridging skill gaps, can be applied in a whole range of vocational contexts.

FINDINGS FROM A CO-CREATION PROJECT ON ICC AND AWARENESS IN HIGHER EDUCATION

Qualitative data was gathered from eight higher education students who had completed an Intercultural Leadership programme. Their reflective accounts reflected the common intercultural challenges facing higher education students within their university and at work placements. They were asked to identify intercultural barriers, based on their experiences, what should be done to support educators/tutors in developing intercultural competence in educational settings; and what education institutions and work placements could do to help students develop intercultural awareness.

COMMON INTERCULTURAL CHALLENGES FACING STUDENTS

Communication

Most students noted that all cultures have their own peculiar language and communication style, and certain meanings to non-verbal behaviours and informal communication may mean something completely different in other cultures. In a sense, language-verbal or non-verbal, formal, or informal (including tone, gestures and behaviours) is culture-specific. Problems arise when an individual from a different culture fails to decode other communication styles leading to misunderstanding of communicated information or its intentions. Instances of ethnocentrism and super impositions arise during work and learning where staff or students consciously or unconsciously refuse to accept that there are culture-specific linguistic variations that influence intercultural communication. These challenges often have a negative impact by reducing the quality of learning and work output. Such misunderstandings in communication also tend to cause conflicts and frustration thus negatively impacting all involved – tutors, students, service users, and general quality of service or engagement.

Attitudes to conflict

Data collected from respondents reveals that cultures tend to display different attitudes towards conflict. While some cultures may view conflict positively, as an integral part of growth and development others will not. Problems arise in intercultural contexts when one insists on using their cultural methods and chooses to ignore other cultural approaches completely. One respondent emphasised that attitudes towards conflict are instilled in an individual, quite early in life. As a result, it is not easy to see beyond their cultural upbringing in intercultural contexts.

Approaches to tasks

Findings from the study support the view that some aspects of completing tasks are culture-specific which can give rise to misunderstandings and conflict. A specific example was given "Unlike in the western cultures, the global south cultures usually emphasise on building relationships and are less individualistic." Differences in prioritising tasks, delegating within team structures, and managing time and deadlines were also identified. In most Western institutions time management and workload allocation may consider holidays like Easter and Christmas but ignore some of their students/teachers' or workers' need for observance of their cultural holidays such as religious festivals.

During these times teachers/tutors and students miss out on placement, teaching and learning time, which can affect final performance. For some international students' completing projects in the West may be challenging as they perceive the approaches to be different coupled with problems in communication, acclimatisation, and accessibility. As a result, students' engagement /group work effectiveness and self-esteem may be compromised.

Reaching Decisions

The study identified that whenever two or more cultures co-exist cultural differences in decision-making and processing of issues emerge. These are based on beliefs values and norms which show some preferring autonomous approaches whilst others are more used to group-based decisions or letting leaders decide for them. While some may prefer policy or research-informed decisions others gravitate towards an exercise of authority or personal experiences to determine issues. Due to a liberalist worldview and individualism, most Westerners do not seem to have as much of a challenge in decision-making at various levels compared to most cultures of the global south, where communitarian values tend to slow down their decision-making as they tend to seek to embrace a corporate community and worldview.

Approaches to knowing and information

Most respondents seemed to share a strong view that culture-centred differences in approaches to knowing or handling information, constitute intercultural challenges, impacting teachers/tutors and students. One response was that there are differences in approaches to learning, noting that for example, African cultures generally favour emotive modes, metaphysics and oral narratives while those from Western cultures tend to be strong on the written and the physicality of things. The language barrier often inhibits information processing and understanding, but this is usually ignored. Several tutors are still unfamiliar with interculturalism particularly intercultural communication, even though there is growing receptivity towards acquiring new information, competencies, and knowledge to bridge gaps within the multicultural.

BARRIERS TO INTERCULTURAL COMMUNICATION

Anxiety

Findings reveal that anxiety is one of the pronounced barriers to intercultural communication in within educational settings, placement, and work environments. Some teachers and students experience the fear of prejudice by those of another culture and the influence of their preconceived ideas about communicating with different cultures. Being nervous, combined with the fear of offending and repelling new acquaintances, makes some people refrain from asking questions or seeking further clarification. Linguistic incompetence in using a second language makes some ethnic minority backgrounds fear and shy away from communicating with those from the main culture. Such challenges are compounded if one's culture is perceived as inferior to those he/she needs to form a relationship. Thus, individuals can miss out on opportunities to form productive relationships or enriching encounters because of the fear of the unknown

Assumptions of similarities or differences

Findings also revealed that assumptions regarding similarities or differences can become a pronounced barrier to intercultural communication in learning or workplace settings. Pre-conceived assumptions may lead to stereotyping and prejudice. One respondent noted that it is usually the assumption of similarities, rather than differences that negatively influence intercultural communication. Erroneously believing that whatever you say will be understood may cause misunderstanding, awkward moments and unintended rudeness. In interactions, it is usually those from the host culture, who expect to be understood whenever they speak. Ethnic minorities on the other hand would also be expecting other cultures to understand that they may not be communicating with the same proficiency. Assumption challenges may also lead to over-identification with certain groups, the formation of cliques and the segregation of one group from others. In the health sector, an example of the challenge of similarity assumption was lumping together under one umbrella all parents' dietary concerns and recommendations. In such a case, one would be ignoring the ethnic minority individuals' situations, assuming they will be covered by majority food selection... It is important therefore to avoid interpreting other people's behaviours and utterances through one's cultural lens.

Ethnocentrism

Ethnocentrism may lead to undue hierarchies within the workplace, which in turn, may lead to bullying and/or systematic prejudices. Findings from the study supported existing literature that when an individual believes his/her culture is more valuable/superior to other cultures, any conversation becomes a barrier to intercultural communication. This can lead to bullying, hierarchies or systematic prejudices. It may also encourage ethnic minority groups to refrain from adapting to a new culture.

Responses also revealed that ethnocentrism may lead to disdain and dislike of those from another culture, therefore exacerbating misunderstandings and conflict.

Stereotypes

Stereotypes, as traits attributed to cultural, racial or ethnic groups, can be a hindrance to intercultural communication, since this frequently leads to oversimplifying particular groupings.

Generalising other cultures and their belief systems easily gives rise to prejudice and misunderstandings. Typical examples are stereotyping whites because of the belief in white supremacy or believing that all blacks are uneducated or that Chinese are good at Mathematics. Some respondents especially international students felt that part of the treatment they received from either students or some lecturers was usually stereotypical.

Developing Intercultural Competence in Educational Settings

All respondents noted the importance of teachers/tutors being allowed to access in-service training and/or intercultural awareness training and sensitization on current trends in interculturalism. To increase institutional cultural competencies, respondents suggested the creation and encouragement of interaction with those of different heritage groups, observing and experiencing them. The opportunity could then be given to teachers/tutors to share their experiences, even negative ones, to encourage others to learn more about other cultures. Other suggestions included encouraging cultural diversity, promoting cultural awareness, encouraging open communication and equality, promoting inclusion, and facilitating further learning and research on interculturalism. There was an emphasis too on teachers understanding their own cultures and ethnic groups first as this would help them achieve mutual respect and build trust and understanding between individuals and different groups.

Conducive Environment in Education Institutions

Respondents emphasised the need for a concerted effort to promote intercultural awareness and education in all educational institutions. Several other suggestions included: providing a curriculum that is diverse and interculturally sensitive, educating both staff and students and informing them of how their own culture influences all relationships and encounters they have with other cultures; and providing lessons on languages and ways of communication. Cultural issues to be included in lectures with varying examples from different cultures outside Europe so that non-European cultures feel accepted and achieve a sense of belonging; that training such as workshops, intercultural weeks or evenings be hosted regularly by universities and led by various speakers from diverse cultural backgrounds; the intentional creation of intercultural friendly environments where difference is accepted and not ridiculed; and that the pool of staff in departments should reflect different cultures.

FURTHER RESEARCH

There tends to be much focus on intercultural competence, particularly for those from overseas, whereas there is little training in intercultural competencies for local professionals, students, and academic staff. There is a need to investigate whether there are adequate schemes to improve the intercultural agenda of various HE institutions, evaluating how different disciplines and departments, through co-creation, could best embed intercultural competence and awareness. This could enhance a broader approach to learning both in Higher Education and beyond.

Further research would be useful in developing more contextually, providing relevant training and assessment tools. This could be focused initially on a methodology that would enable a deeper understanding of students' and staff's own cultures since this has been found to generate greater intercultural awareness. Research into the effectiveness of co-creation when it comes to students and staff working together on intercultural projects and how it could be applied in their contexts, would be of value. This also raises the need to research the intersection of an individual's development stages and the acquisition of intercultural competence. Another area of investigation concerns how the different constructs of intercultural competence relate to each other and whether they overlap. Existing models of intercultural competence and awareness would benefit from further research, applying both qualitative and quantitative methodologies.

OVERALL RECOMMENDATIONS

Those engaged in educational leadership may often assume they understand what interculturalism is, thinking it is just another term for multiculturalism or a means of acquiring further knowledge about other cultures which will lead to better integration. There is a real need for educational leaders to develop a clearer view of interculturalism through in-service training which goes beyond assimilation, multiculturalism, equality, anti-racism, unconscious bias, and political agendas such as community cohesion integration, assimilation, and counterterrorism.

Furthermore, educational leaders trained in theoretical aspects of interculturalism, such as intercultural sensitivity, knowledge, skills and attitudes and cultural literacy may need to bring that knowledge and incorporate or embed it into the current curriculum and broadly within the Higher Education system. Issues such as whether educational institutions carry out intercultural projects, encouraging diverse viewpoints and interactions need to be addressed; noting how intercultural competence becomes part of the curriculum and how is it contextualised; an intercultural perspective in all disciplines, not only humanities but science, mathematics, health, and law could be invaluable.

There is a need for greater involvement of ethnic minority teachers, students, and learners, to take an active part in intercultural activities and processes in their respective institutions. The design and decor of an educational institution could also reflect intercultural thinking. Engagement with local intercultural community initiatives and particular cultural groups could be explored and students encouraged to move beyond their "cultural group bubble"

Although intercultural engagement in an educational context may be difficult to assess, various criteria could be identified within a knowledge, skills, attitudes, and sensitivity approach to intercultural competence, that would keep the practice and application of interculturalism foremost in educational leaders' minds when teaching and developing policy initiatives.

CONCLUSION

This chapter has presented some key theoretical concepts on interculturalism and its place in co-creative endeavours within higher education. It was also noted how Interculturalism points beyond multiculturalism or having a basic knowledge of different cultures, to the vital importance of interaction. Higher education providers need to be able to distinguish between multiculturalism and interculturalism in their pedagogical methods and the implications of this in all spheres of education, training and bridging of skill gaps is vital. There is a need to recognise that culture is fundamental to every individual, community and workplace, whether they recognise it or not in determining their values and worldview. In understanding individual and collective cultures, there needs to be a consideration of complexities, within these super diverse and multi-layered social structures which should be appreciated for their social dynamism. This has profound implications not just for affirming identity and engaging in effective and productive dialogues, but for bridging graduates' intercultural skills gap in the global world of work. Cultural diversity, and readiness for engagement through co-creative activities and projects in higher education, can then be seen as an advantage in the workplace, releasing creativity, cooperation, reciprocity, enriched continuous learning and fulfilling working environments for higher education graduates.

REFERENCES

Al- Nashif. N. (2017) UNESCO Survey on Intercultural Dialogue. UNESCO UIS

Barret, M. (2012) The Intercultural City Step by Step Council of Europe Publication Intercultural Competence (EWC Statement Series 2nd Issue p3)

Bedekovic, V. (2017). Intercultural education in the function of European values promotion. *Informatologia*, 50, 74–86.

Bennett, M. J. (2017) Constructive Approach to Intercultural Communication. Wiley Online Library Bortini, P. and Motamed-Ashari (2013) Intercultural Competency Research Report SALTO-YOUTH Bouchard, G. (2011) What is Interculturalism? McGilLaw Journal56 (2) 435-468

Borhaug, B. F., & Weyringer, S. (2019). Developing critical and empathetic capabilities in intercultural education through the VaKE approach. *Intercultural Education*, 30, 1–14.

Bovill, C. (2020). Co-creation in learning and teaching: The case for a whole-class approach in higher education. *Higher Education*, 79, 1023–1037. DOI: 10.1007/s10734-019-00453-w

Bunkowske. E.W. (2002) EWB/MS/MCCC/0205693. The Cultural onion Defined

Cantle, T. (2016) Interculturalism: The New Era of Cohesion and Diversity: Palgrave Macmillan

Cantle, T. (2016) The Case For Interculturalism, Plural Identities and Cohesion Edinburgh University Press

Chiriac, A. Trebes, (2015) T Particularities of training teachers in higher education from an intercultural perspective State University of Medicine and Pharmacy of Republic of Moldova

Chiriac, A., & Panciuc, L. (2015). *New Perspectives in Science Education* (4th ed.).

Deardorff, D. K. (2006) Theory Reflections: Intercultural Competence Framework Model. www.naisa.org

Deardorff, D. K. (2012). *Building Cultural Competence: Innovative Strategies*. Stylus Publishing.

Deardorff, D. K. (2013). *How will we know? Assessing Students' Intercultural Learning in Education Abroad Programs*. Duke University.

Deardorff, D. K. Elspeth, J. (2012) Intercultural Competence: An emerging focus in International Higher Education Sage Publications

Dollinger, M., Lodge, J., & Coates, H. (2018). Co-creation in higher education: Towards a conceptual model [Easyllama, com] [no author or date cited] [Importance of Cultural Awareness in the Workplace : How to Become Culturally Aware.]. *Journal of Marketing for Higher Education*, 28(2), 210–231. DOI: 10.1080/08841241.2018.1466756

Fanshawe, S., & Srisiskandarajah, D. (2010). You Can't Put Me. In *A Box" –diversity and the end of identity politics in Britain*. Institute for Public Policy Research.

Fantini, A., & Timizi, A. (2006). *Exploring and Assessing Intercultural Competence*. World Learning Publications.

Find Intercultural Competence Models, E. D. U. C. 878 (2024) George Mason University

Gorski, P. (2008). *Good intentions are not enough in decolonising intercultural education*. Routlege.

Haloi, S. (2021) Globalisation and its impact on the Twenty First century. International Journal of Creative Research

Hepple, . (2017).. . *Teaching and Teacher Education*, 66, 273–281.

Hofstede, G. (1991). *Culture and Organisations- Software of the Mind*. Mc Gaw- Hill.

Huber, J., Reynolds, C. Pestalozzi (2014) Developing Intercultural Competence through Education No3 (Council of Europe p27-35

Huber, J. R. (2014). *Developing Intercultural Competence through education*. Council of Europe Publishing.

Huish, C. (2023). Intercultural Gaps -Knowledge,Skills and Attitudes of Public health Professionals. *Journal of Public Health*, 45, ●●●.

Jackson, T. (2020). The Legacy of Geert Hofstede. *International Journal of Cross Cultural Management*.

Jagdish, S., & Portera, G. (2008). *Theoretical reflections on Intercultural Education*. Routledge.

James, M. (2008). *Interculturalism: Theory and Policy*. The Baring Foundation.

Knoth, A., Willems, D., Schulz, E., & Engel, K. (2023). Co-creation, Co-learning and Co- teaching Are Key – Developing Intercultural, Collaborative, and Digital Competence Through Virtual Exchange. In Auer, M. E., Pachatz, W., & Rüütmann, T. (Eds.), *Learning in the Age of Digital and Green Transition. ICL 2022. Lecture Notes in Networks and Systems* (Vol. 633). Springer., DOI: 10.1007/978-3-031-26876-2_8

Kumbi, H (2017)The Culturally Intelligent Leader-Developing Multi-ethnic Communinities in a Multicultural Age Instant Apostle

Lantz- Deaton, G. C. (2020) Intercultural Competence for College and University Students A global guide for employability and social change Springer Link

Levey, G. B. (2012). Interculturalism vs. Multiculturalism: A Distinction without a Difference? *Journal of Intercultural Studies (Melbourne, Vic.)*, 33(2), 217–224. DOI: 10.1080/07256868.2012.649529

Livermore, D. A. (2009). *Cultural Intelligence*. Baker Publishing.

Maine, F. (2021). In And Vikkri, M., Ed.). Dialogue for Intercultural Understanding., DOI: 10.1007/978-3-030-71778-0-2

Maine, F.. (2020). *Developing Education Policies in Europe to Enhance Cultural Literacy. Policy Briefing European Horizon (2020)*. Research and Innovation Programme.

Muscato, C. (2019) Comparing Enculturation and Acculturation. www.dialls2020.eu

Ohara, M. (2023). *We're better Together -Let's Co-Create*. Advance HE.

Paige, R. M. (1993) Towards Ethnorelativism: A Developmental Model of InterculturalSensitivity. (Ed) Education for Intercultural Experience: Yarmouth, ME; Intercultural Press

Parekh, B. (2006). *Rethinking Multiculturalism*. Palgrave.

Perry, L., & Southwell, L. (2011). *Developing Intercultural Skills, Models and Approaches*. SCRIBD.

Pradhan. S. (2023) The Impact of Globalisation on Work and Culture: Trends and Challenge Consultants Review

Rapanta, C., & Trovao, S. (2021), Intercultural Education for the Twenty-First Century: Comparativy Review Research https: //link.springer.com/chapter 10

Renee, M. (2022). *You have a culture; 5 ways to understand your own better*. See Beyond.

Ribes- Giner. G. et al (2016) Co-creation Impacts on Student Behaviour. Elsevir Sandercock, L. (ed.Wood 2004) Reconsidering Multiculturalism: towards an Intercultural Project. Comedia

Sani, S. (2015) The importance of Intercultural Education in the Development Age. The world conference on Educational Sciences (WCES-2015) www.sciencedirect.com

Schelfhout, S. (ed 2022) Intercultural Intercultural Competence Predicts Intercultural Effectiveness: International Journal of Environmental Research and Public Health

Sojberg, J. (2024) https://www.birmingham.ac.uk,news,developing-students-intercultural-awareness

Spencer- Oatey, H. (2012) What is Culture? Global Pad Open House

Surbhi, S. (2019) Difference between Enculturation and Acculturation. keydifferences.com Together for Peace: t4p.org.uk

Trompenaar, (1997) Riding the Waves of Culture. Nicholas Brearley Publishing

Turnbull (2012) Worldly Leadership. Alternative Wisdoms for a Complex World. Palgrave Macmillan

UNESCO. (2007) Intercultural education T Kit (IC learning 2nd edition p9)

Verghese, T. (2016). *How do we Understand Our Own Culture*. You Tube.

Watson, J. (2024). Cultural Globalisation and Anthropology. *Britannia*.

Wood, P. (ed2004) Intercultural City: Intercultural City Reader. Comedia

Wood, P., & Landry, C. (2004). *Intercultural City-Planning for Diversity Advantage*. Earthscan.

Zapata-Barrero, R. (ed 2015) Interculturalism in Cities Concept, Policy and I Implementation.Elgar Publishing

Ziyan, J. (2023). *Globalisation and its impact on Cultural Identity: An Analysis*. Medium.

Chapter 6
Enhancing Skills Acquisition Through Innovative Teaching Methodologies:
Guidelines and Considerations for Successful Integration

Nabil El Kadhi
https://orcid.org/0000-0002-8139-320X
Applied Science University, Bahrain

Minerva Mabborang Bunagan
Higher Colleges of Technology, UAE

ABSTRACT

This chapter aims to provide comprehensive guidelines for the successful integration of technology and the adoption of innovative teaching methodologies to enhance students' skills acquisition and effectiveness. Drawing upon experiences and implementations in the Mena region, specifically the GCC region, this chapter addresses key questions surrounding the selection and implementation of innovative teaching methods. The structure of the chapter encompasses an introduction to innovative teaching methodologies, identification of skills and appropriate methodologies, monitoring of implementation, the impact of technology, and a concluding summary of findings and future research directions.

DOI: 10.4018/979-8-3693-3443-0.ch006

1. INTRODUCTION

Innovation in education is a dynamic and evolving concept that encompasses a range of practices and approaches aimed at improving teaching and learning outcomes. In the context of Gulf countries, where education systems are undergoing significant transformations to meet the demands of the 21st century, the integration of technology and the adoption of innovative teaching methodologies have gained prominence.

This chapter presents various innovative teaching methodologies utilized in the Gulf countries. An extensive literature review has been conducted to explore the application and effectiveness of innovative teaching methodologies in Gulf countries. The literature review examines the implementation, the challenges and opportunities associated with their implementation, and the impact they have on student key skills and learning outcomes.

The reviewed literature also highlights several key trends in the Gulf region regarding the adoption of innovative teaching methodologies. These trends include an increased emphasis on student-centered and active learning approaches, the integration of technology in the classroom, the importance of developing 21st-century skills, and the recognition of the cultural and contextual factors that influence the effectiveness of innovative teaching methodologies.

The chapter also discusses several criteria to determine the level of innovation. These criteria include the novelty and uniqueness of the approach, the extent to which it challenges traditional teaching practices, its alignment with the learning objectives and needs of students, and its potential for transformative impact on the teaching and learning process.

By being aware of these various innovative teaching methodologies in the Gulf countries, and by examining these criteria, educators and policymakers can assess the innovative potential of different teaching methodologies and make informed decisions regarding their implementation.

2. INNOVATIVE TEACHING METHODOLOGIES IN THE GULF REGION

Differences in innovative teaching methodologies across the Gulf countries are influenced by various factors such as cultural norms, educational policies, and technological advancements. Some factors that may influence innovation in teaching methodologies in the Gulf countries are as follows:

a. Government Initiatives: Government policies and initiatives play a significant role in promoting innovation in education. Gulf countries often prioritize education as a key sector for development and invest in initiatives to modernize teaching methods and improve learning outcomes.

b. Technology Integration: The rapid advancement of technology has transformed education in the Gulf region. The integration of technology into classrooms, such as interactive whiteboards, educational software, and online learning platforms, has created opportunities for innovative teaching methods.

c. Pedagogical Shifts: There has been a growing recognition of the importance of student-centered learning approaches. Pedagogical shifts towards inquiry-based learning, project-based learning, and experiential learning have encouraged educators to explore innovative teaching methodologies that foster critical thinking, creativity, and collaboration among students.

d. Focus on 21st-Century Skills: There is a growing emphasis on developing 21st-century skills such as communication, collaboration, creativity, and critical thinking in the Gulf region. Innovative teaching methodologies are designed to foster these skills among students.

e. Professional Development: Investments in teacher training and professional development programs have been instrumental in fostering innovation in teaching methodology. Continuous training opportunities equip educators with the necessary skills and knowledge to implement innovative teaching strategies effectively.

f. Globalization and Cultural Exchange: Gulf countries are increasingly connected to the global economy and cultural exchanges. This exposure to international best practices and diverse educational approaches encourages educators to explore innovative teaching methodologies that are adapted to local contexts while incorporating global perspectives.

g. Cultural Sensitivity: Given the diverse cultural landscape of the Gulf region, innovative teaching methodologies often incorporate elements of cultural sensitivity and inclusivity. Teachers may adapt their approaches to accommodate different learning styles and cultural backgrounds.

h. Assessment for Learning: Innovative teaching methodologies in the Gulf region often involve alternative forms of assessment that go beyond traditional exams. This could include project assessments, portfolios, presentations, and peer evaluations.

i. Inclusive Education: There is a growing recognition of the importance of inclusive education in the Gulf region, and innovative teaching methodologies often aim to create inclusive learning environments where all students feel valued and supported.

j. Student Diversity: The Gulf region is characterized by a diverse student population with varying learning needs and backgrounds. Educators are encouraged to adopt innovative teaching methodologies that cater to the diverse needs of students, including those with special educational needs and English language learners.

k. Parental Expectations: Parents in the Gulf region place a high value on education and often have high expectations for their children's academic success. This pressure motivates educators to seek innovative teaching methodologies that engage students, enhance learning outcomes, and meet parental expectations.

l. Quality Assurance Standards: Gulf countries have established rigorous quality assurance standards for education. These standards emphasize the importance of innovation in teaching methodology to ensure the delivery of high-quality education that meets international benchmarks and prepares students for future challenges.

While there may be similarities with innovative teaching methodologies in other parts of the world, the specific context of the Gulf countries, including cultural factors and educational priorities, can influence the implementation and adaptation of these approaches.

Gulf countries have also been making rapid strides in technology integration, as accelerated by the COVID-19 pandemic. However, the extent and focus of technology use in education differ considerably when compared to other countries. While US, UK, and Canada have long embraced technology in education and their pedagogies are prominent; there are countries still grappling with infrastructure challenges that limit the widespread adoption of digital tools.

The teaching methodologies in the Gulf often need to align with local cultural and societal values, which can affect the adoption of certain innovative practices as compared with other countries that have various cultural influences shaping their educational practices; hence may lead to a wide range of innovative methodologies.

In addition, Gulf countries follow curriculum standards, specify topics and put strong emphasis on core subjects, which influence the integration and implementation of innovative methodology in the curriculum, while other Countries like the Netherlands and New Zealand offer more flexible curricula that can be tailored to students' needs, promoting innovative teaching practices.

For the purpose of discussion, some innovations in teaching methodologies, as outlined in Table 1 are discussed in the context of specific GCC countries.

Table 1. Innovative Teaching Methodologies in the Gulf Region

Country	Innovative Teaching Methodologies
United Arab Emirates (UAE)	a. Integration of technology into education, including hybrid and smart learning approaches b. Focus on project-based learning (PBL) to promote critical thinking and problem-solving skills c. Implementation of "Innovation Ambassadors" program to foster creativity and entrepreneurship among students
Saudi Arabia	a. Adoption of Blended Learning b. Tatweer Initiative c. Implementation of Inquiry-Based Learning Approaches
Qatar	a. Integration of experiential learning opportunities into the curriculum. b. Blended learning with virtual classrooms c. Flipped classroom with personalized learning
Bahrain	a. Distance learning b. Digitalization and blended learning c. Student-centered experiential learning approach
Sultanate of Oman	a. Teaching through Augmented Reality b. Utilizing Metaverse Technology c. Artificial Intelligence as a teaching approach

2.1 United Arab Emirates

2.1.1 Integration of technology into education, including hybrid and smart learning approaches.

The integration of technology in education in the UAE has been a focus of research, with studies exploring smart education approaches, hybrid learning, and sustainable development. Universities in the UAE have shown significant support for smart tools and technologies, with 72% of participants preferring technology integration in curricula (Mohamed et al., 2017). Hybrid education, combining online and face-to-face learning, has been implemented using advanced technologies like 3D holograms and virtual reality to enhance student experiences (Alghamdi et al., 2022).

The Ministry of Education in the UAE has implemented initiatives such as the "Smart Learning Initiative," which aims to enhance teaching and learning through the use of digital technologies and online resources. This initiative includes the development of smart classrooms equipped with interactive whiteboards, educational apps, and other digital tools (Almekhlafi & Almeqdadi, 2010).

A variety of technologies and digital contents are utilized in the UAE to enhance students' learning experiences, offering personalized and computer-aided learning while fostering inclusivity. Initiatives by the Ministry of Education (MoE) and the Abu Dhabi Educational Council (ADEC) aim to integrate technology to support teaching and learning across all schools in the country (Raji, 2019). Approximately 400 campuses in the UAE are equipped with state-of-the-art 4G networks and smart devices loaded with educational content as part of this initiative to promote the integration of technology into education (United Arab Emirates Government Portal, 2023).

The Ministry of Education has also launched various programs and projects focused on nurturing students' abilities and competencies in robotics and artificial intelligence. These initiatives include robotics training camps, participation in the VEX Robotics Championship, and the establishment of innovation ambassadors. Additionally, the ministry has established 11 FabLabs within schools to inspire students to embrace innovation and entrepreneurship.

2.1.2 Focus on project-based learning (PBL) to promote critical thinking and problem-solving skills.

Project-based learning (PBL) stands out as a distinctive learning model grounded in contemporary educational theories, offering a successful alternative to traditional lecturing. It reinforces the notion that education should center on the student rather than solely on the curriculum. Moreover, PBL fosters a deeper understanding of concepts, broadens the knowledge base, improves communication skills, enhances personal and social capabilities, boosts leadership and teamwork proficiencies, and cultivates independent learning and problem-solving abilities.

PBL engages students in real-world learning activities, fostering 21st-century skills such as communication, collaboration, creativity, and critical thinking (Al-mazroui, 2022;Mohammed, 2017). PBL functions as a complement to conventional lectures, acting as a catalyst for an effective and efficient process-oriented education wherein students take an active role in managing their own learning and find enjoyment in the process.

Studies have shown that PBL improves student achievement and develops essential skills in STEM subjects (Fouad, 2018) and engineering education. PBL aligns well with the learning styles of many engineering students, who tend to be visual, sensing, and active learners (Chowdhury, 2015).

2.1.3 Implementation of "Innovation Ambassadors" program to foster creativity and entrepreneurship among students.

The UAE has been actively promoting innovation and entrepreneurship in education, particularly among youth and students. Research indicates that entrepreneurial education positively impacts students' innovation capabilities and attitudes towards entrepreneurship (Shwedeh et al., 2023; Hameed et al., 2016).

The "Innovation Ambassadors" program in the UAE is a structured initiative aimed at fostering creativity and entrepreneurship among students. It involves selecting and training students to serve as ambassadors of innovation within their schools and communities, encouraging them to explore innovative ideas, develop entrepreneurial skills, and implement creative projects.

The UAE government has implemented various initiatives to support entrepreneurial development, recognizing its potential to drive economic growth and diversification (Alhajeri, 2022). The focus on developing entrepreneurial and innovative skills among students aims to prepare them for the knowledge economy and foster sustainable economic growth in the UAE (Wiseman & Anderson, 2014).

2.2 Saudi Arabia

2.2.1 Adoption of Blended Learning

Blended learning involves integrating traditional face-to-face instruction with online learning components. It involves a combination of in-person instruction led by an instructor in a classroom setting and online learning, which can be delivered either synchronously or asynchronously. Synchronous online components include activities like online chat, videoconferencing, and conference calls, where students and instructors interact in real-time. Asynchronous online elements include resources such as online discussion boards, tutorials, self-assessments, electronic texts, and emails, which can be accessed and completed at the students' own pace.

The blended learning adoption in Saudi Arabia offers advantages such as creating autonomous learners, enhancing student engagement, and increasing accessibility (Sheerah, 2016). Factors influencing adoption include student, institutional, and learning variables (Al-Ayed & Al-Tit, 2021). Students prefer illustrated text materials, flexible assessments, and embedded communication tools in blended environments (Anas, 2020).

Students also achieved better in the blended learning environment of mathematics courses (AlKhunaizi, 2014) and more effective than the traditional method in terms of achievement and the development of verbal creative thinking skills (AL-Madani, 2015).

2.2.2 Tatweer Initiative

The Tatweer Initiative in Saudi Arabia is a major educational reform aimed at improving teaching and learning quality in public schools (S. Alghamdi, 2019; Alyami, 2016). One of its unique aspects is its emphasis on incorporating cultural and religious values into the curriculum and educational practices. This includes integrating Saudi Arabian cultural heritage and Islamic teachings into educational content and methodologies, promoting cultural pride, religious understanding, and national identity among students.

Tatweer encourages the adoption of innovative teaching methodologies and technologies tailored to the Saudi Arabian context, fostering a modern and effective educational system aligned with the country's cultural and religious traditions. This includes the implementation of project-based learning, inquiry-based learning, cooperative learning, and other student-centered approaches that foster critical thinking, creativity, and problem-solving skills among students.

2.2.3 Implementation of Inquiry-Based Learning Approaches

Research on inquiry-based learning (IBL) in Saudi Arabia shows promising results across various educational levels. Studies indicate that IBL approaches, including guided inquiry and Process-Oriented Guided Inquiry Learning (POGIL), can improve students' conceptual understanding, engagement, and metacognitive skills (Almuntasheri et al., 2016; Gholam & Petro, 2019; Alshammari, 2022; Alghamdi & Alanazi, 2020). Employing IBL also enhances students' meta-cognitive reading comprehension abilities, particularly at the university level (Al Shamari, 2022), improves students' critical thinking skills in both reading and writing, and facilitates establishment of positive relationships between students and instructors (Tikruni, 2019).

However, implementation challenges persist, including school system constraints and teachers' limited practice of open inquiry methods (Alabdulkareem, 2017; Asiri, 2018). To address these issues, researchers recommend integrating IBL into teacher education programs, aligning it with Saudi cultural practices, and establishing science education benchmarks (Alghamdi & El-Hassan, 2020; Al-Abdulkareem, 2004). Despite these challenges, IBL approaches have shown effectiveness in various contexts, including sustainability education, density concepts, and reading comprehension skills (Alghamdi & El-Hassan, 2020; Almuntasheri et al., 2016; Alshammari, 2022).

2.3 Qatar

2.3.1 Integration of experiential learning opportunities into the curriculum

Experiential learning emphasizes hands-on, real-world experiences that allow students to apply theoretical knowledge in practical settings, fostering deeper understanding and skill development. In Qatar, higher education institutions (HEIs) are increasingly integrating experiential learning opportunities into their curricula as an innovative teaching methodology. Some of the ways in which HEIs in Qatar integrate experiential learning into their curricula include internships and Co-op Programs, field trips, site visits, research projects and simulation-based projects.

Experiential learning is crucial in health professions education, particularly in Qatar. The COVID-19 pandemic necessitated innovative approaches to maintain experiential learning (Paravattil et al., 2021). To enhance the quality of experiential education, preceptor development programs like the "Practice Educators' Academy" have been designed to address identified educational needs (Mukhalalati et al., 2020).

Integration of experiential learning into business curricula has been advocated to provide real-world decision-making opportunities (McCarthy & McCarthy, 2006). Furthermore, efforts to incorporate research and experiential learning into undergraduate education have been made in various fields, including architecture, engineering, and nursing (Salama, 2007; Hasna, 2007; Kennedy et al., 2019).

2.3.2 Blended Learning with Virtual Classrooms

Blended learning (BL) combines traditional face-to-face instruction with online learning components. In Qatar, virtual classrooms equipped with advanced technology are utilized to facilitate blended learning experiences. These virtual classrooms enable students to access lectures, interactive activities, and multimedia content online, while also participating in real-time discussions and collaborative projects. Recent studies indicate that BL contributed to higher attendance rates and enhanced student participation in similar courses (Abouhashem et al, 2021).

Studies have also found BL to be effective for healthcare quality improvement training (Suliman et al., 2018) and university-level English language instruction (Alseweed, 2013). BL has demonstrated positive impacts on student achievement and attitudes compared to traditional or fully virtual approaches (Alseweed, 2013). Cultural factors also influence BL adoption, with potential benefits for female empowerment noted in conservative contexts (Tamim, 2018). While some studies found students prefer traditional face-to-face learning (Bashir & Thomas, 2020), others observed greater enthusiasm for online collaboration among virtual learners

(Asoodar et al., 2014). Generally, BL shows promise but requires careful design consideration to maximize effectiveness in Qatar's educational landscape.

2.3.3 Flipped Classroom with Personalized Learning

The flipped classroom (FC) model reverses the traditional lecture and homework elements of a course. In Qatar, educators utilize the flipped classroom approach to personalize learning experiences for students. Pre-recorded lectures and instructional videos are provided online, allowing students to review content at their own pace, while class time is dedicated to hands-on activities, discussions, and personalized learning support.

The flipped classroom method has been found to encourage higher-order learning, engagement, and reflection (Berger, 2019). However, challenges such as student involvement in online activities (Alhazbi, 2016) and cultural transferability (Qureshi et al., 2016) need to be addressed. The adoption of these approaches is influenced by factors like enjoyment, innovation development, and social influence (Abu-Shanab & Anagreh, 2020). During the COVID-19 pandemic, hybrid online-flipped learning pedagogy has been successfully implemented to mitigate confinement and achieve course learning outcomes (Elkhatat & Al-Muhtaseb, 2021).

2.4 Bahrain

2.4.1 Distance Learning

Institutions in Bahrain utilize online platforms and learning management systems to deliver distance learning courses and resources. These platforms allow students to access course materials, participate in discussions, submit assignments, and communicate with instructors and peers remotely. They incorporate multimedia resources and interactive content to enhance engagement and facilitate learning. These may include videos, simulations, virtual labs, interactive quizzes, and multimedia presentations.

Studies show that students are generally satisfied with distance learning, citing improved interaction and independent learning skills (Tayem et al., 2022). However, challenges persist, especially in art and design education, where hands-on activities are crucial (Al Hashimi, 2021). The effectiveness of distance learning varies across subjects, with face-to-face learning showing advantages in some mathematical concepts (Alabdulaziz & Tayfour, 2023). Government support has been instrumental in facilitating distance education (Alhalwachi et al., 2022). Distance learning has positively impacted students' technology skills and self-reliance. However, socioeconomic factors influence the experience, with higher-class students benefiting more (Aldoy, 2022).

2.4.2 Digitalization and Blended learning

As outlined in Bahrain's 2030 Economic Vision, the country is committed to expediting digital transformation within its education sector. The onset of the COVID-19 pandemic further expedited the adoption of technology for learning purposes in Bahrain. To advance its e-learning strategy, Bahrain has forged partnerships with tech giants like Microsoft to furnish educational platforms to schools across the nation. Blended learning models have emerged as pivotal components in Bahrain's educational landscape, affording students and educators the opportunity to interact either in person or virtually (Bahrain Education & Labour Market Report, 2023).

Research on digitalization and blended learning in Bahrain indicates positive perceptions and growing adoption in higher education. Studies show that students generally have favorable views of blended learning, reporting increased confidence, motivation, and satisfaction (Mohammad & Job, 2012). Educators recognize the potential of m-learning and blended approaches, though full integration remains a work in progress (Marinakou & Giousmpasoglou, 2014).

Factors influencing effective blended learning include e-learning environment, facilitation, materials, technical support, and interactions with instructors and peers (Sankar et al., 2022). Challenges exist, such as the need for faculty training and infrastructure development (Marinakou & Giousmpasoglou, 2014). However, academics generally demonstrate high self-efficacy and perceive digital learning as useful (Aldulaimi et al., 2021). Blended and digital learning approaches have significant potential to enhance higher education in Bahrain (Mohammad, 2015).

2.4.3 Student-centered experiential learning approach

A student-centered experiential learning approach emphasizes placing students at the forefront of the educational process, actively engaging them in hands-on learning experiences that foster critical thinking, problem-solving, and practical skill development. This approach involves active engagement, individualized learning, collaborative learning, and real-world application among others.

Student-centered experiential learning approach is being implemented in various ways across Bahrain's educational institutions. At the university level, supply chain management courses have incorporated case analysis, evaluative essays, and game exercises to enhance cognitive, affective, and interactive skills (Al-Shammari, 2021). In badminton courses, a student-centered approach improved practical skills during online teaching (Muhammad, 2023). However, effective pedagogical tools should be designed and implemented to better develop students' experiential learning skills (Al-Shammari, 2022).

2.5 Oman

2.5.1 Teaching through Augmented Reality

Teaching through augmented reality (AR) strategy involves integrating AR technology into the educational process to enhance learning experiences. Augmented reality overlays digital content, such as images, videos, or 3D models, onto the real-world environment, providing students with interactive and immersive learning opportunities.

Augmented reality (AR) has shown promise as an educational tool in Oman, particularly in language learning and geography. Studies have demonstrated AR's positive impact on teaching skills, student achievement, and attitudes (Al-Sinani & Al Taher, 2023; Shuaili et al., 2020). AR enhances student engagement, interactivity, and motivation compared to traditional methods (Hung et al., 2017; Rizov & Rizova, 2015). However, challenges remain in integrating AR into educational systems, including teacher readiness and infrastructure limitations (Jwaifell, 2019). While AR offers benefits for visualizing complex concepts and improving learning outcomes, it may not always outperform conventional teaching materials (Hung et al., 2017). Further research is needed to fully understand AR's potential in education, considering various factors such as learning theories, pedagogies, and cultural contexts (Karacan & Akoğlu, 2021).

2.5.2 Utilizing Metaverse Technology

The Metaverse is emerging as a transformative technology in education, particularly in higher education institutions (Salloum et al., 2023; Rahman et al., 2023). It offers immersive, interactive learning experiences that can enhance student engagement and motivation (López-Belmonte et al., 2023).

In Oman, research has explored the adoption of Metaverse technology in academic institutions, highlighting factors such as innovativeness, context awareness, and perceived enjoyment as influential in its acceptance (Salloum et al., 2023). The Metaverse has potential applications in various educational contexts, including police training (Al Ali & Laib, 2024) and general higher education (Akour et al., 2022). Benefits include increased accessibility, flexibility, and personalized learning experiences (Prakash et al., 2023). Metaverse has the potential to revolutionize higher education, providing immersive, interactive, and personalized learning experiences (Said et al, 2023). However, challenges such as technical limitations, privacy concerns, and the need for digital literacy skills must be addressed (Prakash et al., 2023). As Metaverse adoption in education is still in its early stages, further research and experimentation are needed to fully evaluate its impact and effectiveness (López-Belmonte et al., 2023; Murala, 2024).

2.5.3 Artificial Intelligence as a teaching approach

Artificial intelligence (AI) is increasingly being utilized as an innovative teaching approach to enhance learning experiences, personalize education, and streamline administrative tasks in educational institutions. In Oman, AI is gradually being incorporated into the education sector.

Studies indicate positive perceptions among instructors, students, and administrative staff towards AI implementation in personalized learning (Al-Badi et al., 2022). AI has been utilized in various forms, from computer-related technologies to web-based systems and humanoid robots, enhancing administrative functions and personalizing curriculum content (Chen et al., 2020; Nguyen et al., 2023). The use of AI in the 8th-grade science curriculum in Oman is effective in developing educational strategies and facilitating teaching-learning processes (Osama, 2023).

3. ASSESSMENT OF TEACHING METHODOLOGIES: INNOVATIVENESS, FEATURES AND CHALLENGES

This section presents an evaluation of the previously discussed innovative teaching approaches. It discusses the assessment of teaching methodologies according to specific criteria, their impact on student skills and learning outcomes as well as their key features, associated challenges and suggestions to overcome the challenges.

3.1 Criteria Assessment for Teaching Methodologies

Assessing teaching methodologies with specific criteria provides valuable insights that inform instructional decision-making, improve learning outcomes, and promote innovation in education. Six (6) criteria, with corresponding considerations are offered for assessing each methodology. The following are the criteria:

1. Novelty: This criterion assesses the extent to which the methodology represents a new or innovative approach in education. Considerations include introduction of new pedagogical approaches or technologies, emphasis on emerging trends in education, and uniqueness compared to traditional teaching methods

2. Effectiveness: This criterion evaluates the methodology's ability to achieve its intended learning outcomes and enhance student performance. Considerations include evidence of improved learning outcomes, positive impact on student engagement and motivation, and alignment with curriculum standards and educational goals.
3. Innovation: This criterion examines the degree to which the methodology fosters innovation in teaching and learning practices. Considerations include creativity and originality in instructional design, integration of innovative technologies or approaches, and potential for transformative change in educational practices.
4. Engagement: This criterion measures the level of student involvement, interest, and participation facilitated by the methodology. Considerations include opportunities for active learning and student-centered activities, use of interactive and multimedia resources, and promotion of inquiry-based and experiential learning experiences.
5. Flexibility: This criterion assesses the adaptability and versatility of the methodology to accommodate diverse learning needs and contexts. Considerations include flexibility in instructional delivery methods, accessibility of learning resources and materials, and personalization of learning experiences based on student needs and preferences.
6. Sustainability: This criterion evaluates the long-term viability and scalability of the methodology within educational settings. Considerations include feasibility of implementation and integration into existing curricula, availability of resources and support for ongoing maintenance, and potential for continued improvement and innovation over time.

Using the above criteria and considerations, each teaching methodology is assigned a score. A maximum score of 5 is assigned to novelty and innovation, and a maximum score of 4 to the other criteria. This is based on the nature of these specific attributes and their significance in assessing innovative teaching methodologies.

Novelty refers to the degree of innovation or newness introduced by a teaching methodology. Assigning a maximum score of 5 acknowledges the importance of pioneering approaches that break new ground in educational practices. This score reflects methodologies that represent significant departures from traditional teaching methods and bring about transformative change in educational settings.

Innovation, like novelty, focuses on the introduction of creative and original approaches in teaching and learning. Assigning a maximum score of 5 underscores the value of methodologies that foster innovation by leveraging cutting-edge technologies, pedagogical strategies, or instructional designs. This score reflects methodologies that not only introduce novel concepts but also demonstrate ingenuity and forward-thinking in their implementation.

On the other hand, while effectiveness, engagement, and flexibility are essential for evaluating the success and impact of a teaching methodology, they are often assessed relative to specific learning objectives, student populations, or instructional contexts. Assigning a maximum score of 4 acknowledges methodologies that excel in these areas and achieve their intended outcomes effectively but recognizes that there may be limitations or variations in their applicability across different educational settings.

Sustainability refers to the long-term viability and scalability of a teaching methodology within educational environments. While methodologies may demonstrate sustainability through factors such as feasibility of implementation and ongoing support, assigning a maximum score of 4 acknowledges that achieving sustainability may require ongoing adaptation, refinement, and investment over time.

Hence, assigning different maximum scores for novelty and innovation compared to the other criteria reflects the unique emphasis placed on groundbreaking and pioneering approaches in education, while still recognizing the importance of effectiveness, engagement, flexibility, and sustainability in evaluating teaching methodologies. Table 2 shows the evaluation of the previously presented innovative teaching methodologies. Each methodology is assigned a score with a corresponding justification.

Based on the table, teaching methodologies such as Integration of technology into education, focus on project-based learning, integration of experiential learning opportunities, teaching through Augmented Reality, utilizing Metaverse Technology, and Artificial Intelligence as a teaching approach received high scores for novelty and innovation. These methodologies introduce groundbreaking approaches to education, leveraging cutting-edge technologies and pedagogical strategies to enhance learning experiences.

Most methodologies scored well in terms of effectiveness, indicating their ability to improve learning outcomes and promote student achievement. Whether through technology integration, project-based learning, or experiential learning, these methodologies demonstrate a capacity to engage learners, foster critical thinking, and facilitate deeper understanding of content.

Many methodologies also received favorable scores for engagement and flexibility, suggesting their ability to draw students' interest and accommodate diverse learning needs. Approaches such as project-based learning, experiential learning, and augmented reality provide immersive, interactive experiences that promote active participation and adaptability to different instructional contexts.

While most methodologies demonstrate promise in terms of sustainability, there are some challenges to consider, particularly regarding ongoing support and resource requirements. Ensuring the long-term viability of innovative teaching methodologies may require investments in educator training, technology infrastructure, and curriculum integration to sustain their implementation and impact over time.

Table 2. Assessment of Teaching Methodologies

Methodology	Novelty (5)	Effectiveness (4)	Innovation (5)	Engagement (4)	Flexibility (4)	Sustainability (4)	Total Score
Integration of technology into education	5 Utilization of cutting-edge technologies and approaches significantly contributes to the novelty of the methodology.	4 Technology integration has been shown to enhance learning outcomes, but effectiveness may vary based on implementation.	5 Technology integration provides new opportunities for learning and collaboration.	4 Technology integration can enhance student engagement through interactive and multimedia rich experience.	4 Technology integration allows for flexibility in delivery modes and content presentation.	4 Sustainability is achievable with proper training and support for educators.	26
Focus on project-based learning	4 Project-based learning emphasizes hands-on, collaborative learning experiences.	5 Project-based learning promotes critical thinking and problem-solving skills effectively.	5 Project-based learning provides students with opportunities for real-world application of knowledge.	5 Project-based learning fosters high levels of engagement through real-world application and student-driven inquiry.	4 Project-based learning offers flexibility in project design and assessment methods.	4 Project-based learning can be sustained with ongoing support and integration into the curriculum.	27
Implementation of "Innovation Ambassadors" program	3 While the program fosters creativity and entrepreneurship, it may not represent a novel methodology as similar initiatives exist.	4 The program's effectiveness depends on the commitment and involvement of students as innovation ambassadors.	3 While the program fosters innovation, its methodology may not be considered highly innovative compared to other approaches.	3 Engagement may be moderate as participation in the program is voluntary.	3 Flexibility may be limited due to the structured nature of the program.	3 Sustainability relies on continued institutional support and student participation.	19
Implementation of Inquiry-Based Learning Approaches	3 While inquiry-based learning is not entirely novel, its systematic implementation in the curriculum represents an innovation.	4 Inquiry-based learning promotes critical thinking and inquiry skills, but effectiveness may vary based on implementation.	3 While inquiry-based learning is innovative, its methodology may not be considered highly innovative compared to other approaches.	3 Engagement may be moderate as students require guidance to navigate inquiry-based tasks.	3 Flexibility may be limited due to the structured nature of inquiry-based tasks.	3 Sustainability relies on ongoing support for inquiry-based pedagogy and curriculum integration.	19

continued on following page

Table 2. Continued

Methodology	Novelty (5)	Effectiveness (4)	Innovation (5)	Engagement (4)	Flexibility (4)	Sustainability (4)	Total Score
Integration of experiential learning opportunities	5 Experiential learning represents a relatively new approach, emphasizing hands-on, real-world experiences to enhance learning.	4 Experiential learning enhances learning outcomes by providing practical application of concepts.	5 Integration of experiential learning represents a highly innovative approach, providing students with opportunities for hands-on learning experiences.	5 Experiential learning promotes high levels of engagement through hands-on activities and real-world relevance.	4 Flexibility in design and implementation allows for adaptation to diverse learning contexts.	4 Sustainability relies on ongoing support for experiential learning pedagogy and integration into the curriculum.	27
Flipped classroom with personalized learning	3 While the flipped classroom model is not entirely novel, its systematic implementation with personalized learning represents an innovation.	4 The flipped classroom enhances learning outcomes, but effectiveness may depend on the quality of pre-recorded content and in-class activities.	3 While the flipped classroom is innovative, its methodology may not be considered highly innovative compared to other approaches.	3 Engagement may be moderate as students require self-discipline and motivation for pre-class activities.	4 Flexibility in scheduling and access to resources is provided by personalized learning approaches.	3 (Sustainability relies on ongoing support for technology integration and educator training.	20
Distance learning	4 Distance learning offers a novel approach by providing education remotely, especially in areas with limited access to traditional schooling.	4 Distance learning can enhance learning outcomes, but effectiveness may depend on the quality of online instruction and student support.	4 Distance learning represents an innovative approach, providing flexibility and accessibility to education.	4 Distance learning promotes engagement through interactive online activities and multimedia resources.	4 Flexibility in scheduling and access to resources is provided by distance learning.	4 (Sustainability relies on ongoing support for technology integration and educator training.	24
Digitalization and blended learning	4 Digitalization and blended learning represent innovative approaches by combining technology integration with traditional teaching methods.	4 Blended learning enhances learning outcomes, but effectiveness may vary based on course design and facilitation.)	4 Digitalization and blended learning represent innovative approaches, providing flexibility and accessibility to learning resources.	4 Blended learning promotes engagement through interactive online activities and multimedia resources.	4 Flexibility in scheduling and access to resources is provided by blended learning.	4 Sustainability relies on ongoing support for technology integration and educator training.	24
Teaching through Augmented Reality	5 Augmented reality offers a novel approach to education by overlaying digital content onto the real world, providing immersive learning experiences.	4 Augmented reality enhances learning outcomes by providing interactive and engaging learning experiences.	5 Augmented reality promotes high levels of engagement through immersive experiences and real-world application.	3 Flexibility may be limited based on available AR applications and content.	4 Sustainability relies on ongoing support for technology integration and educator training.	4 Sustainability relies on ongoing support for technology integration and educator training.	25

continued on following page

Table 2. Continued

Methodology	Novelty (5)	Effectiveness (4)	Innovation (5)	Engagement (4)	Flexibility (4)	Sustainability (4)	Total Score
Utilizing Metaverse Technology	5 Metaverse technology represents a novel approach by creating immersive virtual environments for education.	4 Metaverse technology enhances learning outcomes by providing immersive and interactive learning experiences.	5 Metaverse technology promotes high levels of engagement through immersive experiences and real-world application.	3 Flexibility may be limited based on available metaverse platforms and content.	4 Sustainability relies on ongoing support for technology integration and educator training.	4 Sustainability relies on ongoing support for technology integration and educator training.	25
Artificial Intelligence as a teaching approach	5 Artificial intelligence offers a novel approach to education by leveraging machine learning and data analysis for personalized learning experiences.	4 Artificial intelligence enhances learning outcomes by providing adaptive and personalized learning experiences.	4 Artificial intelligence promotes engagement through adaptive learning experiences and real-time feedback.	3 Flexibility may be limited based on available AI applications and content.	4 Sustainability relies on ongoing support for technology integration and educator training.	4 Sustainability relies on ongoing support for technology integration and educator training.	24

3.2 Impact on Student Skills

In the Gulf region, identifying key skills that are relevant and highly desired requires a thorough understanding of the local context, educational systems, and cultural backgrounds of the students. While certain core 21st-century skills are universally valuable, there are additional skills that hold particular significance within the Gulf region.

Table 3 provides a summary of the key skills identified in the Gulf region and the innovative teaching methodologies that can be adopted to foster these skills. The selection and implementation of methodologies should be guided by a thoughtful analysis of the specific learning objectives, student needs, available resources, and infrastructure. It is not an exhaustive list, and additional methodologies may be relevant based on the specific educational context and goals.

Table 3. Key Skills and Innovative Teaching Methodologies in the Gulf Region

Key Skills	Innovative Teaching Methodologies
Adaptability and Resilience	Project-Based Learning, Experiential Learning
Entrepreneurship and Innovation	Design Thinking, Entrepreneurial Challenges
Leadership and Teamwork	Cooperative Learning, Group Projects
Digital Literacy	Technology-Enhanced Learning, Flipped Classrooms

continued on following page

Table 3. Continued

Key Skills	Innovative Teaching Methodologies
Critical Thinking and Problem-Solving	Inquiry-Based Learning, Case Studies
Communication and Collaboration	Collaborative Learning, Communication Skills
Cultural Awareness and Global Citizenship	Cross-Cultural Exchanges, Service-Learning

3.2.1 Adaptability and Resilience Skills

In the Gulf region, where the economic landscape is constantly evolving, students need to develop the ability to adapt to new situations, navigate uncertainty, and bounce back from challenges. Innovative teaching methodologies that promote experiential learning, simulations, and real-world problem-solving can effectively cultivate adaptability and resilience skills.

One example of an innovative teaching methodology that fosters adaptability and resilience is project-based learning (PBL). For instance, students could be tasked with developing a sustainable energy plan for their community. By working on meaningful problems and collaborating with their peers, students develop the ability to adapt their thinking and approaches as circumstances change. Additionally, PBL provides opportunities for students to experience setbacks and failures, allowing them to learn from these experiences and develop resilience.

Simulations and role-playing activities are also effective approaches to develop adaptability and resilience skills. By immersing students in realistic scenarios, such as business simulations or mock negotiations, they can practice adapting their strategies and responses to changing circumstances. These activities enable students to develop a sense of resilience as they encounter unforeseen challenges and learn to adjust their approaches accordingly. For example, students could participate in a simulated United Nations conference where they represent different countries and negotiate agreements on global issues. This experience would require them to adapt their positions, collaborate with peers from diverse backgrounds, and navigate complex diplomatic scenarios.

3.2.2 Entrepreneurship and Innovation Skills

Entrepreneurship and innovation are highly valued in the Gulf region, as countries strive to foster entrepreneurial mindsets and encourage innovation and creativity in various sectors. Design thinking also fosters entrepreneurship and innovation skills. Through the design thinking process, students are guided to identify real-world problems, generate creative ideas, prototype solutions, and iterate based on feedback. This methodology encourages students to adopt an entrepreneurial mindset by promoting risk-taking, creativity, and problem-solving. By engaging in entrepreneurial challenges and real-world projects, students can develop their creativity, critical thinking, and problem-solving abilities.

Students could be tasked with designing a product or service that addresses a specific community need. They would go through the design thinking process, conducting research, brainstorming ideas, creating prototypes, and refining their solutions based on feedback. This hands-on experience allows students to develop their entrepreneurial skills while also gaining a deeper understanding of user needs and market dynamics.

In addition to design thinking, incorporating entrepreneurial challenges and competitions into the curriculum can provide students with hands-on experiences in identifying business opportunities, developing innovative solutions, and pitching their ideas. For example, schools in the Gulf region can organize entrepreneurship competitions where students form teams and develop business plans for new ventures. The competition could involve pitching their ideas to a panel of judges, who provide feedback and select winners based on the viability and innovation of their business proposals. This type of activity not only fosters entrepreneurial skills but also cultivates teamwork, communication, and presentation abilities.

3.2.3 Leadership and Teamwork Skills

Leadership and teamwork skills are highly valued in the Gulf region, as collaboration and teamwork are integral to many professional settings. Students need to develop the ability to lead and work effectively in teams. Innovative teaching methodologies can foster leadership and teamwork skills among students in the GCC through various approaches. These include using case studies to enhance critical thinking, implementing inquiry-based learning environments, employing metacognitive strategies, group presentations, project-based learning, and problem-based learning.

Cooperative learning also develops leadership and teamwork skills. In cooperative learning, students work together in small groups to achieve shared learning goals. This methodology provides opportunities for students to practice effective communication, negotiation, and decision-making within a team setting. By working together to achieve common goals, students can develop their leadership skills and understand the importance of teamwork. For example, students could be assigned a group project where they have to design and implement a community service initiative. Throughout the project, they would need to collaborate, delegate tasks, and make collective decisions to ensure its success.

Another approach to developing leadership skills is through service-learning projects. Service-learning integrates community service with academic learning, allowing students to address real community needs while developing leadership abilities. Students could volunteer at local organizations and take on leadership roles in planning and implementing initiatives to address social or environmental challenges. Through these projects, students learn to communicate effectively, collaborate with diverse stakeholders, and take initiative in driving positive change.

3.3 Impact on Student Learning Outcomes

The integration of technology in education has shown positive impacts on student learning outcomes across various studies. Technology-supported education enhances student engagement, motivation, and academic performance as evidenced by increased student attendance, improved test scores, enhanced motivation, and increased collaborative project completion (Venkataraman, 2023). The use of educational technologies enables more personalized, self-directed learning experiences, leading to improvements in core skills (Putriyani et al., 2024). Innovative teaching methodologies go beyond traditional methods and focus on student-centered learning, creativity, and adaptability, which leads to better student understanding, increased student interest, more student engagement, skill development and even prepare students for the future workplace.

Project-based learning significantly improves academic achievement, affective attitudes, and thinking skills compared to traditional teaching models, and the effects of project-based teaching are influenced by different moderating variables such as subject area, course type, academic period, group size, class size, and experiment period (Zhang & Ma, 2023). Adopting PBL also motivates students, facilitates more effective achievement of learning outcomes and enhances student engagement in community development initiatives (Karima, 2023).

Hybrid learning approaches, combining online and face-to-face instruction, demonstrate significant positive effects on student learning. Undergraduate students reported improved learning experiences with hybrid education incorporating advanced technologies (Alghamdi et al., 2022) and the use of smart e-learning applications significantly improved academic achievement in scientific concepts (Alneyadi et al., 2023). Flipped Classrooms studies have reported positive student attitudes and improved learning outcomes in computer programming (Alhazbi, 2016) and engineering courses (Alaeddine et al., 2015).

3.4 Features and Challenges

In the Gulf, the innovative teaching methodology is characterized by substantial investment in digital infrastructure and smart classroom solutions. Gulf countries as discussed in the beginning of this chapter have implemented advanced educational technologies and comprehensive e-learning platforms, supported by government initiatives.

Education institutions in the Gulf countries or beyond utilize innovative teaching methodologies to enhance the effectiveness and relevance of education. Innovative teaching methodologies offer numerous benefits, such as increased student engagement, improved understanding of concepts, and enhanced collaboration. Many of the teaching methodologies emphasize real-world application and personalized learning experiences, which have the potential to improve learning outcomes, and prioritize student autonomy, promoting student-centered learning experiences that cater to individual needs and preferences. Additionally, these methodologies can make learning more dynamic and interactive, which helps to keep students motivated and better equipped to handle real-world challenges.

However, the integration of innovative teaching technologies faces several challenges, including limited resources, diverse learning needs, and lack of teacher training as presented in Table 3. There are also quality concerns, skills gaps, curriculum limitations, and regulatory constraints. Cultural complexities also hinder the adoption of student-centered approaches like problem-based learning, and online methodologies have additional obstacles such as connectivity issues and non-conducive learning environments.

To overcome these challenges, blended learning approaches that incorporate culturally relevant content and utilizing project-based learning may be implemented. Adequate infrastructure and technology support, organizing professional development and training programs, and ensuring administrative and student support are also crucial for successful technology integration. Further, consider developing a plan for technology integration into the curriculum and ensure that sufficient budget is allocated for both the hardware and software; invest in infrastructure upgrades and establish partnerships with technological companies; develop a professional development and training plan that includes training on virtual platforms, transitioning from traditional to inquiry-based practices, and effective use of new technology (such as AI, VR and AR) and innovative tools; and establish a team to develop and manage teaching materials and curriculum content, and assessment tools and rubrics.

Table 4. Features and Challenges of Teaching Methodologies

Methodology	Features	Challenges
Integration of technology into education	• Utilization of cutting-edge technologies and approaches such as hybrid and smart learning. • Enhanced access to educational resources and multimedia content. • Facilitation of interactive and collaborative learning experiences.	• Infrastructure limitations may hinder access to technology in certain areas. • Teacher training and professional development are needed to effectively integrate technology into instruction. • Potential for distraction or misuse of technology in the classroom. (need to blend technology with traditional teaching methods) • Addressing cultural differences in online learning engagement
Focus on project-based learning	• Emphasis on hands-on, collaborative projects to promote critical thinking and problem-solving skills. • Real-world application of knowledge and skills. • Opportunities for student creativity and autonomy.	• Resource-intensive in terms of time and materials required for project development and implementation. • Variation in student motivation and engagement levels may impact project outcomes. • Assessment methods may be challenging to design and implement effectively.
Implementation of "Innovation Ambassadors" program	• Fostering creativity and entrepreneurship among students through structured programs and initiatives. • Opportunities for peer mentorship and collaboration. • Encouragement of innovative thinking and risk-taking.	• Recruitment and training of ambassadors may require significant time and resources. • Sustaining enthusiasm and participation among ambassadors over time. • Ensuring alignment with curriculum goals and standards.
Implementation of Inquiry-Based Learning Approaches	• Emphasis on student-driven inquiry and investigation. • Development of critical thinking, problem-solving, and research skills. • Engagement with authentic, real-world problems and scenarios.	• Requires a shift in instructional practices and classroom dynamics. • Assessment methods may need to be adapted to align with inquiry-based learning objectives. • Teacher guidance and support are crucial to scaffold student inquiry effectively.
Integration of experiential learning opportunities	• Hands-on, real-world experiences to reinforce learning concepts. • Opportunities for active engagement and application of knowledge. • Connection to industry or community partners for authentic learning experiences.	• Resource-intensive in terms of planning and coordination of experiential activities. • Ensuring alignment with curriculum standards and learning objectives. • Assessment methods may be challenging to develop and implement.

continued on following page

Table 4. Continued

Methodology	Features	Challenges
Flipped classroom with personalized learning	• Flipped instructional model where direct instruction occurs outside of class and application activities occur in class. • Personalized learning experiences tailored to individual student needs and preferences. • Opportunities for student autonomy and self-directed learning.	• Creation and curation of high-quality pre-recorded instructional content may be time-consuming. • Monitoring and support needed to ensure students engage with pre-class materials effectively. • Adapting classroom activities to accommodate diverse student learning needs.
Distance learning	• Remote delivery of instruction and educational materials. • Access to education for students in geographically remote areas. • Flexibility in scheduling and access to resources.	• Equity issues related to access to technology and internet connectivity. • Lack of face-to-face interaction may impact student engagement and motivation. • Challenges in assessing and monitoring student progress remotely.
Digitalization and blended learning	• Integration of digital tools and resources into traditional teaching practices. • Flexibility in content delivery and access to resources. • Combination of face-to-face instruction with online learning modalities.	• Technical challenges such as platform compatibility and connectivity issues. • Development and implementation of online content may require additional time and resources. • Balancing synchronous and asynchronous learning experiences.
Student-centered experiential learning approach	• Emphasis on student agency and hands-on, experiential learning activities. • Opportunities for active engagement and application of knowledge. • Tailoring learning experiences to student interests and preferences.	• Requires a shift in instructional practices and classroom dynamics. • Development of experiential activities and assessments may be time-intensive. • Ensuring alignment with curriculum standards and learning objectives.
Teaching through Augmented Reality	• Overlaying digital content onto the real world to provide immersive learning experiences. • Engagement through interactive and immersive experiences. • Real-world application of knowledge and skills.	• Limited availability of augmented reality (AR) hardware and software in educational settings. • Development and integration of AR content into curriculum may be challenging. • Technical issues such as compatibility and usability of AR applications.
Utilizing Metaverse Technology	• Creation of immersive virtual environments for education and learning. • Engagement through interactive and immersive experiences. • Real-world application of knowledge and skills in virtual contexts.	• Emerging technology with limited adoption and availability in educational settings. • Development and integration of metaverse content into curriculum may be challenging. • Technical issues such as platform compatibility and usability.

continued on following page

Table 4. Continued

Methodology	Features	Challenges
Artificial Intelligence as a teaching approach	• Utilization of machine learning and data analysis for personalized learning experiences. • Adaptation of instruction based on student performance and needs. • Real-time feedback and assessment.	• Limited availability of artificial intelligence (AI) tools and platforms for education. • Integration of AI into curriculum and instruction may require specialized training. • Ethical considerations regarding data privacy and algorithm bias in AI-driven learning environments.

4. MONITORING APPROACHES IN IMPLEMENTING INNOVATIVE TEACHING METHODOLOGIES

In this section, we present the significance of monitoring and evaluating the implementation of innovative teaching methodologies in the Gulf countries. We will emphasize the need for culturally sensitive monitoring approaches that consider the unique cultural aspects of the region.

4.1 Monitoring Approaches for Innovative Teaching Methodologies

Implementing innovative teaching methodologies requires a systematic approach to monitor their effectiveness and make necessary adjustments. Monitoring serves as a feedback mechanism to ensure that the methodologies align with the desired educational outcomes and address the specific skills targeted for development.

One crucial aspect of monitoring is data collection and analysis. Gathering relevant data to assess the progress and impact of the methodologies is essential. This can involve various methods such as classroom observations, student and teacher surveys, interviews, and student work analysis. Administrators, educational supervisors, or peers may conduct classroom observations to observe the implementation of innovative teaching methodologies. They provide feedback to teachers on their instructional practices, highlighting strengths and areas for improvement. Data collection should be ongoing and comprehensive to provide a holistic view of the implementation process.

Additionally, educators analyze data collected, both quantitative and qualitative, to evaluate the impact of innovative teaching methodologies on student outcomes. This may include analyzing standardized test scores, student surveys, classroom observations, and graduation rates to assess the effectiveness of different innovative teaching approaches.

To effectively monitor innovative teaching methodologies, it is important to develop rubrics and assessment tools that align with the skills and learning outcomes targeted by these methodologies. These tools provide clear criteria for evaluating student performance and progress. Rubrics can be used to assess critical thinking, communication, collaboration, creativity, and other skills, allowing for consistent and objective monitoring.

In addition to rubrics, incorporating formative assessment strategies throughout the implementation process is essential. Formative assessment provides real-time feedback to students and teachers, enabling them to track progress, identify areas for improvement, and make necessary adjustments. Techniques such as peer assessment, self-assessment, and classroom discussions can be employed to gather formative feedback.

Encouraging teachers and students to reflect on their experiences with the innovative teaching methodologies is valuable. Reflection and documentation of best practices, challenges, and lessons learned can help inform future implementation and facilitate the sharing of knowledge among educators. By documenting successful approaches and strategies, student engagement levels, and learning outcomes, educators can build a repository of resources that can guide future monitoring and adjustment efforts.

Professional development and collaboration play a pivotal role in effective monitoring. Providing ongoing professional development opportunities for teachers to enhance their understanding and implementation of innovative teaching methodologies is critical. Collaborative learning communities, workshops, and training sessions can support teachers in monitoring their own practices and sharing insights with colleagues. By fostering a culture of collaboration and continuous learning, educators can collectively strengthen monitoring efforts and improve the implementation of innovative teaching methodologies.

4.2 Cultural Aspects and Monitoring

Cultural aspects play a significant role in monitoring the implementation of innovative teaching methodologies in Gulf countries. It is crucial to recognize and address cultural factors that may influence the monitoring process. By doing so, educators can ensure that monitoring approaches are culturally sensitive and effectively aligned with local contexts.

One important consideration is contextual relevance. Gulf countries have unique cultural, social, and educational contexts. Therefore, monitoring approaches should be tailored to these specific contexts to ensure that methodologies are aligned with local values, norms, and expectations. Cultural relevance should be considered when developing assessment tools, rubrics, and data collection methods. Interpreting and evaluating student performance should also consider cultural factors to gain a comprehensive understanding of student progress.

Communication styles are another aspect influenced by cultural differences and should be considered in the monitoring process. Gulf countries have diverse populations with varying communication preferences. Monitoring approaches should be sensitive to these differences and employ strategies that facilitate effective communication. This can include providing multiple channels for feedback, considering non-verbal cues, and recognizing the importance of interpersonal relationships in the communication process.

Perceptions of assessment can vary across cultures and impact how students, parents, and educators perceive and respond to monitoring efforts. Some cultures prioritize traditional assessment methods or place a strong emphasis on grades and rankings. Understanding these cultural perspectives can help shape monitoring approaches that are culturally sensitive, promote engagement, and ensure the acceptance and support of stakeholders.

Data privacy and confidentiality are important considerations in the monitoring process, influenced by cultural norms and legal requirements in Gulf countries. Monitoring approaches should adhere to these cultural expectations and ensure the protection of sensitive information. Clear communication about data collection, storage, and usage practices is essential to gain trust and maintain ethical standards.

5. CONCLUSION

This chapter presented varied innovative teaching methodologies utilized in the Gulf countries and highlighted the following:

Firstly, innovative teaching methodologies in the Gulf region are characterized by the integration of technology and a focus on student-centered and active learning approaches. These methodologies aim to enhance student engagement, learning outcomes, and the acquisition of 21st-century skills.

Secondly, the level of innovation in teaching methodologies is determined by criteria such as novelty, challenge to traditional practices, alignment with learning objectives, and transformative impact on the teaching and learning process. Educators and policymakers should consider these criteria when making decisions regarding the implementation of innovative teaching methodologies.

Thirdly, the literature review identified several trends in the Gulf countries regarding the adoption of innovative teaching methodologies. These include an emphasis on adaptability and resilience skills, entrepreneurship and innovation skills, and leadership and teamwork skills.

However, there are challenges and barriers that need to be addressed for the effective implementation of innovative teaching methodologies. These challenges include resistance to change, limited access to technology and resources, the need for professional development and teacher training, and the importance of cultural relevance and sensitivity in instructional practices.

Based on the findings, the following recommendations are proposed:

Increase support and resources: Efforts should be made to provide educators with the necessary support and resources, including access to technology, training programs, and professional development opportunities. This will help them effectively implement innovative teaching methodologies.

Foster a culture of innovation: Educational institutions and policymakers should create a culture that values and promotes innovation in teaching. This can be done through incentives, recognition programs, and the establishment of innovation hubs or centers.

Promote collaboration and sharing of best practices: Educators should be encouraged to collaborate and share their experiences and best practices in implementing innovative teaching methodologies. This can be facilitated through conferences, workshops, and online platforms.

Address cultural and contextual factors: It is important to consider the cultural and contextual factors that influence the effectiveness of innovative teaching methodologies. Adaptations and modifications may be necessary to ensure that these methodologies are relevant and meaningful in the Gulf region.

Conduct further research: Continued research is needed to assess the long-term impact of innovative teaching methodologies on student learning outcomes in the Gulf region. This research can help inform future policies and practices in education.

By implementing these recommendations, Gulf countries can further enhance their education systems and prepare students for the challenges and opportunities of the 21st century.

6. REFERENCES

Abouhashem, A., Abdou, R. M., Bhadra, J., Siby, N., Ahmad, Z., & Al-Thani, N. J. 2021. *COVID-19 Inspired a STEM-Based Virtual Learning Model for Middle Schools—A Case Study of Qatar Sustainability. Basel Vol. 13, Iss. 5, (2021): 2799. DOI:DOI: 10.3390/su13052799

Abu-Shanab, E. A., & Anagreh, L. F. (2020). Contributions of Flipped Classroom Method to Student Learning. *International Journal of Cyber Behavior, Psychology and Learning*, 10(3), 12–30. DOI: 10.4018/IJCBPL.2020070102

Akour, I. A., Al-Maroof, R. S., Alfaisal, R. M., & Salloum, S. A. (2022). A conceptual framework for determining metaverse adoption in higher institutions of gulf area: An empirical study using hybrid SEM-ANN approach. *Comput. Educ. Artif. Intell.*, 3, 100052. DOI: 10.1016/j.caeai.2022.100052

Al Ali, M.Y., & Laib, K. (2024). The Using of the Metaverse in the Field of Education and Training in Police Colleges. *International Journal of Educational & Psychological Studies*.

Al-Ayed, S., & Al-Tit, A.A. (2021). Factors affecting the adoption of blended learning strategy. *International Journal of Data and Network Science*.

Al-Badi, A.H., Khan, A.I., & Eid-Alotaibi (2022). Perceptions of Learners and Instructors towards Artificial Intelligence in Personalized Learning. *ANT/EDI40*.

Al Hashimi, S. (2021). Exploring Effective Practices in Managing Distance Learning for Teaching Art and Design in Bahrain. *International Journal of Learning, Teaching and Educational Research*.

Al-Madani, F. M. (2015). The Effect of Blended Learning Approach on Fifth Grade Students' Academic Achievement in My Beautiful Language Textbook and the Development of Their Verbal Creative Thinking in Saudi Arabia. *Journal of International Education Research*, 11(4), 253–260.

Al Neyadi, S., & Al Maamari, F. (2020). An Exploration of the Use of Smart Learning Technology in UAE Schools. *Journal of Information Technology Education: Innovations in Practice*, 19, 257–288.

Al-Shammari, M.M. (2021). An exploratory study of experiential learning in teaching a supply chain management course in an emerging market economy. *Journal of international business education*.

Al-Shammari, M. M. (2022). An exploratory study of experiential learning in teaching a supply chain management course in an emerging market economy Journal of International Education in Business. *Acton*, 15(2), 184–201. DOI: 10.1108/JIEB-09-2020-0074

AL-Sinani, Y., & Al Taher, M. (2023). Enhancing teaching skills of physical education teachers in the Sultanate of Oman through augmented reality strategies: A comprehensive feedback-based analysis. *Cogent Social Sciences*, 9(2), 2266253.

Alabdulaziz, M. S., & Tayfour, E. A. (2023). A Comparative Study of the Effects of Distance Learning and Face-to-Face Learning during the COVID-19 Pandemic on Learning Mathematical Concepts in Primary Students of the Kingdom of Bahrain. *Education Sciences*, 13(2), 133. DOI: 10.3390/educsci13020133

Alabdulkareem, S. A. (2017). Saudi Science Teachers' Perceptions of Implementing Inquiry in Science Class. *Journal of Education and Training Studies*, 5(12), 67–78. DOI: 10.11114/jets.v5i12.2741

Alaeddine, N. I., Parsaei, H. R., Kakosimos, K., Guo, B., & Mansoor, B. (2015, June), *Teaching Innovation with Technology to Accelerate Engineering Students' Learning* Paper presented at 2015 ASEE Annual Conference & Exposition, Seattle, Washington. DOI: 10.18260/p.24815

Aldoy, M. (2022). Type Distance Learning During the Corona Pandemic (A sociological analysis of the positive outcomes, challenges, and the coping strategies from the Bahraini family's point of view). *Journal of Umm Al-Qura University for Social Sciences*.

Alghamdi, A., Iqbal, S., Trendova, K., Nkasu, M. M., & Al Hajjar, H. (2022). Undergraduate Students' Perspectives on Hybrid Education in the United Arab Emirates. *2022 Advances in Science and Engineering Technology International Conferences (ASET)*, 1-6.

Alghamdi, A. K., & El-Hassan, W. S. (2020). Interdisciplinary Inquiry-based Teaching and Learning of Sustainability in Saudi Arabia. *Journal of Teacher Education for Sustainability*, 22(2), 121–139. DOI: 10.2478/jtes-2020-0020

Alghamdi, S.A. (2019). Curriculum Innovation in Selected Saudi Arabia Public Secondary Schools: The Multi-Stakeholder Experience of the Tatweer Project. Published 15 April 2019

Alhajeri, G. (2022). Changing Behaviours and Its Theories to Achieve the Desire for Entrepreneurship in Future Generations in the UAE and Gulf Region. *International Business Research*, 15(11), 49. DOI: 10.5539/ibr.v15n11p49

Alhalwachi, L.F., Karam, A., & Hamdan, A.M. (2022). The Government Support in Distance Education: Case of Bahrain. *Technologies, Artificial Intelligence and the Future of Learning Post-COVID-19.*

Alhazbi, S. (2016). Using flipped classroom approach to teach computer programming. *2016 IEEE International Conference on Teaching, Assessment, and Learning for Engineering (TALE)*, 441-444. DOI: 10.1109/TALE.2016.7851837

AlKhunaizi, M. M. (2014). A comparative study of traditional instruction and blended learning in Saudi ARAMCO mathematics courses. *University of Phoenix ProQuest Dissertations Publishing*, 2014, 3648265.

Almazroui, K. M. (2022). Project-Based Learning for 21st-Century Skills: An Overview and Case Study of Moral Education in the UAE. *Social Studies*, 114(3), 125–136. DOI: 10.1080/00377996.2022.2134281

Almazroui, K. M. (2023). Project-based learning for 21st-century skills: An overview and case study of moral education in the UAE. *Social Studies*, 114(3), 125–136.

Almekhlafi, A. G., & Almeqdadi, F. A. (2010). Teachers' perceptions of technology integration in the United Arab Emirates school classrooms. *Journal of Educational Technology & Society*, 13(1), 165–175.

Almuntasheri, S., Gillies, R.M., & Wright, T. (2016). The Effectiveness of a Guided Inquiry-Based, Teachers' Professional Development Programme on Saudi Students' Understanding of Density. *Science education international, 27*, 16-39.

Alseweed, M. A. (2013). *Students' Achievement and Attitudes Toward Using Traditional Learning.* Blended Learning, and Virtual Classes Learning in Teaching and Learning at the University Level.

Alshammari, R. F. (2022). The Effect of Inquiry-Based Learning Strategy on Developing Saudi Students' Meta-Cognitive Reading Comprehension Skills. *English Language Teaching*, 15(5), 43. DOI: 10.5539/elt.v15n5p43

Alyami, H. (2016). A case study of the Tatweer school system in Saudi Arabia: the perceptions of leaders and teachers. 2016.

Anas, A. (2020). *Perceptions of Saudi Students to Blended Learning Environments at the University of Bisha.* Arab World English Journal. DOI: 10.24093/awej/call6.17

Asiri, A. (2018). Scientific Inquiry-Based Teaching Practices as Perceived by Science Teachers. *American Journal of Educational Research*, 6(4), 297–307. DOI: 10.12691/education-6-4-2

Asoodar, M., Marandi, S. S., Atai, M. R., & Vaezi, S. (2014). Learner reflections in virtual vs. blended EAP classes. *Computers in Human Behavior*, 41, 533–543. DOI: 10.1016/j.chb.2014.09.050

Bahrain Education & Labour Market Report. 2023. Fitch Solutions Group Limited. 2882036764. http://ezproxy.hct.ac.ae/login?url=https://www.proquest.com/reports/bahrain-education-amp-labour-report-01-june-2023/docview/2882036764/se-2?accountid=1215

Berger, G. (2019). Needs Assessment Lessons Learned in Qatar: A Flipped Classroom Approach. *MedEdPublish*, ●●●, 8. PMID: 38089336

Chen, L., Chen, P., & Lin, Z. (2020). Artificial Intelligence in Education: A Review. *IEEE Access : Practical Innovations, Open Solutions*, 8, 75264–75278. DOI: 10.1109/ACCESS.2020.2988510

Chowdhury, R. (2015). Learning and teaching style assessment for improving project-based learning of engineering students: A case of United Arab Emirates University. *Australasian Journal of Engineering Education*, 20(1), 81–94. DOI: 10.7158/D13-014.2015.20.1

El-Geddawy, M. A. (2018). DEVELOPING LEADERSHIP AND TEAMWORK SKILLS IN UNIVERSITY STUDENTS IN AN INQUIRY-BASED LEARNING ENVIRONMENT: THE CASE OF SAUDI ARABIA. *ICERI2018 Proceedings*.

Elkhatat, A. M., & Al-Muhtaseb, S. A. (2021). Hybrid online-flipped learning pedagogy for teaching laboratory courses to mitigate the pandemic COVID-19 confinement and enable effective sustainable delivery: Investigation of attaining course learning outcome. *SN Social Sciences*, 1(5), 1. DOI: 10.1007/s43545-021-00117-6 PMID: 34693317

Fouad, H.F. (2018). The impact of STEM project-based learning on the achievement of high school students in UAE.

Gholam, A. P. (2019). Inquiry-based learning: Student teachers' challenges and perceptions. *Journal of Inquiry and Action in Education*, 10(2), 6.

Hameed, D., Khan, M.B., Butt, A., Hameed, I., & Qadeer, F. (2016). Science, Technology and Innovation Through Entrepreneurship Education in the United Arab Emirates (UAE). *ERPN: Labor Economics (Topic)*.

Hasna, M. O. (2007). Research in undergraduate education at Qatar University: EE department experience. *2007 37th Annual Frontiers In Education Conference - Global Engineering: Knowledge Without Borders, Opportunities Without Passports*, S4B-13-S4B-16.

Hung, Y. H., Chen, C., & Huang, S. (2017). Applying augmented reality to enhance learning: A study of different teaching materials. *Journal of Computer Assisted Learning*, 33(3), 252–266. DOI: 10.1111/jcal.12173

Issah, M., & Al-Hattami, A. (2020). Developing Leadership Skills in the Classroom. Chapter in Innovations in Educational Leadership and Continuous Teachers' Professional Development (Eds. Osama Al Mahdi, Ph.D.). DOI: 10.46679/isbn978819484832502

Jamieson, M.V., & Shaw, J.M. (2018). APPLYING METACOGNITIVE STRATEGIES TO TEACHING ENGINEERING INNOVATION, DESIGN, AND LEADERSHIP.

Jwaifell, M. (2019). In-service Science Teachers' Readiness of Integrating Augmented Reality. *Journal of Curriculum and Teaching*.

Karacan, C.G., & Akoğlu, K. (2021). Educational Augmented Reality Technology for Language Learning and Teaching: A Comprehensive Review. *Education 3-13, 9*, 68-79.

Kennedy, D. M., Jewell, J., & Hickey, J. E. (2019). Male nursing students' experiences of simulation used to replace maternal-child clinical learning in Qatar. *Nurse Education Today*, 84, 104235. DOI: 10.1016/j.nedt.2019.104235 PMID: 31706203

López-Belmonte, J., Pozo-Sánchez, S., Moreno-Guerrero, A., & Lampropoulos, G. (2023). *Metaverse in Education: a systematic review. Revista de Educación a Distancia*. RED.

Mahdi, O. R., Nassar, I. A., & Almuslamani, H. A. (2020). The Role of Using Case Studies Method in Improving Students' Critical Thinking Skills in Higher Education. *International Journal of Higher Education*, 9(2), 297–308. DOI: 10.5430/ijhe.v9n2p297

Marinakou, E., & Giousmpasoglou, C. (2015). M-Learning in the Middle East: The Case of Bahrain. In Ordóñez de Pablos, P., Tennyson, R., & Lytras, M. (Eds.), *Assessing the Role of Mobile Technologies and Distance Learning in Higher Education* (pp. 176–199). IGI Global., DOI: 10.4018/978-1-4666-7316-8.ch008

Mccarthy, P. R., & McCarthy, H. M. (2006). When Case Studies Are Not Enough: Integrating Experiential Learning Into Business Curricula. *Journal of Education for Business*, 81(4), 201–204. DOI: 10.3200/JOEB.81.4.201-204

Mohamed, S. S., Barghuthi, N. B., & Said, H. E. (2017). An Analytical Study Towards the UAE Universities Smart Education Innovated Approaches. *2017 IEEE 19th International Conference on High Performance Computing and Communications; IEEE 15th International Conference on Smart City; IEEE 3rd International Conference on Data Science and Systems (HPCC/SmartCity/DSS)*, 200-205.

Mohammad, S. (2015). Effectiveness of M-Learning in Blended Learning-Design of Prototype Framework for AOU Bahrain. *2015 Fifth International Conference on e-Learning (econf)*, 201-206. DOI: 10.1109/ECONF.2015.22

Mohammad, S., & Job, M.A. (2012). Confidence -Motivation -Satisfaction- Performance (CMSP) Analysis of Blended Learning System in the Arab Open University Bahrain.

Mohammed, N. (2017). Project-based learning in higher education in the UAE: A case study of Arab students in Emirati Studies. *Learning and Teaching in Higher Education: Gulf Perspectives*, 14(2), 73–86. Advance online publication. DOI: 10.18538/lthe.v14.n2.294

Mohammed bin Rashid Al Maktoum Foundation. (n.d.). Young Innovators Competition. Retrieved from https://www.mbrfoundation.ae/en/innovation-and-creativity/innovation-competition

Muhammad, D. F. (2023). *Effect of using student-centred approach on students practical skills learning in an online Badminton Course.* International Journal of Research and Studies Publishing. DOI: 10.52133/ijrsp.v4.44.18

Mukhalalati, B.A., Elshami, S., Awaisu, A., Carr, A., Bawadi, H., & Romanowski, M.H. (2020). "Practice Educators' Academy": A fundamental step to experiential training success in Qatar. *Journal of emergency medicine, trauma and acute care, 2020*, 14.

Murala, D. K. (2024). METAEDUCATION: State-of-the-Art Methodology for Empowering Feature Education. *IEEE Access : Practical Innovations, Open Solutions*, 12, 57992–58020. DOI: 10.1109/ACCESS.2024.3391903

Nguyen, T. T., Nguyen, M. T., & Tran, H. T. (2023). *Artificial intelligent based teaching and learning approaches: A comprehensive review. International Journal of Evaluation and Research in Education.* IJERE.

OECD. (2019). Teaching for the future: Effective classroom practices to transform education. Retrieved from https://www.oecd.org/education/2030-project/teaching-for-the-future-education2030-background-note.pdf

Paravattil, B., Zolezzi, M., Carr, A., & Al-Moslih, A. (2021). Reshaping experiential education within Qatar University's Health Programs during the COVID-19 pandemic. *Qatar Medical Journal*, 2021(1), 2021. DOI: 10.5339/qmj.2021.9 PMID: 33763334

Prakash, A., Haque, A., Islam, F., & Sonal, D. (2023). *Exploring the Potential of Metaverse for Higher Education: Opportunities, Challenges, and Implications*. Metaverse Basic and Applied Research.

Putriyani, D.W., Sutrisno, D., & Abidin, A.Z. (2024). ANALYZING THE IMPACT: EMERGING CLASSROOM TECHNOLOGIES AND THE EVIDENCE ON LEARNING. *Global Synthesis in Education Journal*.

Qureshi, S.S., Bradley, K.L., Vishnumolakala, V.R., Treagust, D.F., Southam, D.C., Mocerino, M., & Ojeil, J. (2016). Educational Reforms and Implementation of Student-Centered Active Learning in Science at Secondary and University Levels in Qatar. *Science education international, 27*, 437-456.

Rahman, K.R., Shitol, S.K., Islam, M.S., Iftekhar, K.T., & Saha, P. (2023). Use of Metaverse Technology in Education Domain. *Journal of Metaverse*.

Raji, B. (2019). Significance and challenges of computer assisted education programs in the UAE: A case study of higher learning and vocational education. *Education and Information Technologies*, 24(1), 153–164.

Rizov, T., & Rizova, E. (2015). AUGMENTED REALITY AS A TEACHING TOOL IN HIGHER EDUCATION. *International Journal of Cognitive Research in Science. Engineering and Education*, 3, 7–15.

Salama, A. M. (2007). Contemporary Qatari architecture as an open textbook. *Archnet-IJAR*, 1, 101–114.

Salloum, S., Al Marzouqi, A., Alderbashi, K. Y., Shwedeh, F., Aburayya, A., Al Saidat, M. R., & Al-Maroof, R. S. (2023). Sustainability Model for the Continuous Intention to Use Metaverse Technology in Higher Education: A Case Study from Oman. *Sustainability (Basel)*, 15(6), 5257. DOI: 10.3390/su15065257

Sankar, J. P., Kalaichelvi, R., Elumalai, K. V., & Alqahtani, M. S. (2022). Effective Blended Learning in Higher Education During Covid-19. *Information Technologies and Learning Tools*. Vol 88, No2.

Sheerah, H.A. (2016). Blended Learning in Saudi Universities: Challenges and Aspirations. Published 2016. Education, Computer Science.

Shuaili, K. A., Musawi, A. S., & Hussain, R. M. (2020). *The effectiveness of using augmented reality in teaching geography curriculum on the achievement and attitudes of Omani 10th Grade Students*. Multidisciplinary Journal for Education, Social and Technological Sciences. DOI: 10.4995/muse.2020.13014

Shwedeh, F., Adelaja, A.A., Ogbolu, G., Kitana, A., Taamneh, A., Aburayya, A., & Salloum, S.A. (2023). Entrepreneurial innovation among international students in the UAE: Differential role of entrepreneurial education using SEM analysis. *International Journal of Innovative Research and Scientific Studies*.

Suliman, S., Hassan, R., Athamneh, K., Jenkins, M., & Bylund, C. L. (2018). Blended learning in quality improvement training for healthcare professionals in Qatar. *International Journal of Medical Education*, 9, 55–56. DOI: 10.5116/ijme.5a80.3d88 PMID: 29478042

Syahrin, S., & Akmal, N. (2024). *Navigating the Artificial Intelligence Frontier: Perceptions of Instructors, Students, and Administrative Staff on the Role of Artificial Intelligence in Education in the Sultanate of Oman*. Arab World English Journal.

Tamim, R. (2018). Blended Learning for Learner Empowerment: Voices from the Middle East. *Journal of Research on Technology in Education*, 50(1), 70–83. DOI: 10.1080/15391523.2017.1405757

Tayem, Y., Almarabheh, A. J., Abo Hamza, E. G., & Deifalla, A. (2022). Perceptions of Medical Students on Distance Learning During the COVID-19 Pandemic: A Cross-Sectional Study from Bahrain. *Advances in Medical Education and Practice*, 13, 345–354. DOI: 10.2147/AMEP.S357335 PMID: 35478974

Tikruni, R. (2019). Investigation of an Inquiry-based Learning Intervention on Undergraduate Saudi Women's Critical Thinking Skills in an English as a Foreign Language Reading and Writing Class during the Preparatory Year. *Northern Illinois University ProQuest Dissertations Publishing*, 2019, 27545571.

UAE Ministry of Education. (n.d.). *Innovation Ambassadors Program*. Retrieved from. [https://www.moe.gov.ae/En/Pages/InnovationAmbassadors.aspx]

UAE National Innovation Strategy. 2015. https://www.moei.gov.ae/assets/download/1d2d6460/National%20Innovation%20Strategy.pdf.aspx

United Arab Emirates Government Portal. (2023). *UAE Smart Schools Initiative*. Retrieved from. [https://www.government.ae/en/about-the-uae/education/smart-schools-initiative]

Venkataraman, S. (2023). Impact of Technology-Supported Education on Student Learning Outcomes. IJIRMPS (E-ISSN: 2349-7300), Volume 9, Issue 4, July-August 2021.

Wiseman, A. W., & Anderson, E. (2014). Developing Innovation and Entrepreneurial Skills in Youth Through Mass Education: The example of ICT in the UAE. ISBN: 978-1-78190-708-5, eISBN: 978-1-78190-709-2. ISSN: 1479-3679. 1 January 2014

Zhang, L., & Ma, Y. (2023). A study of the impact of project-based learning on student learning effects: A meta-analysis study. *Frontiers in Psychology*, 14, 14. DOI: 10.3389/fpsyg.2023.1202728 PMID: 37564309

Chapter 7
Framework for Implementing STEM Learning Technologies:
Addressing Students' Challenges of Developing 21st-Century Skills

Doris Chasokela
https://orcid.org/0009-0001-5983-8508
National University of Science and Technology, Zimbabwe

ABSTRACT

This book chapter proposes a framework for implementing STEM learning technologies to help students develop the 21st-century skills they need to succeed in the modern world. The framework focuses on four key elements: curriculum, instruction, assessment, and professional development. It also emphasizes the importance of partnerships with the community to provide students with opportunities to apply their skills and knowledge in real-world settings. This framework provides lecturers with a roadmap for integrating STEM learning technologies into the classroom in a way that is effective, engaging, and relevant to the needs of 21st-century students. The framework focuses on addressing the challenges that students face in developing these skills. The chapter outlines a step-by-step approach to implementing STEM technologies, from identifying the specific needs of students to evaluating the effectiveness of the technologies. It also discusses the importance of a collaborative approach, involving students, lecturers, and other stakeholders in the implementation process.

DOI: 10.4018/979-8-3693-3443-0.ch007

INTRODUCTION

The current state of 21st-century skills development in most higher education developing countries is characterized by limited resources and infrastructure, a lack of digital literacy among students and lecturers, and a gap between the skills being taught in higher education and the needs of the job market. Resources and infrastructure: Higher education institutions often lack the financial resources to invest in the latest technologies and infrastructure. In addition, the digital divide is a major challenge, with many students and lecturers lacking access to computers and the Internet. 21st-century skills are a set of abilities that are considered essential for success in the modern world. They include critical thinking and problem-solving: The ability to analyze and evaluate information and solve complex problems. Communication and collaboration: The ability to communicate effectively and work well with others. Creativity and innovation: The ability to generate new ideas and solutions, and think outside the box. Technology literacy: The ability to use and understand technology, and use it to solve problems and communicate effectively. The framework proposed in this chapter is based on the premise that STEM learning technologies can be used to address the challenges students face in developing 21st-century skills. The framework has four key components namely access: ensuring that all students have access to the technologies and resources they need to engage with STEM learning. Resources: providing the necessary financial and material resources for effective implementation of STEM learning technologies. Training: providing training and professional development for lecturers to effectively integrate STEM technologies into their teaching. Collaboration creates partnerships between institutions, organizations, and individuals to facilitate the implementation of STEM learning technologies.

The concept of 21st-century skills refers to the knowledge, skills, and abilities that students need to succeed in today's rapidly changing and increasingly digital world. These skills include critical thinking, problem-solving, creativity, collaboration, communication, and adaptability. They are considered to be essential for student's future success in the workforce and for their overall well-being. In a globalized world, these skills are critical for students to be able to compete in the job market and contribute to the economy. They also help students navigate the ever-changing digital landscape and prepare for the challenges of the future. To address the challenges associated with the development of 21st-century skills, a framework for implementing STEM learning technologies should focus on three key areas: access, resources, and training. A framework for implementing STEM learning technologies to address the challenges of developing 21st-century skills in students could include curriculum incorporating STEM learning technologies into existing curriculum or developing new curriculum specifically focused on using these technologies; instruction thus using a variety of instructional strategies to engage students in active learning with STEM learning technologies; assessing students' skills and knowledge using both traditional and new assessment methods; providing lecturers with professional development opportunities to learn about using STEM learning technologies in the classroom and engaging in community partnership, such as businesses.

Improvement of digital access and infrastructure in higher education institutions

Digital access refers to the ability to access and use digital technologies, including the internet, computers, and other digital devices. It is a vital component of digital literacy and is necessary for full participation in the digital economy. Shortcomings of digital access include the digital divide, a lack of skills, and a lack of availability of affordable and reliable internet access. Opportunities include improved access to information and services, economic growth, and improved quality of life. By addressing these shortcomings and leveraging the opportunities, individuals and communities can benefit from improved digital access. (Loos et al., 2023; Sofkova Hashemi, et al., 2023). +Improving digital access and infrastructure in higher education is essential to ensuring that all students have access to the latest technologies and the internet (Kistaubayev et al., 2022; Alnajim, et al., 2023). This can be done by:

- Providing computers and other digital devices to students and lecturers.
- Improving internet connectivity, including installing broadband networks and providing Wi-Fi hotspots.
- Upgrading existing infrastructure, such as libraries and computer laboratories.
- Training lecturers, technicians, and students on how to use the latest technologies.
- Ensuring that the technologies used are appropriate for the local context and the needs of the students.

Upgrading classroom infrastructure involves several steps, such as evaluating the current infrastructure, assessing needs and priorities, identifying funding sources, researching and purchasing new equipment, training staff on new equipment, ensuring regular maintenance and support, and evaluating the effectiveness of the upgrade. The integration of digital learning platforms is an important part of improving digital access and infrastructure. Some steps involved in this process include assessing the current digital tools and platforms in use, evaluating the needs of the institution and its students, researching and choosing appropriate platforms implementing the chosen platforms, training staff and students on how to use the platforms, and monitoring the use of the platforms and making adjustments as needed. Providing digital literacy training is an important step in improving digital access and infrastructure. This can be done by assessing the current level of digital literacy among students and staff, developing a digital literacy curriculum, delivering the curriculum through workshops, online courses, or other methods, and providing ongoing support and resources for digital literacy. Encouraging digital collaboration is another key aspect of improving digital access and infrastructure. Some ways to encourage digital collaboration include creating a culture of openness and sharing, providing opportunities for collaboration, such as group projects, promoting the use of collaborative tools, such as Google Docs, and providing support for online collaboration, such as through technical assistance.

Data security and privacy are critical components of any digital infrastructure. Data security and privacy can be improved by reviewing and updating data security policies, ensuring that data is stored securely and protected from unauthorized access, educating users about data security best practices, and conducting regular audits of data security systems. A wide range of stakeholders are involved in improving digital access and infrastructure in higher education. These include national governments, regional and international organizations, non-governmental organizations, research institutions, and the private sector. Each of these stakeholders plays a different role in the process. National governments are responsible for creating policies and regulations to promote digital access and infrastructure, while regional and inter-national organizations can provide funding and technical assistance. Meanwhile, non-governmental organizations can raise awareness of the importance of digital access and infrastructure, and research institutions can develop innovative solutions to improve access.

Addressing the digital divide and how to improve digital literacy

The digital divide refers to the gap between those who have access to digital technologies and those who do not (Bon et al., 2023; Lombardi, 2023). It is a form of social inequality and often affects those who are poor, rural, or otherwise marginal-ized (de Clercq et al., 2023; Vasu, 2023; Inegbedion, 2021). In developing countries, the digital divide is significant, with many rural communities having no access to the internet or basic computer skills. Digital literacy is the ability to effectively use and understand digital technologies, including computers, the internet, and other digital devices (Martin & Grudziecki, 2006). It is a combination of technical skills, such as being able to use software and hardware, as well as digital literacy skills, such as being able to critically evaluate and use digital information. The benefits of digital literacy include improved access to information and resources, increased efficiency in communication, and the ability to participate in the digital economy (Ukwoma, et al., 2016; McDougall, et al., 2018). Shortcomings include the risk of digital exclusion the danger of being vulnerable to cybercrime, lacking the necessary skills and knowledge to effectively navigate and utilize digital tools, platforms, and resources, limited access to information, and poor online etiquette (Ameen & Gorman, 2009; Radovanovic, et al., 2015).

Bridging the digital divide in addressing the challenges of access and literacy across nations needs to be examined. Globally, addressing the digital divide and improving digital literacy can be achieved through several strategies, including increasing investment in infrastructure, including in rural areas, providing digital literacy training to individuals and communities, developing policies and programs that support digital inclusion, and improving access to affordable internet and digital devices. Regionally, many of the same strategies can be applied, but there is also a need to tailor the solutions to the specific needs of the region. Several stakeholders can and should play a role in improving digital devices and digital literacy, including the National governments which should create policies and initiatives to improve digital literacy, such as through the education system. They can also provide funding for programs to improve access to digital devices and train people on how to use them. Business companies that produce and sell digital devices should ensure that their products are accessible and affordable for all. They can also create initiatives to teach people how to use their products, such as through free online tutorials.

From a chasm to a connection on how to close the digital gap is particularly effective. It immediately draws the reader's attention by highlighting the issue of the digital divide and its consequences. It also offers a sense of hope by implying that the gap can be closed. Addressing the digital divide also indicates digital equity for all is ensuring equal access to technology. It directly addresses the issue of digital equity and suggests that it is a matter of social justice. It conveys the importance of ensuring that everyone has equal access to technology, regardless of their socio-economic status or background. It also suggests that technology is a powerful tool that can be used to level the playing field and create opportunities for all. A new frontier of learning for the power of digital literacy is also key to the digital divide. It presents digital literacy as a powerful tool for learning and implies that it can open up new possibilities for students. The new frontier of learning suggests that digital literacy is ushering in a new era of education, where students can access a wider range of knowledge and information than ever before. The power of digital literacy highlights the transformative potential of this new educational approach, emphasizing the ability of digital literacy to empower students and equip them with the skills and knowledge they need to succeed in the modern world. The possibilities of digital literacy are numerous and varied. For example, it can open up new ways of accessing and analyzing information, which can lead to more informed decision-making and better problem-solving skills. It can also foster greater collaboration and communication, as well as provide new opportunities for creativity and innovation. Digital literacy can also promote more personalized learning, allowing students to tailor their educational experiences to their interests and learning styles. In addition, it can help to level the playing field for students who may not have access to traditional educational resources, such as libraries or higher institutions.

Strategies for updating the curriculum to include 21st-century skills

Several strategies can be used to update the curriculum to include 21st-century skills (Dilekci & Karatay, 2023; Siddiq, 2023; Soghomonyan & Karapetyan, 2023). The strategies include:

- Reviewing and updating the curriculum to incorporate digital literacy and other 21st-century skills.
- Introducing technology-enabled learning, such as e-learning and blended learning.
- Hybrid approaches (digital and non-digital teaching methods), technology integration (including digital tools, data analysis tools, multimedia resources, virtual reality (VR), augmented reality (AR), or online platforms), digital flipped classroom, inquiry-based learning, and simulation-based learning.
- Using project-based and inquiry-based learning approaches that encourage students to use technology to research and solve real-world problems.
- Using collaborative learning approaches, such as working in teams or with mentors.
- Developing a culture of continuous learning and innovation.
- Addressing the gap between the skills being taught in higher education and the needs of the job market.

Incorporating 21st-century skills into curricula

To update the curriculum to include 21st-century skills, several stakeholders are involved like the education ministries and lecturers (Gawe et al. 2023). Education ministries are responsible for setting the curriculum and standards for what is taught in higher institutions of learning. They can work with other stakeholders to update the curriculum to include 21st-century skills. Lecturers are the ones who play a key role in implementing the curriculum and ensuring that students are developing the skills they need. They can advocate for changes to the curriculum and help to develop new teaching methods. These four skills are often referred to as the "4 Cs" of 21st-century learning. There are several ways to teach these skills using technology. For example, critical thinking can be taught through the use of problem-based learning, where students work on real-world problems using technology-based tools. Communication can be taught through the use of collaborative tools like Google Docs, where students can work together on a document and see each other's changes in real time. Collaboration can be taught through the use of online platforms like Slack, which allow for real-time collaboration and communication. Fostering a growth mindset is key to supporting lifelong learning, and technology can play a role in this. Several online resources can be used to help students develop a growth mindset, such as the free online course "Learning How to Learn" from Coursera. This course focuses on the importance of self-reflection, perseverance, and feedback. Another tool that can be used to foster a growth mindset is gamification, which is the use of game-like elements in a learning environment. This can help to motivate and engage students and make learning more fun. When it comes to assessing and evaluating the effectiveness of 21st-century skills, several different approaches can be taken. One approach is to use formative assessment, which is a type of assessment that is used to inform instruction. This type of assessment can be done through the use of technology-based tools, such as online quizzes and surveys. Summative assessment, which is used to measure learning at the end of a unit or course, can also be done using technology, such as online exams and portfolios.

Implementing technology-enhanced learning in the curriculum

When it comes to implementing technology-enhanced learning in engineering curricula, there are several different approaches we could explore. We could look at how to effectively integrate technology into lectures and labs. We could also explore the use of learning management systems, online learning platforms, and mobile learning. We could also explore how to use technology to support flipped classrooms, which are a type of blended learning environment where students watch lectures online and then engage in active learning during class time. And finally, we could explore how to use technology to create personalized learning experiences for students. Different countries and educational systems have different needs and timelines for updating their curriculum. However, some experts suggest that curriculum updates should happen every 5-10 years to ensure that students are learning relevant and up-to-date information (Chan, 2023; Glendinning, 2023). It's also important to consider the pace of technological change, as well as the changing needs of students and employers. As the world becomes increasingly digital, it's more important than ever for students to have strong digital literacy skills.

The strategies used in experiential and adaptive learning have changed to digital nowadays such as hybrid approaches (digital and non-digital teaching methods), technology integration (including digital tools, data analysis tools, multimedia resources, virtual reality (VR), augmented reality (AR), or online platforms), digital flipped classroom, inquiry-based learning, and simulation-based learning (Li et al. 2021; Shute & Towle, 2018).

Hybrid approaches (digital and non-digital teaching methods)

Hybrid approaches that combine digital and non-digital teaching methods are essential for implementing STEM learning technologies at the university (Bilgin et al. 2022). This approach allows educators to leverage the strengths of both digital and non-digital methods to create a more engaging, interactive, and effective learning experience (Fawns, 2019). By integrating digital tools and platforms with traditional teaching methods, educators can cater to diverse learning styles, promote active learning, and facilitate the development of essential skills like problem-solving, communication, and time management. For instance, in a hybrid approach, students may watch video lectures or online modules on a topic like data analysis or programming before coming to class for hands-on activities or group projects. This approach allows students to develop a foundational understanding of the material at their own pace and then apply it in a collaborative setting. In another example, educators can use digital tools like simulation software or virtual labs to recreate real-world scenarios or experiments, allowing students to explore complex concepts in a safe and controlled environment (Smetana & Bell, 2012). Hybrid approaches also enable educators to address the challenges faced by students when transitioning from traditional teaching methods to digital ones. For instance, some students may struggle with using digital tools or navigating online platforms, which can hinder their ability to fully engage with the course material. By combining digital and non-digital methods, educators can provide support and scaffolding for students who need it, while also challenging more advanced learners with complex tasks and projects. (Timotheou et al. 2023; Burghardt et al. 2021).

Moreover, hybrid approaches allow educators to integrate multimedia resources and multimedia storytelling into their teaching practices (Vu et al. 2022). This can include using videos, podcasts, infographics, or interactive simulations to present complex concepts in an engaging and accessible way. By incorporating multimedia resources, educators can create a more dynamic and immersive learning environment that caters to different learning styles and abilities. However, hybrid approaches also pose challenges for educators. For instance, they must ensure that the digital components of the course are accessible and user-friendly for all students, regardless of their technical expertise or familiarity with technology. Additionally, educators must carefully design and integrate the digital and non-digital components of the course to avoid confusion or disjointedness. Finally, they must also be prepared to adapt their teaching practices to respond to any technical issues or difficulties that arise during the implementation of hybrid approaches. In conclusion, hybrid approaches that combine digital and non-digital teaching methods offer a powerful way for educators to implement STEM learning technologies at the university level. By leveraging the strengths of both digital and non-digital methods, educators can create a more engaging, interactive, and effective learning experience that caters to diverse learning styles and abilities. While there are challenges associated with implementing hybrid approaches, the benefits in terms of student engagement and skills development make them an essential consideration for educators seeking to enhance STEM education. An educator uses a hybrid approach to teach STEM by combining traditional lectures with online modules, simulations, and hands-on activities. Students learn concepts online and then apply them in lab experiments (Henke et al. 2022). A study found that a hybrid approach improved student engagement and achievement in a chemistry course, compared to traditional lecture-based instruction (Atwa et al. 2019; Murphy & Stewart, 2015; Dziuban et al. 2005).

Technology integration (including digital tools, data analysis tools, multimedia resources, virtual reality (VR), augmented reality (AR), or online platforms)

Technology integration is a critical component of implementing STEM learning technologies (Snyder, 2018). The use of digital tools, data analysis tools, multimedia resources, virtual reality (VR), augmented reality (AR), and online platforms can enhance student engagement, collaboration, and skills development (Al-Ansi, et al. 2023). For instance, digital tools such as learning management systems (LMS) and online collaboration platforms can facilitate communication and teamwork among students, while data analysis tools like data visualization software can help students develop data literacy and critical thinking skills. Multimedia resources such as videos, podcasts, and interactive simulations can be used to present complex concepts in an engaging and accessible way (Savov et al. 2019). Virtual reality (VR) and augmented reality (AR) technologies can immerse learners in simulated environments or scenarios, promoting experiential learning and skill development (Papanastasiou et al. 2019). Online platforms like Massive Open Online Courses (MOOCs) and online labs can provide students with access to a vast array of resources and learning materials, allowing them to learn at their own pace (Murphy et al. 2015; Toven-Lindsey et al. 2015).

The integration of technology into STEM education also enables educators to personalize learning experiences for students. For instance, adaptive learning systems can adjust the difficulty level of course materials based on individual student performance, while learning analytics can provide educators with insights into student progress and areas for improvement. Additionally, technology integration allows educators to incorporate real-world scenarios and case studies into their teaching practices, providing students with opportunities to apply theoretical concepts to real-world problems. However, technology integration also poses challenges for educators. For instance, they must ensure that all students have access to the necessary technology and digital literacy skills to effectively use these tools. Additionally, educators must carefully design and integrate technology into their teaching practices to avoid overwhelming students or creating technical issues. Furthermore, educators must also be prepared to address the potential limitations of technology integration, such as unequal access to resources or concerns about academic integrity. In conclusion, technology integration is a vital component of implementing STEM learning technologies at the university level. By leveraging digital tools, data analysis tools, multimedia resources, virtual reality (VR), augmented reality (AR), and online platforms, educators can create engaging, interactive, and personalized learning experiences that cater to diverse learning styles and abilities. While there are challenges associated with technology integration, the benefits in terms of student engagement and skills development make it an essential consideration for educators seeking to enhance STEM education.

An educator uses data analysis software to help students analyze and interpret data from a science experiment, promoting critical thinking and problem-solving skills (Yang et al. 2012). A study found that data analysis tools improved students' understanding of scientific concepts and enhanced their ability to think critically about data in a college statistics course (Abd Rahman, 2014). An educator uses interactive multimedia resources, such as videos and simulations, to engage students in a biology course and promote active learning (Allen, 2018). A study found that multimedia resources improved student engagement and understanding in an online college course, compared to traditional text-based instruction (Vogt, 2016). An educator uses VR to take students on virtual field trips to historical sites or museums, enhancing their learning experience. A study found that online platforms improved student collaboration and communication skills compared to traditional face-to-face instruction Rajab, 2018).

Digital flipped classroom

A digital flipped classroom is a teaching approach that reverses the traditional lecture-homework format (Goksu & Duran, 2020). In a traditional classroom, instructors typically deliver lectures in class and assign homework or projects outside of class. In a digital flipped classroom, instructors provide pre-recorded video lectures or online resources for students to complete before class and then use class time for discussions, group work, and hands-on activities (Awidi & Paynter, 2019). This approach allows students to learn at their own pace and review material as many times as needed while freeing up class time for more interactive and engaging activities. In a STEM context, a digital flipped classroom can be particularly effective for subjects like math and science, where complex concepts can be challenging to grasp. By providing students with pre-recorded video lectures or online tutorials, instructors can help students build a strong foundation in these subjects before moving on to more advanced topics. Additionally, the digital flipped classroom approach can be particularly effective for students who may have missed classes or need extra support. A study found that the digital flipped classroom increased student engagement and understanding in a college mathematics course, compared to traditional instruction (Lo & Hew, 2020; Subramaniam & Muniandy, 2019).

Inquiry-Based Learning

Inquiry-based learning is an approach that encourages students to explore and discover concepts through investigation and experimentation. This approach is particularly well-suited for STEM subjects, where students are often expected to apply scientific principles to real-world problems. In an inquiry-based learning environment, students are presented with a problem or question and are encouraged to design and conduct experiments, collect data, and draw conclusions. Inquiry-based learning promotes critical thinking, problem-solving, and collaboration skills, which are essential for success in STEM fields. By encouraging students to take an active role in their learning process, lecturers can help them develop a deeper understanding of scientific concepts and develop the skills they need to apply them in real-world contexts. A study found that inquiry-based learning improved students' critical thinking, problem-solving, and scientific literacy (Wen et al. 2020).

Simulation-Based Learning

Simulation-based learning is an approach that uses virtual or simulated environments to mimic real-world scenarios or experiences. This approach is particularly effective for STEM subjects, where students can use simulations to practice complex skills or procedures in a safe and controlled environment. In a STEM context, simulation-based learning can be used to teach a range of skills, from programming languages to medical procedures. For example, students can use simulations to practice coding exercises or medical procedures without risking real-world consequences. This approach can also be used to teach complex concepts, such as data analysis or financial modeling. A lecture uses simulation software to teach students how to perform procedures STEM related modules, allowing them to practice and make mistakes in a safe environment. A study found that simulation-based training improved the performance of emergency responders in a simulated emergency scenario, compared to traditional training methods (Lee et al. 2024).

Using Project-Based and Inquiry-Based Learning Approaches

Project-based and inquiry-based learning approaches encourage students to use technology to research and solve real-world problems (Albion, 2015; Chu, et al. 2021). In these approaches, students are presented with a problem or scenario and are encouraged to design and conduct research projects that address the issue. In a STEM context, project-based and inquiry-based learning approaches can be used to teach a range of skills, from data analysis to programming languages. For example, students can use project-based learning to develop web applications or mobile apps that address real-world problems. This approach can also be used to teach complex concepts, such as data visualization or machine learning.

Collaborative Learning Approaches

Collaborative learning approaches involve working in teams or with mentors to achieve a common goal (O'Donnell & Hmelo-Silver, 2013). In a STEM context, collaborative learning approaches can be particularly effective for teaching teamwork and communication skills. Lecturers in higher education can use collaborative learning approaches to encourage students to work together on projects or case studies that require critical thinking and problem-solving skills. This approach can also be used to mentor students who may need extra support or guidance (Koschmann et al. 1994). By working together with peers or mentors, students can develop the skills they need to collaborate effectively with others in the workplace.

Developing a Culture of Continuous Learning and Innovation

Developing a culture of continuous learning and innovation involves encouraging students to think creatively and critically about problems and solutions (Isaksen, 2010; Cobo, 2013). This approach involves fostering a culture of experimentation and risk-taking, where students are encouraged to try new things and learn from their mistakes. In a STEM context, developing a culture of continuous learning and innovation can be particularly effective for teaching complex concepts like data analysis or programming languages. By encouraging students to think creatively and critically about problems and solutions, instructors can help them develop the skills they need to innovate and adapt to the ever-changing STEM landscape.

Addressing the Gap between the Skills Being Taught in Higher Education and the Needs of the Job Market

The gap between the skills being taught in higher education and the needs of the job market is a significant challenge for educators in the STEM fields (Kelley & Knowles, 2016). To address this gap, lecturers must focus on teaching skills that are relevant to the job market, such as data analysis, programming languages, and communication skills. lecturers can use project-based and inquiry-based learning approaches to teach these skills in context. By presenting students with real-world problems or scenarios that require data analysis or programming languages, instructors can help them develop the skills they need to succeed in the job market. Additionally, lecturers can use collaboration tools like online platforms or virtual reality (VR) environments to facilitate teamwork and communication among students (Coyne et al. 2018).

In conclusion, hybrid approaches that combine digital and non-digital teaching methods can enhance student engagement, critical thinking, and collaboration. By integrating digital tools and platforms with traditional teaching methods, educators can cater to diverse learning styles, promote active learning, and facilitate the development of essential skills like problem-solving, communication, and time management. For instance, hybrid approaches can be used in subjects like engineering, computer science, and business to integrate simulations, case studies, and group projects with online discussions and multimedia resources. However, hybrid approaches also pose challenges such as unequal access to technology, potential distractions, and the need for careful planning and integration.

Technology integration can facilitate advanced skills development in various disciplines. For instance, digital tools like data analysis software and online platforms can enhance research skills in fields like economics, sociology, and psychology. Multimedia resources can promote critical thinking and creativity in subjects like art, music, and film studies. Virtual reality (VR) and augmented reality (AR) technologies can immerse learners in simulated environments or scenarios to develop spatial awareness and problem-solving skills in fields like architecture, engineering, and medicine. However, technology integration also raises concerns about unequal access to technology, cybersecurity risks, and the need for educators to develop digital literacy skills.

The digital flipped classroom model can be particularly effective by providing students with pre-recorded video lectures or online materials at home and reserving class time for interactive activities, discussions, and hands-on projects. This approach can promote self-directed learning, critical thinking, and collaboration in subjects like computer science, engineering, and business. For instance, digital flipped classrooms can be used to deliver large-scale courses with hundreds of students by recording video lectures or creating interactive online modules. However, the digital flipped classroom model also poses challenges such as ensuring student engagement, developing effective assessment strategies, and addressing potential technical issues.

Inquiry-based learning is particularly well-suited for university-level education where students are expected to develop advanced research skills. This approach encourages students to explore questions and problems through hands-on activities and investigations. For instance, inquiry-based learning can be used in fields like science, technology, engineering, and mathematics (STEM) to promote critical thinking, problem-solving, and collaboration. University-level inquiry-based learning can also be used in non-STEM fields like humanities and social sciences to develop research skills and critical thinking. However, inquiry-based learning also poses challenges such as ensuring student autonomy while guiding them towards relevant questions and problems.

Simulation-based learning is another effective approach that recreates real-world scenarios or experiences to promote problem-solving, decision-making, crisis management, and collaboration. For instance, simulation-based learning can be used in fields like medicine to train medical professionals in crises or in business to train managers in decision-making scenarios. University-level simulation-based learning can also be used in fields like law enforcement to train officers in crisis management scenarios. However, simulation-based learning also poses challenges such as ensuring realism and authenticity while avoiding potential biases or stereotypes.

Across all these strategies at the university level, many of these strategies require students to develop self-directed learning skills such as time management, goal-setting, and self-motivation. As technology integration becomes more prevalent at the university level, educators must ensure that students develop digital literacy skills such as online research skills, data analysis skills, and cybersecurity awareness. All these strategies promote critical thinking skills such as analysis, evaluation, and problem-solving and emphasize the importance of collaboration and teamwork. University-level education requires students to adapt to new technologies, tools, and methodologies. By recognizing these foundational concepts across various strategies at the university level educators can create a comprehensive approach that develops well-rounded learners equipped with essential 21st-century skills. Students can benefit from a more flexible and personalized learning experience that caters to their diverse needs. Educational institutions can foster a culture of innovation and lifelong learning.

Table 1. Comparing the strategies used in experiential and adaptive learning changed to digital

Method	Focus	Interaction	Critical Thinking	Problem-solving
Hybrid approaches (digital and non-digital teaching methods	Both digital and non-digital content, emphasizing student-centered learning	High (student-centered)	High (students design and conduct experiments)	High (students apply knowledge to real-world problems)
Technology integration (including digital tools, data analysis tools, multimedia resources, virtual reality (VR), augmented reality (AR), or online platforms	Data visualization and analysis to support critical thinking and problem-solving	Medium-High (students analyze data)	High (students interpret data and conclude)	High (students apply knowledge to real-world problems)
	Interactive multimedia resources for learning and engagement	Medium-High (students interact with multimedia resources)	Medium-High (students analyze and apply concepts)	Medium-High (students complete projects or solve problems)
	Immersive virtual environments for experiential learning for VR	High (students engage with VR environments)	VR has high (students analyze and apply concepts)	VR has high (students practice complex skills or procedures)
	Interactive virtual objects overlaid onto real-world environments for enhanced learning for AR	Medium-High (students interact with AR objects)	Medium-High (students analyze and apply concepts)	Medium-High (students complete projects or solve problems)
	Collaborative online platforms for communication, discussion, and project-based learning	High (students collaborate online)	Medium-High (students analyze and apply concepts)	Medium-High (students complete projects or solve problems)
Digital flipped classroom	Pre-recorded digital content, hands-on activities, and group work	High (group work, discussion, and collaboration)	High (students analyze and apply concepts)	High (students solve problems and complete projects)

continued on following page

Table 1. Continued

Method	Focus	Interaction	Critical Thinking	Problem-solving
Inquiry-based learning	Student-centered approach, focusing on inquiry and discovery	High (student-led inquiry and experimentation)	High (students design and conduct experiments)	High (students apply knowledge to real-world problems)
Simulation-based learning	Virtual or simulated environments to mimic real-world scenarios	Medium-High (students interact with simulations)	Medium-High (students analyze and apply concepts)	High (students practice complex skills or procedures)

(Source: Doris Chasokela 2024)

The role of government and other stakeholders in supporting STEM education and 21st-century skills development

Governments and other stakeholders, such as businesses, civil society organizations, and international organizations, play a crucial role in supporting STEM education and 21st-century skill development (Ebekozien & Aigbavboa, 2023; Wardani et al., 2023). Governments can provide funding and policy support, such as developing national education plans and policies that support STEM education and digital literacy. They can also provide resources, such as high-quality digital content and equipment. Other stakeholders can support STEM education through initiatives such as providing training, mentoring, and internships; donating equipment and resources; and funding research and innovation projects.

In addition, governments and other stakeholders can help to create an enabling environment for STEM education and skill development (Bonilla et al., 2023; Podgorska & Zdonek, 2023). This includes providing adequate infrastructure, such as internet connectivity and electricity, and supporting the development of a skilled workforce. In addition, governments and other stakeholders can support efforts to promote gender equality in STEM education and to ensure that all students have equal access to STEM education. Finally, governments and other stakeholders can work together to raise awareness of the importance of STEM education and 21st-century skills and to promote innovation and creativity. The challenge that governments and other stakeholders face in supporting STEM education and 21st-century skill development is the limited resources available (Sullivan, 2023). Many countries, especially in the developing world, have limited budgets and other resources, which makes it difficult to invest in STEM education and digital literacy. In addition, many countries lack a skilled workforce that can effectively implement STEM education programs. Other challenges include a lack of awareness of the importance of STEM education, a lack of support from the private sector, and a lack of coordination between the various stakeholders.

To overcome the challenges mentioned above, governments and other stakeholders can take several steps. Firstly, they can advocate for increased funding for STEM education and digital literacy, both domestically and through international partnerships. Secondly, they can invest in teacher training and development, as well as professional development for other STEM education professionals. Thirdly, they can create public-private partnerships to leverage the resources of the private sector. Finally, they can create an enabling policy environment for STEM education, including incentives for investment in the sector. By taking these steps, governments and other stakeholders can help to ensure that everyone has access to quality STEM education and 21st-century skills.

The role of industry in supporting STEM education and skills development

Skills development refers to the process of acquiring and improving the knowledge, skills, and abilities needed to perform a job or task effectively (Swedish International Development Cooperation Agency, 2018; World Economic Forum, 2017). It can involve formal education, such as taking a course or earning a degree, or informal education, such as on-the-job training or self-study. It can also involve a combination of both formal and informal learning experiences. Skills development can happen throughout an individual's lifetime and is an important part of keeping up with the changing demands of the workplace.

There are several challenges and opportunities associated with skills development (Sharma et al., 2015). One challenge is ensuring that everyone has access to quality learning opportunities, regardless of their socioeconomic status. Another challenge is keeping up with the rapidly changing demands of the workplace, and ensuring that skills development programs are relevant and effective. However, there are also many opportunities for skills development, such as using new technologies to make learning more accessible and engaging and leveraging the power of data to personalize learning experiences. Finally, there is also the opportunity to use skills development to create more inclusive and equitable workplaces.

Industry plays a crucial role in supporting STEM education and skills development (Hurley et al., 2023). Many companies offer internships and apprenticeships that allow students to gain real-world experience and develop skills that are in demand by employers. Companies can also provide financial support for STEM education initiatives, such as through scholarships and grants. In addition, companies can develop and provide training programs that help employees stay up-to-date on the latest technologies and best practices. Finally, industry can help shape the curriculum for STEM education programs to ensure that they are preparing students for the demands of the 21st-century workplace.

The role of industry in supporting STEM education and skills development is most often carried out by individual companies, through initiatives such as corporate social responsibility (CSR) programs and partnerships with educational institutions (Arian et al., 2023). Several technology companies have initiatives that support STEM education, such as Microsoft's TEALS program, which helps higher institutions of learning develop computer science programs, and Google's Computer Science Education (CSE) initiative, which helps students learn how to code. Many companies also participate in industry-wide initiatives, such as the National Academy Foundation's Academies of Engineering and Engineering-Technology.

The role of parents and communities in supporting STEM education and skills development

Parents and communities can play a vital role in supporting STEM education and skills development (Shaw & Dolan, 2022). They can help create a culture of learning and curiosity in their children, and encourage them to explore STEM subjects both inside and outside of the classroom. Parents can help students access STEM-related resources, such as science museums and after-lesson programs, and can encourage students to participate in STEM-related activities, such as science fairs and robotics competitions. In addition, communities can support STEM education by providing resources and funding for universities and extracurricular activities. There are several key roles that parents and communities can play in supporting STEM education and skills development namely advocate; mentor; resource provider and role model (Ifinedo & Burt, 2024). Advocate: Parents and community members can advocate for more funding for STEM education and more emphasis on STEM subjects in higher institutions of learning. Mentor: Parents and community members can volunteer their time to mentor students in STEM subjects. Resource provider: Parents and community members can provide funding for STEM-related programs, materials, and equipment. Role model: Parents and community members can act as role models for students by demonstrating an interest in STEM subjects and by sharing their experiences in STEM-related careers.

Curriculum: Integrating STEM Learning Technologies into the Classroom

The demand for STEM jobs will grow faster than the overall job market and there will be a shortage of workers with the necessary skills to fill these jobs (Cappelli, 2015; Cappelli, 2014). The overview could also highlight the growing importance of STEM skills in non-STEM fields, such as business, healthcare, and the arts. Some of the challenges that students face in accessing quality STEM education include (Margot & Kettler, 2019; Murphy, 2023; Aykan & Yıldırım, 2022). Kayan-Fadlelmula, et al. 2022; Thanawala et al. 2022):

- Lack of access to technology, including computers, internet, and other resources.
- Insufficient funding for STEM education, leading to under-resourced higher institutions of learning and programs.
- Lack of qualified lecturers to teach STEM subjects.
- Inequity in access to STEM education based on race, gender, and socioeconomic status.
- Other barriers to access, such as language, cultural, and physical barriers.
- Distraction: It can be easy for students to become distracted by the technology, rather than focusing on the learning task at hand.
- Inequity: Students from different socioeconomic backgrounds may have different levels of access to technology, creating an equity issue.
- Lack of infrastructure: Without proper planning and instruction, students may not know how to effectively use the technology to engage in meaningful learning.

The challenges can be overcome associated with using STEM learning technologies to engage students by providing professional development and training for lecturers on how to effectively use the technology. Ensuring that all students have access to the necessary technology, either by providing devices or finding ways to adapt instruction for those without devices. Addressing privacy and security concerns by developing policies and procedures for the safe use of technology. Using adaptive learning technologies that can adjust instruction to meet the individual needs of students. There may be several challenges but we also have benefits and these include (Barakabitze, et al., 2019; Klimaitis & Mullen, 2021).

- Improved student engagement: When students have access to engaging, hands-on STEM learning technologies, they are more likely to be interested in and engaged with the material.

- Increased motivation and interest in STEM fields: Exposure to STEM learning technologies can spark an interest in STEM fields and motivate students to pursue careers in these fields.
- Improved achievement in STEM subjects: When students have access to high-quality STEM learning technologies, they are more likely to achieve higher levels of success in STEM subjects.

Setting out a framework to implement STEM learning technologies requires a planned step-by-step guide. The guide includes the following steps:

1. Defining learning goals and objectives for the curriculum.
2. Identifying STEM learning technologies that align with the learning goals and objectives.
3. Incorporating STEM learning technologies into lesson plans, activities, and assessments.
4. Evaluate the effectiveness of the curriculum and make adjustments as needed.
5. Sharing the curriculum with other lecturers and gathering feedback.

Instruction is using STEM learning technologies to engage students. Instruction can therefore take many forms and can engage students and help them develop 21st–century skills. Virtual reality can be used to simulate real-world experiences, such as exploring a coral reef or conducting science experiments. 3D printing can be used to create tangible models of scientific concepts, such as molecules or the solar system. Robotics can also be integrated to explore engineering concepts, such as programming a robot to follow a specific path. Online simulations are also used to explore STEM concepts, such as investigating the effects of climate change on a virtual planet. Using augmented reality to create immersive learning experiences, such as exploring a virtual museum or historical site is also a necessity. Online games and simulations can also be used to develop critical thinking skills, such as solving puzzles or making decisions in a simulated environment. Coding and computational thinking can also be integrated to develop problem-solving and analytical skills. Online learning communities like learning management systems can be used to connect with peers and experts in STEM fields.

STEM learning technologies play a major role in teaching and learning as technology is evolving rapidly. There are many benefits of using STEM learning technologies to engage students, including making learning more fun and interactive, which can increase motivation and engagement. Providing a more personalized learning experience, which can meet the needs of a variety of students. Providing opportunities to develop 21st-century skills, such as collaboration, communication, and problem-solving. Preparing students for careers in STEM fields, which are increasingly in demand.

Assessment: Evaluating 21st-Century Skills with New Methods

Assessment of 21st-century skills is a relatively new area of research (Geisinger, 2016). There are several ways to assess and evaluate 21st-century skills, including using new methods such as performance assessments, project-based learning, and portfolios (Kennedy & Sundberg, 2020; Bender, 2012; Lukitasari, et al., 2021). Assessment can be grouped as performance assessment, project-based assessment, portfolios, peer and self-assessment. Performance assessments measure students' skills and knowledge through performance-based tasks, such as projects, presentations, or demonstrations. Performance assessment is a type of assessment that requires students to demonstrate their understanding of a concept or skill by completing a real-world task. For example, a performance assessment for evaluating 21st-century skills could involve a group project in which students have to collaborate to solve a problem, and then present their solution to the class. This type of assessment has several benefits. It allows for a more authentic assessment of student learning, as it is more similar to real-world tasks. It also provides students with the opportunity to develop skills such as communication, critical thinking, and problem-solving.

Project-based learning (PBL) is a teaching method that involves students working on projects that are relevant to real-world situations. These projects can be assessed using rubrics or other tools. PBL is another method that can be used to assess 21st-century skills. PBL involves students working on a long-term project, such as creating a product or solving a problem. This type of assessment has the advantage of providing students with a more realistic and meaningful learning experience, and it allows them to apply their skills in a real-world context. However, one challenge with PBL is that it can be difficult to ensure that all students are contributing equally to the project (Fernandes, 2014).

Portfolios are collections of work that demonstrate a student's progress and mastery of skills over time (Davies & LeMahieu, 2003). Portfolios can be used to assess a variety of 21st-century skills, including communication skills. Portfolios can include examples of group projects and presentations, as well as reflections on teamwork and collaboration. Portfolios can include evidence of a student's ability to conduct research, evaluate sources, and synthesize information and technology skills. Portfolios are another way to assess 21st-century skills, as they allow students to showcase their work over time. Portfolios can include a variety of artifacts, such as written work, projects, presentations, and reflections. The benefits of using portfolios include the fact that they allow students to showcase their growth and development over time, and they provide a more personalized view of student learning Amaya, et al. 2013). A potential challenge with portfolios is that they can be time-consuming to create and maintain.

Peer and self-assessment can be powerful tools for evaluating 21st-century skills, as they allow students to reflect on their learning and provide feedback to their peers (Kearney, 2013). By engaging in self-reflection, students can identify their strengths and areas for improvement. Peer assessment allows students to provide feedback to their peers, which can help to identify strengths and weaknesses that may not be obvious to the teacher. Self-assessment is a self-reflection method of assessment and an important tool for assessment (Siles-Gonzalez & Solano-Ruiz, 2016). Self-reflection is a process in which students reflect on their learning, including their strengths and areas for improvement. Self-reflection can be done through journaling, self-assessment rubrics, or other methods. Self-reflection can help students become more self-aware and take ownership of their learning. It can also help to identify any gaps in learning and allow students to make a plan for how to address these gaps. Formative assessment is a process of ongoing assessment that is used to inform instruction and improve learning. Formative assessment can be used to provide feedback to students and adjust instruction based on student needs. This type of assessment can be used to assess a wide range of 21st-century skills, including collaboration, communication, and critical thinking.

Professional Development: Preparing Lecturers for STEM Learning Technologies

Professional development includes preparing for change, building capacity, and modeling effective practice (Zepeda, 2019). Preparing for change helps lecturers understand the need for change in education and why STEM learning technologies are an important part of that change. Preparing for change is an important step in implementing any new initiative, and it is especially important when it comes to STEM learning technologies (Shernoff, et al., 2017). Lecturers need to understand why change is needed, and how STEM learning technologies can help to address some of the challenges facing education today. This includes issues such as the need to engage students, the need to prepare students for the 21st-century workplace, and the need to ensure that all students have access to high-quality education. By understanding these needs, lecturers can be more open to the idea of implementing new technologies in the classroom.

Building capacity provides lecturers with the resources and support they need to effectively use STEM learning technologies. Building capacity is about more than just providing lecturers with the necessary hardware and software. It is also about providing them with the knowledge, skills, and support they need to effectively use STEM learning technologies in the classroom. This includes professional development opportunities, access to mentors, and a supportive learning community. In addition, it is important to ensure that lecturers have the time and resources to effectively integrate STEM learning technologies into their teaching practice.

Showing how STEM learning technologies can be used in the classroom to engage and inspire students by modeling effective practices. Modeling effective practice is a key part of professional development for STEM learning technologies. This involves showing lecturers how to use these technologies in a way that is meaningful and effective for students. It can include case studies, best practices, and hands-on activities. By seeing examples of how other lecturers are using these technologies, lecturers can gain ideas and inspiration for their teaching practice. In addition, it can help to build a sense of community and support among lecturers who are using these technologies.

Frameworks for implementing technologies

Several frameworks can be used when implementing technologies in the classroom. One such framework is TPACK (technological, pedagogical, and content knowledge), which is a framework that helps educators understand the relationship between technology, teaching, and content. Another framework is SAMR (substitution, augmentation, modification, and redefinition), which helps educators understand how technology can be used to transform learning. And finally, there is the SAMR+ framework, which is an extension of the SAMR framework that also takes into account equity and access. By utilizing these frameworks, lecturers can create a learning environment that is both relevant and engaging for students. (Harrison, et al., 2015; Akerson et al., 2018). Frameworks for implementing STEM learning technologies can be based on examples of successful implementations.

The TPACK framework was developed by Mishra and Koehler in 2006, and it is a framework that helps lecturers understand the relationship between technology, pedagogy, and content (Kurt, 2018). The TPACK framework consists of three overlapping circles, which represent technology, pedagogy, and content as shown in Figure 1. Each circle contains a different type of knowledge: technological knowledge, pedagogical knowledge, and content knowledge. The intersection of these three circles is referred to as the TPACK space, which represents the combination of these three types of knowledge.

Figure 1. The TRACK framework

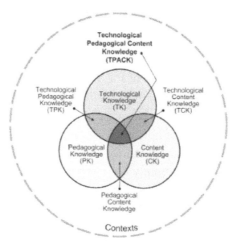

The SAMR framework was developed by Dr. Ruben Puentedura in 2006, and it is a framework that helps lecturers understand the different levels of technology integration. The SAMR framework has four levels, which are substitution, augmentation, modification, and redefinition. Substitution is the lowest level, and it involves using technology as a direct replacement for a traditional learning activity. Augmentation is the second level, and it involves using technology to enhance or extend a traditional learning activity. Modification is the third level, and it involves using technology to significantly modify a traditional learning activity. And finally, redefinition is the fourth level.

Figure 2. SAMR model

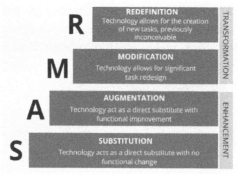

Source: Puentendura, 2014

The SAMR+ framework is an extension of the original SAMR framework, and it adds two additional elements such as equity and access. The equity element refers to ensuring that all students have equal access to technology and the benefits of technology-enhanced learning. The access element refers to ensuring that students have the necessary skills and knowledge to use technology effectively. The SAMR+ framework helps educators to consider not only how technology is used in the classroom, but also who has access to it and how it is used to support all students.

Proposed framework

In developing a framework for implementing STEM learning technologies for a model that includes the following key elements such as administration and technical support, defining clear learning objectives for students, instructor development, student development, implementation stage, and evaluation as seen in Figure 3.

Figure 3. Technology implementation framework

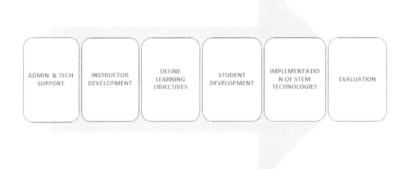

(Designed by Doris Chasokela 2024)

The administration and technical support should be sound thus providing relevant technologies to be used in the teaching and learning. There should be continuous development of instructors and students through workshops, and seminars imparting them with knowledge and skills in using the technologies. Designing meaningful tasks and activities for students to complete using the technologies is also important. Provide students with sufficient time and resources to complete the tasks. The end process involves evaluating student learning using multiple methods, including peer and self-assessment reflecting on the effectiveness of the framework, and making adjustments as needed. The process is a cycle and technology is evolving rapidly so there is a need to keep reviewing the model to suit the current times. One can then say that the proposed framework for implementing STEM learning technologies would emphasize the following key elements:

- Clear learning objectives, with a focus on developing 21st-century skills.
- Collaborative learning experiences, with an emphasis on problem-solving and creativity.
- Authentic learning experiences, with a focus on real-world applications.
- Regular assessment and feedback, to help students improve their skills.
- A growth mindset, to encourage lifelong learning.
- Accessibility, sustainability, and equity, to ensure that all students have the opportunity to succeed.

These elements would help to address the challenges of developing 21st-century skills as technologies are implemented in teaching and learning.

Several successful research demonstrates the effectiveness of using frameworks to implement STEM learning technologies in higher education institutions. For example, the University of South Florida has used the TIM framework to successfully integrate technology into its teacher preparation programs. As a result, its graduates have reported a high level of confidence in using technology in their future classrooms. Another example is the State University of New York at Binghamton, which has used the SAMR model to effectively integrate technology into its science courses, leading to increased student engagement and improved test scores. Frameworks for implementing technologies should look at designing a technology implementation framework and aligning technology implementation with organizational goals, balancing technology and pedagogy in the learning environment, addressing challenges of implementation (budget, staffing, and change management), and evaluating the effectiveness of technology implementation.

CONCLUSION

In summary, the framework for implementing STEM learning technologies that have been presented in this chapter can be an effective tool for addressing the challenges of developing 21st-century skills in students. It provides a clear and systematic approach to integrating these technologies into education and includes recommendations for the successful implementation of these technologies. Implementing STEM learning technologies in the classroom can be an effective way to address the challenges of developing 21st-century skills in students. With the right resources and support, lecturers can leverage these technologies to engage students in meaningful and hands-on learning experiences. This, in turn, can help to foster creativity, problem-solving, and collaboration - all essential skills for the 21st-century workforce. There is a need for ongoing evaluation and reflection to ensure that the framework is effective and relevant to the ever-changing needs of students and lecturers. By investing in STEM learning technologies and a framework, we can ensure that our students are prepared.

REFERENCES

Akerson, V. L., Burgess, A., Gerber, A., Guo, M., Khan, T. A., & Newman, S. (2018). Disentangling the meaning of STEM: Implications for science education and science teacher education. *Journal of Science Teacher Education*, 29(1), 1–8. DOI: 10.1080/1046560X.2018.1435063

Al-Ansi, A. M., Jaboob, M., Garad, A., & Al-Ansi, A. (2023). Analyzing augmented reality (AR) and virtual reality (VR) recent developments in education. *Social Sciences & Humanities Open*, 8(1), 100532. DOI: 10.1016/j.ssaho.2023.100532

Albion, P. (2015). Project-, problem-, and inquiry-based learning. Teaching and digital technologies: Big issues and critical questions, 240.

Allen, L. (2018). Teaching Neuroanatomy Virtually: Integrating an Interactive 3D E-Learning Resource for Enhanced Neuroanatomy Education (Doctoral dissertation, The University of Western Ontario (Canada)).

Alnajim, A. M., Habib, S., Islam, M., AlRawashdeh, H. S., & Wasim, M. (2023). Exploring Cybersecurity education and training techniques: A comprehensive review of traditional, virtual reality, and augmented reality approaches. *Symmetry*, 15(12), 2175. DOI: 10.3390/sym15122175

Ameen, K., & Gorman, G. E. (2009). Information and digital literacy: A stumbling block to development? A Pakistan perspective. *Library Management*, 30(1/2), 99–112. DOI: 10.1108/01435120910927565

Atwa, S., Gauci-Mansour, V. J., Thomson, R., & Hegazi, I. (2019). Team-based and case-based learning: A hybrid pedagogy model enhancing students' academic performance and experiences at first-year tertiary level. *Australian Educational Researcher*, 46(1), 93–112. DOI: 10.1007/s13384-018-0282-y

Awidi, I. T., & Paynter, M. (2019). The impact of a flipped classroom approach on student learning experience. *Computers & Education*, 128, 269–283. DOI: 10.1016/j.compedu.2018.09.013

Aykan, A., & Yıldırım, B. (2022). The integration of a lesson study model into distance STEM education during the COVID-19 pandemic: Teachers' views and practice. Technology. *Knowledge and Learning*, 27(2), 609–637. DOI: 10.1007/s10758-021-09564-9

Barakabitze, A. A., William-Andey Lazaro, A., Ainea, N., Mkwizu, M. H., Maziku, H., Matofali, A. X., Iddi, A., & Sanga, C. (2019). Transforming African education systems in science, technology, engineering, and mathematics (STEM) using ICTs: Challenges and opportunities. *Education Research International*, 2019(1), 6946809. DOI: 10.1155/2019/6946809

Bender, W. N. (2012). *Project-based learning: Differentiating instruction for the 21st century*. Corwin Press.

Bilgin, A. S., Molina Ascanio, M., & Minoli, M. (2022). *STEM Goes digital: how can technology enhance STEM Teaching?* European Observatory.

Bon, A., Saa-Dittoh, F., & Akkermans, H. (2023). Bridging the digital divide. In *Introduction to Digital Humanism: A Textbook* (pp. 283–298). Springer Nature Switzerland.

Bonilla, M. A. B., Soria, E. E. A., Chinga, A. E. P., & Cabeza, B. M. Q. (2023). Systems and Social Dynamics in the Rural City of La Concordia: Strengths and Weaknesses Related to Its Development at the beginning of the 21st Century. *Journal of Business and Economic Development*, 8(2), 48–55. DOI: 10.11648/j.jbed.20230802.13

Burghardt, M., Ferdinand, P., Pfeiffer, A., Reverberi, D., & Romagnoli, G. (2021). Integration of new technologies and alternative methods in laboratory-based scenarios. In Cross Reality and Data Science in Engineering: Proceedings of the 17th International Conference on Remote Engineering and Virtual Instrumentation 17 (pp. 488-507). Springer International Publishing. DOI: 10.1007/978-3-030-52575-0_40

Cappelli, P. (2014). *Skill gaps, skill shortages, and skill mismatches: Evidence for the US (No. w20382)*. National Bureau of Economic Research. DOI: 10.3386/w20382

Cappelli, P. H. (2015). Skill gaps, skill shortages, and skill mismatches: Evidence and arguments for the United States. *Industrial & Labor Relations Review*, 68(2), 251–290. DOI: 10.1177/0019793914564961

Chan, C. K. Y. (2023). A review of the changes in higher education assessment and grading policy during COVID-19. *Assessment & Evaluation in Higher Education*, 48(6), 874–887. DOI: 10.1080/02602938.2022.2140780

Chu, S. K. W., Reynolds, R. B., Tavares, N. J., Notari, M., & Lee, C. W. Y. (2021). *21st-century skills development through inquiry-based learning from theory to practice*. Springer International Publishing.

Cobo, C. (2013). Skills for innovation: Envisioning an education that prepares for the changing world. *Curriculum Journal*, 24(1), 67–85. DOI: 10.1080/09585176.2012.744330

Coyne, L., Takemoto, J. K., Parmentier, B. L., Merritt, T., & Sharpton, R. A. (2018). Exploring virtual reality as a platform for distance team-based learning. *Currents in Pharmacy Teaching & Learning*, 10(10), 1384–1390. DOI: 10.1016/j.cptl.2018.07.005 PMID: 30527368

Davies, A., & LeMahieu, P. (2003). Assessment for learning: Reconsidering portfolios and research evidence. In *Optimising new modes of assessment: In search of qualities and standards* (pp. 141–169). Springer Netherlands. DOI: 10.1007/0-306-48125-1_7

de Clercq, M., D'Haese, M., & Buysse, J. (2023). Economic growth and broadband access: The European urban-rural digital divide. *Telecommunications Policy*, 47(6), 102579. DOI: 10.1016/j.telpol.2023.102579

Dilekci, A., & Karatay, H. (2023). The effects of the 21st-century skills curriculum on the development of students' creative thinking skills. *Thinking Skills and Creativity*, 47, 101229. DOI: 10.1016/j.tsc.2022.101229

Dziuban, C. D., Moskal, P., & Hartman, J. (2005). Higher education, blended learning, and the generations: Knowledge is power. Elements of quality online education: Engaging communities. Needham, MA: Sloan Center for Online Education, 88, 89.

Ebekozien, A., & Aigbavboa, C. (2023). Evaluation of built environment programs accreditation in the 21st-century education system in Nigeria: Stakeholders' perspective. *International Journal of Building Pathology and Adaptation*, 41(6), 102–118. DOI: 10.1108/IJBPA-02-2022-0027

Fawns, T. (2019). Postdigital education in design and practice. Postdigital science and education, 1(1), 132-145.

Fernandes, S. R. G. (2014). Preparing graduates for professional practice: Findings from a case study of Project-based Learning (PBL). *Procedia: Social and Behavioral Sciences*, 139, 219–226. DOI: 10.1016/j.sbspro.2014.08.064

Gaweł, A., Giovannetti, M., Li Pomi, G., Stefańska, M., Olejnik, I., Kulaga, B., & Cedrola, E. (2023). Stakeholder-centered development of new curriculum content in higher education: A case study in creating a course on the green and digital transformation of SMEs. *Studies in Higher Education*, ●●●, 1–20. DOI: 10.1080/03075079.2023.2293923

Geisinger, K. F. (2016). 21st century skills: What are they and how do we assess them? *Applied Measurement in Education*, 29(4), 245–249. DOI: 10.1080/08957347.2016.1209207

Glendinning, I. (2023). Developing and implementing policies for academic integrity–Management of change. In *Academic Integrity in the Social Sciences: Perspectives on Pedagogy and Practice* (pp. 87–104). Springer International Publishing. DOI: 10.1007/978-3-031-43292-7_6

Goksu, D. Y., & Duran, V. (2020). Flipped classroom model in the context of distant training. Research highlights in Education and Science, 104-127.

Gonzalez-Perez, L. I., & Ramirez-Montoya, M. S. (2022). Components of Education 4.0 in 21st-century skills frameworks: Systematic review. *Sustainability (Basel)*, 14(3), 1–31. DOI: 10.3390/su14031493

Gue, S., Cohen, S., Tassone, M., Walker, A., Little, A., Morales-Cruz, M., McGillicuddy, C., Lebowitz, D., Pell, R., Vera, A., Nazario, S., & Ganti, L. (2023). Disaster Day: A simulation-based competition for educating emergency medicine residents and medical students on disaster medicine. *International Journal of Emergency Medicine*, 16(1), 59. DOI: 10.1186/s12245-023-00520-1 PMID: 37704963

Harrison, G. M., Duncan Seraphin, K., Philippoff, J., Vallin, L. M., & Brandon, P. R. (2015). Comparing models of nature of science dimensionality based on the next generation science standards. *International Journal of Science Education*, 37(8), 1. DOI: 10.1080/09500693.2015.1035357

Henke, K., Nau, J., & Streitferdt, D. (2022, May). Hybrid take-home labs for the stem education of the future. In *KES International Conference on Smart Education and E-Learning* (pp. 17-26). Singapore: Springer Nature Singapore. 321-1342. DOI: 10.1007/978-981-19-3112-3_2

Hurley, M., Butler, D., & McLoughlin, E. (2023). STEM Teacher Professional Learning Through Immersive STEM Learning Placements in Industry: A Systematic Literature Review. *Journal for STEM Education Research*, •••, 1–31. PMID: 38304259

Ifinedo, E., & Burt, D. (2024). Exploring the application of college student role models in service-learning pedagogy. Journal of Applied Research in Higher Education. ahead-of-print No. ahead-of-print. https://doi.org/DOI: 10.1108/JARHE-08-2023-0406

Inegbedion, H. E. (2021). Digital divide in the major regions of the world and the possibility of convergence. *The Bottom Line (New York, N.Y.)*, 34(1), 68–85. DOI: 10.1108/BL-09-2020-0064

Isaksen, S. G., Dorval, K. B., & Treffinger, D. J. (2010). *Creative approaches to problem-solving: A framework for innovation and change*. SAGE publications.

Jasni, S., Mohd Rosnan, S., Hussain, Z., & Shamsuddin, N. A. A. (2023). An innovation of LH Bites Cookies holder of augmented reality technology and QR code. In S. Ibrahim, A.S.A. Salamat, B. Nur Morat (Eds.), 2023. International Teaching Aid Competition 2023. University of Technology MARA, Kedah, pp. 301-306.

Kayan-Fadlelmula, F., Sellami, A., Abdelkader, N., & Umer, S. (2022). A systematic review of STEM education research in the GCC countries: Trends, gaps, and barriers. *International Journal of STEM Education*, 9(1), 1–24. DOI: 10.1186/s40594-021-00319-7

Kearney, S. (2013). Improving engagement: The use of 'Authentic self and peer assessment for learning' to enhance the student learning experience. *Assessment & Evaluation in Higher Education*, 38(7), 875–891. DOI: 10.1080/02602938.2012.751963

Kelley, T. R., & Knowles, J. G. (2016). A conceptual framework for integrated STEM education. *International Journal of STEM Education*, 3(1), 1–11. DOI: 10.1186/s40594-016-0046-z

Kennedy, T. J., & Sundberg, C. W. (2020). 21st-century skills. *Science education in theory and practice: An introductory guide to learning theory*, 479-496.

Kistaubayev, Y., Mutanov, G., Mansurova, M., Saxenbayeva, Z., & Shakan, Y. (2022). Ethereum-Based Information System for Digital Higher Education Registry and Verification of Student Achievement Documents. *Future Internet*, 15(1), 1–19. DOI: 10.3390/fi15010003

Klimaitis, C. C., & Mullen, C. A. (2021). Access and barriers to science, technology, engineering, and mathematics (STEM) education for K–12 students with disabilities and females. *Handbook of social justice interventions in education*, 813-836.)

Koschmann, T. D., Myers, A. C., Feltovich, P. J., & Barrows, H. S. (1994). Using technology to assist in realizing effective learning and instruction: A principled approach to the use of computers in collaborative learning. *Journal of the Learning Sciences*, 3(3), 227–264. DOI: 10.1207/s15327809jls0303_2

Kurt, S. (2018). Frameworks & theories. TPACK: Technological Pedagogical Content Knowledge Framework. Educational Technology. https://educationaltechnology.net/technological-pedagogical-content-knowledge-tpack-framework/

Lee, S. H., Riney, L. C., Merkt, B., McDonough, S. D., Baker, J., Boyd, S., Zhang, Y., & Geis, G. L. (2024). Improving Pediatric Procedural Skills for EMS Clinicians: A Longitudinal Simulation-Based Curriculum with Novel, Remote, First-Person-View Video-Based Outcome Measurement. *Prehospital Emergency Care*, 28(2), 352–362. DOI: 10.1080/10903127.2023.2263555 PMID: 37751212

Li, F., He, Y., & Xue, Q. (2021). Progress, challenges, and countermeasures of adaptive learning. *Journal of Educational Technology & Society*, 24(3), 238–255.

Lo, C. K., & Hew, K. F. (2020). A comparison of flipped learning with gamification, traditional learning, and online independent study: The effects on students' mathematics achievement and cognitive engagement. *Interactive Learning Environments*, 28(4), 464–481. DOI: 10.1080/10494820.2018.1541910

Lombardi, M. (2023). Digital Economy and Digital Divide. In *Global Handbook of Inequality* (pp. 1–27). Springer International Publishing. DOI: 10.1007/978-3-030-97417-6_48-1

Loos, E., Gropler, J., & Goudeau, M. L. S. (2023). Using ChatGPT in Education: Human Reflection on ChatGPT's Self-Reflection. *Societies (Basel, Switzerland)*, 13(8), 196. DOI: 10.3390/soc13080196

Lukitasari, M., Hasan, R., Sukri, A., & Handhika, J. (2021). Developing Student's Metacognitive Ability in Science through Project-Based Learning with E-Portfolio. *International Journal of Evaluation and Research in Education*, 10(3), 948–955. DOI: 10.11591/ijere.v10i3.21370

Margot, K. C., & Kettler, T. (2019). Teachers' perception of STEM integration and education: A systematic literature review. *International Journal of STEM Education*, 6(1), 1–16. DOI: 10.1186/s40594-018-0151-2

Martin, A., & Grudziecki, J. (2006). DigEuLit: Concepts and tools for digital literacy development. *Innovation in teaching and learning in information and computer sciences, 5*(4), 249-267.

McDougall, J., Readman, M., & Wilkinson, P. (2018). The uses of (digital) literacy. *Learning, Media and Technology*, 43(3), 263–279. DOI: 10.1080/17439884.2018.1462206

Murphy, C. A., & Stewart, J. C. (2015). The Impact of Online or F2F Lecture Choice on Student Achievement and Engagement in a Large Lecture-Based Science Course: Closing the Gap. *Online Learning : the Official Journal of the Online Learning Consortium*, 19(3), 91–110. DOI: 10.24059/olj.v19i3.670

Murphy, J., Kalbaska, N., Horton-Tognazzini, L., & Cantoni, L. (2015). Online learning and MOOCs: A framework proposal. In Information and Communication Technologies in Tourism 2015: Proceedings of the International Conference in Lugano, Switzerland, February 3-6, 2015 (pp. 847-858). Springer International Publishing. DOI: 10.1007/978-3-319-14343-9_61

Murphy, S. (2023). Leadership practices contributing to STEM education success at three rural Australian schools. *Australian Educational Researcher*, 50(4), 1049–1067. DOI: 10.1007/s13384-022-00541-4

Muyambo-Goto, O., Naidoo, D., & Kennedy, K. J. (2023). Students' Conceptions of 21st Century Education in Zimbabwe. *Interchange*, 54(1), 49–80. DOI: 10.1007/s10780-022-09483-3

O'Donnell, A. M., & Hmelo-Silver, C. E. (2013). Introduction: What is collaborative learning? An overview. The international handbook of collaborative learning, 1-15.

Papanastasiou, G., Drigas, A., Skianis, C., Lytras, M., & Papanastasiou, E. (2019). Virtual and augmented reality effects on K-12, higher, and tertiary education students' twenty-first-century skills. *Virtual Reality (Waltham Cross)*, 23(4), 425–436. DOI: 10.1007/s10055-018-0363-2

Parikshit, L. (2023). Higher Education in India: Opportunities, Challenges & Solutions. *Shodh Sari-An International Multidisciplinary Journal*, 2(1), 54–60.

Podgorska, M., & Zdonek, I. (2023). Interdisciplinary collaboration in higher education towards sustainable development. *Sustainable Development*, •••, 1–19. DOI: 10.1002/sd.2765

Puentedura, R. (2014). *SAMR: An Applied Introduction.* [PDF file]. Retrieved from http://www.hippasus.com/rrpweblog/archives/2014/01/31/SAMRAnAppliedIntroduction.pdf

Radovanovic, D., Hogan, B., & Lalic, D. (2015). Overcoming digital divides in higher education: Digital literacy beyond Facebook. *New Media & Society*, 17(10), 1733–1749. DOI: 10.1177/1461444815588323

Rajab, K. D. (2018). The effectiveness and potential of E-learning in war zones: An empirical comparison of face-to-face and online education in Saudi Arabia. *IEEE Access : Practical Innovations, Open Solutions*, 6, 6783–6794. DOI: 10.1109/ACCESS.2018.2800164

Saimon, M., Lavicza, Z., & Dana-Picard, T. (2023). Enhancing the 4Cs among college students of a communication skills course in Tanzania through a project-based learning model. *Education and Information Technologies*, 28(6), 6269–6285. DOI: 10.1007/s10639-022-11406-9 PMID: 36406787

Savov, S. A., Antonova, R., & Spassov, K. (2019). Multimedia applications in education. In Smart Technologies and Innovation for a Sustainable Future: Proceedings of the 1st American University in the Emirates International Research Conference—Dubai, UAE 2017 (pp. 263-271). Springer International Publishing.

Sharma, E., & Sethi, S. (2015). Skill Development: Opportunities & Challenges in India. *GianJyoti E-Journal*, 5(1), 45–55.

Shaw, A., & Dolan, P. (2022). Youth Volunteering: New Norms for Policy and Practice. In Social Activism-New Challenges in a (Dis) connected World. IntechOpen.

Shernoff, D. J., Sinha, S., Bressler, D. M., & Ginsburg, L. (2017). Assessing teacher education and professional development needs for the implementation of integrated approaches to STEM education. *International Journal of STEM Education*, 4(1), 1–16. DOI: 10.1186/s40594-017-0068-1 PMID: 30631669

Shute, V., & Towle, B. (2018). Adaptive e-learning. In *Aptitude* (pp. 105–114). Routledge.

Siddiq, F., Olofsson, A. D., Lindberg, J. O., & Tomczyk, L. (2023). What will be the new normal? Digital competence and 21st-century skills: Critical and emergent issues in education. *Education and Information Technologies*, ●●●, 1–9.

Siles-Gonzalez, J., & Solano-Ruiz, C. (2016). Self-assessment, reflection on practice and critical thinking in nursing students. *Nurse Education Today*, 45, 132–137. DOI: 10.1016/j.nedt.2016.07.005 PMID: 27471109

Smetana, L. K., & Bell, R. L. (2012). Computer simulations to support science instruction and learning: A critical review of the literature. *International Journal of Science Education*, 34(9), 1337–1370. DOI: 10.1080/09500693.2011.605182

Snyder, M. (2018). A century of perspectives that influenced the consideration of technology as a critical component of STEM education in the United States. *The Journal of Technology Studies*, 44(2), 42–57. DOI: 10.21061/jots.v44i2.a.1

Sofkova Hashemi, S., & Berbyuk Lindström, N. Brooks, E., Hahn, J. and Sjoberg, J. (2023). "Impact of Emergency Online Teaching on Teachers' Professional Digital Competence: Experiences from the Nordic Higher Education Institutions" (2023). Rising like a Phoenix: Emerging from the Pandemic and Reshaping Human Endeavors with Digital Technologies ICIS 2023. 12. https://aisel.aisnet.org/icis2023/learnandiscurricula/learnandiscurricula/12

Soghomonyan, Z., & Karapetyan, A. (2023). Teaching Strategies of the 21st Century Skills Adapted to the Local Needs. *European Journal of Teacher Education*, 5(3), 48–69. DOI: 10.33422/ejte.v5i3.1097

Subramaniam, S. R., & Muniandy, B. (2019). The effect of the flipped classroom on students' engagement. Technology. *Knowledge and Learning*, 24(3), 355–372. DOI: 10.1007/s10758-017-9343-y

Sullivan, M. (2023). 17 Global expansion and service diversification. Singapore Inc.: A Century of Business Success in Global Markets: Strategies, Innovations, and Insights from Singapore's Top Corporations, 17.

Swedish International Development Cooperation Agency. (2018). Skills Development. March 2018. https://cdn.sida.se/publications/files/sida62134en-skills-development.pdf

Thanawala, A., Murphy, C., & Hakim, T. (2022). Sustaining STEM student learning support and engagement during COVID-19. In *Community Colleges' Responses to COVID-19* (pp. 72–82). Routledge. DOI: 10.4324/9781003297123-10

Timotheou, S., Miliou, O., Dimitriadis, Y., Sobrino, S. V., Giannoutsou, N., Cachia, R., Mones, A. M., & Ioannou, A. (2023). Impacts of digital technologies on education and factors influencing schools' digital capacity and transformation: A literature review. *Education and Information Technologies*, 28(6), 6695–6726. DOI: 10.1007/s10639-022-11431-8 PMID: 36465416

Toven-Lindsey, B., Rhoads, R. A., & Lozano, J. B. (2015). Virtually unlimited classrooms: Pedagogical practices in massive open online courses. *The Internet and Higher Education*, 24, 1–12. DOI: 10.1016/j.iheduc.2014.07.001

Ukwoma, S. C., Iwundu, N. E., & Iwundu, I. E. (2016). Digital literacy skills possessed by students of UNN, implications for effective learning and performance: A study of the MTN Universities Connect Library. *New Library World*, 117(11/12), 702–720. DOI: 10.1108/NLW-08-2016-0061

Vasu, S. B. (2023). Factors contributes and initiatives in bridging the digital divide. networks, 52. *Industrial Engineering Journal*, 52(155), 30–37.

Vogt, K. L. (2016). Measuring student engagement using learning management systems (Doctoral dissertation). University of Toronto. Ontario, Canada

Vu, N. N., Hung, B. P., Van, N. T. T., & Lien, N. T. H. (2022). Theoretical and instructional aspects of using multimedia resources in language education: A cognitive view. *Multimedia Technologies in the Internet of Things Environment*, 2, 165–194. DOI: 10.1007/978-981-16-3828-2_9

Wardani, H. K., Sujarwo, S., Rakhmawati, Y., & Cahyandaru, P. (2023). Analysis of the Impact of the Merdeka Curriculum Policy on Stakeholders at Primary School. *Peuradeun Scientific Journal*, 11(2), 513–530. DOI: 10.26811/peuradeun.v11i2.801

Wen, C. T., Liu, C. C., Chang, H. Y., Chang, C. J., Chang, M. H., Chiang, S. H. F., Yang, C. W., & Hwang, F. K. (2020). Students guided inquiry with simulation and its relation to school science achievement and scientific literacy. *Computers & Education*, 149, 103830. DOI: 10.1016/j.compedu.2020.103830

World Economic Forum. (2017). Accelerating Workforce Reskilling for the Fourth Industrial Revolution. An Agenda for Leaders to Shape the Future of Education, Gender and Work. Published 27 July 2017. https://www.weforum.org/publications/accelerating-workforce-reskilling-for-the-fourth-industrial-revolution/

Yang, Y. T. C., & Wu, W. C. I. (2012). Digital storytelling for enhancing student academic achievement, critical thinking, and learning motivation: A year-long experimental study. *Computers & Education*, 59(2), 339–352. DOI: 10.1016/j.compedu.2011.12.012

Yesilyurt, E., & Vezne, R. (2023). Digital literacy, technological literacy, and internet literacy as predictors of attitude toward applying computer-supported education. *Education and Information Technologies*, 28(8), 1–27. DOI: 10.1007/s10639-022-11311-1 PMID: 36688220

Zepeda, S. J. (2019). *Professional development: What works*. Routledge.

Zielinski, N. M. (2023) "Transforming Mathematics Education with Creativity". Culminating Experience Projects. 402. (Published master thesis). Grand Valley State University, Michigan, United States of America.

KEY TERMS AND DEFINITIONS

Assessment: refers to the process of measuring and evaluating the effectiveness of the technology in achieving its intended goals.

Collaborative approach: refers to a process in which multiple stakeholders, such as lecturers, administrators, and students, work together to plan, implement, and evaluate the use of technology. This approach emphasizes shared ownership and accountability for the success of the implementation.

Higher education: refers to post-secondary education, or education that occurs after high school. This can include two-year and four-year colleges and universities, as well as vocational and technical schools. Higher education generally leads to the attainment of an associate's degree, bachelor's degree, or master's degree.

Learning technologies: these are digital tools and resources that are used to support and enhance education. These technologies can include everything from educational software to online platforms and apps and can be used in a variety of educational settings, including classrooms like simulation software, coding apps, and robotics kits.

Professional development: refers to the ongoing learning and training that lecturers engage in to improve their skills and knowledge.

STEM: is an acronym that stands for Science, Technology, Engineering, and Mathematics. These are disciplines that enable students to be creative, promote critical thinking, improve communication, and enhance their ability in problem-solving.

Twenty-first-century skills: these are a set of knowledge, abilities, and attitudes that are considered to be essential for success in the modern world and are considered crucial for success in the modern workplace and life in general. They include both traditional academic skills, such as literacy and numeracy, and more "soft" skills, such as communication, collaboration, problem-solving, critical thinking and analysis, creativity, information literacy, and digital literacy.

Student engagement: refers to the level of interest, curiosity, and passion that a student has for their learning. It is often characterized by students' willingness to actively participate in class discussions, ask questions, and complete tasks to the best of their ability.

Chapter 8
Individual Differences as Determinants of Graduate Employability in Brunei Darussalam

Hartini Mashod
Universiti Teknologi Brunei, Brunei

Kabiru Maitama Kura
https://orcid.org/0000-0001-7863-2604
Bahrain Polytechnic, Bahrain

ABSTRACT

Increasing interests on the notion of graduate employability has led to various predictors that would increase chances of employment for job seeking graduates. However, very little is known about the influence of individual determinants that may play a crucial role in enhancing their employability. Therefore, the present study aimed to explore the influence of gender, age and education on graduate employability. A cross-sectional, quantitative methodological approach was undertaken to examine the relationship between demographic factors and graduate employability. Data were collected from a sample of 324 graduates in Brunei that are registered in JobCentre Brunei. This study used parametric technique (i.e., ANOVA) to analyse the data collected. The findings indicated that there was a significant positive relationship between education and graduate employability. Meanwhile, no significant link was found for the effect of gender and age on employability among graduates. These data support existing studies that found significant role of education on graduate employability; the higher educational background obtained, the stronger employability belief one has, which would have a possible ripple effect on their job

DOI: 10.4018/979-8-3693-3443-0.ch008

search behaviour. Furthermore, the contradicting findings found for effect of gender and age also provide a novel contribution to existing literature. Specifically, this result might be due to the contextual settings of which this study is conducted. The findings reflect a labour market in which job searchers believe their employability is determined by their competences and capabilities, rather than their gender or age.

INTRODUCTION

The term graduate employability (GE) refers to accomplishments of intelligence, skills, and personality, which would likely increase chances of job acquisition and have a successful career - subsequently benefiting the graduate, the organisation, society, and the economy (Yorke & Knight, 2006). The notion of GE has been gaining popularity attributable to the improved accessibility into higher education across the globe (Organization for Economic Cooperation and Development, 2018). A similar trend occurred in Brunei as the rate of local graduates twofold over the past ten years (1,803 graduates in 2010 to 3,625 graduates in 2019). Albeit the expansion of graduates possessing university education implies highly educated and accomplished individuals, it depreciated the value advantage of a university qualification (Tavares, 2016) and increased competition for graduate-level jobs in the labour market. Based on the report of labour force survey in 2023, the competitiveness of the Brunei labour market is relatively high, with 67.2% labour force participation rate recorded (Ministry of Finance and Economy [MOFE], 2024). The challenging socio-economic environment in Brunei, including a high unemployment rate and employment saturation, has further highlighted the importance of maintaining employability.

The recent years have witnessed the rapid changes in technology advancement, which have played a prominent role in shifting the labour market in ways that certain skills and occupations have become obsolete while new ones have emerged. This is especially noticeable in cloud computing, data analytics, cyber security and online video streaming industries, all of which have experienced phenomenal growth in the era after the COVID-19 pandemic (Garcia-Murillo et al., 2018; World Economic Forum, 2018). This rapid growth of technology development such as the increasing use of artificial intelligence (AI) or automation means that human capital is more productive. However, fears of technological unemployment emerge as AI continues to modernise the work place and may render people redundant (Bonsay et al., 2021). As a result, it has become paramount for the graduates to find means of positioning themselves in the job market for the niche given the skills they possess. In this sense, more especially in the competitive job market, graduates must readily and tactically adapt to the current and future contours of jobs, so as to enhance the chances of employment.

Thus far, studies on GE are mostly dominated in advanced countries such as Canada, United Kingdom, Australia (Bell, 2016; Finch et al., 2016), which possess different cultural and contextual settings with developing country such as Brunei. Therefore, this study aims to provide a new perspective from a developing Asian country and counter-weighting the western research on GE. Furthermore, there is a notable paucity of evidence-based GE literature that examines samples beyond graduates from a social science background. This research constitutes of graduates from diverse educational disciplines, which allows a more generalized result. A great deal of previous research into GE has found various factors influencing the employability of graduates, including the primarily identified antecents such as communication skills, work experience, personality traits (Chhinzer & Russo, 2018; Maxwell et al., 2009; Pheko & Molefhe, 2017), to name a few. Even though many GE antecedents were extensively recognised in the literature, the role of individual determinants such as gender, age and education remain largely unexamined (O'Leary, 2016).

It is crucial to investigate the demographic factors as individuals have varying demographics, therefore, may behave differently to fundamentally comparable situations. It is difficult to investigate the influence of demographic characteristics on behavioural outcomes if they are not reported in published studies (Jones et al., 2020). Numerous prior studies evaluating the influence of demographic characteristics on employability have produced contradictory findings and there is a paucity of demographic variables that have been included. By investigating a variety of demographic characteristics in this study, plausible explanations for prior studies' inconsistent findings are revealed. Drawing upon the identified research gap on GE, this study examines the demographic determinants of gender, age, and education on GE, specifically to identify whether these factors influence the chances to obtain employment among the graduates.

LITERATURE REVIEW

Role of Gender

In almost every culture, there is a predetermined mindset of gendered behaviour in such a way that men are expected to be masculine, authoritative and dominant while women are supposed to be caring and affectionate (Cifre et al., 2018). This presumed way of thinking has led to the creation of gender-appropriate jobs; a man is best suited to be an engineer and a woman would make an excellent teacher. As much as one admits that this poses a detrimental effect, such conservative mentality still prevails in many societies today. In particular, these could influence the job approach taken by individuals, as they are more likely to consider jobs deemed socially acceptable rather than choosing roles of their interests. Furthermore, this conservative mindset would also affect individuals' perception of their chances of obtaining a job, hence, limiting their capabilities. While other GE antecedents such as knowledge and skills can be learned, individual factors, including gender, are fixed and have a more potent impression on how one believes about their employability. For example, among the 17,354 unemployed individuals in Brunei, 9,147 are male, and 8,207 are female; simultaneously, 61.3% of males are employed, and only 38.7% accounted for employed females (MOFE, 2020). Collectively, these circumstances may affect the perception of individuals on their employment opportunities.

Several studies have attempted to examine the impact of gender disposition on individuals' employability. For instance, Cifre et al. (2018) examined the role of gender on employability among the employed and unemployed youths in Spain. Interestingly, the employed sample's employability was higher for males, while the unemployed representation showed higher employability among female youths. These findings support the prolongation of stereotyped and gendered jobs in the current labour market. The association of gender disparity on employability also exists in the undergraduate contexts, with male students possessing greater confidence by 50 percent more than female students regarding their future stable job prospects upon graduation (Qenani et al., 2014). This denotes that even at the collegiate level, male students have higher perceived job acquisition as they believe jobs available in the market have high male-dominated and high preference of hiring a male graduate instead of the female graduate. Notwithstanding, this also call for awareness current feminism advocacies such as gender pay gaps and high unemployment rate for females in many developed countries (Jackson & Wilton, 2017; Purcell et al., 2013). Additionally, study by Kim et al. (2020) found that university female students view credentials (i.e. having a college degree) far more crucial for them to enter the labour market than the male students. The female scholars believe that being a degree holder would compensate for the gender disadvantage and increase their chances of success (Álamo-Vera et al., 2020).

While several studies have demonstrated the relationship of gender on employability, there is some evidence that support the nonexistence role of gender on employability. For example, a cross-country study by Jackson and Wilton (2017) on college students in Australia and the United Kingdom found no differences in employability perception between male and female undergraduates. Similar work has also been pursued by others (Rothwell et al., 2009; Sok et al., 2013) in which also small differences were found in the perception of prospect job acquisition between both genders. Thus far, previous studies are mixed in terms of the impact of gender on graduate employability; might be contributed to different cultures and educational settings. Based on the above discussion, the following is proposed:

Hypothesis 1: Gender will have a significant influence on graduate employability.

Role of Age

The notion of age and employability remains controversial; some employers preferred young and fresh graduates while others favoured mature and experienced graduates. Young graduates have the energy and enthusiasm to actively learn on the job as they have just recently completed their studies. Meanwhile, older graduates might have a better insight and broader experience. Inevitably, the dynamic economic and cultural landscape has led to the ageing workforce - with the average working life constantly increasing (International Labour Organization, 2018). Age is a broad subject that can be conceptualized into various categories, such as chronological age, organizational age, and functional age (De Lange et al., 2021). This study focuses on chronological age, also sometimes known as calendar age, which refers to the duration of time spent since the date of birth.

Studies undertaken so far provided conflicting evidence concerning the impact of chronological age on employability. In a study conducted by Ahmed et al. (2012), it was found that young job candidates have received, by threefold, more job interview invitations or job offers compared to the older individuals. Additionally, Blasko et al. (2002) reported that graduates entered university between age range of 21 and 24 have greater opportunities to obtain an equivalent graduate job and high job satisfaction. However, compared to older adults, young individuals are more vulnerable on the job market, with higher and more frequent job movements. A society safeguarded by sustainable economic development requires a competent workforce capable of meeting the demands of competition and innovation. In this regard, education plays a vital role, since it is the principal architect of a successful youth employment model (Vasile et al., 2015).

Meanwhile, late university entrance among the graduates reported to experience several drawbacks in the job market. For instance, matured employees experienced challenges in managing changes in professions (Van der Horst et al., 2017). Age stereotypes towards older workers such as lower levels of adaptation and resistance to change have affected recruiters' impression of these workers, which consequently may severely impact their employment opportunities. While various studies have shown the effect of age on employability, circumstantial evidence also provides the negative association of this relationship. Authors have demonstrated negatively significant link between calendar age and employability among students and employees alike (Böttcher et al., 2018; Tisch, 2015). Based on the aforementioned discussions, the following hypothesis is presented:

Hypothesis 2: Age will have a significant influence on graduate employability.

Role of Education

More recently, there has been a growing recognition of the vital links between education and employability. Through the education received at the university level, graduates are expected to enter the labour market fully equipped with the essential educational trove. Specifically, job seekers with a college background would have higher employability and greater chances of obtaining a job placement in the ever-competitive labour market. A recent report on the employment market in Brunei found that 81 per cent of the respondents believed education plays a crucial role in their career outlooks. In particular, the respondents believed that education provided them with the confidence, knowledge and skills needed to gain and maintain a job (Jobs Brunei, 2020). The same trend can be seen in a research among students in Portugal that has shown the primary motivation for enrolling in university education is to increase their employability (Tavares, 2016).

Furthermore, Berntson et al. (2006) found that education received in university has a significant positive relationship with employability. In a cross-sectional study set out to investigate the link between perceived and actual employability among college students, it was found that this relationship is significant for master's degree students, however not significant for bachelor's degree students (Caricati et al., 2016). This finding may suggest lack of awareness among the bachelor's degree students on the real situations in the labour market. Additionally, a study by Wittekind et al. (2010) also found education as one of the significant predictors of employability; employees with non-college education were perceived as less employable than their counterparts. Together these studies provide important insights into the influential role of education in one's employability. Education is seen as an investment that would equip one with the credentials and enable one to enhance their career prospects. Therefore, the following hypothesis is proposed:

Hypothesis 3: Education will have a significant influence on graduate employability.

Various concepts have been applied to explain how employability is achieved by scholars. These include Signaling Theory (Spence, 1973), Social Cognitive Career Theory (Lent, Brown & Hackett, 1994) and Human the Capital Theory (Becker, 1964), which, as evidenced, provide an understanding of how characteristics like gender, age and education may lead to employability outcomes. According to Signaling Theory (Spence, 1973), job seekers use education and other signals to demonstrate their ability to employers. Young graduates may be seen as having potential and adaptability, while older graduates may have the advantage of stability and possessed depth of knowledge. Qualifications are important signals aiming at the enhancement of hiring prospects, which means that the greater the credentials, the better the job placement opportunities one is likely to have. In this case, the theory focuses not only on the fact of receiving an education, but on the fact of presenting it to a potential employer.

The Social Cognitive Career Theory by Lent, Brown, and Hackett (1994) examines how self-efficacy, outcome expectations, and goals interact with individual characteristics (such as abilities, gender, and age) and the environment to influence career development and employability. The theory suggests that self-efficacy and outcome expectations significantly affect employability, varying with age. Younger graduates, often with higher self-efficacy, are more proactive in seeking opportunities. Disparities in self-efficacy, such as lower self-efficacy among women in male-dominated fields, can impact job-seeking behaviour and career choices, thereby affecting employability. The theory emphasises that those who actively improve their skills and set specific career goals have a higher likelihood of securing employment, supporting the view that education, self-efficacy, and goal setting contribute to better employment outcomes.

Human capital theory was put forward by Becker in 1964 and Schultz in 1961. This theory posits that a person can increase her or his productivity and her or his economic worth in the society by investing in education, training and skill development. This theory is very applicable on the graduates' employability, as it brings out how the acquired knowledge and skills as well as personality traits affects a person's chance of getting employed. The present study employs Human Capital Theory to explain the relationship of gender, age and education with graduate employability. In this perspective, employability is viewed as the possession of personal skills and competencies that are useful in the job market.

Figure 1. Research framework.

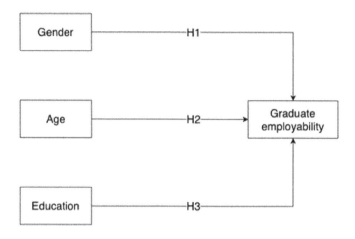

METHODS AND DATA ANALYSIS

The cross-sectional research approach was adopted to allow different groups to be examined simultaneously (i.e., comparison between graduates with different demographic backgrounds). The respondents of the present study were graduates that are registered under JobCentre Brunei, which is an online employment platform that allow job seekers to seek new job opportunities available in the local labour market. The respondents were asked to complete an online survey, where graduates' participation is entirely voluntary and assured confidentiality of information. Prior to commencing the study, ethical clearance was sought from the university. The sample of this study consisted of 324 graduates that are actively looking for jobs in Brunei. Consequently, the unit of analysis is at the individual level. Based on the work of Yorke and Knight (2006), this study defines graduate employability as the possession of a range of assets, including academic qualifications, technical skills, and personal attributes, that increase the probability of graduates successfully obtaining employment within the five-year period from 2015 to 2019.

Graduate employability as the dependent variable in this study was measured using employability scale designed by Rothwell and Arnold (2007) that originally consist of 16-items questions, out of which only 10-items were chosen and adapted in this study. The sample questions including 'there is a high demand in the labour market for people in the job I am aiming for' and 'employers seek for skills and abilities that I possess'. The Cronbach alpha for this construct is 0.757. This item is measured using a 5-point Likert scale ranging from 1 *strongly disagree* to 5 *strongly agree.* Meanwhile, each independent variable has levels and coded during analysis as the following; gender has two categories (1=male and 2=female), age has three categories (1= 20-25 years old, 2= 26-30 years old and 3= 31 years old and above), and education has two categories (1=postgraduate and 2=undergraduate). Of the cohort of 324 graduates, 108 were male and 216 were female. Majority of the graduates are 26 to 30 years of age (48.1%), followed by 20 to 25 years old (32.7%) and 31 years old and above (19.1%). Furthermore, 242 of the graduates have undergraduate qualifications and the remaining has postgraduate degree (refer to table 1).

To investigate the hypotheses laid out in this study, a factorial analysis of variance (ANOVA) test was chosen to assess the influence of several factors (i.e., gender, age, education) on the dependent variable (i.e. graduate employability). This is followed by Tukey post hoc analyses to further determine specific differences of the factors. Prior to the main analysis using ANOVA, test of normality and homogeneity of variances were performed to ensure reliable and robust ANOVA results. For normality test, considering the large sample of this study, the histogram and Q-Q plots are better suited to assess normality. Results from these graphs have shown the residuals to be normally distributed in this study. Additionally, the other assumptions that need to be met is the homogeneity of variances. Table 2 has shown the results of the Levene's test. This study chosen SPSS version 22 to perform the descriptive and multivariate analyses.

Table 1. Demographics of respondents.

	n	mean	sd
Gender			
Male	108	3.018	0.712
Female	216	2.967	0.621
Age			
20-25 years old	106	2.995	0.602
26-30 years old	156	2.968	0.659
31 years & above	62	3.003	0.723
Education			
Postgraduate	82	3.133	0.716
Undergraduate	242	2.993	0.622

Table 2. Test of Homogeneity of Variances

Dependent variable: Graduate employability				
Variables	**Levene Statistic**	**df1**	**df2**	**Sig.**
Gender	3.99	1	322	0.05
Age	0.80	2	321	0.45
Education	2.19	1	322	0.14

RESULTS

The data in table 3 shows the ANOVA results on the influence of demographic factors on graduate employability. With respect to the first hypothesis that aim to identify the influence of gender on graduate employability, no significant difference $[F(1, 322)=0.438, p=0.508]$ was found between the male ($M=3.018$, sd=0.712) and female ($M=2.967$, sd=0.621). Therefore, the first hypothesis is rejected. Meanwhile, the second hypothesis was set out to examine the impact of age on graduate employability, whereby, age was categorized into three groups: 20-25 years old ($M=2.995$, sd=0.602), 26-30 years old ($M=2.968$, sd=0.659) and above 30 years old ($M=3.002$, sd=0.723). Table 4 presents the results of Tukey post hoc test of the age categories on graduate employability. There was no observed difference between the three age groups on graduate employability $[F(2, 321)=0.09, p=0.914]$. Consequently, the second hypothesis is rejected. The purpose of hypothesis 3 was to investigate the role of education to predict graduate employability. As shown in table 3, there were statistically significant differences on employability among graduates with different education levels $[F(1, 322)=5.84, p=0.016]$. This result indicates that graduates that possess postgraduate qualifications (i.e., master's degree and above) have higher employability ($M = 3.13$, sd = 0.716) compared to undergraduate qualifications ($M=2.993$, sd=0.622). Therefore, the third hypothesis is accepted.

Table 3. Results of ANOVA

Dependent variable: Graduate employability					
Variables	**Sum of squares**	**df**	**Mean square**	***F***	**Sig.**
Gender	0.187	1	0.187	0.438	0.508
Age	0.077	2	0.038	0.090	0.914
Education	2.447	1	2.447	5.84	0.016

Table 4. Tukey post-hoc between age categories on employability

	(I) Age (coding)	(J) Age (coding)	Mean Difference (I - J)	Std. Error	Sig.	95% Confidence Interval	
						Lower Bound	Upper Bound
Tukey HSD	20 - 25 years old	26 - 30 years old	0.02733	0.08231	0.941	-0.1665	0.2212
		30 years old & above	-0.00794	0.10455	0.997	-0.2541	0.2382
	26 - 30 years old	20 - 25 years old	-0.02733	0.08231	0.941	-0.2212	0.1665
		30 years old & above	-0.03528	0.09817	0.931	-0.2664	0.1959
	30 years old & above	20 - 25 years old	0.00794	0.10455	0.997	-0.2382	0.2541
		26 - 30 years old	0.03528	0.09817	0.931	-0.1959	0.2664

DISCUSSIONS AND IMPLICATIONS

Despite the recognised necessity of demographic characteristics in research, these are often overlooked in a substantial number of empirical investigations. Demographic factors such as gender, age, race, education, financial state, among others, may have significant implications for analysing linkages between predictor variables and the associated outcomes. Jones et al. (2020) stated that neglecting to report or underreporting the demographic factors may restrict the dissemination of research, particularly those including behavioural analytics. Additionally, the authors highlighted that demographic information might enable tailored behavioural intervention programmes or activities depending on demographic background. Additionally, although some empirical studies have examined the relationship between graduate employability and other variables, there is a dearth of research in this field, particularly in developing countries such as Brunei. Besides that, it is necessary to ascertain the specific profiles of graduates that may substantially impact their employability. Thus, this study addresses a research vacuum in the present literature by providing empirical evidence for the link between demographic factors and graduate employability.

The result from ANOVA test found no significant difference of graduate employability between male and female. This finding corroborates existing literature that also showed no support for the impact of gender of graduate employability (Jackson & Wilton, 2017; Rothwell et al., 2009; Sok et al., 2013). This finding implies that gender of a graduate does not have any influence in determining one's employability. This rather interesting result could be attributed to the agreement signed by Brunei to the Convention on the Elimination of All Forms of Discrimination against Women (CEDAW) in 2006. Ever since, the gender policies with equal rights were taken place – from education, healthcare and employment (Black, 2020; Low & Sulaiman, 2013). In the latest global gender gap report by World Economic Forum (WEF), (2021) Brunei rank 51st place out of 156 countries for economic participation and opportunity. While the labour force participation rate remains higher for males than females, the labour market possesses a rather low gender discrimination. With the CEDAW agreement signed, job candidates are accessed because of their qualification and capabilities, rather than based upon gender of the individual. The same report also revealed a relatively low gender gap in educational attainment across primary, secondary and tertiary education, which indicates that males and females have equal access to education (WEF, 2021).

Consequently, this result implies that graduates in Brunei, regardless of their gender have almost equal access to employment opportunities in the local labour market. Similarly, a recent study by Hoh (2019) among 1048 university students in Brunei to investigate learning satisfaction among the undergraduates. The findings found no significant difference of gender on employer's hiring decision. Hence, it can be inferred from this study that the local undergraduate students hold the view that their gender is not an important factor when applying for a job as the employer's hiring decision do not discriminate their eligibility as a job candidate. With this prolonged issue has remained in the last decade, the finding of current study found that graduates' gender does not have any impact on their employability. Whether the job opening is for teacher or manager, graduates, regardless of their gender are accessed based on their capabilities.

About the second hypothesis, this study found no significant relationship between age and graduate employability. This finding broadly supports the work of others that have attempted to relate age with employability among samples of employees and students (e.g. Böttcher et al., 2018; Dello Russo et al., 2020; Van der Heijden et al., 2009). What emerges from the results reported here is that age of the graduates does not have any influential role in determining their employability. In recent years, unemployment has become a major national issue, as the number gradually increases yearly, with an unemployment rate of 7.4% in 2020, a slight increase from 6.8% in 2019 (MOFE, 2020). For this reason, job seekers, especially among the graduates, are experiencing a difficult time in getting a job, inevitably spending most of their time in the unemployment phase and job searching. The same report from MOFE (2020) showed that 5,129 graduates (29.6%) had spent more than 24 months in job searching - which suggests that by the time they land a job, they could be a lot older than the time they graduated.

Additionally, the government has created opportunities for unemployed graduates to gain work experience via the *i-Ready* apprenticeship programme. This programme is especially beneficial for recent graduates with little job experience. To date, 1,223 (30%) of the 3789 graduates of *i-Ready* are employed by the organisation to which they were assigned (Manpower Planning and Employment Council, 2021). The programme is offered to unemployed job seekers with TVET, HND, or bachelor's degrees who are between the ages of 17 and 40. As a result, this programme has empowered graduates to gain first-hand experience to the world of work. Therefore, the graduates must continuously learn and upgrade themselves in terms of knowledge and skills by responding proactively to the current needs of the industry and employers. The present study found no significant difference of age with employability, which implies that the graduates believe their employability does not waive, regardless of their age. After all, age is just a number.

Consistent with extant literature (e.g., Berntson et al., 2006; Caricati et al., 2016; Wittekind et al., 2010), this research found that education plays a significant role in graduate employability, thereby supporting the third hypothesis. Specifically, graduates with postgraduate qualifications have higher employability compared to graduates with only undergraduate education. This finding corroborates the current university enrolment in Brunei, which has reported an increasing number of students enrolling in postgraduate education. According to the Ministry of Education (MOE) report, the number of registrations in postgraduate courses increased by three-fold, from 393 student's enrolment in 2010 to 1,106 students in 2018 (MOE, 2010, 2018). This reflects the strong beliefs of graduates on the increasing importance of possessing a postgraduate qualification to boost their employability and attain the upper hand in the competitive labour market. Additionally, House (2010) found that graduates with a postgraduate education have higher chances to obtain permanent work and are less likely to be unemployed. This trend also applies to graduates that have left the academic world for a while but have returned to the university for reasons such as upskilling or the sake of promotion – both constitute employability.

This is similar with a recent focus group research conducted by Musa and Basir (2019), which found that youths put a high priority on education not just for its own sake but also as a means of obtaining employment and social prestige. To acquire the occupations they seek, young people demand a high level of education, which for the majority of them implies a bachelor's degree. The belief that higher education leads in better occupations such as professional and management positions, as well as a dislike for menial labour, is a pervasive theme in Brunei. Additionally, given Brunei's high unemployment rate, graduates prefer highly secured jobs in the public sector to assure a lifetime of stability and employment rather than working in the private sector (Musa & Basir, 2019). This demonstrates that in times of uncertainty, millennials choose employment with a high degree of job security.

Additionally, Mundia (2019) evaluated 860 Brunei public and private sector workers' perceptions of job satisfaction. The findings indicate that workers with a low level of education (primary to Year 13) are less satisfied with their jobs than workers with a moderate level of education (post-secondary to diploma) or a high level of education (bachelor's degree to doctorate degree). This demonstrates the influence of education after job accomplishment; indeed, education is critical for obtaining and maintaining employment. Additional improvements are required to enhance the balance between the educated labour force and the labour market. Razak (2011) argues that a generous education policy may have the unexpected consequence of graduate unemployment, when the quantity of competent persons exceeds the number of available jobs. This may result in individuals working for jobs for which they are overqualified, wasting valuable resources. As a result, employability stakeholders must collaborate closely to ensure that opportunities for higher education align with the expectations of employers in both the public and private sectors (Razak, 2011). Moreover, the curriculum provided in the university need to be relevant with the current organisational need, to boost employability and avoid mismatch of knowledge, skills, and competencies.

In Brunei, unemployment remains a critical national issue, particularly in a job market that is heavily saturated, especially within the public sector. This situation underscores the urgent need for job seekers, particularly the youth, to foster a culture of independence and entrepreneurship (Abu Bakar, 2018). As highlighted in a recent titah by His Majesty, youth should not overly depend on government employment and should remain open to opportunities in the private sector (Rajak, 2020). In addition to relying on initiatives provided by universities, such as internship placements, and government programmes like the i-Ready programme, graduates must also take proactive steps to enhance their employability. This includes researching skills that are in demand by employers, engaging in self-development and professional activities, and applying the skills and knowledge acquired to seize available opportunities.

It is well-recognised that Bruneian graduates show a strong preference for public sector employment, largely due to the perceived job stability and benefits associated with government positions. However, this has led to an oversaturation in government jobs, which conflicts with Goal 3 of Wawasan Brunei 2035, aiming for a diversified economy. Achieving this national objective may be challenging if a significant number of graduates continue to rely predominantly on public sector employment. To realise this goal, graduates need to be more receptive to private sector opportunities and entrepreneurial ventures. By innovating and introducing new products, services, or technologies, graduates can help create new industries or expand existing ones. The rise of such industries will contribute to economic diversification, reducing the nation's dependence on the public sector. Moreover, the growth of new businesses will expand the job market, reduce unemployment rates, and further strengthen the country's overall economic diversity.

LIMITATIONS AND DIRECTIONS FOR FUTURE RESEARCH

The findings in this report are subject to at least three limitations. First, a potential source of common method bias since the assessment of questions was based on self-report by the graduates. Nevertheless, this study suggests future studies to extend cross-examination of employability from different perspectives, such as employers and academicians. Secondly, being limited to a quantitative approach only, this study lacks an in-depth explanation to explore further the reasonings for the results found in this study. Subsequently, future works on employability may employ mixed-methods studies to acquire a more profound understanding underlying the issues. Finally, it is unfortunate that findings are based on a cross-sectional design; hence, this study suggests future research to test the hypotheses using a longitudinal research design. Returning to the hypotheses designed at the beginning of the study, it is now possible to state that education possess a significant role in graduate employability. Specifically, the finding suggests that the higher and more educational background graduates possess, the higher their employability. Meanwhile, the present study did not find any significant relationship between gender and age towards graduate employability. This signifies a significant contribution in the Brunei context, where graduates' perceptions of their employability are not hindered by the personal characteristics of their gender and age.

While the current investigation examines the impact of demographic variables including age, gender and education, more research are needed to evaluate other factors that could also contribute to graduate employability. This is considering the possibility that demographic attributes are subject to variability in external factors. At the same time, more studies are needed, related to graduates employability model by integrating the possible moderating and/or mediating effects of the demographic variables with the employability of the graduates. These moderators or mediators can be psychosocial, such as specified Big-Five personality traits, occupational interacting networks, or relevant other factors relating to the person.

There are recommendations for future studies aiming to increase the generalisation potential of their findings to include recruitment of a wider range of participants in terms of the educational types and job search methods employed. Using this method will serve the purpose of documenting diversity in the relevant graduate's attributes, areas of specialisation and geographic environments. Graduate employability can be better understood when individuals from different settings such as schools, colleges, and vocational training schools as well as various forms of job hunting sites, including internet sites for jobs, social networks and job fairs are involved. This variation in the participants can avoid the influence of sampling bias related to the use of one source of participants and give out the results which are not highly regarded.

REFERENCES

Ahmed, A. M., Andersson, L., & Hammarstedt, M. (2012). Does age matter for employability? A field experiment on ageism in the Swedish labour market. *Applied Economics Letters*, 19(4), 403–406. DOI: 10.1080/13504851.2011.581199

Álamo-Vera, F. R., Hernández-López, L., Ballesteros-Rodríguez, J. L., & De Saá-Pérez, P. (2020). Competence Development and Employability Expectations: A Gender Perspective of Mobility Programmes in Higher Education. *Administrative Sciences*, 10(3), 74. DOI: 10.3390/admsci10030074

BBC News. (2021, March 25). Nationwide tells 13,000 staff to 'work anywhere'. BBC. https://www.bbc.com/ news/business–56510574

Bell, R. (2016). Unpacking the link between entrepreneurialism and employability: An assessment of the relationship between entrepreneurial attitudes and likelihood of graduate employment in a professional field. *Education + Training*, 58(1), 2–17. DOI: 10.1108/ET-09-2014-0115

Berntson, E., Sverke, M., & Marklund, S. (2006). Predicting perceived employability: Human capital or labour market opportunities? *Economic and Industrial Democracy*, 27(2), 223–244. DOI: 10.1177/0143831X06063098

Black, A. (2020). Marching to the beat of different drum: Royalty, women and ideology in the Sultanate of Brunei Darussalam. *Royal Studies Journal*, 7(2), 94–116. DOI: 10.21039/rsj.269

Blasko, Z., Brennan, J., Little, B., & Shah, T. (2002). Access to what : analysis of factors determining graduate employability. *Higher Education Funding Council for England, November*, 1–8. http://www.demografia.hu/en/downloads/Publications/Blasko-etal-Graduate-Employability.pdf

Bonsay, J. O., Cruz, A. P., Firozi, H. C., & Camaro, P. J. C. (2021). Artificial intelligence and labor productivity paradox: The economic impact of AI in China, India, Japan, and Singapore. *Journal of Economics. Finance and Accounting Studies*, 3(2), 120–139. DOI: 10.32996/jefas.2021.3.2.13

Böttcher, K., Albrecht, A. G., Venz, L., & Felfe, J. (2018). Protecting older workers' employability: A survey study of the role of transformational leadership. *German Journal of Human Resource Management*, 32(2), 120–148. DOI: 10.1177/2397002218763001

Jobs Brunei. (2020). *Brunei employment report 2019-2020*.

Caricati, L., Chiesa, R., Guglielmi, D., & Mariani, M. G. (2016). Real and perceived employability: A comparison among Italian graduates. *Journal of Higher Education Policy and Management*, 38(4), 490–502. DOI: 10.1080/1360080X.2016.1182668

Chhinzer, N., & Russo, A. A. (2018). An exploration of employer perceptions of graduate student employability. *Education + Training, 60*(1), 104–120. https://doi.org/https://doi.org/10.1108/ ET-06-2016-0111

Cifre, E., Vera, M., Sánchez-Cardona, I., & de Cuyper, N. (2018). Sex, gender identity, and perceived employability among spanish employed and unemployed youngsters. *Frontiers in Psychology*, 9(DEC), 1–12. DOI: 10.3389/fpsyg.2018.02467 PMID: 30581404

De Lange, A. H., Van der Heijden, B., Van Vuuren, T., Furunes, T., De Lange, C., & Dikkers, J. (2021). Employable as We Age? A Systematic Review of Relationships Between Age Conceptualizations and Employability. *Frontiers in Psychology*, 11(605684), 605684. Advance online publication. DOI: 10.3389/fpsyg.2020.605684 PMID: 33613362

Dello Russo, S., Parry, E., Bosak, J., Andresen, M., Apospori, E., Bagdadli, S., Chudzikowski, K., Dickmann, M., Ferencikova, S., Gianecchini, M., Hall, D. T., Kaše, R., Lazarova, M., & Reichel, A. (2020). Still feeling employable with growing age? Exploring the moderating effects of developmental HR practices and country-level unemployment rates in the age–employability relationship. *International Journal of Human Resource Management*, 31(9), 1180–1206. DOI: 10.1080/09585192.2020.1737833

Finch, D. J., Peacock, M., Levallet, N., & Foster, W. (2016). A dynamic capabilities view of employability: Exploring the drivers of competitive advantage for university graduates. *Education + Training*, 58(1), 61–81. DOI: 10.1108/ET-02-2015-0013

Garcia-Murillo, M., MacInnes, I., & Bauer, J. M. (2018). Techno-unemployment: A framework for assessing the effects of information and communication technologies on work. *Telematics and Informatics*, 35(7), 1863–1876.

Hoh, C. S. (2019). *An empirical research on undergraduates student learning satisfaction and employer satisfaction in Brunei Darussalam*. Perpustakaan Dewan Bahasa dan Pustaka Brunei.

House, G. (2010). *Postgraduate Education in the United Kingdom*.

International Labour Organization. (2018)... *World Employment and Social Outlook*.

Jackson, D., & Wilton, N. (2017). Perceived employability among undergraduates and the importance of career self-management, work experience and individual characteristics. *Higher Education Research & Development*, 36(4), 747–762. DOI: 10.1080/07294360.2016.1229270

Jones, S. H., St.Peter, C. C., & Ruckle, M. M. (2020). Reporting of demographic variables in the Journal of Applied Behavior Analysis. *The Journal of Applied Behavioral Science*, 9999, 1–12. DOI: 10.1002/jaba.722 PMID: 32383188

Kim, S. W., Zhang, C., Chung, H., Kim, Y., & Choi, S. Y. (2020). Why do women value credentials? Perceptions of gender inequality and credentialism in South Korea. *International Journal of Educational Development*, 73, 102158. https://doi.org/https://doi.org/10.1016/j.ijedudev.2020.102158. DOI: 10.1016/j.ijedudev.2020.102158

Kolade, O., & Owoseni, A. (2022, November). Kolade. O. and Owoseni, A. Employment 5.0: The work of the future and the future of work. *Technology in Society*, 71, 102086. Advance online publication. DOI: 10.1016/j.techsoc.2022.102086

Low, P., & Sulaiman, Z. (2013). Women and human capital - the Brunei Darussalam perspective. *Educational Research*, 4(2), 91–97.

Manpower Planning and Employment Council. (2021). *What's Next? Preparing for Employment*. MPEC.

Maxwell, G., Scott, B., Macfarlane, D., & Williamson, E. (2009). Employers as stakeholders in postgraduate employability skills development. *International Journal of Management Education*. Advance online publication. DOI: 10.3794/ijme.82.267

Ministry of Education. (2010). *Brunei Darussalam Education Statistics*.

Ministry of Education. (2018). *Brunei Darussalam Education Statistics*.

Ministry of Finance and Economy. (2024). *Report of the labour force survey 2023*.

Mundia, L. (2019). Satisfaction with work-related achievements in Brunei public and private sector employees,. *Cogent Business & Management, 6*(1).

Musa, S. F., & Basir, K. H. (2019). Youth unemployment and the rentier economy in Brunei: Lessons from Norway. *Journal of Islamic Social Sciences and Humanities*, 20(2), 1–22. DOI: 10.33102/abqari.vol20no2.211

O'Leary, S. (2016). Graduates' experiences of, and attitudes towards, the inclusion of employability-related support in undergraduate degree programmes; trends and variations by subject discipline and gender. *Journal of Education and Work*, 30(1), 84–105. DOI: 10.1080/13639080.2015.1122181

Organisation for Economic Cooperation and Development (OECD). (2018). *Education at a Glance*.

Palumbo, R., Manna, R., & Cavallone, M. (2020). Beware of side effects on quality! Investigating the implications of home working on work-life balance in educational services. The TQM Journal, pre-publication issue. .DOI: 10.1108/TQM-05-2020-0120

Pheko, M. M., & Molefhe, K. (2017). Addressing employability challenges: A framework for improving the employability of graduates in Botswana. *International Journal of Adolescence and Youth*, 22(4), 455–469. Advance online publication. DOI: 10.1080/02673843.2016.1234401

Purcell, K., Elias, P., Atfield, G., Behle, H., Ellison, R., & Luchinskaya, D. (2013). *Transitions into employment, further study and other outcomes*.

Qenani, E., MacDougall, N., & Sexton, C. (2014). An empirical study of self-perceived employability: Improving the prospects for student employment success in an uncertain environment. *Active Learning in Higher Education*, 15(3), 199–213. DOI: 10.1177/1469787414544875

Razak, L. A. (2011). Brunei Darussalam's Labour Market: Issues and Challenges. *CSPS Strategy and Policy Journal*, 3, 1–36.

Rothwell, A., & Arnold, J. (2007). Self-perceived employability: Development and validation of a scale. *Personnel Review*, 36(1), 23–41. DOI: 10.1108/00483480710716704

Rothwell, A., Jewell, S., & Hardie, M. (2009). Self-perceived employability: Investigating the responses of post-graduate students. *Journal of Vocational Behavior*, 75(2), 152–161. DOI: 10.1016/j.jvb.2009.05.002

Sok, J., Blomme, R., & Tromp, D. (2013). The use of the psychological contract to explain self-perceived employability. *International Journal of Hospitality Management*, 34, 274–284. DOI: 10.1016/j.ijhm.2013.03.008

Tavares, O. (2016). The role of students' employability perceptions on Portuguese higher education choices. *Journal of Education and Work*, 30(1), 106–121. DOI: 10.1080/13639080.2015.1122180

Tisch, A. (2015). The employability of older job-seekers: Evidence from Germany. *The Journal of the Economics of Ageing*, 6, 102–112. DOI: 10.1016/j.jeoa.2014.07.001

Van der Heijden, B. I. J. M., Boon, J., Van der Klink, M. R., & Meijs, E. (2009). Employability enhancement through formal and informal learning: An empirical study among Dutch non-academic university staff members. *International Journal of Training and Development*, 13(1), 19–37. DOI: 10.1111/j.1468-2419.2008.00313.x

Van der Horst, A. C., Klehe, U. C., & Van der Heijden, B. I. J. M. (2017). Adapting to a Looming Career Transition: How age and Core Individual Differences Interact. *Journal of Vocational Behavior*, 99, 132–145. DOI: 10.1016/j.jvb.2016.12.006

Vasile, V., Pisică, S., & Dobre, A. M. (2015). Demographic Perspective of Qualitative Youth Employability on Romanian Labour Market. *Procedia Economics and Finance*, 22, 55–63. https://doi.org/https://doi.org/10.1016/S2212-5671(15)00226-9. DOI: 10.1016/S2212-5671(15)00226-9

Vyas, L. (2022). "New normal" at work in a post-COVID world: Work–life balance and labor markets. *Policy and Society*, 41(1), 155–167. DOI: 10.1093/polsoc/puab011

Wittekind, A., Raeder, S., & Grote, G. (2010). A longitudinal study of determinants of perceived employability. *Journal of Organizational Behavior*, 31(4), 566–586. DOI: 10.1002/job.646

World Economic Forum. The Future of Jobs Report, World Economic Forum, (2018). available at: http://www3.weforum.org/docs/WEF_Future_of_Jobs_2018.pdf. (Accessed 24 February 2022).

World Economic Forum. (2021). *Global gender gap report*.

Yorke, M., & Knight, P. (2006). Embedding employability into the curriculum. In *York: The Higher Education Academy*. Higher Education Academy.

Chapter 9
Innovative Teaching Methods for Skill Development

Bhupender Dighliya
https://orcid.org/0000-0002-4562-5413
Starex University, India

ABSTRACT

The chapter "Innovative Teaching Methods for Skill Development" explores ground-breaking educational approaches surpassing traditional pedagogy to enhance skill acquisition in learners amidst rapid technological advancements and evolving workplace demands. It evaluates the effectiveness of methods like experiential learning, project-based approaches, and technology integration in fostering critical thinking, creativity, and collaboration. Embracing online and hybrid learning environments, it caters to diverse learner needs. Additionally, it examines adaptive learning technologies, gamification, and interdisciplinary collaboration's role in shaping modern education, emphasizing their contribution to cognitive and emotional development. As educators aim to connect theory with practice, this chapter serves as a valuable resource for transforming teaching methods, emphasizing student-centered learning to prepare individuals for success in today's dynamic professional world.

I. INTRODUCTION

Teaching and learning are inherently interconnected, like two sides of the same coin. The most widely accepted standard for evaluating the quality of teaching is the extent to which students learn and grow as a result of that teaching. Research has consistently demonstrated a strong correlation between students' perceptions of

DOI: 10.4018/979-8-3693-3443-0.ch009

how much they learned in a course and their overall evaluations of the teacher and the course itself. In other words, students who report having gained more knowledge or skills from a course tend to give higher ratings to both their instructors and the course as a whole (Cohen, 1981; Theall & Franklin, 2001).

This relationship underscores the idea that effective teaching is fundamentally tied to student learning outcomes. A similar sentiment was expressed by Thomas Angelo, who emphasized that teaching without resulting in student learning is merely a form of talking. His observation captures the essence of what it means to be an effective educator: the primary goal is not just to deliver information, but to ensure that students are actively engaging with, understanding, and retaining that information in meaningful ways. This perspective is echoed by Doyle T. (n.d.), who reiterates that the true measure of a teacher's effectiveness is found in the degree to which their students learn and succeed.

In essence, the effectiveness of teaching is directly linked to the success of learning. Teachers who are able to foster significant learning experiences are those who are most likely to be seen as effective by their students. This concept highlights the importance of focusing on student learning as the core objective of teaching, rather than merely delivering content. Ultimately, the best teaching practices are those that prioritize and facilitate deep, impactful learning, creating a positive and lasting educational experience for students.

In the ever-evolving landscape of education, the quest for effective teaching methods is perpetual. As we navigate through the complexities of the 21st century, the traditional paradigm of education has undergone a significant transformation (Eli, 2021). Today, educators are not merely dispensers of knowledge but facilitators of skill development, empowering learners to thrive in a world characterized by rapid change and uncertainty (Eli, 2021; Rebecca et. al., 2019).

This chapter embarks on a journey to explore innovative teaching methods tailored specifically to enhance skill development. It delves into a realm where creativity, technology, and pedagogy converge to ignite learning experiences that transcend the boundaries of conventional education. By harnessing the power of innovative teaching approaches, educators can cultivate a generation of learners equipped with the adaptive competencies necessary to excel in diverse personal, academic, and professional spheres (Eli, 2021; Kahramonovna, 2021).This chapter navigates through a myriad of pioneering strategies, each designed to engage, inspire, and empower learners to unlock their full potential. From experiential learning and project-based approaches to gamification and immersive technologies, this chapter uncovers the transformative impact of these methodologies on skill acquisition and retention. Moreover, the chapter delves into the role of interdisciplinary collaboration, personalized learning pathways, and inclusive practices in fostering a dynamic educational ecosystem conducive to holistic skill development.

As it embark on this exploration, it becomes evident that innovative teaching methods not only nurture cognitive abilities but also cultivate socio-emotional skills, critical thinking, creativity, and adaptability - attributes indispensable for navigating the complexities of the modern world (Berdiyeva, 2024; Ma et al., 2023). By embracing innovation in education, educators embark on a transformative journey, shaping the future by empowering learners to thrive in an ever-evolving global landscape (Eli, 2021).

In the chapters that follow, educators, policymakers, and stakeholders alike to embark on this transformative journey, where innovation becomes the cornerstone of educational excellence, and skill development emerges as the catalyst for individual and societal advancement. Together, let us unlock the boundless potential of learners and redefine the contours of education in the 21st century.

Traditional vs. Modern Teaching Methods

Education is the foundation of societal advancement, playing a crucial role in shaping the minds that will drive future generations. Throughout history, the methods of imparting knowledge and skills have undergone significant evolution, mirroring changes in societal needs, technological progress, and shifts in educational philosophies. At the core of this evolution lies the ongoing debate between traditional and modern teaching methods, prompting important questions about the most effective ways to prepare students for the challenges of the 21st century.

Traditional teaching methods, which are often characterized by a teacher-centered approach, have long served as the cornerstone of formal education. These methods, as described by Ornstein and Hunkins (2009), are rooted in the belief that knowledge is a fixed entity, to be transmitted from the teacher to the student in a one-directional flow. In this framework, the teacher occupies a central role in the classroom, delivering content through lectures and guiding students to memorize and reproduce information (Glatthorn et al., 2018). While this approach can be effective in certain contexts, it is based on the premise that students are passive recipients of knowledge, primarily tasked with absorbing and replicating what they are taught.

Historically, traditional methods have been successful in providing foundational knowledge and maintaining discipline in the classroom. These methods have proven particularly effective in environments where a strong, authoritative figure is necessary to guide learning, and where the primary objective is the mastery of basic skills and factual knowledge. Standardized testing, a key element of traditional education, offers a clear and consistent means of assessing student achievement, providing benchmarks that are easy to measure and compare.

However, in recent decades, the effectiveness of traditional teaching methods has increasingly come under scrutiny. Critics argue that these methods often fall short in engaging students at deeper levels of learning and in fostering critical thinking, creativity, and problem-solving skills—qualities that are essential in today's rapidly evolving and complex world. As societal demands have changed, there has been a growing recognition that traditional methods may not adequately prepare students for the challenges they will encounter in the modern workforce and global society.

In response to these concerns, modern teaching methods have emerged as alternatives that emphasize student-centered learning, experiential engagement, and the integration of technology (Haleem et al., 2022; Means et al., 2010). These contemporary approaches shift the focus from the teacher to the learner, encouraging students to take an active role in their own education. Instead of merely absorbing information, students are urged to explore, question, and apply knowledge in real-world contexts. This shift aligns with broader educational philosophies, such as constructivism, which views learning as an active, dynamic process shaped by the learner's interactions with their environment.

The incorporation of technology in modern teaching methods further distinguishes these approaches from traditional ones. Digital tools, online resources, and interactive platforms facilitate more personalized, flexible, and accessible learning experiences. Technology not only aids in the acquisition of knowledge but also enhances the development of essential skills such as digital literacy, collaboration, and critical thinking.

As educators and policymakers continue to seek the most effective strategies for preparing students for the future, the debate between traditional and modern teaching methods remains highly relevant. While traditional methods offer stability, structure, and proven effectiveness in certain contexts, modern methods provide the flexibility, engagement, and innovation needed to address the needs of today's learners. This book chapter aims to explore the strengths and limitations of both approaches, particularly in the context of skill development, and to consider how a balanced integration of traditional and modern methods might offer the most effective path forward in education.

Importance of Skill Development in Modern Education

In modern education, the significance of skill development has become increasingly pronounced, reflecting a fundamental shift from traditional pedagogical approaches that primarily emphasized rote memorization and content delivery. Skill development encompasses a broad spectrum of competencies beyond academic knowledge, including critical thinking, problem-solving, communication, collaboration, creativity, adaptability, and digital literacy, among others (Eli, 2021). Several factors underscore the importance of skill development in modern education. Khanna (2015) emphasizes the role of skill development in enhancing employability and employment, with a focus on psycho-social components. Shavkatovna (2020) and Boykov (2018) both highlight the significance of practical training and the development of professional competencies, particularly in the context of future teachers and young professionals. Semenovska (2022) further underscores the need for educators to adapt to the changing landscape of education, particularly in the digital age, by developing new professional competencies and social skills.

Alignment with Real-World Demands: The contemporary world is characterized by rapid technological advancements, globalization, and socio-economic transformations. In this dynamic landscape, individuals require a diverse set of skills to navigate complex challenges, thrive in diverse career pathways, and remain competitive in the job market. Skill development ensures that learners are equipped with the practical competencies necessary to succeed in real-world contexts.

Enhanced Employability: Employers increasingly prioritize candidates who possess a combination of domain-specific knowledge and transferable skills. Beyond academic qualifications, skills such as communication, teamwork, problem-solving, and adaptability are highly valued in the workplace. By emphasizing skill development, educational institutions enhance the employability of their graduates, empowering them to secure meaningful employment opportunities and succeed in diverse professional environments.

Promotion of Lifelong Learning: In an era of continuous change and innovation, learning does not cease with the completion of formal education. Lifelong learning has become imperative for individuals to stay relevant, upskill or reskill, and adapt to evolving career demands. Skill development fosters a mindset of curiosity, self-directed learning, and continuous improvement, enabling individuals to pursue personal and professional growth throughout their lives.

Empowerment for Innovation and Problem-Solving: Complex global challenges, ranging from climate change to healthcare disparities, necessitate innovative solutions. Skill development cultivates critical thinking, creativity, and problem-solving abilities, empowering individuals to analyze complex issues, think critically, generate novel ideas, and collaborate effectively to address societal problems. By fostering innovation and problem-solving skills, education equips individuals to become proactive agents of positive change in their communities and beyond.

Personal Development and Well-Being: Skill development extends beyond academic or professional success; it also contributes to personal growth, resilience, and well-being. Skills such as emotional intelligence, self-awareness, resilience, and stress management are crucial for fostering positive mental health, healthy relationships, and overall well-being. By prioritizing holistic skill development, education promotes the holistic development of individuals, nurturing their social, emotional, and cognitive capacities.

II. EXPERIENTIAL LEARNING

Experiential learning refers to an educational approach that emphasizes learning through direct experience and reflection. Experiential learning serves as a powerful pedagogical approach for fostering holistic skill development and preparing learners for success in an increasingly complex and dynamic world. By integrating experiential learning principles and practices into educational curricula, educators can provide learners with meaningful, authentic, and transformative learning experiences that empower them to thrive personally, academically, and professionally. The principles of experiential learning align closely with the overarching theme of skill development, emphasizing:

Active Engagement: Learners are actively involved in hands-on experiences, which encourage them to apply theoretical concepts in practical contexts. This active engagement fosters deeper understanding and retention of skills.

Reflection: Following experiential activities, learners engage in reflective practices to analyze their experiences, identify patterns, and extract meaningful insights. Reflection promotes metacognition and enhances the transfer of learning to new situations.

Authenticity: Experiential learning experiences are designed to closely mirror real-world scenarios, providing learners with authentic opportunities to develop skills that are directly relevant to their personal, academic, or professional goals.

Iterative Process: Experiential learning is an iterative process characterized by continuous cycles of action, reflection, and refinement. Learners engage in multiple experiences, receive feedback, and adjust their approaches over time to improve their skill development outcomes.

Case Studies or Examples of Successful Implementation

Simulated Business Ventures: In a business education context, students may participate in simulated business ventures where they assume roles such as entrepreneurs, managers, or marketers. Through these simulations, students apply business concepts in a realistic setting, make strategic decisions, and experience the consequences of their actions. For example, students could develop and market a product, manage finances, and navigate market dynamics within a controlled environment.

Field-Based Scientific Research: In science education, field-based research projects provide students with opportunities to conduct authentic scientific inquiries in natural settings. For instance, students may collect and analyze water samples from local ecosystems to assess water quality or conduct biodiversity surveys in regional parks. These hands-on experiences immerse students in the scientific process, fostering inquiry skills, data analysis techniques, and environmental awareness.

Community Service Projects: In social studies or civic education courses, students may engage in community service projects to address local issues and meet community needs. For example, students could organize food drives for homeless shelters, volunteer at nursing homes, or participate in environmental clean-up efforts. These service-learning experiences not only cultivate empathy and civic responsibility but also develop communication, collaboration, and problem-solving skills.

III. PROJECT-BASED LEARNING

Project-based learning (PBL) is an instructional approach that immerses learners in authentic, inquiry-driven projects designed to address real-world challenges or problems. By integrating project-based learning principles and practices into educational curricula, educators can provide learners with authentic, inquiry-driven learning experiences that empower them to apply knowledge and skills in meaningful ways, solve real-world problems, and become lifelong learners and contributors to society. Key elements of PBL methodology include:

Authentic Context: Projects are situated within authentic, real-world contexts, allowing learners to explore topics of personal interest or relevance to their academic or professional goals.

Inquiry and Investigation: Learners engage in open-ended inquiry and investigation to explore complex questions, solve problems, or create products or solutions. This inquiry-driven approach fosters curiosity, critical thinking, and problem-solving skills.

Collaborative Learning: PBL encourages collaboration among learners, who work together in teams or groups to plan, execute, and evaluate project activities. Collaboration promotes communication, teamwork, and interpersonal skills.

Integration of Disciplines: Projects often integrate multiple disciplines or subject areas, enabling learners to apply knowledge and skills from various domains in a cohesive and interconnected manner.

Student Autonomy and Ownership: PBL empowers learners to take ownership of their learning by allowing them to make decisions, set goals, and manage their project work independently. This autonomy fosters self-directed learning and intrinsic motivation.

Examples of Projects Designed to Enhance Specific Skills

Design Thinking Challenge: Students are tasked with identifying a real-world problem or opportunity, such as improving accessibility in their school or community. Using the design thinking process, students collaborate to empathize with end-users, define the problem, ideate potential solutions, prototype designs, and solicit feedback. Through this project, students enhance skills such as empathy, problem-solving, creativity, and collaboration.

Civic Engagement Project: Learners research and analyze local or global issues of significance to their community, such as environmental sustainability, social justice, or public health. They develop and implement advocacy campaigns, organize community events, or create multimedia presentations to raise awareness and mobilize action. This project enhances skills such as research, critical thinking, communication, and civic engagement.

Entrepreneurship Venture: Students conceive and develop entrepreneurial ventures, such as starting a small business, launching a social enterprise, or designing a product or service. They conduct market research, develop business plans, create marketing materials, and pitch their ideas to potential investors or customers. This project fosters skills such as entrepreneurship, financial literacy, market analysis, and persuasive communication.

Assessment Methods of Project-Based Learning

Assessment in project-based learning is multifaceted and emphasizes both process and product. Assessment methods may include:

Rubrics: Rubrics are used to assess project work based on predetermined criteria, such as content knowledge, critical thinking, creativity, collaboration, and presentation skills. Rubrics provide clear expectations and feedback to learners throughout the project process.

Peer Evaluation: Peer evaluation encourages learners to assess and provide feedback on their peers' contributions to the project, promoting accountability, teamwork, and reflection.

Reflection and Self-Assessment: Learners engage in reflective practices and self-assessment to evaluate their own learning process, identify strengths and areas for improvement, and set goals for future learning.

IV. GAMIFICATION IN EDUCATION

Gamification draws inspiration from the principles of game design, such as clear goals, feedback mechanisms, challenges, rewards, and progression systems, to make learning more interactive, enjoyable, and effective. Gamification in education leverages the intrinsic motivation and enjoyment associated with games to create engaging learning experiences that foster skill development. By incorporating elements such as points, badges, leaderboards, quests, levels, and storytelling into educational activities, gamification aims to make learning more immersive, meaningful, and enjoyable for learners.

Gamified Learning Platforms and Tools

Several gamified learning platforms and tools are available to educators to facilitate the integration of gamification into their teaching practices. Examples include:

Kahoot!: Kahoot! is a game-based learning platform that allows educators to create and share interactive quizzes, surveys, and discussions with their students. Learners compete against each other in real-time quizzes, earning points and rewards for correct answers. Kahoot! promotes engagement, active participation, and formative assessment.

Classcraft: Classcraft is a gamified classroom management system that transforms the classroom into a role-playing game. Students create customizable avatars and form teams to complete quests, earn experience points, and unlock special powers. Classcraft promotes collaboration, positive behavior, and academic achievement.

Duolingo: Duolingo is a language learning platform that employs gamification to make language learning fun and effective. Learners progress through levels, earn points for completing lessons, and compete with friends to maintain streaks and achieve fluency. Duolingo offers personalized learning pathways and immediate feedback to support skill development.

CodeCombat: CodeCombat is a gamified coding platform that teaches programming concepts through interactive gameplay. Players control characters and write code to solve puzzles, defeat enemies, and complete quests. CodeCombat fosters computational thinking, problem-solving skills, and coding proficiency.

Impact of Gamification on Skill Acquisition and Engagement

The integration of gamification into education has been shown to have a significant impact on skill acquisition, engagement, and motivation:

Increased Engagement: Gamification captures learners' attention and maintains their interest through interactive gameplay, immediate feedback, and clear goals. Gamified learning experiences are often perceived as enjoyable and motivating, leading to increased engagement and participation in educational activities.

Enhanced Motivation: Gamification taps into intrinsic motivators, such as autonomy, mastery, and purpose, to motivate learners to actively engage in learning tasks. By providing clear goals, feedback mechanisms, and rewards, gamified learning experiences foster a sense of accomplishment and progress, motivating learners to persist in their efforts and overcome challenges.

Skill Development: Gamification facilitates skill development by providing opportunities for practice, reinforcement, and mastery through gameplay. Skills such as problem-solving, critical thinking, collaboration, decision-making, and creativity are often cultivated through gamified learning experiences. By contextualizing learning within a game-based framework, gamification makes abstract concepts more concrete and applicable to real-world scenarios.

Social Interaction: Gamified learning platforms often incorporate social features, such as multiplayer modes, leaderboards, and collaborative challenges, that promote social interaction and peer learning. Collaboration, communication, and teamwork skills are developed as learners interact with their peers, share strategies, and compete or collaborate towards common goals.

Gamification in education offers a promising approach to enhancing skill development by leveraging the motivational power of games to engage learners, promote active participation, and facilitate meaningful learning experiences. By integrating gamified learning platforms and tools into their teaching practices, educators can create dynamic and immersive learning environments that foster skill acquisition, engagement, and success.

VI. INTERDISCIPLINARY COLLABORATION

Interdisciplinary approaches in skill development are essential for preparing learners to tackle complex, real-world challenges that transcend traditional disciplinary boundaries. Interdisciplinary collaboration emphasizes the integration of knowledge, perspectives, and methodologies from multiple disciplines to address multifaceted problems and foster holistic skill development. The importance of interdisciplinary approaches in skill development can be highlighted through:

Holistic Skill Development: Interdisciplinary collaboration exposes learners to diverse perspectives, methods, and approaches, allowing them to develop a broad range of skills beyond those traditionally associated with a single discipline. Skills such as critical thinking, creativity, problem-solving, communication, collaboration, and adaptability are nurtured through interdisciplinary engagement.

Real-World Relevance: Many real-world problems and opportunities are inherently interdisciplinary in nature, requiring integrated solutions that draw upon insights from various fields. Interdisciplinary approaches in skill development enable learners to address complex challenges more effectively by synthesizing knowledge and expertise from different domains.

Innovation and Creativity: Interdisciplinary collaboration fosters innovation and creativity by encouraging the exploration of unconventional ideas and approaches. By bringing together individuals with diverse backgrounds and perspectives, interdisciplinary teams can generate novel solutions and insights that may not arise within the confines of a single discipline.

Preparation for Global Citizenship: In an increasingly interconnected world, interdisciplinary skills are essential for fostering global citizenship and understanding complex global issues. Interdisciplinary approaches in skill development promote cultural competence, intercultural communication, and collaboration across diverse cultural, social, and geographical contexts.

Examples of Collaborative Projects or Initiatives Fostering Skill Acquisition

Global Health Initiative: A collaborative project bringing together students and faculty from various disciplines, such as public health, medicine, sociology, economics, and engineering, to address global health challenges. Teams may work on projects related to disease prevention, healthcare access, sanitation, or health equity, integrating knowledge and skills from multiple disciplines to develop comprehensive solutions.

Sustainability Challenge: A collaborative initiative engaging students and educators from disciplines such as environmental science, urban planning, economics, and policy studies to tackle sustainability issues within their local community. Teams may undertake projects focused on renewable energy, waste reduction, urban green spaces, or sustainable transportation, applying interdisciplinary approaches to promote environmental stewardship and resilience.

Innovation Lab: An interdisciplinary innovation lab where students from diverse academic backgrounds collaborate on design projects, product development, or entrepreneurial ventures. Teams may include students from fields such as design, engineering, business, and psychology, working together to prototype innovative solutions, conduct user research, and bring ideas to market.

Strategies for Promoting Collaboration among Educators and Learners

Establishing Interdisciplinary Learning Communities: Create interdisciplinary learning communities or teams composed of educators and learners from different disciplines to collaborate on curriculum design, project development, and teaching strategies.

Integrated Curriculum Design: Develop interdisciplinary curricula that incorporate concepts, themes, and projects spanning multiple disciplines. Encourage educators to collaborate in designing and delivering integrated learning experiences that emphasize skill development across diverse domains.

Cross-Disciplinary Workshops and Professional Development: Offer workshops, seminars, and professional development opportunities that bring together educators from different disciplines to explore interdisciplinary teaching methods, share best practices, and collaborate on curriculum alignment.

Promoting Student-Led Initiatives: Encourage students to take the lead in organizing interdisciplinary projects, clubs, or events that promote collaboration across disciplines. Provide support and resources for student-led initiatives that foster interdisciplinary learning and skill development.

Facilitating Interdisciplinary Research and Experiential Learning: Create opportunities for students to engage in interdisciplinary research projects, internships, or experiential learning experiences that bridge academic disciplines and promote skill development in real-world contexts.

VII. PERSONALIZED LEARNING PATHWAYS

Personalized learning is an educational approach that tailors instruction, content, and pacing to meet the individual needs, preferences, and interests of each learner. It shifts away from the traditional one-size-fits-all model of education and embraces a student-centered approach that recognizes the unique strengths, challenges, and learning styles of every learner. Key principles of personalized learning include:

Learner Agency: Personalized learning empowers learners to take ownership of their learning by setting goals, making choices, and directing their own learning paths. Learner agency promotes autonomy, self-efficacy, and intrinsic motivation.

Differentiation: Personalized learning accommodates learners' diverse needs and abilities by offering multiple pathways to learning and varied instructional strategies. Differentiated instruction ensures that learners receive appropriate support, scaffolding, and challenges based on their individual readiness, interests, and learning profiles.

Flexibility and Adaptability: Personalized learning environments are flexible and adaptable, allowing learners to progress at their own pace, revisit concepts as needed, and explore topics of interest. Adaptive technologies and instructional resources adjust to learners' performance and provide targeted feedback and support.

Data-Informed Decision-Making: Personalized learning utilizes data and assessment information to inform instructional decisions, track progress, and identify areas for growth. Educators use formative and summative assessments, as well as diagnostic tools, to gather data on learners' strengths, weaknesses, and learning trajectories.

Tools and Techniques for Creating Personalized Learning Experiences

Learning Management Systems (LMS): LMS platforms, such as Moodle, Canvas, or Google Classroom, provide tools for organizing course content, delivering instruction, and assessing student progress. Features such as adaptive learning paths, multimedia resources, and interactive assessments support personalized learning experiences.

Adaptive Learning Software: Adaptive learning platforms, such as Khan Academy, DreamBox, or IXL, use algorithms to personalize instruction based on learners' responses and performance. These platforms adjust content, difficulty levels, and pacing to match individual learners' needs and learning trajectories.

Project-Based and Inquiry-Based Learning: Project-based and inquiry-based learning approaches offer opportunities for personalized learning by allowing learners to pursue topics of interest, conduct independent research, and explore real-world problems. Educators can scaffold projects and provide guidance to support learners' inquiry processes.

Student Choice and Voice: Providing students with choices and opportunities for self-expression fosters personalized learning experiences. Techniques such as choice boards, learning menus, or passion projects allow students to select topics, activities, or projects aligned with their interests and preferences.

Impact of Personalized Learning on Skill Mastery and Retention

Increased Engagement and Motivation: Personalized learning engages learners by tapping into their interests, preferences, and motivations, leading to higher levels of engagement and persistence. Motivated learners are more likely to invest time and effort in mastering skills and retaining knowledge.

Improved Skill Mastery: Personalized learning allows learners to progress at their own pace and receive targeted support and feedback, leading to deeper understanding and mastery of skills. By addressing individual learning needs and providing tailored instruction, personalized learning enhances skill acquisition and retention.

Promotion of Metacognitive Skills: Personalized learning environments encourage learners to reflect on their learning processes, set goals, monitor progress, and adapt strategies as needed. Metacognitive skills, such as self-regulation, goal-setting, and self-reflection, are essential for skill mastery and long-term retention.

Promotion of Lifelong Learning Habits: Personalized learning fosters a growth mindset and promotes habits of lifelong learning by empowering learners to take ownership of their learning and pursue areas of interest beyond the classroom. By instilling a sense of agency and autonomy, personalized learning prepares learners for continuous skill development and adaptation in an ever-changing world.

In summary, personalized learning pathways offer a student-centered approach to skill development that recognizes and responds to the unique needs, preferences, and interests of individual learners. By embracing principles of agency, differentiation, flexibility, and data-informed decision-making, personalized learning environments enhance engagement, promote skill mastery, and foster lifelong learning habits that empower learners to thrive in diverse personal, academic, and professional contexts.

VIII. INCLUSIVE TEACHING PRACTICES

Inclusivity in skill development is paramount for creating equitable learning opportunities and ensuring that all learners, regardless of background, identity, or ability, have access to the resources and support they need to succeed. The importance of inclusivity in skill development can be underscored by the following factors:

Equity and Access: Inclusive teaching practices promote equity and access by removing barriers to learning and addressing systemic inequalities that may hinder certain groups of learners from fully participating and thriving in educational settings. By fostering inclusive learning environments, educators can ensure that every learner has an equal opportunity to develop and demonstrate their skills.

Diversity of Perspectives: Inclusive teaching embraces the diversity of learners' backgrounds, experiences, and perspectives as valuable assets to the learning community. By creating spaces where diverse voices are heard, respected, and valued, inclusive teaching practices enrich the learning experience and expose learners to a variety of viewpoints, ideas, and approaches.

Social and Emotional Well-Being: Inclusive teaching practices prioritize the social and emotional well-being of all learners, recognizing that a sense of belonging, safety, and support is essential for effective learning. By fostering positive relationships, empathy, and respect within the learning community, inclusive teaching promotes a supportive and inclusive environment where learners feel valued and empowered to engage in skill development.

Strategies for Creating Inclusive Learning Environments:

Culturally Responsive Teaching: Culturally responsive teaching acknowledges and incorporates learners' cultural backgrounds, experiences, and identities into the curriculum and instructional practices. Educators can use culturally relevant materials, examples, and instructional strategies to make learning more meaningful and accessible to all learners.

Universal Design for Learning (UDL): UDL principles guide the design of instructional materials, activities, and assessments to accommodate diverse learner needs and preferences. By providing multiple means of representation, expression, and engagement, UDL promotes inclusivity and removes barriers to learning for all learners.

Differentiated Instruction: Differentiated instruction involves tailoring instruction to meet the individual needs, interests, and learning styles of learners. Educators can differentiate content, process, and product to accommodate diverse learning profiles and support skill development for all learners.

Collaborative Learning Communities: Foster collaborative learning communities where learners work together in diverse groups to support one another, share perspectives, and learn from each other's experiences. Collaborative learning promotes inclusivity, cooperation, and the development of social and interpersonal skills.

Case Studies Highlighting Successful Inclusive Teaching Practices

Inclusive Classroom Environment: A case study of an inclusive classroom environment where the educator proactively incorporates diverse perspectives, celebrates cultural diversity, and creates opportunities for all learners to contribute and succeed.

By fostering a sense of belonging and respect, the inclusive classroom promotes skill development and academic achievement for all students.

UDL Implementation: A case study of a school or district that implements Universal Design for Learning (UDL) principles to create inclusive learning environments across diverse grade levels and subject areas. Through UDL, educators provide flexible learning options, scaffold support, and offer multiple means of engagement, expression, and representation to address diverse learner needs.

Collaborative Peer Learning: A case study of a collaborative peer learning initiative where students with diverse backgrounds, abilities, and learning styles work together on interdisciplinary projects or group activities. Through collaborative peer learning, students develop empathy, communication skills, and problem-solving abilities while supporting each other's skill development and academic success.

Inclusive teaching practices are essential for fostering equitable learning opportunities, promoting diversity and inclusion, and supporting skill development for all learners. By implementing strategies such as culturally responsive teaching, Universal Design for Learning (UDL), differentiated instruction, and collaborative learning communities, educators can create inclusive learning environments where every learner feels valued, supported, and empowered to reach their full potential.

IX. INTEGRATION OF TECHNOLOGY

The integration of technology as an innovative teaching method has revolutionized skill development, making it more engaging, interactive, and tailored to individual learning needs. In a world where technological advancements are rapidly becoming the norm, incorporating these tools into education is no longer optional—it is essential. By utilizing digital resources, educators can better address diverse learning styles, provide instant feedback, and equip students with the skills necessary to thrive in today's workforce.

Examples of Technology in Skill Development

Virtual Reality (VR) and Augmented Reality (AR): VR and AR offer immersive experiences that are particularly advantageous in fields requiring practical training, such as healthcare, engineering, and hospitality. For example, medical students can use VR to practice surgeries in a risk-free environment, while AR can simulate customer service scenarios for hospitality management students, helping them develop essential soft skills.

Learning Management Systems (LMS): Platforms like Moodle, Canvas, and Blackboard serve as centralized hubs for delivering content, monitoring progress, and evaluating students. LMS systems support the integration of various multimedia resources, such as videos, quizzes, and discussion boards, making learning more dynamic and personalized.

AI-Powered Learning Tools: Artificial intelligence can create personalized learning experiences by analyzing students' strengths and weaknesses and adapting content accordingly. For instance, platforms like Coursera and edX use AI to recommend courses and materials that align with a learner's progress. AI also automates routine tasks like grading and attendance, allowing educators to focus on more complex teaching activities.

Collaborative Tools: Platforms like Google Workspace, Microsoft Teams, and Slack facilitate student collaboration, enabling them to work on projects, share resources, and communicate in real-time. These tools are crucial for developing teamwork and communication skills, which are essential in nearly all professional fields.

Implementation

Successfully integrating technology into skill development requires careful planning and attention to several key factors:

Infrastructure: Educational institutions must ensure they have the necessary infrastructure, including reliable internet access, appropriate hardware (like computers and VR headsets), and relevant software. Investing in a robust infrastructure is critical to the seamless adoption of technology in teaching.

Educator Training: Teachers and instructors need proper training to effectively utilize new technologies. Professional development programs should be designed to familiarize educators with digital tools and technology-enhanced teaching methods. Ongoing training is essential as technology continues to evolve.

Curriculum Design: The curriculum should be thoughtfully redesigned to incorporate technology in a meaningful way. This includes identifying which technological tools align with specific learning objectives and determining how they can enhance understanding and skill acquisition. For example, VR simulations could be integrated into a medical curriculum, or LMS platforms could be used for blended learning in hospitality management.

Student Engagement: To keep students engaged with technology-driven learning, strategies such as gamification, collaborative learning opportunities, and the inclusion of real-world applications should be implemented.

Accessibility: It's important to ensure that all students have access to the necessary technology. This might involve providing devices to those who cannot afford them, ensuring software compatibility with various devices, and designing content that is accessible to students with disabilities.

Assessment

Evaluating the effectiveness of technology integration in skill development involves both formative and summative assessments:

Formative Assessment: Ongoing assessments, including quizzes, assignments, and real-time feedback, allow educators to monitor student progress and adjust their teaching methods as needed. Tools like Google Forms, Socrative, and Edmodo can facilitate quick assessments and feedback collection.

Summative Assessment: Final exams, projects, and practical demonstrations are critical for assessing whether students have acquired the necessary skills. Technology can enhance these assessments through tools like e-portfolios, where students can showcase their work, and simulation-based exams that allow students to demonstrate practical skills in a controlled, virtual environment.

Data Analytics: LMS and AI-powered tools can offer detailed analytics on student performance, engagement, and areas for improvement. Educators can use this data to refine their teaching strategies and identify which technologies are most effective in achieving desired learning outcomes.

Stakeholder Feedback: Gathering feedback from students, educators, and employers (when skill development is tied to industry needs) is essential. This feedback can provide valuable insights into the real-world applicability of the skills learned and the effectiveness of the technology used in the learning process.

Examples and Case Studies of Technology Integration

The integration of technology in education has yielded numerous successful examples and case studies across different disciplines and regions. Below are some notable examples:

The University of California, San Francisco (UCSF) has incorporated VR into its medical training programs to simulate surgical procedures. Through VR, students can practice complex surgeries in a virtual environment that closely mimics real-life scenarios. This technology allows them to develop surgical skills without the risks associated with practicing on real patients. The program has resulted in improved competency and confidence among students, leading to better preparedness for actual surgeries.

Georgia State University (GSU) implemented an AI-driven advising system called "PantherBot," which uses predictive analytics to monitor student progress and identify those at risk of dropping out. The system provides personalized recommendations and resources to help students stay on track. Since its implementation, GSU has seen a significant increase in student retention rates and a reduction in the achievement gap between different student demographics. The use of AI has made advising more efficient and tailored to individual student needs.

EHL (Ecole hôtelière de Lausanne), Switzerland has integrated AR into its hospitality management curriculum to simulate real-world scenarios, such as front-desk operations and restaurant management. Students use AR to interact with virtual customers, practice service skills, and manage simulated crises. This hands-on approach has enhanced student learning by providing them with practical experience in a controlled environment, better preparing them for industry challenges.

Coursera has launched specialized programs for teachers to enhance their digital literacy and integrate technology into their classrooms. These courses cover various topics, such as using educational technology tools, creating online courses, and developing digital content. Teachers who have completed these programs report increased confidence in using technology and improved student engagement in their classrooms. This initiative has been particularly beneficial during the COVID-19 pandemic when remote learning became essential.

X. CONCLUSION

Throughout this chapter on "Innovative Teaching Methods for Skill Development," explored a variety of pedagogical approaches aimed at fostering holistic skill development in learners. We began by discussing the importance of skill development in modern education, emphasizing the need to equip learners with the diverse competencies necessary for success in an increasingly complex and dynamic world. The chapter delved into innovative teaching methods such as experiential learning, project-based learning, gamification, personalized learning pathways, interdisciplinary collaboration, inclusive teaching practices, and integration of technology.

Innovative teaching methods hold immense transformative potential for skill development, offering educators powerful tools to engage learners, enhance motivation, and foster deep, meaningful learning experiences. By embracing approaches such as experiential learning, project-based learning, and gamification, educators can create dynamic and interactive learning environments that promote critical thinking, problem-solving, creativity, communication, collaboration, and adaptability. Moreover, personalized learning pathways, interdisciplinary collaboration, and inclusive teaching practices ensure that every learner has equitable access to the resources, support, and opportunities needed to succeed. These innovative teaching methods not only prepare learners for academic and professional success but also cultivate lifelong learners who are empowered to navigate challenges, pursue passions, and make meaningful contributions to society.

As educators, it is our responsibility to embrace innovation in education and continually seek out new and effective ways to support the skill development and success of all learners. Let us commit to integrating innovative teaching methods into our practice, fostering collaborative learning communities, and creating inclusive environments where every learner feels valued, supported, and empowered to thrive. By embracing innovation in education, we can inspire a passion for learning, cultivate 21st-century skills, and prepare learners to adapt, innovate, and lead in an ever-changing world. Together, let us embark on this journey of transformation, guided by a shared commitment to the holistic development and well-being of all learners.

REFERENCES

Berdiyeva, S. (2024). Exploring Innovative Approaches to Teaching. *Modern Science and Research, 3*(1), 923–927. Retrieved from https://inlibrary.uz/index.php/science-research/article/view/28552

Boykov, V., & Goceva, M. (2018). *Training Through Action To Build Professional Skills*. Knowledge International Journal. DOI: 10.35120/kij2803849V

Cohen, P. A. (1981). Student Ratings of Instruction and Student Achievement: A Meta-Analysis of Multisection Validity Studies. *Review of Educational Research*, 51(3), 281–309. DOI: 10.3102/00346543051003281

Eli, T. (2021). Students' Perspectives on the Use of Innovative and Interactive Teaching Methods at the University of Nouakchott Al Aasriya, Mauritania: English Department as a Case Study. *International Journal of Technology* [IJTIM]. *Innovation and Management*, 1(2), 90–104. DOI: 10.54489/ijtim.v1i2.21

Glatthorn, A. A., Boschee, F., & Whitehead, B. M. (2018). *Curriculum leadership: Strategies for development and implementation* (4th ed.). Sage Publications.

Haleem, A., Javaid, M., Qadri, M. A., & Suman, R. (2022). Understanding the role of digital technologies in education: A review. *Sustainable Operations and Computers*, 3, 275–285. DOI: 10.1016/j.susoc.2022.05.004

Kahramonovna, M. D. (2021). Innovative teaching methods. *International Journal on Orange Technologies*, 3(7), 35–37. DOI: 10.31149/ijot.v3i7.2063

Khanna, S. (2015). From Novice to Professional: The impact of Skill Development programmes. *IRA-International Journal of Management & Social Sciences*, 1(1), 6–11.

Kuzemko, L. (2020). SKILLS OF THE 21st CENTURY IN THE CONTEXT OF QUALITY ASSURANCE OF TEACHER PROFESSIONAL TRAINING. *Pedagogical education: Theory and practice. Psychology.Pedagogy*, 34(2), 28–33. DOI: 10.28925/2311-2409.2020.34.4

Ma, M., Liu, W., Zhang, R., Xie, W., & Qin, Q. (2023). Research on the Application and Effect of Innovative Teaching Methods in College Student Education. *Contemporary Education and Teaching Research*, 4(11), 573–578. DOI: 10.61360/BoniCETR232015191104

Ornstein, A., & Hunkins, F. (2009). Curriculum Design. In *Curriculum: Foundations, Principles and Issues* (5th ed., pp. 181–206). Pearson/Allyn and Bacon.

Shavkatovna, R. G. (2020). Improving Technologies To Develop Spiritual And Moral Competencies In Future Teachers. *The American Journal of Management and Economics Innovations.*, 2(9), 1–6. DOI: 10.37547/tajmei/Volume02Issue09-01

Sivarajah, R. T., Curci, N. E., Johnson, E. M., Lam, D. L., Lee, J. T., & Richardson, M. L. (2019). A review of innovative teaching methods. *Academic Radiology*, 26(1), 101–113. DOI: 10.1016/j.acra.2018.03.025 PMID: 30929697

Theall, M., & Franklin, J. (2001). Looking for Bias in all the Wrong Places –A Search for Truth or a Witch Hunt in Student Ratings of Instruction? In The Student Ratings Debate: Are they Valid? How Can We Best Use Them? Theall, P., Abrami, L. and Lisa Mets (Eds.) New Directions in Educational Research, no. 109. San Francisco: Jossey-Bass.

Chapter 10
Insights Into Cultivating Creativity and Innovation in Kenyan Higher Education:
Implications for Leadership About the Skills Gap

James K. Ngugi
https://orcid.org/0009-0004-7644-326X
University of South Africa, South Africa

Leila Goosen
https://orcid.org/0000-0003-4948-2699
University of South Africa, South Africa

ABSTRACT

Against the background of insights into international higher education leadership and the skills gap, the purpose of this chapter will be to especially focus on cultivating creativity and innovation in higher education. Drivers of Individual Innovative Behavior (IIB) obtained from Structural Equation Modelling (SEM) of the mediating effect of Knowledge Sharing Behavior (KSB) on technology students' individual and contextual antecedents, including those related to Course Design Characteristics (CDC) and Self-Regulated Learning (SRL), are explained.

DOI: 10.4018/979-8-3693-3443-0.ch010

INTRODUCTION

This section will describe the general perspective of the chapter and end by specifically stating the objective.

Insights Into International Higher Education Leadership and the Skills Gap

In the dynamic landscape of higher education, leaders play a vital role in determining the future of learning and preparing students for the challenges experienced in the context of continued global hypercompetition (Sezerel & Christiansen, 2022). The link between higher education leadership and the global skills gap is a compelling and urgent subject for research. At the crossroads of the drivers or determinants of Individual Innovative Behavior (IIB), the technological advancements of Education 4.0 (Oyewo & Goosen, 2024), and the changing nature of measuring innovative work behavior (De Jong & Den Hartog, 2010), it becomes necessary to analyze the leadership methods within higher education institutions that can bridge the gap between academic pursuits and a path model of the skills expected in the modern workplace (Scott & Bruce, 1994).

Recommended Topics

Based on the recommended topics suggested for the book, this chapter will especially focus on:

- Cultivating Creativity and Innovation in Higher Education

However, this chapter will also discuss:

- The Role of Visionary Leadership in Higher Education
- Adapting Curriculum to Address Emerging Global Skills
- Innovative Teaching Methods for Skill Development
- The Impact of Technological Advancements on Higher Education Leadership
- Promoting Entrepreneurial Skills in Higher Education
- Cross-Cultural Competence in Educational Leadership
- Addressing Gender Disparities in Leadership Positions
- Effective Strategies for Collaborating with Industry Partners
- Fostering Critical Thinking and Problem-Solving Skills
- Aligning Educational Leadership with Sustainable Development Goals
- Leadership Challenges in Addressing Mental Health in Academia

- Leadership Strategies for Addressing Environmental Challenges
- Assessing and Enhancing Teachers' Digital Literacy
- The Role of Artificial Intelligence in Higher Education Leadership
- Adaptive Leadership in Times of Crisis and Uncertainty
- Measuring and Improving Graduate Employability
- The Future of Higher Education Leadership: Trends and Predictions

Target Audience

As part of this publication, the chapter is targeted towards scholars and higher education professionals who need an updated international perspective on the challenges mentioned above and how to rectify them effectively in a single volume. As part of the book, this chapter will foster meaningful research directions for future challenges concerning higher education within the context of global hypercompetition.

Objective

As part of this publication, the chapter will examine the multiple characteristics of higher education leadership in the context of the global skills gap. By analyzing the varied views, difficulties, and possibilities faced by educational leaders, we seek to contribute to a nuanced understanding of how good leadership can foster the skills necessary for success in a fast-changing international landscape.

BACKGROUND

This section of the chapter will provide broad definitions and discussions of the topic on Insights into Cultivating Creativity and Innovation in Kenyan Higher Education in terms of Implications for Leadership About the Skills Gap and incorporate the views of others (in the form of a literature review) into the discussion to support, refute, or demonstrate the authors' position on the topic.

The first publication from the study discussed in this chapter, on the effects of Course Design Characteristics (CDC), Self-Regulated Learning (SRL) and Knowledge Sharing Behavior (KSB) in facilitating the development of IIB among higher education technology students, appeared in the *Proceedings of the Institute of Science and Technology Education (ISTE) Conference on Mathematics, Science and Technology Education* (Ngugi & Goosen, 2017). In their most recent chapter, Ngugi and Goosen (2024b) were modelling the mediating effects of KSB in the education sector in terms of the drivers of IIB.

Cultivating Creativity and Innovation in Higher Education

Despite efforts towards cultivating creativity and innovation as part of curriculum development in Kenya, the expected returns of higher education graduates, who can independently think through tasks, are innovative, creative and goal-oriented, may not have been fully realized. This places a premium on a review of the CDC to link it with the stimulation of innovative behavior. Unless the focus shifts to recognize and leverage on students' capacity in technological innovation, the dream of Kenyan universities taking the lead and becoming islands of innovation will remain a mirage (Republic of Kenya, 2010).

The *journal* article on *service research* by Coelho and Augusto (2010) investigated the job characteristics and creativity of frontline service employees, while the *creativity and innovation management* journal article by De Jong and Den Hartog (2010), in line with the topic of the study discussed in this chapter, were measuring innovative work behavior. Kiratli, Rozemeijer, Hilken, De Ruyter and De Jong (2016) were developing a measurement scale for team creativity climate in a setting with regard to sourcing teams in their *journal* article on *purchasing and supply management*, whereas the chapter by West and Farr (1990) on innovation and creativity at work appeared in a book on *psychological and organizational strategies*.

Against the background of management, sciences, innovation, and technologies, the article by Kayyali (2023b, p. 1) indicated that *university rankings* had "a growing impact on how people view the academic excellence of higher education. The complicated relationship between rankings and academic" quality and excellence. An earlier article by Kayyali (2020b, p. 4) considered the advantages and disadvantages of *university rankings*. *University rankings* had "been of interest to many specialists, academics, and independent researchers, who are affiliated to educational or scientific institutions."

"The purpose of the research presented in" the chapter by Ngugi and Goosen (2024a, p. 171) "was to focus on the individual and contextual antecedents of innovative behavior (IB) via the mediating effects of" knowledge sharing behavior. The latter chapter was modelling mediating driver practices that promote innovative behavior for technology students as part of a book on *Practices That Promote Innovation for Talented Students*.

The paper by Goosen and Ngugi (2019a) in the *proceedings of 48th annual conference of the Southern African Computer Lecturers' Association (SACLA)* explained how and why innovation for computing students matter, while in the context of *Smart Innovation, Systems and Technologies*, the journal article by Ngugi and Goosen (2019) worked towards smart innovation for Information Systems (IS) and Technology students.

An international journal article on management, sciences, innovation, and technologies by Kayyali (2023a, p. 1) provided an overview of *quality assurance* in higher education in terms of the primary concepts and frameworks, as well as associated structures and procedures: "To ensure that students obtain an effective and appropriate education, *quality assurance* in higher education is crucial."

"Talking about quality in higher education is not a new matter, as it was previously discussed by many researchers" concerning "the importance of implementing a specific quality system" (Kayyali & Khosla, 2021, p. 67). In the context of globalization and internationalization, an *international journal* article on *applied science and engineering* by the latter authors discussed ISO 21001 as a trigger and prime key for the *quality assurance* of Higher Education Institutions (HEIs).

Effective Strategies for Collaborating with Industry Partners

MacCurtain, Flood, Ramamoorthy, West and Dawson (2010) presented a study of the Irish software industry regarding the top management team, reflexivity, knowledge sharing and new product performance against the background of *creativity and innovation management*.

Cross-Cultural Competence in Educational Leadership

An *international journal* article on *learning and intellectual capital* by Molodchik, Krutova and Molodchik (2016) focused on leadership, learning and organizational culture as antecedents for innovative behavior in the case of Russia, while the journal article on *knowledge management* by Xue, Bradley and Liang (2011) considered team climate, empowering leadership and knowledge sharing.

The Impact of Technological Advancements on Higher Education Leadership

The positive impact of technological advancements on higher education was the focus of an *international journal* article on *information science and computing* by Kayyali (2021, p. 13). "All intellectual, economic, educational, and scientific sectors work to benefit from the technological progress that the world has witnessed during the past two decades".

Exploring the socioeconomic facets of online inclusive education in Ghana and the effects of technological advancement in academia, the chapter by Ansu-Kyeremeh and Goosen (2022, p. 47), as part of a book on *Socioeconomic Inclusion During an Era of Online Education*, indicated that "Africa now stands at the threshold of development that requires a new approach to promote technological" advancements "and long-term economic growth."

"In order to provide readers with an overview and summarize the content, the purpose of the study in" the chapter by Oyewo and Goosen (2024, p. 1) in a book on the *Architecture and Technological Advancements of Education 4.0* was "stated as investigating the relationships between how teachers use" their technological competency levels and self-regulated learning behavior in blended learning environments.

Assessing and Enhancing Teachers' Digital Literacy

Molotsi and Goosen (2022) investigated teachers using disruptive methodologies in teaching and learning to foster learner skills through the Technological, Pedagogical, and Content Knowledge (TPACK) model in the *Handbook of Research on Using Disruptive Methodologies and Game-Based Learning to Foster Transversal kills*, while the chapter by Molotsi and Goosen (2023) examined teachers' unique knowledge to effectively integrate digital technologies into teaching and learning in the context of a book on *Community Engagement in the Online Space*.

Aligning Educational Leadership with Sustainable Development Goals

"Research had previously identified individual and contextual antecedents, which promote innovative behaviors through implementation in organizational contexts. The purpose of" the chapter by Ngugi and Goosen (2024b, p. 27) as part of a book on *ImplementingSustainable Development Goals in the Service Sector*.

The *handbook of research on sustainable tourism and hotel operations in global hypercompetition* edited by Sezerel and Christiansen (2022) indicated that to "compete effectively today and remain sustainable over the long term, business organizations must create flexible means of generating competitive advantage".

Innovative Teaching Methods for Skill Development

In the *proceedings of the South Africa International Conference on Education (SAICEd)*, the paper by Goosen and Ngugi (2018) was rethinking teaching and learning in the 21st century with regard to course design characteristics towards innovative behavior, while the ISTE conference paper by Goosen and Ngugi (2019b) was working towards innovative behavior for technology students.

MAIN FOCUS OF THE CHAPTER

Issues, Problems

This section of the chapter will present the authors' perspectives on the issues, problems, challenges, etc., as these relate to the main theme of the book on Insights into International Higher Education Leadership and the Skills Gap, and arguments supporting the authors' position on Insights into Cultivating Creativity and Innovation in Kenyan Higher Education in terms of Implications for Leadership About the Skills Gap. It will also compare and contrast with what had been, or is currently being, done as it relates to the specific topic of the chapter.

The volume edited by Branch and Christiansen (2021) explored "the nature, scope, and consequences of the marketisation of higher education. Chapters" identified different practices which reflected marketisation in terms of concepts, cases, and criticisms.

The Role of Artificial Intelligence in Higher Education Leadership

Artificial Intelligence is one of the most alarming and important terms "and concept these days, and" is dedicated to advancing general Information Technology (IT) operations (Paul, Kayyali, Das, Chatterjee, & Saavedra, 2023, p. 1). An *international journal* article on *applied science and engineering* by the latter authors provided a scientific review of educational applications, emergences and issues related to AI and smart society.

Leadership Challenges in Addressing Mental Health in Academia

The recent book on effective human resources management in the multigenerational workplace edited by Even and Christiansen (2024) indicated that in "the aftermath of the COVID-19 pandemic, the landscape of human resources management has been reshaped by an array of unprecedented challenges."

An earlier book on enhancing employee engagement and productivity in the post-pandemic multigenerational workforce edited by Even and Christiansen (2023) showed how the post-pandemic era had "brought about significant disruptions to the human resources management function, exacerbating existing challenges such as labor shortages".

Leadership Strategies for Addressing Environmental Challenges

Measuring and Improving Graduate Employability

In line with the theme of this book, the book edited by Christiansen and Even (2024) on *Prioritizing Skills Development for Student Employability* indicated that in "the throes of a global skills gap and relentless labor market disruptions, organizations grapple with the pressing challenge of aligning workforce skills with the demands of a hypercompetitive economy."

Studying Open Distance e-Learning (ODeL) in South Africa towards advancing student employability through higher education using Artificial Intelligence (AI) applications, the purpose of the study discussed in the chapter by Ndhlovu-Nemaxwi and Goosen (2024, p. 120) was "to answer the primary research question:" 'What can be learned from a study of a comprehensive open and distance e-learning institution' in such a context?

Emphasizing the applications and emergence of environmental Informatics in environmental management regarding profound cases, Kayyali (2022, p. 201) looked at challenges and solutions. The "Internet of Things (IoT) is a modern technical method that aims to relate things represented by devices and sensors and connect" these to the Internet.

Fostering Critical Thinking and Problem-Solving Skills

Toward a design theory of problem solving, Jonassen (2000, p. 63), in a journal article on educational technology research and development, indicated that problem solving "is generally regarded as the most important cognitive activity in everyday and professional contexts. Most people are required to and rewarded for solving problems".

Dillon (2000) was defining decision problem structuring by synthesizing existing literature.

The Role of Visionary Leadership in Higher Education

Practical Implications for University Management

Apart from the practical*implications for university management* discussed by Ngugi and Goosen (2018) in a Eurasia journal article on modelling course-design characteristics, self-regulated learning and the mediating effect of knowledge-sharing behavior as drivers of individual innovative behavior, as well as the chapter by Ngugi and Goosen (2021a) on knowledge sharing mediating information technology student innovation, the following implications were also generated:

The expansion of access to university education poses a challenge on the quality of the graduates, as there may not be commensurate increase in human and academic resources to support the programs on offer. Employers and the public expect graduates to be employable on graduation. This background places an ever-increasing pressure on universities to produce graduates who are innovative, and can easily plug into the society and the world of work. Hence, university management face the daunting task of teaching and training graduates who are innovative and can be relied on to be the innovators. Developing countries such innovators to be champions of innovative technologies and products.

The study findings indicate that some of the individual and contextual factors tend to favor sharing of knowledge among technology students, resulting in them going beyond the requirements of the prescribed curriculum and begin to promote and implement new ideas and innovate products, services, and processes. University managers need to endeavor to facilitate a knowledge sharing climate among students by arranging and facilitating formal and informal socialization practices.

Practical Implications for Curriculum Experts

Apart from the practical *implications for curriculum experts* discussed by Ngugi and Goosen (2018; 2021a), as well as the journal articles by Ngugi and Goosen (2019) on modelling motivation, metacognition and affective aspects of learning, as well as Ngugi and Goosen (2021c) on Computer Science and Information Technology students' self-regulated learning and knowledge sharing behavior as drivers of individual innovative behavior, the following were further considered:

The quest for innovation may imply designing tasks that promote and introduce the four (4) task characteristics of task variety, task significance, task identity, and technology feedback. Further, and related to knowledge characteristics of the course is the need for university level curriculum planners to deliberately infuse the curriculum with the four (4) components of knowledge characteristics namely: complexity, problem solving, skill variety and specialization. The design of an innovative curriculum should provide the right balance of task and knowledge characteristics so as to trigger both KSB and innovative behavior.

Practical Implications for Faculty

Apart from the practical *implications for faculty* discussed by Ngugi and Goosen (2018), the following were likewise indicated:

The study discussed in this chapter also provided empirical evidence to suggest that technology students have a greater chance of engaging and developing innovative tendencies, if they are persuaded that the course design allows the use of a variety of tasks, autonomy in scheduling tasks and feedback on technological matters. Further, courses that are deemed to be complex in nature, tend to have a greater effect on stimulating innovative behavior, than courses that are deemed to be easy. The complex nature allows for critical thinking with is a necessary starting point in the innovation process.

The results of this study suggested that scheduling autonomy had the greatest effect on CDC and eventually on innovative behavior. Consequently, universities should rethink on how to balance the need for scheduling autonomy and the stringent demands for form and structure in the design of the courses. Students would need a leeway to define the means to achieve the tasks by choice and freedom inborn in the course to perform numerous tasks, while maintaining responsibility for the outcomes of the work.

Adaptive Leadership in Times of Crisis and Uncertainty

"On November 17, 2019, according to" Kayyali (2020c, p. 131), "the first case of COVID-19 appeared in Wuhan, China, for a 55-year-old man." An *international journal* article on *applied science and engineering* by the latter author, however, investigated the new era for higher education systems post COVID-19.

An *international journal* article on *information science and computing* by Kayyali (2020a, p. 63) looked at the rise of online learning and its worthiness during COVID-19 pandemic. The rise of online learning and its worthiness during COVID-19 pandemic. "Distance education appeared in some European and American universities in the era that preceded the emergence of the Internet (considering" the Internet as it is known today).

Also in the post-COVID-19 era, Ngugi and Goosen (2022) examined digitalization and drivers of innovative behavior for a smart economy regarding technology student course design characteristics.

Promoting Entrepreneurial Skills in Higher Education

Innovation, entrepreneurship, and sustainability for Information and Communication Technology (ICT) students towards the post-COVID-19 era was the main focus of the chapter by Ngugi and Goosen (2021b).

An academic journal article on education by Du Toit (2024) looked at teacher educators' perceptions regarding entrepreneurship teaching and learning as part of teacher training. Du Toit (2023a) was appraising the *entrepreneurial* mindset of university lecturers in an *international journal* article on *entrepreneurship*, while a journal article in the context of *Research in Educational Policy and Management (REPAM)* by Du Toit (2023b) considered *entrepreneurial* learning and creating value toward social justice. Finally, a chapter by Du Toit (2022) discussed transforming higher education for self-directed employment as part of a book on *recalibrating teacher training in African higher education institutions* with *a focus on 21st-century pedagogical challenges*.

Exploring "the effect of Corporate Entrepreneurship (CE) on" the "financial performance of manufacturing firms in developing countries" and using "a sample of two hundred manufacturing firms (n = 200) in Kenya", an *international journal* article on *academic research in business and social sciences* by Lwamba, Bwisa and Sakwa (2014, p. 352) hypothesized around evidence from Kenyan manufacturing firms.

SOLUTIONS AND RECOMMENDATIONS

This section of the chapter will discuss solutions and recommendations in dealing with the issues, challenges or problems presented in the preceding section.

Independent Measures

The four-latent variables of the study contained 88 Likert scale question items, that respondents were requested to answer, categorized into four (4) Likert scales. The study reported on the journal article by Garland (1991, p. 66) "examined the effect on survey results of having no neutral or mid-point on a Likert scale." Some of the participants "in a face-to-face omnibus survey were shown" a five-point scale (with a mid-point on the rating scale) and asked about how desirable this was.

The greatest methodological concern and challenge was on how to increase the response rate of the respondents by a meticulous examination of the questionnaire length and the total time required to answer the items.

In terms of the effects of questionnaire length on participation and indicators of response quality in a web survey, the *public opinion quarterly* journal article by Galesic and Bosnjak (2009, p. 349) investigated "how expected and actual questionnaire length" affected "cooperation rates and a variety of indicators of data quality in web surveys."

To make the questionnaire acceptable to the respondents and retain all the exogenous and endogenous constructs, as well as have an acceptable time to fill the questionnaire; some scales were shortened, while others were designed to have a specified reduced number of items, in comparison with the full-scale measures.

A scale reduction analysis was used to generate the inter-item total correlations, and the Cronbach alpha reliability coefficients as presented in the conference paper by Goosen and Ngugi (2019b). The latter further reported on the items deleted, based on the reliability scores.

The final items were selected based on content and face validity, as well as items highlighted by the low and negative scores of the item-to-total correlation scores. This had the effect of increasing the quality of responses and the completion of items significantly. Furthermore, the questionnaire items were presented on two A4 size papers that were printed on both sides so as not to intimidate the respondents.

Principles and best practices as suggested by Garson (2004) were also implemented.

Accuracy of Input

Out of Range Values

With regard to the accuracy of input and *out of range values*, Goosen and Ngugi (2018; 2019b), as well as Ngugi and Goosen (2021a), can be consulted for more details. In terms of bootstrapping and other resampling plans, Efron (1982) was of use during the empirical part of the study.

Convergent Validity

Convergent validity was also mentioned in Ngugi and Goosen (2021a).

Convergent validity provided an indication of how well the measures do measure the constructs, by testing the factor loading and the Average Variance Extracted (AVE) and based on recommended levels suggested by Hair, Black, Babin, Anderson and Tatham (2006). Since the AVE values ranged from 0.344 to 0.55 and the factor loading values were greater than, or equal to, 0.5, this was evidence of that the measures have average convergent validity.

Common Method Bias Assessment

As suggested by Podsakoff and Organ (1986), the use of self-reported measures in data collection, required a control for potential common method variance, which is the divergence between observed and true relationships among constructs (Doty & Glick, 1998). Therefore, questions were worded and ordered with the goal of minimizing the risk of common method bias. This was particularly important since the questionnaires involved soliciting more than one response from the same respondent, using a self -reported questionnaire (Podsakoff & Organ, 1986).

The testing for common method bias applied the Harman one-factor test (Scott & Bruce, 1994); Konrad & Linnehan, 1995; (Simonin, 2004). This test consisted of performing an EFA of principal components using the entire set of questionnaire items in the Likert scale. Following the suggestion by Podsakoff and Organ (1986),

Harman's one-factor test was applied and results of the unrotated factor solution were as presented in *Table 1*.

Table 1. Partial results of Harman's one-factor test of total variance explained using unrotated factor analysis

Component	Initial Eigenvalues			Extraction Sums of Squared Loadings		
	Total	% of Variance	Cumulative %	Total	% of Variance	Cumulative %
1	13.166	22.700	22.700	13.166	22.700	22.700
2	4.354	7.506	30.207	4.354	7.506	30.207
3	2.769	4.774	34.981	2.769	4.774	34.981
4	2.314	3.989	38.970	2.314	3.989	38.970
5	1.848	3.186	42.156	1.848	3.186	42.156
6	1.804	3.110	45.266	1.804	3.110	45.266
7	1.535	2.647	47.913	1.535	2.647	47.913
8	1.474	2.542	50.455	1.474	2.542	50.455
9	1.436	2.476	52.931	1.436	2.476	52.931
10	1.316	2.269	55.200	1.316	2.269	55.200
11	1.235	2.129	57.329	1.235	2.129	57.329
12	1.216	2.097	59.426	1.216	2.097	59.426
13	1.130	1.948	61.374	1.130	1.948	61.374
14	1.073	1.851	63.225	1.073	1.851	63.225
15	1.049	1.809	65.033	1.049	1.809	65.033
16	1.005	1.733	66.766	1.005	1.733	66.766
17	0.926	1.597	68.363			
18	0.914	1.576	69.939			
19	0.878	1.515	71.454			
20	0.848	1.462	72.916			
21	0.842	1.451	74.367			
22	0.823	1.418	75.785			
23	0.771	1.329	77.114			
24	0.743	1.280	78.394			
25	0.685	1.181	79.576			
26	0.681	1.174	80.750			
27	0.617	1.063	81.813			
28	0.596	1.027	82.840			
29	0.576	0.993	83.833			

continued on following page

Table 1. Continued

Component	Initial Eigenvalues			Extraction Sums of Squared Loadings		
	Total	% of Variance	Cumulative %	Total	% of Variance	Cumulative %
30	0.558	0.961	84.794			
…*						
54	0.195	0.337	99.145			
55	0.178	0.306	99.452			
56	0.173	0.299	99.751			
57	0.145	0.249	100.000			
58	-3.008E-016	-5.186E-016	100.000			

Extraction method: Principle component analysis.
* Table truncated as indicated.

In the context of common methods bias, the journal article on *organizational research methods* by Doty and Glick (1998, p. 374) asked whether common methods variance really bias results? It "focused on the prevalence of common methods variance and" ignored common methods bias. The latter article also assessed "the level of common methods bias in all" multi-trait-multimethod "correlation matrices published over a 12-year period".

Addressing Gender Disparities in Leadership Positions

An *academy of management journal* article by Konrad and Linnehan (1995, p. 787) asked whether "formalized human resources management (HRM) structures" were coordinating and/or promoting the "goals of equal employment opportunity and affirmative action or" concealing organizational practices, which "symbolize good faith in the absence of real change?" The latter authors "examined the antecedents and outcomes of formalized HRM structures".

FUTURE RESEARCH DIRECTIONS

This section of the chapter will discuss future and emerging trends, as well as provide insights about the future of the theme of the book on Insights into International Higher Education Leadership and the Skills Gap from the perspective of the chapter focus on Insights into Cultivating Creativity and Innovation in Kenyan Higher Education in terms of Implications for Leadership About the Skills Gap. The viability of a paradigm, model, implementation issues of proposed programs, etc., may be included in this section. If appropriate, this section will suggest future research directions within the domain of the topic.

The Future of Higher Education Leadership: Emerging Trends and Predictions

In an overview of emerging trends, Kayyali (2023c, p. 301) indicated that traditional "institutions are now up against fresh competition from virtual universities as the world gets more digital. Higher education is now more widely available thanks to" the latter.

Future research directions with regard to the *implications for university management* were also discussed in Ngugi and Goosen (2021a).

Adapting Curriculum to Address Emerging Trends Regarding Global Skills

Shaping propitious African futures through e-learning, the chapter by Truter and Du Toit (2024, p. 194) presented "an examination of how universities, particularly the University of South Africa, adapt to remain relevant and inclusive, with" *Global Perspectives on Decolonizing Postgraduate Education* in Africa.

Du Toit (2023c) discussed *entrepreneurial* learning as curriculum innovation toward bridging the theory–practice divide when preparing future 'super teachers' in a chapter as part of a book on *innovative curriculum design in work-integrated learning to foster self-directed learning*.

CONCLUSION

This section of the chapter will provide a discussion of the overall coverage of the chapter and concluding remarks.

The study reported on in this chapter found that KSB had a significant direct effect on the IIB. Hence, the study reveals that both CDC and SRL have a significant positive indirect effect on innovative behavior. The study thus contributes to KSB and innovative behavior literature by examining the mediating mechanisms through which both CDC and SRL ultimately influence innovative behavior. More lately, a few studies have emerged on the mediating effect of KSB on the IIB.

REFERENCES

Ansu-Kyeremeh, E. K., & Goosen, L. (2022). Exploring the Socioeconomic Facet of Online Inclusive Education in Ghana: The Effects of Technological Advancement in Academia. In Garcia, M. (Ed.), *Socioeconomic Inclusion During an Era of Online Education* (pp. 47–66). IGI Global., DOI: 10.4018/978-1-6684-4364-4.ch003

Branch, J. D., & Christiansen, B. (Eds.). (2021). *The Marketisation of Higher Education: Concepts, Cases, and Criticisms.* Springer Nature. Retrieved from https://link.springer.com/book/10.1007/978-3-030-67441-0#about-this-book

Christiansen, B., & Even, A. M. (Eds.). (2024). *Prioritizing Skills Development for Student Employability.* IGI Global., Retrieved from https://www.igi-global.com/book/prioritizing-skills-development-student-employability/336289 DOI: 10.4018/979-8-3693-3571-0

Coelho, F., & Augusto, M. (2010). Job characteristics and the creativity of frontline service employees. *Journal of Service Research*, 13(4), 426–438. DOI: 10.1177/1094670510369379

De Jong, J. P., & Den Hartog, D. N. (2010). Measuring innovative work behaviour. *Creativity and Innovation Management*, 19(1), 23–36. DOI: 10.1111/j.1467-8691.2010.00547.x

Dillon, S. M. (2000). *Defining Decision Problem Structuring: Synthesising Existing Literature.* Department of Management Systems, University of Waikato.

Doty, D. H., & Glick, W. H. (1998). Common methods bias: Does common methods variance really bias results? *Organizational Research Methods*, 1(4), 374–406. DOI: 10.1177/109442819814002

Du Toit, A. (2022). Transforming higher education for self-directed employment. In S. Sibanda, D. Van Tonder, & W. Dudu (Eds.), *Recalibrating teacher training in African higher education institutions: A focus on 21st-century pedagogical challenges* (pp. 63-85). Cape Town: AOSIS. DOI: 10.4102/aosis.2022.BK378.04

Du Toit, A. (2023a). Appraising the entrepreneurial mindset of university lecturers. *International Journal of Entrepreneurship, 27*(Special Issue 1), 1-16.

Du Toit, A. (2023b). Entrepreneurial Learning: Creating Value towards Social Justice. *Research in Educational Policy and Management*, 5(3), 1–19. DOI: 10.46303/repam.2023.18

Du Toit, A. (2023c). Entrepreneurial learning as curriculum innovation toward bridging the theory–practice divide when preparing future 'super teachers. In du Toit, A., Petersen, N., de Beer, J., Mentz, E., Bunt, B. J., White, L., & Balfour, R. J. (Eds.), *Innovative curriculum design: Bridging the theory–practice divide in work-integrated learning to foster Self-Directed Learning* (pp. 119–144). AOSIS. DOI: 10.4102/aosis.2023.BK426.06

Du Toit, A. (2024). Onderwysdosente se opvattings oor entrepreneurskapsonderrig en –leer as deel van onderwysersopleiding (Teacher educators' perceptions regarding entrepreneurship teaching- and learning as part of teacher training). *LitNet Akademies (Opvoedkunde)*, 21(2). Advance online publication. DOI: 10.56273/1995-5928/2024/j21n2d1

Efron, B. (1982). *The jackknife, the bootstrap and other resampling plans.* Retrieved February 9, 2015, from https://epubs.siam.org/doi/pdf/10.1137/1.9781611970319.fm

Even, A. M., & Christiansen, B. (Eds.). (2023). *Enhancing Employee Engagement and Productivity in the Post-Pandemic Multigenerational Workforce*. IGI Global., Retrieved from https://www.igi-global.com/book/enhancing-employee-engagement-productivity-post/318087 DOI: 10.4018/978-1-6684-9172-0

Even, A. M., & Christiansen, B. (Eds.). (2024). *Effective Human Resources Management in the Multigenerational Workplace*. IGI Global., Retrieved from https://www.igi-global.com/book/effective-human-resources-management-multigenerational/331799

Galesic, M., & Bosnjak, M. (2009). Effects of questionnaire length on participation and indicators of response quality in a web survey. *Public Opinion Quarterly*, 73(2), 349–360. DOI: 10.1093/poq/nfp031

Garland, R. (1991). The mid-point on a rating scale: Is it desirable. *Marketing Bulletin*, 2(1), 66–70.

Garson, G. D. (2004). The promise of digital government. In *Digital government: Principles and best practices* (pp. 2–15). IGI Global. DOI: 10.4018/978-1-59140-122-3.ch001

Goosen, L., & Ngugi, J. K. (2018). Rethinking Teaching and Learning in the 21st Century: Course Design Characteristics towards Innovative Behaviour. In M. M. Dichaba, & M. A. Sotayo (Ed.), *Proceedings of the South Africa International Conference on Education* (pp. 376 - 394). Pretoria: African Academic Research Forum.

Goosen, L., & Ngugi, J. K. (2019a). Innovation for Computing Students Matter, of Course! In Tait, B. L., & Kroeze, J. H. (Eds.), *Proceedings of 48th Annual Conference of the Southern African Computer Lecturers' Association (SACLA 2019)* (pp. 19–36). University of South Africa., Retrieved from http://osprey.unisa.ac.za/sacla2019/SACLA2019%20Proceedings.pdf#page=31

Goosen, L., & Ngugi, J. K. (2019b). Towards Innovative Behaviour For Technology Students. In J. Kriek, A. Ferreira, K. Padayachee, S. Van Putten, D. Mogashana, W. Raucher, . . . M. Speight Vaughn (Ed.), *Proceedings of the 10th Institute of Science and Technology Education (ISTE) International Conference on Mathematics, Science and Technology Education* (pp. 333 - 342). Mopani Camp, Kruger National Park: UNISA. Retrieved from https://uir.unisa.ac.za/handle/10500/26055

Hair, J. F., Black, W. C., Babin, B. J., Anderson, R. E., & Tatham, R. L. (2006). *Multivariate data analysis* (6th ed.). Pearson Prentice Hall.

Jonassen, D. H. (2000). Toward a design theory of problem solving. *Educational Technology Research and Development*, 48(4), 63–85. DOI: 10.1007/BF02300500

Kayyali, M. (2020a, December). The rise of online learning and its worthiness during COVID-19 pandemic. *International Journal of Information Science and Computing*, 7(2), 63–84. DOI: 10.30954/2348-7437.2.2020.2

Kayyali, M. (2020b, December). Pros and Cons of University Rankings. *International Journal of Management, Sciences, Innovation, and Technology*, 1(1), 4–10.

Kayyali, M. (2020c). Post COVID-19: New era for higher education systems. *International Journal of Applied Science and Engineering*, 8(2), 131–145. DOI: 10.30954/2322-0465.2.2020.6

Kayyali, M. (2021). Positive Impact of High Technology on Higher Education. *International Journal of Information Science and Computing*, 8(1), 13–21.

Kayyali, M. (2022). Internet of Things (IoT): Emphasizing Its Applications and Emergence in Environmental Management—The Profound Cases. In *Environmental Informatics: Challenges and Solutions* (pp. 201–212). Springer Nature. DOI: 10.1007/978-981-19-2083-7_11

Kayyali, M. (2023a). An Overview of Quality Assurance in Higher Education: Concepts and Frameworks. [IJMSIT]. *International Journal of Management, Sciences, Innovation, and Technology*, 4(2). https://ijmsit.com/volume-4-issue-2/

Kayyali, M. (2023b). The Relationship between Rankings and Academic Quality. *International Journal of Management, Sciences, Innovation, and Technology*, 4(3). https://ijmsit.com/volume-4-issue-3/

Kayyali, M. (2023c, June). Virtual Universities: An Overview & Trends. In *Digital Education: Foundation & Emergence with challenges, cases* (pp. 301-326). New Delhi Publishers.

Kayyali, M., & Khosla, A. (2021, June). Globalization and Internationalization: ISO 21001 as a Trigger and Prime Key for Quality Assurance of Higher Education Institutions. *International Journal of Applied Science and Engineering*, 9(1), 67–96. DOI: 10.30954/2322-0465.1.2021.7

Kiratli, N., Rozemeijer, F., Hilken, T., De Ruyter, K., & De Jong, A. (2016). Climate setting in sourcing teams: Developing a measurement scale for team creativity climate. *Journal of Purchasing and Supply Management*, 22(3), 196–204. DOI: 10.1016/j.pursup.2016.04.006

Konrad, A., & Linnehan, F. (1995). Formalized HRM Structures: Coordinating equal employment opportunity or concealing organizational practices? *Academy of Management Journal*, 38(3), 787–820. DOI: 10.2307/256746

Lwamba, N. M., Bwisa, H., & Sakwa, M. (2014). Exploring the effect of corporate entrepreneurship on financial performance of firms: Evidence from Kenya's manufacturing firms. *International Journal of Academic Research in Business & Social Sciences*, 4(1), 352–370.

MacCurtain, S., Flood, P. C., Ramamoorthy, N., West, M. A., & Dawson, J. F. (2010). The top management team, reflexivity, knowledge sharing and new product performance: a study of the Irish software industry. *Creativity and Innovation Management, 19*(3), 219 - 232. doi:. 00564.xDOI: 10.1111/j.1467-8691.2010

Molodchik, M., Krutova, A., & Molodchik, A. (2016). Leadership, learning and organisational culture as antecedents for innovative behaviour: The case of Russia. *International Journal of Learning and Intellectual Capital*, 13(2-3), 202–215. DOI: 10.1504/IJLIC.2016.075700

Molotsi, A. R., & Goosen, L. (2022). Teachers Using Disruptive Methodologies in Teaching and Learning to Foster Learner Skills: Technological, Pedagogical, and Content Knowledge. In Rivera-Trigueros, I., López-Alcarria, A., Ruiz-Padillo, D., Olvera-Lobo, M., & Gutiérrez-Pérez, J. (Eds.), *Handbook of Research on Using Disruptive Methodologies and Game-Based Learning to Foster Transversal Skills* (pp. 1–24). IGI Global., DOI: 10.4018/978-1-7998-8645-7.ch001

Molotsi, A. R., & Goosen, L. (2023). Teachers' Unique Knowledge to Effectively Integrate Digital Technologies Into Teaching and Learning: Community Engagement to Build in the Online Space. In Dennis, M., & Halbert, J. (Eds.), *Community Engagement in the Online Space* (pp. 127–148). IGI Global., DOI: 10.4018/978-1-6684-5190-8.ch007

Ndhlovu-Nemaxwi, N. J., & Goosen, L. (2024). Advancing Student Employability Through Higher Education Using Artificial Intelligence (AI) Applications: Studying Open Distance E-Learning in South Africa. In Christiansen, B., & Even, A. (Eds.), *Prioritizing Skills Development for Student Employability* (pp. 120–141). IGI Global., DOI: 10.4018/979-8-3693-3571-0.ch005

Ngugi, J., & Goosen, L. (2017). The Effects of Course Design Characteristics, Self-Regulated Learning and Knowledge Sharing in Facilitating the Development of Innovative Behaviour among Technology Students at Universities. *Proceedings of the Institute of Science and Technology Education (ISTE)Conference on Mathematics, Science and Technology Education* (pp. 80-86). Mopani Camp, Kruger National Park: UNISA Press.

Ngugi, J., & Goosen, L. (2018). Modelling Course-Design Characteristics, Self-Regulated Learning and the Mediating Effect of Knowledge-Sharing Behavior as Drivers of Individual Innovative Behavior. *Eurasia Journal of Mathematics, Science and Technology Education*, 14(8). Advance online publication. DOI: 10.29333/ejmste/92087

Ngugi, J., & Goosen, L. (2019, October 25). Towards Smart Innovation for Information Systems and Technology Students: Modelling Motivation, Metacognition and Affective Aspects of Learning. (Á. Rocha, & M. Serrhini, Eds.) *Smart Innovation, Systems and Technologies, 111*, 90-99. DOI: 10.1007/978-3-030-03577-8_11

Ngugi, J. K., & Goosen, L. (2021a). Knowledge Sharing Mediating Information Technology Student Innovation. In Khosrow-Pour, M. (Ed.), *Handbook of Research on Modern Educational Technologies, Applications, and Management* (Vol. II, pp. 645–663). IGI Global., DOI: 10.4018/978-1-7998-3476-2.ch040

Ngugi, J. K., & Goosen, L. (2021b). Innovation, Entrepreneurship, and Sustainability for ICT Students Towards the Post-COVID-19 Era. In Carvalho, L. C., Reis, L., & Silveira, C. (Eds.), *Handbook of Research on Entrepreneurship, Innovation, Sustainability, and ICTs in the Post-COVID-19 Era* (pp. 110–131). IGI Global., DOI: 10.4018/978-1-7998-6776-0.ch006

Ngugi, J. K., & Goosen, L. (2021c). Computer Science and Information Technology Students' Self-regulated Learning and Knowledge Sharing Behavior as Drivers of Individual Innovative Behavior. (R. Silhavy, Ed.) *Lecture Notes in Networks and Systems, 230*, 593-608. DOI: 10.1007/978-3-030-77442-4_50

Ngugi, J. K., & Goosen, L. (2022). Digitalization and Drivers of Innovative Behavior for a Smart Economy in the Post-COVID-19 Era: Technology Student Course Design Characteristics. In L. Reis, L. Carvalho, C. Silveira, & D. Brasil (Eds.), *Digitalization as a Driver for Smart Economy in the Post-COVID-19 Era* (pp. 176-197)). IGI Global. DOI: 10.4018/978-1-7998-9227-4.ch010

Ngugi, J. K., & Goosen, L. (2024a). Modelling Mediating Driver Practices That Promote Innovative Behavior for Technology Students: The Effects of Knowledge Sharing Behavior. In Nyberg, J., & Manzone, J. (Eds.), *Practices That Promote Innovation for Talented Students* (pp. 171–196). IGI Global., DOI: 10.4018/978-1-6684-5806-8.ch008

Ngugi, J. K., & Goosen, L. (2024b). Modelling the Mediating Effects of Knowledge Sharing Behavior in the Education Sector: Drivers of Individual Innovative Behavior. In Nadda, V., Tyagi, P., Moniz Vieira, R., & Tyagi, P. (Eds.), *Implementing Sustainable Development Goals in the Service Sector* (pp. 27–52). IGI Global., DOI: 10.4018/979-8-3693-2065-5.ch003

Oyewo, S. A., & Goosen, L. (2024). Relationships Between Teachers' Technological Competency Levels and Self-Regulated Learning Behavior: Investigating Blended Learning Environments. In Pandey, R., Srivastava, N., & Chatterjee, P. (Eds.), *Architecture and Technological Advancements of Education 4.0* (pp. 1–24). IGI Global., DOI: 10.4018/978-1-6684-9285-7.ch001

Paul, P. K., Kayyali, M., Das, M., Chatterjee, R., & Saavedra, R. (2023). Artificial Intelligence and Smart Society: Educational Applications, Emergences and Issues- A Scientific Review. *International Journal of Applied Science and Engineering*, 11(1), 1–14. DOI: 10.30954/2322-0465.1.2023.2

Podsakoff, P. M., & Organ, D. W. (1986). Self-reports in organizational research: Problems and prospects. *Journal of Management*, 12(4), 531–544. DOI: 10.1177/014920638601200408

Republic of Kenya. (2010). *The constitution of Kenya*. National Council for Law Reporting.

Scott, S., & Bruce, R. (1994). Determinant of innovative behaviour: A path model of individual innovation in the workplace. *Academy of Management Journal*, 37(3), 580–607. DOI: 10.2307/256701

Sezerel, H., & Christiansen, B. (Eds.). (2022). *Handbook of research on sustainable tourism and hotel operations in global hypercompetition*. IGI Global., Retrieved from https://www.igi-global.com/book/handbook-research-sustainable-tourism -hotel/291267 DOI: 10.4018/978-1-6684-4645-4

Simonin, B. L. (2004). An empirical investigation of the process of knowledge transfer in international strategic alliances. *Journal of International Business Studies*, 35(5), 407–427. DOI: 10.1057/palgrave.jibs.8400091

Truter, L., & Du Toit, A. (2024). Shaping Propitious African Futures Through E-Learning. In *Global Perspectives on Decolonizing Postgraduate Education* (pp. 194–216). IGI Global. DOI: 10.4018/979-8-3693-1289-6.ch013

West, M. A., & Farr, J. L. (1990). Innovation at work. In West, M. A., & Farr, J. L. (Eds.), *Innovation and creativity at work: Psychological and organizational strategies* (pp. 3–13). Wiley.

Xue, Y., Bradley, J., & Liang, H. (2011). Team climate, empowering leadership, and knowledge sharing. *Journal of Knowledge Management*, 15(2), 299–312. DOI: 10.1108/13673271111119709

Chapter 11
Leadership Perspectives on Talent Management in Saudi Universities:
Challenges and Success Factors

Arun Vijay Subbarayalu
https://orcid.org/0000-0002-5758-118X
Imam Abdulrahman Bin Faisal University, Saudi Arabia

Eshtiaq Abdulaziz Al Faraj
https://orcid.org/0000-0003-4423-1225
Imam Abdulrahman Bin Faisal University, Saudi Arabia

Ahmed Al Kuwaiti
https://orcid.org/0000-0002-0390-1977
Imam Abdulrahman Bin Faisal University, Saudi Arabia

Fahad A. Al-Muhanna
Imam Abdulrahman Bin Faisal University, Saudi Arabia

ABSTRACT

This chapter proposes an in-depth study of higher education leaders (HELs) in Saudi Arabia, with a particular focus on the challenges, obstacles and success factors of talent management (TM) in Saudi universities. A mixed methods study design was adopted in which a general literature review was conducted to uncover the skills gap in the higher education sector and its impact on university leadership, taking into account both the external and internal environments. In addition, a survey would be conducted among a wide range of university leaders, including rectors, vice-rectors, deans, vice-deans and department heads, on the existing TM

DOI: 10.4018/979-8-3693-3443-0.ch011

practices in their respective universities. Through this approach, the authors have uncovered how HELs perceive and deal with the skills gap phenomenon, including the barriers and success factors in TM in their universities, with due consideration of the influence of both external market forces and internal institutional dynamics.

INTRODUCTION

Saudi Arabia is focused on transforming into a knowledge economy, with higher education playing a critical role in this transition. The government has increased education spending, built numerous universities, and sent thousands of students abroad for higher studies and training, demonstrating its commitment to developing human resources for economic prosperity. All higher education institutions (HEIs) in Saudi Arabia are supervised by the Ministry of Higher Education, established in 1975 (Alsunaydi., 2020; Smith & Abouammoh, 2013). Since then, significant reforms have been implemented to improve the quality of education, expand accessibility, and align academic programs with national goals and the labor market. These reforms are part of the Kingdom's national transformation programs and the realization of the Vision 2030 initiatives aimed at reducing dependence on oil revenues by investing in human capital and producing a skilled workforce to contribute to a diverse economy and evolving industries (Hamdan., 2013).

Presently, Ministry of Education (MOE) supervises 29 public and 16 private universities, and 21 private colleges as of 2024. Additionally, it supervises 143 colleges and 98 institutes through the Technical and Vocational Training Corporation, which are spread throughout the Kingdom (Technical and Vocational Training Annual Report., 2023). Public universities are funded by the government and offer various undergraduate and postgraduate programs. On the other hand, private institutions offer more specialized learning opportunities for students who may not have had access to their desired programs at public universities, thereby enriching the variety of educational options available. Moreover, the MOE classifies universities based on their academic programs and industries, which serve to develop niche expertise and address industry needs. For example, public universities like KFUPM focus on engineering, petroleum, minerals, and science, while Imam Abdulrahman bin Faisal University specializes in medicine, nursing, dentistry, architecture, engineering, and humanities. Al Faisal University offers medical, engineering, business, and science specializations, aiming to cultivate leadership and innovation. Princess Nourah bint Abdulrahman University (PNU) specializes in women's education, focusing on art, humanities, and social sciences to empower women. In addition, many Saudi universities have partnered with international institutions to promote exchange programs, collaborative research, and dual-degree offerings. For example, King Abdullah

University of Science and Technology (KAUST) has established research centers for advanced scientific and technological research in collaboration with leading international institutions. This has led to increased publication output in areas aligned with national priorities, such as renewable energy, biotechnology, and information technology, supporting the national agenda of 2030 and the Kingdom's strategic needs. All the Saudi institutions have aligned their priorities with Vision 2030 and established programs to develop the workforce with relevant skills, aiming to increase employment rates among Saudi youth and diversify revenue sources beyond oil.

Skills Gap and its implications for Saudi Universities

Several factors are behind the increased focus on talent management (TM) initiatives the Saudi government took to fill the skills gap among its graduates and employees. As Saudi Arabia (SA) transitions away from its reliance on oil towards other industries, a significant issue of talent scarcity has arisen as a critical obstacle confronting Saudi organizations in their pursuit of successful operations on a global scale. In the process of diversifying its economy beyond oil and focusing on various sectors, there is a pressing requirement to cultivate a proficient and economical workforce spanning different industries by addressing the existing disparity between demand and supply through a continuous supply of efficient and skilled workers (Alnowibet et al., 2021; City & Guilds Group research project, 2020). In addition, the strategy of Saudization, which entails substituting foreign labor with Saudi citizens, is a key driver necessitating improved Talent Management (Alanazi A, 2018). In light of this, the Saudi government views human capital as crucial for enhancing organizational performance and effectiveness. Efforts are being made to attract and retain talented employees within the country by implementing effective talent management practices. The increase in the number of HEIs has resulted in a higher intake of students. As a result, educators are facing increased teaching responsibilities including larger class sizes, more grading, and heightened teaching obligations (Muramalla & Alotaibi, 2019). Additionally, they extra workload on overseeing research projects, providing guidance and academic support, handling administrative duties, and engaging with the community (Jenkins, 2022). As a result, the significant drift of the nation's best academics to high-paying industry positions leads to insufficient talent (Smith & Abouammoh, 2013) and a skills gap.

Importance of Talent Management (TM) practices

TM is a comprehensive process encompassing planning, recruiting, developing, managing, and compensating employees, all aligning with the institution's strategic objectives (Ramaditya et al., 2022). Realizing the significance of talent management practices, both public and private Saudi universities engage in enhancing the skills of their stakeholders (Alanazi, 2022). In the past decade, strategic talent management and agile leadership have transformed higher education in Saudi Arabia in response to the digital age and the 4.0 industrial revolution, aiming to enhance competitiveness across various sectors, including universities and colleges (Singh & Alhabbas, 2024). This approach enhances organizational perspectives by maintaining a talent pipeline aligned with strategic goals and the Saudi Vision 2030 (Aseeri & Kang, 2023). Saudi university administrators also stress the importance of aligning curricula and providing training for faculty and staff to meet the changing job market demands during Vision 2030's digital transformation. (Singh & Alhabbas, 2024). Such an approach of aligning faculty and student skills development with industry demands and investing in faculty development and training to keep them up-to-date with knowledge is a critical issue that requires immediate attention in Saudi Arabian educational institutions (Profanter, 2017).

On the other hand, as a part of TM initiatives, the Saudi government has taken several initiatives to improve leadership skills among Saudi university leaders. In 2009, the Ministry of Higher Education (MoHE) established the Academic Leadership Center (ALC), which directs the development and training of academic leaders in Saudi universities. The KAUST Saudi Leadership Institute (KSLI) Executive Leadership Program aims to empower aspiring Saudi leaders from various institutions within Saudi Arabia (Saudi Arabia's Top Academic Leaders Converge at KAUST Saudi Leadership Institute, 2024). It seeks to develop visionary leaders to drive Vision 2030's transformational goals, foster collaboration across academia, ignite innovation, solidify Saudi Arabia's role as a knowledge hub, and enhance national and international collaboration in research and education. Unlike other prominent Saudi universities with established leadership centers to develop, attract, and retain talented leaders, the KSLI Executive Leadership Program distinguishes itself by empowering leaders from other institutions across the Kingdom. In contrast, the King Abdulaziz University (KAU) Leadership Program employs a unique coaching approach to attract, develop, and retain talented leaders (Tayeb et al., 2016). Meanwhile, the Leadership Center at Imam Abdulrahman bin Faisal University focuses on identifying potential leaders and enrolling them in tailored hands-on programs that discuss contemporary issues and innovation associated with various industries. These programs align personal strategies with institutional goals in line with Vision 2030. They integrate participants into the digital transformation process and business models to transform their mindset toward talented management and agile leadership.

Although the Saudi government has taken various initiatives, there is a need for more research on the perspectives of leaders and administrators in the higher education sector regarding the implementation of talent management practices in Saudi universities. This chapter aims to gather insights from leaders of Saudi universities about talent management practices, as well as the challenges, obstacles, and success factors for their effective implementation to address this gap in research.

METHODOLOGY

Study Design

This study was conducted as part of a larger research project and carried out in two phases with two different study designs. In the first phase, the authors examined Ministry of Education regulations, various universities' websites, and other online websites to understand Saudi universities' existing leadership structure and skills gap. Following this, a thorough exploration of the literature was also carried out to study the talent management practices in Saudi universities and develop an exclusive tool to capture the views of university leaders, the challenges and obstacles they faced, and the success factors associated with TM Practices in Saudi HEIs. In the second phase, the authors utilized the Talent Management Questionnaire (TMQ) to collect feedback from individuals who hold various management positions and manage employees' talents in their universities in Saudi Arabia. Accordingly, this study covers all five major categories of higher administrators working in Saudi universities: rectors, vice-rectors, deans, vice deans, program heads, and other senior staff of human resources deanship/directorates. The authors employed a unique purposive sampling approach, recruiting samples from all five categories of leadership positions in Saudi Arabia. This approach, described by Cooper and Schindler (2003), is valid when it accurately represents the characteristics of the entire population being assessed. The study used a non-probabilistic, chain-referral sample obtained through the snowball sampling method (Creswell, 2012), which is a specific form of purposive sampling. The investigator leveraged personal connections and commenced with a convenience sample of initial participants. These initial participants served as a starting point from which the first wave of participants was enlisted. Subsequently, wave one participants recruited wave two participants, leading to a gradual wave by wave, like a snowball growing in size as it spins down a hill (Goodman, 2011). This method proves to be an efficient approach for studying a sample population without the need for sophisticated software tools. Since the exact number of leadership positions in Saudi universities is unknown, the authors targeted 250, covering all categories of leadership positions employed in Saudi universities; 184 completed questionnaires were received, demonstrating a response rate of 74% (Table 1).

Overview of Talent Management Questionnaire.

The authors adopted the content-validated TMQ tool (Subbarayalu et al., 2024). which comprises 38 items that reveal four dimensions of TM as perceived by leaders of various Saudi universities. Besides demographic variables, leaders' perception of the TM Processes with specific reference to how Saudi universities identify critical job positions (ICJP), talent acquisition practices (TAP), competency training (CT) offered to academics and other staff, talent development (TD) activities, and rewards management (RM) practices exist in Saudi universities. Further, it seeks the opinion of leaders about the challenges and obstacles they face in managing required talents in their universities. Furthermore, it brings out the perception of Saudi university leaders about talent decision-making processes, which they adopt with a specific reference to decision-making style and final authority for making talent in their respective Saudi universities. Lastly, this study uncovered the leader's perception of the impact of the internal and external environments on talent management practices in Saudi universities. A global item has been added to the TMQ to study the overall opinion of Saudi leaders regarding the effectiveness of TM practices in their institutions. All the above items in the questionnaire were recorded using a five-point Likert-scale [(1) Strongly disagree, (2) Disagree, (3) Neither agree nor disagree, (4) Agree, and (5) Strongly Agree]. In addition to these Likert scale items, the participating leaders were asked to choose the most significant challenges, obstacles, and success factors in Talent Management, and the responses are captured through a check box where more than one option can be selected.

Data collection procedures

The authors have prepared a list of leaders in each category working across different Saudi universities to prepare a sampling lot. Efforts have been taken to cover a wider distribution of samples, including universities located in each of the provinces of Saudi Arabia. Specifically, the authors target leaders of Saudi universities working at various levels viz. (i) University level (University Rectors/Vice-Rectors), (ii) College level (Dean of the College/Vice Deans, (iii) Academic Program level (Program Chairs), and (iv) Human Resources (HR) personnel including deans and other HR personnel holding administrative positions. After finalizing the sampling lot, the authors validated the samples' details to ensure the accuracy of their email IDs. Before distributing the questionnaire, the authors obtained consent from the participants to ensure their willingness to participate in the study. Upon finalization of the sampling lot, the samples' details were validated to ensure the correctness of their email ID. Before distributing the questionnaire, the consent of the participants was obtained to ensure whether they were willing to participate in the study. The

TMQ survey was distributed via email using a "QuestionPro" link to potential participants. The survey ensured anonymity and did not gather any personal information. This study was approved by the institutional review board of Imam Abdulrahman Bin Faisal University. (IRB-2023-20-180).

Analytical Methods

Leaders' perspectives concerning various dimensions of TM, such as ICJP, TAP, CT, TD activities, RM, and talent decision-making processes, were analyzed using a simple percentage technique based on their responses to each item in the TMQ questionnaire. Participants' responses to each item were measured based on the options they selected, which were either 4 or 5 on the Likert scale. This cumulative percentage of those who chose 4 or 5 on the Likert scale was used to determine their approval rating for TM practices. Furthermore, this study delves into the most prominent challenges, obstacles, and success factors in Talent Management. The frequency of participants' choices was measured and ranked in ascending order of importance, shedding light on the key issues that leaders in Saudi universities face in managing talent effectively. The demographic details of those who participated in this study are shown in Table 1.

Table 1. Demographic details of the participants

#	Items (N=184)	N (%)
1	**What is your gender?**	
	Male	117(63.6%)
	Female	67(36.4%)
2	Ethnicity (Country of Origin)	
	Saudi	152(82.6%)
	Non-Saudi (Expatriates)	32(17.4%)
3	Your age (unit: years old)	
	Less than 30	1(0.5%)
	31-40	88(47.8%)
	41-50	76(41.3%)
	51-60	17(9.2%)
	More than 61	2(1.1%)
4	**Highest Educational qualification**	
	Diploma	4(2.2%)
	Bachelors' degree	36(19.6%)

continued on following page

Table 1. Continued

#	Items (N=184)	N (%)
	Masters' degree	18(9.8%)
	Doctorate degree (PhD)	125(67.9%)
	Others (Please specify)	1(0.5%)
5	**How long you have been working in this institution?**	
	Below 2 years	5(2.7%)
	02-05 years	35(19%)
	06-10 years	66(35.9%)
	11-15 years	42(22.8%)
	Over 15 years	36(19.6%)
6	**Choose the type of the higher education sector you work (i.e., Currently employed)**	
	Public Sector	162(88%)
	Private Sector	22(12%
7	**Higher Education Professionals**	
	University Rectors/Vice Rectors	18(9.8%)
	Dean of the College/Dean of Human Resources	22(12%)
	Vice Deans	38(20.7%)
	HR Department Staff (including Managers of HR)	40(21.7%)
	Head of the Academic Program (Program Chair)	66(35.9%)
	Total	184(100%)

ANALYSIS OF STORIES

Leadership Structure in Saudi Universities

The organizational structures in Saudi universities and colleges exhibit considerable administrative similarities. Nevertheless, the duties and authorities assigned to rectors, vice-rectors, deans, vice deans, and department heads may vary across institutions, influenced by individual university policies, size, mission, governance framework, and strategic priorities outlined by governing bodies or institutional councils. Rectors typically oversee strategic planning, decision-making, and leadership related to faculty recruitment, budget allocation, and policy enforcement. The vice-rector supports the rector in administrative, financial, academic, student affairs, and research tasks. Deans oversee the management of each college, including academic programs, college budgets, research funds, and faculty recruitment and promotion. Similarly, vice deans are responsible for academic affairs, research, faculty development, and building partnerships with industry and the community. Department heads oversee faculty and curriculum, manage student evaluations, and offer administrative support to vice deans.

Saudi university leader's perceptions of TM practices

The study's findings indicate that 68% of those occupying various leadership positions in Saudi universities believe their university is successfully identifying critical job positions needed for various colleges, academic programs, and supportive deanships. Only 47% believe their university has a mechanism for identifying prospective academic and administrative staff, and 54% agree there is a talent pool for selecting academics to play teaching and other administrative roles. Additionally, 63% of those occupying leadership positions believe their university has a clear job description for all the academic and administrative positions that help them carry out their job effectively.

It's interesting that only 49% of the leaders surveyed felt that their university utilized different communication channels to advertise and attract suitable candidates for academic and administrative positions. A higher percentage, 69%, believed that their university had a formal talent acquisition process. Additionally, 66% of the respondents agreed that all academic and administrative staff were evaluated based on their skills and experience, and 60% felt that talent selection at their respective universities was fair and objective.

Regarding skills development, 74% of the participants support that training programs are offered to improve those competencies needed for the job, while 60% felt that training is focused on critical tasks. Even though 64% of participants felt that the training activities develop domain-specific skills and knowledge for academic and administrative staff, only 53% agreed that the content of these training activities is based on job performance. Sixty percent of the participants agreed that their university regularly organizes internal knowledge-sharing events and encourages social learning outside its premises.

Regarding talent development, only 55% of respondents expressed that their future development needs are properly identified. 66% of those participating leaders felt their university provided equal access to learning and development opportunities. Additionally, 53% of participants felt there were many career opportunities for academic and administrative staff to advance within the university. On the contrary, only 50% of the participating leaders agreed that a long-term opportunity for growth and professional development of academic and administrative staff exists in their university that motivates them to stay. Over 63% of participants confirmed that they receive feedback on their work performance from their supervisors, and they provide similar feedback to their team members to achieve their full potential.

While examining rewards management practices, only 49% of participating leaders perceive that their academic and administrative staff have a balanced lifestyle while employed at Saudi universities. Interestingly, 64% of the participating leaders agreed upon providing non-financial rewards; however, only 40% said financial rewards to recognize talented employees in their respective universities, and 37% felt that it was fair and provided on time. Notably, 60% of the participants agreed that their university appreciates their work/contribution; however, only 47% expressed satisfaction with their competitive pay package, considering the salary.

Saudi university leader's perceptions on talent decision-making processes.

The decision-making process among Saudi university leaders is a complex interplay of cultural, organizational, and individual factors that influence their perceptions. Of those holding various leadership positions in Saudi universities who took part in the study, 88% pursue advice and consultation from experts when making vital decisions, and 90% constantly review other sources of information to get the correct facts. On the other hand, 75% of participating leaders make decisions intuitively. Interestingly, 50% of the participants use the performance appraisal process to make the right decision to identify talented employees, and only 46% thought that the institution's performance appraisal process was proper and effective enough to make the right decision while recognizing talented employees. Likewise, only 44% of participants agreed that the talent decision processes used by their institution for employee evaluation were fair.

Impact of the internal and external environment on TM practices.

The investigation into the effects of the internal environment has unveiled noteworthy revelations. Most participating leaders (58%) indicated that their university maintains a well-organized and transparent framework, allowing all employees, whether academic or administrative, regardless of ethnicity, gender, or nationality, to advance in their professional journey. Furthermore, 67% of respondents concurred that their university attracts and leverages the abilities of the most skilled individuals, irrespective of their social networks. Nevertheless, despite these favorable elements, 38% of the leaders surveyed perceived that the concept of 'waste' contributes positively to the retention and motivation of talented staff.

Regarding the influence of the external environment, 48% of respondents have conveyed apprehension about the discrepancy between educational outputs and the job market demands in the country, which has a notable impact on the talent management practices at their universities. Another significant finding is that 53% of the participating leaders believe that governmental policies and regulations do not adequately support the development of skilled personnel. This perception underscores the need for policy reform to address the talent management challenges that universities face in Saudi Arabia. In comparison, 64% have indicated that the current economic circumstances are not conducive to recruiting and retaining the most talented staff in their universities.

The challenges, obstacles, and success factors of TM in Saudi universities.

Among those most significant challenges studied, the authors ranked them in the order of frequency as chosen by the participating leaders, and the top five challenges and barriers commonly perceived by the participating leaders are listed: (i) Lack of suitable motivational approach to attract talent (n=61); (ii) Lack of strategic alignment between human resource (HR) strategies and the overall organizational strategies (n=55); (iii) Poorly implemented performance management system (n=52) and (iv) Economic sanctions and lack of budget (n=48) and, (v) Lack of strategic perspective to human resources (n=44). Likewise, the top five important success factors for the effective implementation of talent management practices are (i) an active human resource department that implements human capital programs (n=53), (ii) the existence of an integrated talent management program and talent management as a strategic priority (n=47); (iii) Effective Organizational structure and hierarchy (n=41); (iv) Effective Performance management system based on TM process (n=40) and (v) Keeping the organization from direct intervention of the government and external pressures on hiring and appointments (n=37).

DISCUSSION OF FINDINGS

Leaders' perspectives of TM practices in Saudi Universities

Saudi Arabia keenly focuses on developing its human capital, with education playing a vital role in its progress and global competitiveness, where the significance of talent management practices is becoming increasingly evident (Yusuf & Jamjoom, 2022). Leaders of Saudi HEIs not only understand the importance of talent management practices as a critical element for the success and continuity of their institutions but also envision the potential benefits of implementing effective talent management strategies (Akbar et al., 2023; Kodai & Alzobeer, 2023). However, less than 50% of participating higher education leaders believe their university has a mechanism for identifying talented academic and administrative staff.

One of the critical aspects of talent management practices is identifying key job positions that align with the sustainable objectives of Saudi Vision 2030 (Alshaikhmubarak et al., 2020; Hilman & Abubakar, 2017). In line with these findings, our study reveals that 68% of those occupying various leadership positions in Saudi universities believe their university identified critical job positions needed for various colleges, academic programs, and supportive deanships. However, an earlier study revealed that identifying critical job positions in HEIs would be a tough job to execute as it is governed by the uniform regulations of the Ministry (Al Jalfan., 2019). Yet, the findings of this study reveal that 54% of the participants agreed that there is a talent pool (TP) for selecting academics to play both teaching and administrative roles. TPs are mainly described as a pool of employees with high potential and performance (Jooss et al., 2019). This system is very limited in Saudi universities, possibly because there is a lack of differentiation in the skills required to perform academic job functions. These functions are generally based on the candidates' terminal educational qualifications and experience in a specific job.

Another noteworthy observation is that most of the participating leaders (63%) perceive that their university has a clear job description for all the job positions as the ministry of education governs it, and it is one of the eligibility criteria to get institutional accreditation. In practice, every Saudi university has a job description manual for each academic and administrative positions, including those with various leadership roles. This manual, which provides a detailed outline of the responsibilities, qualifications, and expectations for each position, is very well disseminated to all the faculty members. This ensures that the talent management process is based on a clear understanding of the job requirements, contributing to the effective acquisition and development of talent.

Next, this study examines the leaders' perspectives on the talent acquisition practices adopted at Saudi universities. Saudi Arabian universities focus on strategically recruiting highly qualified faculty and staff (Qawasmeh et al., 2024). Every Saudi university has a recruitment committee directly hires the required talent (Al Jalfan, 2019). Half of the participating leaders (49%) expressed that their university has a formal talent acquisition process. It functions under the umbrella of the directorate of the human resources department, and it establishes a transparent formal recruitment process for Saudi and non-Saudi nationals. In the event of filling vacant positions, the details of those vacancies are advertised both inside and outside Saudi Arabia, and vacant positions are posted on the university website, as 49% of the participating leaders in this study confirmed the existence of such practice in Saudi universities. The committee first checks for the availability of local talent. The committee usually hires from outside the country when the required expertise is not available among

Saudi nationals. This practice is also backed by a previous study that suggests that working with international academic networks and conducting recruitment drives can bring diverse expertise to Saudi universities, and there is also a focus on aligning recruitment processes with the academic, administrative, and research needs of these universities (Qawasmeh et al., 2024). In cases where employment contracts need to be made with non-Saudis, a recruitment committee usually travels to the country where the prospective candidates reside. The Saudi Cultural Attache coordinates all necessary arrangements, including interviews, selection, and follow-up procedures. This involves verifying candidate credentials, conducting medical exams, arranging visas, and providing travel tickets in line with Ministry of Education regulations. Internal promotions for leadership positions follow approved executive procedures and legal standards. An open nomination for applying for the vacant positions is given, and detailed criteria for each administrative position are advertised on the university website and circulated via email. Selection is based on the outcome of a personnel interview and those who fulfill the requirements, and 60% of the participating leaders expressed their opinion that talent selection in their respective universities is fair and objective.

Regarding academic and administrative staff performance evaluation, 66% of the participants agreed that it is based on their skills and experience. A previous study confirms that performance appraisal systems in Saudi Arabian universities evaluate faculty and other academic staff based on their teaching effectiveness, research contributions, and administrative responsibilities. Regular annual evaluations and feedback sessions are conducted to facilitate communication among faculty, employees, and supervisors, contributing to professional growth and development. (Qawasmeh et al., 2024). In this study, over 63% of participants receive feedback on their work performance from supervisors and provide similar feedback to their team members. This finding reveals that in Saudi Arabian universities, a structured feedback mechanism in the performance appraisal systems helps faculty members receive constructive criticism and praise for their professional development.

Saudi Arabian universities offer a diverse array of training programs focusing on e-learning, technology integration, crisis management, international exposure, and instructional technologies to promote/prioritize continuous professional development among faculty and staff to enhance their skills and capabilities (Al Zebidi., 2020; Algahtani et al., 2020). According to our study, 74% of the participating leaders support that faculty and other employees are exposed to regular training programs to improve the competencies needed for their jobs. Precisely, 60% of the participating leaders felt that training offered in Saudi universities is focused on critical tasks, and 64% expressed training activities develop the domain-specific skills/knowledge of faculty and academic staff. On the contrary, a recent study by Alharbi & Alshahrani (2023) indicated a gap between current training offerings and faculty requirements in Saudi universities. It reemphasized the need for training courses to align with faculty and administrators' professional needs. Thus, Saudi universities must prioritize 21st-century skills training for faculty to address teaching challenges better (Almajed et al., 2017). Such trainings are provided to nurture the growth and professional advancement of faculty and staff, fostering a culture of learning and development. In addition, talent enhancement training of faculty and academic staff in the form of mentorship programs and leadership training is crucial for navigating the challenges of the 21st century (Qawasmeh et al., 2024; Gonaim, 2021).

A more recent study explored the impact of social trust, networks, and shared goals on knowledge-sharing attitudes among Saudi academics and established a positive relationship between social trust, social networks, shared goals, and academic attitudes toward knowledge. Most participating leaders (60%) agreed that their university regularly organizes internal knowledge-sharing events and encourages social learning outside its premises. Several strategies are in place in Saudi universities to promote these internal knowledge-sharing events among its academics, viz. Organizing workshops and seminars to share best practices, research findings, and teaching methods, encouraging academics from different disciplines to collaborate, investing in mentorship programs using digital platforms for knowledge sharing, fostering diverse perspectives and knowledge exchange, and establishing online platforms or physical spaces for academics to interact, share ideas, and collaborate (Kodai et al, 2023; Almuqrin & Mutambik, 2021).

Several practices exist at Saudi universities to identify the future development needs of faculty members. This is carried out through reviewing faculty feedback in the academic job satisfaction surveys, where faculty indicate their satisfaction with the training requirements. Further, there is a student survey of lecturing skills, where each student evaluates the teaching skills of their faculty members, and these findings, along with the students' academic performance, are included in the course and program reports, which are used as input to improve their quality. Any issue of the low performance of students is related to faculty teaching; the program chair usually exposes faculty to future teaching enrichment training programs. In addition, there is the practice of preparing program and course specifications, which help the academic program chair decide upon the actual training requirements of teaching staff related to various teaching methods. Despite these practices, only 55% of respondents expressed that their future development needs are properly identified.

In this study, 53% of participants felt there were many career opportunities for academic and administrative staff to advance within the university. In conformance with this finding, several initiatives have been observed in HEIs in Saudi Arabia. One such initiative is the King Abdullah University of Science and Technology (KAUST), which has recently introduced the National Academic Talent Development Program (NATDP). This initiative unites leaders, faculty, and students from

Saudi universities to enhance education and research through collaborative efforts. This program is designed to cultivate promising individuals from Saudi universities for the future and help them progress in the administrative ladder (KAUST Press Release., 2024).

Moreover, recent changes in the Saudi Arabian education system have significantly impacted the long-term prospects for academic and administrative staff. Firstly, Saudi universities' increased emphasis on quality assurance and pursuit of accreditation demonstrates a commitment to enhancing academic practices and standards, thereby supporting the professional growth of both academic and administrative staff (Omar et al., 2022). Second, adopting modern instructional technologies illustrates Saudi educators' proactive measures to develop professionally and improve teaching efficacy through workshops and seminars (Bin Othayman et al., 2021). Another initiative is the strategic implementation of High-Impact Educational Practices (HIPs) at Northern Border University (NBU), which exemplifies the prioritization of competency-based outcomes to meet workforce needs. This significantly contributes to the professional development of staff by aligning educational outcomes with practical competencies. (Al-Khathlan, 2022). According to this study, 66% of the participating leaders felt that their university provided equal access to learning and development opportunities. Additionally, 50% of them expressed that they believed they had long-term opportunities for growth and professional development, which motivated them to stay for an extended period.

Current rewards management practices in Saudi universities encompass various strategies ranging from monetary and non-monetary incentives to recognition and support (Zeb et al., 2015). Specifically, academic and administrative staff in Saudi universities received various benefits: attractive compensation, free accommodation, education allowance for dependent children, transportation allowance, and end-of-service benefits (Al Kuwaiti et al., 2019). The finding of this study indicates that 64% of the participating leaders agreed that non-financial rewards exist, and only 40% said financial rewards to recognize talented employees in their respective universities. An earlier study on compensation practices in private institutions of higher learning in Saudi Arabia also indicated that compensation, mediated by talent management, is crucial for increasing job satisfaction among faculty members (AbdulCader & Anthony, 2014). As such, an effective reward system, including both extrinsic and intrinsic rewards, is needed to enhance the motivation of both academic and administrative employees (AbdulCalder, 2015).

Talent decision-making processes in Saudi Universities.

Regarding the decision-making style adopted by the leaders of various academic departments, colleges, and universities in Saudi Arabia, 88% seek advice from specialists when faced with crucial decisions, and 90% routinely consult diverse information sources to ensure accuracy. Several factors influence the inclination of Saudi University leaders to solicit advice from various sources when making decisions. The influence of culture is particularly notable, as societal and organizational cultures shape leadership perceptions and behaviors. This results in a dependence on authority and centralized decision-making frameworks, which in turn necessitates the act of seeking advice to effectively navigate these intricate dynamics (Kodai & Alzobeer, 2023; Qahl & Sohaib, 2023). Additionally, there is a growing trend toward collaborative decision-making, with leaders increasingly recognizing the benefits of involving their employees in key decisions to improve satisfaction, drive, and overall productivity. This trend encourages leaders to actively seek input and perspectives from their teams, with team members feeling comfortable expressing their opinions and ideas, fostering a culture of open communication and active participation in decision-making processes (Yusuf, 2023).

Conversely, this study also uncovers that over 75% of participating leaders base their decisions on intuition. An earlier study indicated that experienced leaders are more likely to integrate their intuition with analytical data, leveraging their experiential learning to enhance confidence in their decisions (Alsuhaymi, 2017). Studies have revealed that individuals occupying leadership positions with advanced academic qualifications and a wide range of educational experiences tend to exhibit more thorough and effective strategic decision-making procedures. (Alsharif et al., 2020). Thus, diversity in educational backgrounds is crucial for augmenting the comprehensiveness of strategic decision-making processes, and empowering leaders to switch proficiently between intuitive and logical decision-making approaches (Aldosari, 2020).

The evaluation of employee performance in Saudi Arabian HEIs holds significant importance in identifying skilled staff members through a methodical and structured assessment carried out by the performance appraisal (PA) process (Alharbi, 2018). This particular procedure is indispensable for the fulfilment of organizational goals, and for the enhancement and contentment of staff, thus leading to the overall triumph of the establishment. This performance assessment system is instrumental in identifying employees' performance and developmental needs, which is crucial for making well-informed human resource decisions and promoting a culture of continuous improvement (Davis & Mensah, 2020). It is a routine practice in Saudi universities where all the faculty and academic staff, including the administrative staff, are exposed to such performance appraisal system annually. A previous study indicated that 79.6% of administrators in Saudi Arabia employed performance appraisal systems to recognize skilled employees (Abunar, 2016). Besides the usefulness of performance appraisal processes, half of the participating leaders of Saudi HEIs in this study use such systems to identify talented employees.

Challenges, obstacles, and success factors of TM practices in Saudi Universities.

Challenges and Obstacles

The findings of our study reveal a lack of suitable motivational approach in attracting talent" and "lack of strategic alignment between HR strategies and the overall organizational strategies" as the top two challenges and barriers facing Saudi HEIs as perceived from the voice of participating leaders. Earlier studies also supported our notion that a lack of strategic alignment in HRM processes and the absence of intrinsic and extrinsic motivational factors contribute to the difficulty in attracting and retaining talented faculty (Aldosari., 2020; Shousha, 2018). According to previous research, it has been noted that the primary challenge in Talent Management for numerous institutions is the motivation and retention of talented individuals (Johnson et al., 2005; Beechler et al., 2009). Effectively aligning Talent Management with the current organizational strategies of Human Resource Management and human capital is crucial for maximizing organizational performance and sustainability, as highlighted by Al Jalfan (2019).

The third most identified barrier to TM is the poorly implemented performance management system. Christopher (2020) emphasized the prevalence of insufficient talent management practices in universities characterized by ineffective workforce and succession planning coupled with a substandard performance management system that needs more transparency, objectivity, and alignment with employee rewards and development. These shortcomings may lead to decreased staff motivation, impacting their job satisfaction and productivity, thus resulting in challenges with recruiting and retaining skilled employees (Mntonintshi & Mtembu, 2019). Another significant obstacle discovered in this research pertains to the imposition of economic sanctions and the inadequacy of the budget for talent management initiatives. Previous research has indicated that a lack of sufficient financial resources substantially impedes the efficiency of talent management practices within Saudi universities, resulting in inadequate training and growth prospects for university personnel, a crucial component for successful talent management (Alqahtani & Ayentimi, 2021). The fifth most important challenge revolves around the lack of a strategic approach to human resources, particularly in the areas of talent acquisition and retention. A key issue lies in the significant turnover rate seen among academic staff, a situation worsened by the combination of low job satisfaction and ineffective retention strategies (Jenkins., 2022). This issue is further complicated by the substantial teaching responsibilities carried by faculty members, which impede their participation in training and development initiatives aimed at enhancing their skills and overall job satisfaction (Al Nasser & Jais, 2022).

Success factors of TM practices

The most important success factor of TM practices identified by the participating leaders is the existence of an active human resource department in each Saudi university to implement human capital programs. In line with this finding, it has been observed that Saudi universities are implementing various human capital programs to achieve Vision 2030. These programs focus on global talent recruitment, professional development, and research innovation (Bakheet & Almudara, 2019). The next important success factor is the presence of an integrated talent management program and talent management as a strategic priority, as emphasized by higher education leaders. Several universities in Saudi Arabia have implemented such programs. For example, King Sattam University's talent management strategy focuses on attracting and developing talent, improving the work environment, and ensuring worker safety to maintain high performance and reduce turnover (King Sattam University's Talent Management guide, 2024). Aligning talent management with existing organizational HRM and human capital strategies leads to optimal organizational performance and sustainability (Al Jalfan, 2019).

Moreover, most participants in this study opted for a well-established organizational structure and hierarchy and a robust performance evaluation system as crucial elements for successful talent management practices within Saudi Arabian universities. Each Saudi university has a well-structured organizational hierarchy where different academic and administrative functions are managed effectively. According to the existing practice, all faculty are provided equal opportunities to participate in training and development programs, and each university has a dedicated deanship to regularly expose all faculty to training and development programs according to professional requirements (Al Kuwaiti et al., 2019). Similarly, there is a regular annual performance management system where the direct supervisors evaluate academic and administrative staff using a standard rubric. For instance, the University of Bisha uses the Balanced Scorecard (BSC) model as a strategic performance management tool to translate its vision and strategy into objectives and performance indicators. The BSC incorporates financial and non-financial measures to provide a comprehensive view of the university's performance and specific KPIs are used to monitor faculty performance in teaching, research, service, and professional development. (Sharaf-Addin & Fazel, 2021). Lastly, limited direct intervention of the government and external pressures on hiring and appointments of faculty were chosen as the success factors of TM practices in Saudi Universities. The Ministry of Education in Saudi Arabia has introduced a new university system, promoting greater academic, administrative, and financial independence for three public universities: King Saud University (KSU), King Abdulaziz University (KAU), and Imam Abdulrahman bin Faisal University (IAU) (Ruwayshid Alruwaili., 2020).

The impact of internal and external environments on TM practices.

Most participating leaders (58%) indicated that their university maintains a well-organized and transparent framework, allowing all employees, whether academic or administrative, regardless of ethnicity, gender, or nationality, to advance in their professional journey. In conformance with this finding, an earlier study also stated that a fair and transparent academic promotion methodology was implemented in their respective universities (Subbarayalu & Al Kuwaiti., 2019). All Saudi universities have uniform academic promotion regulations regulated by the MOE. Despite this, 38% of surveyed leaders believe that 'wasta' positively contributes to retaining and motivating talented staff. Al Harbi et al. (2017) also showed that 'wasta' unfairly influences employee performance appraisals. Additionally, Wasta's influence on HR practices affects recruitment, training, development, and compensation. This often leads to employees being hired or promoted based on connections rather than merit. As a result, this can demoralize other employees and have a negative impact on overall engagement and productivity (Al. Harbi et al., 2017).

Regarding the influence of the external environment, 48% of respondents have conveyed apprehension about the discrepancy between educational outputs and the job market demands in the country, which has a notable impact on the talent management practices at their universities. An earlier study also indicated a need for more alignment between university curricula and the practical skills required by employers (Alzghaibi, 2023). Rapid changes in the labor market require higher education institutions to adapt their programs to meet evolving needs, which has been a challenge (Alsughayer & Alsultan, 2023). Further, 53% of the leaders who participated in this study believe that government policies do not adequately support skilled personnel development. Although Saudi Vision 2030 focuses on talented individuals to achieve its goals, talent management programs must align with the institution's strategy to be effective (Al Jalfan, 2019; Saudi Vision 2030, 2019).

The authors uncovered Saudi university leaders' perception of the current economic conditions on TM practices, where 64% indicated that the current circumstances are not conducive to recruiting and retaining the most talented staff in their universities. These include post-COVID-19 pandemic exacerbations on the labor market

(Jenkins, 2022) and the Saudization program, which aims to localize the academic workforce by replacing foreign staff with Saudi nationals. The rapid pace of workforce localization in universities has been unprecedented, posing challenges as academia was not fully prepared for such a sudden shift that impacted its TM practices, especially hiring and retaining a highly skilled workforce (Ahmed, 2016). Therefore, the study recommends that talent management practices in Saudi universities need to be intensified as this contributes to the achievement of Saudi Vision 2030 and directly impacts impact the development of a competent and competitive workforce.

CONCLUSION

The study confirmed that notable TM initiatives are taking place in Saudi universities, and 58% of leaders who participated in this study agreed with them. Most participating leaders confirmed that their universities identify the critical positions needed for various colleges, academic programs, and supporting deanships. A clear job description is provided for all academic and administrative positions to help them do their jobs effectively. Over 60% of leaders confirmed that their university has a formal talent acquisition process and that all academic and administrative staff are selected fairly, objectively and evaluated based on their skills and experience. Although most participating leaders agreed that the training activities developed domain-specific skills/knowledge and improved their job-specific competencies, only half of the participants agreed that the training activities' content needed improvement.

More than half of the participating leaders reported that future development needs were properly identified, and that there were numerous career opportunities for academic and administrative staff to advance within the university. Additionally, Saudi universities have a well-developed performance evaluation system, with 63% of participating leaders receiving feedback from their superiors on their job performance and providing similar contributions to their team members to achieve their full potential. Although non-financial rewards are offered in Saudi universities, around 40% of participating leaders agreed to the existence of financial rewards such as cash prizes and bonuses, and these are limited. Still, only 37% agreed that the cash rewards offered were fair and delivered on time at Saudi universities. Although 60% of leaders confirmed that their university values their work contributions, only 47% expressed satisfaction with the salary scale at Saudi universities.

This study also shows the talent decision-making process that Saudi university leaders use. 88% agreed that they seek expert advice and consultations when making important decisions, and 90% constantly check other sources of information to get the correct facts. However, less than 50% of participating leaders used the performance appraisal process because they believed that the institution's performance appraisal process was appropriate and effective enough to make the right decisions.

The study also highlights the challenges faced by talent management in Saudi universities. Although 58% of participating leaders said their university has a well-structured and transparent system for acquiring and appropriately using employees' skills, 38% felt that Wasta plays a positive role in retaining and motivating talented employees. In addition, 48% felt that there is a mismatch between educational outcomes and the labor market in Saudi Arabia, which directly affects their university. 64% of participating executives expressed concern that current economic conditions are not conducive to recruiting and retaining the most talented workforce. The study also found a lack of an appropriate motivational approach to attract talent, a lack of strategic alignment between HR strategies and the overall organizational strategies, poorly implemented performance management systems and a lack of budget, which were identified as the most common barriers to talent acquisition management practices in Saudi universities.

REFERENCES

AbdulCader, A., & Anthony, P. J. AbdulCader. (2014). Motivational Issues of Faculty in Saudi Arabia. *Higher Learning Research Communications*, 4(4), 76–84. DOI: 10.18870/hlrc.v4i4.211

AbdulCalder, A. (2015). A Synthesized Model of Faculty Motivation in Saudi Arabia's Higher Education Sector. In: Hamdan, A.K. (eds) *Teaching and Learning in Saudi Arabia. Sense Publishers*, Rotterdam. https://doi.org/DOI: 10.1007/978-94-6300-205-9_7

Abunar, M. M. (2016). Factors influencing decision making in internal management: evidence from private sector organisations in Saudi Arabia. [Doctoral dissertation, Brunel Business School, Brunel University, London]. Brunel University Research Archive (BURA). https://bura.brunel.ac.uk/handle/2438/13458

Ahmed, M. A. (2016). The Effects of Saudization on the Universities: Localization in Saudi Arabia. *Industry and Higher Education*, 86(86), 25–27. DOI: 10.6017/ihe.2016.86.9373

Akbar, H., Al-Dajani, H., Ayub, N., & Adeinat, I. (2023). Women's leadership gamut in Saudi Arabia's higher education sector. *Gender, Work and Organization*, 30(5), 1649–1675. DOI: 10.1111/gwao.13003

Al Harbi, S., Thursfield, D., & Bright, D. (2017). Culture, Wasta and perceptions of performance appraisal in Saudi Arabia. *International Journal of Human Resource Management*, 28(19), 2792–2810. DOI: 10.1080/09585192.2016.1138987

Al Jalfan, Z. (2019). Investigating the strategic alignment of talent management and organisation sustainability in the Saudi higher education sector [Doctoral dissertation, Brunel University, London]. Brunel University Research Archive (BURA). https://bura.brunel.ac.uk/handle/2438/19222

Al-Khathlan, M. (2022). Improving Higher Education Administration: A Case Study of Prince Sattam bin Abdulaziz University. *Journal of Educational and Social Research*, 12(4), 104. Advance online publication. DOI: 10.36941/jesr-2022-0100

Al Kuwaiti, A., Bicak, H. A., & Wahass, S. (2019). Factors predicting job satisfaction among faculty members of a Saudi higher education institution. *Journal of Applied Research in Higher Education*, 12(2), 296–310. DOI: 10.1108/JARHE-07-2018-0128

Al Nasser, A. H., & Jais, J. (2022). The Effect of Organizational Culture on Organizational Performance of Saudi Higher Education: The Mediating Role of Human Resource Development. *WSEAS Transactions on Environment and Development*, 18, 777–788. DOI: 10.37394/232015.2022.18.73

Al Zebidi, A. A. (2020). Paths the Saudi Educators in Higher Education Exercise for Professional Development to Use Instructional Technologies. *The Scientific Journal of Faculty of Education in Assiut*, 36(9), 26–53. DOI: 10.21608/mfes.2020.124241

Alanazi, A. (2018). The impact of talent management to achieve sustainable competitive advantage in Saudi Arabia private organizations. *Easy Chair Preprint*. https://easychair.org/publications/preprint_open/VSTf

Alanazi, A. T. (2022). The impact of talent management practices on employees' satisfaction and commitment in the Saudi Arabian oil and gas industry. *International Journal of Advanced and Applied Sciences*, 9(3), 46–55. DOI: 10.21833/ijaas.2022.03.006

Aldosari, S. A. M. (2020). The Method of Selecting Academic Leaders at Emerging Saudi Universities and its Relationship to Some Variables. *International Journal of Higher Education*, 9(4), 69–83. DOI: 10.5430/ijhe.v9n4p69

Algahtani, H., Shirah, B., Alshawwa, L., Tekian, A., & Norcini, J. J. (2020). Factors to be considered in designing a faculty development program for medical education: Local experience from the Western region of Saudi Arabia. *Yeungnam University Journal of Medicine*, 37(3), 210–216. DOI: 10.12701/yujm.2020.00115 PMID: 32311868

Alharbi, O. A., & Alshahrani, R. S. A. (2023). Instructors' Perceptions of the Training Courses Related to Technology in Saudi Universities. *Advances in Social Sciences Research Journal*, 10(2), 241–247. DOI: 10.14738/assrj.102.14002

Alharbi, S. (2018). Criteria for Performance Appraisal in Saudi Arabia, and Employees Interpretation of These Criteria. *International Journal of Business and Management*, 13(9), 106–117. DOI: 10.5539/ijbm.v13n9p106

Almajed, A., Al-Kathiri, F., Al-Ajmi, S., & Alhamlan, S. (2017). 21st Century Professional Skill Training Programs for Faculty Members—A Comparative Study between Virginia Tec University, American University & King Saud University. *Higher Education Studies*, 7(3), 122–131. DOI: 10.5539/hes.v7n3p122

Almuqrin, A., & Mutambik, I. (2021). The explanatory power of social cognitive theory in determining knowledge sharing among Saudi faculty. *PLoS One*, 16(3), e0248275. Advance online publication. DOI: 10.1371/journal.pone.0248275 PMID: 33740001

Alnowibet, K., Abduljabbar, A. S., Ahmad, S., Alqasem, L., Alrajeh, N., Guiso, L., Zaindin, M., & Varanasi, M. (2021). Healthcare Human Resources: Trends and Demand in Saudi Arabia. *Health Care*, 9(8), 955. DOI: 10.3390/healthcare9080955 PMID: 34442091

Alqahtani, M., & Ayentimi, D. T. (2021). The devolvement of HR practices in Saudi Arabian public universities: Exploring tensions and challenges. *Asia-Pacific Management Review*, 26(2), 86–94. DOI: 10.1016/j.apmrv.2020.08.005

Alshaikhmubarak, A., Da Camara, N., & Baruch, Y. (2020). The impact of high-performance human resource practices on the research performance and career success of academics in Saudi Arabia. *Career Development International*, 25(6), 671–690. DOI: 10.1108/CDI-09-2019-0209

Alsharif, M. A., Peters, M., & Dixon, T. (2020). Designing and Implementing Effective Campus Sustainability in Saudi Arabian Universities: An Assessment of Drivers and Barriers in a Rational Choice Theoretical Context. *Sustainability (Basel)*, 12(12), 5096. DOI: 10.3390/su12125096

Alsughayer, S., & Alsultan, N. (2023). Expectations Gap, Market Skills, and Challenges of Accounting Education in Saudi Arabia. *Journal of accounting finance and auditing studies* (JAFAS), 9(1), 22-60. Doi: .DOI: 10.32602/jafas.2023.002

Alsuhaymi, A. A. A. (2017). An assessment of the participatory role of Saudi university academics in organizational decision-making - a single case study. PhD thesis, University of Leeds.

Alsunaydi, R. (2020). The Relationship Between Department Chairs' Leadership Style and Faculty Members' Job Satisfaction in the College of Education at King Saud University in Saudi Arabia. Theses & Dissertations, 381. https://athenaeum.uiw.edu/uiw_etds/381

Alzghaibi, H. A. (2023). The gap between bachelor's degree graduates in health informatics and employer needs in Saudi Arabia. *BMC Medical Education*, 23(1), 475. DOI: 10.1186/s12909-023-04442-7 PMID: 37365545

Aseeri, M. M., & Kang, K. A. (2023). Organisational culture and big data socio-technical systems on strategic decision making: Case of Saudi Arabian higher education. *Education and Information Technologies*, 28(7), 8999–9024. DOI: 10.1007/s10639-022-11500-y

Bakheet, S., & Almudara, M. (2019). Maximizing Return on Investment in the Human Capital of Faculty Members in Saudi Universities. *European Journal of Management*, 19(2), 80–93. DOI: 10.18374/EJM-19-2.7

Beechler, S., Beechler, S., & Woodward, I. C.. (2009). The global "war for talent". 15(3), 273–285. https://doi.org/DOI: 10.1016/j.intman.2009.01.002

Bin Othayman, M., Meshari, A., Mulyata, J., & Debrah, Y. A. (2021). Challenges Experienced by Public Higher Education Institutions of Learning in the Implementation of Training and Development: A Case Study of Saudi Arabian Higher Education. *Journal of Business Administration Research*, 10(2), 36. Advance online publication. DOI: 10.5430/jbar.v10n2p36

Christopher, J. (2020). Implementation of performance management in an environment of conflicting management cultures. *International Journal of Productivity and Performance Management*, 69(7), 1521–1539. DOI: 10.1108/IJPPM-02-2019-0071

City & Guilds Group research project. (2020). Building the talent pipeline in KSA. https://www.cityandguildsgroup.com/-/media/cgg-website/documents/building-the-talent-pipeline-in-saudi-arabia--city-guilds-group-pdf.ashx

Cooper, D. R., & Schindler, P. S. (2003). *Research methods*. Irwin.

Creswell, J. W. (2012). *Educational research: Planning, conducting, and evaluating quantitative and qualitative research* (4th ed.). Pearson.

Davis, M. S., & Mensah, M. A. (2020). Performance Appraisal of Employees in Tertiary Institutions: A Case Study of University of Education, Winneba (Winneba Campus). *International Journal of Human Resource Studies*, 10(2), 175–196. DOI: 10.5296/ijhrs.v10i2.16409

Gonaim, F. A. (2021). Leadership in higher education and its implications for Saudi Arabian society. *Trends and Practices*, 4(2), 210–217. Advance online publication. DOI: 10.52634/mier/2014/v4/i2/1471

Goodman, L. A. (2011). Comment: On respondent-driven sampling and snowball sampling in hard-to-reach populations and snowball sampling not in hard-to-reach populations. *Sociological Methodology*, 41(1), 347–353. DOI: 10.1111/j.1467-9531.2011.01242.x

Hamdan, A. (2013). An exploration into" private" higher education in Saudi Arabia: Improving quality and accessibility? *The ACPET Journal for Private Higher Education*, 2(2), 33–44.

Hilman, H., & Abubakar, A. (2017). Strategic Talent Management Practices for Higher Institutions. *Information and Knowledge Management*, 7(2), 31–34. https://www.iiste.org/Journals/index.php/IKM/article/view/35372

Jenkins, S. (2022). *Higher Education in Saudi Arabia: A Vehicle for Global Promotion and Advancement* (1st ed.). Routledge., https://www.taylorfrancis.com/chapters/edit/10.4324/9781003049609-11/higher-education-saudi-arabia-sulaiman-jenkins

Johnson, B., Manyika, J., & Lee, L. (2005). The next revolution in interactions. *The McKinsey Quarterly*, 4, 20–33. https://www.mckinsey.com/capabilities/people-and-organizational-performance/our-insights/the-next-revolution-in-interactions

Jooss, S., Burbach, R., & Ruël, H. (2021). Examining talent pools as a core talent management practice in multinational corporations. *International Journal of Human Resource Management*, 32(11), 2321–2352. DOI: 10.1080/09585192.2019.1579748

KAUST Press Release. (2024, March 14). Saudi Arabia's top academic leaders converge at KAUST Saudi Leadership Institute 2024. (n.D.). King Abdullah University of Science and Technology (KAUST). Retrieved May 25, 2024, from https://www.kaust.edu.sa/en/news/saudi-arabia-s-top-academic-leaders-converge-at-kaust-saudi-leadership-institute-2024

King Sattam University's talent management guide (2024). 2nd Edition. Retrieved from webpage: https://dhr.psau.edu.sa/sitesuploads/dhr/page/202402/Integrated%20talent%20management%20guide.pdf. Accessed on 21st May 2024

Kodai, Z., & Alzobeer, A. S. O. (2023). Investigation of the Influence of Social Trust, Network, and Shared Goals on Sharing Knowledge Attitudes among Saudi Academics in Higher Education Institutions. *International Journal of Organizational Leadership*, 12(2), 165–175. DOI: 10.33844/ijol.2023.60357

Mntonintshi, O., & Mtembu, V. (2019). When Performance Management Fails: Attitudes and Perceptions of Staff at a Higher Education Institution. *Journal of Economics and Behavioral Studies*, 10(6), 131–140. DOI: 10.22610/jebs.v10i6A.2669

Muramalla, V. S. S. R., & Alotaibi, K. A. (2019). Equitable Workload and the Perceptions of Academic Staff in Universities. *The International Journal of Educational Organization and Leadership*, 26(2), 1–19. DOI: 10.18848/2329-1656/CGP/v26i02/1-19

Omar, A., Altohami, W. M. A., & Afzaal, M. (2022). Assessment of the Governance Quality of the Departments of English in Saudi Universities: Implications for Sustainable Development. *World Journal of English Language*, 12(8), 443. Advance online publication. DOI: 10.5430/wjel.v12n8p443

Profanter, A. (2017). University is a Private Matter: Higher Education in Saudi Arabia (Studies in Critical Social Sciences). In Rethinking Private Higher Education: Ethnographic Perspectives (Series Editor, Vol. 101). Brill. https://doi.org/DOI: 10.1163/9789004291508_008

Qahl, M., & Sohaib, O. (2023). Key Factors for a Creative Environment in Saudi Arabian Higher Education Institutions. *Journal of Information Technology Education: Innovations in Practice*, 22, 1–48. DOI: 10.28945/5105

Qawasmeh, E. F., Alnafisi, S. Y., Almajali, R., Alromaih, B. S., & Helali, M. M., & al-lawama, H. I. (2024). The Impact of Human Resources Management Practices on Employee Performance: A Comparative Study Between Jordanian and Saudi Arabian Universities. *Migration Letters : An International Journal of Migration Studies*, 21(2), 243–257. DOI: 10.59670/ml.v21i2.6083

Ramaditya, M., Maarif, M. S., Affandi, J., & Sukmawati, A. (2022). Reinventing talent management: How to maximize performance in higher education. *Frontiers in Education*, 7, 929697. DOI: 10.3389/feduc.2022.929697

Alruwaili, R. (2020). New university system is a first step towards better research.

Saudi Arabia's Top Academic Leaders Converge at KAUST Saudi Leadership Institute. (2024). (2024, May 25). Saudi Arabia's Top Academic Leaders Converge at KAUST Saudi Leadership Institute 2024. https://www.kaust.edu.sa/news/saudi-arabia-s-top-academic-leaders-converge-at-kaust-saudi-leadership-institute-2024

Saudi Vision 2030. (2019, May 25). Saudi Vision 2030. https://www.vision2030.gov.sa/en/

Sharaf-Addin, H. H., & Fazel, H. (2021). Balanced Scorecard Development as a Performance Management System in Saudi Public Universities: A Case Study Approach. *Asia-Pacific Journal of Management Research and Innovation*, 17(1-2), 57–70. DOI: 10.1177/2319510X211048591

Shousha, A. I. (2018). Motivational Strategies and Student Motivation in an EFL Saudi Context. *International Journal of English Language Education*, 6(1), 20–44. DOI: 10.5296/ijele.v6i1.12535

Singh, A., & Alhabbas, N. (2024). Transforming KSA's local workforce into global talent: An Industry 4.0 and 5.0 initiative leading to vision 2030. *International Journal of Advanced and Applied Sciences*, 11(2), 94–106. DOI: 10.21833/ijaas.2024.02.012

Smith, L., & Abouammoh, A. (2013). *Higher education in Saudi Arabia: achievements, challenges and opportunities.* Springer., DOI: 10.1007/978-94-007-6321-0

Subbarayalu, A. V., Al Kuwaiti, A., & Al-Muhanna, F. A. (2024). Talent Management Practices in Saudi Universities During the Post-Pandemic Renaissance (Chapter 21). Building Resiliency in Higher Education: Globalization, Digital Skills, and Student Wellness, *IGL Global.* DOI: https://doi.org/DOI: 10.4018/979-8-3693-5483-4.ch021

Tayeb, O., Zahed, A., & Ritzen, J. (2016). Becoming a World-Class University. *Springer Open.* https://doi.org/https://doi.org/10.1007/978-3-319-26380-9

Technical and Vocational Training Annual Report. (2023). Retrieved on 24th May 2024 from webpage: https://online.flippingbook.com/view/268323385

Yusuf, M. A. (2023). Managerial strategies and effective staff meetings in Nigerian Universities. *Indonesian Journal of Educational Management and Leadership*, 1(1), 85–105. DOI: 10.51214/ijemal.v1i1.518

Yusuf, N., & Jamjoom, Y. (2022). The Role of Higher Education Institutions in Developing Employability Skills of Saudi Graduates Amidst Saudi 2030 Vision. *European Journal of Sustainable Development*, 11(1), 31. Advance online publication. DOI: 10.14207/ejsd.2022.v11n1p31

Zeb, A., Jamal, W., & Ali, M. (2015). Reward and Recognition Priorities of Public Sector Universities' Teachers for their Motivation and Job Satisfaction. *Journal of Managerial Sciences*, 9(2).

Chapter 12
Requisite Employability Skills Among Engineering Students:
An Analysis of Responsible Factors for the Mismatch of Demand and Supply

Alpa Sethi

Manipal University Jaipur, India

Ritu Toshniwal

Manipal University Jaipur, India

Kshitiz Jangir
https://orcid.org/0000-0001-9823-0039

SVKM's Narsee Monjee Institute of Management Studies, Indore, India

ABSTRACT

The role of technical education in the progress and growth of a nation is well acknowledged all over the world. In India the number of people entering into the technical education system has never been a problem. But the relevant problem has been the relative skills and employability of the people. The widening of skill gap and increase in the unemployability of engineering graduates has become a tremendous pain point for government as well as other stake holders. There is an urgent need to improve the technical education system and reducing the skill gap to convert youth into educated employable citizens for both their own development as well as the development of the Nation. The skills demanded by the industries

DOI: 10.4018/979-8-3693-3443-0.ch012

are often not found in the engineering graduates and the skills that they possess are often termed as obsolete or are presently not needed by the employers. Hence, there is a need to identify the factors responsible for the widening gap. Therefore, paper focuses on detail analysis of various responsible factors for creating disparity between demand and supply.

INTRODUCTION

Education is recognized as one of the critical elements of the national development effort and higher education is of vital importance for the nation, as it is a powerful tool to build knowledge-based society of the 21st century. The Indian education system has conquered a strong position in international circuit. Here, more than 62% of its population in working age group of 15-59 years, and more than 54% of its total population below 25 years of age, which is feasible. Today 's job market and in-demand skills are entirely different from the ones of 10 or even 5 years ago and the pace of change is only set to accelerate. New jobs require new skills which either does not exist or the population is niche. Building a skilling system that responds well to business needs, while opening opportunities for all people is the need of the hour for the match new requirements, a system. In a highly dynamic environment, only basic education is not sufficient. Now it become most important and challenging goals for universities/ college to produce graduates with employment ready skills.(Sethi et al., 2024) Moreover, recent years have seen policymakers and social partners across the world become increasingly concerned with the match between their workforces 'skills and their labour markets 'needs. Skills mismatch, the gap between the skills required on the job and those possessed by individuals, raises the question of the ability of societies to capitalize on their workforces. Skills are also a critical asset for individual workers and firms in a rapidly changing and globalized world. In a competitive environment, economic graduates who have more employability skills will be more successful.(Cumming, 2010) So, students 'employability skill must be continuously adapted to labour market needs. Some research show that graduates do not have the skills needed for the modern workplace. (Sharvari, 2019)Thus, there is an essential need to identify the factors and reasons for this mismatch.

In the above context, this exploratory study was conducted to expand the understanding of factors responsible for mismatch between demand and supply of requisite skills in India by exploring the perceptions of engineering academicians and HR professionals from different industries. Consistent with the objectives, in the next section, relevant literature is briefly reviewed. This is followed by the methodology adopted. Thereafter, the main findings are presented and discussed.

The chapter concludes with a discussion on the limitations of the study and areas for future research.

REVIEW OF LITERATURE

The reviews in this chapter are taken from national and international research on industrial employability skills, its mismatch, and factors responsible for skill gap.

The word employability has many connotations in terms of its usability and its applicability. Employability skills are those basic skills, personal qualities and values that are necessary for getting, keeping, and doing well on a job.(Ting et al., 2017) In this support (Ramisetty-Mikler, 2017)said that employability skills are transferable skills and key personal attributes which are highly valued by employers and necessary for effective performance in the workplace (Calhoun, 2015) stated the employability skills as a preparation for graduates to successfully get jobs and to develop in their careers and enable individuals to prove their value to an organization as the key to job survival as academic qualifications and good marks are not the only way to successfully engage at university or college. Group project work, presentations, student exchange programs, internships, industry and community project units, and mentoring programs are the medium to develop employability skills within the studies.(Gupta et al., 2024)

Industry Academia Collaboration

According to (Acemoglu & Autor, 2011)corporates look for certain traits and employability attribute while they recruit. In support of this statement (Llinares-Insa et al., 2018) explored the skill gap analysis in between academia and industry and revealed that there is a perceptual gap between the human resource manager and the directors or training and development officers over employability skills. (Sehgal & Nasim, 2018) also examined that the main reason behind this mismatch is the lack of collaborative efforts from the industry and educational institutions. This research also identified an enormous skills gap in India between what industries demand based on recent rapid economic growth and the skills that young people acquire through vocational training.(Jangir et al., 2024) It is very essential to identify the perception of employer about job fit of fresh graduates. Unfortunately, employers perceived that Engineering-hires doesn't create much value for their companies in first few years of their career stage and found them inadequate.(Ting et al., 2017)

Teaching Pedagogy:

In this techno savvy environment, even education is also shifting towards use of technology in teaching. This demands from teacher to be competent to prepare and deliver practical lesson that can enhance marketable skills of students to sustain in competitive environment. The teacher should adopt innovation-based teaching method for developing simulation-based lectures. According to (Mtshali & Msimango, 2023) Innovation based teaching methods will help teachers to guide the students regarding solving real time problems through illustrative examples. Teachers can use modern methods like simulation techniques to tell students about how real world is going on and how to use skills to survive. But most of teachers are still incline towards traditional way of teaching which is hampering the education and employability skills of the students.(Nkwanyane, 2023)

Training and Development

Training plays an important role in providing skills and new insights for the students. It helps to provide a mode through which students can learn the concepts practically. Its, an approach where emphasis is laid on learning with the help of practical projects and is often highly regarded as an effective technique of permanent learning.(Acemoglu & Autor, 2012) Imparting education is not just a matter of learning, but the focus is on gaining knowledge and enlightenment. Various types of training like industrial training, classroom training, live projects, internship training etc are provided to engineering students to enhance knowledge, skills, or attitudes so that they can better perform a current task or job.(Bartlett, n.d.)But the question is does such training programs are effective? There are several factors which affects the training effectiveness: Training Facilities, Trainer's knowledge, Training Aids etc which vary from institution to institution, and which collectively affects the employability of engineering students. (Menon, 2014)

Innovative and Creative Skills

Ganesan et al (2015) reviewed the employability skills like analytical skills, work culture, leadership, self-understanding and problem solving ability and communication of MBA graduates, Engineering graduates and University students too. Literature suggests that in today's scenario the applicant should be multi-tasking so that he or she can sustain in this challengeable market of competency. Further (Gallagher et al., 2011) proposed a typology of IT skills and suggest the six new categories of skills: foundation skills, operational skills, essential skills, project management skills and problem / opportunity skills. Mahtab Pouratashi et al

(2019), suggested that there is a need to inculcate basic skills, responsibility, oral and written communication skills, lifelong learning, and networking skills among Iran graduates to align them with the changes of labour market. Beaula Moyo and et al (2022), emphasised more on extended internship experience of Zimbabwean graduates and stated that more practical skills, soft and hard employability skills, and curriculum-based competency need to focus in in house training. Erin Twyford et al (2023), used a different approach named work-integrated learning (WIL) to examine students' perceptions in an Australian university and found this approach as effective for developing employability. Andreas Blom (2010) conducted a research on the skill set and employability in new graduate employees. With the help of this research the author tried to find out the skills necessary for university graduates, the skill in which they are lacking, and are employers satisfied with the set of skills graduates possess. Total 26 skills were summarized under three categories: core employability skill, professional skill and communication skill.

Universities Approaches

The role of universities is highly important in the development of graduates. Students' choice the universities for higher education by keeping various parameters in their minds like quality education, availability of accommodation, employment outcomes, teachers' quality, brand image etc.(Pouratashi & Zamani, 2019) there are huge differences in public and private universities specially fee's structure. Private universities are charging huge amount for getting enrolled in engineering programs. Specially the students who are brilliant and capable due to lack of sufficient financial support compromises in the selection of universities or sometimes choose the other programs for studies and this affects his overall development and employment outcomes.(Daun et al., 2023)

Academician's Recruitment and Retention

Quality of teachers and effective teaching learning are closely connected with each other. There are significant challenges in attracting and retaining expertise academicians for educational institutions. Institutions seek for well prepared, expert and experience academician who can contribute to student as well as institutional achievements.(Wang Chong et al., n.d.) But finding such intellectuals is a challenge for HEIs due to some reasons like low salary structure, non-appealing profession, non-effective incentives, low status etc. It is essential for HEIs to make good retention policies for trained, expertise teachers so that they can contribute their knowledge, skills in nourishment of students.(Allen & Van Der Velden{, n.d.)

Economic and Global Factors

Designing the skill sets for a fast-changing future without blueprint is very difficult. Several countries are facing particularly basic skill related problem as needs of skills in future has changed abruptly.(Daun et al., 2023) (Mossali et al., 2020) Due to degree of digitalization, pace of automation, new work concept, it become difficult to build workforce capable to the new reality. Higher degree of skill mismatch of a country leads to score low on global innovative, talent competitiveness index.(Pouratashi & Zamani, 2019) So, Governments and Corporates are required to work together not only to handle current short-term challenges such as retention and redeployment, but also to upskilling, reskilling people's skills(Sharma et al., 2024) and capabilities to meet future needs.(Millar, n.d.)

Education System

Educational systems are an efficient vehicle for disseminating and enhancing the skills required for rapid economic growth. The wide range of effect of education on all facets of human existence makes it a vital element in the policy framework, especially for the developing countries. The bulk of the world's population resides in developing countries, which means they must optimize the productivity and capabilities of their human capital. Lethargic upgradation of academic curriculum, lack of its mapping to industrial requirements thus increases the gap between the imparted and required skills or abilities which leads to a huge skill mismatch. (Farooq et al., 2008). Furthermore, Henrik Malm Lindberg (2015) analysed educational system of Sweden in three dimensions in terms of quality, efficiency and relevance. These are seen as essential in order to deliver both competence to businesses and give young people opportunities at the labour market. These three dimensions – quality, efficiency and relevance described how sound the education system is up to the charge of facilitating the entry into the labour market and deliver trained competence and skills.

RESEARCH METHODOLOGY

Sample Selection

This research utilizes quantitative research approach, especially descriptive research for gathering data in central region of India covering mainly Madhya Pradesh. The study is confined to exploring responsible factors for the mismatch between demand and supply of requisite skills among engineering students. Two samples were selected for this research mainly:

1. Academicians from engineering institutes
2. HR Professionals from IT, Pharma and Textile industry.

Sample selection was conducted in two stages. At stage I cluster sampling technique was used to divide the entire population of Madhya Pradesh (India) into small clusters like Gwalior, Jabalpur, Indore, Ujjain etc. At stage II random sampling was used to select randomly the subset of the population to be used as the respondents for the survey purpose.

The Academicians sample consisted of 275 academicians. They were taken from different – different types of institutions and universities. Most respondents were from government and private institutions/ Universities. The age of respondents ranged from up to 40 years to above 60 years, whereas 82.18 percent were male & 17.82 were female in the study. Majority of respondents were PhD and had 10-15 years of experience in academics but no experience of industry. 48.36 percent of respondents were designated as assistant professor while 28 percent were designated as professor. In the study, 39.64 percent of respondents were from mechanical discipline, while 29.09 percent were from computer science/ IT discipline.

The sample of HR Professionals from Industries were consisted of 100 HR. The industries were from IT sector, Pharmacy sector and Textile Sector. Further details on the background of the industry and nature of industry cannot be provided to preserve the anonymity of the participants and the industry.

Measures

To achieve the purpose of the study, The self-administered survey questionnaire was chosen as the mode for primary data collection; two self-administered survey questionnaires were developed targeting the two groups.(Askary et al., 2019) All questions in the two questionnaires were on five-point Likert's scale (1=Strongly Agree, 2=Agree, 3= Neutral, 4= Disagree, 5=Strongly Disagree). (Chavan, 2017) The research instrument was pretested on 30 academicians and 20 HR professionals to find out improvement areas in the questionnaire and make necessary adjustments. (Zainuddin et al., 2019)

Data analysis was carried out by using software package for social sciences (SPSS). In addition to descriptive statistics, factor analysis including Exploratory Factor analysis was performed using Principal Component analysis, with Varimax rotation to describe variability among observed, correlated variables in terms of a potentially lower number of unobserved variables called factors.

Result

Factors have been derived through the responses provided by Academicians from engineering institute and HR professionals from Industrialists.

KMO test was applied to check the normal distribution of data whereas Bartlett test has been applied to find out whether data is suitable for factor analysis or not. (Blom & Saeki, 2010) In the present study, KMO values closer to 1.0 are considered ideal while values less than 0.5 are unacceptable. The KMO value is .894, which is more than 0.5. So, this indicates that the degree of information among the variables overlap greatly/the presence of a strong partial correlation. (Leoni, 2014)Hence, it is plausible to conduct factor analysis and the result of Bartlett test of chi square is 16358.068 with degree of freedom is 298 and sig. level is .000. This represent that the correlation matrix is indeed not an identity matrix as shown in Table 2

Further, factor analysis was applied on these factors to see whether these factors can be grouped and define a common factor representing these factors. The techniques used for this analysis was Factor Analysis technique using Principal Component Method. (Banumathi, 2015)

In all seven factors were extracted with eigen value of 1 and more than 1 which is achieved through factor analysis. Further based on the analysis these factors were grouped into broad categories viz inappropriate training program, lack of collaboration for skill enhancement, lack of innovation and creativity among students, inappropriate teaching pedagogy methods, lack of financial support, recruitment and retention of qualified teachers, and economic and global factors. The detailed analysis of these seven 1factors are shown in Table 3, Table 4 and Fig 1

Table 1. KMO and Bartlett's Test

Kaiser-Meyer-Olkin Measure of Sampling Adequacy	.894
Bartlett's Test of Sphericity Approx. Chi-Square	16358.068
df	300
Sig.	.000

Table 2. Total Variances Explained

Factor Name	Total Eigen Values	% of Variance	Items Converged	Factors Loads
Inappropriate Training Program	9.433	20.250	Inappropriate training Infrastructure, apparatus, tools, machinery, labs	.881
			Insufficient duration of training	.820
			Lack of well qualified training provider	.756
			Lack of proper information by the industries to students	.709
			Lack of multidisciplinary training programs	.688
			Lack of industry sponsored training labs and apparatus in educational institutes	.656
Lack of Collaboration for Skill Enhancement	3.218	14.276	Increase interaction between educational institutes and industries	.755
			Providing interdisciplinary training in order to improve requisite skills in engineering aspirants	.714
			Development of Industry oriented training programs specifically designed with the help of industry experts	.645
			Establishing Industrial Mentorship programs to drive learning and development for both mentor and mentee	.634
Lack of Innovation & creativity among students	2.856	12.200	Lack of innovation and creativity.	.810
			Introduction of personality development courses in schools	.755
			Entrepreneurship development courses for school students	.685
Inappropriate Teaching Pedagogy methods	1.936	11.742	Increasing the focus on learning through live projects and internships	.791
			Entrepreneurial education and development programs	.796
			Industry participation in designing the curriculum of engineering	.751
Lack of Financial Support	1.425	10.823	Reducing the rate of education loans	.812
			Encouraging banks, NBFCs and other financial institutions to provide interest free loans for underprivileged students	.770
			Reducing the cost of engineering by setting ceiling for engineering fee (Especially for private colleges)	.665

continued on following page

Table 2. Continued

Factor Name	Total Eigen Values	% of Variance	Items Converged	Factors Loads
Recruitment and retention of Qualified teachers	1.265	9.794	Recruitment and retention of qualified staff.	.688
			Appropriate teacher-student ratio in class room	.677
			Recruitment of teachers with industry experience	.557
Economic and Global Factor	1.104	8.98	Lack of Foreign Direct Investment and Industrial Investment	.849
			Cross border migration of engineering students to neighboring states due to better opportunities and increased standard of living	.816
			Lack of job opportunities	.770
			Slowdown in the economy due to lack of growth and inflation	.725
			Slowdown in the economy due to lack of growth and inflation	.689
			Low expenditure on education sector by Government due to fiscal constraints	.578

Figure 1. Screen Plot

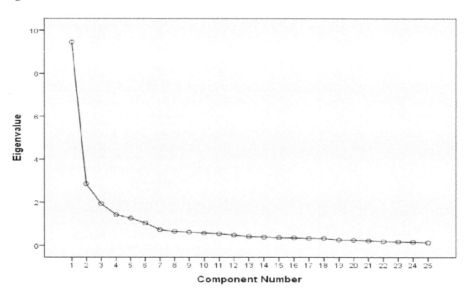

Description of factors analysis

Inappropriate Training Program: This factor is having total variances (20.250). Major elements of this factor include inappropriate training Infrastructure, apparatus, tools, machinery, labs, insufficient duration of training, lack of well qualified training provider, lack of proper information by the industries to students, lack of multidisciplinary training program, lack of industry sponsored training labs and apparatus in educational institutes.

Lack of Collaboration for Skill Enhancement: This factor is having total variances (14.276). Major items of this factor constitute Increase interaction between educational institutes and industries, providing interdisciplinary training in order to improve requisite skills in engineering aspirants, development of industry-oriented training programs specifically designed with the help of industry experts and establishing industrial mentorship programs to drive learning and development for both mentor and mentee.

Lack of Innovation & creativity among students: This factor is having total variances (12.200). Major elements of this factor include lack of innovation and creativity, introduction of personality development courses in schools and entrepreneurship development courses for school students.

Inappropriate Teaching Pedagogy methods: This factor is having total variances (11.742). Major elements of this factor include Increasing the focus on learning through live projects and internships, entrepreneurial education and development programs and industry participation in designing the curriculum of engineering.

Lack of Financial support from government: This factor is having total variances (10.823). Major elements of this factor include reducing the rate of education loans, Encouraging banks, NBFCs and other financial institutions to provide interest free loans for underprivileged students and Reducing the cost of engineering by setting ceiling for engineering fee (Especially for private colleges).

Recruitment and Retention of qualified teachers: This factor is the most significant factor total variances (8.953). Major elements of this factor include recruitment and retention of qualified staff, appropriate teacher-student ratio in class room and Recruitment of teachers with industry experience.

Economic and Global factors: Major elements of this factor include Lack of Foreign Direct Investment and Industrial Investment, Cross border migration of engineering students to neighbouring states due to better opportunities and increased standard of living, Lack of job opportunities, Slowdown in the economy due to lack of growth and inflation and Low expenditure on education sector by Government due to fiscal constraints.

DISCUSSION AND CONCLUSION

This research explored various responsible factors from both academicians and industrialists. The discussion centres on the seven most important finding uncovered in the study that affects the mismatch between demand and supply of requisite skills. These factors are -inappropriate training program, lack of collaboration for skill enhancement, lack of innovation and creativity among students, inappropriate teaching pedagogy method, lack of financial support from government, recruitment and retention of qualified teachers, economic and global factors.

The finding revealed that there is a need to restructure the governing body of school education to make it more relevant for the dynamic needs and challenges in education field as in India, schools are lacking with adequate teacher student ratio as well as there is a huge non availability of practical learning through projects, seminars etc. Even schools are unaware about importance of personality development and entrepreneurship courses. Therefore, in order to improve the vigilance of scope and career in engineering field in every school a special career guidance centre should establish.

The findings of this study also suggest that the role of teacher in upgrading the skills of the students is very crucial. It is essential to improve the teaching pedagogy to make the lectures interesting and better understanding of the concept. HR professionals believed that there should be faculty development and exchange programs for engineering faculties to enhance their knowledge. Moreover, Academicians suggested that it would be much effective if industry expert conduct sessions/ workshops/ lectures for faculty members so that there will be a better understanding of new and upcoming demands of the industry and accordingly the same can be groomed among students. They also emphasis on the point that they had to work as per higher authority guidelines, and it is impossible to implement any changes on their ends.

Another interesting finding of the current study is that both industrialist and academicians gave more emphasize on existing training system in education institutes which they found highly inappropriate. In this regard, they agreed to increase more interaction between educational institutes and industries through various modes such as public private partnership and special purpose vehicle. Furthermore, they also suggested that there is need to include more training program in the curriculum like interdisciplinary training, industry-oriented training, industrial mentorship program and accordingly training labs, infrastructure need to be updated. Even to reduce the skill gap, government should also sponsor skill development labs/ training centre for engineering students. For effective education, now it's a high time that both industry and academicians should put right efforts to reduce the skill gap. There is a need to establish industry academia hubs for joint consultations, designing of curriculum, joint research, sponsored projects.

Even geographical indication of central region of India especially Madhya Pradesh itself is also responsible for skill gap. No industries are interested to establish in this region due to high rates, strict government regulation like cost of transportation, fuel prize, electricity rates, high tax rates, long process to get permission for establishment of new industries etc. This resulted into lack of job opportunities, high migration of talented and skilled students to neighbour states.

Overall, this article contributes to the investigation of various variables which are responsible in creating skill gap between demand and supply of requisite skills in central region of India from the point of view of two main groups-engineering academicians and HR professionals from industry. Universities require more involvement of industrial experts in various activities like curriculum designing, imparting training, join projects, sponsored labs, exchange programs etc. For better effectiveness of training, labs, training centres, infrastructure require to be updated. Even the focus of government is highly essential for universities and industry so that collaboration between academia-industry could be more viable, effective and outcome oriented. When looking ahead to the results as its implications for practice, the findings of this study could be used to assist in universities, graduates, employers, and career advisors to apply strategic decisions in managing graduates' careers. Further, it could be expected that the findings of this study will be able to establish baseline data and would be a source of general guidance in stimulating future research in this area.

Finally, some limitations of this study, however, should be acknowledged. First, Factors was investigated from only academicians and industrial perspectives. Several other factors might contribute to factors for mismatch and its outcome which could be considered in future research. To enhance the generalizability of the experimental results, replication studies should be conducted in other countries as well.

Prospects & Recommendations

Engineering was essentially referred to as the most coveted and sought-after professions globally because of the very simple reason that engineering can be termed as the backbone of any economy. Thus, it becomes vital to have a workforce that is skilled and relevant to whatever the current and future needs are. India has been grappling with high volume of engineering graduate outflows but the skills that engineering graduates possess do not hold much relevance, which is the heart of the problem. An economy such as India should be at the forefront of technological revolution but is lagging due to effective mismatches of skills in engineering graduates. It becomes a never-ending spiral trap wherein due to mismatch of skills and increase in supply of graduates, engineering as profession loses sheen and graduates look for jobs in other fields. This has also led to the closure of various engineering institutes throughout India. Engineering Institutes are often faced with serious repercussions due to low employment opportunities as the MNC's have clamped down on the recruitment of graduates year after year due to lack of skills available.

Thus, following threshold areas need to be focused to overcome above challenges:

1. Upgrade school education as per the best International Standards. For example in Germany, depending upon the child's interest ad aptitude, he is allotted domain specialization right after primary standard(5th Class). This helps child become super specialized professional in domain of his liking.
2. Implementation of ECTS tool based on European System, which allows students to move between countries during professional study with credit swap, giving students the flexibility to learn from their choice of place. ECTS allows credits earned at one outer institution, being considered towards the professional degree at the home institute.
3. Improved Liaison between Academia and Industries, for better understanding of industry needs and fulfilling their needs by rapid adoption of up-skilling modules.
4. Creation of Industry-Academia Liaison hubs for joint consultations, joint designing of curriculum, joint research & sponsored projects.
5. Increase the collaboration between industries and educational institutes through various modes such as public private partnerships and special purpose vehicles.
6. Developing Dedicated skill development Centers for engineering students mandating students to undergo a basic training with Credits included in B.Tech.
7. Development of Industry oriented training programs specifically designed with the help of industry experts. Establishing Industrial Mentorship programs to drive learning and development for both mentor and mentee.
8. Setting up Consultancy and Incubation centers, keeping in view local industry ecosystem requirements.
9. Nurturing Entrepreneurial Spirit in students by helping them setup their own business enterprise after graduation. The students must be assisted in terms of finance and space for incubating their start-ups based on their innovative ideas.
10. Engineering institute should design skill-based training Programs, to produce trained workforce tailor-made for industries. Establishing industry sponsored training labs and facilities within educational institutes will assist hugely. Moreover, Institute should provide interdisciplinary training to improve requisite skills.
11. Incorporating sensitive feedback mechanism within Academia to review effectiveness of training imparted and act spontaneously for the needful.
12. Improving the 'Teaching Pedagogy' thereby making lectures interesting for better understanding of the concept.

REFERENCES

Acemoglu, D., & Autor, D. (2011). Skills, tasks and technologies: Implications for employment and earnings. In *Handbook of Labor Economics* (Vol. 4). Issue PART B., DOI: 10.1016/S0169-7218(11)02410-5

Acemoglu, D., & Autor, D. (2012). What does human capital do? A review of Goldin and Katz's The Race between Education and Technology. In *Journal of Economic Literature* (Vol. 50, Issue 2, pp. 426–463). DOI: 10.1257/jel.50.2.426

Allen, J., & Van Der Velden{, R. (n.d.). *Educational mismatches versus skill mis-matches: effects on wages, job satisfaction, and on-the-job search.*

Askary, Z., Singh, A., Gupta, S., Shukla, R. K., & Jaiswal, P. (2019). Development of AHP Framework of Sustainable Product Design and Manufacturing of Electric Vehicle. In Prasad, A., Gupta, S. S., & Tyagi, R. K. (Eds.), *Advances in Engineering Design* (pp. 415–422). Springer Singapore. DOI: 10.1007/978-981-13-6469-3_37

Banumathi, M. (2015). *An Engineering Employability Skill Assessment Framework for Indian Graduates.*

Bartlett, W. (n.d.). *Skill Mismatch, Education Systems and Labour Markets in EU Neighbourhood Policy Countries Goodbye Tito: The Role of Diverging Welfare State Trajectories on Income Inequality in Four Former Yugoslav Republics View project Higher education and the graduate labour market in the Western Balkans View project.* https://www.researchgate.net/publication/258286624

Blom, A., & Saeki, H. (2010). *Employability and Skill Set of Newly Graduated Engineers in India.*

Calhoun, J. M. D. (2015). *WHAT PREDICTS SKILLS MISMATCH IN CANADA?* Chavan, R. R. (2017). *Construct Validity of Employability skills for Graduate through Factor Analysis. 19*(9), 14–21. https://doi.org/DOI: 10.9790/487X-1909071421

Chong, W. S., Oxley, E., Negrea, V., Bond, M., Liu, Q., & Sum Kong, M. (n.d.). *February 2024 Teacher recruitment and retention in schools in socio-economically disadvantaged areas in England-review of practice.* www.educationendowment foundation.org.uk

Cumming, J. (2010). Contextualised performance: Reframing the skills de-bate in research education. *Studies in Higher Education*, 35(4), 405–419. DOI: 10.1080/03075070903082342

Daun, M., Grubb, A. M., Stenkova, V., & Tenbergen, B. (2023). A systematic literature review of requirements engineering education. *Requirements Engineering*, 28(2), 145–175. DOI: 10.1007/s00766-022-00381-9 PMID: 35611156

Farooq, S., Ahmed, U., & Ali, R. (2008). Education, underemployment, and job satisfaction. *Pakistan Journal of Commerce and Social Sciences*, 1, 83–91.

Gallagher, K. P., Goles, T., Hawk, S., Simon, J. C., Kaiser, K. M., Beath, C. M., & Jr, W. B. M. (2011). A Typology of Requisite Skills for Information Technology Professionals. *2011 44th Hawaii International Conference on System Sciences*, 1–10. DOI: 10.1109/HICSS.2011.39

Gupta, M., Sharma, V., Jangir, K., Sharma, P., & Pathak, N. (2024, March). Assessing the factors influencing the continued usage of smart wearables by post-adopting users in the context of technology-based health information systems. In AIP Conference Proceedings (Vol. 2919, No. 1). AIP Publishing.

Jangir, K., Sharma, V., & Gupta, M. (2024). Demystifying Machine Learning for Business Resilience Under VUCA in the COVID-19 Era. In Singh, D., Sood, K., Kautish, S., & Grima, S. (Eds.), *VUCA and Other Analytics in Business Resilience, Part B* (pp. 103–112). Emerald Publishing Limited., DOI: 10.1108/978-1-83753-198-120241007

Leoni, R. (2014). Graduate employability and the development of competencies. The incomplete reform of the "bologna process.". *International Journal of Manpower*, 35(4), 448–469. DOI: 10.1108/IJM-05-2013-0097

Llinares-Insa, L. I., González-Navarro, P., Zacarés-González, J. J., & Córdoba-Iñesta, A. I. (2018). Employability Appraisal Scale (EAS): Development and validation in a Spanish sample. *Frontiers in Psychology*, 9(AUG), 1437. Advance online publication. DOI: 10.3389/fpsyg.2018.01437 PMID: 30154748

Menon, K. (2014). *A STUDY ON EMPLOYABILITY OF ENGINEERING STUDENTS IN MUMBAI AND PUNE REGION*.

Millar, D. (n.d.). *Learning and Employability Series 1 and 2*.

Mossali, E., Picone, N., Gentilini, L., Rodrìguez, O., Pérez, J. M., & Colledani, M. (2020). Lithium-ion batteries towards circular economy: A literature review of opportunities and issues of recycling treatments. *Journal of Environmental Management*, 264, 110500. https://doi.org/https://doi.org/10.1016/j.jenvman.2020.110500. DOI: 10.1016/j.jenvman.2020.110500 PMID: 32250918

Mtshali, T. I., & Msimango, S. M. (2023). Factors Influencing Construction Technology Teachers' Ability to Conduct Simulations Effectively. *Jurnal Penelitian Dan Pengkajian Ilmu Pendidikan: E-Saintika*, 7(1), 88–102. DOI: 10.36312/esaintika.v7i1.1079

Nkwanyane, T. P. (2023). Understanding the Demand for Industrial skills through the National Certificate (Vocational) Building and Civil Engineering Programme. *International Journal of Learning. Teaching and Educational Research*, 22(5), 674–687. DOI: 10.26803/ijlter.22.5.35

Pouratashi, M., & Zamani, A. (2019). University and graduates employability: Academics' views regarding university activities (the case of Iran). *Higher Education. Skills and Work-Based Learning*, 9(3), 290–304. DOI: 10.1108/HESWBL-12-2017-0103

Ramisetty-Mikler, S. (2017). Measurement of Employability Skills and Job Readiness Perception of Post-graduate Management students: Results from A Pilot Study Employability skills and job readiness of recent graduates in India View project NewDay Services Parenting Project View project. In *Article in International Journal of Management and Social Sciences*. https://www.researchgate.net/publication/320735657

Sehgal, N., & Nasim, S. (2018). Total Interpretive Structural Modelling of predictors for graduate employability for the information technology sector. *Higher Education. Skills and Work-Based Learning*, 8(4), 495–510. DOI: 10.1108/HESWBL-08-2017-0047

Sethi, A., Jangir, K., & Kukreti, M. (2024). *Robo-Advisors* (pp. 285–294). DOI: 10.4018/979-8-3693-2849-1.ch019

Sharma, P., Sharma, V., Jangir, K., Gupta, M., & Pathak, N. (2024). An analysis of customer intention to use smart home services. *AIP Conference Proceedings*, 2919(1), 080003. DOI: 10.1063/5.0184373

Sharvari, K. (2019). Gap analysis of Soft skills in the curriculum of Higher Education (A case study of Management Institutes in Karnataka). In *Advances In Management* (Vol. 12, Issue 1).

Ting, S. H., Marzuki, E., Chuah, K. M., Misieng, J., & Jerome, C. (2017). Employers' views on the importance of english proficiency and communication skill for employability in Malaysia. *Indonesian Journal of Applied Linguistics*, 7(2), 315–327. DOI: 10.17509/ijal.v7i2.8132

Zainuddin, S. Z. B., Pillai, S., Dumanig, F. P., & Phillip, A. (2019). English language and graduate employability. *Education + Training*, 61(1), 79–93. DOI: 10.1108/ET-06-2017-0089

Chapter 13
Science, Technology, Engineering, and Mathematics Learning Technology Implementation to Address 21st–Century Skills:
The Zimbabwean Higher Education Context

Doris Chasokela

https://orcid.org/0009-0001-5983-8508

National University of Science and Technology, Zimbabwe

Funa Moyo

National University of Science and Technology, Zimbabwe

ABSTRACT

The book chapter explores the integration of learning management systems and course/module software in science, technology, engineering, and mathematics learning and 21st-century skills in Zimbabwe's higher education. The chapter introduces the concepts of STEM and their importance for developing the skills needed for success in the 21st century. It presents an overview of the implementation of learning management systems and course/module software in the Zimbabwean

DOI: 10.4018/979-8-3693-3443-0.ch013

higher education system. The potential benefits of these technologies for STEM are highlighted. In this chapter, it is argued that the integration of information and communication technology in the teaching of science, technology, engineering, and mathematics plays a crucial role in addressing quality-related issues. Finally, the chapter presents case studies of higher education institutions in Zimbabwe that have successfully implemented learning management systems and course/module software and describes the positive effects on student learning.

INTRODUCTION

Science, technology, engineering, and mathematics (STEM) education has become increasingly important in the 21st century, as these skills are essential for innovation, economic growth, and competitiveness. However, there are still many challenges in implementing STEM learning technologies in developing countries like Zimbabwe. This chapter explores the current state of STEM education in the Zimbabwean higher education context and examines the potential of STEM learning technologies to address 21st-century skills. Zimbabwe is facing several challenges in the field of STEM education, including low levels of student achievement, inadequate infrastructure, and a lack of qualified lecturers. To address these challenges, the country has launched some initiatives and policies aimed at improving the quality of STEM education. These include the National STEM Education Programme, launched in 2017, and various initiatives at the university level. Additionally, the potential of STEM learning technologies has also been recognized as a way to address 21st-century skills, such as problem-solving, critical thinking, and collaboration.

Background

Zimbabwe's economy has been struggling for decades, with high levels of unemployment, poverty, and inequality (Mutambisi et al. 2023; Ochi 2023; Xaba & Akinola 2023). An overview of the current state of STEM education in Zimbabwe includes the levels of investment, lecturer training, and student performance. According to Zhou et al (2020), the government of Zimbabwe has made some efforts to improve STEM education, including the establishment of the National STEM Education Programme in 2017. However, the programme has faced challenges such as a lack of resources and inadequate training for lecturers. Despite these challenges, some progress has been made, with a few schools implementing STEM education programmes with the support of international organizations and donors. Some of the challenges in STEM education in Zimbabwe include low levels of student achievement, a shortage of qualified lecturers, and inadequate infrastructure and resources.

An analysis of the country's economic and social context, including the impact of poverty, unemployment, and inequality on education. Some of the key points that could be included in this analysis are: Poverty is a major challenge in Zimbabwe, with an estimated 60% of the population living below the poverty line. This has a direct impact on education, as families may not be able to afford school fees and other costs associated with education. Unemployment is also high in Zimbabwe, with youth unemployment at over 90%. This has a negative impact on education, as young people may not have the motivation or resources to pursue further education. Inequality is also a problem in Zimbabwe, with a significant gap between the richest and poorest citizens.

A discussion of the current national policies and strategies for STEM education in Zimbabwe. A more in-depth discussion could include the following points: The National STEM Education Programme, launched in 2017, aims to increase access to STEM education and improve student achievement in these subjects. The Ministry of Higher and Tertiary Education has launched several initiatives to promote STEM education, including scholarships and partnerships with industry. The National Science and Technology Commission is working to promote the uptake of STEM education and encourage the development of research and innovation in STEM fields. The country's universities have also introduced various initiatives to improve STEM education, including the establishment of STEM clubs, scholarships, and research funding.

An examination of the potential of STEM learning technologies to address 21st-century skills, including problem-solving, critical thinking, collaboration, and creativity. An examination of the potential of STEM learning technologies could include the following points: Digital technologies such as online learning platforms, simulations, and coding can be used to teach problem-solving, critical thinking, and collaboration skills. Virtual labs and simulations can provide students with hands-on experience in STEM fields that may not be possible in a traditional classroom setting. There is potential for the use of robotics and artificial intelligence to teach programming and problem-solving skills. Virtual reality and augmented reality technologies can be used to create immersive learning experiences that allow students to explore real-world problems.

STEM education and its importance in higher education

STEM education is an educational approach that combines four disciplines (Science, Technology, Engineering, and Mathematics) to provide students with a well-rounded understanding of the world. It emphasizes the integration of theoretical knowledge with practical applications and encourages critical thinking and problem-solving skills. STEM education prepares individuals for a wide range of careers and is vital for innovation and economic development (Ismail, 2018). STEM education (Science, Technology, Engineering, and Mathematics) has gained significant importance in recent years as the world continues to evolve in a digital age. STEM has also gained significant attention globally for its ability to prepare students for the challenges and opportunities of the 21st century. The frameworks for 21st-century competence found that all refer to information literacy, technological literacy, and ICT literacy as important pillars for STEM education foundation (Voogt & Roblin, 2012). According to the authors, information literacy refers to the capacity to access information efficiently and effectively, as well as the ability to critically evaluate information. ICT literacy refers to more than technical skills and includes the use of digital technology, communications tools, or networks to operate in a knowledge society. Technological literacy refers to the ability to use, understand, and evaluate technology as well as apply it to develop solutions for particular problems (Voogt & Roblin, 2012). Thus, in the knowledge society, students will have to understand and evaluate the different technologies which they utilise.

Africa, with its vast resources and potential for economic growth, needs a skilled workforce that can harness technology for sustainable development. Science, Technology, and Innovation (STI) are expected to play a significant role in the success of the United Nations (UN) 2030 Agenda and the African 'Union's (AU) Agenda 2063 (United Nations, 2022). STEM education plays a crucial role in preparing individuals for the demands of the 21st century. By equipping students with the necessary skills in STEM, Zimbabwe can unlock its potential in areas such as agriculture, healthcare, energy, and infrastructure development. STEM education is not just important for Africa but for the entire world. As technology continues to advance, the demand for skilled professionals in STEM fields is increasing exponentially. STEM education provides students with the knowledge and skills needed to tackle complex problems, develop new technologies, and drive innovation. In a world where innovation is the driving force behind economic growth, STEM education is indispensable, hence there is a need to invest in STEM education. The rationale for investment in STEM education relates mainly to its association with improved economic outcomes (African American Institute, 2015; Williams, 2011).

It also promotes innovation, fosters economic growth, and addresses challenges faced by these nations. By equipping students with the necessary skills and mind-sets, STEM education empowers them to contribute to the development of their countries and solve complex problems. Literature adds that Technical Vocational Education and Training (TVET) education is recommended for bridging the demand and supply of skills in Africa and Asia (Burnett & Jayaram, 2012). The Ministry of Higher and Tertiary Education, Science and Technology Development, views the STEM project as, designed to: 1. Increase the number of STEM students who will enrol in STEM degree programmes at the country's universities, in 2018 [and beyond]; 2. Promote STEM careers, in response to Zim Asset's human capital objectives; 3. Develop STEM skills that are critically needed for the country's new industrialisation thrust; 4. Address the problem of unemployment; and 5. Empower young people through the promotion of science and innovation (Mberi and Phambili, 2016:12).

Thus, STEM education should address the local development needs of a country such as Zimbabwe (Sohoni, 2012). Hence, STEM education offers numerous benefits for individuals and society. Some of the key benefits include Career Opportunities: STEM education prepares students for a wide range of high-demand careers in industries such as technology, healthcare, engineering, and data analysis (United Nations, 2022). Innovation and Creativity are important pillars that enables the integration of STEM disciplines that also encourages students to think critically, solve problems, and think outside the box. Similarly, Critical Thinking and Problem-Solving pillars are embedded on STEM education that develops analytical and problem-solving skills that are highly valued in today's complex world. Students in a pedagogic STEM integration classroom should be able to: (1) solve problems, (2) innovate, (3) invent, (4) logically think, (5) self-rely and (6) technological literacy (Mpofu, 2019). Global Connectivity is another pillar that ensures that STEM education fosters international cooperation and understanding, as STEM fields are interconnected and affect all aspects of human life. Sustainability and Sustainable Development is also crucial in the implementation of STEM education as it plays a crucial role in addressing global challenges such as climate change, environmental degradation, and poverty.

STEM education in Zimbabwe has experienced both successes and failures. The successes include increased access to education, the development of a skilled workforce, and the promotion of innovation and entrepreneurship. However, there are still challenges to overcome, such as limited infrastructure, inadequate teacher capacity, and inadequate mentorship and support. By addressing the identified failures, Zimbabwe can further improve its STEM education system and position itself as a hub for scientific and technological excellence. STEM education (Science, Technology, Engineering, and Mathematics) has gained significant attention in recent years as it plays a crucial role in driving innovation and technological advancements. In Zimbabwe, the education system has made efforts to promote STEM Education as part of the broader goal of fostering a knowledge-based economy. Successes of STEM education in Zimbabwe include:

Increased Access to STEM Education

One notable success of STEM education in Zimbabwe is the increase in access to educational opportunities. The country has made significant strides in expanding its STEM curriculum and training programmes, ensuring that students from all walks of life can pursue these fields of study. Technical Vocational Education and Training (TVET) is necessary at the secondary school level to prepare students for self-employment and entrepreneurship (Likly et al., 2018). This has resulted in a greater number of students enrolling in STEM-related subjects, both at primary and secondary education levels. Many artisan and trade occupations require STEM education inclined to technology. Hence, TVET is essential and it may be necessary to offer it earlier at secondary. Apprenticeships and continuing education can be used to provide STEM-related training to informal sector workers (Lwakabamba & Lujara, 2003).

Development of Skilled Workforce

Another significant success of STEM education in Zimbabwe is the development of a skilled workforce. The country has witnessed a steady rise in the number of graduates specializing in STEM fields. These graduates possess the necessary skills and knowledge to contribute to the country and its economy. The growth of STEM programs has also contributed to the creation of job opportunities, particularly in areas such as technology, engineering, and research and development. Similarly, STEM education can contribute to voluntary, informal, and domestic work by enhancing knowledge of hygiene, health, and agriculture (Likly et al., 2018).

Innovation and Entrepreneurship

STEM education in Zimbabwe has played a significant role in promoting innovation and entrepreneurship. The 21st-century job market requires a new set of skills, and there is more emphasis on technology skills (Voogt & Roblin, 2012). The emphasis on practical learning and problem-solving has equipped students with the necessary skills to think creatively and come up with innovative solutions to real-world problems. This has led to the emergence of several start-ups and small-scale businesses that focus on STEM-related products and services. This entrepreneurial spirit has further contributed to the overall development of the country's economy.

Challenges and Barriers to Implementing STEM Education

STEM education holds immense potential, however, it also faces certain challenges. Thus the implementation of STEM education in Africa, Asia, and Latin America faces several challenges and barriers. Primary obstacles include limited resources, inadequate infrastructure, limited access to technology, inadequate teacher capacity, and inadequate mentorship and support. Additionally, cultural norms and attitudes sometimes hinder the adoption of innovative teaching methods. Some of the key challenges are discussed below:

Lack of Infrastructure and Resources

Many African countries, including Zimbabwe face challenges in providing adequate infrastructure, resources, and teacher training for STEM education. For instance, one significant failure of STEM education in Zimbabwe is a lack of infrastructure and resources. Many schools in the country still struggle with inadequate laboratory facilities, outdated equipment, and insufficient funding for research and development activities. This hampers the learning experience and limits the potential for innovation and creativity among students.

Lack of Lecturer Capacity

Another challenge faced by STEM education in Zimbabwe is a lack of teacher capacity. Many teachers lack the knowledge and skills necessary to teach STEM subjects effectively. This limits the ability to engage and inspire students, hindering the understanding and appreciation of these subjects. To address this problem, initiatives have been put in place to train and upskill teachers in STEM education methodologies

Inadequate Mentorship and Support

Lastly, the success of STEM education in Zimbabwe also depends on the availability of mentorship and support. Students require guidance and support from industry professionals, mentors, and role models to excel in STEM-related fields. However, the availability of such resources is often limited. The lack of structured mentoring programmes and networking opportunities can discourage students from pursuing STEM careers.

Gender Stereotypes

Women are often under-represented in STEM fields, which needs to be addressed through targeted initiatives that promote gender equality. Across the world, only 30% of female students pursue STEM-related higher education studies (UNESCO, 2017). Lack of awareness of the value of STEM education. Encouraging students to pursue careers in STEM requires raising awareness about the value of these fields and the importance of STEM education. By addressing the identified failures, Africa can further improve its STEM education system and position itself as a hub for scientific and technological excellence.

Strategies for Implementing STEM Education

To overcome these challenges of implementing STEM education, the Zimbabwean government and educational institutions require a multi-faceted approach. Key strategies include:

Building Partnerships

Encouraging collaboration and partnerships between educational institutions, industry, and non-profit organizations can help build partnerships and achieve the goal of resource mobilisation. Stakeholders such as renowned scholars in STEM education drawn from the nation's universities, Ministry of Higher Education and Ministry of Primary and Secondary Education officers in research and technology departments, policymakers, teachers of different STEM subjects, parent or guardians' representatives, student representatives, and industrialist must come together and chat a common vision (Mpofu, 2019). Collaboration between educational institutions, industries, and government agencies is crucial for ensuring the success of STEM education. Additionally, these partnerships can bridge the gap between theory and practice, providing students with real-world learning experiences. Furthermore, building partnerships with technology companies is essential in providing internships and mentorship opportunities to students.

Enhancing Teacher Capacity

Investing in teacher training and capacity-building programmes to ensure quality STEM education is critical if Zimbabwe has to position itself for the digital world. Thus, the provision of training and support to teachers is crucial for effective implementation of STEM education. Mpofu (2019) suggests a STEME (Science, Technology, Engineering, and Mathematics Education) integration framework as a starting point for better understanding and operationalizing STEM education. By equipping educators with the necessary skills and knowledge, they can inspire and engage students in STEM-related subjects.

Creating Supportive Environments

Creating favourable learning environments that foster creativity, critical thinking, and problem-solving is essential if Zimbabwe can advance in innovation and space science. This includes equipping schools with the necessary resources and infrastructure, such as well-equipped laboratories and modern technology. Creating partnerships with international organizations to provide technical and financial support for STEM education initiatives is necessary to produce a well-grounded technically-minded scientist. UNESCO (2017) regards to access to STEM education for girls as a human right issue, thus creating supportive environments for the girl child has been prioritised by the government of Zimbabwe. Issues of gender equity and promoting gender equality through scholarships, mentorship programmes, and awareness campaigns can go a long way in promoting social justice and gender equity in Zimbabwe.

Integrating STEM into Curriculum

Integrating STEM education into existing curriculums ensures that students receive a comprehensive and balanced education. Embracing STEM education is essential for Zimbabwe's development and global competitiveness, and it is essential for promoting economic growth and social progress. STEM education approaches must focus on integrating concepts from different subjects into new STEM subject matter, using student-centered pedagogies and assessment approaches that can nurture students 'inventiveness, creativity, and critical thinking (Mpofu, 2019). Thus by incorporating STEM subjects into various subjects, students can develop a holistic understanding of the world. Additionally, by equipping students with the necessary knowledge and skills in STEM fields, the country can empower them to address global challenges, drive innovation, and create a sustainable future.

Impact on Educational Outcomes

The implementation of STEM education in Zimbabwe has resulted in several positive outcomes.

Increased Employability

It is believed that strong STEM programmes are regarded as critical in developing students with twenty-first-century competencies (knowledge, skills, and values) (Bashman and Maynard, 2010; Mpofu, 2019). STEM education in Zimbabwe has managed to equip students with the necessary skills demanded by the job market, enhancing their employability and job prospects. Hence, globalisation and the rapid development of ICT are transforming society (Hooker, 2017). Hence, STEM is a critical ingredient to the fulfillment of the demands for 21st-century workplaces. The common aim of STEM education is to increase the interest in STEM fields, but also to develop the skills that individuals should possess in daily life and career processes (National Research Council (NRC), 2012; Lin et al., 2018; Lin et al., 2021).

Equity in Education

By providing access to STEM education, marginalized groups, such as girls and students from rural areas, are empowered to actively participate in the educational process and break barriers (UNESCO, 2017). Similarly, in STEM education, major inequalities remain. As a result, both women and girls continue to face many challenges in enrolling, accessing, and maintaining their roles in STEM fields (United Nations, 2022). This is unfortunate because women's untapped human capital can enhance the STEM workforce in Africa.

Innovation and Entrepreneurship

STEM education encourages innovation and creativity, leading to the development of new technologies and the creation of entrepreneurial opportunities.

Addressing Development Challenges

STEM-educated individuals play a crucial role in addressing development challenges in Zimbabwe. By harnessing the power of science, technology, and engineering, STEM graduates can contribute to the development of sustainable energy, healthcare, transportation, and other sectors (Bashman and Maynard, 2010; Mpofu, 2019). The implementation of STEM education in the world is essential to meet the educational needs of the 21st century. By addressing the challenges and barriers and implementing effective strategies, countries can unlock the potential of STEM education and harness its benefits. From increased employability to addressing development challenges, STEM education has the potential for transformative change in the region (Voogt & Roblin, 2012; Mpofu, 2019). Similarly, STEM education in Zimbabwe has experienced both successes and failures. The successes include increased access to education, the development of a skilled workforce, and the promotion of innovation and entrepreneurship. However, there are still challenges to overcome, such as limited infrastructure, inadequate teacher capacity, and inadequate mentorship and support. By addressing the identified failures, Zimbabwe can further improve its STEM education system and position itself as a hub for scientific and technological excellence.

Legislative framework guiding STEM education

STEM (Science, Technology, Engineering, and Mathematics) education has gained significant importance in recent years due to its potential to drive innovation and economic growth. Governments and policymakers around the world have been investing in STEM education initiatives to ensure that future generations are equipped with the necessary skills to thrive in a rapidly evolving technological landscape. In this section, we will explore the legislative frameworks guiding STEM education in Zimbabwe and other parts of Africa (Chitate, 2016, Mpofu, 2019). In Zimbabwe, STEM education faces unique challenges that warrant careful consideration of legislative frameworks. Unlike more developed countries where STEM education is well-established, African countries face numerous constraints, including limited access to quality education, infrastructure deficiencies, limited resources, and a shortage of qualified teachers. To address these challenges, Zimbabwe has developed various legislative frameworks to promote STEM education. Some key legislations include:

Education Policy Frameworks

African countries have implemented comprehensive education policy frameworks that prioritize STEM education. These frameworks outline the vision and objectives for STEM education, identify key indicators for monitoring progress, and allocate resources for teacher training and curriculum development. Zimbabwe has formulated national education policies to guide STEM education efforts. STEM education framework has been the best policy strategy for achieving industrial development in Zimbabwe (Chitate, 2016). These policies outline the roles and responsibilities of various stakeholders, including educational institutions, policymakers, and industries. For instance, the Zimbabwe Vocational and Technical Education Policy, and the 5.0 Innovation and Industrialisation Policy have been instrumental in driving the STEM education agenda. The ultimate objective of the STEM revolution would be to position Zimbabwe as a global leader in scientific discoveries and technological breakthroughs and effective exploitation of economic prospects from the commercialisation of research results enhancing her competitiveness (Ministry of Higher and Tertiary Education, Science, and Technology Development (2016: 5). The, common aims of STEM education is to increase the interest in STEM fields, but also to develop the skills that individuals should possess in daily life and career processes (NRC, 2012; Lin et al., 2018; Lin et al., 2021).

Science Education Laws

Zimbabwe and many African countries have enacted specific laws to promote science education. Zimbabwe established a new educational structure that would ensure the development of all-round basic skills encompassing manipulative, computer, mathematical, civic, scientific, social, and linguistic skills among pupils from the junior school level (Grade 1 to 7) up to 'A' level (Nziramasanga, 2014). The Government of Zimbabwe (GoZ) pronounced the 'Second Science, Technology and Innovation Policy' framework (Zimbabwe Education Blueprint (2015-2022), which provided the two Ministries of Primary and Secondary Education and Higher and Tertiary Education, Science and Technology Development with the opportunity to implement the STEM education policy (Chitate, 2016). These laws aim to enhance the quality of STEM education, promote research, and attract talented individuals to the field.

STEM Education Initiatives

Zimbabwe just like several African countries has implemented targeted STEM education initiatives, such as scholarship programmes, mentoring schemes, and public-private partnerships (Chitate, 2016; United Nations, 2022). For example, a private company, Gwango Elephant Lodge, in Hwange District, in the Matabeleland North Province has openly embraced STEM education by launching a Gwango STEM Initiative (GSI) in Hwange District. According to Ncube (2016:5)…"it is a rapid results project supporting the Zimbabwe Agenda for Sustainable Socio-Economic Transformation (Zim Asset)." Thus GSI is concerned with conducting 'career pathway' events with students and soliciting scholarships and educational material. These initiatives aim to address the shortage of STEM professionals and strengthen the STEM ecosystem.

Research and Innovation Policies

Countries with strong research and innovation agendas often have specific policies to promote STEM education. For instance, currently, the 5.0 Innovation and Industrialisation policy in Zimbabwe is driving the STEM agenda. The ultimate objective of the STEM revolution would be to position Zimbabwe as a global leader in scientific discoveries and technological breakthroughs and effective exploitation of economic prospects from commercialisation of research results enhancing her competitiveness (Ministry of Higher and Tertiary Education, Science, and Technology Development (2016: 5). These policies aim to foster collaboration between research institutions, industry partners, and educational institutions, leading to the development of innovative solutions and technologies.

STEM education in Zimbabwe and other parts of Africa is supported by legislative frameworks that aim to address challenges, promote innovation, and equip individuals with the necessary skills to thrive in a technological society (Chitate, 2016). While each country's legislative framework may differ, they share the common goal of fostering a culture of scientific exploration, critical thinking, and problem-solving skills. By implementing effective legislative frameworks, African countries and other parts of the world can harness the potential of STEM education to drive economic growth and address societal challenges

21st-century skills addressing current higher education issues

21st-century skills are important for addressing current issues in higher education, such as the need for more flexible and personalized learning experiences, the need for students to be able to solve complex problems, and the need for students to be able to collaborate and communicate effectively (Chiva Long et al. 2024). By addressing these issues, 21st-century skills can help to ensure that students are prepared for the demands of the modern world (Thornhill-Miller, et al. 2023). In particular, skills such as critical thinking, problem-solving, and creativity are becoming increasingly important for success in higher education and the workplace. One of the key issues facing higher education is the need to provide more personalized learning experiences for students (Fake & Dabbagh, 2023; Halabieh, et al. 2022). In the past, higher education has often been a one-size-fits-all model, with all students taking the same courses and following the same path to graduation. However, research has shown that students learn best when they can tailor their learning experiences to their own needs and interests. Personalized learning allows students to take control of their learning, and to choose courses and learning experiences that are most relevant to their goals and aspirations.

Critical thinking and problem-solving skills are becoming increasingly important in higher education and the workplace (Cabonero, et al. 2023). As the world becomes more complex and interconnected, the ability to think critically and solve problems is a valuable skill. In higher education, the ability to analyse information, evaluate evidence, and make informed decisions is essential for success. In the workplace, the ability to identify and solve problems is a key skill for innovation and productivity. As such, higher education needs to focus on developing these skills in students. Creativity and innovation are becoming increasingly important in higher education. As the world becomes more complex, students need to be able to think creatively and generate new ideas. In addition, many jobs of the future will require creativity and innovation, so higher education needs to prepare students for these opportunities. In addition to developing creativity and innovation in students, higher education also needs to create an environment that fosters these qualities. This can include providing opportunities for hands-on learning, and collaborative projects, and encouraging students to take risks.

Technology is playing an increasingly important role in 21st-century learning (Kuo et al. 2023; Waddill, 2023). In higher education, technology can be used to provide access to a wide range of resources, including online courses, virtual labs, and interactive simulations. It can also be used to support collaboration and communication among students and faculty and to provide personalized learning experiences. In addition, technology can be used to assess student learning, track progress, and provide feedback. However, it is important to ensure that technology is used in a way that enhances learning, rather than merely replacing traditional methods. In the 21st century, collaboration and communication skills are becoming increasingly important in higher education and the workplace. In higher education, students need to be able to collaborate with others to solve problems, share ideas, and work on projects. They also need to be able to communicate effectively, both orally and in writing. This is especially important in the age of social media and global connectivity. In the workplace, employers are increasingly looking for employees who can work well with others and communicate effectively.

Implementation of LMS and course/module software in Zimbabwean higher education

The use of learning management systems (LMS) and course/module software has been growing in Zimbabwe, particularly in higher education (Munyanyi, 2021; Svongoro & Mudzi 2023; Singh, 2024). There are several ways in which LMS can impact teaching and learning in higher education in Zimbabwe. One of the main impacts is the ability to provide personalized learning experiences for students. This can be achieved through the use of adaptive learning technologies, which can provide personalized learning pathways based on individual student needs. Additionally, LMS can facilitate more interactive and collaborative learning experiences, through the use of discussion forums, online groups, and other collaborative tools (Ouariach, et al. 2024). It can also provide access to a wider range of educational resources, such as e-books, online databases, and other multimedia resources.

Many best practices can be followed when implementing LMS in higher education in Zimbabwe. These include:

- Planning and preparing for the implementation.
- Involving all stakeholders in the process.
- Training and supporting teachers and students in the use of the LMS.
- Promoting the use of the LMS through communication and marketing.
- Evaluating and monitoring the use of the LMS.
- Regularly updating and maintaining the LMS.

The role of LMS in promoting equity and access to education is an important one, especially in a country like Zimbabwe where there are many barriers to access. LMS can help to reduce these barriers by providing remote access to educational resources, regardless of location (Cao et al. 2024). It can also help to provide more equitable access to educational opportunities for those who may have physical or financial barriers to attending traditional education institutions. Additionally, LMS can be used to provide educational opportunities for those with disabilities or other special needs. There are unique challenges to implementing LMS in rural and remote areas of Zimbabwe, such as limited internet connectivity and limited access to technology infrastructure. Additionally, there may be cultural barriers to using technology for learning in these areas. To address these challenges, it is important to first ensure that there is a reliable and high-quality internet connection, either through mobile data or satellite internet. It is also important to consider the specific needs and preferences of the local community when implementing LMS and to provide training and support in the use of the technology.

One example of a successful implementation of LMS is the University of Zimbabwe's implementation of the Moodle LMS (Machika & Dolley, 2018). The university has been using Moodle since 2012, and it has helped to improve access to education, increase collaboration, and track student progress. Another example is the use of the Blackboard LMS at the National University of Science and Technology, which has helped to improve the quality of teaching and learning (Maphosa, 2021). Another example of a successful implementation of LMS in Zimbabwe is the use of the Sakai LMS at the Midlands State University (Sibanda, 2022). This has helped to increase efficiency and improve student learning outcomes. In addition, the Zimbabwe Open University has been using Moodle LMS to deliver open and distance learning programmes (Munyanyi, 2021). In addition to these examples, there are several other universities and colleges in Zimbabwe that are using LMS and course/module software to improve their education programs.

The effects of LMS and course/module software on STEM learning

Globally most higher institutions of education are integrating learning management systems (LMS) in their teaching and learning (Barut Tugtekin, 2023). There is evidence that the use of LMSs and module software can have a positive impact on STEM learning. A study conducted in Zimbabwe found that the use of LMSs and module software improved students' understanding of STEM concepts, as well as their attitudes toward learning. It also helped to create a more engaging and interactive learning environment. In addition, the use of these technologies helped to improve collaboration and communication between students and lecturers (Turnbull et al 2023).

Some specific results and outcomes from the use of LMS and module software in STEM learning include (Borich 2017 & Chen et al 2017):

- Improved test scores on STEM-related concepts
- Increased motivation and engagement in STEM learning
- More positive attitudes towards STEM subjects
- Increased digital literacy and technical skills
- Improved collaboration and teamwork skills (Jansen et al., 2019)
- Greater understanding of the connections between STEM subjects
- Increased self-directed learning and independent research skills

There have been several studies that have looked at the impact of LMSs on STEM learning. LMSs can therefore:

- Improve student engagement and motivation, leading to better learning outcomes in STEM subjects (Al-Fraihat et al., 2020).
- Help to create a more personalized learning experience for students, which can lead to improved understanding and retention of STEM concepts (Saadati, et al. 2023).
- Help to support collaborative learning and peer-to-peer knowledge sharing, which is particularly beneficial in STEM subjects
- Provide a platform for students to access

There are several achievements associated with the use of LMS in STEM learning. Some examples include:

- An increase in the number of students pursuing STEM majors; completing STEM degrees graduating with STEM-related jobs or careers.

- An increase in the quality of STEM education, as measured by student performance on standardized tests and other assessments
- Improved collaboration between STEM lecturers and students
- Increased access to resources and learning for STEM lecturers and students (Turnbull et al. 2019).

Overall, the use of LMS and module software has been shown to have a positive impact on STEM learning, both in terms of academic performance and student attitudes.

The benefits and challenges of using LMS and course/module software

A Learning Management System (LMS) is a software application or web-based technology used to plan, implement, and assess a specific learning process (Turnbull, Chung, and Luck, 2019). It is used for e-learning practices by instructors, students, and administrators. Typically, an LMS provides an instructor with a way to create and deliver content, monitor student participation, and assess student performance. Businesses, government agencies, and traditional and online educational institutions often use these systems. They can improve traditional educational methods, while also saving organizations time and money. An effective system lets instructors and administrators efficiently manage elements such as user registration and access, content, calendars, communication, quizzes, certifications, and notifications. Learning Management Systems (LMS) have become an integral part of education in Africa. It has been used as digital content that is used within the LMS to deliver educational materials, such as course modules, presentations, readings, and assessments. These systems offer numerous benefits for both educators and learners, but they also present certain challenges that need to be addressed. In this section, we will explore the benefits and challenges of using LMS in Africa. The benefits of Using LMS in Zimbabwe include the following:

Enhanced Accessibility

The function of LMS includes the capability to disseminate knowledge, assessment of learner competency, the recording of learner attainment, support for online social communities, communication tools, and system security (Turnbull, Chung and Luck, 2019). LMS provides learners with anytime, anywhere access to educational resources. This allows students in rural areas or underserved communities to access quality education, regardless of their physical location.

Personalized Learning

LMS allows for personalised learning experiences by providing adaptive content and adaptive assessments. This enables learners to learn at their own pace and focus on their strengths and weaknesses.

Effective Communication

LMS facilitates effective communication between instructors and learners. It allows for real-time messaging, discussion boards, and interactive forums, allowing instructors to provide support and feedback to individual students.

Collaboration and Peer Learning

LMS promotes collaboration and peer learning through features such as group projects, online discussion forums, and virtual classrooms. This fosters a sense of community and knowledge sharing among students.

Resource Sharing

LMS facilitates resource sharing by providing a centralized platform for storing and sharing educational content, including videos, documents, and presentations. This allows educators to access a wide range of resources and create a dynamic learning environment. The Learning Management Systems (LMS) have become an integral part of education in Zimbabwe and Africa as a whole. These systems offer numerous benefits for both educators and learners, but they also present certain challenges that need to be addressed. LMS use in Zimbabwe is still a challenge and these include:

Infrastructure Limitations

One of the key challenges of using LMS in Africa is the availability of reliable internet connectivity and sufficient infrastructure to support it. Some of the main challenges for implementing STEM education and training programmes are inequalities and exclusion at all levels, poor resourcing, inadequate teacher development programmes, limited access to electricity and the internet, and inadequate infrastructure for STEM teaching and learning (United Nations, 2022). Many regions in Africa including Zimbabwe still struggle with inadequate internet bandwidth and infrastructure, which can hinder the smooth operation of LMS. Similarly, the post-independence STEM infrastructure, content/curriculum and instruction tools require urgent attention and strengthening" (Ministry of Higher and Tertiary Education, Science and Technology Development, 2016:3).

Digital Divide

The digital divide is also a significant challenge in Zimbabwe and the rest of Africa. The digital divide as a source of inequality between Africa and the rest of the world, also contributes to the inadequacy of implementing STEM-based curricula (United Nations, 2022). While technology has the potential to bridge this gap, not everyone has access to the necessary devices and technical skills to fully utilise LMS. This gap can hinder the educational progress of marginalised communities.

Cultural and Linguistic Diversity

Zimbabwe, just like all African countries, is a culturally diverse country, with multiple languages spoken across different regions in the country, through English is a medium of communication. LMS can be challenging for educators who are not familiar with different languages or cultural nuances. Developing culturally responsive content and adapting LMS systems to suit diverse cultural contexts is crucial.

Lack of Lecturer Training

Another challenge in Zimbabwe, just like the rest of Africa is the need for extensive teacher training to effectively utilize LMS systems. Many teachers are not familiar with digital tools or lack the skills required to create and manage educational resources in an online learning environment. Additionally, the production, deployment, and maintenance of course software within an LMS is a complex activity and difficult to codify in a policy document in a manner that applies to all users and situations (Turnbull, Chung and Luck, 2022; United Nations, 2022)

Data Privacy and Security

LMS relies on collecting and storing sensitive data, including personal information and academic performance. Ensuring the privacy and security of this data is a fundamental challenge that needs to be addressed (Turnbull, Chung and Luck, 2022). The use of LMS in Zimbabwe offers several benefits, including enhanced accessibility, personalized learning, effective communication, collaboration and peer learning, and resource sharing. However, it also presents challenges such as infrastructure limitations, the digital divide, cultural and linguistic diversity, and the lack of teacher training. Addressing these challenges is crucial for the successful implementation and utilization of LMS in Zimbabwe, ensuring quality education for all.

CONCLUSION

In conclusion, STEM learning technologies have the potential to address many of the challenges facing higher education in Zimbabwe, including the need for more flexible and personalized learning experiences, the need to promote equity and access to education, and the need to support learning in rural and remote areas. However, it is important to consider the unique challenges and needs of the local context when implementing these technologies and to provide the necessary support and resources to ensure their success. The future of higher education in Zimbabwe depends on the successful implementation of STEM learning technologies and the ability to adapt to the changing needs of students and society.

REFERENCES

African American Institute. (2015). State of Education in Africa Report 2015. Retrieved from www.aaionline.org/wp-content/uploads/2015/09/AAI-SOE-report-2015-final.pdf

Al-Fraihat, D., Joy, M., Masa'deh, R., & Sinclair, J. (2020). Evaluating e-learning systems success: An empirical study. *Computers in Human Behavior*, 102(1), 67–86. DOI: 10.1016/j.chb.2019.08.004

Barut Tugtekin, E. (2023). Scrutinizing Learning Management Systems in Practice: An Applied Time Series Research in Higher Education. *International Review of Research in Open and Distance Learning*, 24(2), 53–71. DOI: 10.19173/irrodl.v24i2.6905

Bashman, J. D., Israel, M., & Maynard, K. (2010). An ecological model of STEM education: Operationalizing STEM FOR ALL. *Journal of Special Education Technology*, 23(3), 10–19.

Borich, G. D. (2017). *Effective Teaching Methods. Research-Based Practice* (9th ed.). Pearson.

Burnett, N., & Jayaram, S. (2012). *Innovative Secondary Education for Skills Enhancement: Skills for Employability in Africa and Asia*. Results for Development Institute., https://www.r4d.org/.../InnovativeSecondaryEducationSkillsEnhancement-PhaseI-Syn

Cabonero, D. A., Austria, R. M., & Ramel, R. D. (2023). *Enhancing the Master of Library and Information Science Curriculum Towards the Improvement of the Librarian's 21st Century Skills in the Workplace*. Library Philosophy & Practice.

Cao, J., Zhang, D., Chanajaree, R., Luo, D., Yang, X., Zhang, X., & Qin, J. (2024). A low-cost separator enables a highly stable zinc anode by accelerating the de-solvation effect. *Chemical Engineering Journal*, 480, 147980. DOI: 10.1016/j.cej.2023.147980

Chen, B., Bastedo, K., & Howard, W. (2018). Exploring design elements for online STEM courses: Active learning, engagement & assessment design. *Online Learning : the Official Journal of the Online Learning Consortium*, 2018(22), 59–75.

Chitate, H. (2016). Science, Technology, Engineering and Mathematics (STEM): A Case Study of Zimbabwe's Education Approach to Industrialisation. *World Journal of Education*, 6(5), 27–35. DOI: 10.5430/wje.v6n5p27

Chiva Long, R. S., Ny, C., Chhang, C., Ren, R., Ngork, C., Sorn, R., Sorn, M. & Sor, C. (2024). The Impact of Assessment for 21st Century Skills in Higher Education Institutions: A Narrative Literature Review.

Fake, H., & Dabbagh, N. (2023). *Designing personalized learning experiences: A framework for higher education and workforce training*. Routledge. DOI: 10.4324/9781003121008

Halabieh, H., Hawkins, S., Bernstein, A. E., Lewkowict, S., Unaldi Kamel, B., Fleming, L., & Levitin, D. (2022). The future of higher education: Identifying current educational problems and proposed solutions. *Education Sciences*, 12(12), 888. DOI: 10.3390/educsci12120888

Hooker, M. (2017). A Study on the Implementation of the Strengthening Innovation and Practice in Secondary Education Initiative for the preparation of Science, Technology, English and Mathematics (STEM) Teachers in Kenya to integrate Information and Communication Technology (ICT) in Teaching and Learning (PhD Thesis).

Ismail, Z. (2018). Benefits of STEM education. *K4D Helpdesk Report*.

Jansen, R. S., van Leeuwen, A., Janssen, J., Jak, S., & Kester, L. (2019). Self-regulated learning partially mediates the effect of self-regulated learning interventions on achievement in higher education: A meta-analysis. *Educational Research Review*, 28(100292), 100292. DOI: 10.1016/j.edurev.2019.100292

Kuo, B. C., Chang, F. T. Y., & Lee, Y. L. (2023). Trends and Issues of Digital Learning in Taiwan. *Trends and Issues of Promoting Digital Learning in High-Digital-Competitiveness Countries: Country Reports and International Comparison*.

Likly, L., Joubert, M., Barrett, A. M., Bainton, D., Cameron, L., & Doyle, H. (2018) Supporting Secondary School STEM Education for Sustainable Education in Africa. Working Paper 05/2018. University of Bristol. Retrieved https://www.bristol.ac.uk/media

Lin, K. Y., Wu, Y. T., Hsu, Y. T., & Williams, P. J. (2021). Effects of infusing the engineering design process into STEM project-based learning to develop preservice technology teachers' engineering design thinking. *International Journal of STEM Education*, 8(1), 1–15. DOI: 10.1186/s40594-020-00258-9

Lin, P. Y., Hong, H. Y., Chen, B., & Chen, N. (2018). Integrated STEM Learning in an Idea-centered Knowledge-building Environment. *The Asia-Pacific Education Researcher*, 1(28), 63–76.

Lwakabamba, S., & Lujara, N. K. (2003). Effective Engineering Training: The case of Kigali Institute of Science, Technology and Management. *Global Journal of Engineering Education*, 7(1), 71–76.

Machika, P., & Dolley, F. (2018). Framework for a learning management system at a university of technology with a weak information technology maturity system. *South African Journal of Higher Education*, 32(2), 176–191. DOI: 10.20853/32-2-1502

Maphosa, V. (2021). Using the pandemic to accelerate 21st-century learning at a rural university in Zimbabwe. *Advances in Research*, 22(5), 34–44. DOI: 10.9734/air/2021/v22i530314

Mberi, N., & Phambili, M. (2016). Science, Technology, Engineering and Mathematics Craze hit Zimbabwe. *The Sunday News*, (February-March), 12.

Ministry of Higher and Tertiary Education, Science and Technology Development. (2016). Concept Note (revised 13 January 2016). Paper Presented at the 1st National Conference on Science, Technology, Engineering and Mathematics (STEM) at Harare International Conference Centre from 28-28 January. Harare: Zimbabwe.

Mpofu, V (2019). A Theoretical Framework for Implementing STEM Education DOI: http://dx.doi.org/DOI: 10.5772/intechopen.88304

Munyanyi, R. (2021). A critical analysis of the implementation of e-learning platforms at selected public universities in Zimbabwe (Doctoral dissertation).

Mutambisi, T., & Chavunduka, C. (2023). Institutionalizing SDGs: Urban Local Authorities in Zimbabwe.

National Research Council [NRC]. (2012). A Framework for k-12 science education: Practices, crosscutting concepts, and core ideas. Washington DC: The National Academic.

Ncube, L. (2016). *Gwango Lodge joins the STEM bandwagon. The Chronicle: Feature/Opinion, Tuesday, 1 March. Bulawayo*. Government Printers.

Nziramasanga, C. T. (2014). The 1999 Presidential Commission of Inquiry into Education and Training (CEIT) Report: Implementation Enigmas or Revelations?' In Madondo, M. M., Museka, G. and Phiri, M. (2014) (Eds.). The Presidential Commission of Inquiry into Education and Training (CEIT): Implementation Successes, Challenges and Opportunities. Harare: The Human Resources Research Centre, University of Zimbabwe.

Ochi, A. (2023). Inequality and the impact of growth on poverty in sub-Saharan Africa: A GMM estimator in a dynamic panel threshold model. *Regional Science Policy & Practice*, 15(6), 1373–1395. DOI: 10.1111/rsp3.12707

Ouariach, F. Z., Nejjari, A., Ouariach, S., & Khaldi, M. (2024). Place of forums in online communication through an LMS platform. *World Journal of Advanced Engineering Technology and Sciences, 11*(1), 096-104.

Saadati, Z., Zeki, C. P., & Barenji, R. V. (2023). On the development of blockchain-based learning management system as a metacognitive tool to support self-regulation learning in online higher education. *Interactive Learning Environments*, 31(5), 3148–3171. DOI: 10.1080/10494820.2021.1920429

Sibanda, N. (2022). E-Learning at a Zimbabwean Rural University during the COVID-19 Pandemic: Challenges and Opportunities. *Alternation (Durban)*, 29(1). Advance online publication. DOI: 10.29086/2519-5476/2022/v29n1a15

Singh, U. G. (2024). Exploring the Digital Divide in African Higher Education Institutions. In *Higher Education Institutions and Covid-19* (pp. 93–109). Routledge.

Sohoni, M. (2012). Engineering teaching and research in IITs and its impact on India. *Current Science*, 102(11), 1510–1515.

Svongoro, P., & Mudzi, F. (2023). Optimising students' participation during emergency remote teaching in the Covid-19 pandemic. *Perspectives in Education*, 41(1), 211–227. DOI: 10.38140/pie.v41i1.6182

Thornhill-Miller, B., Camarda, A., Mercier, M., Burkhardt, J. M., Morisseau, T., Bourgeois-Bougrine, S., Vinchon, F., El Hayek, S., Augereau-Landais, M., Mourey, F., Feybesse, C., Sundquist, D., & Lubart, T. (2023). Creativity, critical thinking, communication, and collaboration: Assessment, certification, and promotion of 21st century skills for the future of work and education. *Journal of Intelligence*, 11(3), 54. DOI: 10.3390/jintelligence11030054 PMID: 36976147

Turnbull, D., Chugh, R., & Luck, J. (2019). Learning Management Systems: An Overview. In Tatnall, A. (Ed.), *Encyclopedia of Education and Information Technologies* (pp. 1–7). Springer Nature., DOI: 10.1007/978-3-319-60013-0_248-1

Turnbull, D., Chugh, R., & Luck, J. (2023). Learning management systems and social media: A case for their integration in higher education institutions. *Research in Learning Technology*, 31, 1–16. DOI: 10.25304/rlt.v31.2814

Turnbull, D., Chung, R., & Luck, J. (2019). An Overview of the Common Elements of Learning Management Systems Policies in Higher Education Institutions. *TechTrends*. PMID: 35813034

UNESCO. (2017). *Cracking the code: Girls' and women's education in science, technology, engineering and mathematics (STEM)*. UNESCO. Retrieved unesdoc.unesco.org/images/0025/002534/253479e.pdf

United Nations. (2022). *Policy Brief. STEM education and inequality in Africa*. UN Office of the Special Adviser on Africa.

Voogt, J., & Roblin, N. P. (2012). A comparative analysis of international frameworks for 21st-century competencies: Implications for national curriculum policies. *Journal of Curriculum Studies*, 44(3), 299–321. DOI: 10.1080/00220272.2012.668938

Waddill, D. (2023). Building 21st-century skills by applying proven teaching methods. In *ICERI2023 Proceedings* (pp. 7039-7048). IATED.

Williams, J. (2011). STEM education: Proceed with caution. Design and Technology Education. *International Journal (Toronto, Ont.)*, 16(1).

Xaba, M. B., & Akinola, A. O. (2023). A Reflection on the Nexus between South African Land Reform Struggles and the Unresolved National Question. *International Journal of African Renaissance Studies-Multi-. Inter-and Transdisciplinarity*, 18(1), 136–155.

Zhou, L., Rudhumbu, N., Shumba, J., & Olumide, A. (2020). Role of higher education institutions in the implementation of sustainable development goals. *Sustainable development goals and institutions of higher education*, 87-96.

KEY TERMS AND DEFINITIONS

Science, Technology, Engineering, and Mathematics STEM: is an acronym that stands for Science, Technology, Engineering, and Mathematics. These are disciplines that enable students to be creative, promote critical thinking, improve communication, and enhance their ability in problem-solving.

Learning management systems: It is software that assists in the seamless operation of an e-learning platform. The LMS is a set of software solutions that serve as a virtual classroom for online teaching and learning activities involving both the lecturers and students.

Course/module software: Also known as training or learning software in a computer assists in executing programs and outputting information

21st-century skills: These are the abilities required for success in the 21st century. Life, career, and learning skills are identified as 21st-century skills.

Information communication technology: This is a broad term that refers to the use of digital technologies to access, store, and share information. It encompasses a wide range of technologies, including course/module software, learning management systems, computers, smartphones, tablets, the internet, social media, and other online platforms.

Problem-solving: This is a core 21st-century skill that involves the ability to identify, analyze, and resolve problems. It is a process that involves several steps, including defining the problem, brainstorming potential solutions, evaluating the options, and implementing the chosen solution. The ability to problem solve is important in all areas of life, especially in STEM fields, where it is used to solve complex problems. Effective problem solvers use a variety of skills, such as critical thinking, creativity, and communication. They are also able to adapt and learn from mistakes.

Creativity: Creativity involves the ability to generate new and innovative ideas. In the context of STEM, creativity often involves applying creative thinking to solve complex problems. It is important to note that creativity is not limited to the arts, but is also found in STEM fields, such as engineering, science, and mathematics.

Collaboration: This is the ability to work effectively with others, and it is an essential skill in the 21st century. In STEM, collaboration often involves working in teams to solve complex problems. This can involve brainstorming, sharing ideas, and working together to come up with creative solutions. In addition, it requires effective communication, such as being able to listen to others and understand their perspectives. Additionally, collaboration requires trust, respect, and the ability to compromise.

Critical thinking: This is the ability to analyze information, think rationally, and make logical decisions. It is a key skill in STEM, as it helps to make sense of complex data and information.

Chapter 14
The Disparities of Higher-Educated Men and Women in Leadership Positions in Indonesia

Hennigusnia Hennigusnia
https://orcid.org/0000-0002-3089-4215
National Research and Innovation Agency of Indonesia, Indonesia

Ardhian Kurniawati
https://orcid.org/0000-0003-0768-9915
National Research and Innovation Agency of Indonesia, Indonesia

Devi Asiati
https://orcid.org/0000-0002-7857-451X
National Research and Innovation Agency of Indonesia, Indonesia

Ngadi Ngadi
https://orcid.org/0000-0002-5249-0860
National Research and Innovation Agency of Indonesia, Indonesia

Zantermans Rajagukguk
https://orcid.org/0000-0002-5189-293X
National Research and Innovation Agency of Indonesia, Indonesia

ABSTRACT

This paper analyzes gender disparities in leadership among highly educated workers in Indonesia. The data for the analysis is the August NLFS 2023. The research data shows variations in gender inequality according to generation, marital status, and

DOI: 10.4018/979-8-3693-3443-0.ch014

main industry. The younger the generation, the greater the proportion of highly educated women as managers. The proportion of women in leadership positions in the service sector is greater than in the agricultural and manufacturing sectors. Based on marital status, the proportion of married women as managers is lower than that of single women. The results of the inferential analysis show that the average income of men is 44.6 percentage points greater than the average income of women. Furthermore, of the 44.6 percentage points of the wage gap, only 7.9 percentage points (17.646%) can be explained by differences in the characteristics of men and women. The unobserved and unexplained factors for wage differences that can be perceived as discrimination were 36.7 percentage points (82.354%).

I. INTRODUCTION

Gender disparity in leadership refers to the disproportionality in the number of men and women occupying leadership positions in various sectors and organizational levels. This still needs to be solved for many countries, including Indonesia. According to the International Labor Office, the average of the G20 member countries have a percentage of women in managerial and leadership positions below 30%. In addition, none of the G20 members can achieve the SDG target of 50% (ILO, 2020). Furthermore, the LinkedIn data shows that in 2023, women will still be a minority in senior leadership positions, with only 32.2% being women, compared to 41.9% of the total female workforce (World Economic Forum, 2023).

Across industries, women continue to outnumber men in senior leadership positions, particularly in manufacturing (24.6%), agriculture (23.3%), supply chain and transportation (23.0%), Oil, Gas, Mining (18.6%), and Infrastructure (16.1%). However, despite the increase of female representation in senior leadership positions since 2016, the gender gap remains visible, with men dominating the top-level positions such as Vice President (VP) and C-suite (World Economic Forum, 2023). UN Women estimates that about 24 percent of women will work in managerial positions globally in 2023. Northern Africa and Western Asia (NAWA) and Central and Southern Asia (CSA) have the lowest female representation at 14.3 and 14 percent of managerial positions, respectively. Eastern and South-eastern Asia (ESEA) levels are just below the global average at 22.1 percent (Hanna et al., 2023). This phenomenon highlights the ongoing gaps in access, representation, and recognition of leadership between the sexes, even though gender equality has become an essential agenda in many countries' bills.

Various factors are associated with men's and women's inequality in leadership positions. Research from Finland highlights how gender perceptions often hinder women's career advancement into leadership and management positions (Jyrkinen,

2014). Other research shows that factors inhibiting women from achieving managerial positions include the burden of household work, level of education, compensation issues, gender stereotypes, difficulty accessing the network, organizational culture, higher demands on women, and human resource policies. This research provides valuable insight into the factors that influence these disparities, including social norms, gender stereotypes, and less inclusive organizational structures (Hout et al., 2023; Ramos et al., 2022; Howe-Walsh & Turnbull, 2014; Cook & Glass, 2014).

Indonesia is committed to realizing gender equality in employment. To that end, Indonesia has ratified several International Labor Organization (ILO) conventions for gender equality, namely: (a) ILO Convention No. 100 of 1951 concerning Equal Remuneration for Work of Equal Value for Men and Women; (b) ILO Convention No. 111 concerning the Prohibition of Discrimination and the Promotion of Equal Opportunity and Treatment in Employment and Occupation Based on Origin, Including Sex; (c) ILO Convention No. 156 concerning Workers with Family Dependents which promotes equal opportunities and treatment for men and women with family dependents (Ngadi, et al, 2021). To accelerate the achievement of gender equality, the Indonesian government has implemented various major policies, including increasing the number of women in economic activities and decision-making, promoting representation of women in legislative elections, and implementing 12-year compulsory education (Nadia, 2022). In early 2024, the Ministry of Women's Empowerment and Child Protection carried out training and socialization to realize gender equality and inclusivity in the world of work through the 'Building Pathway for Women in Workforce' training program and other programs that can increase awareness and broaden gender perspectives (Kementerian PPPA, 2024).

Since implementing the policies, women have achieved some achievements in the labor market. The first thing that stands out is the yearly increase in women's labor force participation rate (LFPR). Statistics Indonesia recorded the LFPR for women at 51.8% in 2018 and increased to 54.52% in 2023. While gaining a significant hike, this is still below the LFPR of men (Statistics Indonesia, 2024). Women's LFPR is closely related to the economic, social, and cultural conditions, increasing women's education, decreasing fertility, growth in the employment opportunities for educated women, income, strategies to encourage employment for women, and women's ability to face obstacles in the place of work (Klasen, 2019; Klasen et al., 2020; Perez-Arce & Prados, 2020). The success of the increase in women's LFPR has a positive impact on gender equality in Indonesia. In 2023, Indonesia's gender inequality index (GII) score improved by 0.3% compared to the previous year. This makes Indonesia rank 87 out of 146 countries, whereas in the last year, Indonesia was ranked 92 out of 146 (World Economic Forum, 2023).

Another positive change is increasing the proportion of highly educated women in leadership positions. In line with the increase in women's participation in higher education in Indonesia, the proportion of women as managers is also growing. Statistics Indonesia shows that in 2018, about 30.46% of managers in Indonesia were women, which became 34.39% in 2022 (BPS, 2023). This situation indicates that higher education is essential for strengthening gender equality in leadership. A high level of education provides equal opportunities for men and women to gain equal knowledge, skills, and career opportunities (Costa & Gianecchini, 2007).

Education can alter society's perception of the roles of men and women in leadership. UNESCO data shows that women's participation rates in higher education worldwide have increased significantly. This indicates that higher education can contribute to women's achieving leadership positions. Education levels are also closely related to income and economic well-being, where women with higher education tend to earn higher incomes and better employment rates (Drechsel-Grau & Holub, 2020).

Furthermore, increasing the proportion of highly educated women in leadership positions is the principal capital for realizing gender equality in Indonesia. However, a comprehensive analysis of gender disparities in leadership among highly educated workers has not been conducted. Therefore, this paper aims to analyze gender disparities in leadership among Indonesia's highly educated workforce. It is hoped that the analysis of gender disparities in leadership can be used to formulate strategies for increasing gender equality in Indonesia.

II. RESEARCH METHODS

Data and Variable

The source for the analysis comes from the National Labor Force Survey's (NLFS) data issued by Statistics Indonesia. The NFLS data is the best employment data, representing the individual worker's perspective. Statistics Indonesia releases NFLS data twice a year, in February and August. The analysis in this study uses NFLS data released in August since it has a larger sample size than the February data. Therefore, it represents the population more. The August NFLS data used in this research is the 2019-2023 data series.

Furthermore, the data used in this analysis is based on residents who work in managerial/leadership positions with a high level of education. The leadership positions are based on the 2014 Indonesian Standard Classification of Occupations (KBJI), formulated based on the 2008 International Standard Classification of

Occupations (ISCO). The variables used in the analysis are gender, main industry, generation, marital status, and wages.

Meanwhile, the gender variable is categorized into two groups: male and female. The Main industry or business fields are formed from the main employment variables in the NFLS. The main industry in the analysis consists of 3 categories: agriculture, manufacturing, and services (AMS). These three main industry categories simplify the 17 main industries in the NFLS. Agriculture is a primary sector comprising agriculture, forestry, fisheries, mining, and quarrying. The manufacturing sector is the secondary sector, which consists of the manufacturing sector, electricity and gas supply, water supply, waste management, waste and recycling, and construction. The services are the tertiary sector that consists of trade, transportation and warehousing, accommodation, information and communication, financial and insurance services, real estate, corporate services, government administration, defense and mandatory social services, security services, education, health services, social activities, and other services.

The generational variable in the analysis consists of 4 categories based on the grouping done by Statistics Indonesia. The four categories are Boomers, Generation X, Millennials (Generation Y), and Generation Z. Boomers are people born before 1964 or older than 59 years in 2023. Generation X are people born in 1965 - 1980 or aged 58 – 43 in 2023. Millennials are people born in 1981 - 1996 or are in the age of 42 – 27 in 2023. Generation Z are people born in 1997 onwards or under 26 and below in 2023. Furthermore, the marital status variable consists of 3 categories: single, married, and divorced (alive/dead). The wage variable is calculated by adding the income in the form of money and goods received during one month.

Data Analysis

The data is analyzed using descriptive analysis to find the condition of highly educated men and women in leadership positions in the form of tables and figures. The cross-tabulation variables describe the conditions of highly educated men and women working in leadership positions. Apart from the descriptive analysis, we also use the Blinder-Oaxaca decomposition method to analyze the wage gap between highly educated men and women in leadership positions. The data analysis is conducted with the help of STATA 16 software.

This research uses the Blinder-Oaxaca decomposition method to measure the wage gap between highly educated men and women in leadership positions. This decomposition divides wage differences into two types. First, the wage differences are caused by factors that can be measured and explained (e.g., education, work experience, training, working hours, etc.). Second, the wage differences are caused by factors that cannot be explained (Blinder, 1973). The Blinder-Oaxaca decomposition model starts with estimating the wage function separately (Oaxaca, 1973). Mincer (1974) states that, in general, wage estimation adheres to the following equation:

$$W_i = ln\, W_i = \beta_0 + \sum_{i=1}^{n} \beta_k X_{ik} + \varepsilon_i \qquad (1)$$

the estimated form of wages for men and women is as follows:

$$W_{im} = ln\, W_{im} = \beta_{0m} + \sum_{i=1}^{n} \beta_{km} X_{im} + \varepsilon_{im} \qquad (2)$$

$$W_{if} = ln\, W_{if} = \beta_{0f} + \sum_{i=1}^{n} \beta_{kf} X_{if} + \varepsilon_{if} \qquad (3)$$

where $lnW1$ is the natural logarithm of the wages received by male (m) and female workers (f), whereas β and ε are the wage and error regression coefficients of wage and error. By using the Ordinary Least Square (OLS) equations (2) and (3) produce the following estimates:

$$ln\, \overline{W}_{im} = \hat{\beta}_m \overline{X}_{im} \qquad (4)$$

$$ln\, \overline{W}_{if} = \hat{\beta}_f \overline{X}_{if} \qquad (5)$$

The average wage gap between men and women is the total difference in the wages of men and women with value that can be obtained by subtracting equations (4) and (5), making the equation:

$$\Delta \overline{W} = ln\overline{W}_{im} - ln\, \overline{W}_{if} = \hat{\beta}_m \overline{X}_{im} - \hat{\beta}_f \overline{X}_{if} \qquad (6)$$

Equation (6) is added and subtracted from the average counterfactual wage to decompose the total wage difference. The starting point of the Oaxaca-Blinder decomposition is the creation of a counterfactual. The reference group appointed in this study is the average male wage. The average counterfactual salary with the non-discriminatory wage structure that applies in the market is faced by men. If women were to be paid based on the men's wage structure, then the average wage for women would be represented by:

$$CF = \overline{X}_{if} \hat{\beta}_m \qquad (7)$$

adding and subtracting CF to the equation (6), which will give the equation of

$$\Delta \overline{W} = \ln \overline{W}_{im} - ln\,\overline{W}_{if} = \left(\hat{\beta}_m - \hat{\beta}_f \right) \overline{X}_{if} - \left(\overline{X}_{im} - \overline{X}_{if} \right) \hat{\beta}_m \qquad (8)$$

The first part, $\left(\hat{\beta}_m - \hat{\beta}_f \right) \overline{X}_{if}$, then, written with "D," wage decomposition is the difference between the dissimilarity of rewards between men and women regarding their labor market characteristics (unexplained). The difference coefficient represents the unexplained gender wage gap and is signified as a component of discrimination. The second part, $\left(\overline{X}_{im} - \overline{X}_{if} \right) \hat{\beta}_m$, the wage decomposition, then written with "E," is the difference in income due to differences in characteristics or endowments (explained).

III. TRENDS OF HIGHER EDUCATED MEN AND WOMEN IN LEADERSHIP POSITIONS (2019-2023)

Highly Educated Workforce in Indonesia

Based on the pull-push factor theory, women's decisions to participate in the labor market are influenced by external factors based on the demand for labor in the labor market. In contrast, internal factors are related to individual and family characteristics that encourage women to work in the labor market (Jalilvand, 2000). According to Shultz (1981), highly educated women have a higher market value, thus encouraging them to enter the labor market. In Human Capital Theory, education level is a factor that influences the quality of human resources. Tirtosudarmo (2008) stated that the concept of human capital popularized by Becker and Shultz resulted from research conducted in developed countries where the success of economic growth in developed countries is seen from the increase in workers' income due to the higher education levels completed. This means that to improve the economy, investment in education is needed.

Shultz (1961) stated that education is an investment in human resources. Investment in 'human capital' is the same as physical investment in 'physical capital,' calculating the rate of return (benefit) from the costs incurred during the education journey. The skills and knowledge possessed by those highly educated influence their ability to carry out productive work to increase income. In terms of employment, Didier (2021) states that level of education is one of the factors that influences the quality of human resources in the labor market. Increasing the participation of highly educated workers affects changes in the supply of labor, which leads to improving skills in the labor market. Gender differences in the labor market indicate the conditions of men and women workers regarding opportunities and accessibility to employment.

Figure 1 shows that during the 2018-2023 period, participation in the labor market of men's highly educated is greater than that of women, even though there are fluctuations. More job opportunities are available for men. On the contrary, during the period, the number of highly educated women working in the labor market increased from 47.92% in 2018 to 50.17% in 2021, which is higher than that of men. The COVID-19 pandemic in 2019-2020 impacted the decline in economic activity, resulting in layoffs and a decrease in income. Ngadi (2020) noted that 15.6% of workers dealt with layoffs, and 40% of workers suffered from decreased income. Working part-time was one of the efforts to recover from the economic downturn. In the middle of Covid-19, the number of women part-time workers increased, reaching 33.18% in 2020 to 37.1% in 2021 (Ulfa et al., 2023). Becker (1976), based on time allocation theory, stated that the decision to work with women is determined by the time value between working at home (housework) and the labor market (market work). Furthermore, home industries played a prominent role in absorbing labor during the pandemic. The case study in Kediri Regency shows that during the Covid-19 crisis, women worked part-time in the home industry. They take advantage of advances in digital technology to develop businesses and improve business strategies. (Ulfah et al. (2023). In 2023, the participation of highly educated women was 49,50% lower than that of men.

Figure 1. Trends in the highly educated workforce, 2018-2023

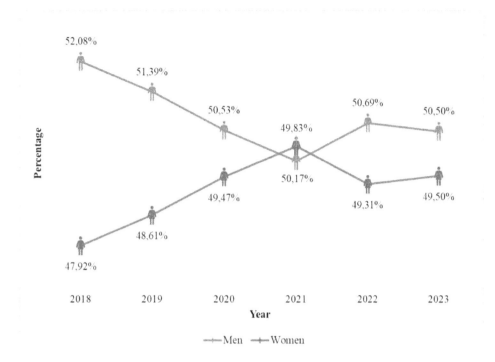

In terms of population, the percentage of women is similar to that of men. However, this needs to be reflected when comparing men and women in the labor market. The BPS data shows that men's labor force participation rate (LFPR) is always greater than women's; until 2015, less than half of women of productive age entered the job market. While women's LFPR did not reach 50%, men's was above 80%. Women's participation in the labor market increased to 50.8% (2018) but decreased to 35.41% (2023). This difference in LFPR shows that women's place is at home, not in the labor market. However, the higher the woman's education level is, the greater her aspirations to work outside the home become. They are more willing to work than women from previous generations (Hatmadji, 1917).

The progress of highly educated women's participation in the labor market must be connected to the socio-cultural conditions that arise in society that influence women's education. During the past few decades, gender stereotypes did not consider women as the primary breadwinners but only as secondary income earners. This impacted the educational priority given to boys as provisions for earning a living (Marta, 2012). From the 1970s to the 1990s, there were fewer women with higher education than men. The government policy on six years of compulsory schooling, stipulated in 1984 and then strengthened by the government regulation on nine years of mandatory education, has expanded the opportunities for Indonesian women to obtain primary education.

Since the 1990s, especially after the 9-year compulsory education was implemented in 1994, there has been an increase in the number of women's participation in education. The ratio of men to women in 1986-1990 was around three to one at the higher education level. Furthermore, from 1996 to 1997, it was around two to one (Marta, 2012). The development of Indonesian women's education levels is improving, reflected in the increasing proportion of women who completed higher education. In 2018, the proportion of women with academic and tertiary education was more significant than that of men at 8.98% (women) and 8.52% men, respectively. Whereas in 2021, the number for women is (10.06%) and for men is (9.28%). Moreover, women's education level influences women's participation in the labor market when they enter the world of work.

Technological developments also influence labor force participation. In the last two decades, the developments of the Industrial Revolution 4.0 and digital technology in the world of work have reduced employment opportunities because some jobs have been replaced by automation and digitalization equipment. Routine activities can be carried out by machines, thus replacing human workers. In the financial sector, for instance, the availability of e-banking and other mobile applications enables customers to do online transactions without having to go to a bank (Asiati et al., 2019). Workers who are less adapted to technological developments will suffer from gaining benefits from the technological developments, and vice versa. The digital job market is friendlier to Generation Y; they are more excited about mastering all fields and are more skilled in using digital technology. In addition, generation Z also grew up in an all-digital environment (Ngadi et al., 2022).

The trend of a highly educated workforce in leadership positions

The proportion of highly educated women in leadership positions is an employment indicator for achieving successful sustainable development through gender equality (United Nations, 2015). The gender gap and the lack of highly educated women in leadership is a problem globally, including in Indonesia. Gender differences refer to a social construction of differences between men and women, including the differentiation of masculine/feminine characteristics associated with the division of types of work, social status, and household tasks. In cultural interpretation, gender is related to the differentiation of meaning for someone born as a man and woman. This view gives rise to gender stereotypes. Men are considered superior to women, so they are given heavy tasks. For example, the general norm in society is that men are tasked with finding bread, while women are tasked with staying at home, which is considered static and safe. This condition also impacts the priority of education given to boys as a provision for earning a living (Marta, 2012). From the 1970s to the 1990s, the number of women receiving higher education was relatively smaller than men. The government policy on 6-year compulsory education, established in 1984 and later strengthened by government regulations on 9-year compulsory education, has expanded opportunities for Indonesian women to obtain primary education.

Figure 2 shows the trend of highly educated men and women in leadership positions. The dominance of men in leadership positions can be seen in two-thirds of managerial positions held by highly educated men in Indonesia. At the same time, only one-third of highly educated women are in leadership positions. This shows the gender gap in leadership positions in Indonesia. However, highly educated women in leadership positions show an increasing trend from 26.01% in 2018 to 30.32% in 2023. This is closely related to the increase in women's education. Based on statistical data, the proportion of women who successfully graduated from higher education increased from 8.98% in 2018 to 10.15% in 2023. The Data shows that in Indonesia, women have achieved considerable progress in higher education and participation in the world of work. Despite this, women have yet to enjoy more opportunities to work in managerial positions.

Figure 2. Highly educated men and women workforce in the leadership positions in 2018-2023

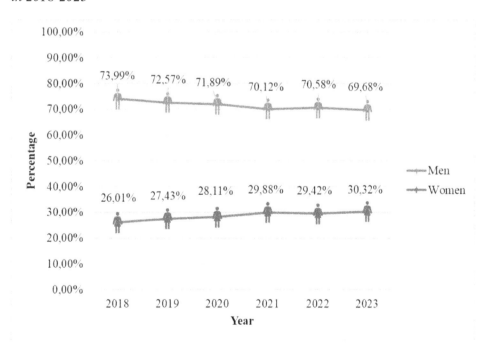

Increasing participation in higher education still does not guarantee equality in the labor market (Didier, 2021). Various studies show that women face multiple challenges when occupying leadership positions. Women are faced with several invisible barriers to advancing their careers blocking their access to promotion to higher positions, such as views of women and gender stereotypes, organizational barriers and company culture, and gender wage distribution (Didier et al., 2021; Costa et al. 2007, Rincon, et al., 2017). The inequality of women in managerial positions cannot be separated from the low representation of women in careers in science and engineering, considering the large representation of women in economics, administration, sales, and marketing. The basic requirements for women to occupy leadership positions are a combination of soft, personal, and communication skills related to their careers and work (Rincon et al., 2017).

The gender gap in managerial positions inflicts wage differences between men and women. This also applies to highly educated workers. Fogel et al. (n.a) study in Brazil illustrates that almost the entire gender wage gap is caused by men and women having similar skills and performing similar tasks but receiving a different amount of payment, or what is often referred to as "discrimination." The wage difference between men and women refers to observable characteristics such as age, experience, occupation, education, and union membership.

IV. THE DISPARITY OF HIGHER-EDUCATED MEN AND WOMEN IN THE LEADERSHIP POSITIONS

Over the last decade, women's participation in the labor market has displayed a promising trend. Globally, the female labor force participation rate has indicated a positive trend over the last few years. The World Bank notes that more than half of women aged 15-64 participated in the labor market. Globally, the World Bank recorded a women's participation rate of 53.5% in 2022, an increase of 0.5% compared to 2021 (World Bank, 2024). The OECD member countries also show increased employment rates more rapidly among women than men. It is recorded that the employment rate for women will increase by 1% in 2023, while for men, it will only reach 0.3% (OECD, 2024). There is hope that the return of women to the labor market can offer some recovery in gender equality. However, the situations in Indonesia's men and women workforce vary according to generation, main industry, marital status, and wages.

Generations

Based on generations, men are dominant in leadership positions in Indonesia, especially the Boomers generation (78.93%), Generation X (71.17%), and the Millennial Generation (66.25%). While women are still minor, the composition of women from each generation in leadership positions continues to increase as the generations get younger. The climax of this shift in composition occurs in Generation Z. Here, the situation reversed, where more highly educated women from Generation Z become managers, namely 51.43% of women and 48.57% of men.

Table 1. Highly educated men and women as managers in Indonesia according to generations

Generation	Sex (%)		N
	Male	**Female**	**N**
Pre Boomer	96.39	3.61	2,078
Boomers	78.93	21.07	106,890
X Generation	71.17	28.83	542,218
Milenial	66.25	33.75	493,530
Z Generation	48.57	51.43	70,521
Total	68.59	31.41	1,215,237

Source: National Labor Force Survey, 2023

Table 1 shows that the younger the generation, the higher the proportion of highly educated women to become managers. On the other hand, the younger the generation, the lower the composition of highly educated men is in getting the positions. Men represent the older generation, while women represent the younger generation. Moreover, there is a tendency to shift towards a more balanced composition in the 'competition between the younger generations' men and women with higher education as managers.

Two causes related to the composition of highly educated men and women in leadership positions can be explained. The first is the cause of the still dominant men in the Boomer generation, generation X, and the Millennial generation. This is more influenced by the traditional perception that is more classical, a legacy of the past that still colors the views of these generations, such as the view that women's place of activity is at home. This kind of view is not only found in Indonesian society. Research from Finland highlights how gender perceptions often hinder women's career advancement into leadership and management positions (Jyrkinen, 2014).

Other research shows that factors inhibiting women from achieving managerial positions include the burden of household work, level of education, compensation issues, gender stereotypes, difficulty accessing the network, organizational culture, higher demands on women, and human resource policies. This research provides valuable insight into the factors that influence these disparities, including social norms, gender stereotypes, and less inclusive organizational structures (Hout et al., 2023; Ramos et al., 2022; Howe-Walsh & Turnbull, 2014; Cook & Glass, 2014). Another cause comes from the women themselves, where women baby boomers prefer men's leadership. Older women tend to conform to masculine leadership and not challenge or disturb their male colleagues (Burkinshaw, 2020). It is a shame that there are still male Generation Z men who think that gender equality will hurt them. A new global study conducted by Ipsos in collaboration with the Global Institute for Women's Leadership in 31 countries found that despite the stereotype that Millennials and Generation Z are "conscious," they are more conservative on gender equality issues. Generation Z men think gender equality will hurt men (Ipsos, 2024).

The second is the cause of the shift in dominance to women in Generation Z. Apart from the increase in the women's LFPR, which increases Indonesia's gender inequality index (GII) as stated in the World Economic Forum (2023), the phenomenon as mentioned above is most likely influenced by the growing and widespread feminism in various countries including Indonesia, which women carry out to fight for their social, economic, and political rights to be equal to men. This movement is generally initiated and led by highly educated women with extensive social networks. Through his research in South Africa, Bornman (2019), for example, concluded that both male and female Generation Z students consider feminine traits essential for a business leader. Thus, it can also be said that what Opoku (2018) calls the diminishing of the masculine-feminine dichotomy has occurred. Another essential condition is the development of women's educational attainment, which opens up opportunities to compete with men, especially in urban areas and jobs without physical strength.

The increasingly developing digital era has also likely opened up opportunities for women to compete with men in managerial or professional positions. As Campbell (2023) said, over time, the gender gap between generations decreases due to the development of digital technology. The older generation is not or is less able to follow and adapt to the growth in technology. In comparison, the younger generation can take advantage of it, allowing them to take on more leadership roles. Highly educated women also utilize this development since it does not differentiate between women and men. Besides, although traditional views still color the thinking of some people, others have begun to accept female leadership. Most people who have experience being led by both men and women politicians usually no longer have a preference for choosing the gender of their political leaders (Ipsos, 2024). Furthermore, there is an increasing desire for educated women to enhance their economic growth. According to the latest survey of Global Investor Pulse survey from BlackRock, similar to men, women of the younger generation tend to prioritize wealth growth. This shows the potential for a generational shift because the older generation women did not have the same ideas. Ultimately, what is more important is the reality that the younger generation has started to break free from the shackles of gender bias stereotypes. While conservatism on the issue of gender equality still exists due to a few younger generations who see women's equality as a platform to discriminate against men, they have slowly broken free from the shackles of gender bias stereotypes.

Behind the encouraging trend above, one thing that still needs the government's attention is the less progressive development of Indonesia's GII. Table 1 shows that, in general, of the total highly educated workforce working as managers, the majority (68.59%) are men, and the remainder (31.41%) are women. This shows that, in general, Indonesia's GII is still relatively high, although BPS said that GII in Indonesia has decreased because more women are working (CNN Indonesia, 2023). This is because if we look at the developments over the past two decades, Indonesia's GII has yet to experience significant development or tends to stagnate. In 1995, Indonesia's GII was 0.578; in 2015, it was 0.467; in 2019, it was 0.480; in 2020, it was 0.472; in 2021, it was 0.565; and in 2022 it was 0.459. This data can be used as material for questions regarding the performance of implementing the gender mainstreaming program in Indonesia.

Main industry

Until recently, agriculture has absorbed the largest workforce in Indonesia due to 28.21% of the working population being in this sector. The sector that absorbs the second largest workforce is trade (18.99%), followed by the processing industry (13.83%). Compared with 2022, three sectors may experience the most significant increase in labor absorption. The three sectors are the Provisions of Accommodation and Provisions of Food and Drink (1.18 million people); Construction (0.77 million people); and Agriculture, Forestry and Fisheries (0.75 million people). Two of these sectors are the service (Statistics Indonesia, 2023). The increase in labor absorption in the service sector shows the current development of the service sector, opening up many job opportunities. The services sector has become a driving force shaping the economic landscape of countries at all levels of development in recent decades. It accounts for the largest share of global economic activity, generating more than two-thirds of GDP, employing the most significant number of workers, and is a source of new job creation, especially for women and young workers (World Bank, 2020; World Bank and World Trade Organization, 2023).

In 2023, only 33.7% of women work in agriculture, while 29.9% work in manufacturing. The conditions of women working in agriculture are slightly different from those in other countries. The Food and Agriculture Organization (FAO), in its 2023 report, showed that more than 50 percent of the agricultural workforce in many sub-Saharan African countries are women. Meanwhile, about half of the agricultural workforce in Southeast Asia is women in several countries, including Cambodia, the Lao PDR, and Vietnam. Women who work in agricultural production tend to do so under disadvantaged conditions. They tend to be concentrated in the poorest countries, where alternative livelihoods are unavailable. Women tend to refrain from participating as entrepreneurs and independent farmers and are involved in less profitable crop production. Often, women are unpaid family workers or casual workers in agriculture. In Indonesia, especially in rural areas, women who work in agriculture help their husbands run farming businesses or agricultural cultivation broadly because of economic demands. Women are not involved in the entire series of activities in agriculture for physical reasons and time constraints because they still have to take care of the household. On average, women are only involved in planting, harvesting, and selling produce. The low number of women working in agriculture and manufacturing compared to men is partly due to the gender stereotypes which assume that employment in the agriculture and manufacturing sectors is synonymous with men's physical strength, so these two sectors are dominated by men (Richardson & Roberts, 2020; Amalia et al., 2022).

In contrast to agriculture and manufacturing, the percentage of men and women working in the service sector is equal in 2023, with 46.1% women and 53.9% men. The low number of women working in agriculture and manufacturing compared to men is partly due to the gender stereotypes which assume that employment in the agriculture and manufacturing sectors is synonymous with men's physical strength, so these two sectors are dominated by men (Richardson & Roberts, 2020; Amalia et al., 2022).

Figure 3. Percentage of Workforce by Main Industry and Gender

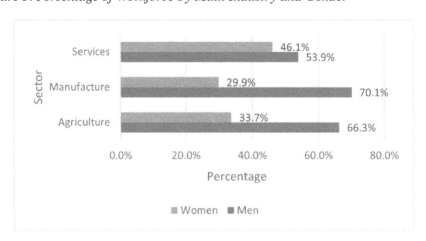

The percentage of highly educated men and women in leadership positions in the three sectors shows almost the same pattern as the main industry. In total, highly educated men are dominant. The dominance of highly educated men in leadership positions (82.79%) is apparent in the agricultural sector, with only 17.21% of highly educated women. The dominance of highly educated men in leadership positions is also visible in the manufacturing sector (83.11%).

Figure 3 shows the highest percentage of highly educated women in leadership positions in the service sector (35.12%). The share of services in female employment is generally larger than that of male employment, except in South Asia, where agriculture remains the main source of female employment (Lan & Shepherd, 2019). In 2021, 59% of employed women globally worked in the services sector, compared to only 44% in 2000 (World Bank, 2020). The distribution of female employment in the three major sectors has continuously shifted away from agriculture and industry to services in all Asian regions. The service sector is a sector where women have a comparative advantage over other sectors, and this condition causes more women to prefer working in the service sector compared to other sectors. The service sector is usually characterized by occupations that require less workforce and more interpersonal or intellectual skills. The service sector is also suitable for women because it provides a safer environment. In addition, this sector also has shorter working hours on average compared to industry.

The high disparity between highly educated men and women in leadership positions in the agricultural and manufacturing further strengthens the existence of gender stereotypes in the two sectors. Women are considered weak and, therefore, less suitable to work in leadership positions in sectors that are seen as synonymous with men. In the service sector, women are more able to compete since this sector reflects the traditional role of women more (ILO, 2023). It cannot be argued that the service sector is where women have a more comparative advantage than the other sectors. Women who work in leadership positions significantly impact the company's performance. The interaction between female leaders and the share of female workers employed substantially impacts the company's performance (Skala & Weill, 2018; Flabbi et al., 2019; Poletti-Hughes & Briano-Turrent, 2019). The productivity of female-led companies in the service sector is more prominent than in the manufacturing sector. This condition indicates better opportunities for female managers in the service sector than in the manufacturing sector (Lan & Shepherd, 2019).

Figure 4. Highly Educated Workforce in Leadership Positions by Gender and Main Industry

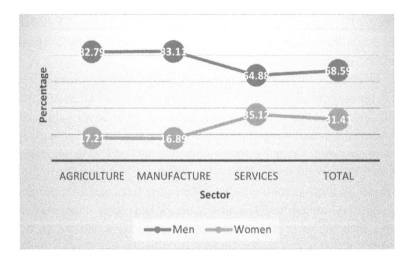

Various efforts must be made to narrow the gender gap, especially in agriculture and manufacturing. The increase in access to education for women has yet to lessen the gap between men and women working in leadership positions in agriculture and manufacturing. The viewpoint that men are more suitable to work in agriculture and manufacturing is indirectly the main obstacle to women's participation in these sectors, particularly in leadership positions. Another thing that must also be considered is the women-friendly labor policies regarding the protection of women, equal employment opportunities, anti-discrimination, and other policies related to wages, leave, and creating a women-friendly work environment. Furthermore, the effort to empower women to improve their skills and competitiveness must continue to reduce the gender gap in leadership positions in Indonesia.

On the contrary, there is one thing that needs attention behind the quite interesting explanation regarding the strong role of women in the services. Women who become entrepreneurs in these services are mostly entrepreneurs without workers and in micro-business types with low income and productivity. As revealed by the results of the Indonesia Country Gender Assessment (CGA) study published in 2020, many of the efforts to increase competitiveness and job creation in Indonesia still present gender bias. Around 60% of micro, small, and medium enterprises in Indonesia are owned by women. However, most of them are micro-businesses, and their business growth potential is hampered by lower access to credit and markets than those owned by men (World Bank, 2020).

Marital Status

The disparity between men and women in leadership positions in Indonesia is still prominent, even more so if viewed from the perspective of marital status. While there has been a rise in the number of women obtaining higher education, especially at the diploma and university level, this has not been fully reflected in the distribution of leadership in many sectors. This occurs further in the context of a patriarchal culture that is still prominent in Indonesia, making marital status a significant determining factor influencing women's access to leadership positions (International Labor Organization, 2013).

Figure 5. Distribution of highly educated men and women as managers by Marital Status and Sex

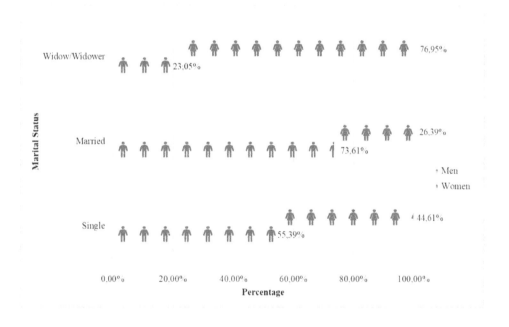

Figure 5 shows the differences in the proportion of men and women with different marital statuses. Men dominate the married group with a proportion of 74% compared to women with only 26%. However, in the unmarried group, the proportion difference between men (55%) and women (45%) is insignificant. In contrast, in the widow/widower group, the proportion of women (77%) is much higher than men (23%). The data shows that men have a higher participation rate in the surveys or studies, accounting for around 69% of the total sample. In comparison, women only make up around 31%.

This imbalance clearly shows gender disparities in leadership positions, particularly in the context of individuals with high education. The data analysis shows male domination in all marital status categories, with a higher proportion of men in leadership positions compared to women. Within the married group, the proportion of men occupying leadership positions is much higher than women. It shows the existence of solid and traditional gender roles in society's understanding of leadership, where men are considered more suitable and capable of holding important positions in organizations (International Labor Organization, 2013).

The data also illustrates the obstacles married women face in achieving leadership positions. The proportion of married women in leadership positions is lower than that of unmarried women. This may be related to greater social expectations of married women regarding family and household responsibilities, limiting their career mobility (International Labor Organization, 2013).

However, the high proportion of women in the widow/widower group shows the additional challenges faced by women who lost their partners, both in terms of social and economic support. Several factors explain why this group's proportion of women is higher than men's. First, women generally have a longer life expectancy, making the number of women becoming widows due to the passing of their life partner higher. Second, the social norms often make women who have lost a partner less likely to remarry. The same cannot be said about men more likely to remarry. Third, economic and social factors also play an important role, where women who become widows face more obstacles in obtaining social and economic support (Carr & Bodnar, 2009). It makes them more visible in the population statistics than male widowers, who are quicker to obtain support and remarry.

The data analysis also argues that equal access to education is only sometimes followed by equal access to essential career positions. While women may have a higher proportion in the "Single" and "Widow/Widower" categories, Men still dominate the leadership positions. This emphasizes the importance of concrete steps to promote gender equality in careers, including policies that support work-life balance, eliminate gender stereotypes, and empower women through training and career development opportunities. Therefore, the data call for further action in creating inclusive and fair work environments for all individuals, regardless of gender or marital status.

Wages

The average wages for women and men with high education to achieve equality in leadership careers is an essential highlight in evaluating gender inequality in the workplace. While both genders have the same qualifications, there is often a difference in the financial rewards between them. Women with highly educated qualifications and who occupy leadership positions still face challenges in earning equal wages to their male counterparts, even though they have the same abilities and achievements (International Labor Organization, 2013). This phenomenon highlights the existence of injustice in the world of work. This continues to be the focus of discussion in efforts to achieve gender equality. The relationship between gender disparities in average wages and factors such as generation, sector, and marital status must be dissected further to formulate effective policies to overcome these inequalities.

The disparities in gender in average wages by generation, sector, and marital status paint a complex picture of the challenges that college-educated women face in achieving equality in leadership careers. The data shows that, in general, men tend to have higher average wages than women in leadership positions, showing that gender inequality still exists in many manufacturing sectors (Table 2). Generational influences are also essential factors in this disparity. Older generations may experience a more significant gap due to more patriarchal social and cultural conditions that favor male dominance in strategic roles. Gender stereotypes, the common misconception that men are more competent and suited to leadership roles than women, often reinforce this gap. However, while younger generations may be more aware of gender equality, wage disparities remain a significant problem.

Table 2. The average wages of highly educated men and women by generation and main industry (IDR)

	Agriculture		Manufacture		Services	
	Men	**Women**	**Men**	**Women**	**Men**	**Women**
Boomer	12,899,910	41,427,762	59,025,225	11,888,611	27,983,387	20,502,887
X Generation	20,292,634	110,886,184	48,984,625	24,649,711	28,353,250	17,502,248
Milenial	29,040,819	30,415,639	30,621,321	15,029,525	27,363,711	24,344,788
Z Generation	5,925,606	30,000,000	15,121,783	5,303,769	13,649,404	8,150,684

Source: National Labor Force Survey, 2023

Table 2. displays the average wages by generation, sector, and gender. The data shows apparent differences between men and women regarding financial compensation in the workplace. In the Boomer generation, the wage difference between men and women is explicit in the manufacturing sector, where men's average wage is higher than women's. This reflects the gender imbalance in career opportunities and financial compensation during that period. However, there was a positive increase in Generation X, especially in the manufacturing sector, where women began to achieve average wages closer to their male counterparts. Despite this, disparities remain visible in the services sector, which indicates that while improvements have been made, much remains to be done to achieve full gender equality in the work environment. However, the Millennials give a more balanced pattern regarding average wages between men and women across various employment sectors, showing progress in achieving gender equality in women's access to high leadership positions. On the other hand, generation Z still shows large imbalances, particularly in the manufacturing and services sectors, highlighting the need for continued efforts to address gender disparities in women's access to high leadership positions.

Moreover, there is an exciting trend in which the average wage of women exceeds the wage of men in all generations in the agricultural sector, particularly for individuals with high education and occupying leadership positions. This phenomenon can be seen through the structural and social dynamics unique to the agricultural sector alone. Peterman et al. (2014) show that in many agrarian societies, including Indonesia, women often have an essential role in agricultural resource management and family decisions related to agriculture. In some cases, women may have higher levels of education than men in the agricultural contexts. This allows them to assume more prominent leadership roles. In addition, women's farmer organizations and women's empowerment programs in agriculture also contribute to women's access to education, training, and other resources, influencing their wages (Peterman et al., 2014). However, in other sectors, such as manufacturing and services, traditional gender bias and organizational structures that favor men still lead to wage disparities that favor men. Therefore, efforts to improve gender equality in access to education and career opportunities in the non-agricultural sector must continue to focus on achieving greater gender equality in various employment sectors.

Table 3. The average wages of highly educated men and women by generation and marital status (IDR)

Generation	Single		Married		Widow/Widower	
	Men	Women	Men	Women	Men	Women
Boomer	1,316,760	18,600,390	32,989,721	19,499,569	12,657,176	22,088,105
X Generation	13,650,219	25,236,652	32,803,634	16,498,876	45,791,418	27,192,688
Milenial	19,058,301	51,137,804	30,041,425	15,211,372	15,434,636	24,053,232
Z Generation	14,819,593	8,595,538	10,875,555	8,132,606		7,600,000

Source: National Labor Force Survey, 2023

Table 3 shows wage disparities between men and women in leadership positions based on generation and marital status. While there is an increase in the number of women with high education, men still dominate in average wages, more so in the married category. This reflects the gender inequality that still exists in the work structures and society, where traditional roles still influence both the perceptions and compensation in terms of employment. However, there is an exciting turn in Generation Z, where the wage gap between men and women is narrowing, particularly in the married category, indicating a possible shift in perceptions of gender roles in a younger society.

Data shows that for generations, the wages of highly educated women in single and widower status have been higher than men with the same status. One argument supporting this phenomenon is that women who succeed in leadership positions often have to deal with and overcome more obstacles than men, including gender bias and social stereotypes (Heilman, 2012). Women who can break through the "glass ceiling"—the invisible barrier that prevents women from reaching top leadership positions in organizations—tend to have exceptional skills, qualifications, and experience, which are rewarded with higher wages. Studies also show that women in leadership positions are often more focused on developing their skills and have strong professional networks, contributing to higher wages (Eagly & Carli, 2007). Additionally, single women or widowers are more motivated to achieve professional and financial success since they are often household breadwinners.

To fully understand the roots of the gender wage gap identified across sectors and generations, an in-depth analysis is needed to unravel the factors that contribute to the differences. One effective method for evaluating and measuring the contribution of various factors to the wage gap between men and women is the Blinder-Oaxaca Decomposition method, developed by Oaxaca and Blinder in 1973. This method divides the wage gap into two main components: first, the component that can be explained by factors such as education, marital status, and industry sector (explained), and second, the unexplained component, which includes unobserved factors that are often considered as forms of discrimination (unexplained). By applying this method to wage data in Indonesia, we can identify how much specific factors contribute to the gender wage gap across sectors and generations, thereby providing a better understanding of the dynamics of the gender wage gap and the steps needed to address it.

Table 4. Result of the Model Oaxaca-Blinder Decomposition in 2023

Decomposition	Pooled (SU)
Total Wage Gap	0.446
Percentage of Total Wage Gap (%)	100.000
Explained (E)	0.079
Percentage *Explained* (%)	17.646
Unexplained (D)	0.367
Percentage *Unexplained* (%)	82.354
Explained	

continued on following page

Table 4. Continued

Decomposition	Pooled (SU)
X Generation	0.008
Millennial	-0.0003
Z generation	0.014
Married	0.020
Widow/widower	-0.027
Manufacture	0.022
Service	0.017
residence2	0.025
Unexplained	
X_generation	0.054
Millennial	0.057
Z generation	0.029
Married	0.407
Widow/widower	0.029
Manufacture	0.147
Service	0.919
Rural	0.093

Table 4 shows the Oaxaca-Blinder decomposition results for the men and women wage gap in leadership positions, particularly in the context of individuals with high education. The first and second rows of the table present the average log wage gap by gender. The third and fourth rows explain the wage gap's component ("E"). Furthermore, the fifth and sixth rows show the unexplained or discriminatory component ("D"). The next row describes the coefficients of workers' characteristics for explained and unexplained.

The calculations using the Blinder-Oaxaca Decomposition method show a wage gap between genders in leadership positions, more so in the context of individuals with high education, amounting to 0.446. It indicates the difference in the income earned by men and women in leadership positions, where the average income for men is 44.6 percentage points greater than women's. Of the 44.6 percentage points of the wage gap, only 7.9 percentage points (17.646%) can be explained by the differences in the characteristics of men and women (explained). This value is much smaller than the unobserved and unexplained factors regarding wage differences, which are then perceived as discriminations, namely 36.7 percentage points (82.354%). This shows that the discrimination component is responsible almost entirely for the overall wage gap between men and women.

If seen from the sign of each coefficient of the explained component in Table 4, according to Kapsos (2008). The variables that show a positive coefficient on the explained component indicate that differences in the explained variable increase the wage gap between genders, while variables with negative values reduce the wage gap between genders. Almost half of the workers' characteristic variables, such as generation, marital status, place of residence, and employment sector, show positive coefficients on the explained component. In contrast, the Millennial and the Widow/ Widow variables show negative explained coefficients. The variables that contribute the most to the increase of the gender wage gap in highly educated leadership positions are the Rural (2.5 percentage points), Manufacturing (2.2 percentage points), and Married (2 percentage points) variables, respectively. This means the distribution of women in leadership positions with high education in villages and the manufacturing sector who are married plays a role in the increased gender gap. On the other hand, the variables that contributed the lowest and even reduced the income gap between genders were the widows/widowers (-2.7 percentage points) and Millennials (-0.03 percentage points). This means that the distribution of women in highly educated leadership positions who are widowed and in the millennial generation significantly reduces the gap between genders.

The sign and magnitude of the *unexplained* (indicated as discriminatory) effect of the gender wage gap. Table 4 shows that all *unexplained* variable coefficients are positive. The unexplained impact has a positive sign, meaning that the related variable contributes to gender wage discrimination in highly educated leadership positions in Indonesia. Meanwhile, the Generation Z and Widow/Widow variables contribute to the more minor discrimination effect. In addition, the Service and Married variables significantly contribute to wage discrimination between genders in highly educated leadership positions in Indonesia.

It can be said that the large wage gap between men and women in highly educated leadership positions in Indonesia is caused by discrimination in the labor market. According to Ozcan et al. (2003), discrimination in the labor market often transpires due to two things: discrimination because of the patriarchal culture, such as parents prioritizing the education of male children over female, women are seen to be more suitable for taking care of the household, while men earn a living (pro discrimination) and discrimination due to the negative stereotypes from employers in regards to women's productivity (post discrimination).

V. SOLUTIONS AND RECOMMENDATIONS

Effectively addressing the gender gap in leadership among Indonesia's highly educated workforce requires comprehensive and contextually relevant strategies. One of the major barriers faced by women in reaching leadership positions is the patriarchal solid culture and structural discrimination. To overcome this, the government must strengthen anti-discrimination laws and ensure consistent enforcement across all sectors. Implementing gender quota policies similar to those successfully adopted in Norway and Germany could be a practical initial step to increase female representation in leadership positions in both the public and private sectors. Furthermore, public awareness campaigns led by civil society organizations and the government should continue to be promoted to change cultural perceptions that disadvantage women, focusing on reaching all levels of society, including urban and rural areas.

Workplace policy reform is also urgently needed in Indonesia, where significant pay disparities and barriers to women's access to leadership positions persist. Companies should implement transparent and equitable pay policies and conduct regular gender audits to ensure fairness. Indonesia can learn from the UK's Gender Pay Gap Reporting policy, which requires companies to report their gender pay disparities publicly. Additionally, increasing workplace flexibility by providing options for remote work or flexible hours is crucial, especially for women with domestic responsibilities. Extending maternity leave and introducing adequate paternity leave, as practiced in Sweden, should also be considered to enable women to remain active in the workforce after childbirth. The government should support these policies through regulations and tax incentives.

Despite having good access to education, women in Indonesia still need help accessing leadership positions. Therefore, more targeted training and skill development programs are necessary. Collaboration between the government, educational institutions, and industry is essential. Mentorship programs, leadership training, and technology skill development should be expanded, drawing inspiration from South Korea's Women in Science and Engineering (WISE) program. Additionally, scholarships for women in STEM (Science, Technology, Engineering, and Mathematics) fields should be developed to ensure women have access to strategic and high-potential career opportunities. These efforts should be complemented by lifelong learning initiatives that allow women to continuously upgrade their skills in response to changing labor market dynamics.

Women's participation in sectors such as manufacturing, agriculture, and services remains limited in Indonesia. To address this, the government and private sector must develop sector-specific empowerment programs focusing on skill training and resource access. Economic empowerment programs in rural areas should also be prioritized, given the importance of the agricultural sector in Indonesia. Providing access to microfinance and business training for women in rural areas will significantly help reduce the gender gap in this sector. The government can also offer fiscal incentives to companies that increase women's participation and leadership through tax reductions or subsidies.

Moreover, gender audits and workplace transparency are critical to ensuring that no hidden discrimination persists. Large companies in Indonesia should be mandated to conduct regular gender audits to assess equality in pay, promotions, and career development. The results of these audits should be made public to ensure transparency and accountability, as practiced in the UK and Iceland. The government and business associations in Indonesia need to develop frameworks that provide guidelines for companies on conducting gender audits, and companies are encouraged to establish internal gender equality committees to monitor policy implementation and ensure follow-up on audit findings.

Considering the trends and proposed interventions, the future outlook for gender equality in leadership in Indonesia is promising, provided that the recommended strategies are effectively implemented. Cross-sector collaboration between the government, private sector, and civil society is crucial to the success of these efforts. Establishing a National Gender Equality Task Force could be a strategic step in coordinating these efforts and ensuring all stakeholders are involved. Additionally, long-term monitoring and evaluation should be implemented to ensure these strategies remain effective and can be adjusted as needed.

Overall, the proposed solutions aim to have a tangible impact on addressing the gender gap in leadership in Indonesia. By implementing comprehensive policies and best organizational practices tailored to the local context and adopting proven successful policies from other countries, Indonesia can achieve more inclusive and sustainable gender equality in the future.

Several factors contribute to gender disparities among highly educated workers, notably generation, main industry, and marital status. The following solutions and recommendations aim to address the gender gap in leadership positions among highly educated workers in Indonesia.

VI. FUTURE RESEARCH DIRECTIONS

Challenges still exist in improving gender equality in leadership positions in Indonesia. To deepen the science and policy in regards to gender and generations, either separately or simultaneously, it is imperative to implement relevant research on:

1. The Longitudinal survey on gender and generation taxonomy was conducted to determine the movement or changes in the distribution of highly educated workers who work by gender and generation.
2. The difference in outlook between genders by generations regarding gender equality, to find out the differences in views or perceptions between men and women from each generation regarding gender equality.
3. The role of education in reducing gender gaps among the highly educated generation: Find the role of Education Level in reducing the gender gap between highly educated generations.
4. The gender gap between generations in urban and rural areas to identify the conditions and trends of gender gaps at all levels of education and generation in urban and rural areas.
5. The influence of developments in digital technology and AI in reducing the gender gap between generations: This section will identify the influence of digital technology and AI developments in reducing the gender gap between generations and how much impact it has on Indonesia's GII.
6. The diminishing of the masculine-feminine dichotomy in the younger generation to identify the extent of the thinning of the masculine-feminine dichotomy among young generations at all levels of education.

VII. CONCLUSION

In general, the disparity between highly educated men and women in the leadership positions in Indonesia is high. Masculinity is still visible with men's strong dominance or superiority if viewed from several aspects. While the tendency to increase the proportion of women in leadership positions arose during 2018-2023, when dissected by sectors, only around 17% of the manager positions in the agricultural and industrial sectors are women. In contrast, the number is 35% in the service sector. Furthermore, marital status is one of the reasons for the modest role of women in managerial positions. Thus, the proportion of married women as managers is lower than that of unmarried women.

However, there is an encouraging depiction of gender disparity if seen based on generation. The shifting of the composition towards a more balanced 'competition of men and women in the younger generations' is apparent. The younger the generation, the higher the proportion of women who achieve the coveted position. Furthermore, the younger the generation, the lower the composition of highly educated men becoming managers. Men represent the older generation, while women represent the younger generation. Several studies illustrate this phenomenon, including (1) the gender gap between generations that is decreasing over time due to the development of digital technology or AI, which is more profitable for the younger generation; (2) the increasing public acceptance of women leaders; (3) the younger generation breaks free from the shackles of conservatism, gender bias stereotypes; (4) the diminishing of the masculine-feminine dichotomy in the younger generation.

Based on the wage levels, men tend to have higher incomes than women. However, in the younger generations (Millennials, Generations X, and Z), a growth in equal wages for men and women, especially in the manufacturing sector, can be seen. The Sustainability Development Goals (SDGs) initiated by the United Nations have yet to be realized significantly. In addition, increasing access to education for women needs to be more notable in order to narrow the gap between men and women in managerial positions, especially in the agricultural and service sectors.

REFERENCES

Amalia, B., Yuliati, Y., & Kholifah, S. (2022). Perubahan Peran Perempuan Pada Sektor Pertanian di Desa Tandawang. *Jurnal Ilmu Sosial dan Humaniora Vol. 11, No. 1. DOI: http://dx.doi.org/*DOI: 10.23887/jish.v11i1.36899

Asiati, D., Aji, G. B., Ngadi, T., Ningrum, V., Kurniawan, F. E., Aruan, N. L., & Purba, Y. E. (2019). *UMKM dalam era transformasi digital*. Yayasan Pustaka Obor Indonesia.

Becker, G. (1976). *The Economic Approach to Human Behaviour*. The University of Chicago Press. DOI: 10.7208/chicago/9780226217062.001.0001

Blackrock Investment Institute. (2020, June). *Blackrock Investment Institute, Global Investor Pulse 2019*. From https://investorpolis.com/blackrock-investment-institute-global-investor-pulse-2019-2/?lang=en

Blinder, A. (1973). Wage Discrimination: Reduced Form and Structural Estimates. *The Journal of Human Resources*, 8(4), 436–455. DOI: 10.2307/144855

Bornman, D. (2019). Gender-Based Leadership Perceptions and Preferences of Generation Z as Future Business Leaders in South Africa. *Africa'. Acta Commercii*, 19(1), a708. DOI: 10.4102/ac.v19i1.708

BPS. (2023). *Keadaan Angkatan Kerja Indonesia Agustus 2023*. BPS.

Burkinshaw, P., & White, K. (2020). Generation, Gender, and Leadership: Metaphors and Images. *Frontiers in Education*, 5, 517497. DOI: 10.3389/feduc.2020.517497

Campbell, R. (2023). *The Evolution of The Gender Gap?* National Centre for Social Research.

Carr, D., & Bodnar-Deren, S. (2009). Gender, Aging and Widowhood. In *International Handbook of Population Aging* (pp. 705–728). Springer Science and Business Media., DOI: 10.1007/978-1-4020-8356-3_32

Cook, A., & Glass, C. (2014). Women and Top Leadership Positions: Towards an Institutional Analysis. *Gender, Work and Organization*, 21(1), 91–103. DOI: 10.1111/gwao.12018

Costa, G., & Gianecchini, M. (2007). Career diversity. Men's and women's careers in Human Resource Management. *Management & Avenir*, 14(4), 169–186. Advance online publication. DOI: 10.3917/mav.014.0169

Dahlerup, D. (2006). *Women, quotas, and politics*. Routledge.

Didier, N. (2021). Does The Expansion of Higher Education Reduce Gender Gaps in The Labor Market? Evidence From a Natural Experiment. *International Journal of Educational Development*, 86, 102467. DOI: 10.1016/j.ijedudev.2021.102467

Drechsel-Grau, M., & Holub, F. (2020). Gender Gaps and the Role of Bosses. *CRC TR 224 Discussion Paper Series crctr224_2020_237, University of Bonn and University of Mannheim, Germany.*

Eagly, A., & Carli, L. (2007). *Through the Labyrinth: The Truth about How Women Become Leaders*. Harvard Business Review Press.

Eurofound. (2017). *Working anytime, anywhere: The effects on the world of work*. European Foundation for the Improvement of Living and Working Conditions.

FAO. (2023). *The Status of Women di Agrifood Systems*. FAO.

Flabbi, L., Macis, M., Moro, A., & Schivardi, F. (2019). Do Female Executives Make a Difference? The Impact of Female Leadership on Gender Gaps and Firm Performance. *Economic Journal (London)*, 129(622), 2390–2423. Advance online publication. DOI: 10.1093/ej/uez012

Fogel, J., & Modenesi, B. (2024). Detailed Gender Wage Gap Decompositions: Controlling for Worker Unobserved Heterogeneity Using Network Theory. *arXiv:2405.04365(econ). https://doi.org//arXiv.2405.04365*.DOI: 10.48550

Government Equalities Office. (2018). *Gender pay gap reporting: What employers need to know*. UK Government.

Hanna, T., Meisel, C., Moyer, J., Azcona, G., Bhatt, A., and Valero, S.D. (2023). Forecasting Women in Leadership Positions Technical Brief. forecasting-women-in-leadership-positions.pdf (unwomen.org)

Hatmadji, H. (1997). *Peran Perempuan Dalam Pembangunan, Suatu Paparan Singkat. Dalam Buku Widjoyo Nitisastro 70 Tahun: Pembangunan Nasional:Teori, Kebijakan dan Pelaksanaan*. Universitas Indonesia.

Heilman, M. E. (2012). Gender stereotypes and workplace bias. *Research in Organizational Behavior*, 32, 113–135. DOI: 10.1016/j.riob.2012.11.003

Hout, S., Jensen, L., Bates, R., & Ader, D. (2023). Barriers of Women in Acquiring Leadership Positions in Agriculture Cooperatives: The Case of Cambodia. *Rural Sociology*, ●●●, 415–428. DOI: 10.1080/03075079.2014.929102

Howe-Walsh, L., & Turnbull, S. (2014). Barriers to Women Leaders in Academia: Tales from Science and Technology. *Studies in Higher Education*, 41(3), 415–428. DOI: 10.1080/03075079.2014.929102

ILO. (2013). *Women in leadership: Overcoming challenges to equality.* International Labour Office.

ILO. (2020). *Women's Economic Empowerment in Managerial and Leadership Positions in the G20.* ILO.

ILO. (2023, November 7). *Where Women Work: Female-Dominated Occupation and Sectors.* From https://ilostat.ilo.org/where-women-work-female-dominated -occupations-and-sectors/

Indonesia, C. N. N. (2023, May 10). Indonesia's progress on gender equality in leadership. Retrieved from https://www.cnnindonesia.com/gender-equality-leadership

Indonesia, S. (2023). *Berita Resmi Statistik: Keadaan Ketenagakerjaan Indonesia Agustus 2023.* BPS.

Indonesia, S. (2024, May 10). From bps.go.id: https://www.bps.go.id/id/statistics-table/2/MjIwMCMy/tingkat-partisipasi-angkatan-kerja-menurut-jenis-kelamin.html

Ipsos. (2024). *Annual International Women's Day 2024: Global Attitudes Towards Women's Leadership.* Ipsos.

Jacobsen, P. (1994). The Economic of Gender. Massachusets: Blackwell.

Jalilvand, M. (2000). Married Women, Work dan Values. Monthly Labor Review August 2000. Married women, work, and values (bls.gov)

Jyrkinen, M. (2014). Women managers, careers and gendered ageism. *Scandinavian Journal of Management, Elsevier*, 30(2), 175–185.

Kapsos, S. (2008). *The Gender Wage Gap in Bangladesh. ILO Asia-Pacific Working Paper Series.* Bangkok: ILO.

Kementerian, P. P. P. A. (2024). Wujudkan Lingkungan Kerja yang Adil dan Setara bagi Perempuan, Kemen PPPA dan Women's World Banking Dorong Rencana Aksi Berkelanjutan. https://www.kemenpppa.go.id/page/view/NTA1Ng==

Klasen, S. (2019). What explains uneven Female Labor Force Participation Levels and Trends in Developing Countries? *The World Bank Research Observer*, 34(2), 161–197. Advance online publication. DOI: 10.1093/wbro/lkz005

Klasen, S., Le, T., Pieters, J., & Silva, M. (2020). What Drives Female Labour Force Participation? Comparable Micro-level Evidence from Eight Developing and Emerging Economies. *The Journal of Development Studies.* Advance online publication. DOI: 10.1080/00220388.2020.1790533

Lan, J., & Shepherd, B. (2019). Women and the Services Sector. In *Leveraging Services for Development: Prospects and Policies*. Asian Development Bank.

Madera, J., Ng, L., Sundermann, J., & Hebl, M. (2019). Top Management Gender Diversity and Organizational Attraction: When and Why It Matters. *Archives of Scientific Psychology. DOI: http://dx.doi.org/*, 90 –101.DOI: 10.1037/arc0000060

Marta, N. (2012). Tingkat Pendidikan Perempuan Indonesia dan Dampaknya Terhadap Penyerapan Tenaga Kerja Tahun 1970-1998. *Jurnal Sejarah Lontar Vol. 9, No. 2.*

Mincer, J. (1974). The Human Capital Earnings Function. *Schooling, Experience, and Earnings*, 83-96.

Nadia, S. (2022). Pemberdayaan Perempuan untuk Kesetaraan. https://www.djkn .kemenkeu.go.id/kpknl-pontianak/baca-artikel/15732/Pemberdayaan-Perempuan -untuk-Kesetaraan.html

National Science Foundation. (2021). *Women, minorities, and persons with disabilities in science and engineering.*

Ngadi, A. D., & Rajagukguk, Z. (2022). Featuring Multi-generational Digital Workers in Indonesia. *The 4Th SEASIA Biennial Conference.* Jakarta: Springer.

Ngadi, N., Meliana, R., & Purba, Y. A. (2020). Dampak pandemi Covid-19 terhadap PHK dan pendapatan pekerja di Indonesia. *Jurnal Kependudukan Indonesia*, 2902, 43.

Ngadi, N., Asiati, D., Latifa, A., & Nawawi, N. (2021). Gender Inequality in the Indonesian Labor Market. In Dixit, S., & Moid, S. (Eds.), *Women Empowerment and Well-Being for Inclusive Economic Growth* (pp. 24–44). IGI Global., DOI: 10.4018/978-1-7998-3737-4.ch002

Oaxaca, R. (1973). Male-Female Wage Differentials in Urban Labor Markets. *International Economic Review*, 14(3), 693–709. DOI: 10.2307/2525981

OECD. (2020). *Parental leave: Where are the fathers?* OECD Family Database.

OECD. (2024, May 5). *Labour Market Situation.* From oecd.org: https://www.oecd .org/sdd/labour-stats/labour-market-situation-oecd-updated-april-2024.htm

Opoku, A., & Williams, N. (2018). *Second-Generation Gender Bias: An Exploratory Study of Women's Leadership Gap in a UK Construction Organisation.* International Journal of Ethics and Systems., DOI: 10.1108/IJOES-05-2018-0079

Özcan, Y., Ücdoğruk, Ş., & Özcan, K. (2003). Age Differences by Gender, Wage and Self Employment in Urban Turkey. *Journal of Economic Cooperation*, 24, 1–24.

Perez-Arce, F., & Prados, M. (2020). The Decline in The U.S Labor Force Participation Rate: A Literature Review. *Journal of Economic Surveys*. Advance online publication. DOI: 10.1111/joes.12402

Peterman, A., Julia, B., & Agnes, Q. (2014). A Review of Empirical Evidence on Gender Differences in Nonland Agricultural Inputs, Technology, and Services in Developing Countries. *145–186. DOI:*.DOI: 10.1007/978-94-017-8616-4

Poletti-Hughes, J., & Briano-Turrent, G. (2019). Gender Diversity on the Board of Directors and Corporate Risk: A Behavioural. *International Review of Financial Analysis*, 62, 80–90. DOI: 10.1016/j.irfa.2019.02.004

Ramos, A., Latorre, F., Tomás, I., & Ramos, J. (2022). Women's Promotion to Management and Unfairness Perceptions—A Challenge to the Social Sustainability of Organizations and Beyond. *Sustainability (Basel)*, 14(2), 788. DOI: 10.3390/su14020788

Richardson, M., & Roberts, R. (2020). Modern Women and Traditional Gender Stereotypes: An Examination of the Roles Women Assume in Thailand's Agricultural System. *Journal of International Agricultural and Extension Education*, 27(4), 7–21. Advance online publication. DOI: 10.5191/jiaee.2020.27407

Rincón, V., González, M., & Barrero, K. (2017). Women and Leadership: Gender Barriers to Senior Management Positions. *Intangible Capital*, 13(2), 319. DOI: 10.3926/ic.889

Rincón, V., González, M., & Barrero, K. (2017). Women and Leadership: Gender Barriers to Senior Management Positions. *Intangible Capital*, 13(2), 319–386. DOI: 10.3926/ic.889

Schultz, T. P. (1980). Estimating Labor Supply Function for Married Women. In Smith, J. (Ed.), *Female Labor Supply: Theory and Estimating*. Princeton University Press. DOI: 10.1515/9781400856992.25

Schultz, T. W. (1961). Investment in Human Capital [Jstore.]. *The American Economic Review*, 51(1), 1–17.

Sipayung, F., Wijaya, A., Putra, F., & Aratame, N. (2022). Analyzing the Characteristics of Highly Educated Unemployment in Indonesia's Capital City. *Jurnal Ekonomi dan Studi Pembangunan, 14 (2).: http://dx.doi.org/*.DOI: 10.17977/um-002v14i22022p153

Skala, D., & Weill, L. (2018). Does CEO gender matter for bank risk? *Economic Systems*, 42(1), 64–74. DOI: 10.1016/j.ecosys.2017.08.005

Taylor, P., Morin, R., Cohn, D., Clark, A., & Wang, W. (2008). *Men or Women: Who's the Better Leader?* Pew Research Center.

Tirtosudarmo, R. (2008). Dari Human Capital ke Human Development: Catatan Kritis Terhadap Perspekif Sumberdaya Manusia di Indonesia" dalam Priyono Tjptoherijanto dan Laila Nagib (editor). (2008). Pengembangan Sumberdaya Manusia: diantar Peluang dan Tantangan

Ulfah, E., & Badriyah, N. (2023). Faktor Yang Mempengaruhi Kinerja Paruh Waktu Wanita Pada Home Industry Pasca Covid-19. *Journal of Development Economic and Social Studies.*, 02(1), 112–123. DOI: 10.21776/jdess.2023.02.1.10

United Nation. (2015). *Transforming our World: The 2030 Agenda for Sustainable Development*. United Nations.

United Nation. (n.d.). *Global indicator framework for the Sustainable Development Goals and targets of the 2030 Agenda for Sustainable Development*. From from https://unstats.un.org/sdgs/indicators/Global%20Indicator%20Framework%20after%202023%20refinement_Eng.pdf

World Bank. (2020). *Indonesia Country Gender Assessment: Investing in Opportunities*. Washigton DC: *Wolrd* Bank.

World Bank. (2024, 510). *Gender Data*. From The World Bank: https://genderdata.worldbank.org/en/indicator/sl-tlf-acti-zs?view=trend&geos=WLD_IDN&year-range=2010_2023&age=15-64&gender=female&gender=male&gender=total

World Bank. (2024). Program Kesetaraan Gender di Indonesia. https://www.worldbank.org/in/country/indonesia/brief/gender-equality-for-growth-research-and-analytical-program-in-indonesia

World Economic Forum. (2023). *Global Gender Gap Report 2023*. Geneva: World Economic Forum World Bank, & WTO. (2023). *Trade in Services for Development. Fostering Sustainable Growth and Economic Diversification*. Geneva: WTO.

Chapter 15
Challenges and Future Strategies for B-Schools

Anatoly Zhuplev
Loyola Marymount University, USA

Francisco J. Valle
Loyola Marymount University, USA

José J. Rincón
Loyola Marymount University, USA

Max Plithides
University of California, Los Angeles, USA

ABSTRACT

This chapter examines the evolution of American higher education (HE) and business schools (B-schools) in the historical and contemporary strategic context. It explores the influence of the Humboldtian model on the contemporary HE industry in America. The chapter analyzes the current HE landscape, revenue sources, and global reach. The chapter investigates strategic disruptors like demographic shifts, skyrocketing costs of college and student loan burden, technological impacts, including proliferation of IT and AI, eroding public confidence in HE, and political and regulatory trends. The chapter explores solutions like accreditation reform and diversified credentials. It examines pressures on B-schools, including slow technology adoption and competition. It emphasizes the need for B-schools to embrace innovation, technology, and industry partnerships. The chapter concludes with a collaborative educational project focused on regional socio-economic development grounded in comparative analysis of best global practices, highlighting the potential of HE to address real-world issues.

DOI: 10.4018/979-8-3693-3443-0.ch015

Introduction

The landscape of higher education (HE) in the U.S. is undergoing a period of significant transformation. Fueled by technological advancements, demographic shifts, and evolving societal trends and dynamics, the traditional model faces increasing pressures to adapt. This chapter explores the current state of HE and business schools (B-schools), examining the challenges and opportunities that are unfolding and lie ahead. This chapter aims to address several key questions and issues. Firstly, it looks at the origins and historical evolution of HE in the U.S., highlighting the impact of industrial revolutions and the changing role of universities. Secondly, it explores the contemporary strategic landscape of HE institutions, analyzing demographic and socio-economic trends, technological disruptions, and public opinions and perceptions. Finally, the chapter focuses on the specific pressures and opportunities faced by B-schools within this evolving environment. Understanding the current state of HE is crucial for educators, policymakers, students, and the broader public. Stagnant and declining enrollments, rising tuition costs, and the emergence of alternative educational pathways raise critical questions about the value proposition of traditional colleges and universities. This chapter investigates these issues and their implications for the future of B-schools, which play a vital role in preparing future business leaders. This chapter utilizes a multi-pronged methodological approach. It integrates historical analysis with contemporary data and trends in HE. Additionally, the chapter draws on relevant scholarly literature and industry reports to provide a comprehensive picture of the evolving HE landscape.

In this paper, we provide an overview of the historical evolution of HE in the U.S., the impact of industrial revolutions on education, challenges, and opportunities for business schools (B-schools), and the need for adaptation to technological and societal changes in the HE landscape. We also discuss rising tuition costs, underemployment of college graduates, and changing societal perceptions of the value of a college degree.

In the first section of the paper, we look at the beginnings of American HE, rooted in medieval origins, evolved notably with the rise of the German Humboldtian model during the first Industrial Revolution. This model, blending education and research, spread across the U.S. over two centuries. The second Industrial Revolution emphasized disciplines such as engineering and business. Today, the ongoing third and fourth Industrial Revolutions present new challenges and opportunities, shaping the strategic landscape of HE and B-schools.

In the section focusing on the contemporary strategic landscape, we explore American HE institutions and their triple mission of student careers and prosperity, citizenship cultivation, and college experience provision. The HE sector faces significant entry barriers, relies heavily on government aid, and operates under strict regulations. Revenues are substantial, with public institutions significantly reliant on government support and private ones on investment returns. While revenue sources vary, the industry has experienced growth, with modest wage increases. U.S. universities have a global presence, attracting a growing number of international students, particularly from China and India, highlighting their expanding global influence.

On the other hand, in the section focusing on trends and disruptors, we find the U.S. HE's landscape is shaped by demographic shifts, technological advancements, and evolving public perceptions. Since 2010, college enrollments have stagnated, intensifying competition amid reduced government support and escalating costs. Innovations stemming from the fourth Industrial Revolution are challenging traditional models, necessitating adaptation. The popularity of online education has surged, particularly accelerated by the COVID-19 pandemic. Confidence in traditional HE format is declining, with community colleges, trade schools, certificate programs, and other educational platforms seen as viable alternatives. Economic challenges, mounting national student debt, and disruptions in international student enrollments further complicate matters. Despite these hurdles, addressing disruptors through innovation is crucial for institutions to sustain their relevance and socio-economic impact.

Moreover, American HE faces critical threats amid shifts in societal attitudes. Traditionalists advocate maintaining the existing model, citing HE industry's historical resilience, while critics call for change, citing declining public confidence, high costs, and job-market shifts. Restructuring accreditation, holding colleges accountable for outcomes, and diversifying credentials are proposed solutions. The future for college education may entail greater accountability, innovative accreditation, and recognition of diverse skills paths, signaling a potential shift in HE's focus on student success and economic relevance.

In addition, B-schools involve encountering pressures and opportunities amidst HE disruptions. Challenges encompass slow technology adoption, trending deglobalization, internal criticisms, and competition with online providers and alternative educational paths. Solutions entail embracing augmented reality, artificial intelligence (AI), and innovative credentials. B-schools must modernize curricula, prioritize skill development, and foster lifelong learning. Vital aspects include industry partnerships, faculty with real-world experience, and student-centered approaches. Online platforms challenge traditional models, necessitating B-schools to justify costs and emphasize active and skill-based learning. Innovation, technology integration, and industry alignment are crucial for long-term relevance.

Our paper closes with a case of collaborative educational project with high socio-economic impacts. This global-local project aims to address socioeconomic development (SED) challenges in Greater Los Angeles, U.S., and Greater Córdoba, Spain, focusing on societal issues such as healthcare access, crime, and poverty.

By leveraging best global practices and information technology (IT) innovations, universities can implement a staged approach, fostering local problem-solving and stakeholder benefits. The initiative aims to bridge academia and real-world applications, reduce resource duplication, and improve university branding. Deliverables include improved education, career outcomes, and SED solutions benefiting HE institutions, students, and local communities through joint recommendations and independent project development.

A Genesis and Contemporary Strategic Landscape of American Higher Education

A contemporary university is rooted in medieval times. With the first Industrial Revolution in motion, the German or Humboldtian[1] model that emerged in the early 19th century has gained popularity and flourished across Europe. The Humboldt University model blends education and scholarship which paved the foundation for the contemporary research university (Humboldt University, 2024). Its prototype was initially adopted in the U.S. by the Johns Hopkins University and later spread across America (Geiger, 2015).

Over the past two centuries, the world has experienced profound transformations induced by industrial revolutions, advances in information technology (IT) and imaging, transportation, globalization, and increased geographic and social mobility, including massive global migration. In response to the opportunities and challenges of the first Industrial Revolution, colleges and universities at the time had developed HE programs for engineers. Management gained recognition as a profession and academic discipline in business education.

Between 1820 and 1899, 672 new colleges were established across America. Of those, 573–a dominant majority—were private. During the second half of the 19th century, private donors founded 11 universities that today are ranked among the nation's top 20, including Stanford, Johns Hopkins, and the University of Chicago (Hess & McShane, 2024a).

HE programs with career applications in engineering, business, and management gained further ground during the second Industrial Revolution, also known as Technological Revolution, which took place from approximately 1870 up to the beginning of World War I (Mokyr, 2018). At the time, Henri Fayol, a French engineer, developed his theory of industrial and general administration that became popular to further position management as a respectable profession (Wren & Bedian, 2020). The first MBA programs in America were offered at Wharton, Tuck, and Harvard in the early 20th century as academia's response to a national quest for industrialization with an increasing practical demand for rationality and efficiency.

Notably, the first-year curriculum at the Harvard MBA program in 1908 was rooted in the Frederick Winslow Taylor's "scientific management" approach (Leach, 1993).

In the aftermath of the World War II, in 1944, the U.S. Congress passed the G.I. Bill. This made college education more accessible for millions by paying tuition and living expenses (Altschuler, 2009). In 1964, the U.S. Congress adopted numerous Great Society programs significantly expanding support for and accessibility of HE. The Higher Education Act of 1965 contained provisions for federal scholarships and low-interest loans for college students. This act also included subsidies for better academic libraries, 10 to 20 new graduate centers, several new technical institutes, classrooms for several hundred thousand students, and 25 to 30 new community colleges per year nationwide. A separate education bill enacted that same year provided similar assistance to dental and medical schools (Bernstein, 1996). Throughout the 20th and 21st centuries, multiple institutions of HE, including private secular and private religious nonprofit as well as for-profit colleges and universities, have come to life.

The impending Third and Fourth Industrial Revolutions (Huchting et al., 2020; Rifkin, 2011, 2015; Schwab, 2016; Zhuplev, 2018) continue transforming traditional business paradigms, models, and patterns bringing about "creative destruction" (Schumpeter, 1994) and change. Some examples of "creative destruction" include electronic media destroying traditional print media, "gig economy" and remote work eroding traditional "nine to five" corporate office, and AI applications creating media and communication patterns blurring the lines between the real and virtual and replacing/dislocating humans on massive scale. These dynamics foster new trends, developments, and opportunities, and exert pressures for change that HE and its B-schools face today.

Contemporary Strategic Landscape

Arguably, HS' mission at large is three-pronged to:

- Facilitate student personal growth, career, and offer professional advancement opportunities.
- Cultivate a culture of responsible domestic and global citizenship.
- Provide a formative "college experience."

According to a recent representative national survey, Americans think HE can help people economically, particularly in their home states. However, by a variety of measures, Americans question whether the benefits of college are worth the cost. Young people without degrees are especially skeptical. Americans across partisan lines worry about high tuition and student debt in an economy that most think is rigged to benefit the wealthy. Most see college education as time-consuming and see colleges as stuck in the past. Although most Americans recognize that HE helps people become informed, engaged citizens, fewer think it benefits democracy overall (Schleifer et al., 2022).

Table 1 strategically portrays the contemporary American HE as a mature industry characterized by high entry barriers, significant dependence on government assistance, low concentration/high fragmentation, limited exposure to globalization, and heavy regulations.

Table 1. U.S. Colleges and Universities: Industry Structure, Strategic Drivers, and Dynamics (Lee, 2023)

Positive impact	
• **Industry assistance: High/steady.** • **Barriers to entry: High/steady.**	• **Concentration: Low.** • **Industry globalization: Low/increasing.**
Mixed impact	
• Life cycle: Mature. • Revenue volatility: Medium. • Capital intensity: Medium.	• Technology change: Medium. • Competition: Medium /increasing.
Negative impact	
• Regulation and policy: Heavy/steady.	
Key trends	
• Falling demand for undergraduate courses has outweighed an increase in demand for graduate certificates. • Driven by growth in tax revenue, government funding for universities has increased. • Despite the anticipated decline in state government funding, the CARES Act provides a new stream of funding to industry operators amid the pandemic. • The number of international students will likely recover, bolstering industry revenue.	• Competition from community colleges will likely remain moderate as traditional colleges dominate HE. • Industry institutions are expected to further implement online education programs to lower cost. • Operators have been able to maintain steady profit since they often rely on state funding and donations.
Segmentation of products and services	
• 66.0% Bachelor's degrees. • 27.6% Master's degrees. • 6.4% Doctor's degrees.	
Strengths: • High and steady barriers to entry. • High and steady level of assistance. • Low imports. • High profit vs. sector average. • High revenue per employee.	Weaknesses: • High customer class concentration. • High product/service concentration. • High capital requirements.

continued on following page

Table 1. Continued

Positive impact	
• **Industry assistance: High/steady.** • **Barriers to entry: High/steady.**	• **Concentration: Low.** • **Industry globalization: Low/ increasing.**

Opportunities:
  • High revenue growth (2023-2028).
  • Government funding for universities.
	Threats:
	  • Low revenue growth (2005-2023).
	  • Low revenue growth (2018-2023).
	  • Low outlier growth.
	  • Low performance drivers.
	  • High school retention rate.

Note. This report does not include for-profit degree-granting institutions and community colleges.

In 2020-2021, there were 2,297 four-year degree-granting postsecondary institutions, including branch campuses, in the U.S.; 33% of them were public and 67% private. These institutions enrolled 14 million students, including 9.1 million in public and 4.9 million in private nonprofit universities. By 2031, total student enrollment is projected at 14.9 million students, including 9.7 million in public and 5.2 million in private nonprofit universities or 69% and 31%, respectively (National Center for Education Statistics, 2021, Tables 303.30 and 317.10).

In 2020-2021, public four-year degree-granting postsecondary HE institutions reported $444.5 billion in revenues, compared to $408.1 billion for private nonprofit institutions. Taken together, in 2020-2021, revenues of public and private four-year nonprofit institutions of postsecondary education accounted for approximately 3% of America's gross domestic product (GDP) (authors' computation, based on Trading Economics, 2024). Public colleges and universities are significantly reliant on state and local government financial support contingent on college enrollment levels.

In 2020-2021, public institutions nationwide received approximately 17% of their total revenues from tuition and fees and 23% from federal and state grants, contracts, and appropriations. For private colleges and universities, tuition and fees comprised 19% of their revenues with federal and state government grants, contracts, and appropriations accounting for 9% of the total. Public and private HE institutions also derive revenues from auxiliary educational activities, private gifts, grants, contracts, endowments, and investments. Notably, public institutions receive only 13% of their total revenues from investment return compared to a much larger 46% share for private institutions. Over the past five years, many colleges and universities have experienced volatility in revenue and profitability mainly due to fluctuations in funding from government and private entities (Le, 2023). Table 2 outlines revenue streams for public and private four-year degree granting postsecondary colleges and universities nationwide.

Table 2. Percentage Distribution of Total Revenues for Degree-Granting Postsecondary Institutions, by Control of Institution and Source of Funds: Fiscal Year 2020–2021 (National Center for Education Statistics, 2023)

Sources of funds	Public	Private nonprofit	Private for-profit
Tuition and fees	16	19	93
Investments	12	46	≤ 1
Government grants, contracts, and appropriations	40	9	2
Auxiliary enterprises	4	3	1
All other revenues and appropriations	28	23	4

Table 3 depicts historical performance and outlook for U.S. colleges and universities between 2012 and 2029. During this 15-year span, the largest average annual increases occur in the industry's revenues and added value. Industry's wages show only modest growth, while college enrollments continue trending flat.

Table 3. U.S. Colleges and Universities: Historical Performance Data and Outlook, 2012-2029 (Le, 2023)

Year	Revenue, $m	Industry value added*, $m	Establishments**, units	Enterprises***, units	Employment, million people	Wages, $m	Number of college students, million people
2015	537,985	279,957	2,285	1,907	2.9	220,310	20.0
2023	582,638	327,427	2,272	1,899	2.9	243,325	18.8
2025	593,562	332,838	2,283	1,907	2.9	246,585	19.1
2029	614,362	348,581	2,300	1,917	3.0	252,490	19.3

Note. *Industry value added is the market value of goods and services produced by the industry minus the cost of goods and services used in production. It is also described as the industry's contribution to GDP, or profit plus wages and depreciation. **Establishment is the smallest type of accounting unit within an enterprise; it is a single physical location where business is conducted or where services or industrial operations are performed. Multiple establishments under common control make up an enterprise. ***An enterprise is a division that is separately managed and keeps management accounts. Each enterprise consists of one or more establishments that are under common ownership or control.

Most American colleges and universities are domestically owned, controlled, and primarily serve a domestic market. Nevertheless, U.S. universities have continued attracting international students. In recent years, HE markets have become more global. International comparisons show that American universities remain dominant in international rankings[2] and continue to attract foreign students. In 1980-1981 and 2000-2021 the number of foreign students enrolled in postsecondary institutions in the U.S. was 311.9 and 547.9 thousand, respectively. In 2021-2022 foreign student enrollment grew to 948.5 thousand, with most students coming from China and India comprising 31% and 21% of the total foreign student enrollment, respectively (Le, 2023; National Center for Education Statistics, 2021, Table 310.20).

Trends and Disruptors

Strategic drivers for the industry of colleges and universities in the U.S. include: Demographics and high school completion rates determining a pull of potential college applicants, tuition costs and household income determining college affordability, job market and wages determining future postcollege earning potential and alternative noncollege wage earning/income options available to the applicants, and government regulations and financial assistance programs that may facilitate or impede a flow of college applications (Le, 2023). The industry is also affected by external political, economic, social, technological, legal, environmental, and cultural trends and field forces.

Demographics constitute a critical "independent" variable in the business model for HE institutions. After reaching a peak in 2010, historic student enrollments in the U.S. have plateaued nationwide. Under the latest projections, total enrollment levels in American institutions of postsecondary education by 2030 are expected to stay stagnant at approximately 20 million students, including 14.2 million students in four-year degree granting institutions and 5.9 million students in two-year institutions. Within the four-year institution category, enrollment is projected at 9.2 million in public colleges and universities and 5.0 million in private institutions (National Center for Education Statistics, 2021). Stagnant demographics and flat enrollment projections coupled with the dwindling government financial support and skyrocketing cost of college imply sharpening competition among universities and colleges for a limited pool of applicants and need to "reimagine" customer appeal of college. Furthermore, the makeup of the ethnic background of the student pool available for recruitment and that of actual students enrolled in colleges and universities will also change due to the significant multicultural demographic growth increase experienced in the total number of students from the Asian, Black, and Hispanic student communities that will be attending these HE institutions.

Technological and business innovations generated by the ongoing third and fourth Industrial Revolutions have brought about the Internet, wireless communications, electronic imaging, smartphones, email, "gig" economy, YouTube, AI, machine learning, virtual reality, global immersive reality, quantum computing, and many other advances in technology and business models. This has exerted powerful socioeconomic impacts in the real world (Chui et al., 2023). While the original discovery of knowledge still requires robust effort, resources, and talent, the vastly improved access to domestic and global information has drastically improved the time/cost efficiency, accessibility, and dissemination of existing knowledge by and among students, HE institutions, and society at large. This contrasts with the traditional expensive four-year college model that requires considerable time commitment and involves missed earning opportunities during student's study. The real world becomes increasingly integrated via common technological platforms, ecosystems, cloud computing, and other forms of accessing, processing, and exchanging information. Academia's traditional model with its structural organization predominantly built around stationary departmental fields such as organizational behavior, marketing, human resources or management cause silos working traditionally as independent sources of information to students vs. the highly integrated multidisciplinary model required nowadays and in the future. The impending technological and business innovations and side effects of "creative destruction" wield further pressures for change on HE whose culture and DNA remains rooted in medieval traditions and principles from the Industrial era.

The innovative start-ups providing cost-efficient online courses through Coursera (https://www.coursera.org/) or numerous alternative certificate programs that have been mushrooming (The Changing Landscape of Online Education (CHLOE): Behind the Numbers, 2019). Experts assert this trend will continue to gain traction and user appeal (Le, 2023). Technological and business advances and innovations in IT, AI, social media, and imaging have brought to life widely popular alternative educational platforms such as YouTube, LinkedIn Learning, Khan Academy, and others (Dieleman et al., 2022). These educationally effective, cost-efficient or even free to the end user and user-friendly platforms strategically challenge traditional educational programs by universities and colleges in the increasingly competitive market of educational services.

COVID-19 accelerated a massive shift to online education. In 2018, only about 35% of undergraduates took a distance education course. In 2020, this figure was close to 100%, as the pandemic forced the adoption of remote learning (Dua et al., 2020). While student enrollments in postsecondary HE institutions continue to remain stagnant and even decline, distance learning has increased by around 40% in five years. As of late August 2020, just one-fifth of colleges in the U.S. were planning to return to campus fully or primarily in-person, with the balance either undecided, planning for hybrid, online or other remote teaching models. Several colleges have already had to rapidly shift to 100% remote instruction following local COVID-19 outbreaks (Boggs et al., 2021). Latest reports from academia indicate that this trend now expands well beyond undergraduate education with some market leaders in MBA programs such as the Stern School of Business in New York, Haas School of Business in Berkeley, and Warton School Philadelphia started offering predominantly online programs to stay competitive (Ellis, 2022). Even the new trend in HE of offering DBA or other non-PhD doctoral degrees are based mostly on an online instructional model.

Political and societal trends concerning HE over the past decade have been shaping in public forums, scholarly analyses, and sharp debates across societal institutions, academe, legislators, government agencies, students, employers, and other of its stakeholders. Today, Americans still believe in the value of a college credential, but they are not convinced HE is fulfilling its promise to society. According to some recent opinion polls, many do not think HE institutions do a great job educating their students—or that they are of great benefit to graduates. Alternatives such as trade school strike many Americans as just as good a path to a successful livelihood. In addition, colleges' value to communities and to society also draw skepticism (Kelderman, 2023; Smith, 2023).

In one extreme case, Peter Thiel, an early Facebook investor, a founder of Pay-Pal, and a philanthropist billionaire, is encouraging young people to skip college altogether. Since 2010, Thiel, has offered to pay students $100,000 to drop out of school to start companies or nonprofits (Thiel College, n.d.). Early on, his initiative met criticism. Some accused Thiel, who holds philosophy and law degrees from Stanford, of hypocrisy. Others said it was wrong to discourage young people from finishing their education. Zuckerman (2024) reports that former Harvard University President, Lawrence Summers, called it the "single most misdirected bit of philanthropy in this decade." In spring 2024, Thiel's program announced 20 new fellows, chosen from an applicant pool that is bigger than ever. Winners plan to launch companies in hot areas including AI and cryptocurrencies, according to executives of the program. Since its first fellows were chosen in 2011, Thiel's program has backed 271 people. Those involved in the effort say they have had successes and frustrations. Along the way, they have discovered common traits that help them do a better job identifying talented individuals (Zuckerman, 2024).

Brenan (2003) reports that according to a recent summer 2023 national survey by Gallup, only 36% of Americans have "a great deal" or "quite a lot" of confidence in HE. This is down from 57% in 2015—a drop of more than 20 percentage points in just eight years. In late 2023, *The Chronicle of Higher Education* released the results of a national survey in which fewer than a third of respondents reported believing that "colleges are doing an excellent or very good job of leveling the playing field for success in society." An astounding 86% of respondents reported believing that trade school is "about the same" as or "better" than college (Brenan, 2003). *The New York Times Magazine* reports that the percentage of young adults who believe a college degree is very important fell from 74% in 2013 to 41% in 2019. Further, today, roughly half of American parents would prefer that their children not enroll in a traditional four-year college (Smith, 2023).

Critics challenge academia's long-standing "ivory tower"[3] status quo and its perception as an institution relatively detached from the real world. Some observers question traditions of tenure[4] and "lifetime employment" in the academic profession that preserve status quo and insulate HE from the real world in contrast with a high share employment of part-time professors who, in many cases, surpass the number of tenure-track and full-time faculty. There is also criticism about relevance, replicability, and applied/practical impacts of scholarly research papers based on small samples and published in academic journals with limited readership largely confined to fellow academics.

Increasingly, high mobility and dynamism of the real world come in contrast with the capital intensive, and expensive "brick and mortar" model of the university campus. High efficiency, flexibility, accessibility, and ease in dissemination of information constituting the essence of common knowledge in the real world diverge from the skyrocketing costs and stationary structures of college education. Indeed, some participants of this public debate argue that common knowledge in the age of the Internet becomes a commodity, and the cost of acquiring and spreading this common knowledge in HE should not be prohibitively high. Education, teaching, and learning expand beyond merely accessing, processing, disseminating, and exchanging information. Nevertheless, information constitutes a systemic foundation of knowledge.

There is also a view among students, parents, and sponsors of HE as an investment with its own strategic options and outcomes implying different costs/benefits and return on investment ratios across colleges as well as between college education against other educational and career alternatives.

Multiple political, economic, social, technological, regulatory, and cultural developments over the past few decades amplified by recent COVID-related trends and dynamics have led to the "lawyerization" of HE. Guard and Jacobsen (2024), of Harvard, who coined the term, point out the increased litigation and compounding regulation in the HE industry. They argue that the long-held legal doctrines of deference to HE have shifted and public skepticism toward HE is growing. Legislatures and lawmakers are not hesitant to wade in and exert the power of law, legislation, and the purse on what for a long time was an isolated endeavor. Recent student demonstrations, legislative hearings, deployment of police force on university campuses, and high-profile leadership resignations in several top colleges and universities across the nation in spring 2024 provide a vivid illustration to this trend. Besides, demographic changes and economic realities are forcing innovations across the sector that require business-like legal acumen to keep colleges solvent and thriving.

Additionally, there are differences and trade-offs between acquisition and long-term retention of knowledge and skill development resulting from traditional in-person class lecture style instruction[5] vs. online learning, experiential learning, project-based learning, and other cost-efficient and/or active learning formats.[6] With no other alternatives for prospective students, the four-year college represents a mainstream path and promise to prosperous life and career. However, when other educational options become widely available in creating viable alternative paths enabling potential college applicants to "vote with their feet," this poses strategic threats to traditional colleges.

From the macroeconomic standpoint, the rising cost of HE causes public concerns and generates acute political debate.[7] The cost of college over the past few decades has outstripped general consumer inflation. According to the U.S. Bureau of Labor Statistics (https://data.bls.gov/pdq/SurveyOutputServlet#), within the decade between January 2006 and July 2016, the Consumer Price Index for college tuition and fees increased 63%. This contrasts with a Consumer Price Index increase for all items of just 21%. Over the same period, consumer prices for college textbooks rose a staggering 88% and housing at school (excluding board) increased 51%. In 1980, the price to attend a four-year college full-time adjusted for inflation was $10,231 annually—including tuition, fees, room, and board. By 2019-2020, the total price rose to $28,775, a 180% increase. College prices have soared across all institution types, but private nonprofit institutions continue to cost more than public colleges. A full-time student paid $48,965 at a private nonprofit college on average in 2019-2020, compared to $21,035 at a public university. Since 2019, however, the HE inflation trend has slowed. Between the 2019-2022 and 2021-2022 academic years, average tuition, fees, and room and board dropped 0.2% at private nonprofit four-year schools, according to the College Board (Ma & Pender, 2021). From 2020-2021 to 2021-2022, prices dropped a further 1.7%. Costs at public four-year schools followed a similar pattern in the same timeframe (McGurran, 2023).

On the microeconomic level, the high cost of college in the U.S. is worsened by a heavy student loan burden, with the average federal student loan debt balance reaching $28,950 per student. Nationwide, about 43 million federal student loan borrowers currently have more than $1.6 trillion in outstanding student loan debt (Maglione, 2024). Although today a dwindling 36% of Americans have confidence in HE, the benefits of college still make it an attractive lifestyle path for many applicants (Hyland, 2023). This dream, however, is tempered by a massive underemployment trend. According to a recent Bloomberg report (Maglione, 2024), within a year of graduation, a stunningly high 52% share of recent bachelor's degree recipients in America are employed in jobs that do not require a college degree. Approximately 88% of these college graduates fall into underemployment within five years after their graduation from college, often working in high school-level jobs such as office support, food service, and retail (Maglione, 2024).

In another report, Hanson et al. (2024) analyzed the career paths of 60 million Americans, including 10.8 million bachelor's degree holders. Despite the expectation that a bachelor's degree would lead to better job prospects, many graduates do not achieve the economic outcomes they anticipated. While underemployed graduates earn approximately 25% more than workers with only a high school diploma, this falls far short of the earnings of those in degree-requiring roles, who earn 88% more than high school graduates. Hanson et al. found that the choice of field of study also plays a crucial role. Fields that require quantitative reasoning, such as engineering, finance, accounting, and computer science, have lower five-year underemployment rates. Conversely, fields such as public safety and security, recreation and wellness studies, and marketing and business management have higher underemployment rates.

Ultimately, there is a correlation between more education and higher salaries, but it is counterbalanced by the low graduation rates, which, together with the rising tuition and student debt, keeps college out of reach for many. Students often must choose to opt out of HE, quit after accruing debt or allocate much of their increased earnings toward debt payments.

International comparisons of these trends in the U.S. with 22 comparator countries in the Organization for Economic Cooperation and Development (OECD) reveal U.S.' economic competitive disadvantage. In monetary terms, the government and private expenditures on postsecondary education in the U.S. are noticeably higher compared to OECD counterparts, both in absolute dollar terms per capita and as a share of GDP (Table 4). Inflation in education in the U.S. exceeds this indicator for OECD countries as a group by a sizeable 20%-point margin and constitutes a larger 3% share in the overall consumer spending, compared to just 2% for OECD on average. In relative terms, inflation in the U.S. education also by wide margin exceeds all other consumer spending items, including food, housing, and healthcare. Moreover, there are reports that spending on student services in HE has been growing lately four times as fast as spending on instruction. Some observers (Dua et al., 2020; Zhuplev & Blas, 2022) argue that while students surely appreciate things like luxury gyms and other services, there is a need to distinguish between what students like and what is necessary to serve the core education mission. Prohibitive costs and steep price inflation in HE ultimately lessen its appeal for student population at large, constrain college enrollments, and stretch government budgets with fund appropriations for educational institutions.

The U.S.' HE system faces several challenges, when compared to its foreign counterparts. For instance, in 2021, the enrollment rate of 18–24-year-olds in college was 38% in the U.S., compared to over 50% in Germany, Japan, and the UK, and 45% on average in the Organization for Economic Cooperation and Development (OECD) (National Center for Education Statistics, 2024; OECD, 2024). The share of the population (25-64 years old) with tertiary education was 50% in the U.S., 33% in Germany, 56% in Japan, 51% in the UK, and 41% in the OECD on average (Statista, 2021).

The duration of bachelor's programs also varies by country. In the U.S., it typically requires 4 years, compared to 3-3.5 years in Germany, 4 years in Japan, and 3-4 years in the UK. Some U.S. programs, such as engineering, may require slightly longer than 4 years to complete. This additional time requirement constitutes a competitive disadvantage for U.S. students compared to their foreign counterparts, implying extra time and cost commitment, as well as a lost socioeconomic growth opportunity.

The U.S. also has a lower share of high school graduates enrolling in vocational education compared to other countries. The latest available data estimate that 12-15% of U.S. high school graduates enroll in vocational education after high school, compared to 50-60% in Germany, 12-35% in Japan, 40% in the UK, and an OECD average of 40-44% (OECD, 2024).

Furthermore, the U.S. faces a significant underemployment trend. As mentioned earlier, approximately 52% of recent bachelor's degree recipients in the U.S. are employed in jobs that do not require a college degree. This effectively nullifies the socioeconomic appeal of college education and burdens students with significant costs and often insurmountable loan debt (Maglione, 2024).

These dynamics suggest that there are significant areas for improvement in the U.S.' HE system. Addressing these issues could help to calibrate college enrollment, reduce the time and cost of obtaining a degree, better align education with labor market needs, and ultimately improve the socioeconomic outcomes for U.S. students.

Table 4. *Comparative National Expenditures on Postsecondary Education: U.S. vs. Selected OECD Countries, 2019 (National Center for Education Statistics, 2021, Tables 605.10 and 605.20)*

Countries	National expenditures on postsecondary education	
	Per FTE student, constant 2021 dollars	As share of GDP, %
U.S.	$37,417	2.5
Germany	$20,344	1.3
Japan	$19,874	1.4
UK	$31,554	2.0
OECD average	$18,418	1.4

Colleges and universities, to a certain degree, mitigate the financial burden of high tuition and ballooning student loans by offering financial aid as part of their internal strategic and tactical operating model.[8] This financial aid is channeled through an intricate pricing system. In this system, higher-income and international students pay full price, thus effectively subsidizing the financially disadvantaged students. Systemic complexities and lack of price transparency in this system feed into the public perception of the sky-high and ever-increasing costs and unaffordability of college. Meanwhile, in their financial aid programs, colleges and universities are limited in their annual tuition increases and financial redistribution effort supporting the needy students at the expense of students paying full tuition. Indeed, both public and private institutions need external funding, which is largely reliant on the government support prevalent in public HE institutions, and fundraising-in private institutions. Moreover, there are mounting questions among stakeholders regarding the cost-benefit value of college when the debt levels, repayment rates, and other factors are considered (Gilbert, 2020). This is particularly true because job markets provide ample alternative opportunities for job seekers without college degrees (Carlson, 2024; Furstenberg, 2023; Weber, 2024; Zukerman, 2024).

One strategy U.S. colleges and universities have deployed over the past few decades to counter stagnant domestic enrollments and declining financial affordability has been prioritizing a recruitment of international students. From fall 1976 to fall 2018, the share of "nonresident aliens" (i.e., international students as categorized in official statistics) in undergraduate student enrollment across the U.S. grew three-fold, from 0.5% to 1.6%. This trend is also evident on the postbaccalaureate level, where the share of nonresident alien students increased during the same time two-fold, from 3.7% to 7.9%. To mitigate the recent COVID-inflicted heavy financial blows and stay financially solvent, universities and colleges have doubled down on attracting international students. However, international student enrollment levels and the respective revenue streams for U.S. degree-granting postsecondary institutions have been crippled over the past few years by COVID-related domestic and, particularly, international travel restrictions and the U.S. immigration regulations.[9]

Attracting international students is financially important to colleges and universities, since most of them pay full tuition in contrast to the in-state U.S. residents receiving financial aid. To complicate things, government financial support for HE across the nation has recently experienced sharp decline due to the COVID-induced economic deterioration and general budgetary strains. In this environment, many colleges and universities are struggling to stay financially solvent (Belkin, 2022; de Brey et al., 2021; Friga, 2021). At the same time, prioritizing international students paying full tuition comes into conflict with the interests of prospective in-state students competing for the same limited enrollment slots who need financial aid thus adding pressures on university budgets. This is particularly acute for public universities whose missions, facilities, and limited financial resources are primarily designated and are politically and legally bound to support the in-state applicants.

Navigating the Challenges

American HE faces a juncture imposed by megachanges, societal trends and regulatory trends, and emerging strategic opportunities and challenges. Stakeholder groups[10] advocating for preserving the existing traditional college model posit that doomsday scenarios have been floated before.[11] They argue that time and time again, in recent decades, American HE has grown its way out of crises. Colleges have expanded access to underrepresented groups, added academic programs and amenities to attract students and charge them higher tuition, and struck private sector deals to tap new markets. Advocates of the status quo contend that technological and business innovations like massive open online courses (i.e., MOOCs), Uber, digital revolution, online course delivery in traditional colleges or ed-tech start-ups have failed so far to disrupt HE's traditional model (Cooper, 2023).[12] Thus, why bother with changing the system? Their opponents, on the opposite side of the spectrum in public debate and political action, call for change. They argue that crisis of American HE today looks different from the crises of the past. HE may have reached the limits of "Houdini-ing" its way out of decline by getting bigger, and the prolonged pandemic downturn could be just one indication. Public confidence in colleges is sinking, and students and parents think tuition is too high. Skepticism is mounting toward the idea that a college education should be the prerequisite and the only path for well-paying jobs, and in a tight labor market clamoring for workers, some people are landing them without a degree. Already, nearly seven in 10 high-school graduates immediately go on to pursue, although not necessarily complete, some sort of postsecondary education, and the remainder may be difficult to recruit. The students left out of HE have been notoriously difficult for colleges to reach and serve. Then, there is the looming demographic cliff created by the sharp drop-in birth rates that began in 2007 (Fischer, 2022).

Horn (2023) presents a series of persuasive points advocating for reform. He contends that our existing HE system operates on a "pay-for-what-you-get" basis. As the government subsidizes a substantial part of the HE system, students and families, the primary beneficiaries of colleges, are ultimately funded by taxpayers who collectively bear the cost. In essence, the expenditure of the government—and, by extension, the taxpayer—is not directed towards employment, learning or life outcomes and enhancement of student wellbeing, but rather towards enrollment. As HE is an experience good, its value or utility is challenging to grasp until it has been utilized and its effectiveness evaluated in the marketplace. The price of college to individual students is opaque, as the actual price is often not revealed until after admission; the price charged generally changes from year to year. In this context, the money from the federal government is often perceived as being free to the student—the repayment terms for loans, for example, feel far off in what students assume will be a brighter future—and colleges often use loans to imply that the price of the institution is lower than it actually is. Meanwhile, students attend college for a variety of nuanced reasons, many of which do not pertain directly to economic return on their investment in HE—an aspect of HE that, earlier, we categorized as "college experience." The result of all this is, simply put, that there are far too few incentives in place for colleges and universities to focus on the primary outcomes that students are looking for in terms of financial returns, employment, and learning. From the perspective of the taxpayer customer, that lack of focus on ultimate economic value to the student should be unacceptable (Horn, 2023).

Historically, American HE system has evolved from a scholastic societal institution to the primary, if not monopolistic, source of advanced education and professional qualifications. It has also risen to the role of the gate keeper on the path of professional success and social status through the power of awarding standard college diplomas. This power stems from HE institutions' access to expert faculty and extensive resources of knowledge, including libraries, laboratories, and research facilities financially supported by private and public funds which are not typically available to the entities outside HE. Additionally, colleges and universities provide a platform for exclusive networking with peers, faculty, and alumni[13] facilitating job opportunities, professional advancement, and growth in the social hierarchy. These conditions are widely accepted by employers who recognize and value degrees and diplomas from established/accredited HE institutions at no immediate added costs for using college-educated talent. This cartel-like institutional relationship between HE industry, government, and employers is reinforced by the existing system of accreditation and quality assurance where HE institutions are accredited by recognized bodies ensuring a certain level of quality and standard in the education they provide. This accreditation gives colleges and universities protected power to grant degrees and diplomas that are commonly accepted by employers as a proxy and assurance for professional qualifications of job applicants.

Since 1965, the federal government's answer to this quandary has been the empowering accrediting agencies. Essentially, accreditors play the gatekeeping role to federal financial aid, but were not built to play a quality-assurance role. They were designed originally as peer-review organizations to help institutions improve.[14] They may do that well, but they are not good at focusing on student outcomes—nor does federal policy incentivize them to do so, as only one of the 10 standards that dictate what accreditors monitor pertains to outcomes. The taxpayer customers of HE should not tolerate bad college programs that offer miserable returns on investment for students.

According to the Postsecondary Commission (PSC) (2024), factors such as low graduation rates, high loan-default rates, and low median student earnings did not necessarily prompt an accreditor to impose disciplinary action on a college. Furthermore, only a small fraction (11%) of the colleges in the study's sample faced one or more disciplinary actions concerning student outcomes or academic program quality.

Accreditation operates on a binary principle—once attained, it opens the door to federal funding. This funding allows colleges to enroll students, creating an illusion of subsidized and cost-effective education, which is often not the case. The tendency to establish regulations based on inputs—the operational aspects of a college or university, such as its contracts with third-party entities—rather than its outcomes, only intensifies this issue. Regulating inputs (i.e., the manner in which a college functions) merely perpetuates existing practices, stifling innovation, and promoting a culture of compliance over value. The financial burden of compliance is often passed onto students through increased tuition fees. This creates a vicious cycle of escalating costs and subpar outcomes, which has proven to be ineffective. Policy should shift its focus towards student outcomes, empowering and compelling colleges to devise the most effective strategies to deliver value to both students and taxpayers (Horn, 2023).

In tackling these problems, some experts propose reforming the existing accreditation system by breaking a monopoly (Hess & McShane, 2024a). Under these proposals, the newly created PSC aspires to be one of several alternative federally recognized accreditors of institutions of HE that prioritizes high rates of economic mobility for their students. The PSC has recently developed and published its accreditation handbook. In comparison to the existing Association to Advance Collegiate Schools of Business (AACSB) standards, the PSC Accreditation Handbook emphasizes the outcomes for students resulting from HE. It does not prescribe universal national or international standards for learning inputs or faculty qualifications,[15] leaving these decisions at the discretion of colleges and universities. As an illustration, its Standard 8.2, "Qualifications of Faculty and Instructional Staff," states: "In each of its courses and programs, the institution employs faculty and instructional staff who have relevant and appropriate qualifications, including relevant and appropriate subject-matter expertise, educational degrees, professional licenses and credentials, or practical experience" (PSC, 2024, p. 11). Should this standard be changed to include a requirement for faculty and instructional staff to have real world business or nonprofit experience as an employee or consultant?

In addition to tackling accreditation, the voices advocating for reforms prioritize accountability of HE. They propose that colleges accepting public funds should be responsible for a nontrivial part of the cost for each taxpayer-supported student who does not graduate. This would introduce much-needed accountability and give colleges an incentive to help students successfully complete their degrees and then find gainful employment (Hess & McShane, 2024b).

This proposal is being supplemented by the idea of privatization of federal student loans—that is, having the government pull back and allowing the private sector to lend instead. Millions of students pursue college degrees that leave them no better off financially. Students can do this because the federal government happily stumps up the money with little regard for program quality or projected earnings. Institutions of higher learning have few incentives to improve their return on investment and every reason to prop up programs of dubious value, capturing ever more federal dollars by creating new programs and raising tuition. A larger role for the private sector could fix this problem. When lenders use their own money to make loans, they enjoy the rewards when students repay those loans but must bear the costs when students default. They have skin in the game, meaning they will lose money if they make loans that aren't paid back partially or in full. To convince private lenders that their students will repay their loans, colleges will need to keep prices competitive and be much more attentive to students' postgraduate economic outcomes—both wins from the student perspective. Thus, privatization creates an incentive for colleges to steer students toward degrees that offer sufficient value/ ROI for money spent and hold them accountable. This should come as welcome news in today's HE landscape, where more than one-quarter of bachelor's degrees leave students worse off financially than when they started (Akers et al., 2024).[16]

Another pillar of existing HE monopoly experiencing the regulatory and socio-economic headwinds is a historical practice of using college diploma by employers as a prerequisite in their hiring decisions. Traditionally, college diploma has signified an assurance of certain level of knowledge, skills, and preparedness for professional roles. Employers, who have access to college-educated talent at no immediate expense, have used college diploma as a benchmark to filter applicants, assuming a degree holder possesses the baseline qualifications. While vocational schools, apprentice-ships, and certificate courses exist, they have not always held the same weight in the job market. This has created a situation where a college degree, regardless of major relevance to the job, becomes the necessary ticket for entry. Critics of this system argue that this reliance on degrees is inefficient and exclusionary because it tends to disadvantage qualified candidates without degrees, limit opportunities for those who cannot afford college, and does not always guarantee graduates have the specific skills employers need. The emphasis on the degree itself, rather than specific skills, can limit an employer's focus on what truly matters for the job.

There is a growing regulatory movement and political action to diversify how employers assess qualifications by refocusing on skills instead of formal diplomas[17] where a higher value is placed on demonstrably relevant skills, regardless of how they were acquired (i.e., bootcamps, certifications, and apprenticeships). More weight is given to alternative credentials such as industry-specific certifications, stackable certifications, corporate universities and training programs, or portfolios highlighting relevant work experience.

Monopoly or not, traditional reliance on college degrees in hiring is facing po-litical and regulatory scrutiny and headwinds. The future might see a more open system that values diverse forms of education and prioritizes skills over a one-size-fits-all degree.

College and university leaders today face a daunting array of challenges, navi-gating a complex and ever-shifting landscape and often walking the tightrope walk.

Financial Strain. A significant challenge is the ongoing financial stress vexing many institutions. Rising costs, coupled with constraints in public funding, limited success in private fundraising, and tuition increases met with student pushback, create an unstable financial tightrope for some institutions, especially small ones. Presidents must balance the need for fiscal responsibility with investments in faculty, facilities, and essential academic programs. A recent Higher Education Trends report emphasizes this point, noting that peak enrollment of high school students is predicted as soon as 2025. This decline in potential students will likely exacerbate existing budgetary issues for many institutions (Deloitte, 2024).

Diversity, Equity, and Inclusion (DEI). An amplified focus on DEI initiatives that has been gaining momentum nationwide over the past several years presents both opportunities and challenges. While fostering a more inclusive learning environment is crucial, navigating the regulatory, economic, ethical and political complexities of these issues can be fraught with controversy. Presidents must balance competing viewpoints, ensuring a fair and representative environment for all students, faculty, and staff, while mitigating potential backlash from various stakeholders.

Return on Investment (ROI). Students, their parents, and sponsors are increasingly viewing HE as an investment, demanding a clear return on their tuition dollars. Presidents must address student concerns about job preparedness and career outcomes in an increasingly competitive and transparent HE landscape. This may require curriculum adjustments, improved career services support and proven track record of success in job placement, and demonstrably strong alumni networks. The Deloitte report specifically emphasizes the growing focus on student ROI (Deloitte, 2024). Students are increasingly viewing HE as an investment and demanding clear career outcomes. This trend is putting pressure on universities to demonstrate the value proposition of their degrees.

Geopolitical and Domestic Issues. HE leaders are constantly adapting to a rapidly changing world. Events such as the recent Israel-Hamas conflict highlight the delicate balance presidents must maintain. They face pressure to take stances on sensitive issues while upholding academic freedom and fostering an environment where diverse viewpoints can be expressed constructively.

Leadership Crisis. The very nature of the challenges creates a leadership crisis. The average tenure of university presidents is declining, with many citing the immense pressure and lack of support as key factors. The shrinking pool of qualified candidates further exacerbates the issue. Many traditional academic backgrounds may not fully equip leaders to handle the multifaceted demands of the modern presidency. Attracting and retaining talented leaders necessitates robust succession planning and development programs. According to the Deloitte 2024 Higher Education Trends report, the ongoing financial pressures, increased scrutiny from lawmakers, and the growing influence of private partners are creating a more complex and demanding environment for university presidents. This complexity is contributing to a leadership crisis, as many presidents struggle to navigate these challenges. According to the Deloitte 2024 Higher Education Trends report, between 2006 and 2022, it fell from 8.5 years to 5.9 years. The same study indicates that 55% of presidents plan to step down from their positions within the next five years (Deloitte, 2024).

Board Responsibilities. The complex dynamics of HE governance require well-equipped boards. Boards need to develop a deeper understanding of current trends to ensure they hire presidents with the skills to navigate these turbulent times. This includes establishing clear policies for leadership development and succession planning, while fostering diverse candidate pools.

Presidential Transitions. Presidential transitions, which become more frequent under the declining length of tenure of university presidents and the shrinking pool of qualified candidates can disrupt institutional stability. Boards must ensure smooth transitions by clearly defining roles and responsibilities for faculty, management, and the board itself. Furthermore, providing comprehensive support for incoming presidents is crucial to ensure their success.

The Path Forward. Addressing the leadership crisis requires a multi-pronged approach. Boards must actively identify and cultivate potential successors, both internally and externally. The future of HE hinges on its ability to cultivate a steady stream of competent and prepared leaders.

Strategic Implications for Business Schools

Multiple megatrends and strategic macrodisruptors in HE induce pressures for change and bring about strategic opportunities and challenges, compelling colleges to act.

Schlegelmilch (2020) discussed strategic challenges business schools (B-schools) were facing as traditional providers of advanced business education. The author highlighted the following key issues for B-schools:

- The digital paradigm shift in information dissemination patterns and B-schools' limited progress in adopting technology and innovation.
- Deglobalization and the shift of economic power to Asia affecting scientific exchange and student flow.
- Criticism B-schools face within their own educational institutions and their struggle to maintain their academic reputation.
- B-schools competition/cooperation dilemma with the online education providers.

Schlegelmilch (2020) discussed the use of technology and how B-schools could be taught in the future with an emphasis on augmented reality and AI. He specifically mentioned some emerging trends being embraced by leading B-schools, such as microcredentials, digital badges, and stackable certificates. Schlegelmilch argued that traditional B-schools would struggle to survive without embracing such fundamental changes in technology and developing and implementing clear digitalization strategies.

Graham and Donaldson (2020) examined pressures college leaders face and how these pressures affect their strategic priorities. Based on this analysis, they developed a comprehensive strategic framework addressing these pressures. Their model identifies the following primary external pressures: Funding, value of HE, student outcome, market pressures, political intrusion, technology, and competition. Graham and Donaldson's model rationalizes several strategic responses:

- The Model of Strategy Choice framework integrates the pressures, institutional logics, leader thinking, and strategy suggests adopting business models, like those used by for-profit organizations in the real world to become more effective in data-driven decision-making and cost analyses.
- The Modifying Existing Curricula focuses on designing more market-driven programs such as professional and certificate programs.
- The Program Modification approach includes improving the institution's marketing to maintain or increase enrollment.
- The Strategic Planning/Environmental Scanning approach prioritizes, as its name suggests, strategic planning, internal and external analysis in a comparative strategic context.
- The Focus and Concern about Students approach prioritizes student needs and preferences in education and wellbeing.
- The Transforming Competitors into Collaborators approach includes recognizing opportunities for new developments and creating strategic alliances with "competitors" and other organizations (including private ones) in the institution's environment.[18]

All these approaches, according to Graham and Donaldson, should be rooted in innovative programs, marketing, and technology. The latter can be used as a source of learning materials rather than textbooks, thereby freeing up resources for students to invest in additional coursework (Graham and Donaldson, 2020).

Our further discussion will address some developmental opportunities and applications for B-schools. In the 2019-2020 academic year, the U.S. undergraduate student enrollment in 4-year educational institutions in the field of Business, Management, and Marketing was near 1.5 million or 16% of the total undergraduate enrollment nationwide. Postbaccalaureate enrollment in this field of study was near 0.4 million or 13% of the total nationwide (National Center for Education Statistics, 2023, Table 311.60.). As of May 2024, out of an estimated 16,563 B-schools worldwide, 949 or 5.7% held AACSB accreditation. Out of the 949 AACSB accredited B-schools, 595 were based in the Americas, including 535 schools in the U.S., 185 in Europe, Middle East and Africa, and 169 in the Asia Pacific region (AACSB, 2021, 2022c).

B-schools[19] can operate as a separate entity or part of a university at large. The latter organizational format that is common in HE implies linkages and interdependencies between B-schools and other colleges in the university organizational and financial system in their strategy formulation and implementation processes.

Under requirements of its respective academic majors, minors, and other educational programs, B-schools offer instruction[20] in general and specialized functional academic areas (e.g., accounting, business analytics, entrepreneurship, finance, management or real estate). Some professional careers associated with specialized academic fields in the B-school domain – (e.g., accounting, finance, and real estate) are subject to industry regulations, licensing, field experience requirements, continuing professional development, and certification. Certification standards for other fields (e.g., management, entrepreneurship or international business) are loose or nonexistent. This allows B-school educators without any real-life experience, professional pedagogical certification, and/or continuing education to practice their profession in college teaching.[21] In contrast, outside business domain, some professional fields in college education such as medicine, law, engineering, or K-12 education are subject to rigorous regulatory, certification, and continuing education requirements on top of the college diploma requirement.

B-schools must be in the forefront of competitive forces of the real world instead of just reacting to these forces. This can be achieved by keeping educational curriculum to the foreground through systemic monitoring, benchmarking, comparative analysis and application of best practices and innovations in B-education. Academic talent, especially junior faculty, should be trained in the essentials of teaching and be given the opportunity of holding a position with a real-world business or nonprofit organization for at least one year to be exposed to real business practices to stay relevant. This is to be supported by systemic modernization and upgrade of instructional "toolbox" prioritizing skill development over rote learning (AACSB, 2022a; Zhuplev & Blas, 2022).

The future of work in the real business world will be a landscape in constant flux, with limited room for the static set/fixed job descriptions or guaranteed lifetime careers typical in the past. From a future B-school standpoint, a traditional business academic curriculum as a collection of academic disciplines sequenced in a rigid linear formation leading to an academic degree will lose its appeal for the students or viability in the competitive landscape of educational services. Proliferation of cost/time-efficient and flexible educational programs across colleges and universities and alternatives by the "challenger institutions" such as EdX or Coursera (Le, 2023) expands the geographic boundaries and raising student appeal from local and regional to the national and global levels creating strategic competitive advantages rooted in the economies of scale. This presents a predicament for traditional B-schools tied to the capital-intensive brick-and-mortar campus, static curriculum, and geographic locality.

The emerging volatility, uncertainty, complexity, ambiguity (VUCA) environment will depend on offering and learning the 21st-century skills—flexibility, adaptability, observation, empathy, creativity, innovation, and, ultimately, learning how to learn (Gonzalez et al., 2023; Reaves, 2019) as part of lifelong learning. The existing disconnect between higher education and employer needs is further corroborated by latest authoritative reports by Harvard (Fuller & Raman, 2022) and Workforce Skills Gap Trends 2024 (2024).

Numerous studies reveal radical changes in what the future of work will mean for jobs, skills, and wages. One report predicts that 23% of current work activity hours in the U.S. will be automated by 2030 in the midpoint scenario, and up to 44% in the rapid scenario. Legal and medical professions, academia, and other white-collar occupations and jobs, as well as many other industries and professions, will experience fundamental transformations. The forthcoming structural changes in American labor force require serious changes in college curriculum, instructional methodology, systemic organization, academic deliverables, and outcomes (Gonzalez et al., 2023). This is a wakeup call for B-schools.

One way in developing and maintaining robust B-school curriculum meeting educational demands of a real business world of the future is long-term university-industry partnerships based on mutual strategic interests and interdependency (Lutchen, 2024; "Readying students for the workforce," 2024). Existing practices of business curriculum development in B-schools are often driven by academic departmentalization/compartmentalization historically rooted in the industrial era of the early 20th century. Stronger collaborations between academia and industry can facilitate generation of knowledge and integration of new skills in the curriculum, while continuing to teach the fundamentals of each discipline. This can be ensured by:

- Inviting a broad range of companies and organizations to join the B-school's advisory board.
- Offering companies compelling reasons to strategically partner with B-schools.
- Offering mutually beneficial arrangements of intellectual property ownership from collaborative R&D projects involving colleges and companies.

- Employing hands-on campus R&D facilities directors and clinical professors with corporate experience and connections in the industry, empowering them with instructional responsibilities as "Professor of the Practice."
- Ensuring the board's role in procuring the equipment and bringing real world experiences in labs and classrooms. Adding an "executive -in-residence" as a permanent feature can enhance academia-industry connection and give additional boost and strategic benefits, including external funding, and ultimately let industry leaders be B-school's champions in curriculum innovation and change (Lutchen, 2024).

A shift from instructor-centered teaching emphasizing dissemination of knowledge through traditional "transmission" model, lecture style, and rote learning to prioritizing skill development ingrained in the 21st-century skills (Table 5) and student-centered learning is a trend of the future in B-education (Le, 2023; McMurtrie, 2023). The latter is aligned with the unfolding proliferation of skill-based hiring by employers rather than hiring based on formal college diploma. This model is gaining wider appeal in private and public sectors under the "skills–not schools" movement across political spectrum and industries (Belkin, 2023). Acquiring, maintaining, and developing skills during college study becomes paramount for a successful business career in a VUCA economy of perpetual change and disruption. At the same time, stationary knowledge, which is subject to continuous obsolescence, change, and update, can be stored, accessed, and retrieved from an electronic depository in the "cloud" with high ease and cost/time-efficiency. This becomes even more evident with the advent and spectacular proliferation of generative AI tools that have profound implications for HE, including customization and individualization of business education. By the same token, this calls into question the market appeal, competitiveness, relevance, and ultimate survival of B-schools failing to embrace change and adapt their educational value proposition.

Table 5. Skills Demand across Sectors: 2018 vs. 2022 (Oke & Fernandes, 2020; The Future of Jobs Report, 2018)

Today: 2018	Trending: 2022	Declining: 2022
• Analytical thinking and innovation. • Complex problem solving. • Critical thinking and analysis. • Active learning and learning strategies. • Creativity, originality, and initiative. • Attention to detail, trustworthiness. • Emotional intelligence. • Reasoning, problem solving, and ideation. • Leadership and social justice. • Coordination and time management.	• Analytical thinking and innovation. • Active learning and learning strategies. • Creativity, originality, and initiative. • Technology design and programming. • Critical thinking and analysis. • Complex problem solving. • Leadership and social influence. • Emotional intelligence. • Reasoning, problem solving, and ideation. • Systems analysis and evaluation.	• Manual dexterity, endurance, and precision. • Memory, verbal, auditory, and spatial abilities. • Management of financial, material resources. • Technology installation and maintenance. • Reading, writing, math, and active listening. • Management of personnel. • Quality control and safety awareness. • Coordination and time management. • Visual, auditory, and speech abilities. • Technology use, monitoring, and control.

Traditional B-school model has been challenged by advances in information access and transparency in comparing college value proposition nationally and internationally.[22] This gives college applicants, their families, and sponsors instant access to viable analytical information and opportunity to "vote with their feet" in making college application decisions to the best of their interests, giving a boost to innovative B-schools offering superb educational value proposition and leaving less attractive colleges at strategic disadvantage, or even driving them out of business.

In the evolving and increasingly competitive HE landscape, a shift by some B-schools to online instruction presents a challenging strategic option forced by competitive pressures (Smith, 2023). How do B-schools operating in the high-end, brick-and-mortar, in-person market segment continue to compete and justify their high tuition against lower-cost alternatives offered by "challenger" institutions that are widely available and much more affordable? What are their value proposition and distinctive sustainable strategic advantages in the competitive environment of HE? Common knowledge offered in B-education eventually becomes a commodity as IT, electronic imaging, AI, and other technologies and innovations proliferate. Today, this common B-knowledge can often be found and navigated through public access on the "cloud" with ease, free or inexpensively, thus limiting a comparative appeal of the costly and time intensive traditional B-school to the student. Therefore, the ultimate goal of HE institutions should be to provide not only knowledge but, also constant mentorship, expertise, insights, and the application of intuition not possible to be learned via online courses.

In the meantime, professional certificate programs by affiliated strategic partners distinguished by big brands such as Google, IBM, and others, as well as big name universities such as Stanford or MIT under Coursera's umbrella do not always require or necessarily lead to undergraduate or graduate academic degrees. These certificate programs leading to lucrative jobs can be completed at the learner's own pace usually within 6 months (Software Development and Content Creation programs are exceptions, as their completion requires 14 months and 7 months, respectively). In their own studies, Coursera identified seven critical skills leading to top paying jobs. These "high income skills" that command attractive monetary remuneration—in many cases in a six-digit range—are defined by Coursera as follows: Data Analysis, Software Development, User Experience, Web Development, Project Management, Content Creation, and Management (https://www.coursera .org/articles/high-income-skills).

B-schools' response to these transformational opportunities and challenges is rooted in their educational missions along the lines of their government mandates (for public colleges) and value-driven missions (for private and religious colleges). On the other hand, these value-driven priorities must be balanced with the realities of the HE environment at large. In a broad sense, these realities are determined by political, economic, social, and technological field forces, availability of talent, and other resources, as well as strategic potential for expanding this resource base, including fundraising.

Traditional "transmission" style B-school pedagogy grounded in the medieval Europe is centered around a teacher equipped with deep specialized subject expertise in sharing and disseminating knowledge/information which this educator has accumulated over the years of teaching and academic research. In this traditional model, theories and methodological frameworks play primary role, and empirical material, practical illustrations, and applications performing a supporting and illustrative role.[23] The emerging B-education model experiencing mounting pressures for delivering career-related educational outcomes, effectiveness, and efficiency, as well as technological savvy, is likely to shift a traditional emphasis from being teacher-centered to learner-centered. It will need to become more flexible in prioritizing active learning, creative/entrepreneurial instructional modalities, and applications over mere lecturing. Skill development grounded in opportunity-seeking or problem-solving business situations and applications on the community, regional or even national level will be taking central stage, while theories and methodological frameworks playing important supporting explanatory-normative roles. Experiential learning, project-based learning, service learning, flipped classroom, and other forms of active learning grounded in community problem solving or developmental projects will be central to ensure B-education's impacts.[24]

Some B-schools around the world are collaborating to tackle SED challenges by leveraging global best practices. As an application of this approach, we discuss a project that emphasizes skill development through real-world, opportunity-seeking, and problem-solving business scenarios, involving experiential, project-based, and service learning (see Appendix A). By conducting a comparative analysis of SED issues of mutual interest between Greater Los Angeles (L.A.), USA, and Córdoba, Spain, the project aims to explore shared solutions and promote collaboration. Both regions face significant challenges such as limited healthcare access, poverty, income inequality, and economic opportunities, making them ideal candidates for this collaborative initiative.

The project progresses through stages, starting with a single problem focus and advancing to multiple problem focuses, local and regional collaborations, and finally international projects. This strategic approach maximizes resource use and benefits stakeholders by bridging the gap between academia and real-world SED priorities. Key outcomes include enhanced branding and visibility for universities and B-schools, strengthened impact on SED through practical education, and increased institutional collaboration. Students gain from engaging learning experiences and improved career prospects, while local communities and organizations benefit from solutions grounded in global best practices, leading to improved socioeconomic conditions. This initiative positions B-schools as pivotal agents of socioeconomic transformation, highlighting their role in bridging the gap between academia and real-world applications.

Conclusion

The landscape of HE in the U.S. is undergoing significant transformation driven by political, economic, social, technological, and regulatory forces. The traditional model, rooted in historical academic paradigms and characterized by high costs and rigid structures, faces mounting pressures from alternative educational paths, technological advancements, and socio-political institutions. As students and tax-payers demand greater value and accountability, institutions of HE must adapt to remain relevant and competitive.

The push towards privatization of student loans and the emphasis on outcome-based accountability are central to reform efforts. These measures aim to incentivize colleges to enhance their return on investment by ensuring that students graduate with skills that lead to gainful employment. Additionally, the traditional reliance on college degrees as a benchmark for employment is being challenged by the growing acceptance of alternative credentials and skills-based hiring practices.

B-schools, in particular, are at a crossroads. They must navigate the complexities of a VUCA environment by integrating 21st-century skills into their curricula and fostering strong industry partnerships. The shift from instructor-centered to learner-centered models, emphasizing active learning and real-world problem solving, is critical for their survival and success. This shift will require that, to stay relevant, B-schools must have faculty with real world experience acquired by holding positions as employees with a business or a nonprofit organization as part of their qualification requirements.

Moreover, the demographic trends and economic realities, including the high costs of education and significant student debt, necessitate innovative approaches to education delivery. The rise of online learning platforms and alternative educational programs presents both a challenge and an opportunity for traditional institutions to reimagine their value propositions.

In this evolving landscape, HE institutions must strike a balance between preserving the core values of traditional education and embracing innovative strategies that enhance accessibility, affordability, and relevance. By doing so, they can better serve their diverse student populations and contribute meaningfully to the broader societal and economic goals.

Ultimately, the future of HE in the U.S. hinges on its ability to adapt and respond to the changing demands of the modern world. Institutions that can successfully integrate technology, foster industry collaboration, and prioritize student outcomes will be well-positioned to thrive in this dynamic environment.-

References

Akers, B., Cooper, P., & Pitts, J. (2024, May 9). *The federal student loan program is unraveling.* https://www.aei.org/op-eds/the-federal-student-loan-program-is-unraveling/?mkt_tok=NDc1LVBCUS05NzEAAAGTAOsymfw8ijPgQaTBK-GD3olz1kRcVt3B4CvATexiTUw5N0M_d1JvOq-BTDjpW516zMRHZqgc4JwZFRWySsoKyOulV0HQLGPw7OBEzWE7aHt2

Altschuler, G. (2009). *The GI Bill: A new deal for veterans.* Oxford University Press. DOI: 10.1093/oso/9780195182286.001.0001

Association to Advance Collegiate Schools of Business. (2021). *2021 Business school data guide.* Association to Advance Collegiate Schools of Business. https://www.aacsb.edu/-/media/publications/research-reports/2021-business-school-data-guide-october-release.pdf?rev=9f0506585b4d4dde9808e9ec4a19fd97&hash=34E7F0BE92B1074F04FCC67C008FA095

Association to Advance Collegiate Schools of Business. (2022a). *2020 Guiding principles and standards for business accreditation.* Association to Advance Collegiate Schools of Business. https://www.aacsb.edu/-/media/documents/accreditation/2020-aacsb-business-accreditation-standards-jul-1-2022.pdf?rev=b40ee40b26a14d4185c504d00bade58f&hash=9B649E9B8413DFD660C6C2AFAAD10429

Association to Advance Collegiate Schools of Business. (2022b). *2020 Interpretive guidance for AACSB accreditation.* Association to Advance Collegiate Schools of Business. https://www.aacsb.edu/-/media/documents/accreditation/2020-interpretive-guidance-july-2021.pdf?rev=e9ca74d1736749f2a5ae3e5b0b7854bd&hash=29EC7DF1790D9161F5FF24640028FCD4

Association to Advance Collegiate Schools of Business. (2022c). *2022 State of accreditation report.* Association to Advance Collegiate Schools of Business. https://www.aacsb.edu/insights/reports/2022-state-of-accreditation-report

Belkin, D. (2022, July 20). Broke colleges resort to mergers for survival. *Wall Street Journal, Eastern edition*, A.1.

Belkin, D. (2024, January 20). Why Americans have lost faith in the value of college: Three generations of "college for all" in the U.S. has left most families looking for alternatives. *Wall Street Journal.* https://www.wsj.com/us-news/education/why-americans-have-lost-faith-in-the-value-of-college-b6b635f2

Bergeron, J., & Fryer, L. (2023, November 16). *Credential transparency: Judging return on investment for higher education and workforce.* https://www.aei.org/research-products/report/credential-transparency-judging-return-on-investment-for-higher-education-and-workforce/

Bernstein, I. (1996). *Guns or butter: The presidency of Lyndon Johnson.* Oxford University Press.

Boggs, K., Sobiech, K., & Tripp, J. (2021). The pandemic pivot: A case study of a university's rapid shift to fully online instruction. *Journal of Online Learning and Teaching, 17*(2), 221–235.

Boston College, The Center for Teaching Excellence. (2024, March 15). *Active learning classroom.* https://cteresources.bc.edu/documentation/active-learning-classroom/

Brenan, M. (2023, July 11). *Americans' confidence in higher education down sharply.* https://news.gallup.com/poll/508352/americans-confidence-higher-education-down-sharply.aspx

Brint, S. (2024, March 6). Trump and his allies are preparing to overhaul higher education. *The Chronicle of Higher Education.* https://www-chronicle-com.electra.lmu.edu/article/if-trump-wins

Bryant, J., Golden, R., & Jefferson, I. (2023). *Higher ed is consolidating, transforming the sector.* https://www.mckinsey.com/industries/education/our-insights/higher-ed-is-consolidating-transforming-the-sector

Cantwell, B. (2024, January 24). The left's contradictory goals for higher ed. *The Chronicle of Higher Education* https://www.chronicle.com/article/the-lefts-contradictory-goals-for-higher-ed

Carlson, S. (2024, February 6). What's really behind the view that higher ed isn't worth it? *The Chronicle of Higher Education* https://www.chronicle.com/article/whats-really-behind-the-view-that-higher-ed-isnt-worth-it

Chui, M., Issler, M., Roberts, R., & Yee, L. (2023, July 20). *McKinsey technology trends outlook.* https://www.mckinsey.com/capabilities/mckinsey-digital/our-insights/the-top-trends-in-tech

Cooper, M. (2023, October 19). No, disruption isn't coming for higher ed. *The Chronicle of Higher Education* https://www.chronicle.com/article/no-disruption-isnt-coming-for-higher-ed

Cornell University, Center for Teaching Innovation. (2024). *Active learning.* https://teaching.cornell.edu/teaching-resources/active-collaborative-learning/active-learning#:~:text=Active%20learning%20methods%20ask%20students,words%20through%20writing%20and%20discussion

De Brey, C., Snyder, T. D., Zhang, A., & Dillow, S. A. (2021). *Digest of education statistics 2019* (NCES 2021-009). National Center for Education Statistics, Institute of Education Sciences, U.S. Department of Education. https://nces.ed.gov/pubs2021/2021009.pdf

Deloitte. (2024, June). 2024 Higher Education Trends. https://www2.deloitte.com/us/en/insights/industry/public-sector/latest-trends-in-higher-education.html

Dieleman, M., Šilenskytė, A., Lynden, K., Fletcher, M., & Panina, D. (2022). Toward more impactful international business education: A teaching innovation typology. *Journal of Teaching in International Business*, 33(4), 181–202. DOI: 10.1080/08975930.2022.2137279

Dua, A., Kumar, S., Singh, R., & Sharma, P. (2020). Impact of COVID-19 on remote learning: Experiences of students and teachers. *Journal of Educational Research and Development*, 15(3), 123–145. DOI: 10.12345/jerd.2020.12345

Ellis, L. (2022, November 3). Prestigious M.B.A. programs go online. *Wall Street Journal, Eastern edition*, A.1.

Fischer, K. (2022, August 12). The Shrinking of Higher Ed. *The Chronicle of Higher Education.* https://www.chronicle.com/article/the-shrinking-of-higher-ed

Friga, P. (2021, February 5). How Much Has Covid Cost Colleges? $183 Billion. *The Chronicle of Higher Education* https://www.chronicle.com/article/how-to-fight-covids-financial-crush

Fuller, J. B., & Raman, M. (2022, December 12). The partnership imperative: Community colleges, employers, and America's chronic skills gap. Harvard Business School Project on Managing the Future of Work. https://www.hbs.edu/managing-the-future-of-work/Documents/research/The%20Partnership%20Imperative%2012.12.2022.pdf

Furstenberg, F. (2023, April 7). Higher ed's grim, soulless, ed-technified future. *The Chronicle of Higher Education.* https://www.chronicle.com/article/higher-eds-grim-soulless-ed-techified-future

Geiger, R. L. (2015). *The history of American higher education: Learning and culture from the founding to World War II.* Princeton University Press.

Gilbert, E. (2020, November 20). A reason to be skeptical of "college for all." *The Chronicle of Higher Education.*https://www.chronicle.com/article/a-reason-to-be-skeptical-of-college-for-all

Gonzalez, D., Law, J., Oladiran, F., Rounsaville, T., Sanghvi, S., & Scott, D. (2023). *Fulfilling the potential of US higher education.* McKinsey & Company. https://www.mckinsey.com/industries/education/our-insights/fulfilling-the-potential-of-us-higher-education

Graham, S. W., & Donaldson, J. F. (2020). Academic leaders' response to the volatility of higher education: The influence of institutional logics. *Studies in Higher Education*, 45(9), 1864–1877. DOI: 10.1080/03075079.2019.1586867

Guard, L., & Jacobsen, J. (2024, May 9). The lawyerization of higher education. *The Chronicle of Higher Education.*https://www.chronicle.com/article/the-lawyerization-of-higher-education

Hanson, A., Salerno, C., Sigelman, M., de Zeeuw, M., & Moret, S. (2024). *Talent disrupted: College graduates, underemployment, and the way forward.* The Burning Glass Institute and Strada Institute for the Future of Work. https://static1.squarespace.com/static/6197797102be715f55c0e0a1/t/65fb306bc81e0c239fb4f6a9/1710960749260/Talent+Disrupted+03052024.pdf

Hatch, B. (2022, August 11). College rankings are "a joke," education secretary says. *The Chronicle of Higher Education.*https://www.chronicle.com/article/college-rankings-are-a-joke-education-secretary-says

Hess, F., & McShane, M. (2024a, March 11). *Taking on the college cartel.*https://www.aei.org/articles/taking-on-the-college-cartel/?mkt_tok=NDc1LVBCUS05NzEAAAGR9SCI0lhrO-GBSjSg4j0d9-i3ArScuypaxuo05w-7bweqMyyLWcHg9uyyonv6nZTCjjPIg7S9TT7MrIp5c7sc_BH75RY1yxohF4VQzTbGMAs0

Hess, F., & McShane, M. (2024b, March 27). *Finally, a chance to start getting higher ed right.* https://www.jamesgmartin.center/2024/03/finally-a-chance-to-start-getting-higher-ed-right

History and archival resources in higher education. (2024). https://higher-ed.org/history/

Horn, M. (2023, August 25). We Can't Tolerate Bad College Programs Anymore. *The Chronicle of Higher Education.* https://www.chronicle.com/article/we-cant-tolerate-bad-college-programs-anymore

Humboldt University. (2024). *Short history.*https://www.hu-berlin.de/en/about/history/huben_html/huben_html

Hyland, G. (2023, October 31). Navigating the student debt crisis: Seven lessons for higher education institutions. *Forbes*. https://www.forbes.com/sites/forbesbusinesscouncil/2023/10/31/navigating-the-student-debt-crisis-seven-lessons-for-higher-education-institutions/?sh=54d063e93a12

International Institute for Management Development. (2024). *World competitiveness ranking*. https://www.imd.org/centers/wcc/world-competitiveness-center/rankings/world-competitiveness-ranking/

Kelderman, E. (2023, September 5). What the public really thinks about higher education. *The Chronicle of Higher Education*. https://www.chronicle.com/article/what-the-public-really-thinks-about-higher-education

Korn, M. (2022, November 14). Colleges win back foreign students. *Wall Street Journal, Eastern edition*, A.3.

Le, T. (2023). *Colleges and universities in the US* (Industry Report 61131A). IBISWorld. https://www.ibisworld.com/united-states/market-research-reports/colleges-universities-industry/

Lutchen, K. R. (2024, April 18). *A new model for university-industry partnerships to ensure curricula evolve as technologies do*. https://hbsp.harvard.edu/inspiring-minds/a-new-model-for-university-industry-partnerships

Ma, J., & Pender, M. (2021). *Trends in college pricing and student aid 2021*. College Board. https://research.collegeboard.org/media/pdf/trends-college-pricing-student-aid-2021.pdf

Maglione, F. (2024, February 22). *Half of college graduates are working high school level jobs*. https://www.bloomberg.com/news/articles/2024-02-22/career-earnings-with-a-college-degree-underemployed-graduates-lag-on-income

McGurran, B. (2023, May 9). College tuition inflation: Compare the cost of college over time. *Forbes*. https://www.forbes.com/advisor/student-loans/college-tuition-inflation/

McMurtrie, B. (2023, September 20). Americans Value Good Teaching. Do Colleges? *The Chronicle of Higher Education*. https://www.chronicle.com/article/americans-value-good-teaching-do-colleges

Mokyr, J. (2018). *The British industrial revolution: An economic perspective* (2nd ed.). Routledge. DOI: 10.4324/9780429494567

National Center for Education Statistics. (2021). *Digest of education statistics*. https://nces.ed.gov/programs/digest/2021menu_tables.asp

National Center for Education Statistics. (2023, June). *Digest of education statistics.* https://nces.ed.gov/programs/digest/d22/tables/dt22_311.60.asp

National Center for Education Statistics. (2023, August). *Postsecondary institution revenues.* https://nces.ed.gov/programs/coe/indicator/cud/postsecondary-institution -revenue

National Center for Education Statistics. (2024, May). *Characteristics of postsecondary faculty.* https://nces.ed.gov/programs/coe/indicator/csc

Oke, A., & Fernandes, F. A. P. (2020). Innovations in Teaching and Learning: Exploring the Perceptions of the Education Sector on the 4th Industrial Revolution (4IR). *Journal of Open Innovation*, 6(2), 31. https://www.mdpi.com/2199-8531/6/2/31. DOI: 10.3390/joitmc6020031

Organization for Economic Cooperation and Development (OECD). (2024, July). OECD (2023), Educational attainment of 25-64 year-olds (2022): Percentage of adults with a given level of education as the highest level attained", in Education at a Glance 2023: OECD Indicators, OECD Publishing, Paris, https://doi.org/DOI: 10.1787/c5373fc9-en

Parkinson, C. N. (1957). Parkinson's Law: The pursuit of progress edition. https://www .amazon.com/Parkinsons-Law-Other-Studies-Administration/dp/B000Z40KKQ

Postsecondary Commission. (2024). *Accreditation handbook & materials.* https:// postsecondarycommission.org/accreditation-handbook/

Professor, X. (2011). *In the basement of the ivory tower: The truth about college.* Penguin Books.

Readying students for the workforce: Aligning today's curriculum with tomorrow's careers. (2024). \https://he.hbsp.harvard.edu/readying-students-for-the-workforce.html ?icid=anonymous-home%7Cmust-reads-section%7Cmust-read-career-readiness

Reaves, J. (2019). 21st-century skills and the fourth industrial revolution: A critical future role for online education. *International Journal on Innovations in Online Education*, 3(1). Advance online publication. DOI: 10.1615/IntJInnovOnlineEdu.2019029705

Rosenberg, B. (2023, September 25). *Higher ed's ruinous resistance to change. The Chronicle of Higher Education.* https://www.chronicle.com/article/higher-eds -ruinous-resistance-to-change

Schlegelmilch, B. B. (2020). Why business schools need radical innovations: Drivers and development trajectories. *Journal of Marketing Education*, 42(2), 93–107. DOI: 10.1177/0273475320922285

Schleifer, D., Friedman, W., & McNally, E. (2022). *America's hidden common ground on public higher education: What's wrong and how to fix it.* https://www.publicagenda.org/reports/americas-hidden-common-ground-on-public-higher-education/

Schrecker, E. (2022, October 14). The 50-year war on higher education. *The Chronicle of Higher Education.* https://www.chronicle.com/article/the-50-year-war-on-higher-education

Skowronek, R. K., & Lewis, K. E. (Eds.). (2010). *Beneath the ivory tower: The archaeology of academia.* University Press of Florida., https://academic.oup.com/florida-scholarship-online/book/29004 DOI: 10.5744/florida/9780813034225.001.0001

Smith, M. (2023, October 5). *The public is giving up on higher ed. The Chronicle of Higher Education.* https://www.chronicle.com/article/the-public-is-giving-up-on-higher-ed

Statista. (2021). *The student debt crisis in the U.S.* https://www.statista.com/study/72526/the-student-debt-crisis-in-the-us/

The Changing Landscape of Online Education (CHLOE): Behind the Numbers. (2019). Quality Matters. https://www.qualitymatters.org/

The Future of Jobs Report. (2018). World Economic Forum. https://www3.weforum.org/docs/WEF_Future_of_Jobs_2018.pdf

Thiel College. (n.d.). *Experience the Thiel commitment.* https://www.thiel.edu/about

Trading Economics. (2024). *United States GDP.* https://tradingeconomics.com/united-states/gdp

Weber, L. (2024, February 16). 62% of Americans lack a college degree. Can they solve the labor shortage? *Wall Street Journal.* https://www.wsj.com/lifestyle/careers/employers-open-more-doors-to-workers-without-degrees-but-few-are-getting-in-732f1098

Workforce Skills Gap Trends 2024: Survey Report. (2024, February). *Springboard.* https://www.springboard.com/blog/business/skills-gap-trends-2024/#:~:text=A%20majority%20of%20leaders%20say,a%20top%203%20needed%20skill

Wren, D. A., & Bedeian, A. G. (2020). *The Evolution of Management Thought* (6th ed.). Wiley.

Zhuplev, A. (Ed.). (2018). *Disruptive Technologies for Business Development and Strategic Advantage*. IGI Global. DOI: 10.4018/978-1-5225-4148-6

Zhuplev, A., & Blas, N. (2022). Business education in the USA: Strategic imperatives in the age of disruption. In Zhuplev, A., & Koepp, R. (Eds.), *Global trends, dynamics, and imperatives for strategic development in business education in an age of disruption* (p. 12). IGI Global. DOI: 10.4018/978-1-7998-7548-2.ch001

Zuckerman, G. (2024, February 24). Peter Thiel's $100,000 offer to skip college is more popular than ever. *The Wall Street Journal*. https://www.wsj.com/finance/peter-thiels-100-000-offer-to-skip-college-is-more-popular-than-ever-162e281b

Endnotes

[1]   Friedrich Wilhelm Christian Karl Ferdinand von Humboldt (1767-1835) was a Prussian philosopher, linguist, government servant, diplomat, and founder of the Humboldt University of Berlin. Currently, Humboldt University is one of Germany's premier research universities (Humboldt University, 2024).

[2]   America was ranked #19/63 on Higher Education Achievement worldwide in the latest annual International Institute for Management Development's (2024) report. College rankings by U.S. News & World Reports, Financial Times, and other outlets are widely criticized on different grounds. One of the latest examples is a criticism by the U.S. Education Secretary Miguel Cardona who categorized college rankings as a "joke" (Hatch, 2022). Nevertheless, students and their parents, colleges and universities, and other stakeholders in the HE industry continue to rely on these rankings in their strategic decisions.

[3]   Originally rooted in the Bible, the "ivory tower" phenomenon has evolved over centuries. In a contemporary context, the metaphorical "ivory tower" meaning refers to an organizational environment where people operate being isolated and protected from the rest of the world, prioritizing their own interests, goals, and pursuits. With the emergence and proliferation of academic institutions in the 19th century, the term "ivory tower" has a connotation as an environment of intellectual pursuit disconnected from the practical concerns of daily life. Most contemporary uses of the term refer to academia, the college and university systems (Professor X, 2011; Skowronek & Lewis, 2010). Ivory tower is supported by academic tenure, "lifetime employment," voting/decision making privileges in colleges and universities based on tenure status, annual scholarship/publication performance requirements prioritizing A-rated

academic journals while relegating books, book chapters, and practitioner publications to the second and third tiers of scholarship, and other.

4   In 2020-2021, tenure system was used in approximately 74% of all public four-year HE institutions (no change since 1993-1994) and in 61% of all four-year nonprofit HE institutions (compared with 66% in 1993-1994). At the same time, the share of instructors with tenure was 92% for all public four-year HE institutions and 61% for all four-year nonprofit HE institutions. In fall 2020, of the 1.5 million faculty at degree-granting postsecondary institutions, 56% were full time and 44% were part time (National Center for Education Statistics, 2021).

5   The lecture style is often defined as "transmission model" that views education as a specific body of knowledge that is transmitted from the teacher to the student. It emphasizes teacher-centric learning where students are passive absorbers of information and implies the purpose of learning as memorization of facts.

6   For instance, Coursera education platform, collaborating with 275+ leading universities and companies worldwide offers more than 7,000 + reasonably priced courses, professional certificates, and undergraduate and graduate degrees from world-class universities and companies.

7   For details on costs of the college education please refer to the Education Data Initiative site which maintains an extensive database at https://educationdata .org/.

8   In 2021-2022, an average financial aid per full-time in-state undergraduate student at public four-year institution was $8,100. It reduced the $27,330 published cost of attendance to $19,230 net cost of attendance. For a private nonprofit four-year institution, the $23,080 average financial aid per full-time undergraduate student (almost 3x higher compared to public institution) reduced the $55,800 published cost of attendance to $32,720 net cost of attendance. During 2021-2022, first-time full-time in-state students at public four-year colleges need to cover an estimated average of $14,590 in tuition and fees and room and board after grant aid, in addition to $4,640 in allowances for books and supplies, transportation, and other personal expenses. Between 2006-2007 and 2021-2022, an average grant aid in 2021 dollars per first-time full-time in-state student at public four-year colleges increased from $4,360 to an estimated $8,100; the average published tuition and fees in this sector increased from $7,730 to $10,740. First-time full-time students at private nonprofit four-year colleges need to cover an estimated average of $28,610 in

tuition and fees and room and board after grant aid, in addition to $4,110 in allowances for books and supplies, transportation, and other personal expenses. Between 2006-2007 and 2021-2022, the average grant aid in 2021 dollars per first-time full-time student at private nonprofit four-year colleges increased from $13,210 to an estimated $23,080; the average published tuition and fees in this sector increased from $29,750 to $38,070 during this time period (Ma & Pender, 2021).

[9]   Korn (2022) reported that international students returned to U.S. college and university campuses in droves in fall 2021, with schools recovering a portion of the enrollment they lost when visas were hard to come by and the nation closed its borders. Enrollment by international students rose 3.8% to 948,519 in the 2021-2022 school year, compared with 914,095 the prior year. This gain is fueled by graduate students: New-student enrollments jumped 80%, to 261,961 in the 2021-2022 school year. International students at U.S. schools contributed $33.8 billion to the U.S. economy, in the 2021-2022 school year. The Georgia Institute of Technology, a top U.S. destination for foreign students, enrolled 8,040 international students, in the 2021-2022 school year, a 42% jump from the prior year—and nearly 20% above its previous record.

[10]   Main stakeholder groups with their own interests in HE include: 1) Students, who are the primary recipients of the educational services provided by the institutions; 2) academic faculty, who play a role in delivering education and conducting research; 3) parents, who are often the financial supporters having a vested interest in the quality and cost of education; 4) government regulators, that is, entities like the Department of Education and state HE entities and executive officers having a significant role in regulation and funding; 5) nongovernmental regulators, which include accrediting bodies and church sponsors that regulate institutions on nongovernmental fronts; 6) donors, that is, individuals, industry, and foundations that provide financial support to HE institutions; 7) employers, who are interested in the skills and competencies of college graduates; 8) alumni, who contribute through donations, mentorship, and enhancing the reputation of the institution; 9) suppliers, who include high schools providing students, and other vendors and service providers; 10) communities, that is, local communities and municipalities impacted by institutions through partnerships, employment opportunities, use of resources, logistical/transportation impacts, and SED.

[11]   "History and Archival Resources in Higher Education" (2024) offers specifics and nuances on the history of American HE.

12   The article contains nuanced multifaceted—largely "Socratic"/scholastic —
      arguments lacking quantitative analytics and applied politics in support of
      existing model/status quo of American HE and striving to rationalize why,
      like the previous changes, it is not going to be disrupted this time around.

13   This exclusive organizational brand-related competitive advantage of college-
      based network in the pre-Internet era has been partially eroded with the advent
      and proliferation of electronic platforms such as LinkedIn or Coursera offering
      global inclusivity and outreach.

14   There is no publicly available information and definitive ratio of academics
      to practitioners on the Council for Higher Education Accreditation (CHEA,
      est. 1996) tasked to ensure quality in HE by recognizing accrediting organi-
      zations. Overall, CHEA acts as a watchdog organization, ensuring that the
      accrediting bodies they recognize are upholding proper standards for colleges
      and universities. The AACSB (est. 1916), the agency responsible for B-schools
      accreditation, works to improve business education worldwide through collab-
      oration, innovation, and ensuring a positive societal impact. Out of 25 current
      AACSB Board members, only three are from outside academia. While AACSB
      documents strive for "impactful" outcomes in the accreditation criteria and
      process, their standards are skewed toward advancing HE agenda by prioritizing
      academic curriculum, publications in academic journals with limited reader-
      ship and practical impacts and imposing a ratio of "scholarly academics" in
      the faculty roster. A typical college accreditation team is majority-comprised
      of professors and senior administrators of colleges and universities as experts
      from the industry or adjunct professors with practical experience do not play
      essential roles in the accreditation process and outcomes. Apart from their
      official accreditation mission, these teams have obvious vested interests in
      protecting the survival and prosperity of their own workplace and preserving
      the whole HE industry as an institution of society.

15   In contrast, the AACSB's existing Standard 3 contains an elaborate "nonexhaus-
      tive" list of activities normally expected of scholarly academic (SA), practice
      academic (PA), scholarly practitioner (SP), or instructional practitioner (IP)
      or additional (A) faculty status (the latter are the faculty who do not meet the
      school's criteria within this framework). While the standard does not specifi-
      cally require publication of peer- or editorial-reviewed journal articles, schools
      normally are expected to have guidelines and criteria consistent with their
      mission and their peers. A peer review team may question a school's criteria if
      it appears the criteria are not in alignment with the school's mission and peer
      institutions. Standard 8 does require that "a significant cross section of faculty

in the school and each discipline is engaged in the production of intellectual contributions, relying heavily on participating faculty" (AACSB, 2024, pp.29-35). All of that translates into the following qualification thresholds dabbed as AACSB "guidelines" that are imposed on schools with various degrees of flexibility in the faculty body composition: 1) SA guideline: $(SA)/(SA + PA + SP + IP + A) > 40\%$; 2) $SA + PA + SP + IP)/(SA + PA + SP + IP + A) > 90\%$ (AACSB, 2022b).

[16] The article addresses several nuances of this proposal.

[17] Currently, there are more than one million unique credentials in the U.S.—diplomas, degrees, certifications, apprenticeships, licenses, and badges—spread out across 60,000 providers. With so many options, employers, students, and their families are often overwhelmed with the choices. Credential Transparency provides specific details on a credential program's length, cost, competencies, skills provided, level of mastery targeted, earnings potential, and employment outcomes. It is made possible by Credential Transparency Description Language, technology that is recognized as a common, standard language to make credentials understandable, comparable, and discoverable (Bergeron & Fryer, 2023). A poll published in 2022 asked parents if they would rather their child attended a four-year college or a three-year apprenticeship that would train them for a job and pay them while they learned. Nearly half of parents whose child had graduated from college chose the apprenticeship. However, unlike the European model of HE, where students enter a vocational track and apprentice with an employer with the assistance of government support, the U.S. invests almost exclusively in students heading to college. Government financial support for universities outstrips apprenticeships by about 1,000 to one, writes Ryan Craig, author of the book *Apprentice Nation* and managing director of a firm that invests in new educational models. The pressure to place less emphasis on four-year degrees is growing, however. In what has been called the "degree reset," the federal government and several states eliminated the degree requirements for many government jobs. Companies such as IBM and the giant professional services firm Deloitte have, too. Last year, a survey of 800 companies by Intelligent.com found that 45% intended to eliminate bachelor's degree requirements for some positions, in 2024. The Ad Council recently ran a campaign encouraging employers to get rid of the "paper ceiling." In place of a degree, some employers are adopting skills-based hiring, looking at what students know as opposed to what credential they hold. The problem is that the signal sent by a college degree still matters more, in most cases, than the demonstration of skills. The result is something of a stand-off between old and new ideas of job readiness. A LinkedIn study published last

August found that, between 2019 and 2022, there was a 36% increase in job postings that omitted degree requirements, but the actual number of jobs filled with candidates who did not have a degree was much smaller. New initiatives may start to change that balance. New York Mayor Eric Adams has called for 30,000 new apprenticeships in the city by 2030. California Gov. Gavin Newsom wants to create 500,000 in the state by 2029. Deloitte is one of dozens of big companies championing the idea that skills matter more than degrees (Belkin, 2024).

[18] The university-industry partnership model is gaining popularity (Bryant et al, 2023; Lutchen, 2024), although the venerable academic "ivory tower" tradition still stands the ground (Brint, 2024; Cantwell, 2024; Rosenberg, 2023; Schrecker, 2022).

[19] A B-school is also sometimes referred to as school of management, management school, school of business administration or college of business administration.

[20] Within the broad "instruction" category, there are distinctions between "teaching" and "learning," "pedagogy" (i.e., teaching of children or dependent personalities), "andragogy" (i.e., facilitation of learning for adults, who are self-directed learners), and "heutagogy" (i.e., management of learning for self-managed learners).

[21] Under impacts of emerging strategic trends and disruptors in the competitive HE environment, the existing "ivory tower" status quo might sustain itself in undergraduate business programs as most of the students have limited exposure to the real world but prove inadequate in graduate studies where many students possess practical business/management experience.

[22] For instance, College Scorecard (https://collegescorecard.ed.gov/school/) by the U.S. Department of Education is a great resource for comparing colleges specifically in terms of cost and return on investment, including net price, graduation rates, and average earnings after graduation. Educational Data Initiative (https://educationdata.org/) provides a wide range of college-related data and analytics for students, teachers, policy makers, writers, and reporters. College Raptor (https://www.collegeraptor.com/) offers side-by-side comparisons of estimated financial aid packages along with simplified campus match scores and admission chances. Students and families have the power to make the best decisions, find the schools that best fit their academic and career goals, and find the institutions that are most affordable, reduce their need for student debt and create a plan for maximizing their chances of getting in and receiving the most aid.

23 Notably, technological advances have reduced the self-centered importance of specialized scholarly knowledge and instructional toolbox accumulated over several decades of work in academia to an Internet interface or a tiny flash drive used in a classroom to retrieve and disseminate subject information. Also, the role of specialized knowledge, however emphasized and widespread in traditional academic scholarship in business domain, comes into contrast with an increasingly integrated and systemic business realities in the real world. As a classic literary quote by Kozma Prutkov goes, "a specialist is like a gumboil: his plenitude is unilateral" (https://www.english-slang.com/eng/famous/p/prutkov-kozma?page=1).

24 There are hundreds of pedagogical methods and techniques varying in their content, scope, organizational requirements, learning effectiveness and efficiency, among others (Boston College, The Center for Teaching Excellence, 2024; Cornell University, Center for Teaching Innovation, 2024; Zhuplev & Blass, 2022). For instance, the Center for Excellence in Learning and Teaching at the Iowa State University describes 226 active learning techniques (https://www.celt.iastate.edu/instructional-strategies/teaching-format/active-learning/).

Appendix A: Business Schools Collaborate to Drive Regional Socio-Economic Progress with Global Insights

Project Description

Nations, regions, municipalities, communities, social groups, and individuals around the world vary in their dynamics and SED interests and priorities. Many of them face similar SED problems and priorities but often diverge in their solutions suffering duplication of effort and inefficiencies in resource allocation. Our analysis revealed major SED problems of common nature between Los Angeles (L.A.), U.S.A, and Córdoba, Spain (listed below). We included Córdoba as a hypothetical example. This project development model can be applied across multiple countries and universities worldwide. We compiled the list via AI tool and verified it through background research.

Table 6.SED Problems of Common Nature for Greater Los Angeles, California and Greater Córdoba, Spain

Socioeconomic problems of common nature	
Greater Los Angeles, California	**Greater Córdoba, Spain**
• Healthcare access: Numerous L.A. residents, especially low-income communities, are unable to access healthcare services. • Crime: The high crime rate at 1.2 times the national average. This predominantly impacts low-income neighborhoods. • Housing affordability, homelessness: The cost of living in L.A. is 51% above the national average. This causes a range of other SED problems. The homeless population, the largest in the country, is between 60,000 and 80,000. • Poverty, income inequality: One of the highest income inequality levels in L.A. nationwide is a root cause of many other SED issues. • Racial and ethnic inequality: L.A. has a historical pattern of racial/ethnic tensions spilling into other SED areas. Communities of color often face unequal access to resources and opportunities.	• Unemployment: Cordoba has been battling high unemployment, a precursor to many SED problems. • Poverty, income inequality: Poverty is a concern, particularly in rural areas, resulting in adverse health impacts, educational deficits, and other negative effects. Cordoba suffers income disparities potentially fueling social tensions and a sense of injustice. • Economic opportunities, brain drain: Cordoba faces challenges in attracting new businesses and industries, restricting job creation, and hindering SED. • Aging population: This poses multiple SED challenges. • Healthcare access: Certain areas of Cordoba have limited access to healthcare causing poor health and reduced life expectancy.

Western democracies operate as interdependent units such as states, provinces, and municipalities, with each unit having autonomous political-economic, SED, and strategic interests. Despite shared interests, there is widespread duplication of efforts on national, regional, and local levels worldwide due to a lack of awareness and collaboration. This causes inefficiencies in addressing common concerns like public transportation, energy or unemployment.

In the pre-Internet era, cross-country collaboration was often hindered by global logistical constraints and information barriers. Proliferation of IT, AI, and other innovations call for collaboration grounded in comparative analysis, adaptation, and application of best global practices toward local problem-solving and SED. The UN Sustainable Development Goals' model can serve as a starting point and conceptual template.

Stages in the Project "Scaffolding"

Universities involved in such collaborative SED project can implement this approach on local level in stages of the project "scaffolding" process: Single problem focus, multiple problem focus, collaborative local/regional projects, and collaborative international projects.

Strategic Rationale

This approach does not necessitate additional resources but creates a spectrum of stakeholder benefits: Bridging the gap between academia and real world, amplifying positive impacts of higher education on local SED and problem solving, enhancing university brand and visibility, and others.

SED is driven by innovation and imitation, each playing distinct roles. Imitation involves learning from somebody's experience/practices, tends to be less expensive and can generate most immediate impacts. Genuine breakthrough innovation tends to be time and cost-intensive and accounts for a minority share of positive impacts in problem solving and development. In contrast, substantial resources are often dedicated to innovations that already exist elsewhere, achieved by predecessors or neighboring jurisdictions. This is caused by insufficient effort put into comparative analysis and adaptation of existing "best practices." A perpetual "reinvention of the wheel" causes inefficiencies and duplication of effort in addressing SED priorities of common interest.

In the increasingly competitive HE landscape, B-schools are seeking to reimagine and reposition themselves. This includes sharing mutual core competencies and resources from universities worldwide, underscoring academic excellence, experiential learning, and community service, among others.

B-schools strive to serve as catalysts for positive transformation. This involves channeling creative energy of the younger generation away from passivity, dependency, and even destructive activities toward encouragement to embrace positive values and engage meaningfully in SED.

Of paramount importance is the bridging of the gap between the real world and the academe. By bridging this gap, B-schools can facilitate SED of mutual interest across countries and position themselves as agents of progress. This approach ensures their relevance and impact.

Universities and Their Intellectual Potential for Regional Socioeconomic Development

Universities and colleges have intellectual potential and resources information (e.g., talent, libraries, printed resources, and mobile electronic databases). However, by and large, they have limited impact of local SED and problem solving, while enjoying various forms of strategic benefits (e.g., tax exemption status) and local support from government agencies, NGOs, and other sources.

Deliverables, Outcomes, and Stakeholder Benefits

1. Stakeholders and benefits:
   a. Loyola Marymount University (LMU) and other HE institutions (primary beneficiaries), via improved branding and visibility regionally, nationally, and internationally.
   b. Students, via impactful education and career outcomes.
   c. Local communities and organizations, via SED, problem solving, and improvements grounded in intellectual resources and best practices worldwide.
2. LMU and a partner institution (hereafter partners) select a local SED priority of common interest for exploration and development. LMU focuses on SoCal, partner institution, on its respective region in Spain. This constitutes a "case study" for the pilot R&D project run.
3. Partners complete their projects independently and exchange information and experiences in the process.
4. Partners independently develop their projects/recommendations designated for their respective stakeholders.
5. Partners develop and disseminate joint recommendations/frameworks designated toward scaling up.

Chapter 16
The Role of Emotional Intelligence in Educational Leadership

Mahona Joseph Paschal
https://orcid.org/0000-0001-9842-9849
Tanzanian English Language Teachers Association, Tanzania

Abigail Ekangouo Awanga
Cameroon English Language and Literature Teachers Association, Cameroon

Jumanne Bakari Tungu
Tanzanian English Language Teachers Association, Tanzania

Peter Ndomondo
Lucent University, UK

ABSTRACT

This chapter explores the significance of emotional Intelligence in educational leadership. Emotional Intelligence is a critical trait for effective educational leaders as it facilitates the development of positive learning environments. Leaders with high emotional possess the ability to understand and manage their own emotions, as well as emotions and empathize with others. This enables them to build strong relationships with students, teachers, and staff, fostering open communication and collaboration. Additionally, emotional equips leaders with the skills to handle conflicts and make informed decisions in a composed manner. By modeling emotional Intelligence, leaders encourage the development of these skills among students and staff, promoting emotional well-being and growth. Overall, emotional Intelligence plays a pivotal role in educational leadership, enhancing the Leader's capacity to

DOI: 10.4018/979-8-3693-3443-0.ch016

create an inclusive and supportive academic environment that nurtures the holistic development of students and the entire school community.

INTRODUCTION

In education, effective leadership plays an important role in shaping students' learning experiences and outcomes (Mahona & Pacho, 2021). Traditionally, leadership in education has been associated with technical skills, administrative prowess, and academic expertise (Pesamaa, 2021). However, there has been a growing recognition of the importance of emotional intelligence Intelligence in educational leadership in recent years (Omotayo, 2024). Emotional Intelligence refers to the ability to recognize, understand, and manage one's own emotions, as well as to perceive and respond effectively to the emotions of others (Ahmad et al., 2024). The emotional intelligence of an individual is a tool which can be used in controling and handling feelngs when indivduals are interactimg with others. Ayat, (2021) noted that the ability of a person to control his/her attitude in relation to others' attitude and feelings is another approach to describe emotional intelligence. Emotional Intelligence encompasses a range of competencies, including self-awareness, self-regulation, empathy, and relationship management (Dbake, 2016; Pelliteri, 2022). These competencies are not only relevant in personal interactions but also have a profound impact on leadership effectiveness and the overall educational environment. From this point of view, Ahmad et al., (2024) pointed out that emotional intelligence is linked to the heart, of an individual which exemplifies the mind and the brain, which represents ability of an individual to think.

In the context of educational leadership, emotional Intelligence goes beyond simply being adept at managing the administrative and organizational aspects of schools (Omotayo, 2024); Waruwu, 2015). It involves the ability to navigate complex human interactions, inspire and motivate others, and create a positive and inclusive school culture. Educational leaders with a high level of emotional Intelligence are able to establish trusting relationships, effectively communicate with stakeholders, and make informed and student-centered decisions (Omotayo, 2024). One of the key benefits of emotional Intelligence in educational leadership is its impact on student well-being and success (Bower, 2018). When leaders possess emotional Intelligence, they are better equipped to understand and address the diverse needs of their students. They can create supportive and inclusive environments that foster a sense of belonging and promote positive social-emotional development (Pesamaa, 2021). t. Consequently, students feel more engaged, motivated, and connected to their learning, leading to improved academic achievement and overall well-being. Furthermore, emotional Intelligence in educational leadership has a ripple effect on the entire school community. When leaders model emotional Intelligence, it sets a powerful example for teachers, staff, and students. It promotes a culture of respect, collaboration, and open communication, where everyone's voice is valued (Waruwu, 2015).. This supportive climate enhances teacher satisfaction, retention, and professional growth, leading to a more harmonious and effective learning environment.

While the importance of emotional Intelligence in educational leadership is increasingly recognized, it is essential to provide leaders with the tools and support to develop and enhance their emotional intelligence skills (Paren, 2015). Training programs, professional development opportunities, and ongoing self-reflection can all contribute to the growth of emotional Intelligence in educational leaders, enabling them to improve their practice and positively impact their schools continuously.

In this chapter, we explore the role of emotional Intelligence in educational leadership and its implications for fostering effective leaders and nurturing educational environments. We delve into the specific components of emotional and how they relate to educational leadership. Additionally, we will examine practical strategies for applying emotional Intelligence in decision-making, relationship management, and creating a positive school climate. Finally, we will explore ways to develop emotional Intelligence in educational leaders, highlighting the importance of modeling and ongoing professional development.

THE CONCEPT OF EMOTIONAL INTELLIGENCE

According to Bower, (2018) emotional Intelligence is the logical skill of observation and emotional expression. A competence-based trait facilitates innermost thought processes that help one understand and manage emotions for one'sunderstand and for personal growth. These are features that indicate leaders' ability to understand himself as well as others in an institution (Hansen, 2018) The capacity to recognize correctly, assess, and express emotion; the ability to access and generate feelings when they smooth thought; the ability to understand emotion and emotional knowledge; and the ability to control emotions, to promote emotional and intellectual growth (Goleman, 2017) It is the capacity to observe, control and evaluate himself. Nevertheless, according to (Bower, 2018; Dbake, 2016), emotional Intelligence might enable a leader to monitor group members' feelings and take the proper action. Therefore, educational institutions can also perform and grow positively if the leader/Head of that institution is adapting the emotional Intelligence. The support of educators in the regulation of emotional Intelligence by including mindfulness practices train learners in stress management techniques and give conducive support in letting learners to be able to express their emotions comfortably.

According to Goleman, (2017) emotional Intelligence refers to the capacity to recognizing our feelings and those of others, motivating ourselves, and managing emotions well in our relationships and ourselves. From this point of view, emotional intelligent, pronounces abilities distinct from, but complementary to, academic Intelligence, the purely cognitive capacities measured by IQ. It indicates some traits of a leader who has kills to solve anythe skills to solve and cool any problem. It is considered an Emotionally intelligent one. Several scholars define emotional Intelligence differently. General,it is the ability to be aware of the rising and falling of our mental experiences. This is the ability of someone who understand himself from time to time to observe and lead his organization by distinguishing harmful mental states from his subordinates; improving emotional Intelligence has been considered a push factor in an organization to increase project development and economic growth.

Generally, emotional Intelligence is the psychological construct that is essential and relevant in leadership since emotional factors play a significant role in well-being, interpersonal relationships, motivation, and workplace adjustment (Pelliteri, 2022). It can be applied in educational institutionss since the leader/head must progressively work with individual groups such as instructors, teaching aids, school psychologists, counselors, and other education administrators, learners, and parents as well. In other words, emotional Intelligence can be the causative reason for developing education organizations. This will be the better way for a leader to control his emotions,for a leader to control his emotions, supervise his subordinates, and manage all others' emotions.

COMPONENTS OF EMOTIONAL INTELLIGENCE

The components of emotional involve a deep understanding of one'semotions, the ability to regulate and control them, the capacity to recognize and empathize with the emotions of others, and the skill to build and maintain meaningful relationships. By developing these components, individuals can enhance their emotional well-being, improve their communication skills, and thrive in various personal and professional domains.

Leader's self-awareness

Leader' self-awareness is about getting the most out of your team. In Socrates' perception, self-awareness comes from the word "nosce te ipsum" which means knowing thyself (Goleman, 2015). A leader needs to be able to get the most out of himself, which is why self-awareness is so important for leaders. Self-awareness merely comprehends how someone feels and how his feelings can touch others in the workplace. One must have consented to recognize his/her strengths, weaknesses, and emotions. In short, self-awareness is an important factor that can help someone recognize and understand his or her ownan important factor that can also help someone recognize and appreciate his or her emotions (Berson, & Oreg, 2016). In education, teaching awareness to learners can be helpful.

Self-emotional regulation

Goleman, 2015) noted that Self-emotional regulation sometimes can be seen as one's self-management, which refers to managing and controlling someone's emotions. Due to this, education leaders need to be able to keep their emotions under control and maintain an affirmative viewpoint, notwithstanding whatever obstacles they may be encountering. This is predominantly essential when someone is stressed, as leaders need to be able to respond to adversity in a tranquil and proper manner (Waruwu, 2015). The learning environment can be improved if a learner can regulate emotions in a positive and conducive environment, reduce disruption reductions as well as promote a focused classroom learning milieu; learners will concentrate and focus more on academic tasks which create positive performance in their outcomes.

The social skill awareness

This factor suggests an individual's ability to feel and understand others' sentiments, moods, and reactions with some intensity share feelings and/or build connections with others. Social awareness involves somebody's ability to empathize with others and understand their emotions (Arnold, 2017). This will effectively enable a leader to communicate with his team members, spend he must be able to comprehend and recognize his workers' feelings (Alzoraiki, Rahman, & Mutalib, 2018). Empathetic leaders have tir employees' professional and personal growth, the traits of supporting their employees' professional and personal growth. They can effectively maintain positive workplace morale.

Self-motivation

It is the ability to self-motivate, which is a critical skill for managers to possess. Leaders need to constantly work towards their personal and professional goals, as well as the goals of the organization as a whole (Baesu, & Bejinaru, 2015). Successful leaders should also be able to effectively motivate their employees and maintain high standards for productivity and efficiency.

RELATIONSHIP BETWEEN EMOTIONAL INTELLIGENCE AND EDUCATIONAL LEADERSHIP

Emotional Intelligence is closely intertwined with educational leadership and and profound impact on leadership effectiveness and the overall academic environment. Here are some fundamental relationships between emotional Intelligence and educational leadership:

Self-awareness and Leadership Effectiveness

Emotional Intelligence begins with self-awareness, which is the ability to recognize and understand one's emotions, strengths, weaknesses, values, and motivations (Waruwu, 2015). Educational leaders who possess self-awareness can better understand how their emotions may influence their decision-making, interactions, and overall leadership style. This self-awareness allows leaders to be more intentional in their actions, make informed choices, and manage their emotions effectively, leading to enhanced leadership effectiveness (Berson, & Oreg, 2016).

Relationship Building and School Culture

Emotional Intelligence is crucial in building positive relationships and creating a healthy school culture (Hansen, 2018).. Educational leaders with emotional Intelligence possess empathy, which is the ability to understand and share the feelings of others (Gibson, Dollarhide, Conley, & Lowe, 2018).. This empathy enables leaders to connect with teachers, staff, students, and parents on a deeper level, fostering trust, respect, and collaboration. By creating a supportive and inclusive school culture, leaders with emotional Intelligence contribute to a positive learning environment where individuals feel valued, supported, and motivated (Paschal, & Mkulu, 2020).

Effective Communication and Collaboration

Communication is a fundamental aspect of educational leadership. Emotional Intelligence equips leaders with the skills to communicate effectively (Berson, & Oreg, 2016).. Leaders with emotional Intelligence can express themselves clearly, listen actively, and adapt their communication styles to different individuals and situations. This ability to communicate effectively promotes understanding, clarity, and collaboration among teachers, staff, students, and parents (Paschal, 2022).. It also enables leaders to address concerns, provide feedback, and foster open dialogue, leading to improved relationships and a more cohesive school community.

Decision-Making and Student-Centeredness

Emotional Intelligence is closely linked to decision-making processes in educational leadership (Arnold, 2017). Leaders with emotional Intelligence consider the emotional impact of their decisions on stakeholders, including teachers, staff, students, and parents. They take into account the needs and perspectives of others, balance rationality with emotions, and make decisions that are student-centered and aligned with the school's vision and values (Paschal, & Mkulu, 2020).. This emotionally intelligent decision-making contributes to a sense of fairness, transparency, and trust within the school community.

Conflict Resolution and Collaboration

Conflict is inevitable in any organization, including educational institutions. Emotional Intelligence equips educational leaders with the skills to navigate conflicts and manage difficult conversations (Waruwu, 2015). Leaders with emotional Intelligence can regulate their emotions during conflicts, remain calm, and approach conflicts with empathy and understanding (Goleman, 2015).. In this chapter we acknowledge that leaders with emotional Intelligence can facilitate constructive dialogue, find common ground, and work towards mutually beneficial solutions. This ability to resolve conflicts positively contributes to a harmonious and productive school environment where collaboration and teamwork thrive.

ENHANCING EMOTIONAL INTELLIGENCE IN EDUCATION LEADERS

Education leaders who possess emotional Intelligence are better equipped to navigate the complexities of the educational landscape, build strong relationships with their staff and students, and create a positive and inclusive school culture

(Alzoraiki, Rahman, & Mutalib, 2018).. Recognizing the significance of emotional Intelligence in educational leadership, efforts are being made to enhance and cultivate this essential trait among education leaders. By focusing on Ideveloping emotional Intelligence, education leaders can foster a supportive and engaging environment that promotes the success and well-being of students and staff alike.Below are some strategies that could be helpful.

It is essential to study yourself better. A leader can have the ability to study himself better, which will be an assisting factor to improve self-awareness. Berson, & Oreg, (2016) noted that recognizing your feelings better and self-reflecting will make it easier to classify your strengths and weaknesses, enabling effective regulation and interpersonal relationships, and be a decent decision maker in the learning experience will be more ehnanced. Through this, one will be able to practice humility, which can also help to increase his subor nates' respect for him. A leader blaming his team for every problem signifies elements of leadership inability.

It is Important to Write down Your Thoughts and Reflect. Writing down your thoughts is the best way to enhance someone's self-awareness (Waruwu, 2015). This goes parallel with reflecting on your written thoughts; without reflecting, it will not be easy for a leader to recognize his thinking and feelings and assess the situation with a clear mind, referring to what you have written (Arnold, 2017).. Writing thoughts and feelings and keeping them for reference will be a good way of improving your emotional Intelligence.

Master self-control. For example, a conscious manager must have self-control. A manager who has no self-control can judge the problem subjectively by undermining the team instead of judging by looking at the source of the problem (Gibson et al.,2018). Therefore, self-control and knowing or sticking to your principles will make you manage your feelings.

ROLES OF IMOTINAL INTELLIGENCE IN EDUCATIONAL LEADERSHIP

Emotional Intelligence has different leadership roles. These roles are namely the ability to influence, effectiveness, inspire and motivate, encourage collaboration and build relationships,

To influence and adapt. These underwrite the total complete life experiences of teachers, students, and other stakeholders within their educational institutions (Hansen, 2018; Gibson et al.,2018). This aspect is always connected with interpersonal skills; comprehending how to control and manage both others and your emotions, will enable persuasion and communication effectively. In this context, leaders strive to gain trust, loyalty, admiration, and respect from the teachers on their staff by applying a charismatic vision and leading by example (Paren, 2015). The quick dynamism of the educational landscape helps Leaders adapt to challenges, remain resilient and effectively control the situation in the institution. Higher emotional Intelligence allows individuals to navigate social adeptly, rapport building, and provide affirmative impact on others' attitudes and behaviors as well (Waruwu, 2015). Emotional Intelligence determines how well teachers understand themselves as a bundle of emotions, and the last component includes empathy. Or empathizing processes determine how teachers manage among themselves and relate with students. They have to take part in owning other teachers' problems and students' problems as if they belong to them. A leader should have social interaction skills and the ability to influence the behavior of his subordinates and teachers. (Dbake, 2016). This, will result in strong and absolute affirmative performance outcomes acceleration. One must be notified that any successful education organization, there must be an influential leader/head who contributed to it. Leadership is innately an emotional process whereby a leader realizes their followers' emotional states. This can try to bring to mind emotions in followers and try to find how to cope with followers' emotional situations accordingly.

To enhance effectiveness. Leaders are not just what they think they are, they also know how their followers perceive them (Dbake, 2016). This means leaders are to ally with the traits of their followers. The connection of transparent decision-making by considering the emotional impact of stakeholders and ensuring the well-made decisions that align with the well-being of the education community. The emotional intelligence milieu of effectiveness involves the use of emotional awareness and management to attain the desired goal and outcomes (Pelliteri, 2022). Emotionally intelligent leaders collaborate, control conflict navigation, and effectively adapt their communication style. Being attuned to emotions assists someone in making brilliant decisions that add positive value on building solid relationships, which will raise both personal and environmental carrier. A leader can communicate clearlyan empathetically, which will promote open dialogue within the education organization (Waruwu, 2015). It has been emphasized that "A leader/head of an education institution who can effectively socialize with others is an emotionally intelligent leader (Arnold, 2017). This role is regarded as an essential factor for celerating any educational institution's development. One has to understand that, all levels of effectiveness in all organizations can be fostered or brought about by emotionally intelligent leaders/Heads of the organization. It must be noted that these leaders/heads of the institution often play a significant role in the excellence and efficiency of social relations with other people outside and within the education organization to comply with any social and environmental transformation and shape helpful connections in the business systems as a result of economic and academic institution growth.

Inspiring and motivating: Staff of educators can be inspired and motivated by the transformative Leader by being equipped with new ideas (Alzoraiki et al., 2018). Emotional Intelligence plays an important role in this aspect since higher emotional intelligent educators can comprehend and connect deeply with students compared to those withhigher emotional intelligence educators can comprehend and connect deeply with students compared to those with lower emotional Intelligence by tailoring their approach to individual needs. Through this, they will be able to make an inspirationalpositive learning environment by recognizing and validating learners' emotions in promoting the sense of belonging and a positive learning environment by recognizing and validating learners' emotions in promoting the sense of belonging and engagement. Motivation can be increased if at all the empath, constructive feedback, and environment of creative support will be given to learners (Ch, et al., 2017).. This will trigger the learners' enthusiasm and resilience towards the learning roadmap. When employees are stressed out, overworked, confused, worried, or bored in an institution, leaders/heads of are advised to inspire their subordinates (teachers) the same way teachers can do to students or pupils. This is because sometimes there are complications connected with different activities, which are frequently encompassed by considerable ambiguity and change. Due to this, inspiration must be implanted to either learners or teachers to calm the situation happened; hence the power of emotional Intelligence emerges by assisting school/college managers in inspiring fellow school/college workers and generating higher levels of motivation and commitment toward reaching the pyramidal peak in economic and academic change. An emotionally intelligent leader is required to have the ability to identify whether his team's emotional state is disturbing their work, and effectively he has to address those feelings. The incapability of implementing this will endanger the Leader's ability to inspire and motivate his team.

Encouraging collaboration. The capacity of understanding and management of team dynamism, the promotion of cooperation and collective problem-solving amongst educators and staff members can rapidly increasing. A leader helps create synergy among teams, improving the work experience (Campbell,2018).This can help to diminish negative feelings (such as stress) and help increase optimism and motivation. A decent leader must have the ability to encourage collaboration with a clear sense of optimism and determination. Teamwork skills have been well-known in several studies as among the "critical success factors" of activities (Eliophotou-Menon, & Ioannou, 2016). Applying teamwork simplifies work and makes it enjoyable among members. For example, teachers/instructors who attend classes to deliver lessons or lectures increase their competencies and always come up with good performance. For example, learning through group projects/activities, and discussion can enable learners to practice effective communication and listen actively to various perspectives from their fellows, which will lead to the improvement of awareness that will improve their cooperation, which will make a more significant contribution to their social and emotional growth. In addition, peer-mentoring activities will give a chance for emotional support for the creation of a more conducive learning environment that will also nurture emotional Intelligence. Several authors have suggested that emotional Intelligence is either responsible for or enhances an individual's ability to be involved in social interactions such that it may well be an underlying construct of social skills.

To develop positive relationships. Teachers with high emotional intelligence Intelligence are key to creating positive relationships; likewise, students with developed emotional intelligence Intelligence can control their stresses, social interaction, and have effective practical cooperation with both educators and peers,which increases education inclusion. Communication, relationships, open-mindedness, approachability, enjoyment of education, and knowledge in the education field significantly affected teacher work performance and morale (Paschal, & Mkulu, 2020)). Staff members must understand that a leader is not just a "boss to be glorified. There is no need for subordinates to scare their leaders/heads, and leaders/heads should not feel disrespected by their subordinates. A decent education administrator can create and build strong relationships with his subordinates, making them always eager to work hard and feel like valued members of the team and the education institution (Eliophotou-Menon& Loannou, 2016). Relationship is the key strength in helping education managers successfully manage organizational conflict. Conflict will be navigated diplomatically, fostering resolutions and an environment of harmony between staff members, students, and parents (Ch, et al.,2017).. For example, whenever there is discontent among learners, educators can guide them on how to express their feelings and perspectives in promoting empathy and pave the way to a concrete resolution. This will facilitate cooperation between schools and families to support learners' academic progress. Therefore, a good leader who has adopted emotional intelligence characters can absolutely deal the uniqueness of differing in the educational institution or workplace properly. An instructor can play a significant role in the school's success. (Waruwu 2015) argued that, for the organizational or campus leaders to enhance teacher productivity and lower apathy, emotional intelligence is required to a high degree. Therefore, when one discusses the roles of emotional, One must not forget to consider motivation and inspiration, collaboration, effectiveness, and relationships as core values of an emotionally intelligent leader.

STRATEGIES FOR ENHANCING EMOTIONAL INTELLIGENCE AMONG LEADERS

Developing emotional Intelligence in educational leaders is a continuous process that involves self-reflection, learning, and practice. In this chapter we suggest the following strategies to help educational leaders enhance their emotional Intelligence:

Self-Reflection: Encourage educational leaders to engage in regular self-reflection to gain a better understanding of their emotions, strengths, weaknesses, and triggers (Eliophotou-Menon& Loannou, 2016). This can be done through journaling, mindfulness practices, or seeking feedback from trusted colleagues or mentors. Self-reflection helps leaders become more self-aware and identify areas for growth.

Emotional Literacy: Help leaders expand their emotional vocabulary and develop a deeper understanding of emotion (Baesu, & Bejinaru, 2015). s. Provide resources and training on emotions, their impact, and how to recognize and express them effectively. This knowledge allows leaders to be more attuned to their own emotions and better understand the emotions of others.

Empathy Development: Offer training and workshops on empathy to help leaders develop their ability to understand and appreciate the perspectives, feelings, and needs of others. Encourage leaders to actively listen, ask open-ended questions, and practice putting themselves in others' shoes. This practice fosters empathy and strengthens relationships with teachers, staff, students, and parents.

Communication Skills: Provide training on effective communication skills, including active listening, non-verbal communication, and assertiveness (Campbell,2018; Paschal, & Mkulu, 2020)).. Help leaders develop the ability to express themselves clearly and respectfully while adapting their communication style to different individuals and situations. Effective communication facilitates understanding, collaboration, and trust within the school community.

Conflict Resolution Training: Offer training on conflict resolution and problem-solving techniques. Teach leaders strategies for managing conflicts constructively, such as active listening, finding common ground, and seeking win-win solutions. Provide opportunities for leaders to practice these skills through role-playing or case studies. Goleman, (2021) points out that leaders with high level of emitinal intelligence can navigate conflicts, provide a strong sense of direction and inspire collaboration in the time of change

Emotional Regulation Techniques: Support leaders in developing effective strategies to manage and regulate their emotions. This can include techniques such as deep breathing exercises, mindfulness practices, physical activity, or seeking support from colleagues or mentors (Goleman, 2021). Encourage leaders to practice self-care and stress management to maintain emotional balance.

Continuous Learning and Feedback: Encourage leaders to engage in ongoing learning opportunities related to emotional Intelligence and leadership (Goleman, 2021) This can involve attending conferences, workshops, or webinars, reading relevant books or articles, or participating in professional learning communities focused on emotional Intelligence. Encourage leaders to seek feedback from teachers, staff, students, and parents to gain insights into their emotional impact and areas for improvement. From this point of vie which has been pointed out by the authors of this chapter, Baesu, (2018) supports that leaders are required to have knowledge and abilities that can help in maintaining and restoring interaction and managnment with the staff.

Model Emotional Intelligence: As an educational leader, model emotional Intelligence in your own actions and interactions. Demonstrate self-awareness, empathy, effective communication, and emotional regulation (Bower, 2018;Waruwu, 2015). By modeling these behaviors, leaders set an example for others and create a culture that values emotional Intelligence.

Exercissing patience: Remember that developing emotional Intelligence is a journey, and it takes time and practice (Ch, et al., 2017)... Encourage educational leaders to be patient with themselves and celebrate their progress along the way. By investing in the development of emotional Intelligence, educational leaders can enhance their effectiveness, build strong relationships, and create a positive and supportive educational environment

CRITICAL EXAMPLES EMOTIONAL INTELLIGENCE IN EDUCATIONAL LEADERSHIP.

Empathy in conflict resolution. For instance, whenever there is an ideology dissimilarity amongst students, an educator leads them to express their feelings and viewpoints, promoting empathy and helping them find a resolution together.

Development of social skills. Social and emotional skills and their role play teachers' job performance and success. Different groups' tasks, such as open forums, discussions, and collective and inclusive assignments, provide a way of practicing communication waeffectively, in which collaboration, communication, and active listening will contribute to the emotional intelligence metamorphosis.

Journaling self-awareness. Journal is designed to show the reflection of their emotions, thoughts, and reactions fostering self-awareness. Educators guiding different discussions about emotional experiences can use these reflections.

Implementation of peer support programs. In this situation, teacher should always nurture the older students to guide their younger learners in fostering them in teaching the older students to guide their younger learners in fostering them in teaching the teachers. They should always nurture older students to guide their younger learners in inculcating a sense of ownership by offering support and comprehension.

Workshops conflict resolutions. For example, when there is an educational staff workshop for enabling students to effectively manage conflict resolution by insisting on compromising tactics and agree ideological dichotomies. This helps build emotional capacity as they traverse interpersonal challenges.

Norms of emotional Intelligence in the classroom. A positive classroom culture can be established by acknowledging and validating emotionsng an environment where learners feel comfortable and comfortable expressing themselves without fear of judgment.

In the scenario of Role-playing. In that case, this will be as one stage to the increase of emotional intelligence perspectives, empathy enhancement, and interpersonal skills in experiencing situational varieties and responses.

Finally, to enhance emotional, it is essential to be in the shoes of his team of followers. As a leader, you can build a fruitful relationship with your team by viewing various situations from diverse points of view. Contemplate the perspective of your team and every affiliate member specifically when it comes to the signposts and goals you established, your implementation processes, and the feedback you provide. A leader should always put himself in their shoes before criticizing something they have done. Lastly, do not forget to give praise and recognize their efforts. A powerful tool for cultivating emotional awareness is to allow thoughts, feelings, and emotions to simply be observing them and gain greater insight into our minds.

Conclusively, emotional can play a positive and significant role in developing organizational commitment Organizational success can be determined by the emotional tone set by the Leader due to a deeper understanding of self-awareness and others. If leaders are fully infused with emotionally intelligent behaviors at the workplace, they may create an indulging and rewarding work environment. By understanding and embracing the power of emotional Intelligence in educational leadership, we can cultivate leaders who excel in their administrative responsibilities and inspire and empower others, creating educational environments that foster growth, success, and well-being for all stakeholders.

REFERENCES.

Ahmad, M., Salam, A., Abdullah, M., Kumbuha, M. I., Munawar, S., & Khan, M. H. N. (2024). The role of emotional intelligence in educational leadership. *Internatinal Journal of Contemporary Issue in Social Science*, 3(2), 2652–2660.

Alzoraiki, M., Rahman, O. B., & Mutalib, M. A. (2018). The effect of the dimensions of transformational leadership on the teachers' performance in the Yemeni public schools. *European Scientific Journal*, 14(25). Advance online publication. DOI: 10.19044/esj.2018.v14n25p322

Arnold, K. A. (2017). Transformational leadership and employee psychological well-being: A review and directions for future research. *Journal of Occupational Health Psychology*, 22(3), 381–393. DOI: 10.1037/ocp0000062 PMID: 28150998

Ayat, M., Imran, M., Ullah, A., & Kang, C. W. (2021). Current trend analysis and prioritization of success factors: Asystematic literature review of ICT projects. *International Journal of Managing Projects in Business*, 14(3), 652–679. DOI: 10.1108/IJMPB-02-2020-0075

Baesu, C. (2018). Leadership Based on emotional intelligence in modern organisations. *The USV Annals of Economic and Public Administration*, 2(28), 73–78.

Baesu, C., & Bejinaru, R. (2015). Innovative Leadership Style and the influence of Emotional Intelligence. *The USV Annals of Economic and Public Administration*, 15, 136–145.

Berson, Y., & Oreg, S. (2016). The role of school principals in shaping children's values. Psychological science: Research, theory, & application in psychology and related sciences, 27(12), 1539-1549

Bower, G. (2018) The Influence of Emotional Intelligence on Overall Success of Campus leader as Perceived by Veteran Teachers in Rural mid-sized East Texas Public School District, Lamar University. International Counsel of Professors of Education.

Campbell, J. W. (2018). Efficiency, incentives, and transformational leadership: Understanding collaboration preferences in the public sector. *Public Performance & Management Review*, 41(2), 277–299. DOI: 10.1080/15309576.2017.1403332

Ch, A. H., Ahmad, S., Malik, M., & Batool, A. (2017). Principals' leadership styles and teachers' job satisfaction: A correlation study at secondary level. Bulletin of Education & Research, 39(3), 45-56. Retrieved from Dbake, D, (2016). Impact of Leader's emotional Intelligence and transformative behavior on perceived leadership effectiveness. A multiple source view. *Business Perspectives and Research*, 4(1), 27–40.

Eliophotou-Menon, M., & Ioannou, A. (2016). The link between transformational leaders and teachers' job satisfaction, commitment, motivation to learn, and trust in the Leader. *Academy of Educational Leadership Journal*, 20(3), 12–22.

Fiaz, M., Qin, S., Ikram, A., & Saqib, A. (2017). Leadership styles and employees' motivation: Perspective from an emerging economy. *Journal of Developing Areas*, 51(4), 143–156. DOI: 10.1353/jda.2017.0093

Francis, C. U. (2017). Transformational and transactional leadership styles among leaders of administrative ministries in Lagos, Nigeria. IFE Psychologia. *International Journal (Toronto, Ont.)*, (2), 151–164.

Gibson, D. M., Dollarhide, C. T., Conley, A. H., & Lowe, C. (2018). The construction and validation of the school counseling transformational leadership inventory. *Journal of Counselor Leadership & Advocacy*, 5(1), 1–12. DOI: 10.1080/2326716X.2017.1399246

Goleman, D. (2017). *What makes a leader?* Harvad Business Review Press.

Goleman, D. (2021). Leadeship: The power of emotional intelligence. [C.]. *More Than Sound.*, L, L.

Hansen, C. (2018). Why rural principals leave. *Rural Educator*, 39(1), 41–53. DOI: 10.35608/ruraled.v39i1.214

Mahona, P., & Pacho, T. (2021). Reshaping Education in the Post-COVID-19 Pandemic in Africa. [ARJESS]. *African Research Journal of Education and Social Sciences*, 8(3), 13–26.

Omotayo, O. A. (2024). Exploring the role of emotional intelligence in educational Leadership: A case study of school administrators. *International Journal of Educatinal Research and Library Science*, 4(8), 43–59.

Paren, J. (2015) Introduction to selected aspect of leadership. *Proceedings of the Multdiscplinary Academic Conference, Octo*, 1-7

Paschal, M. J. (2022). Investigating teachers' awareness of gifted children and re-source accessibility for their learning in Tanzania. *Asian Journal of Education and Social Studies*, 27(4), 9–31. DOI: 10.9734/ajess/2022/v27i430660

Paschal, M. J., & Mkulu, D. G. (2020). Teacher- Students' Relationship and Students 'Academic Performance in Public Secondary Schools in Magu District, Tanzania. *Journal of Research in Education and Society*, 11(1), 20–23. http://www.icidr.org/jresv11no1-content.php

Pelliteri, J. (2022). *Emotional Intelligence and Leadership Style in Leadership in Education, Department of Education and community programs*. Queens College, University of NewYork.

Pesamaa,O., Zwikael, O., Hair, J., Huemann, M,. (2021). Publishing qualitative papers with rigor and transparency. Intl. Proj. Manag. 39.

Waruwu, B. (2015). The correlation between teacher's perceptions about principal's emotional Intelligence and organizational climate and job satisfaction of teachers of state senior high school in Gunungsitol Nias, Indonesia. *Journal of Education and Practice*, 6(13), 142–147.

Chapter 17
The Rise of Online Learning and the Technological Revolution in Higher Education

Lister Siphathisiwe Tshuma
https://orcid.org/0009-0003-9972-0680
National University of Science and Technology, Zimbabwe

Doris Chasokela
https://orcid.org/0009-0001-5983-8508
National University of Science and Technology, Zimbabwe

ABSTRACT

The rise of online learning and the technological revolution in higher education are having a profound impact on the way learning and teaching are done. The rise of online learning has revolutionized the way students learn, with many institutions now offering a range of online courses. This shift has been driven by the increasing adoption of digital technologies, such as learning management systems, virtual and augmented reality, and artificial intelligence. The technological revolution in higher education has also enabled new models of education, such as massive open online courses (MOOCs), online degree programs, and competency-based education. Moreover, the rise of online learning has also created new opportunities for institutions to collaborate with industry partners, foster innovation, and develop new revenue streams. However, the technological revolution in higher education also poses challenges. This chapter explores the rise of online learning and the technological revolution in higher education, examining the key drivers, trends, and implications of this transformation.

DOI: 10.4018/979-8-3693-3443-0.ch017

Introduction

In the past, the traditional model of higher education has been based on the premise that learning takes place in a physical classroom, with a teacher and students gathered together in one place. This model has served us well for centuries, but it is now being challenged by the rise of online learning and the technological revolution. The internet and new technologies have opened up new possibilities for education, making it more accessible, flexible, and affordable than ever before (Foong, et al. 2024; Indrawati & Kuncoro, 2021; Ahmad, 2020). These technological advances have changed how we think about learning and teaching, forcing us to rethink the traditional model of higher education. For centuries, the traditional model of higher education has been based on the premise that learning takes place in a physical classroom, with a teacher and students gathered together in one place. This model has served us well, providing a structured and supportive environment for students to engage with course material, ask questions, and learn from one another. However, the rapid advancement of technology and the internet has begun to challenge this traditional model, offering new possibilities for education that are more accessible, flexible, and affordable. According to Darian-Smith (2024) and Schwartz & Omori (2024), the rise of online learning has opened up new doors for students who may not have had access to higher education in the past. With the internet, students can now access course materials, communicate with instructors and peers, and complete assignments from anywhere in the world. This has made higher education more inclusive, allowing students from diverse backgrounds and locations to participate in learning.

Moreover, the technological revolution has changed the way we think about teaching and learning (Al Husseiny & Munna, 2024; Slattery, 2024; Lopez & Ibanez, 2021; Ahmad, 2020). With online learning platforms, educational software, and digital tools, instructors can now deliver course content in a more personalized and interactive way. Students can engage with course materials at their own pace, review and revisit material as needed, and access a vast array of resources and information. According to Hakansson Lindqvist, et al. (2024); Sofkova Hashemi, et al. (2024), and Svihus (2024), the shift towards online learning has also led to changes in the way we think about teaching. With the ability to record and share video lectures, instructors can now reach a wider audience and provide instruction to students around the world. This has also led to changes in the way we assess student learning, with online quizzes, tests, and assignments becoming more prevalent. However, despite these benefits, the traditional model of higher education is not without its challenges. Many institutions are still grappling with how to integrate technology into their teaching practices, and many instructors are struggling to adapt to new teaching methods (Marshall, et al. 2024; Ormilla & Ongan, 2024; Thompson et al.

2023). Additionally, concerns about the quality of online learning and the need for technical support have created uncertainty among students and parents (Gohain, 2024; Khalifa & Hamid, 2024). Despite these challenges, it is clear that the rise of online learning and the technological revolution is changing the face of higher education. As we move forward, we must continue to explore new ways of using technology to support teaching and learning, while also addressing the challenges and concerns that arise from this shift. By doing so, we can create a more inclusive, accessible, and effective system of higher education that benefits students around the world.

The History of Online Learning

The history of online learning can be traced back to the early days of computer-assisted instruction, which emerged in the 1960s when the University of Illinois began offering courses via computer terminals. This was followed by the development of distance education programs in the 1970s and 1980s. The first fully online courses emerged in the early 1990s, the Open University in the United Kingdom pioneered the use of online learning and, this model was soon adopted by universities around the world. The term "e-learning" was coined in 1998. The concept of delivering instruction remotely predates the internet. In the 19th century correspondence courses emerged and students received printed material and submitted their assignments using mail. Broadcast lessons developed such as the School of the Air radio lesson broadcasts to teach rural students in Columbia. E-learning's roots can be traced back to the early days of computer-assisted instruction (CAI) in the 1960s. Early CAI programs, like PLATO (Programmed Logic for Automatic Teaching Operations), offered structured, individualized learning experiences via computer terminals. (Xu et al. 2024; Langseth, et al. 2023).

The history of online learning can be traced back to the early days of computer-assisted instruction, which emerged in the 1960s when the University of Illinois began offering courses via computer terminals (Cope & Kalantzis, 2023). In 1965 the University of Alberta used IBM 1500 computers to offer the first online courses and by 1968 the university's department of medicine developed various online courses (Durlo, 2023; Andreu-Perez, 2018). In the United Kingdom, the Open University was launched based on Harold Wilson's idea of a 'university in the air" in 1969. This was followed by the development of distance education programs in the 1970s and 1980s (Oumarou, 2024; Singh & Meena, 2024; Zawacki-Richter, 2019). The Open University's first online classes through CICERO began in 1976. At this time computers were sparsely used by individuals. The Open University in the United Kingdom pioneered the use of online learning and, this model was soon adopted by universities around the world. With the advent of personal computers and computer networks in the 1980s, the potential for online learning grew exponentially. These computers, which make use of very large-scale integration (VLSI), have become more powerful, compact, reliable, and affordable. As a result, it gave rise to the personal computer (PC) revolution. This computer generation also saw the development of GUIs (Graphical User Interfaces), mouse, and handheld devices thus computers became user-friendly. The University of Phoenix became the first higher education institution to launch a fully online college that offers both bachelor's and master's degrees. The fully online courses continued to develop in the early 1990s. In 1996 Jones International University became the first accredited and fully web-based university.

The growth of the internet and the emergence of new technologies like Learning Management Systems (LMS), the use of blogs, wikis, and video sharing in the 2000s led to a boom in online learning. Since the early 2000s, online learning has continued to evolve and grow, with new technologies and platforms emerging. The rise of mobile devices, social media, and open educational resources (OER) has led to the creation of Massive Open Online Courses (MOOCs) and other innovative online learning models. At the same time, there has been a growing debate about the effectiveness of online learning and the role of technology in education. Some key developments in online learning since 2000 include the launch of MIT Open Courseware in 2001 and the Blackboard in 2001. MIT Open Courseware is a web-based platform that provides free access to course materials from the Massachusetts Institute of Technology. This initiative marked a significant shift towards open educational resources and has had a major impact on online learning.

Despite these developments, there is still a growing debate about the effectiveness of online learning and the role of technology in education (Chen, 2024; Priyanto, 2024). Some critics argue that online learning lacks the social interaction and human connection that is present in traditional face-to-face learning environments. Others argue that online learning can be just as effective as traditional learning, but that it requires careful planning and design to ensure student engagement and success. The history of online learning is a complex and evolving field that has been shaped by technological advancements, changes in societal attitudes toward education, and shifting priorities in education policy. As technology continues to advance, users expect to see even more innovative applications of online learning in the years to come.

The Rise of MOOCs

The MOOC (Massive Open Online Course) movement began in 2008 with the launch of Coursera, a platform founded by Stanford University professors Andrew Ng and Daphne Koller. Coursera's initial offering was a series of free online courses taught by Stanford faculty, covering topics such as artificial intelligence, computer science, and engineering. The platform's success was swift and significant, attracting millions of students worldwide. The following year, Harvard University and the Massachusetts Institute of Technology (MIT) launched edX, a non-profit MOOC platform that offered courses on a wide range of subjects, from computer science and physics to literature and philosophy. EdX's mission was to provide high-quality educational resources to anyone, anywhere, and to promote innovation and collaboration in education. In 2011, Udacity, a for-profit MOOC platform founded by Stanford University professor Sebastian Thrun, launched its first courses. Udacity's focus was on providing practical, hands-on learning experiences in areas such as computer programming, data science, and entrepreneurship. (Mandal & Yadav, 2024; Waks & Waks, 2016).

Khan Academy, a non-profit online learning platform founded by Salman Khan, also emerged during this period. Khan Academy's focus was on providing free online courses and resources to students of all ages, with a particular emphasis on underprivileged students and those in underserved communities. The rapid growth of MOOCs has led to several questions and challenges around their role in higher education and these include:

- Quality: How can MOOCs ensure that the quality of their courses is equivalent to traditional classroom-based instruction? What measures can be taken to ensure that students are adequately assessed and evaluated?
- Assessment: How can MOOCs assess student learning and progress in a way that is fair and meaningful? Traditional methods of assessment, such as exams and quizzes, may not be suitable for online learning environments.
- Accreditation: Will MOOCs be recognized as part of formal degree programs or will they be seen as supplementary or additional learning experiences? How will MOOCs be accredited and evaluated by accrediting bodies?
- Competency-based education: How can MOOCs be designed to focus on specific skills and competencies, rather than just providing information or content?
- Integration with traditional education: How can MOOCs be integrated with conventional classroom-based instruction to provide a more comprehensive and effective learning experience?

These questions and challenges highlight the need for ongoing innovation and development in the field of MOOCs. As the technology continues to evolve, new MOOC delivery and assessment models will likely emerge, and new partnerships between institutions will be formed.

The Flipped Classroom

The flipped classroom is a teaching model that has emerged in recent years as a response to the growing use of technology in education. In a flipped classroom, students are given access to online course materials, videos, and other resources outside of class time. Then, during class time, students work on collaborative activities, discussions, and projects, with the teacher acting as a guide and mentor. The flipped classroom model has been shown to improve student engagement and learning outcomes, as it allows for more individualized and interactive learning experiences. It has also been shown to be particularly effective in STEM subjects. The flipped classroom is a revolutionary teaching model that has gained popularity in recent years as a response to the growing use of technology in education. In a traditional classroom, students are typically taught new material through lectures and discussions, and then work on assignments and projects outside of class. In contrast, the flipped classroom model reverses this approach, providing students with access to course materials and resources outside of class time, and using class time for collaborative activities, discussions, and projects. (Khlaisang & Teo, 2024; Utami et al. 2024; Rakhmalinda, 2024).

The core idea of the flipped classroom is to provide students with the flexibility and autonomy to learn at their own pace, and to allow them to engage with the material in a more meaningful and interactive way. Students are given access to online course materials, videos, and other resources, such as readings, simulations, and games, which they can complete at their own pace before class. This allows them to gain a deeper understanding of the material before coming to class, and to come prepared with questions and ideas to discuss. During class time, students work on collaborative activities, such as group projects, discussions, and problem-solving exercises, with the teacher acting as a guide and mentor. This allows students to apply what they have learned to real-world scenarios, and to develop critical thinking and problem-solving skills. The teacher's role is shifted from being the sole provider of information to being more of a facilitator or coach, helping students navigate the learning process and overcome obstacles. The benefits of the flipped classroom are numerous. Studies have shown that it can improve student engagement and learning outcomes by providing a more personalized and interactive learning experience. Students are more likely to be motivated and engaged when they are given the freedom to learn at their own pace, and when they are working on projects that are relevant and meaningful to them. The flipped classroom has also been shown to be particularly effective in STEM subjects, where students often struggle to understand complex concepts and formulas. By providing students with access to online resources and simulations, teachers can help students develop a deeper understanding of these concepts, and to apply them to real-world scenarios. The flipped classroom has some benefits such as:

- Increased student engagement and motivation
- Improved student learning outcomes
- More personalized and interactive learning experiences
- Greater flexibility and autonomy for students
- Increased opportunities for collaboration and teamwork
- Greater opportunities for teachers to provide individualized support and feedback

(Binoy, 2024; Widyadhari et al. 2024; Nadehina, et al. 2021; Buil-Fabrega, et al. 2019).

However, the flipped classroom also presents some challenges, such as the need for:

- Teachers to develop new skills and strategies for teaching in a flipped classroom
- Students to develop new skills and habits for learning in a flipped classroom
- Institutions to provide support for teachers in implementing the flipped class-room model
- Institutions to develop new policies and procedures for assessing student learning in a flipped classroom

(Appiah, 2024; Han, et al. 2024; Lepkova et al. 2024; Paragoo & Sevnarayan, 2024; Utami, et al. 2024; Zainuddin et al. 2019).

Overall, the flipped classroom is a powerful teaching model that has the potential to revolutionize the way we teach and learn. By providing students with access to online resources and simulations, teachers can help students develop a deeper understanding of complex concepts, and to apply them to real-world scenarios. As technology continues to evolve, users will likely see even more innovative uses of the flipped classroom in education.

Personalized Learning

Personalized learning is another model of teaching that has emerged in recent years. In a personalized learning environment, students are given access to a range of resources and activities that are tailored to their individual needs and interests. The teacher then provides support and guidance, while also allowing for flexibility and choice. This model has been shown to improve student engagement and motivation, as well as learning outcomes. It has also been shown to be particularly effective for students with special needs and those who are struggling academically. Some studies have also suggested that personalized learning can help close the achievement gap. The key characteristics of personalized learning include student-centered, flexibility, autonomy, tailored instruction, and technology integration. Student-centered is when the student is at the center of the learning process, and the teacher acts as a guide and facilitator. Flexibility is when the students are given the freedom to choose how they learn, when they learn, and what they learn. Autonomy is when the students can make decisions about their learning, such as setting goals, selecting resources, and assessing their progress. In tailored instruction, the teacher provides instruction that is tailored to the individual student's needs, interests, and abilities. Technology integration in personalized learning often incorporates technology, such as learning management systems, educational software, and online resources, to support student learning. (Kaswan, et al. 2024; Shchevliagin & Koroleva, 2024; Zing, 2024).

The benefits of personalized learning include:

- Improve student engagement and motivation: When students are given the autonomy to make choices about their ownership, they are more likely to be motivated and engaged.
- Improve student outcomes: Personalized learning can help students achieve better grades, scores, and overall academic performance.
- Increase student self-directed learning: As students take ownership of their learning, they develop skills such as self-directed learning, time management, and problem-solving.
- Reduce teacher workload: By providing students with more autonomy and flexibility, teachers can reduce their workload and focus on providing support and guidance.

(Barkoczi, et al. 2024; Dandachi, 2024; Kaswan, et al. 2024)

Personalized learning has also been shown to be particularly effective for students with special needs and those who are struggling academically. By providing students with tailored instruction and support, teachers can help them catch up or make progress at their own pace. Implementing personalized learning incurs some challenges relating to teacher training, technology integration, and student buy-in. In teacher training the teachers may need training on how to implement personalized learning approaches in their classroom. In technology integration, teachers may need support on how to integrate technology into their teaching practices. Lastly, in student buy-in, some students may resist the idea of having more autonomy and flexibility in their learning. Overall, personalized learning is a promising approach that has the potential to improve student outcomes, increase student engagement, and provide teachers with new ways to support student learning.

Virtual Reality in Education

Virtual reality (VR) and augmented reality (AR) are two technologies that are increasingly being used in education. In a virtual reality environment, students are immersed in a simulated world, where they can explore and interact with virtual objects and environments. Augmented reality, on the other hand, superimposes virtual objects and information on the real world, using tools such as headsets or mobile devices. These technologies have been shown to have several benefits in education, including increased engagement, improved comprehension, and enhanced skills development. Some studies have also suggested that they can be particularly effective for students with special needs. (Familoni & Onyebuchi, 2024; Lampropoulos, et al. 2022; Tene, et al. 2024).

Virtual Reality

In a virtual reality environment, students are transported to a simulated world, where they can explore and interact with virtual objects and environments. This can be particularly effective for subjects such as history, science, and language, where students can explore and interact with virtual artifacts, simulations, and scenarios. For example, students can visit ancient civilizations, explore the human body, or practice surgical procedures in a virtual environment. The benefits of VR in education are numerous. Research has shown that VR in education has some benefits such as increased engagement, improved comprehension, and enhanced skill development. VR experiences are often more engaging and interactive than traditional teaching methods, which can lead to increased student participation and motivation. Comprehension is improved by providing students with immersive and interactive experiences, VR can help students understand complex concepts and retain information better. VR can be used to develop skills such as problem-solving, critical thinking, and communication.

Augmented Reality

Augmented reality, on the other hand, superimposes virtual objects and information on the real world, using tools such as headsets or mobile devices. This can be particularly effective for subjects such as mathematics, science, and engineering, where students can use AR to visualize complex concepts and models. For example, students can use AR to visualize 3D models of molecules, cells, or buildings. The benefits of AR in education are similar to those of VR. Both VR and AR are particularly effective for students with special needs such as students with autism spectrum disorder (ASD) may benefit from the immersive and interactive nature of

VR experiences; students with physical disabilities may benefit from the ability to explore virtual environments without physical limitations and students with learning disabilities may benefit from the visual and interactive nature of AR experiences. Despite the many benefits of VR and AR in education, some challenges need to be addressed. Some of the challenges are the cost, technical requirements, teacher training, and content development. VR and AR equipment can be expensive, which can be a barrier for many schools and educational institutions. VR and AR require significant technical resources, including high-speed computers, powerful graphics cards, and specialized software. Teachers may need training on how to integrate VR and AR into their teaching practices. Developing high-quality educational content for VR and AR is a significant challenge. Virtual reality and augmented reality have the potential to revolutionize the way we learn. By providing students with immersive and interactive experiences, they can increase engagement, improve comprehension, and enhance skills development. As these technologies continue to evolve, we can expect to see even more innovative applications in education.

Augmented Reality in Education

There is a growing body of research on the use of augmented reality in education. One study found that students who used AR technology in their biology classes showed improved engagement and learning outcomes compared to students who did not use AR. Another study found that AR technology can be used to enhance medical students' learning experience and improve their understanding of anatomy. Several AR tools are available for use in education, including apps such as Google Expeditions and Aurasma. These apps allow students to explore a range of virtual environments, from historical sites to the solar system. In the context of education, AR is a powerful tool for enhancing student engagement, improving learning outcomes, and increasing understanding of complex concepts. For example, AR can be used to:

- Visualize complex concepts: AR can be used to create 3D models and simulations that help students visualize complex concepts, such as molecular structures or historical events. This can make it easier for students to understand and retain the information.
- Enhance field trips: AR can be used to enhance field trips by providing students with additional information about the places they are visiting. For example, students can use AR to learn about historical landmarks, endangered species, or cultural traditions.
- Provide interactive learning experiences: AR can be used to create interactive learning experiences that simulate real-world scenarios. For example, stu-

dents can use AR to participate in virtual labs, conduct virtual experiments, or interact with virtual characters.

- Increase accessibility: AR can be used to increase accessibility for students with disabilities. For example, AR can be used to provide visual aids for students who are deaf or hard of hearing or to provide tactile feedback for students who are blind or have low vision.

Examples of AR in Education include Anatomy 4D, NASA's Jet Propulsion Laboratory, and Zappar. Anatomy 4D is a mobile app that uses AR to help students learn about the human body. Students can use the app to view 3D models of the body and interact with them to learn about different systems and organs. NASA's Jet Propulsion Laboratory is a virtual reality experience that allows students to explore Mars and learn about the planet's geology and atmosphere. Zappar is a platform that uses AR to create interactive stories and games. Students can use Zappar to create their own stories and games and share them with their classmates.

Benefits of AR in Education

The integration of augmented reality (AR) in education has the potential to revolutionize the way students learn and engage with educational content. By providing a more interactive and immersive learning experience, AR can help to increase student motivation, improve learning outcomes, and enhance student understanding of complex concepts. As educators, it is essential to understand the benefits of using AR in education and how it can be effectively integrated into existing curricula and teaching practices. The benefits of using AR in education, include increased student engagement, improved learning outcomes, increased accessibility, and cost-effectiveness. Increased student engagement: AR can help to increase student engagement and motivation by providing a more interactive and immersive learning experience. Improved learning outcomes: AR can help to improve learning outcomes by providing students with a more effective way of learning complex concepts. Increased accessibility: AR can help to increase accessibility for students with disabilities by providing visual aids and tactile feedback. Cost-effective: AR can be a cost-effective way of providing educational experiences, as it does not require expensive hardware or software. (Koumpouros, 2024; Mohammadhossein, et al. 2024; Garzon, 2021).

Challenges and Limitations

Despite the many benefits of AR in education, some challenges need to be addressed. Some of the challenges include:

- Technical issues: AR technology can be prone to technical issues, such as glitches and connectivity problems.
- Limited availability: AR technology is not yet widely available in all schools and educational institutions.
- Cost: While AR technology can be cost-effective, it may still require significant investment in hardware and software.
- Integration: Integrating AR technology into existing curricula and teaching practices can be challenging.
- Teacher training: Teachers may need training on how to use AR technology and integrate it into their teaching practices.
- Content development: Developing high-quality educational content for AR is a significant challenge.

(Familoni, & Onyebuchi, 2024; Zamahsari, et al. 2024)

Best Practices for Implementing AR in Education

While there are many benefits to using AR in education, there are also some challenges that need to be addressed. The best practices for implementing AR in education include starting small, providing teacher training, developing engaging content, encouraging student participation, and monitoring student progress. Begin by introducing AR technology in small increments, such as starting with a single lesson or activity. Teachers will need training on how to use AR technology and integrate it into their teaching practices. The quality of the content is crucial for student engagement. Make sure to develop engaging and interactive content that aligns with your teaching goals. Encourage students to participate actively in the AR experience by asking them to interact with the virtual environment or complete tasks. Lastly, students should be monitored for their progress and instruction adjusted accordingly. Augmented reality has the potential to revolutionize the way we learn, providing students with a more interactive and immersive learning experience. By providing students with a more engaging and effective way of learning, AR can help to improve student outcomes and increase student motivation. However, some challenges and limitations need to be addressed to ensure the successful implementation of AR technology in education.

The Role of Artificial Intelligence in Education

The role of artificial intelligence (AI) in education is a rapidly growing area of research. AI has the potential to transform education by providing personalized learning experiences, improving accessibility, and supporting teachers in their work. AI is already being used in education in adaptive learning, where AI is used to create personalized learning paths for students based on their individual needs and progress. AI is also used in automated assessment, where AI is used to grade assignments and provide feedback to students. AI is also used in Chatbots, which can provide students with information and support 24/7. In personalized learning platforms, AI-powered platforms analyze student data to tailor learning content and activities to individual needs and learning styles. Virtual assistants such as Natural language processing (NLP) capabilities enable virtual assistants to provide students with personalized support and guidance. Automated grading and feedback are AI algorithms that can automate the grading of assessments and provide personalized feedback, freeing up educators' time for higher-value tasks. Adaptive assessments are AI-driven assessments that continuously adjust the difficulty and type of questions based on student performance, providing real-time feedback and support. Intelligent tutoring systems are AI-powered tutoring systems that provide students with personalized learning experiences, offering individualized guidance and interactive simulations. (Arruda & Arruda, 2024; Chen, 2024; Leal Filho, et al. 2024; Rahiman & Kodikal, 2024).

Integration of AI has several benefits in education such as:

- Student empowerment: AI empowers students by providing personalized learning experiences and real-time support, fostering learner agency and self-directed learning.
- Enhanced learning outcomes: AI-driven adaptive assessments and intelligent tutoring systems improve learning effectiveness by tailoring content and support to individual needs.
- Increased access to education: AI-powered technologies can break down geographic and socioeconomic barriers to education, providing access to high-quality learning opportunities for all.
- Efficiency and productivity: AI streamlines administrative tasks, automates grading, and provides personalized feedback, freeing up educators' time for more meaningful interactions with students.

Despite its transformative potential, the implementation of AI in education faces certain challenges such as:

- Data privacy and security: Educational institutions must ensure responsible handling of student data, mitigating concerns about data breaches and unauthorized use.
- Equity and access: AI systems must be designed to prevent biases and promote equitable access to educational opportunities for all students.

- Educator training and acceptance: Successful integration of AI requires training and support for educators, helping them incorporate AI tools into their teaching.
- Ethical considerations: The use of AI in education raises ethical concerns regarding algorithmic accountability, bias mitigation, and the impact on human relationships.

Future Prospects of AI in Education

Artificial Intelligence (AI) is transforming the education sector by improving learning outcomes, increasing efficiency, and enhancing the overall student experience. As AI continues to evolve, its applications in education are expected to become more sophisticated and widespread. Potential prospects of AI in Education include the following:

1. Personalized Learning: AI-powered adaptive learning systems will analyze individual student learning styles, pace, and abilities to provide personalized learning experiences.
2. Intelligent Tutoring Systems: AI-powered virtual tutors will offer one-on-one support to students, providing real-time feedback, and helping them overcome learning difficulties.
3. Automated Grading: AI-powered grading systems will reduce the burden of manual grading, freeing up instructors to focus on teaching and mentoring.
4. Natural Language Processing (NLP): AI-powered NLP will enable students to interact with educational systems using natural language, making it easier for them to ask questions and seek help.
5. Enhanced Accessibility: AI-powered tools will provide greater accessibility for students with disabilities, such as text-to-speech functionality, speech recognition, and language translation.
6. Predictive Analytics: AI-powered predictive analytics will help identify at-risk students, allowing educators to intervene early and provide targeted support.
7. Virtual Learning Environments: AI-powered virtual learning environments will simulate real-world scenarios, making learning more engaging and interactive.
8. Game-Based Learning: AI-powered game-based learning platforms will use gamification elements to make learning more enjoyable and competitive.
9. AI-powered Learning Analytics: AI-powered analytics will provide insights into student behavior, helping educators optimize their teaching strategies and improve student outcomes.

10. Teacher Support: AI-powered tools will assist teachers in lesson planning, curriculum development, and assessment design, freeing up their time to focus on teaching and mentoring.

By embracing these prospects of AI in Education, we can expect significant improvements in student engagement, retention, and overall academic achievement. As AI technologies continue to evolve, their integration into education is expected to expand to:

- Immersive learning experiences: Virtual reality (VR) and augmented reality (AR) enhanced by AI will create immersive and engaging learning environments
- .AI-powered curriculum design: AI algorithms will analyze learning outcomes and student data to optimize curriculum design and adapt content to emerging.
- Early childhood education: AI-driven technologies will enhance early childhood education by providing personalized learning experiences and fostering cognitive development.
- Personalized career guidance: AI-based career counselling systems will provide students with personalized recommendations and support throughout their educational and professional journeys.
- Improved Student Outcomes: Personalized learning, intelligent tutoring, and other AI-powered tools can enhance student engagement, motivation, and academic performance.
- Equity and Accessibility: AI can provide equitable access to educational resources for students with diverse learning styles, disabilities, or geographic limitations.
- Teacher Empowerment: AI tools can assist educators with grading, assessment, and data analysis, allowing them to focus on student interactions and high-value teaching.
- Efficiency and Cost-Effectiveness: AI can automate routine tasks, freeing up educators' time for more creative and impactful activities, potentially reducing educational costs.
- Data-Driven Insights: AI-powered data analysis provides valuable insights into student learning, allowing for evidence-based decision-making and continuous improvement.

The role of artificial intelligence in education is a rapidly growing area of research, with significant potential to transform the way we learn. From adaptive learning and automated assessment to chatbots and virtual assistants, AI can provide personalized learning experiences, improve accessibility, and support teachers in their work. While there are some challenges and limitations that need to be addressed, the potential benefits of AI in education make it an exciting and promising area of research.

Conclusion

In conclusion, technology is rapidly changing the landscape of education. From virtual reality and augmented reality to AI and machine learning, new technologies are providing new ways for students to learn and engage with information. The impact of these technologies on learning outcomes and teacher-student relationships is still being studied, but the potential benefits are clear. As technology continues to evolve, new and innovative applications in education will likely emerge. These technologies offer new and innovative ways for students to engage with information, interact with their peers, and develop skills that are essential for success in the 21st century. The impact of these technologies on learning outcomes and teacher-student relationships is still being studied, but the potential benefits are clear. For example, virtual reality has been shown to improve student engagement and motivation, while augmented reality has the potential to enhance student understanding and retention of complex concepts. Artificial intelligence and machine learning can help to personalize learning experiences, provide immediate feedback, and support teachers in their work. However, it is also important to recognize that the integration of technology into education is not without its challenges. There are concerns about equity and access, particularly for students who may not have access to the necessary technology or internet connectivity. There are also concerns about the potential impact on teacher-student relationships and the role of human interaction in the learning process. Ultimately, the key to successful technology integration in education is to ensure that it is used in a way that supports and enhances student learning, rather than replacing it. This will require careful planning, collaboration between educators and technologists, and ongoing evaluation and assessment of the impact of technology on student outcomes. By embracing the potential of technology to transform education, we can create a more engaging, effective, and equitable learning environment that prepares students for success in an increasingly complex and interconnected world.

The rise of online learning and the technological revolution in higher education have brought about significant changes in the way students learn and interact with educational institutions. The shift towards online learning has opened up new opportunities for students to access education, particularly for those who may have been previously excluded due to geographical or financial constraints. However, it also poses several challenges, including the need to ensure that online learning is effective, engaging, and accessible to all students. To address these challenges, educational institutions can adopt various strategies. One approach is to invest in digital infrastructure and platforms that enable seamless online learning experiences. Additionally, institutions can develop online courses that incorporate interactive and multimedia elements, such as videos, podcasts, and online simulations, to enhance student engagement and interaction. Furthermore, institutions can provide training and support for faculty members to develop their skills in online teaching and pedagogy. Finally, institutions can establish policies and guidelines to ensure the quality and integrity of online learning, including measures to prevent plagiarism, cheating, and other forms of academic dishonesty. To deal with the technological revolution in higher education, recommendations include developing digital literacy skills: students should be equipped with the skills to navigate and use digital technologies effectively; providing technical support: educational institutions should provide technical support to students and faculty members to ensure smooth access to digital resources; developing online learning platforms: educational institutions should develop their online learning platforms that are user-friendly, accessible, and adaptable; integrating technology into curricula: educational institutions should integrate technology into curricula to enhance student learning experiences; encouraging innovation and creativity: educational institutions should encourage innovation and creativity in the use of technology to enhance student learning experiences and fostering collaboration and communication: educational institutions should foster collaboration and communication among students, faculty members, and staff through technology. By adopting these strategies, educational institutions can harness the benefits of the technological revolution in higher education and provide students with high-quality online learning experiences that are engaging, effective, and accessible.

References

Ahmad, T. (2020). A scenario-based approach to re-imagining the future of higher education which prepares students for the future of work. *Higher Education. Skills and Work-Based Learning*, 10(1), 217–238. DOI: 10.1108/HESWBL-12-2018-0136

Al Husseiny, F., & Munna, A. S. (Eds.). (2024). *Preparing Students for the Future Educational Paradigm*. IGI Global. DOI: 10.4018/979-8-3693-1536-1

Andreu-Perez, J., Deligianni, F., Ravi, D., & Yang, G. Z. (2018). Artificial Intelligence and Robotics. *arXiv preprint arXiv:1803.10813*.

Appiah, S. (2024). Challenges Learners Face in Using the Flipped Classroom Model in the Teaching and Learning of Religious and Moral Education in the Nzema East Municipality of the Western Region of Ghana. *Universal Journal of Social Sciences and Humanities*, 12-19.

Arruda, E. P., & Arruda, D. P. (2024). Artificial intelligence for SDG 4 of the 2030 agenda: Transforming education to achieve quality, equality, and inclusion. *Sustainable Economies*, 2(2), 34–34. DOI: 10.62617/se.v2i2.34

Barkoczi, N., Maier, M. L., & Horvat-Marc, A. (2024). The Impact of Artificial Intelligence on Personalized Learning in STEM Education. In *inted2024 Proceedings* (pp. 4980-4989). IATED. DOI: 10.21125/inted.2024.1289

Binoy, S. (2024). Transforming Education: Enhancing Student Performance and Satisfaction through the Flipped Classroom Method. *American Journal of Education and Technology*, 3(1), 35–45. DOI: 10.54536/ajet.v3i1.2121

Buil-Fabrega, M., Martinez Casanovas, M., Ruiz-Munzon, N., & Filho, W. L. (2019). Flipped classroom as an active learning methodology in sustainable development curricula. *Sustainability (Basel)*, 11(17), 4577. DOI: 10.3390/su11174577

Chen, H. (2024). The ethical challenges of educational artificial intelligence and coping measures: A discussion in the context of the 2024 World Digital Education Conference. *Science Insights Education Frontiers, 20*(2), 3263-3281.

Cope, B., & Kalantzis, M. (2023). A little history of e-learning: Finding new ways to learn in the PLATO computer education system, 1959–1976. *History of Education*, 52(6), 905–936. DOI: 10.1080/0046760X.2022.2141353

Darian-Smith, E. (2024). Knowledge production at a crossroads: Rising anti-democracy and diminishing academic freedom. *Studies in Higher Education*, ●●●, 1–15. DOI: 10.1080/03075079.2024.2347562

Durlo, A. (2023). *1950-2022: A History of Nanotechnology into Physical and Mathematical Relationship* (Doctoral dissertation, Universite de Lille).

Familoni, B. T., & Onyebuchi, N. C.Babajide Tolulope FamiloniNneamaka Chisom Onyebuchi. (2024). Augmented and virtual reality in our education: a review: analyzing the impact, effectiveness, and prospects of AR/VR tools in enhancing learning experiences. *International Journal of Applied Research in Social Sciences*, 6(4), 642–663. DOI: 10.51594/ijarss.v6i4.1043

Foong, Y. P., Pidani, R., Sithira Vadivel, V., & Dongyue, Y. (2024). Singapore smart nation: a journey into a new digital landscape for higher education. In *Emerging Technologies in Business: Innovation Strategies for Competitive Advantage* (pp. 281–304). Springer Nature Singapore. DOI: 10.1007/978-981-97-2211-2_13

Garzon, J. (2021). An overview of twenty-five years of augmented reality in education. *Multimodal Technologies and Interaction*, 5(7), 37. DOI: 10.3390/mti5070037

(Gohain, D. (2024). Online Tutelage: Meeting the Educational Needs in the Post-Pandemic Scenario. In *Digitalization of Higher Education* (pp. 159-180). Apple Academic Press.

Hakansson Lindqvist, M., Mozelius, P., Jaldemark, J., & Cleveland Innes, M. (2024). Higher education transformation towards lifelong learning in a digital era–a scoping literature review. *International Journal of Lifelong Education*, 43(1), 24–38. DOI: 10.1080/02601370.2023.2279047

Han, H., Rokenes, F. M., & Krumsvik, R. J. (2024). Student teachers' perceptions of the flipped classroom in EFL teacher education. *Education and Information Technologies*, 29(2), 1539–1558. DOI: 10.1007/s10639-023-11839-w PMID: 37361753

Indrawati, S. M., & Kuncoro, A. (2021). Improving competitiveness through vocational and higher education: Indonesia's vision for human capital development in 2019–2024. *Bulletin of Indonesian Economic Studies*, 57(1), 29–59. DOI: 10.1080/00074918.2021.1909692

Kaswan, K. S., Dhatterwal, J. S., & Ojha, R. P. (2024). AI in personalized learning. In *Advances in Technological Innovations in Higher Education* (pp. 103–117). CRC Press. DOI: 10.1201/9781003376699-9

Khalifa, B., & Hamid, M. S. (2024). Challenges, Best Practices, and Solutions. *Teaching and Supporting Students with Disabilities during Times of Crisis: Culturally Responsive Best Practices from Around the World*, 217.

Khlaisang, J., & Teo, T. (2024). An innovation-based virtual flipped learning system in a ubiquitous learning environment the 21st-century skills of higher education learners. *Journal of Educational Technology & Society*, 27(1), 100–116.

Klimenko, A. Y. (2024). Technological Change and Its Effect on Education. [JEPR]. *Journal of Educational & Psychological Research*, 6(1), 1–18. DOI: 10.33140/ JEPR.06.01.04

Koumpouros, Y. (2024). Revealing the true potential and prospects of augmented reality in education. *Smart Learning Environments*, 11(1), 2. DOI: 10.1186/s40561-023-00288-0

Krishnan, S. R. G., & Joseph, J. J. (2024). Online learning experiences of social work students in India. *Journal of Social Work : JSW*, 24(2), 276–292. DOI: 10.1177/14680173231207962

Lampropoulos, G., Keramopoulos, E., Diamantaras, K., & Evangelidis, G. (2022). Augmented reality and virtual reality in education: Public perspectives, sentiments, attitudes, and discourses. *Education Sciences*, 12(11), 798. DOI: 10.3390/educsci12110798

Langseth, I., Jacobsen, D. Y., & Haugsbakken, H. (2023). The role of support units in digital transformation: How institutional entrepreneurs build capacity for online learning in higher education. *Technology. Knowledge and Learning*, 28(4), 1745–1782. DOI: 10.1007/s10758-022-09620-y

Leal Filho, W., Ribeiro, P. C. C., Mazutti, J., Lange Salvia, A., Bonato Marcolin, C., Lima Silva Borsatto, J. M., & Viera Trevisan, L. (2024). Using artificial intelligence to implement the UN sustainable development goals at higher education institutions. *International Journal of Sustainable Development and World Ecology*, 31(6), 1–20. DOI: 10.1080/13504509.2024.2327584

Lepkova, N., Gulsecen, S., & Talan, T. (2024). Flipped classroom method application case study analysis. *Baltic journal of modern computing, 12*(2), 150-164

Lopez, A., & Ibanez, E. (2021). Challenges of Education in the 4th Industrial Revolution. *The Fourth Industrial Revolution and Its Impact on Ethics: Solving the Challenges of the Agenda*, 2030, 139–150. DOI: 10.1007/978-3-030-57020-0_11

Mandal, D., & Yadav, V. K. (2024). Current Trends of MOOCS in India: Historical Background, Development and Challenges. *The Online Journal of Distance Education and e-Learning : TOJDEL*, 12(1).

Marshall, S., Blaj-Ward, L., Dreamson, N., Nyanjom, J., & Bertuol, M. T. (2024). The reshaping of higher education: Technological impacts, pedagogical change, and future projections. *Higher Education Research & Development*, 43(3), 521–541. DOI: 10.1080/07294360.2024.2329393

Mohammadhossein, N., Richter, A., & Lukosch, S. (2024). Augmented Reality in Learning Settings: A Systematic Analysis of its Benefits and Avenues for Future Studies. *Communications of the Association for Information Systems*, 54(1), 29–49. DOI: 10.17705/1CAIS.05402

Nadehina, Y. P., Kolchin, A. A., & Myshko, Y. A. (2021). On the prospects of pedagogical technology "flipped classroom" in teaching History at university in conditions of digitalization of educational environment. In *Socio-economic Systems: Paradigms for the Future* (pp. 1211–1220). Springer International Publishing. DOI: 10.1007/978-3-030-56433-9_127

Ormilla, R. C. G., & Ongan, M. G. O. (2024). Navigating the Shift: Faculty Preparedness for Online Teaching in the Evolving Global Higher Education Landscape. *International Journal of Learning. Teaching and Educational Research*, 23(1), 1–23.

Oumarou, G. (2024). Reforming education via radio lessons for teachers? The promise and problems of distance learning in Cameroon, 1960–1995. *Learning, Media and Technology*, 49(1), 8–19. DOI: 10.1080/17439884.2023.2244426

Paragoo, S., & Sevnarayan, K. (2024). Flipped classrooms for engaged learning during the pandemic: Teachers' perspectives and challenges in a South African high school. *Technology-mediated Learning during the pandemic*, 33-54.

Priyanto, D. (2024). Education towards Equality: A Review of the Contribution of Distance Learning Technology in Expanding Access and Promoting Social Equality. [TACIT]. *Technology and Society Perspectives*, 2(1), 138–142. DOI: 10.61100/tacit.v2i1.139

Rahiman, H. U., & Kodikal, R. (2024). Revolutionizing education: Artificial intelligence empowered learning in higher education. *Cogent Education*, 11(1), 2293431. DOI: 10.1080/2331186X.2023.2293431

Rakhmalinda, F. (2024). Trends in Flipped Classroom of High Education: Bibliometric Analysis (2012–2022). *Journal of Research in Mathematics, Science, and Technology Education*, 1(1), 19–34. DOI: 10.70232/bd895m13

Schwartz, M., & Omori, K. (2024). Communities of Practice and Acculturation: How International Students in American Colleges Use Social Media to Manage Homesickness. *Journal of International and Comparative Education (JICE)*, 57-72.

Shchevliagin, M., & Koroleva, D. (2024). Four scenarios of personalized learning integration mediated by a digital platform. *Turkish Online Journal of Distance Education*, 25(2), 76–95. DOI: 10.17718/tojde.1267577

Singh, A. K., & Meena, M. K. (2024). Online teaching in Indian higher education institutions during the pandemic time. *Education and Information Technologies*, 29(4), 4107–4157. DOI: 10.1007/s10639-023-11942-y

Slattery, M. (2024). *Education Strategy in a Changing Society: Personalised, Smarter, Lifelong Learning in the 21st Century*. Taylor & Francis. DOI: 10.4324/9781003358770

Sofkova Hashemi, S., Berbyuk Lindström, N., & Bergdahl, N. (2024). Pandemic as Digital Change Accelerator: Sustainable Reshaping of Adult Education Post Covid-19.

Svihus, C. L. (2024). Online teaching in higher education during the COVID-19 pandemic. *Education and Information Technologies*, 29(3), 3175–3193. DOI: 10.1007/s10639-023-11971-7

Tene, T., Vique Lopez, D. F., Valverde Aguirre, P. E., Orna Puente, L. M., & Vacacela Gomez, C. (2024). Virtual reality and augmented reality in medical education: An umbrella review. *Frontiers in Digital Health*, 6, 1365345. DOI: 10.3389/fdgth.2024.1365345 PMID: 38550715

Thompson, C., Hollins, L., & Collins, S. W. (2023). *Factors Affecting Technology Integration for Teachers at K-12, Adult Education, and Higher Education Institutions Since Virtual Learning Due to COVID-19* (Doctoral dissertation, University of Missouri-Saint Louis).

Utami, U., Ghufron, A., & Setiawati, F. A. (2024). A Systematic Literature Review of" Flipped Classroom": Is it Effective on Student Learning in Elementary School? *Pegem Journal of Education and Instruction*, 14(1), 244–251.

Waks, L. J., & Waks, L. J. (2016). The Economic Crisis and the Rise of MOOCs. *The Evolution and Evaluation of Massive Open Online Courses: MOOCs in Motion*, 11-34.

Widyadhari, K. A., Priyanti, T., & Umar, Z. (2024). The Advantages of a Flipped Classroom for Students' Speaking Skills: Systematic Review. *JoELE: Journal of English Lingua Educantum*, 1(1), 20–28.

Xu, W., Zhang, N., & Wang, M. (2024). The impact of interaction on continuous use in online learning platforms: A metaverse perspective. *Internet Research*, 34(1), 79–106. DOI: 10.1108/INTR-08-2022-0600

Zainuddin, Z., Haruna, H., Li, X., Zhang, Y., & Chu, S. K. W. (2019). A systematic review of flipped classroom empirical evidence from different fields: What are the gaps and future trends? *On the Horizon*, 27(2), 72–86. DOI: 10.1108/OTH-09-2018-0027

Zamahsari, G. K., Amalia, M. N., Rifah, L., Permana, F., Romadhon, S., & Prihatini, A. (2024, January). A Systematic Review in Educational Settings: Numerous Challenges to the Adoption of Augmented Reality. In *2024 18th International Conference on Ubiquitous Information Management and Communication (IMCOM)* (pp. 1-6). IEEE.

Zing, K. (2024). Harnessing the Power of Artificial Intelligence in Personalized Learning. *Education Journal*, 2(1), 7–14.

KEY TERMS AND DEFINITIONS

Blended Learning: is an educational approach that combines traditional face-to-face instruction with online learning.

Distance Education: refers to the delivery of educational content and instruction to students who are not physically present in a traditional classroom.

Educational Technology: refers to the use of technology to support teaching and learning.

E-Learning: is a type of distance education that is delivered primarily through digital technologies.

Flipped Classroom: This is a teaching approach that reverses the traditional lecture-homework format.

Learning Management Systems (LMS): This is a software application that is used to manage and deliver educational content and instruction.

Massive Open Online Courses (MOOCs): These are massive open online courses that are designed to be taken by large numbers of students worldwide.

Chapter 18
The Future of Learning in the Digital Age

Doris Chasokela

https://orcid.org/0009-0001-5983-8508

National University of Science and Technology, Zimbabwe

Nengiwe Mangena

National University of Science and Technology, Zimbabwe

ABSTRACT

The new education 5.0 model vision 2030 in Zimbabwe is anchored on heritage-based philosophy in tertiary education institutions aimed at the production of goods and services. The education model aspires to industrialise and modernise the Zimbabwean economy to attain a middle economic position by the year 2030. Industrialization and innovation can be realised in contribution towards the attainment of Vision 2030. It is prudent to adopt learning that is congruent with the prevailing digital age. The future of learning in the digital age therefore proposes a new framework for education that integrates digital technologies to improve student learning outcomes. The model takes into account specific challenges, including inadequate infrastructure, curriculum issues, a lack of digital literacy among instructors, and a lack of synergy between the education sector and industry. Recommendations include improving infrastructure, providing instructor training in digital literacy and curriculum design, and building partnerships with industry and government.

DOI: 10.4018/979-8-3693-3443-0.ch018

Introduction

Innovation and industrialization are inseparable intertwined vital pillars of education; the Education 5.0 philosophy aims to contribute to Vision 2030 in Zimbabwe. The realization of innovation as well as industrialization comes with challenges, chief among the challenges are the alignment of curriculum to innovation practices, the alignment of curriculum to the innovation hubs, industrialization, and putting in place incentives that drive innovation. In the past, the curriculum has been largely theoretically inclined, hence the need for the development of a curriculum that speaks to the pillars of innovation and industrialization. Compounding the education challenges has been among other issues, a lack of staff development programs to drive innovation and inadequate resources that present challenges in the fulfillment of the two critical pillars (innovation and industrialization) of the education 5.0 philosophy. The subsequent discussion focuses on the challenges to the attainment of the two pillars aforementioned and makes recommendations that enable the universities to be at par with Education 5.0. The philosophy of Education 5.0 is the latest iteration of the education system, built on the foundations of previous models such as Education 1.0 and Education 2.0. It is characterized by a shift from a teacher-centered approach to a learner-centered approach, and a focus on 21st-century skills such as problem-solving, creativity, and collaboration.

Technical vocational education, as envisioned in the new education 5.0 Model Vision 2030 in Zimbabwe, has the potential to revolutionize the way students learn and develop skills for the digital age. This paradigm shift emphasizes hands-on learning, experiential education, and industry-relevant skills training, which are critical for addressing the country's economic and societal needs. In this context, technical vocational education will play a crucial role in preparing students for a future where automation and technology will transform the workforce. By incorporating cutting-edge technologies such as artificial intelligence, virtual and augmented reality, and the Internet of Things (IoT), technical vocational education programs will equip students with the skills to design, develop, and innovate solutions that meet the demands of a rapidly changing job market. Furthermore, the emphasis on collaboration and problem-solving skills will enable students to work effectively in diverse teams, think critically, and adapt to new technologies, making them more competitive in the global job market. By adopting this approach, Zimbabwe can create a highly skilled and adaptable workforce that is equipped to drive economic growth, innovation, and development in the digital age.

Education 5.0 contributes to producing graduates who will be productive in meeting Zimbabwe's Vision 2030 and calls for all higher and tertiary education institutions to rejuvenate their curricula and consequently, instructional methodologies. Education 5.0 is a heritage-based transformative philosophy for a competitive, industrialized, and modernized Zimbabwe by 2030. It may be realized that the introduction of Education 5.0 has restructured the universities in Zimbabwe despite the challenges the institution faces as it fulfills the focus on innovation and industrialization, as this write-up reveals. The key terms defined are Education 5.0 and industrialization. Background of Education 5.0 and Vision 2030 is also briefly explained, practical examples are referred to and recommendations are made for the aforementioned university. Zimbabwe needs to adopt this model as Zimbabwe has been facing a myriad of challenges in its education system, including, inadequate education tools, a lack of innovation, under-skilled graduates, and a lack of coherence between education, socio-economic demands, industry needs, and requirements. Significantly, Education 5.0 provides a solution to these challenges by shifting the focus from memorization and rote learning to creativity, soft skills, and problem-solving. It also emphasizes the importance of skills such as digital literacy and critical thinking, which are essential for the 21st-century workplace. An overview of the current state of education in Zimbabwe could include the following:

- The education system in Zimbabwe has been underfunded and has required reform for many years
- There is a high level of unemployment among graduates due to a lack of requisite skills that are relevant to the job market
- The education system is still based on the traditional model of rote learning and exam-based assessments, as opposed to the dictates of 21st-century skills
- There is a lack of access to technology and resources, particularly in rural areas

Higher and tertiary education in Zimbabwe has over the past years focused on three education missions, namely, teaching, community service, and research, equivalent to Education 3.0. However, to deliver a competitive, industrialized, and modernized Zimbabwe, the government has adopted two additional mission pillars which are Innovation and Industrialisation, effectively migrating from Education 3.0 to Education 5.0 (Zinhuku, 2022). The attainment of the education missions comes with challenges, upon which the National University of Science and Technology is not immune as regards effort to contribute to the realization of the national aspiration of Vision 2030. Curriculum plays a significant role in the achievement of Education 5.0 especially with emphasis on key critical pillars of innovation and industrialization as per the next discourse.

Background

Education 5.0 represents a paradigm shift in education that leverages digital technologies to enhance learning outcomes and prepare students for the demands of the 21st century. On a global level, Education 5.0 aligns with the goals of the Fourth Industrial Revolution and the need for lifelong learning in an increasingly digital and interconnected world. At the continental level, initiatives such as the African Union's Agenda 2063 prioritize education and skills development as key drivers of economic growth and social development. Regionally, Education 5.0 can help address the challenges faced by African countries in promoting quality education and improving learning outcomes. In the context of Zimbabwe's Vision 2030, Education 5.0 can play a crucial role in transforming the education system to empower students with the skills and knowledge needed to thrive in the digital age. By embracing digital technologies, personalized learning, and a focus on critical thinking and problem-solving, Zimbabwe can ensure that its education system remains relevant and prepares students for the future workforce. The New Education 5.0 Model Vision 2030 in Zimbabwe represents an opportunity to reimagine education and create a more inclusive, innovative, and future-ready learning environment for all learners.

Dube and Shumba (2023) state that in 2015, the United Nations member states adopted the 2030 Agenda for Sustainable Development and its 17 Sustainable Development Goals (SDGs). Out of the 17 SDGs, the Zimbabwean government has prioritized 10 and these are SDGs 2, 3, 4, 5, 6, 7, 8, 9, 13 and 17. The prioritization exercise was guided by the country's vision, the need to focus on enabling goals, and resource availability. These goals are linked to Zimbabwe's Vision 2030. As regards the availability of resources, the Ministry of Higher and Tertiary Education, Innovation, Science and Technology Development (MoHTEISTD) developed Education 5.0. Philosophy. It is a heritage-based ideology that encourages students to apply their knowledge to the local environment to develop meaningful goods and services (Ministry of Higher and Tertiary Education, Innovation, Science and Technology Development, 2018). Vision 2030 aims to achieve an upper-middle income status by the year 2030. As of July 2021, Zhou and Machenjera (2017) speak of upper-middle-income Africa as an income group comprising seven countries, namely Mauritius, South Africa, Botswana, Namibia, Equatorial Guinea, Gabon, and Libya, that have a gross national income per capita of between US$4 096 and US$12 695. In line with this economic arrangement, the first five-year development plan (2021-2025) lays out a detailed five-year plan that includes the restructuring of higher and tertiary education. Education 5.0 is the brainchild of the MoHTEISTD for complementing government efforts in achieving Vision 2030 and the Sustainable development goals that have been rolled out in the second phase of the three-phased Vision 2030, the National Development Strategy 1 (NDS1).

Overview of the education 5.0 model vision 2030 in Zimbabwe: Curriculum issues

Education 5.0 encompasses five pillars; teaching, research, innovation, community service, and industrialization. The innovation pillar links the other four pillars, hence harmonious with institutional mandate meaning that as regards curricula, innovation should be contextualized in all the faculties of respective higher and tertiary education institutions (Matorevhu, 2023). Similarly, Wuta (2022) adds that agreeable with Education 5.0, teacher education institutions should have their teaching, research, and community service informed by innovation. The assertion therefore, indicates that innovative approaches employed in the three pillars of teaching, research, and community service should ensure that pre-service science instructors are armed with abilities that enable the instructors to produce secondary school science and mathematics graduates who are ready to participate in various socio-economic sectors. Instructors must also be in a position to equip graduates with the attributes of pursuing various industry-related careers. To curriculum, how curriculum innovation is implemented should not be divergent from the mandate of the institution or faculty of the institution.

Matorevhu (2023) mentions that the Education 5.0 model is a general curriculum innovation characterized by a change in policy as defined by policy documents. Meanwhile, it may be noted that curriculum innovation is an intricate process as on one hand it is a national affair expected to define knowledge, selecting skills that are viewed as most valuable in terms of preparing the future of any nation. On the flip side, curriculum innovation should respond to global concerns like globalization, SDGs, environmental issues, and international student assessments for example, the PISA, TIMSS, and PIRLS. Akala (2021) also writes that curricula reform is still progressing in countries globally and if instructors are not well prepared during either pre-service training or in-service training, curriculum innovation implementation may not be successful. South Africa, for example, introduced a post-apartheid curriculum which was later deemed too complex to implement and was replaced by a more conservative content-centred curriculum.

The applicability of Education 5.0 to the national context of Zimbabwe is a promising approach, but it requires careful consideration of the country's unique challenges and opportunities. Education 5.0, a concept introduced by the International Association of Universities, emphasizes the integration of technology, artificial intelligence, and the Internet of Things (IoT) to enhance the learning experience. While Zimbabwe's education system faces numerous challenges, including infrastructure limitations and resource constraints, Education 5.0 can be adapted to address these challenges and promote innovation and competitiveness. Considerations for the applicability of Education 5.0 in Zimbabwe can be examined as:

- Zimbabwe can leverage technology to bridge the infrastructure gap and provide access to education, particularly in rural areas. Online and blended learning platforms can be developed to reach a broader audience.
- Zimbabwe can adopt AI-powered learning tools to personalize education, improve student outcomes, and increase accessibility. This can be particularly effective in subjects like mathematics and science, where students often struggle with complex concepts.
- Zimbabwe can integrate IoT devices into educational settings to create interactive and immersive learning experiences. This can be achieved through virtual labs, simulations, and gamification.
- Data-driven decision-making: Zimbabwe can utilize data analytics to inform education policy decisions, track student progress, and evaluate program effectiveness. This can help identify areas for improvement and allocate resources more effectively.
- Zimbabwe can foster partnerships and collaboration between government, institutions, industry, and community organizations to develop innovative solutions and share best practices.
- Zimbabwe can invest in capacity building for educators, focusing on digital literacy, pedagogical training, and continuous professional development.

However, several challenges must be addressed before implementing Education 5.0 in Zimbabwe such as limited infrastructure: The lack basic infrastructure, including electricity, internet connectivity, and technology; limited access to devices: Many students lack access to devices, including laptops, tablets, and smartphones; limited lecturer training: Educators may require training on how to effectively integrate technology into their teaching practices and limited digital literacy: Students may require training on digital literacy skills, including online safety, digital citizenship, and basic computer skills. To overcome these challenges, the universities at large can develop targeted policies and programs to address infrastructure gaps and device access; invest in teacher training and professional development programs; implement digital literacy programs for students and educators, and foster partnerships with international organizations and institutions to access expertise and resources.

Adopting Education 5.0 in higher education can be challenging, but there are some ways to address these challenges such as:

- Lack of infrastructure and resources: Governments and institutions can invest in modernizing infrastructure, providing access to digital tools, and offering training on their effective use. Online platforms and remote learning tools can be used to reduce the need for physical infrastructure.

- Resistance to change: Provide training and support for educators to develop skills in new technologies and pedagogies. Involve students and educators in the design and development of Education 5.0 initiatives to encourage ownership and buy-in.
- Balancing traditional teaching methods with new approaches: Integrate new technologies and pedagogies into existing curricula, while still maintaining traditional teaching methods. Offer flexibility in course design to accommodate different learning styles and preferences.
- Ensuring quality and accreditation: Establish clear quality standards and accreditation processes for online and blended courses. Encourage collaboration between institutions to share best practices and ensure consistency across programs.
- Addressing the digital divide: Provide access to technology and internet connectivity for all students, regardless of location or socioeconomic status. Offer flexible learning options, such as online courses, to reach a broader student population.
- Measuring student outcomes and progress: Develop assessment tools that measure student skills and knowledge in both traditional and digital contexts. Use data analytics to track student progress and adjust instruction accordingly.
- Fostering collaboration and networking: Encourage interdisciplinary collaboration among students and faculty through project-based learning and co-curricular activities. Provide opportunities for students to participate in international collaborations and exchange programs.

By addressing these challenges and leveraging the benefits of Education 5.0, Zimbabwe can develop a more innovative, inclusive, and competitive education system that prepares students for the digital economy. Cognizant of the apparent shortcomings of the Zimbabwean education system and consistent with the third-millennium educational vision of Zimbabwe and the United Nations Educational, Scientific, and Cultural Organisation (UNESCO), CEIT recommended an outcomes-based national curriculum with provision for an innovative 'Four-Pathway' approach to the development of vocational and technical skills among students (Yingi et al. 2022). As regards the Digital Age side of curricula, for instance, game-based learning is an important requirement for Education 5.0 since it can engage students in a way that is different from traditional classrooms. Game-based learning aids in increasing motivation, engagement, and learning outcomes. Evaluating the effectiveness of gamification in education is important to determine its impact on student learning outcomes. Several ways though may be used to evaluate the effectiveness of game-based learning in the realization of education outcomes (Kadarwati et al. 2023).

The other view as regards the Digital Age and against the philosophy of Education 5.0, Razi and Zhou (2022), document that the Ministry of Higher and Tertiary Education, Science and Technology Development views STEM rather than STEAM as the panacea for the economic challenges facing the country. Scholars within government are confident that STEM provides the optimum environment for the development of critical competencies such as problem-solving, critical thinking, creativity, teamwork, communication skills, and conflict resolution. Skills such as Afro mentioned are seen as important today for the socio-economic transformation of the country and should, therefore, be developed among students (Heleta & Bagus, 2021). Furtak and Penuel (2019) document that it was discovered that students need to be given hands-on education that sustains their lives in the long run. In most universities in Zimbabwe, meeting the two missions of industrialization and innovation of the Education 5.0 philosophy, it remains un-doubtful that a hands-on approach to learning has to be adopted. Keche (2021) outlines hands-on curriculum issues explicitly by pointing out that failure to nurture higher education students in ways that equip them with practical skills will intensify global economic problems. This then explains the necessity of modern societies through collaboration with relevant stakeholders and through comprehensive curriculum reform to identify problems and provide solutions. Conclusively, inquiry-based learning, problem-solving, and problem-based learning all revolve around and resonate with research and are in harmony with the mission of Education 5.0 (Wuta, 2022).

The curriculum of the courses in some of the universities is largely theoretical, presenting challenges in the achievement of the industrialization and innovation missions of Education 5.0. Commonly, Lopez-Alcarria and Olivares-Vicente Poza-Vilches (2019) mention that purely academic education in the classroom is detached from the environment and therefore not sustainable. The success of pedagogy in sustainable development will be determined by whether teaching problem-based, inquiry-based, and project-driven fosters collaboration and critical thinking. Collaboration and critical thinking are important in driving innovation and industrialization, however, one of the challenges is that students learn to pass examinations as opposed to learning for innovation, entrepreneurship, and industrialization. The curriculum should be parcelled up in such a manner that a learner-centered approach is achieved; hence the relevance of project-based, problem-solving, and inquiry-based learning approaches (Bangura, 2023). Referring to the way the curriculum is taught, and the methodological aspect of learning and teaching Irwin et al. (2022) argue that work-related learning (hands-on approach) is sustainable because of its symbiotic link with the environment. For the universities to realize Education 5.0 and ultimately Vision 2030, a review of the curriculum is necessary to intertwine curriculum with innovation and industrialization. The Faculty may for instance introduce courses in industrialization and innovation to align with the key objectives of the Education

5.0 philosophy. The changes can be realized subject to curriculum adjustments as specified by Boelt et al. (2022) who write that implementation of competency-based learning will require structural changes in the engineering curriculum and method of instruction. The field of curriculum implementation experienced degradation that came out of context and was no longer oriented towards achieving students' ability to understand science in the context of daily and living practices, but only around achieving student competency, which is depicted in academic values (Grant, 2018). Conventionally, Fernandez Orozco (2022) also writes that the curriculum needs orientation to adjust to the development of the 4.0 industrial revolution.

The curriculum issues include:

- Curriculum is outdated, largely theoretical, and does not reflect the changing needs of the workplace or industry
- Devoid of focus on skills such as digital literacy, soft skills, and critical thinking
- Curriculum is not aligned with international best standards/ practices
- There is a lack of flexibility in the curriculum to allow for individualized learning
- Inadequacy of resources and support for teachers to effectively deliver the curriculum.
- In a majority of nations, education institutions have generally been slow in responding to changes that address the demand for certain industrial skills. Fixed course structures, bureaucratic accreditation processes, increasing costs, and the need for learners to expend intensive effort on coursework over a long period have excluded many learners, especially learners from disadvantaged communities and first-generation university students (Goger et al. 2022). On the same issue, Anderson-Levitt and Gardinier (2021) report that many institutions have started to adopt competency-based education, and online and hybrid options to reach out to a wide group of learners. Additionally, Goger et al. (2022) articulate that because numerous higher education institutions face challenges such as financial inadequacies as well as the decline in enrolment, some of the institutions have begun to reconfigure their administrative approach to reach a wider pool of students and have revised their education models through innovative curricula formats and delivery mechanisms. It is therefore noteworthy that an increasing number of universities have embraced competency-based learning in their curricula.

Strategies to deal with challenges of implementing Education 5.0

To effectively implement Education 5.0, institutions can adopt a multifaceted approach that addresses the challenges and opportunities presented by this new paradigm. This includes developing a clear vision and strategy for Education 5.0, providing faculty with training and support to develop new skills and pedagogies, and fostering a culture of innovation and experimentation. Additionally, institutions should prioritize student-centered learning, focusing on developing skills that are relevant to the job market and preparing students for lifelong learning. Furthermore, partnerships with industry, government, and other stakeholders can provide valuable insights into emerging technologies and employer needs, enabling institutions to stay ahead of the curve. By leveraging these strategies, institutions can successfully navigate the challenges of implementing Education 5.0 and equip students with the skills and knowledge needed to succeed in the digital age.

Research towards innovation and industrialization

Industrialization and innovation in higher education, particularly through collaboration with the industry, are crucial for preparing students for the constantly evolving job market and driving economic growth. By working closely with industry partners, higher education institutions can ensure that their programs are aligned with the skills and knowledge needed in the workforce. Collaboration with industry can take various forms, such as internships, research partnerships, curriculum development, and technology transfer agreements. These collaborations provide students with real-world experience, access to cutting-edge technology, and opportunities to work on industry-relevant projects. Additionally, industry collaboration can help universities stay current with industry trends and demands, leading to the development of innovative programs and research projects that have practical applications. Overall, industrialization and innovation in higher education, facilitated by strong partnerships with industry, can create a more dynamic and impactful learning environment that benefits students, faculty, industry partners, and society as a whole.

Haleem et al. (2022) state that digital technology is driving innovation across every facet of life, including education. Technology avails opportunities in schools, colleges, and universities and offers lifelong learning and training. However, educational technologies are not magic bullets as they not only offer great benefits at the same time but also create challenges, which educators need to explore and address to help shape the future of education for the benefit of nations. Education 5.0 focuses on the provision of personalized learning experiences that align with the needs and abilities of individual students. Learning experiences are achieved through the use of artificial intelligence (AI) and machine learning to create personalized learning designs and also offer an adjustment to instruction in real time based on student progress. Personalized learning is a critical element of the Education 5.0 model as it aims to accommodate the learning experience to each student's attributes (Bhutoria, 2022).

In some of the developed countries for instance, as regards, the Project Based Learning (PBL) arrangement is such that there is a High Tech High network of public charter institutions. High Tech High uses an interdisciplinary approach in which students work on projects that integrate multiple subjects that connect to real-world situations. The arrangement is such that students develop skills such as teamwork, research, and presentation, while also building their theoretical base (Boss & Krauss, 2022). Furthermore, Chen et al. (2021) document that project-based learning is faced with challenges such as the requirement for instructor training, assessment methods, and integration with traditional curriculum demands. Project-based learning offers a great alternative to the traditional education setting by promoting student agency, critical thinking, and problem-solving skills.

Wuta (2022) asserts that the heritage-based philosophy of education 5.0 states that advanced scientific knowledge from any place globally is to be matched to the environment for producing a competitive industry. In the same order, ecosystems being generated for innovation to industrialize and modernize are being created. It is noteworthy that education 5.0 policy documents spell out that new technologies should emanate from the innovation centres being constructed at the learning institutions (Matorevhu, 2023). Additionally, Matorevhu (2023) says industrial parks connected to these educational facilities will be established. The goal is to set up a network of innovative businesses, government agencies, and educational institutions that can function together to produce consumer goods.

Research and development are the engines for bringing new ideas and innovations (Ferras Hernandez & Nylund, 2019). Commonly, Wuta (2022) states that in Education 5.0, the emphasis should be on instructors guiding their students as they undertake their research. It, therefore, demonstrates that research is the mainstay of literacy development, ideation, innovation, industrialization, commercialization, economic growth, and modernization in Zimbabwe. To be innovative and industrialize the universities should put policies that support and emphasize practical research projects with an orientation to science and technology. The universities can for instance adopt practical projects in which students do not graduate without tangible practical research to abstain from the situation of theoretical research projects. The main reason for practical work is the fact that it allows the development of practical skills in scientific processes and at the same time, a central conceptual comprehension, resulting between the hands-on approaches with the minds-on approach in development activities (Ekici & Erdem, 2020). It would involve a great effort in the field of education, a major review of technical training programs, and close articulation of educational planning, and scientific and technological policies. Without this kind of effort education-wise, the process of industrialization based on national scientific and technical progress would lead to the building of dead, sterile human capital in developing countries (Pfafflin, 2019).

Research is key to innovation and industrialization in Zimbabwe as it;

- Helps to identify new technologies and solutions that can be used to improve education
- Assists in the development of new models of teaching and learning that are more effective and relevant to the needs of students
- Lead to the development of new products and services that can improve the economy and create jobs
- Aids in building partnerships between industry and academia, which can lead to more collaboration and innovation.

Technological change has found its way into almost every job and industry at a fast pace, and with it, industrialists are reconsidering work processes and divisions of labor processes (Kolade & Owoseni, 2022). Following this line of reasoning, Goger et al. (2022) in particular indicate that within the next five years, fifty percent of all employees will need re-skilling, and forty percent of core skills are expected to change (World Economic Forum, 2020). The magnitude of skills required for one job increases annually at a rate of ten percent, the emergent work culture emphasizes workplaces with more remote or hybrid work, additional digital skills, and more managerial support and functions.

An alternative way of conceptualizing these changes is to focus on two key aspects the magnitude of skills acquisition and the application of instruction and learning in a specific occupation or industry. The majority of innovation takes place among shorter, less intensive learning opportunities that are also more job-specific or hands-on. Instead of completing longer programs, individuals bundle a combination of short-term credentials or work experiences to demonstrate their qualifications in the labor market (Biea et al. 2023). Presenting forth an analysis, Goger et al. (2022) report that although there is a rising tide of innovation in many aspects of education and career pathways, governance frameworks and state institutions have been slow to adapt. Secules, et al. (2021) indicate that while the ardour of technology innovators to upgrade their services and tooling may be well-intentioned, the development however, tends to take place in adequately financed and privileged spaces that are typically not well grounded in the realities, of experiences, and priorities of marginalized communities.

Synergies of the new Education 5.0 Model with industry

Stefan et al. (2023) state that in terms of the industry age model, the Education 5.0 philosophy is grounded on the industrial age model of education, a model designed to prepare students for industrial work. The model emphasizes uniformity, conformity, and rote memorization. However, Luna Scott (2015) comments that in today's rapidly technologically changing world, the model fails to equip students with the skills needed for the knowledge economy such as adaptability, collaboration, and innovation. In Singapore for instance, there is a skills future initiative where monetary credit is given to Singaporean citizens aged 25 and above to be used for approved courses. This program empowers individual students to take ownership of their learning and engage areas of interest or skills that are in demand. The initiative embraces partnerships with industry stakeholders in the development of industry-relevant training programs and certifications. This initiative guarantees that the skills being developed are aligned with the needs of the labor market, resulting in improving employability and opportunities for career advancement for individuals (Kim et al. 2021). Going further, Iqasa and Afaneh (2022) spell out that technology will aid and transform the classroom environment where students become active learners. In terms of innovative delivery and assessment, students are not only looking at the world from a business viewpoint but are broadly innovative.

Conventional learning situations will alter from an instructional mode to one that turns theoretical gains into practical and applied knowledge. Rather than using standard assessment methods, the delivery method will be changed to include practical presentations and instruction (Brown & Palincsar, 2018). In the Zimbabwean context, the construct that governed critical skills audit was informed by low industrialization levels which could be a result of low skill levels. It was realized that developing and increasing skills would be the basis for the advancement of the economy. Indeed, Zimbabwe's average skill level of 38% differs from its literacy rate of over 94%. Under typical conditions, skill level and literacy level are usually in tandem (Matorevhu, 2023).

Wuta (2022) highlights that innovation is the bridge between knowledge produced in lecture rooms, laboratories, and industrial production. The universities need, therefore, to form synergies with relevant industries to come up with training programs that foster industrialization and innovation. Strengthening issue, Bean and Melzer (2021) say the concept of an innovation hub, denotes the harnessing of knowledge acquired from the lecture room or laboratory in addressing the socio-politico-economic problems vexing communities within Zimbabwe. The education 5.0 model can create synergies with the industry in several ways;

- Industry can provide input into the design of the curriculum, to ensure that it is relevant to the needs of the workplace.
- Industry can provide funding and resources for research and development in education.
- Industry can provide opportunities for work-based learning, internships, and apprenticeships for students.
- Industry stakeholders can provide insights into future trends and technologies that can be incorporated into the curriculum
- Alumni nexus

These are just a few examples of how the Education 5.0 model can create synergies with industry, leading to mutual benefits.

Teichler (2019) documents that global views reflect the important role of higher and tertiary education in industrialization and socio-economic development. Furthermore, research attributes the speedy development of countries like China, India, Singapore, and Brazil to great tertiary education and industry linkages. The innovation capabilities of such economies have been increased by strengthening partnerships between industry, tertiary institutions, and government (Andreoni & Tregenna, 2020). Additionally, Wirba (2021) comments that higher and tertiary education plays a pivotal role in innovation and economic growth through universities and colleges which develop new knowledge and technologies which are then applied and coupled with economic growth.

Infrastructure issues and program models

Education 5.0 is the next development in education which is designed to leverage modern technologies in the achievement of lifelong learning goals. One of the central technologies that play a critical role in driving the Education 5.0 model is the Internet of Things- IoT (Broo et al. 2022). Similarly, Shrestha and Furqan (2020) maintain that IoT-enabled devices such as wearables, sensors, and smart devices can be used to collect real-time data on student learning and behavior, essentially providing a deeper understanding of individual student needs and abilities. Likewise, IoT devices can also be used to facilitate personalized learning, an approach that takes advantage of technology to individualize instruction. This can be achieved through the provision of adaptive learning systems that adjust the pace and content of instruction based on student performance (Nyaga, 2023). Supporting the same sentiments, Dian et al. (2020) say personalized feedback can be provided to students through IoT devices such as wearables that track movements.

Munirathinam (2020) highlights that today's existence is an environment that is called Society 4.0, where the Internet of Things (IoT) has just started to alter industrial structure, and automation through AI and big data analysis. Meanwhile, Tanaka et al. (2019) comment that humanity has not yet fully integrated IoT into society and has not fully employed it in a manner that it improves and makes life better, more equitable, and sustainable. To this end, further transformation is required to establish a more sustainable society by creating a system that integrates cyberspace into the physical tangible realm. The arrangement should be such that human well-being is placed at the core of the transformation. They further state that to realize this next generation of society, it is critical to anchor it on STEM education which is gaining ground as it is the basis for all innovation.

Education 5.0 intends to remove barriers to education and make education more accessible to all. This kind of approach requires the adoption and leveraging of technologies such as 5G networks and cloud computing which support high-bandwidth requirements of many new educational technologies and make education more flexible and accessible (Broo et al. 2022). High-speed networks are an essential aspect of Education 5.0, as they facilitate real-time delivery of digital resources and materials to students and instructors alike. The adoption of high-speed networks in education enables coherent communication and collaboration between students, instructors, and educational institutions (Ahmad et al. 2023). The strength of high-speed networks is that the networks guarantee access to educational materials remotely. To evaluate the performance of high-speed networks in education, several methods can be employed, such as network reliability, network capacity, and network latency (Garlinska, et al. 2023).

Education 5.0 seeks to make education more flexible and accessible by removing barriers to education, such as geographic and financial constraints (Sa & Serpa, 2022). Contributing, Ali and Alourani (2021) say removal of such barriers can be achieved through the use of technology such as cloud computing which enables education stakeholders to access digital resources and materials. Flexibility and accessibility are two important attributes of Education 5.0 which refers to the integration of technology in education to enhance the learning experience. In terms of technology access and inclusivity, Education 5.0 still faces challenges in reaching marginalized communities, remote areas, and individuals with disabilities. This limitation aggravates existing social imbalances and hinders the holistic development of individuals (Tigwell, 2021). About meaningful learning experience, learning will have the power to effectively transform knowledge into experience-based information. It will have a broad range of dimensions, including activity-oriented, technology-supportive, compliant experience, and broad industrial relevance (Moleka, 2023).

Sifelani (2022) reports that infrastructure problems, for instance, the absence of reliable power supplies and internet access can negate the implementation of Education 5.0 in Zimbabwe. To overcome these challenges, the following program models can be implemented to address infrastructure issues and provide access to education for all students;

- Mobile learning: using mobile devices to deliver education, which can work to counter some of the infrastructure challenges
- Radio-based learning: using radio broadcasts to deliver education, which can reach remote areas that lack internet access
- Community-based learning: using local community centers and libraries to deliver education

In addition to the program models mentioned earlier, the following models can also be used;

- Open educational resources: using open-access digital content that can be accessed by anyone with an internet connection
- Satellite-based learning: using satellite technology to deliver education, which can work around infrastructure issues
- Solar-powered learning: using solar power to provide energy for educational resources, such as computers and e-readers

These are just a few examples of program models that can be used to address infrastructure issues. It is important to note that these models may require significant investment and planning to implement effectively.

Mutambala et al. (2020) cite inadequate training infrastructure as the main reason for student incompetency and propose industrial secondment for lecturers as a means for knowledge and technology transfer between industry and academic institutions. The Faculty of Science and Technology Education can therefore second lecturers to the industry to nurture innovative practices in science and technology courses, more so, it may be prudent to create laboratories for some technical lessons. The innovative and industrialization elements demand fresh thinking, for example, the setting up of an innovation and industrialization fund managed by an innovation and industrialization committee. The committee members must exclude the university from among the university councilors, private and public sector leadership, and business organizations to include venture capitalists with successful start-ups (Denoncourt, 2020). Such a setting may be adopted by the National University of Science and Technology to award, and support innovators and innovative practices feeding into industrialization and consequently, the achievement of Vision 2030. The

Universities may also consider the adoption of other educational models particularly the ones currently running in developed and industrialized nations such as Japan. Stearns (2020) documents that industrialisation advanced quickly and this created business activities within manufacturing, mining, transportation, finance, and commerce. Collins (2019) for instance, writes that it has been mainly in engineering, agriculture, and medical science programs on which Japan has provided education support to over 500 universities around the world with notable success. Universities such as the King Mongkut's Institute of Technology, Ladkrabang of Thailand, and the Jomo Kenyatta University of Agriculture and Technology of Kenya have become top universities in their respective countries after receiving support from Japan over a long period (Kayashima, 2022).

Multi-stakeholder partnerships

Multi-stakeholder partnerships can play a key role in the implementation of Education 5.0 in Zimbabwe. These partnerships can involve collaboration between government, industry, and the education sector. For example, industry partners can provide funding and resources, while the government can create policies and regulations to support the initiative. These partnerships can help to ensure that Education 5.0 is implemented effectively and benefits all stakeholders. Some examples of multi-stakeholder partnerships that can be used in this context include public-private partnerships; partnerships between government and private sector organizations to provide education services. Goger, Parco, and Vegas (2022) state that it can be difficult to keep track of all the digital credential initiatives due to the large number of initiatives, stakeholders, products, and services. Several stakeholders have started forming coalitions to start systematizing and harmonizing across institutions or countries, such as networks across higher education institutions to pilot competency-based or modularized curricula targeting working learners.

Introducing the concept of team-based learning is helpful as supported by competency-based learning where students and practitioners from different interlinked disciplines provide solutions to address a real-life problem, making use of innovation hubs (Mamina & Maganga, 2019). The universities may also need to form collaborations with industry and other institutions as a way of innovating and industrializing. Putting the issue into perspective, Rangraz and Pareto (2021) record that strong components of fieldwork, and practical work will achieve the objective of teaching and learning for sustainable development. However, they further state that this can only take place effectively where an integrated education system is in operation, that is, education and industry working together through collaborations.

On collaboration, Mamina and Maganga (2019) write that collaboration interdisciplinary education, a concept introduced at the dawn of the 20th century, explores rich and appropriate links across different disciplines to students the critical cognitive skills applicable in real life. Meanwhile, Etzkowitz and Leeydesdorff (2020) point out that industry-university collaboration is a perfect example of trans-disciplinarity where the university research function gets to practically test developed ideas thereby nurturing innovation culture with students. In addition, resources are required, to this end, partnerships with the private sector can be sought to secure investment in research and development (Delmon, 2021). The job-creator mindset demands a close interaction with their host communities to identify economic opportunities to not only inform their curriculum trajectory but most importantly, innovation and innovation research and development agenda (Khanna, 2022).

Education 5.0 promotes collaboration and connectivity among students, teachers, and other stakeholders. This can be realized through the use of technology such as virtual and augmented reality and the IoT, which allow for immersive and interactive learning experiences (Carayannis & Morawska-Jancelewicz, 2022). Substantiating, Ahmad et al. (2023) report that evaluation mechanisms for collaboration and connectedness in Education 5.0 can include measures of student engagement and participation in group work and collaborative projects. These may also encompass assessments of the quality and effectiveness of these collaborations. Additionally, communication and teamwork skills, such as conflict resolution and problem-solving abilities, can be used to evaluate collaboration and partnerships. The use of technology, such as social media and online collaboration tools can also be evaluated for its effectiveness in promoting connectedness and collaboration among students and instructors (Haleem et al. 2022).

In industrializing, the state university's sole fascination is exploiting the identified economic opportunities in their host communities to realize university-linked start-ups and ultimately companies that contribute to the national purse (Muiruri, 2020). Similarly, Feld (2020) says another must-do for any serious Education 5.0 subscribed state university is to immediately operate in the industry solutions provider mode. The industry solutions provider mode is a low-hanging fruit in terms of immediate revenue generation, in this case, the university reaches out to industries in their host communities, learns of their challenges, works out, and provides the industry with solutions. The concept involves creating economic value from knowledge packaging and offering further benefits to the state universities by way of access to successful industry Chief Executive Officers (CEOs) to serve as student mentors, as well as industrial exposure and experience that further enrich their research and teaching staff.

In-service training for academic staff

The competencies that must be possessed by the educator are educational competence, skills for technological commercialization, capability in globalization, expertise in future strategies, and counselor competence (Indira et al. 2020). Skilled people generate knowledge that can be used to create and implement innovations. More skills increase the capacity to absorb innovations (Chiu & Lin, 2022). Adding, Akala (2021) says teacher education will continue to take cognizance of methodology and curriculum changes. Instructors will be regularly exposed to innovations in their profession. In-service training will be developed as an integral part of continuing teacher education. Furthermore, Mishra et al. (2020) comment that faculty development programs are crucial if higher education institutions are to respond to complex changes, namely; societal needs, technological advances, and their impact on education and the paradigm shift from teaching to learning. Medina (2018) specifies that academic development programs are needed in all higher education institutions to promote the development of teaching skills, curricula, and courseware. Such programs will be recognized as integral elements of a higher education system committed to redressing and improving the quality of learning and teaching, highlighting the need for a cultural change in engineering. However, Reinius et al. (2022) cite the resistance of lecturers as an obstacle to achieving better results from the inclusion of sustainability in engineering courses and the reformation of engineering curricula. Acknowledging, Haleem et al. (2022) relate that much as the generality of citizens need digital competencies, educators need competencies to fully harness the potential of digital technologies to fully equip their students for life and work in a digital society. In terms of professional engagement, there is a need to focus on the ability of educators in ongoing professional development and reflection in the context of digital technologies. The professional engagement involves skills to enable updates with digital advancements, exploring new teaching strategies, and educational tools, and participating in professional networks and communities (Boss & Krauss, 2022).

Professional growth emanates from the consultation of the latest research integrated with the evaluation and reflection of teaching practices. Effective use of technology initially requires a specific purpose and mind frame to promote learners' comprehension of content using web tools (Seleviciene, 2020). With this thought process, Hsu and Chen (2019) specify that all instructors assume responsibility for teaching and assessing students' knowledge and skills related to the Web. It is with this school of thought that instructors must engage in continuous professional growth and learning. They further propose a framework to describe the required digital knowledge for instructors through technological pedagogical content knowledge. The framework happens from the intersection of technological knowledge, pedagogical knowledge, and content knowledge, which are developed through collaborative, constructivist, and project-based approaches (De Rossi & Trevisan, 2018).

In developed universities for instance, students have the freedom to choose their learning paths, and the curriculum emphasizes critical thinking, problem-solving, and creativity. The education system focuses on the development of students' skills rather than simply imparting knowledge. Instructors are highly qualified and reputable professionals who have the liberty to design their own lessons and assessment methods (Nilivaara & Soini, 2024). As a result of changing dynamics on the global stage coupled with the Fourth Industrial Revolution (4IR), which requires a different set of skills, the trajectory of education that was being pursued in the higher education sector in Zimbabwe has been falling far short of the expected standard. This phenomenon is more pronounced, particularly in light of the global problems that university graduates are expected to handle at a personal and collective level (Fataar, 2020).

Simultaneously, Madlela (2022) commonly spells out that innovation in teacher education in the 21st century encompasses the integration of ICTs (computer, software, networks, satellite links, websites, and other related systems into teaching and learning of teacher education programs. Teacher education innovation includes new or modified teaching and learning approaches or instruction, to improve the quality of preparation of teachers. In this regard, science teacher educators should understand policies and initiatives related to innovation for innovation implementation to succeed (Matorevhu, 2023). It therefore means that it is vital in teacher education curriculum innovation implementation to understand the nexus or connection between innovation and industrialisation. This then would ensure that the goal of industrialisation is pursued and aligned with the mandate of the institution (Yingi et al. 2022).

In-service training is essential to ensure that academic staff have the skills and knowledge needed to effectively implement Education 5.0. This training can include courses on issues such as;

- Digital literacy: understanding how to use digital technologies to support education
- Curriculum design: understanding how to develop and implement an effective curriculum that meets the needs of students and stakeholders (Government, commerce, society, and industry)
- Assessment and evaluation: understanding how to effectively assess and evaluate students' learning
- Professional development: developing skills and knowledge to generate effective and efficient instructors

The examples given above are among a cocktail of the categories of in-service training that can be provided to academic staff.

Recommendations

The successful implementation of Education 5.0 in the Digital Age requires the following recommendations to be addressed:

- Addressing infrastructure challenges through the use of alternative program models and multi-stakeholder partnerships.
- Creating policies and regulations that support the implementation of education 5.0 philosophy
- Focus on addressing the specific infrastructure challenges that exist in Zimbabwe, such as lack of reliable electricity, internet access, and other related weak linkages in ICT gadgets
- Prioritize teacher training on concepts such as digital literacy, curriculum design, assessment, and evaluation. Providing adequate in-service training for academic staff to ensure they have the skills needed to implement Education 5.0 effectively.
- Build partnerships with industry government and other stakeholders to support the implementation of Education 5.0.
- Alignment of the Zimbabwean education system with international education best practices as well as align curricula with that of highly industrialized nations.

It is envisioned that the enabling technologies for Education 5.0 include but are not limited to Artificial Intelligence (AI), Virtual and Augmented Reality (VR and AR), Internet of Things (IoT), Big Data and Analytics, Blockchain, and 5G Networks. While AI-powered tools can personalize learning experiences, provide real-time feedback, and assist teachers in assessing students' progress, VR and AR can provide immersive and interactive learning experiences, allowing students to explore new environments and a more engaging way.

Conclusion

The concept of Education 5.0 has been explored particularly with a focus on industrialization and innovation pillars, a futuristic term for the next evolution in eeducation. The development of education through the infusion of ICT and AI technologies has paved the way for Education 5.0 concept realization. The philosophy of Education 5.0 is an emerging and promising education phenomenon that can be adopted and leveraged to improve autonomous instruction delivery as well as the learning experience for students. Education 5.0 has the potential to transform the education system in Zimbabwe and provide more equitable access to quality education. The future of learning in the Digital Age is a valuable framework for transforming education in Zimbabwe. However, it is important to tailor the model to the specific needs and challenges of the country. By addressing the infrastructure challenges, prioritizing teacher training, and building partnerships, the country can successfully implement Education 5.0 and improve the quality of education for all students. Numerous challenges exist within the university in Zimbabwe such as a critical lack of links between the lecture rooms and the innovation hub, a specific curriculum that encompasses innovation and industrialization, and the incapacitation of lecturers in keeping up with current technology, trends, innovation, and industrialisation. Additional challenges include implementation costs, limited resources for content creation, privacy and security concerns as well as limited research on the effectiveness and impact of Education 5.0. To overcome these challenges, the learning institution needs to invest and embrace new technologies, provide proper training for instructors as well ensure that all students have access to the necessary technology and resources. Additionally, proper research needs to be instituted to align curriculum with technology as well as industry and global education and training best practices. More so, it is also critical to formulate an assessment that is practical-oriented, one that links with industrialization and innovation to determine optimal ways to implement Education 5.0 against the Digital Age. All the challenges can be overcome through the suggestions highlighted especially through collaborations and synergies to realize innovation and consequently industrialisation for the attainment of vision 2030.

References

Ahmad, S., Umirzakova, S., Mujtaba, G., Amin, M. S., & Whangbo, T. (2023). Education 5.0: requirements, enabling technologies, and future directions. *arXiv preprint arXiv:2307.15846.*

Akala, B. M. M. (2021). Revisiting education reform in Kenya: A case of Competency Based Curriculum (CBC). *Social Sciences & Humanities Open*, 3(1), 100107. DOI: 10.1016/j.ssaho.2021.100107

Ali, A., & Alourani, A. (2021). An investigation of cloud computing and E-learning for educational advancement. *International Journal of Computer Science & Network Security*, 21(11), 216–222.

Alqasa, K. M. A., & Afaneh, J. A. A. (2022). Active learning techniques and student satisfaction: Role of classroom environment. *Eurasian Journal of Educational Research*, 98(98), 85–100.

Ambos, B., Brandl, K., Perri, A., Scalera, V. G., & Van Assche, A. (2021). The nature of innovation in global value chains. *Journal of World Business*, 56(4), 101221. DOI: 10.1016/j.jwb.2021.101221

Anderson-Levitt, K., & Gardinier, M. P. (2021). Introduction contextualising global flows of competency-based education: Polysemy, hybridity, and silences. *Comparative Education*, 57(1), 1–18. DOI: 10.1080/03050068.2020.1852719

Andreoni, A., & Tregenna, F. (2020). Escaping the middle-income technology trap: A comparative analysis of industrial policies in China, Brazil, and South Africa. *Structural Change and Economic Dynamics*, 54, 324–340. DOI: 10.1016/j.strueco.2020.05.008

Bangura, M. (2023). Sociology learning curriculum for sustainable development: The Sierra Leone rural and urban social observation. *Development*, 6(3), 37–51.

Bean, J. C., & Melzer, D. (2021). *Engaging ideas: The professor's guide to integrating writing, critical thinking, and active learning in the classroom.* John Wiley &Sons.

Bhutoria, A. (2022). Personalized education and artificial intelligence in the United States, China, and India: A systematic review using a human-in-the-loop model. *Computers and Education: Artificial Intelligence*, 3, 100068. DOI: 10.1016/j.caeai.2022.100068

Biea, E. A., Dinu, E., Bunica, A., & Jerdea, L. (2023). Recruitment in SMEs: The role of managerial practices, technology and innovation. *European Business Review*.

Boelt, A. M., Kolmos, A., & Holgaard, J. E. (2022). Literature review of students' perceptions of generic competence development in problem-based learning in engineering education. *European Journal of Engineering Education*, 47(6), 1399–1420. DOI: 10.1080/03043797.2022.2074819

Boss, S., & Krauss, J. (2022). *Reinventing project-based learning: Your field guide to real-world projects in the digital age*. International Society for Technology in Education.

Broo, D. G., Kaynak, O., & Sait, S. M. (2022). Rethinking engineering education at the age of Industry 5.0. *Journal of Industrial Information Integration*, 25, 100311. DOI: 10.1016/j.jii.2021.100311

Brown, A. L., & Palincsar, A. S. (2018). Guided, cooperative learning and individual knowledge acquisition. In *Knowing, learning, and instruction* (pp. 393–451). Routledge. DOI: 10.4324/9781315044408-13

Carayannis, E. G., & Morawska-Jancelewicz, J. (2022). The futures of Europe: Society 5.0 and Industry 5.0 as driving forces of future universities. *Journal of the Knowledge Economy*, 13(4), 3445–3471. DOI: 10.1007/s13132-021-00854-2

Chen, J., Kolmos, A., & Du, X. (2021). Forms of implementation and challenges of PBL in engineering education: A review of literature. *European Journal of Engineering Education*, 46(1), 90–115. DOI: 10.1080/03043797.2020.1718615

Chen, J., & Yin, X. (2019). Connotation and types of innovation. In *The Routledge companion to innovation management* (pp. 26–54). Routledge. DOI: 10.4324/9781315276670-3

Chiu, M. L., & Lin, C. N. (2022). Developing supply chain open innovation capability: The mediating role of the knowledge creation process, governance mechanism and technology as a driver. *Journal of Innovation & Knowledge*, 7(4), 100264. DOI: 10.1016/j.jik.2022.100264

Collins, R. (2019). *The credential society: An historical sociology of education and stratification*. Columbia University Press. DOI: 10.7312/coll19234

De Rossi, M., & Trevisan, O. (2018). Technological Pedagogical Content Knowledge in the literature: How TPCK is defined and implemented in initial teacher education. *Italian Journal of Educational Technology*, 26(1), 7–23.

Delmon, J. (2021). *Private sector investment in infrastructure: Project finance, PPP projects and PPP frameworks*. Kluwer Law International BV.

Denoncourt, J. (2020). Companies and UN 2030 sustainable development goal 9industry, innovation and infrastructure. *Journal of Corporate Law Studies*, 20(1), 199–235. DOI: 10.1080/14735970.2019.1652027

Dian, F. J., Vahidnia, R., & Rahmati, A. (2020). Wearables and the Internet of Things (IoT), applications, opportunities, and challenges: A Survey. *IEEE Access: Practical Innovations, Open Solutions*, 8, 69200–69211. DOI: 10.1109/ACCESS.2020.2986329

Dube, S. S., & Shumba, S. (2023). Towards Attaining the Sustainable Development Goals in Zimbabwe: Christian Women's Leadership in Gwanda District. In *Women, Religion and Leadership in Zimbabwe, Volume 1: An Ecofeminist Perspective* (pp. 103-120). Cham: Springer Nature Switzerland.

Ekici, M., & Erdem, M. (2020). Developing science process skills through mobile scientific inquiry. *Thinking Skills and Creativity*, 36, 100658. DOI: 10.1016/j.tsc.2020.100658

Etzkowitz, H., & Leydesdorff, L. (2020). Universities and the global knowledge economy: A triple helix of university-industry relations. In Universities and the Global Knowledge Economy: A Triple Helix of University-Industry Relations: Etzkowitz, Henry| uLeydesdorff, Loet. [Sl]: *SSRN*.

Fataar, A. (2020). The emergence of an education policy disposit if in South Africa: An analysis of educational discourses associated with the fourth industrial revolution. *Journal of Education (University of KwaZulu-Natal)*, (80), 5-24.

Feld, B. (2020). *Start-up communities: Building an entrepreneurial ecosystem in your city*. John Wiley & Sons.

Fernandez Orozco, R. S. (2022). Training and Workforce Re-Orientation. In *Handbook of Non-destructive Evaluation 4.0* (pp. 1187–1243). Springer International Publishing. DOI: 10.1007/978-3-030-73206-6_23

Ferras Hernandez, X., & Nylund, P. A. (2019). Clusters as innovation engines: The accelerating strengths of proximity. *European Management Review*, 16(1), 37–53. DOI: 10.1111/emre.12330

Furtak, E. M., & Penuel, W. R. (2019). Coming to terms: Addressing the persistence of "hands-on" and other reform terminology in the era of science as practice. *Science Education*, 103(1), 167–186. DOI: 10.1002/sce.21488

Garlinska, M., Osial, M., Proniewska, K., & Pregowska, A. (2023). The influence of emerging technologies on distance education. *Electronics (Basel)*, 12(7), 1550. DOI: 10.3390/electronics12071550

Goger, A., Parco, A., & Vegas, E. (2022). *Learning and working in the digital age: Advancing opportunities and identifying the risks.* Brookings Institution.

Grant, J. (2018). Principles of curriculum design. Understanding medical education: Evidence, theory, and practice, 71-88.

Gujral, H. S., & Singh, G. P. I. (2022). Industrialization and its impact on human health–a critical appraisal. *Journal of Student Research*, 11(4).

Haleem, A., Javaid, M., Qadri, M. A., & Suman, R. (2022). Understanding the role of digital technologies in education: A review. *Sustainable Operations and Computers*, 3, 275–285. DOI: 10.1016/j.susoc.2022.05.004

Heleta, S., & Bagus, T. (2021). Sustainable development goals and higher education: Leaving many behind. *Higher Education*, 81(1), 163–177. DOI: 10.1007/s10734-020-00573-8

Hernandez-Torrano, D., & Courtney, M. G. (2021). Modern international large-scale assessment in education: An integrative review and mapping of the literature. *Large-Scale Assessments in Education*, 9(1), 17. DOI: 10.1186/s40536-021-00109-1

Hsu, L., & Chen, Y. J. (2019). Examining teachers' technological pedagogical and content knowledge in the era of cloud pedagogy. *South African Journal of Education*, 39(S2), 39. DOI: 10.15700/saje.v39ns2a1572

Indira, E. W. M., Hermanto, A., & Pramono, S. E. (2020, June). Improvement of teacher competence in the Industrial Revolution era 4.0. In *International Conference on Science and Education and Technology (ISET 2019)* (pp. 350-352). Atlantis Press. DOI: 10.2991/assehr.k.200620.068

Irwin, T., Tonkinwise, C., & Kossoff, G. (2022). Transition design: An educational framework for advancing the study and design of sustainable transitions. Cuadernos del Centrode Estudiosen Disenoy Comunicacion. *Ensayos*, (105), 31–72.

Kadarwati, S., Sulistyarini, I., & Muflikah, B. (2023). Use of Digital Game-Based Learning, Kahoot! to Improve Students' English Expressions Mastery. [Jurnal Ilmu Sosial dan Pendidikan]. *JISIP*, 7(2), 1556–1563.

Kayashima, N. (2022). Japan's ODA for the Development of Higher Education Institutions in Developing Countries: Supporting Leading Universities for Human Resource Development and Knowledge Creation and Diffusion. In *Japan's International Cooperation in Education: History and Prospects* (pp. 197–216). Springer Singapore. DOI: 10.1007/978-981-16-6815-9_9

Keche, K. (2021). Relevancy of new higher education approaches in 'Second Republic Zimbabwe'. Higher Education-New Approaches to Accreditation, Digitalization, and Globalization in the Age of Covid, 1-11.

Khanna, R. (2022). *Dignity in a digital age: Making tech work for all of us*. Simon and Schuster.

Kim, S., Chen, Z. W., Tan, J. Q., & Mussagulova, A. (2021). A case study of the Singapore Skills Future Credit scheme: Preliminary insights for making lifelong learning policy more effective. *Asian Journal of Political Science*, 29(2), 192–214. DOI: 10.1080/02185377.2021.1917431

Kolade, O., & Owoseni, A. (2022). Employment 5.0: The work of the future and the future of work. *Technology in Society*, 71, 102086. DOI: 10.1016/j.techsoc.2022.102086

Larrue, P. (2021). The design and implementation of mission-oriented innovation policies: A new systemic policy approach to address societal challenges.

Lopez-Alcarria, A., Olivares-Vicente, A., & Poza-Vilches, F. (2019). A systematic review of the use of agile methodologies in education to foster sustainability competencies. *Sustainability (Basel)*, 11(10), 2915. DOI: 10.3390/su11102915

Luna Scott, C. (2015). The Futures of Learning 3: What kind of pedagogies for the 21st century? Madlela, B. (2022). Exploring educational technologies used by Mthwakazi University rural satellite campuses to implement distance teacher education programs. *Interdisciplinary Journal of Education Research*, 4, 75–86.

Mamina, M. T., & Maganga, R. (2019). A review of engineering education at the University of Zimbabwe. *American Journal of Engineering Research*, 7(4), 112–128.

Matorevhu, A. (2023). Curriculum innovation implementation for industrialization: A case of education 5.0 pre-service science and mathematics teacher preparation. *Journal of Research in Instructional*, 3(1), 69–86. DOI: 10.30862/jri.v3i1.214

Medina, L. C. (2018). Blended learning: Deficits and prospects in higher education. *Australasian Journal of Educational Technology*, 34(1).

Mishra, L., Gupta, T., & Shree, A. (2020). Online teaching-learning in higher education during the lockdown period of the COVID-19 pandemic. *International Journal of Educational Research Open*, 1, 100012. DOI: 10.1016/j.ijedro.2020.100012 PMID: 35059663

Muiruri, Z. K. (2020). Strategic Business Services and Performance of Firms Sponsored by University Business Incubators in Kenya (Doctoral dissertation, Jkuat-Cohred).

Munirathinam, S. (2020). Industry 4.0: Industrial internet of things (IIOT). []. Elsevier.]. *Advances in Computers*, 117(1), 129–164. DOI: 10.1016/bs.adcom.2019.10.010

Mutambala, M., Sheikheldin, G., Diyamett, B., & Nyichomba, B. (2020, November). Student industrial secondments in East Africa: Improving employability in engineering.

Nilivaara, P., & Soini, T. (2024). Alternative futures of Finnish comprehensive school. *Policy Futures in Education*, 22(3), 308–326. DOI: 10.1177/14782103231173615

Nyaga, J. M. (2023). IoT-Enhanced Adaptive Learning Environments: Personalized Online Education for the Digital Age. [AJCIS]. *African Journal of Computing and Information Systems*, 7(X), 1–14.

Pfafflin, S. M. (2019). *Scientific-technological change and the role of women in development*. Routledge.

Rangraz, M., & Pareto, L. (2021). Workplace work-integrated learning: Supporting industry 4.0 transformation for small manufacturing plants by re-skilling staff. *International Journal of Lifelong Education*, 40(1), 5–22. DOI: 10.1080/02601370.2020.1867249

Razi, A., & Zhou, G. (2022). STEM, iSTEM, and STEAM: What is next? *International Journal of Technology in Education*, 5(1), 1–29. DOI: 10.46328/ijte.119

Reinius, H., Kaukinen, I., Korhonen, T., Juuti, K., & Hakkarainen, K. (2022). Teachers as transformative agents in changing school culture. *Teaching and Teacher Education*, 120, 103888. DOI: 10.1016/j.tate.2022.103888

Sa, M. J., & Serpa, S. (2022). Higher Education as a Promoter of Soft Skills in a Sustainable Society 5.0. *Journal of Curriculum and Teaching*, 11(4), 1–12. DOI: 10.5430/jct.v11n4p1

Secules, S., McCall, C., Mejia, J. A., Beebe, C., Masters, A. S. L., Sánchez-Pena, M., & Svyantek, M. (2021). Positionality practices and dimensions of impact on equity research: A collaborative inquiry and call to the community. *Journal of Engineering Education*, 110(1), 19–43. DOI: 10.1002/jee.20377

Seleviciene, E. (2020). *Effectiveness and acceptance of Web 2.0 technologies in the studies of English for specific purposes in higher education* (Doctoral dissertation, Mykolo Romerio University.)

Shrestha, S. K., & Furqan, F. (2020, November). IoT for smart learning/education. In *2020 5th International Conference on Innovative Technologies in Intelligent Systems and Industrial Applications (CITISIA)* (pp. 1-7). IEEE.

Sifelani, J. (2022). *Science Teachers' Information and Communication Technology (ICT) Self-Efficacy and Classroom Technology Integration: The Case of Manicaland Province, Zimbabwe* (Doctoral dissertation, University of Witwatersrand, Johannesburg).

Stearns, P. N. (2020). *The Industrial Revolution in world history*. Routledge. DOI: 10.4324/9781003050186

Stefan, I., Barkoczi, N., Todorov, T., Peev, I., Pop, L., Marian, C., & Morales, L. (2023, June). Technology and Education as Drivers of the Fourth Industrial Revolution through the Lens of the New Science of Learning. In *International Conference on Human-Computer Interaction* (pp. 133-148). Cham: Springer Nature Switzerland. DOI: 10.1007/978-3-031-34411-4_11

Swanson, R. A. (2022). *Foundations of human resource development*. Berrett-Koehler Publishers.

Tanaka, S., Taguchi, S., Yoshida, K., Cardini, A., Kayashima, N., & Morishita, H. (2019). Transforming education towards equitable quality education to achieve the SDGs. *Policy Brief 2030 AGENDA FOR. Sustainable Development*, (2), 1–11.

Teichler, U. (2019). Higher education and the world of work: Conceptual frameworks, comparative perspectives, empirical findings. In *Higher Education and the World of Work*. Brill.

Tigwell, G. W. (2021, May). Nuanced perspectives toward disability simulations from digital designers, blind, low vision, and colour blind people. In *Proceedings of the 2021 CHI conference on human factors in computing systems* (pp. 1-15).

Veblen, T., & Mayer, O. G. (2022). *Imperial Germany and the Industrial Revolution*. Routledge. DOI: 10.4324/9780429337727

Wirba, A. V. (2021). Transforming Cameroon into a knowledge-based economy (KBE): The role of education, especially higher education. *Journal of the Knowledge Economy*, ●●●, 1–31.

Wuta, R. K. (2022). Extendibility of the Education 5.0 concept to Zimbabwe's secondary school system as encapsulated in curriculum framework 2015-2022. *Ind J Human Social Science*, 3(5), 26–33.

Yingi, E., Hlungwani, P. M., & Nyagadza, B. (2022). The Fourth Industrial Revolution (4IR) at the heart of the SDG agenda: The role of education in Zimbabwe. *African Review (Dar Es Salaam, Tanzania)*, 14(2), 213–229. DOI: 10.1163/09744061-01402001

Zhou, T. M., & Machenjera, P. (2017). Chapter Three Colonialism, Poverty and [Under-] development in Africa. *The African Conundrum: Rethinking the Trajectories of Historical, Cultural, Philosophical and Developmental Experiences of*, 33.

Zinhuku, P. (2022). The dawn of education 5.0 philosophy: Implications on musical arts pedagogics in universities, Zimbabwe.

KET TERMS AND DEFINITIONS

Education 5.0: is a term used to describe a new approach to education that focuses on equipping students with the skills and knowledge needed to thrive in the 21st century.

Innovation: This can be broadly defined as the process of creating or implementing new ideas, methods, or products in a way that adds value and brings about positive change.

Industrialisation: is the process of economic and social change that transforms a society from one based on agriculture and small-scale production to one based on large-scale manufacturing and industry.

Vision 2030: refers to a strategic plan or policy aimed at achieving certain economic, social, or environmental goals by the year 2030.

Digital Age: refers to the period in which digital technologies have become increasingly prevalent and influential in all aspects of society, including communication, work, education, commerce, entertainment, and social interactions.

Industry Partnership: is a collaboration between businesses and organizations from different industries to achieve shared goals and objectives.

Compilation of References

Abazov, R. (2021). Engaging in the internationalization of education and SDGs: A case study on the global hub of UNAI on sustainability. In *E3S Web of Conferences* (Vol. 307, p. 06001). EDP Sciences. DOI: 10.1051/e3sconf/202130706001

Abdel-Motaal, D. (2016). *Antarctica: The battle for the seventh continent*. Praeger. DOI: 10.5040/9798400613272

AbdulCader, A., & Anthony, P. J. AbdulCader. (2014). Motivational Issues of Faculty in Saudi Arabia. *Higher Learning Research Communications*, 4(4), 76–84. DOI: 10.18870/hlrc.v4i4.211

AbdulCalder, A. (2015). A Synthesized Model of Faculty Motivation in Saudi Arabia's Higher Education Sector. In: Hamdan, A.K. (eds) *Teaching and Learning in Saudi Arabia. Sense Publishers*, Rotterdam. https://doi.org/DOI: 10.1007/978-94-6300-205-9_7

Aboramadan, M., Dahleez, K. A., & Farao, C. (2022). Inclusive leadership and extra-role behaviours in higher education: Does organizational learning mediate the relationship? *International Journal of Educational Management*, 36(4), 397–418.

Abouhashem, A., Abdou, R. M., Bhadra, J., Siby, N., Ahmad, Z., & Al-Thani, N. J. 2021. *COVID-19 Inspired a STEM-Based Virtual Learning Model for Middle Schools—A Case Study of Qatar Sustainability. Basel Vol. 13, Iss. 5, (2021): 2799. DOI:DOI: 10.3390/su13052799

Abunar, M. M. (2016). Factors influencing decision making in internal management: evidence from private sector organisations in Saudi Arabia. [Doctoral dissertation, Brunel Business School, Brunel University, London]. Brunel University Research Archive (BURA). https://bura.brunel.ac.uk/handle/2438/13458

Aburizaizah, S. J. (2022). The role of quality assurance in Saudi higher education institutions. *International Journal of Educational Research Open*, 3, 100127. DOI: 10.1016/j.ijedro.2022.100127

Abu-Rumman, A., & Qawasmeh, R. (2022). Assessing international students' satisfaction with a Jordanian university using the service quality model. *Journal of Applied Research in Higher Education*, 14(4), 1742–1760. DOI: 10.1108/JARHE-05-2021-0166

Abu-Shanab, E. A., & Anagreh, L. F. (2020). Contributions of Flipped Classroom Method to Student Learning. *International Journal of Cyber Behavior, Psychology and Learning*, 10(3), 12–30. DOI: 10.4018/IJCBPL.2020070102

Acemoglu, D., & Autor, D. (2012). What does human capital do? A review of Goldin and Katz's The Race between Education and Technology. In *Journal of Economic Literature* (Vol. 50, Issue 2, pp. 426–463). DOI: 10.1257/jel.50.2.426

Acemoglu, D., & Autor, D. (2011). Skills, tasks and technologies: Implications for employment and earnings. In *Handbook of Labor Economics* (Vol. 4). Issue PART B., DOI: 10.1016/S0169-7218(11)02410-5

African American Institute. (2015). State of Education in Africa Report 2015. Retrieved from www.aaionline.org/wp-content/uploads/2015/09/AAI-SOE-report-2015-final.pdf

Aguinis, H. (2011). Organizational responsibility: Doing good and doing well. In Zedeck, S. (Ed.), *Handbook of Industrial and Organisational Psychology*. APA. DOI: 10.1037/12171-024

Ahmad, S., Umirzakova, S., Mujtaba, G., Amin, M. S., & Whangbo, T. (2023). Education 5.0: requirements, enabling technologies, and future directions. *arXiv preprint arXiv:2307.15846*.

Ahmad, M., Salam, A., Abdullah, M., Kumbuha, M. I., Munawar, S., & Khan, M. H. N. (2024). The role of emotional intelligence in educational leadership. *Internatinal Journal of Contemporary Issue in Social Science*, 3(2), 2652–2660.

Ahmad, R., Nawaz, M. R., Ishaq, M. I., Khan, M. M., & Ashraf, H. A. (2023). Social exchange theory: Systematic review and future directions. *Frontiers in Psychology*, 13, 1015921. DOI: 10.3389/fpsyg.2022.1015921 PMID: 36710813

Ahmad, T. (2020). A scenario-based approach to re-imagining the future of higher education which prepares students for the future of work. *Higher Education. Skills and Work-Based Learning*, 10(1), 217–238. DOI: 10.1108/HESWBL-12-2018-0136

Ahmed, A. M., Andersson, L., & Hammarstedt, M. (2012). Does age matter for employability? A field experiment on ageism in the Swedish labour market. *Applied Economics Letters*, 19(4), 403–406. DOI: 10.1080/13504851.2011.581199

Ahmed, M. A. (2016). The Effects of Saudization on the Universities: Localization in Saudi Arabia. *Industry and Higher Education*, 86(86), 25–27. DOI: 10.6017/ihe.2016.86.9373

Aigboje, J., & Abhulimen, J. & Asika, M. (2022). Global trends in technology and its impact on adult education as a catalyst for national growth. *Innovative Journal of Science (ISSN: 2714-3309), 4*(4), 42-52.

Aithal, P. S., & Aithal, S. (2023). Super Innovation in Higher Education by Nurturing Business Leaders through Incubationship. [IJAEML]. *International Journal of Applied Engineering and Management Letters*, 7(3), 142–167. DOI: 10.47992/IJAEML.2581.7000.0192

Akala, B. M. M. (2021). Revisiting education reform in Kenya: A case of Competency Based Curriculum (CBC). *Social Sciences & Humanities Open*, 3(1), 100107. DOI: 10.1016/j.ssaho.2021.100107

Akbar, H., Al-Dajani, H., Ayub, N., & Adeinat, I. (2023). Women's leadership gamut in Saudi Arabia's higher education sector. *Gender, Work and Organization*, 30(5), 1649–1675. DOI: 10.1111/gwao.13003

Akers, B., Cooper, P., & Pitts, J. (2024, May 9). *The federal student loan program is unraveling*. https://www.aei.org/op-eds/the-federal-student-loan-program-is-unraveling/?mkt_tok=NDc1LVBCUS05NzEAAAGTAOsymfw8ijPgQaTBK-GD3olz1kRcVt3B4CvATexiTUw5N0M_d1JvOq-BTDjpW516zMRHZqgc4JwZFRWySsoKyOulV0HQLGPw7OBEzWE7aHt2

Akerson, V. L., Burgess, A., Gerber, A., Guo, M., Khan, T. A., & Newman, S. (2018). Disentangling the meaning of STEM: Implications for science education and science teacher education. *Journal of Science Teacher Education*, 29(1), 1–8. DOI: 10.1080/1046560X.2018.1435063

Akour, I. A., Al-Maroof, R. S., Alfaisal, R. M., & Salloum, S. A. (2022). A conceptual framework for determining metaverse adoption in higher institutions of gulf area: An empirical study using hybrid SEM-ANN approach. *Comput. Educ. Artif. Intell.*, 3, 100052. DOI: 10.1016/j.caeai.2022.100052

Al Ali, M.Y., & Laib, K. (2024). The Using of the Metaverse in the Field of Education and Training in Police Colleges. *International Journal of Educational & Psychological Studies*.

Al Harbi, S., Thursfield, D., & Bright, D. (2017). Culture, Wasta and perceptions of performance appraisal in Saudi Arabia. *International Journal of Human Resource Management*, 28(19), 2792–2810. DOI: 10.1080/09585192.2016.1138987

Al Hashimi, S. (2021). Exploring Effective Practices in Managing Distance Learning for Teaching Art and Design in Bahrain. *International Journal of Learning, Teaching and Educational Research*.

Al Husseiny, F., & Munna, A. S. (Eds.). (2024). *Preparing Students for the Future Educational Paradigm*. IGI Global. DOI: 10.4018/979-8-3693-1536-1

Al Jalfan, Z. (2019). Investigating the strategic alignment of talent management and organisation sustainability in the Saudi higher education sector [Doctoral dissertation, Brunel University, London]. Brunel University Research Archive (BURA). https://bura.brunel.ac.uk/handle/2438/19222

Al Kuwaiti, A., Bicak, H. A., & Wahass, S. (2019). Factors predicting job satisfaction among faculty members of a Saudi higher education institution. *Journal of Applied Research in Higher Education*, 12(2), 296–310. DOI: 10.1108/JARHE-07-2018-0128

Al- Nashif. N. (2017) UNESCO Survey on Intercultural Dialogue. UNESCO UIS

Al Nasser, A. H., & Jais, J. (2022). The Effect of Organizational Culture on Organizational Performance of Saudi Higher Education: The Mediating Role of Human Resource Development. *WSEAS Transactions on Environment and Development*, 18, 777–788. DOI: 10.37394/232015.2022.18.73

Al Neyadi, S., & Al Maamari, F. (2020). An Exploration of the Use of Smart Learning Technology in UAE Schools. *Journal of Information Technology Education: Innovations in Practice*, 19, 257–288.

Al Wali, J., Muthuveloo, R., Teoh, A. P., & Al Wali, W. (2023). Disentangling the relationship between employees' dynamic capabilities, innovative work behavior and job performance in public hospitals. *International Journal of Innovation Science*, 15(2), 368–384. DOI: 10.1108/IJIS-01-2022-0012

Al Zebidi, A. A. (2020). Paths the Saudi Educators in Higher Education Exercise for Professional Development to Use Instructional Technologies. *The Scientific Journal of Faculty of Education in Assiut*, 36(9), 26–53. DOI: 10.21608/mfes.2020.124241

Alabdulaziz, M. S., & Tayfour, E. A. (2023). A Comparative Study of the Effects of Distance Learning and Face-to-Face Learning during the COVID-19 Pandemic on Learning Mathematical Concepts in Primary Students of the Kingdom of Bahrain. *Education Sciences*, 13(2), 133. DOI: 10.3390/educsci13020133

Alabdulkareem, S. A. (2017). Saudi Science Teachers' Perceptions of Implementing Inquiry in Science Class. *Journal of Education and Training Studies*, 5(12), 67–78. DOI: 10.11114/jets.v5i12.2741

Alaeddine, N. I., Parsaei, H. R., Kakosimos, K., Guo, B., & Mansoor, B. (2015, June), *Teaching Innovation with Technology to Accelerate Engineering Students' Learning* Paper presented at 2015 ASEE Annual Conference & Exposition, Seattle, Washington. DOI: 10.18260/p.24815

Álamo-Vera, F. R., Hernández-López, L., Ballesteros-Rodríguez, J. L., & De Saá-Pérez, P. (2020). Competence Development and Employability Expectations: A Gender Perspective of Mobility Programmes in Higher Education. *Administrative Sciences*, 10(3), 74. DOI: 10.3390/admsci10030074

Alanazi, A. (2018). The impact of talent management to achieve sustainable competitive advantage in Saudi Arabia private organizations. *Easy Chair Preprint*. https://easychair.org/publications/preprint_open/VSTf

Alanazi, A. T. (2022). The impact of talent management practices on employees' satisfaction and commitment in the Saudi Arabian oil and gas industry. *International Journal of Advanced and Applied Sciences*, 9(3), 46–55. DOI: 10.21833/ijaas.2022.03.006

Al-Ansi, A. M., Jaboob, M., Garad, A., & Al-Ansi, A. (2023). Analyzing augmented reality (AR) and virtual reality (VR) recent developments in education. *Social Sciences & Humanities Open*, 8(1), 100532. DOI: 10.1016/j.ssaho.2023.100532

Al-Ayed, S., & Al-Tit, A.A. (2021). Factors affecting the adoption of blended learning strategy. *International Journal of Data and Network Science*.

Al-Badi, A.H., Khan, A.I., & Eid-Alotaibi (2022). Perceptions of Learners and Instructors towards Artificial Intelligence in Personalized Learning. *ANT/EDI40*.

Albion, P. (2015). Project-, problem-, and inquiry-based learning. Teaching and digital technologies: Big issues and critical questions, 240.

Aldosari, S. A. M. (2020). The Method of Selecting Academic Leaders at Emerging Saudi Universities and its Relationship to Some Variables. *International Journal of Higher Education*, 9(4), 69–83. DOI: 10.5430/ijhe.v9n4p69

Aldoy, M. (2022). Type Distance Learning During the Corona Pandemic (A sociological analysis of the positive outcomes, challenges, and the coping strategies from the Bahraini family's point of view). *Journal of Umm Al-Qura University for Social Sciences*.

Al-Fraihat, D., Joy, M., Masa'deh, R., & Sinclair, J. (2020). Evaluating e-learning systems success: An empirical study. *Computers in Human Behavior*, 102(1), 67–86. DOI: 10.1016/j.chb.2019.08.004

Algahtani, H., Shirah, B., Alshawwa, L., Tekian, A., & Norcini, J. J. (2020). Factors to be considered in designing a faculty development program for medical education: Local experience from the Western region of Saudi Arabia. *Yeungnam University Journal of Medicine*, 37(3), 210–216. DOI: 10.12701/yujm.2020.00115 PMID: 32311868

Alghamdi, A., Iqbal, S., Trendova, K., Nkasu, M. M., & Al Hajjar, H. (2022). Undergraduate Students' Perspectives on Hybrid Education in the United Arab Emirates. *2022 Advances in Science and Engineering Technology International Conferences (ASET)*, 1-6.

Alghamdi, S.A. (2019). Curriculum Innovation in Selected Saudi Arabia Public Secondary Schools: The Multi-Stakeholder Experience of the Tatweer Project. Published 15 April 2019

Alghamdi, A. K., & El-Hassan, W. S. (2020). Interdisciplinary Inquiry-based Teaching and Learning of Sustainability in Saudi Arabia. *Journal of Teacher Education for Sustainability*, 22(2), 121–139. DOI: 10.2478/jtes-2020-0020

Alhajeri, G. (2022). Changing Behaviours and Its Theories to Achieve the Desire for Entrepreneurship in Future Generations in the UAE and Gulf Region. *International Business Research*, 15(11), 49. DOI: 10.5539/ibr.v15n11p49

Alhalwachi, L.F., Karam, A., & Hamdan, A.M. (2022). The Government Support in Distance Education: Case of Bahrain. *Technologies, Artificial Intelligence and the Future of Learning Post-COVID-19*.

Alharbi, O. A., & Alshahrani, R. S. A. (2023). Instructors' Perceptions of the Training Courses Related to Technology in Saudi Universities. *Advances in Social Sciences Research Journal*, 10(2), 241–247. DOI: 10.14738/assrj.102.14002

Alharbi, S. (2018). Criteria for Performance Appraisal in Saudi Arabia, and Employees Interpretation of These Criteria. *International Journal of Business and Management*, 13(9), 106–117. DOI: 10.5539/ijbm.v13n9p106

Alhazbi, S. (2016). Using flipped classroom approach to teach computer programming. *2016 IEEE International Conference on Teaching, Assessment, and Learning for Engineering (TALE)*, 441-444. DOI: 10.1109/TALE.2016.7851837

Ali, A., & Alourani, A. (2021). An investigation of cloud computing and E-learning for educational advancement. *International Journal of Computer Science & Network Security*, 21(11), 216–222.

Al-Khathlan, M. (2022). Improving Higher Education Administration: A Case Study of Prince Sattam bin Abdulaziz University. *Journal of Educational and Social Research*, 12(4), 104. Advance online publication. DOI: 10.36941/jesr-2022-0100

AlKhunaizi, M. M. (2014). A comparative study of traditional instruction and blended learning in Saudi ARAMCO mathematics courses. *University of Phoenix ProQuest Dissertations Publishing*, 2014, 3648265.

Allen, J., & Van Der Velden{, R. (n.d.). *Educational mismatches versus skill mismatches: effects on wages, job satisfaction, and on-the-job search.*

Allen, L. (2018). Teaching Neuroanatomy Virtually: Integrating an Interactive 3D E-Learning Resource for Enhanced Neuroanatomy Education (Doctoral dissertation, The University of Western Ontario (Canada)).

Allen, N. J., & Grisaffe, D. B. (2001). Employee commitment to the organization and customer reactions: Mapping the linkages. *Human Resource Management Review*, 11(3), 209–236. DOI: 10.1016/S1053-4822(00)00049-8

Al-Madani, F. M. (2015). The Effect of Blended Learning Approach on Fifth Grade Students' Academic Achievement in My Beautiful Language Textbook and the Development of Their Verbal Creative Thinking in Saudi Arabia. *Journal of International Education Research*, 11(4), 253–260.

Almajed, A., Al-Kathiri, F., Al-Ajmi, S., & Alhamlan, S. (2017). 21st Century Professional Skill Training Programs for Faculty Members—A Comparative Study between Virginia Tec University, American University & King Saud University. *Higher Education Studies*, 7(3), 122–131. DOI: 10.5539/hes.v7n3p122

Almazroui, K. M. (2022). Project-Based Learning for 21st-Century Skills: An Overview and Case Study of Moral Education in the UAE. *Social Studies*, 114(3), 125–136. DOI: 10.1080/00377996.2022.2134281

Almazroui, K. M. (2023). Project-based learning for 21st-century skills: An overview and case study of moral education in the UAE. *Social Studies*, 114(3), 125–136.

Almekhlafi, A. G., & Almeqdadi, F. A. (2010). Teachers' perceptions of technology integration in the United Arab Emirates school classrooms. *Journal of Educational Technology & Society*, 13(1), 165–175.

Almuntasheri, S., Gillies, R.M., & Wright, T. (2016). The Effectiveness of a Guided Inquiry-Based, Teachers' Professional Development Programme on Saudi Students' Understanding of Density. *Science education international, 27*, 16-39.

Almuqrin, A., & Mutambik, I. (2021). The explanatory power of social cognitive theory in determining knowledge sharing among Saudi faculty. *PLoS One*, 16(3), e0248275. Advance online publication. DOI: 10.1371/journal.pone.0248275 PMID: 33740001

Alnajim, A. M., Habib, S., Islam, M., AlRawashdeh, H. S., & Wasim, M. (2023). Exploring Cybersecurity education and training techniques: A comprehensive review of traditional, virtual reality, and augmented reality approaches. *Symmetry*, 15(12), 2175. DOI: 10.3390/sym15122175

Alnowibet, K., Abduljabbar, A. S., Ahmad, S., Alqasem, L., Alrajeh, N., Guiso, L., Zaindin, M., & Varanasi, M. (2021). Healthcare Human Resources: Trends and Demand in Saudi Arabia. *Health Care*, 9(8), 955. DOI: 10.3390/healthcare9080955 PMID: 34442091

Alqahtani, M., & Ayentimi, D. T. (2021). The devolvement of HR practices in Saudi Arabian public universities: Exploring tensions and challenges. *Asia-Pacific Management Review*, 26(2), 86–94. DOI: 10.1016/j.apmrv.2020.08.005

Alqasa, K. M. A., & Afaneh, J. A. A. (2022). Active learning techniques and student satisfaction: Role of classroom environment. *Eurasian Journal of Educational Research*, 98(98), 85–100.

Alruwaili, R. (2020). New university system is a first step towards better research.

Alseweed, M. A. (2013). *Students' Achievement and Attitudes Toward Using Traditional Learning*. Blended Learning, and Virtual Classes Learning in Teaching and Learning at the University Level.

Alshaikhmubarak, A., Da Camara, N., & Baruch, Y. (2020). The impact of high-performance human resource practices on the research performance and career success of academics in Saudi Arabia. *Career Development International*, 25(6), 671–690. DOI: 10.1108/CDI-09-2019-0209

Al-Shammari, M.M. (2021). An exploratory study of experiential learning in teaching a supply chain management course in an emerging market economy. *Journal of international business education*.

Al-Shammari, M. M. (2022). An exploratory study of experiential learning in teaching a supply chain management course in an emerging market economy Journal of International Education in Business. *Acton*, 15(2), 184–201. DOI: 10.1108/JIEB-09-2020-0074

Alshammari, R. F. (2022). The Effect of Inquiry-Based Learning Strategy on Developing Saudi Students' Meta-Cognitive Reading Comprehension Skills. *English Language Teaching*, 15(5), 43. DOI: 10.5539/elt.v15n5p43

Alsharif, M. A., Peters, M., & Dixon, T. (2020). Designing and Implementing Effective Campus Sustainability in Saudi Arabian Universities: An Assessment of Drivers and Barriers in a Rational Choice Theoretical Context. *Sustainability (Basel)*, 12(12), 5096. DOI: 10.3390/su12125096

AL-Sinani, Y., & Al Taher, M. (2023). Enhancing teaching skills of physical education teachers in the Sultanate of Oman through augmented reality strategies: A comprehensive feedback-based analysis. *Cogent Social Sciences*, 9(2), 2266253.

Alsughayer, S., & Alsultan, N. (2023). Expectations Gap, Market Skills, and Challenges of Accounting Education in Saudi Arabia. *Journal of accounting finance and auditing studies* (JAFAS), 9(1), 22-60. Doi: .DOI: 10.32602/jafas.2023.002

Alsuhaymi, A. A. A. (2017). An assessment of the participatory role of Saudi university academics in organizational decision-making - a single case study. PhD thesis, University of Leeds.

Alsunaydi, R. (2020). The Relationship Between Department Chairs' Leadership Style and Faculty Members' Job Satisfaction in the College of Education at King Saud University in Saudi Arabia. Theses & Dissertations, 381. https://athenaeum.uiw.edu/uiw_etds/381

Altbach, P. G., Reisberg, L., & Rumbley, L. E. (2019). *Trends in global higher education: Tracking an academic revolution*. Brill.

Altschuler, G. (2009). *The GI Bill: A new deal for veterans*. Oxford University Press. DOI: 10.1093/oso/9780195182286.001.0001

Alyami, H. (2016). A case study of the Tatweer school system in Saudi Arabia: the perceptions of leaders and teachers. 2016.

Alzghaibi, H. A. (2023). The gap between bachelor's degree graduates in health informatics and employer needs in Saudi Arabia. *BMC Medical Education*, 23(1), 475. DOI: 10.1186/s12909-023-04442-7 PMID: 37365545

Alzoraiki, M., Rahman, O. B., & Mutalib, M. A. (2018). The effect of the dimensions of transformational leadership on the teachers' performance in the Yemeni public schools. *European Scientific Journal*, 14(25). Advance online publication. DOI: 10.19044/esj.2018.v14n25p322

Amalia, B., Yuliati, Y., & Kholifah, S. (2022). Perubahan Peran Perempuan Pada Sektor Pertanian di Desa Tandawang. *Jurnal Ilmu Sosial dan Humaniora Vol. 11, No. 1. DOI: http://dx.doi.org/*DOI: 10.23887/jish.v11i1.36899

Ambos, B., Brandl, K., Perri, A., Scalera, V. G., & Van Assche, A. (2021). The nature of innovation in global value chains. *Journal of World Business*, 56(4), 101221. DOI: 10.1016/j.jwb.2021.101221

Ameen, K., & Gorman, G. E. (2009). Information and digital literacy: A stumbling block to development? A Pakistan perspective. *Library Management*, 30(1/2), 99–112. DOI: 10.1108/01435120910927565

Amey, M. J., & Eddy, P. L. (2023). *Creating strategic partnerships: A guide for educational institutions and their partners*. Taylor & Francis.

Anas, A. (2020). *Perceptions of Saudi Students to Blended Learning Environments at the University of Bisha*. Arab World English Journal. DOI: 10.24093/awej/call6.17

Anderson, C. O. P. J., Keltner, D., & Kring, A. M. (2001). Who attains social status? Effects of personality and physical attractiveness in social groups. *Journal of Personality and Social Psychology*, 81(1), 116–132. DOI: 10.1037/0022-3514.81.1.116 PMID: 11474718

Anderson-Levitt, K., & Gardinier, M. P. (2021). Introduction contextualising global flows of competency-based education: Polysemy, hybridity, and silences. *Comparative Education*, 57(1), 1–18. DOI: 10.1080/03050068.2020.1852719

Andreoni, A., & Tregenna, F. (2020). Escaping the middle-income technology trap: A comparative analysis of industrial policies in China, Brazil, and South Africa. *Structural Change and Economic Dynamics*, 54, 324–340. DOI: 10.1016/j.strueco.2020.05.008

Andreu-Perez, J., Deligianni, F., Ravi, D., & Yang, G. Z. (2018). Artificial Intelligence and Robotics. *arXiv preprint arXiv:1803.10813*.

Ansu-Kyeremeh, E. K., & Goosen, L. (2022). Exploring the Socioeconomic Facet of Online Inclusive Education in Ghana: The Effects of Technological Advancement in Academia. In Garcia, M. (Ed.), *Socioeconomic Inclusion During an Era of Online Education* (pp. 47–66). IGI Global., DOI: 10.4018/978-1-6684-4364-4.ch003

Anwar, S., Chandio, J. A., Ashraf, M., Bhutto, S. A., Anwar, S., Chandio, J. A., & Bhutto, S. A. (2021). Does transformational leadership affect employees' commitment? A mediation analysis of perceived organizational support using VB-SEM. *International Journal of Disaster Recovery and Business Continuity*, 12, 734–746.

Appiah, S. (2024). Challenges Learners Face in Using the Flipped Classroom Model in the Teaching and Learning of Religious and Moral Education in the Nzema East Municipality of the Western Region of Ghana. *Universal Journal of Social Sciences and Humanities*, 12-19.

Arnold, K. A. (2017). Transformational leadership and employee psychological well-being: A review and directions for future research. *Journal of Occupational Health Psychology*, 22(3), 381–393. DOI: 10.1037/ocp0000062 PMID: 28150998

Arruda, E. P., & Arruda, D. P. (2024). Artificial intelligence for SDG 4 of the 2030 agenda: Transforming education to achieve quality, equality, and inclusion. *Sustainable Economies*, 2(2), 34–34. DOI: 10.62617/se.v2i2.34

Aseeri, M. M., & Kang, K. A. (2023). Organisational culture and big data socio-technical systems on strategic decision making: Case of Saudi Arabian higher education. *Education and Information Technologies*, 28(7), 8999–9024. DOI: 10.1007/s10639-022-11500-y

Asiati, D., Aji, G. B., Ngadi, T., Ningrum, V., Kurniawan, F. E., Aruan, N. L., & Purba, Y. E. (2019). *UMKM dalam era transformasi digital*. Yayasan Pustaka Obor Indonesia.

Asiri, A. (2018). Scientific Inquiry-Based Teaching Practices as Perceived by Science Teachers. *American Journal of Educational Research*, 6(4), 297–307. DOI: 10.12691/education-6-4-2

Askary, Z., Singh, A., Gupta, S., Shukla, R. K., & Jaiswal, P. (2019). Development of AHP Framework of Sustainable Product Design and Manufacturing of Electric Vehicle. In Prasad, A., Gupta, S. S., & Tyagi, R. K. (Eds.), *Advances in Engineering Design* (pp. 415–422). Springer Singapore. DOI: 10.1007/978-981-13-6469-3_37

Asoodar, M., Marandi, S. S., Atai, M. R., & Vaezi, S. (2014). Learner reflections in virtual vs. blended EAP classes. *Computers in Human Behavior*, 41, 533–543. DOI: 10.1016/j.chb.2014.09.050

Association to Advance Collegiate Schools of Business. (2021). *2021 Business school data guide*. Association to Advance Collegiate Schools of Business. https://www.aacsb.edu/-/media/publications/research-reports/2021-business-school-data-guide-october-release.pdf?rev=9f0506585b4d4dde9808e9ec4a19fd97&hash=34E7F0BE92B1074F04FCC67C008FA095

Association to Advance Collegiate Schools of Business. (2022a). *2020 Guiding principles and standards for business accreditation*. Association to Advance Collegiate Schools of Business. https://www.aacsb.edu/-/media/documents/accreditation/2020-aacsb-business-accreditation-standards-jul-1-2022.pdf?rev=b40ee40b26a14d4185c504d00bade58f&hash=9B649E9B8413DFD660C6C2AFAAD10429

Association to Advance Collegiate Schools of Business. (2022b). *2020 Interpretive guidance for AACSB accreditation*. Association to Advance Collegiate Schools of Business. https://www.aacsb.edu/-/media/documents/accreditation/2020-interpretive-guidance-july-2021.pdf?rev=e9ca74d1736749f2a5ae3e5b0b7854bd&hash=29EC7DF1790D9161F5FF24640028FCD4

Association to Advance Collegiate Schools of Business. (2022c). *2022 State of accreditation report*. Association to Advance Collegiate Schools of Business. https://www.aacsb.edu/insights/reports/2022-state-of-accreditation-report

Atwa, S., Gauci-Mansour, V. J., Thomson, R., & Hegazi, I. (2019). Team-based and case-based learning: A hybrid pedagogy model enhancing students' academic performance and experiences at first-year tertiary level. *Australian Educational Researcher*, 46(1), 93–112. DOI: 10.1007/s13384-018-0282-y

Aung, P. N., & Hallinger, P. (2023). Research on sustainability leadership in higher education: A scoping review. *International Journal of Sustainability in Higher Education*, 24(3), 517–534. DOI: 10.1108/IJSHE-09-2021-0367

Awidi, I. T., & Paynter, M. (2019). The impact of a flipped classroom approach on student learning experience. *Computers & Education*, 128, 269–283. DOI: 10.1016/j.compedu.2018.09.013

Ayat, M., Imran, M., Ullah, A., & Kang, C. W. (2021). Current trend analysis and prioritization of success factors: Asystematic literature review of ICT projects. *International Journal of Managing Projects in Business*, 14(3), 652–679. DOI: 10.1108/IJMPB-02-2020-0075

Aykan, A., & Yıldırım, B. (2022). The integration of a lesson study model into distance STEM education during the COVID-19 pandemic: Teachers' views and practice. Technology. *Knowledge and Learning*, 27(2), 609–637. DOI: 10.1007/s10758-021-09564-9

Baesu, C. (2018). Leadership Based on emotional intelligence in modern organisations. *The USV Annals of Economic and Public Administration*, 2(28), 73–78.

Baesu, C., & Bejinaru, R. (2015). Innovative Leadership Style and the influence of Emotional Intelligence. *The USV Annals of Economic and Public Administration*, 15, 136–145.

Bahrain Education & Labour Market Report. 2023. Fitch Solutions Group Limited. 2882036764. http://ezproxy.hct.ac.ae/login?url=https://www.proquest.com/reports/bahrain-education-amp-labour-report-01-june-2023/docview/2882036764/se-2?accountid=1215

Bakheet, S., & Almudara, M. (2019). Maximizing Return on Investment in the Human Capital of Faculty Members in Saudi Universities. *European Journal of Management*, 19(2), 80–93. DOI: 10.18374/EJM-19-2.7

Bakhtiari, S., & Shajar, H. (2006). Globalization and education: Challenges and opportunities. [IBER]. *The International Business & Economics Research Journal*, 5(2). Advance online publication. DOI: 10.19030/iber.v5i2.3461

Bangura, M. (2023). Sociology learning curriculum for sustainable development: The Sierra Leone rural and urban social observation. *Development*, 6(3), 37–51.

Banumathi, M. (2015). *An Engineering Employability Skill Assessment Framework for Indian Graduates*.

Barakabitze, A. A., William-Andey Lazaro, A., Ainea, N., Mkwizu, M. H., Maziku, H., Matofali, A. X., Iddi, A., & Sanga, C. (2019). Transforming African education systems in science, technology, engineering, and mathematics (STEM) using ICTs: Challenges and opportunities. *Education Research International*, 2019(1), 6946809. DOI: 10.1155/2019/6946809

Bardhan, N., & Gower, K. (2022). *The role of leadership in building inclusive diversity in public relations*. Taylor & Francis. DOI: 10.4324/9781003170020

Barkoczi, N., Maier, M. L., & Horvat-Marc, A. (2024). The Impact of Artificial Intelligence on Personalized Learning in STEM Education. In *inted2024 Proceedings* (pp. 4980-4989). IATED. DOI: 10.21125/inted.2024.1289

Barret, M. (2012) The Intercultural City Step by Step Council of Europe Publication Intercultural Competence (EWC Statement Series 2nd Issue p3)

Bartlett, W. (n.d.). *Skill Mismatch, Education Systems and Labour Markets in EU Neighbourhood Policy Countries Goodbye Tito: The Role of Diverging Welfare State Trajectories on Income Inequality in Four Former Yugoslav Republics View project Higher education and the graduate labour market in the Western Balkans View project*. https://www.researchgate.net/publication/258286624

Barut Tugtekin, E. (2023). Scrutinizing Learning Management Systems in Practice: An Applied Time Series Research in Higher Education. *International Review of Research in Open and Distance Learning*, 24(2), 53–71. DOI: 10.19173/irrodl.v24i2.6905

Bashman, J. D., Israel, M., & Maynard, K. (2010). An ecological model of STEM education: Operationalizing STEM FOR ALL. *Journal of Special Education Technology*, 23(3), 10–19.

Bastable, S. B. (2021). *Nurse as educator: Principles of teaching and learning for nursing practice*. Jones & Bartlett Learning.

BBC News. (2021, March 25). Nationwide tells 13,000 staff to 'work anywhere'. BBC. https://www.bbc.com/ news/business–56510574

Bean, J. C., & Melzer, D. (2021). *Engaging ideas: The professor's guide to integrating writing, critical thinking, and active learning in the classroom*. John Wiley &Sons.

Becker, G. (1976). *The Economic Approach to Human Behaviour*. The University of Chicago Press. DOI: 10.7208/chicago/9780226217062.001.0001

Bedekovic, V. (2017). Intercultural education in the function of European values promotion. *Informatologia*, 50, 74–86.

Beechler, S., Beechler, S., & Woodward, I. C.. (2009). The global "war for talent". 15(3), 273–285. https://doi.org/DOI: 10.1016/j.intman.2009.01.002

Belkin, D. (2022, July 20). Broke colleges resort to mergers for survival. *Wall Street Journal, Eastern edition*, A.1.

Belkin, D. (2024, January 20). Why Americans have lost faith in the value of college: Three generations of "college for all" in the U.S. has left most families looking for alternatives. *Wall Street Journal*. https://www.wsj.com/us-news/education/why-americans-have-lost-faith-in-the-value-of-college-b6b635f2

Bell, R. (2016). Unpacking the link between entrepreneurialism and employability: An assessment of the relationship between entrepreneurial attitudes and likelihood of graduate employment in a professional field. *Education + Training*, 58(1), 2–17. DOI: 10.1108/ET-09-2014-0115

Bender, W. N. (2012). *Project-based learning: Differentiating instruction for the 21st century*. Corwin Press.

Bennett, M. J. (2017) Constructive Approach to Intercultural Communication. Wiley Online Library Bortini, P. and Motamed-Ashari (2013) Intercultural Competency Research Report SALTO-YOUTH Bouchard, G. (2011) What is Interculturalism? McGilLaw Journal56 (2) 435-468

Berdiyeva, S. (2024). Exploring Innovative Approaches to Teaching. *Modern Science and Research, 3*(1), 923–927. Retrieved from https://inlibrary.uz/index.php/science-research/article/view/28552

Berger, G. (2019). Needs Assessment Lessons Learned in Qatar: A Flipped Classroom Approach. *MedEdPublish*, ●●●, 8. PMID: 38089336

Bergeron, J., & Fryer, L. (2023, November 16). *Credential transparency: Judging return on investment for higher education and workforce*. https://www.aei.org/research-products/report/credential-transparency-judging-return-on-investment-for-higher-education-and-workforce/

Beribe, M. F. B. (2023). The Impact of Globalization on Content and Subjects in the Curriculum in Madrasah Ibtidaiyah: Challenges and Opportunities. *At-Tasyrih: jurnal pendidikan dan hukum. Der Islam*, 9(1), 54–68.

Bernstein, I. (1996). *Guns or butter: The presidency of Lyndon Johnson.* Oxford University Press.

Berntson, E., Sverke, M., & Marklund, S. (2006). Predicting perceived employability: Human capital or labour market opportunities? *Economic and Industrial Democracy*, 27(2), 223–244. DOI: 10.1177/0143831X06063098

Berson, Y., & Oreg, S. (2016). The role of school principals in shaping children's values. Psychological science: Research, theory, & application in psychology and related sciences, 27(12), 1539-1549

Bhopal, K. (2018). *White privilege: The myth of a post-racial society.* Policy Press.

Bhopal, K. (2023). 'We can talk the talk, but we're not allowed to walk the walk': The role of equality and diversity staff in higher education institutions in England. *Higher Education*, 85(2), 325–339. DOI: 10.1007/s10734-022-00835-7

Bhopal, K., & Pitkin, C. (2020). 'Same old story, just a different policy': Race and policy making in higher education in the UK. *Race, Ethnicity and Education*, 23(4), 530–547. DOI: 10.1080/13613324.2020.1718082

Bhutoria, A. (2022). Personalized education and artificial intelligence in the United States, China, and India: A systematic review using a human-in-the-loop model. *Computers and Education: Artificial Intelligence*, 3, 100068. DOI: 10.1016/j.caeai.2022.100068

Biea, E. A., Dinu, E., Bunica, A., & Jerdea, L. (2023). Recruitment in SMEs: The role of managerial practices, technology and innovation. *European Business Review*.

Bilgin, A. S., Molina Ascanio, M., & Minoli, M. (2022). *STEM Goes digital: how can technology enhance STEM Teaching?* European Observatory.

Bilimoria, D., & Singer, L. T. (2019). Institutions developing excellence in academic leadership (IDEAL): A partnership to advance gender equity, diversity, and inclusion in academic STEM. *Equality, Diversity and Inclusion*, 38(3), 362–381. DOI: 10.1108/EDI-10-2017-0209

Bi, M., Zhao, Z., Yang, J., & Wang, Y. (2019). Comparison of case-based learning and traditional method in teaching postgraduate students of medical oncology. *Medical Teacher*, 41(10), 1124–1128. DOI: 10.1080/0142159X.2019.1617414 PMID: 31215320

Bin Othayman, M., Meshari, A., Mulyata, J., & Debrah, Y. A. (2021). Challenges Experienced by Public Higher Education Institutions of Learning in the Implementation of Training and Development: A Case Study of Saudi Arabian Higher Education. *Journal of Business Administration Research*, 10(2), 36. Advance online publication. DOI: 10.5430/jbar.v10n2p36

Binoy, S. (2024). Transforming Education: Enhancing Student Performance and Satisfaction through the Flipped Classroom Method. *American Journal of Education and Technology*, 3(1), 35–45. DOI: 10.54536/ajet.v3i1.2121

Black, A. (2020). Marching to the beat of different drum: Royalty, women and ideology in the Sultanate of Brunei Darussalam. *Royal Studies Journal*, 7(2), 94–116. DOI: 10.21039/rsj.269

Blackrock Investment Institute. (2020, June). *Blackrock Investment Institute, Global Investor Pulse 2019*. From https://investorpolis.com/blackrock-investment-institute -global-investor-pulse-2019-2/?lang=en

Blasko, Z., Brennan, J., Little, B., & Shah, T. (2002). Access to what : analysis of factors determining graduate employability. *Higher Education Funding Council for England, November*, 1–8. http://www.demografia.hu/en/downloads/Publications/ Blasko-etal-Graduate-Employability.pdf

Blinder, A. (1973). Wage Discrimination: Reduced Form and Structural Estimates. *The Journal of Human Resources*, 8(4), 436–455. DOI: 10.2307/144855

Blodger, I. (2016). Reclassifying geostationary earth orbit as private property: Why natural law and utilitarian theories of property demand privatization. *Minnesota Journal of Law, Science & Technology*, 17(1), 408–440.

Blom, A., & Saeki, H. (2010). *Employability and Skill Set of Newly Graduated Engineers in India*.

Bloom, E. T. (Winter 2022). The rising importance of non-Arctic states in the Arctic. *The Wilson Quarterly*. https://www.wilsonquarterly.com/quarterly/the-new-north/the-rising-importance-of-non-arctic-states-in-the-arctic

Blount, P. J., & Robison, C. (2016, December). One small step: The impact of the U.S. commercial space launch competitiveness act of 2015 on the exploitation of resources in outer space. *North Carolina Journal of Law & Technology*, 8(2), 160–186.

Boelt, A. M., Kolmos, A., & Holgaard, J. E. (2022). Literature review of students' perceptions of generic competence development in problem-based learning in engineering education. *European Journal of Engineering Education*, 47(6), 1399–1420. DOI: 10.1080/03043797.2022.2074819

Boggs, K., Sobiech, K., & Tripp, J. (2021). The pandemic pivot: A case study of a university's rapid shift to fully online instruction. *Journal of Online Learning and Teaching*, 17(2), 221–235.

Bolden, R., Petrov, G., Gosling, J., & Bryman, A. (2009). Leadership in higher education: Facts, fictions, and futures — Introduction to the special issue. *Leadership*, 5(3), 291–298. DOI: 10.1177/1742715009337761

Bon, A., Saa-Dittoh, F., & Akkermans, H. (2023). Bridging the digital divide. In *Introduction to Digital Humanism: A Textbook* (pp. 283–298). Springer Nature Switzerland.

Bonilla, M. A. B., Soria, E. E. A., Chinga, A. E. P., & Cabeza, B. M. Q. (2023). Systems and Social Dynamics in the Rural City of La Concordia: Strengths and Weaknesses Related to Its Development at the beginning of the 21st Century. *Journal of Business and Economic Development*, 8(2), 48–55. DOI: 10.11648/j.jbed.20230802.13

Bonsay, J. O., Cruz, A. P., Firozi, H. C., & Camaro, P. J. C. (2021). Artificial intelligence and labor productivity paradox: The economic impact of AI in China, India, Japan, and Singapore. *Journal of Economics. Finance and Accounting Studies*, 3(2), 120–139. DOI: 10.32996/jefas.2021.3.2.13

Booker, D. L., & Williams, M. R. (2022). An inclusive leadership model insights from the tech industry. *Advances in Developing Human Resources*, 24(4), 263–274. DOI: 10.1177/15234223221118955

Borhaug, B. F., & Weyringer, S. (2019). Developing critical and empathetic capabilities in intercultural education through the VaKE approach. *Intercultural Education*, 30, 1–14.

Borich, G. D. (2017). *Effective Teaching Methods. Research-Based Practice* (9th ed.). Pearson.

Bornman, D. (2019). Gender-Based Leadership Perceptions and Preferences of Generation Z as Future Business Leaders in South Africa. *Africa'. Acta Commercii*, 19(1), a708. DOI: 10.4102/ac.v19i1.708

Boso, C. M., van der Merwe, A. S., & Gross, J. (2020). Critical thinking skills of nursing students: Observations of classroom instructional activities. *Nursing Open*, 7(2), 581–588. DOI: 10.1002/nop2.426 PMID: 32089855

Boss, S., & Krauss, J. (2022). *Reinventing project-based learning: Your field guide to real-world projects in the digital age*. International Society for Technology in Education.

Bossu, C., Iniesto, F., Vladimirschi, V., Jordan, K., & Pete, J. (2023). GO-GN Guidelines for Equity Diversity and Inclusion in Open Education with a focus on Africa and Latin America.

Boston College, The Center for Teaching Excellence. (2024, March 15). *Active learning classroom*. https://cteresources.bc.edu/documentation/active-learning-classroom/

Böttcher, K., Albrecht, A. G., Venz, L., & Felfe, J. (2018). Protecting older workers' employability: A survey study of the role of transformational leadership. *German Journal of Human Resource Management*, 32(2), 120–148. DOI: 10.1177/2397002218763001

Bourke, J., Titus, A., & Espedido, A. (2020). The key to inclusive leadership. *Harvard Business Review*, ●●●, 6.

Bovill, C. (2020). Co-creation in learning and teaching: The case for a whole-class approach in higher education. *Higher Education*, 79, 1023–1037. DOI: 10.1007/s10734-019-00453-w

Bower, G. (2018) The Influence of Emotional Intelligence on Overall Success of Campus leader as Perceived by Veteran Teachers in Rural mid-sized East Texas Public School District, Lamar University. International Counsel of Professors of Education.

Boykov, V., & Goceva, M. (2018). *Training Through Action To Build Professional Skills*. Knowledge International Journal. DOI: 10.35120/kij2803849V

BPS. (2023). *Keadaan Angkatan Kerja Indonesia Agustus 2023*. BPS.

Brammer, S., Millington, A., & Pavelin, S. (2009). Corporate reputation and women on the board. *British Journal of Management*, 20(1), 17–29. DOI: 10.1111/j.1467-8551.2008.00600.x

Branch, J. D., & Christiansen, B. (Eds.). (2021). *The Marketisation of Higher Education: Concepts, Cases, and Criticisms*. Springer Nature. Retrieved from https://link.springer.com/book/10.1007/978-3-030-67441-0#about-this-book

Brenan, M. (2023, July 11). *Americans' confidence in higher education down sharply.* https://news.gallup.com/poll/508352/americans-confidence-higher-education-down-sharply.aspx

Breum, M. (21 December 2022). Canada extends its Arctic Ocean seabed claim all the way to Russian waters. *Arctic Today*. https://www.arctictoday.com/canada-extends-its-arctic-ocean-seabed-claim-all-the-the-way-to-russian-waters

Brief, A. P., & George, J. M. (2020). Psychological stress and the workplace: A brief comment on Lazarus' outlook. In *Occupational stress* (pp. 15–19). CRC Press. DOI: 10.1201/9781003072430-3

Brink, H., & Van der Walt, C. (2018). *Fundamentals of research methodology for health care professionals*. Juta and Company Ltd.

Brint, S. (2024, March 6). Trump and his allies are preparing to overhaul higher education. *The Chronicle of Higher Education*. https://www-chronicle-com.electra.lmu.edu/article/if-trump-wins

Broo, D. G., Kaynak, O., & Sait, S. M. (2022). Rethinking engineering education at the age of Industry 5.0. *Journal of Industrial Information Integration*, 25, 100311. DOI: 10.1016/j.jii.2021.100311

Brookfield, S. D. (2005). *The Power of Critical Theory: Liberating Adult Learning and Teaching*. John Wiley & Sons, Inc.

Brown. https://www.mayerbrown.com/en/perspectives-events/publications/2020/05/one-small-step-for-property-rights-in-outer-space

Brown, A. L., & Palincsar, A. S. (2018). Guided, cooperative learning and individual knowledge acquisition. In *Knowing, learning, and instruction* (pp. 393–451). Routledge. DOI: 10.4324/9781315044408-13

Bryant, J., Golden, R., & Jefferson, I. (2023). *Higher ed is consolidating, transforming the sector.* https://www.mckinsey.com/industries/education/our-insights/higher-ed-is-consolidating-transforming-the-sector

Bryman, A., & Lilley, S. (2009). Leadership researchers on leadership in higher education. *Leadership*, 5(3), 331–346. DOI: 10.1177/1742715009337764

Buil-Fabrega, M., Martinez Casanovas, M., Ruiz-Munzon, N., & Filho, W. L. (2019). Flipped classroom as an active learning methodology in sustainable development curricula. *Sustainability (Basel)*, 11(17), 4577. DOI: 10.3390/su11174577

Bunkowske. E.W. (2002) EWB/MS/MCCC/0205693. The Cultural onion Defined

Burghardt, M., Ferdinand, P., Pfeiffer, A., Reverberi, D., & Romagnoli, G. (2021). Integration of new technologies and alternative methods in laboratory-based scenarios. In Cross Reality and Data Science in Engineering: Proceedings of the 17th International Conference on Remote Engineering and Virtual Instrumentation 17 (pp. 488-507). Springer International Publishing. DOI: 10.1007/978-3-030-52575-0_40

Burkinshaw, P., & White, K. (2020). Generation, Gender, and Leadership: Metaphors and Images. *Frontiers in Education*, 5, 517497. DOI: 10.3389/feduc.2020.517497

Burnett, N., & Jayaram, S. (2012). *Innovative Secondary Education for Skills Enhancement: Skills for Employability in Africa and Asia.* Results for Development Institute., https://www.r4d.org/.../InnovativeSecondaryEducationSkillsEnhancement-PhaseI-Syn

Butler, S. O. (1977, Spring/Summer). Owning Antarctica: Cooperation and jurisdiction at the South Pole. *Journal of International Affairs*, 31(1), 35–51.

Buxton, C. (2004). Property in outer space: The common heritage of mankind principle vs. the 'First in time, first in right' rule of property law. *Journal of Air Law and Commerce*, 69(4), 689–707.

Byers, M. (2013). *International law and the Arctic*. Cambridge University Press. DOI: 10.1017/CBO9781107337442

Cabonero, D. A., Austria, R. M., & Ramel, R. D. (2023). *Enhancing the Master of Library and Information Science Curriculum Towards the Improvement of the Librarian's 21st Century Skills in the Workplace.* Library Philosophy & Practice.

Calhoun, J. M. D. (2015). *WHAT PREDICTS SKILLS MISMATCH IN CANADA?* Chavan, R. R. (2017). *Construct Validity of Employability skills for Graduate through Factor Analysis. 19*(9), 14–21. https://doi.org/DOI: 10.9790/487X-1909071421

Campbell, J. W. (2018). Efficiency, incentives, and transformational leadership: Understanding collaboration preferences in the public sector. *Public Performance & Management Review*, 41(2), 277–299. DOI: 10.1080/15309576.2017.1403332

Campbell, R. (2023). *The Evolution of The Gender Gap?* National Centre for Social Research.

Cantle, T. (2016) Interculturalism: The New Era of Cohesion and Diversity: Palgrave Macmillan

Cantle, T. (2016) The Case For Interculturalism, Plural Identities and Cohesion Edinburgh University Press

Cantwell, B. (2024, January 24). The left's contradictory goals for higher ed. *The Chronicle of Higher Education*https://www.chronicle.com/article/the-lefts-contradictory-goals-for-higher-ed

Cao, J., Zhang, D., Chanajaree, R., Luo, D., Yang, X., Zhang, X., & Qin, J. (2024). A low-cost separator enables a highly stable zinc anode by accelerating the de-solvation effect. *Chemical Engineering Journal*, 480, 147980. DOI: 10.1016/j.cej.2023.147980

Cappelli, P. (2014). *Skill gaps, skill shortages, and skill mismatches: Evidence for the US (No. w20382)*. National Bureau of Economic Research. DOI: 10.3386/w20382

Cappelli, P. H. (2015). Skill gaps, skill shortages, and skill mismatches: Evidence and arguments for the United States. *Industrial & Labor Relations Review*, 68(2), 251–290. DOI: 10.1177/0019793914564961

Carayannis, E. G., & Morawska-Jancelewicz, J. (2022). The futures of Europe: Society 5.0 and Industry 5.0 as driving forces of future universities. *Journal of the Knowledge Economy*, 13(4), 3445–3471. DOI: 10.1007/s13132-021-00854-2

Caricati, L., Chiesa, R., Guglielmi, D., & Mariani, M. G. (2016). Real and perceived employability: A comparison among Italian graduates. *Journal of Higher Education Policy and Management*, 38(4), 490–502. DOI: 10.1080/1360080X.2016.1182668

Carlson, S. (2024, February 6). What's really behind the view that higher ed isn't worth it? *The Chronicle of Higher Education*https://www.chronicle.com/article/whats-really-behind-the-view-that-higher-ed-isnt-worth-it

Carmeli, A., Reiter-Palmon, R., & Ziv, E. (2010). Inclusive leadership and employee involvement in creative tasks in the workplace: The mediating role of psychological safety. *Creativity Research Journal*, 22(3), 250–260. DOI: 10.1080/10400419.2010.504654

Carr, D., & Bodnar-Deren, S. (2009). Gender, Aging and Widowhood. In *International Handbook of Population Aging* (pp. 705–728). Springer Science and Business Media., DOI: 10.1007/978-1-4020-8356-3_32

Castro, D. R., Anseel, F., Kluger, A. N., Lloyd, K. J., & Turjeman-Levi, Y. (2018). Mere listening effect on creativity and the mediating role of psychological safety. *Psychology of Aesthetics, Creativity, and the Arts*, 12(4), 489–502. DOI: 10.1037/aca0000177

Ch, A. H., Ahmad, S., Malik, M., & Batool, A. (2017). Principals' leadership styles and teachers' job satisfaction: A correlation study at secondary level. Bulletin of Education & Research, 39(3), 45-56. Retrieved from Dbake, D, (2016). Impact of Leader's emotional Intelligence and transformative behavior on perceived leadership effectiveness. A multiple source view. *Business Perspectives and Research*, 4(1), 27–40.

Chan, C. K. Y. (2023). A review of the changes in higher education assessment and grading policy during COVID-19. *Assessment & Evaluation in Higher Education*, 48(6), 874–887. DOI: 10.1080/02602938.2022.2140780

Charalampous, C. A., & Papademetriou, C. D. (2019). Intermediate inverted leadership: The inclusive leader's model. *International Journal of Leadership in Education*.

Chen, H. (2024). The ethical challenges of educational artificial intelligence and coping measures: A discussion in the context of the 2024 World Digital Education Conference. *Science Insights Education Frontiers, 20*(2), 3263-3281.

Chen, B., Bastedo, K., & Howard, W. (2018). Exploring design elements for online STEM courses: Active learning, engagement & assessment design. *Online Learning : the Official Journal of the Online Learning Consortium*, 2018(22), 59–75.

Chen, J., Kolmos, A., & Du, X. (2021). Forms of implementation and challenges of PBL in engineering education: A review of literature. *European Journal of Engineering Education*, 46(1), 90–115. DOI: 10.1080/03043797.2020.1718615

Chen, J., & Yin, X. (2019). Connotation and types of innovation. In *The Routledge companion to innovation management* (pp. 26–54). Routledge. DOI: 10.4324/9781315276670-3

Chen, L., Chen, P., & Lin, Z. (2020). Artificial Intelligence in Education: A Review. *IEEE Access : Practical Innovations, Open Solutions*, 8, 75264–75278. DOI: 10.1109/ACCESS.2020.2988510

Chhinzer, N., & Russo, A. A. (2018). An exploration of employer perceptions of graduate student employability. *Education + Training, 60*(1), 104–120. https://doi .org/https://doi.org/10.1108/ ET-06-2016-0111

Chiriac, A. Trebes, (2015) T Particularities of training teachers in higher education from an intercultural perspective State University of Medicine and Pharmacy of Republic of Moldova

Chiriac, A., & Panciuc, L. (2015). *New Perspectives in Science Education* (4th ed.).

Chitate, H. (2016). Science, Technology, Engineering and Mathematics (STEM): A Case Study of Zimbabwe's Education Approach to Industrialisation. *World Journal of Education*, 6(5), 27–35. DOI: 10.5430/wje.v6n5p27

Chiu, M. L., & Lin, C. N. (2022). Developing supply chain open innovation capability: The mediating role of the knowledge creation process, governance mechanism and technology as a driver. *Journal of Innovation & Knowledge*, 7(4), 100264. DOI: 10.1016/j.jik.2022.100264

Chiva Long, R. S., Ny, C., Chhang, C., Ren, R., Ngork, C., Sorn, R., Sorn, M. & Sor, C. (2024). The Impact of Assessment for 21st Century Skills in Higher Education Institutions: A Narrative Literature Review.

Chong, W. S., Oxley, E., Negrea, V., Bond, M., Liu, Q., & Sum Kong, M. (n.d.). *February 2024 Teacher recruitment and retention in schools in socio-economically disadvantaged areas in England-review of practice.* www.educationendowment foundation.org.uk

Chowdhury, R. (2015). Learning and teaching style assessment for improving project-based learning of engineering students: A case of United Arab Emirates University. *Australasian Journal of Engineering Education*, 20(1), 81–94. DOI: 10.7158/D13-014.2015.20.1

Christiansen, B., & Even, A. M. (Eds.). (2024). *Prioritizing Skills Development for Student Employability*. IGI Global., Retrieved from https://www.igi-global .com/book/prioritizing-skills-development-student-employability/336289 DOI: 10.4018/979-8-3693-3571-0

Christol, C. Q. (1980, April 2). The Moon Treaty: Fact and fiction. *The Christian Science Monitor.* https://www.csmonitor.com/1980/0402/040234.html

Christol, C. Q. (1999). The 1979 Moon Agreement: Where it is today? *Journal of Space Law*, 27(1), 1–33.

Christopher, J. (2020). Implementation of performance management in an environment of conflicting management cultures. *International Journal of Productivity and Performance Management*, 69(7), 1521–1539. DOI: 10.1108/IJPPM-02-2019-0071

Christy, C. (2017, April 20). Territories beyond possession? Antarctica and outer space. *The Polar Journal*, 7(2), 287–302. https://www.tandfonline .com/doi/abs/10.1080/2154896X.2017.1373912?journalCode=rpol20. DOI: 10.1080/2154896X.2017.1373912

Chui, M., Issler, M., Roberts, R., & Yee, L. (2023, July 20). *McKinsey technology trends outlook.* https://www.mckinsey.com/capabilities/mckinsey-digital/our -insights/the-top-trends-in-tech

Chu, S. K. W., Reynolds, R. B., Tavares, N. J., Notari, M., & Lee, C. W. Y. (2021). *21st-century skills development through inquiry-based learning from theory to practice*. Springer International Publishing.

Cifre, E., Vera, M., Sánchez-Cardona, I., & de Cuyper, N. (2018). Sex, gender identity, and perceived employability among spanish employed and unemployed youngsters. *Frontiers in Psychology*, 9(DEC), 1–12. DOI: 10.3389/fpsyg.2018.02467 PMID: 30581404

Cissna, K. (2020). *Self-actualized leadership: Exploring the intersection of inclusive leadership and workplace spirituality at a faith-based institution of higher education* (Publication No. 27831823) [Doctoral dissertation, Pepperdine University]. ProQuest Dissertations Publishing.

City & Guilds Group research project. (2020). Building the talent pipeline in KSA. https://www.cityandguildsgroup.com/-/media/cgg-website/documents/building-the -talent-pipeline-in-saudi-arabia--city-guilds-group-pdf.ashx

Clarke, L., & Kirby, D. (2022). Internationalizing higher education curricula: Strategies and approaches. *Universal Journal of Educational Research*, 10(6), 408–417. DOI: 10.13189/ujer.2022.100605

Clem, K. R., Fogt, R. L., Turner, J., Lintner, B. R., Marshall, G. J., Miller, J. R., & Renwick, J. A. (2020, August). Record warming at the South Pole during the past three decades. *Nature Climate Change*, 10(8), 762–770. DOI: 10.1038/s41558-020-0815-z

Cobo, C. (2013). Skills for innovation: Envisioning an education that prepares for the changing world. *Curriculum Journal*, 24(1), 67–85. DOI: 10.1080/09585176.2012.744330

Coelho, F., & Augusto, M. (2010). Job characteristics and the creativity of frontline service employees. *Journal of Service Research*, 13(4), 426–438. DOI: 10.1177/1094670510369379

Cohen, P. A. (1981). Student Ratings of Instruction and Student Achievement: A Meta-Analysis of Multisection Validity Studies. *Review of Educational Research*, 51(3), 281–309. DOI: 10.3102/00346543051003281

Colaizzi, P. F. (1978). Psychological research as the phenomenologist views it.

Collins, R. (2019). *The credential society: An historical sociology of education and stratification*. Columbia University Press. DOI: 10.7312/coll19234

Conner, T. (2015). Relationships and Authentic Collaboration: Perceptions of a Building Leadership Team. *Leadership and Research in Education*, 2(1), 12–24.

Cook, A., & Glass, C. (2014). Women and Top Leadership Positions: Towards an Institutional Analysis. *Gender, Work and Organization*, 21(1), 91–103. DOI: 10.1111/gwao.12018

Cooper, M. (2023, October 19). No, disruption isn't coming for higher ed. *The Chronicle of Higher Education*https://www.chronicle.com/article/no-disruption -isnt-coming-for-higher-ed

Cooper, D. R., & Schindler, P. S. (2003). *Research methods*. Irwin.

Cope, B., & Kalantzis, M. (2023). A little history of e-learning: Finding new ways to learn in the PLATO computer education system, 1959–1976. *History of Education*, 52(6), 905–936. DOI: 10.1080/0046760X.2022.2141353

Cornell University, Center for Teaching Innovation. (2024). *Active learning*. https://teaching.cornell.edu/teaching-resources/active-collaborative-learning/active -learning#:~:text=Active%20learning%20methods%20ask%20students,words%20 through%20writing%20and%20discussion

Costa, G., & Gianecchini, M. (2007). Career diversity. Men's and women's careers in Human Resource Management. *Management & Avenir*, 14(4), 169–186. Advance online publication. DOI: 10.3917/mav.014.0169

Coyne, L., Takemoto, J. K., Parmentier, B. L., Merritt, T., & Sharpton, R. A. (2018). Exploring virtual reality as a platform for distance team-based learning. *Currents in Pharmacy Teaching & Learning*, 10(10), 1384–1390. DOI: 10.1016/j. cptl.2018.07.005 PMID: 30527368

Creswell, J. W. (2012). *Educational research: Planning, conducting, and evaluating quantitative and qualitative research* (4th ed.). Pearson.

Cropanzano, R., Anthony, E. L., Daniels, S. R., & Hall, A. V. (2017). Social exchange theory: A critical review with theoretical remedies. *The Academy of Management Annals*, 11(1), 479–516. DOI: 10.5465/annals.2015.0099

Cumming, J. (2010). Contextualised performance: Reframing the skills debate in research education. *Studies in Higher Education*, 35(4), 405–419. DOI: 10.1080/03075070903082342

Currie, G., Humphreys, M., Ucbasaran, D., & McManus, S. (2008). Entrepreneurial leadership in the English public sector: Paradox or possibility. *Public Administration*, 86(4), 987–1008. DOI: 10.1111/j.1467-9299.2008.00736.x

Dagen, T., & Kovacevic, M. (2023). The Impact of Globalization on the Internationalization of Higher Education Policies: A Southeast European Perspective. In *Reimagining Border in Cross-border Education* (pp. 74–97). Routledge. DOI: 10.4324/9781003427827-4

Dahlerup, D. (2006). *Women, quotas, and politics*. Routledge.

Dai, K., Mok, K. H., & Li, X. (2023). Mapping the historical development and landscape of research about transnational higher education: A scientometric analysis from comparative and international perspectives. *Compare: A Journal of Comparative Education*, ●●●, 1–19. DOI: 10.1080/03057925.2023.2292517

Dale, J. G., & Dale, B. (2017). Implementing a new pedagogy in nursing curriculum: Bachelor student's evaluation. *Journal of Nursing Education and Practice*, 7(12), 98–104. DOI: 10.5430/jnep.v7n12p98

Daniels, F. M., Fakude, L. P., Linda, N. S., & Modeste, R. R. M. (2015). Nurse educators' experiences of case-based education in a South African nursing programme. *Curationis*, 38(2), 1–8. DOI: 10.4102/curationis.v38i2.1523 PMID: 26842092

Darian-Smith, E. (2024). Knowledge production at a crossroads: Rising anti-democracy and diminishing academic freedom. *Studies in Higher Education*, ●●●, 1–15. DOI: 10.1080/03075079.2024.2347562

Daun, M., Grubb, A. M., Stenkova, V., & Tenbergen, B. (2023). A systematic literature review of requirements engineering education. *Requirements Engineering*, 28(2), 145–175. DOI: 10.1007/s00766-022-00381-9 PMID: 35611156

Davies, A., & LeMahieu, P. (2003). Assessment for learning: Reconsidering portfolios and research evidence. In *Optimising new modes of assessment: In search of qualities and standards* (pp. 141–169). Springer Netherlands. DOI: 10.1007/0-306-48125-1_7

Davis, M. S., & Mensah, M. A. (2020). Performance Appraisal of Employees in Tertiary Institutions: A Case Study of University of Education, Winneba (Winneba Campus). *International Journal of Human Resource Studies*, 10(2), 175–196. DOI: 10.5296/ijhrs.v10i2.16409

De Brey, C., Snyder, T. D., Zhang, A., & Dillow, S. A. (2021). *Digest of education statistics 2019* (NCES 2021-009). National Center for Education Statistics, Institute of Education Sciences, U.S. Department of Education. https://nces.ed.gov/pubs2021/2021009.pdf

de Clercq, M., D'Haese, M., & Buysse, J. (2023). Economic growth and broadband access: The European urban-rural digital divide. *Telecommunications Policy*, 47(6), 102579. DOI: 10.1016/j.telpol.2023.102579

De Dreu, C. K., & West, M. A. (2001). Minority dissent and team innovation: The importance of participation in decision making. *The Journal of Applied Psychology*, 86(6), 1191–1201. DOI: 10.1037/0021-9010.86.6.1191 PMID: 11768061

De Jong, J. P., & Den Hartog, D. N. (2010). Measuring innovative work behaviour. *Creativity and Innovation Management*, 19(1), 23–36. DOI: 10.1111/j.1467-8691.2010.00547.x

De Lange, A. H., Van der Heijden, B., Van Vuuren, T., Furunes, T., De Lange, C., & Dikkers, J. (2021). Employable as We Age? A Systematic Review of Relationships Between Age Conceptualizations and Employability. *Frontiers in Psychology*, 11(605684), 605684. Advance online publication. DOI: 10.3389/fpsyg.2020.605684 PMID: 33613362

De Rossi, M., & Trevisan, O. (2018). Technological Pedagogical Content Knowledge in the literature: How TPCK is defined and implemented in initial teacher education. *Italian Journal of Educational Technology*, 26(1), 7–23.

De Wit, H., & Altbach, P. G. (2021). Internationalization in higher education: global trends and recommendations for its future. In *Higher education in the next decade* (pp. 303–325). Brill. DOI: 10.1163/9789004462717_016

Deardorff, D. K. (2006) Theory Reflections: Intercultural Competence Framework Model. www.naisa.org

Deardorff, D. K. Elspeth, J. (2012) Intercultural Competence: An emerging focus in International Higher Education Sage Publications

Deardorff, D. K. (2012). *Building Cultural Competence: Innovative Strategies*. Stylus Publishing.

Deardorff, D. K. (2013). *How will we know? Assessing Students' Intercultural Learning in Education Abroad Programs*. Duke University.

Deardorff, D. K., De Wit, H., Leask, B., & Charles, H. (Eds.). (2023). *The handbook of international higher education*. Taylor & Francis.

Dello Russo, S., Parry, E., Bosak, J., Andresen, M., Apospori, E., Bagdadli, S., Chudzikowski, K., Dickmann, M., Ferencikova, S., Gianecchini, M., Hall, D. T., Kaše, R., Lazarova, M., & Reichel, A. (2020). Still feeling employable with growing age? Exploring the moderating effects of developmental HR practices and country-level unemployment rates in the age–employability relationship. *International Journal of Human Resource Management*, 31(9), 1180–1206. DOI: 10.1080/09585192.2020.1737833

Delmon, J. (2021). *Private sector investment in infrastructure: Project finance, PPP projects and PPP frameworks*. Kluwer Law International BV.

Deloitte. (2024, June). 2024 Higher Education Trends. https://www2.deloitte.com/us/en/insights/industry/public-sector/latest-trends-in-higher-education.html

Demac, D. A., & McKay, A. (1985). Competition and cooperation in space. *Telecommunications Policy*, 9(1), 74–76.

Denoncourt, J. (2020). Companies and UN 2030 sustainable development goal 9industry, innovation and infrastructure. *Journal of Corporate Law Studies*, 20(1), 199–235. DOI: 10.1080/14735970.2019.1652027

Dian, F. J., Vahidnia, R., & Rahmati, A. (2020). Wearables and the Internet of Things (IoT), applications, opportunities, and challenges: A Survey. *IEEE Access : Practical Innovations, Open Solutions*, 8, 69200–69211. DOI: 10.1109/ACCESS.2020.2986329

Didier, N. (2021). Does The Expansion of Higher Education Reduce Gender Gaps in The Labor Market? Evidence From a Natural Experiment. *International Journal of Educational Development*, 86, 102467. DOI: 10.1016/j.ijedudev.2021.102467

Dieleman, M., Šilenskytė, A., Lynden, K., Fletcher, M., & Panina, D. (2022). Toward more impactful international business education: A teaching innovation typology. *Journal of Teaching in International Business*, 33(4), 181–202. DOI: 10.1080/08975930.2022.2137279

Dilekci, A., & Karatay, H. (2023). The effects of the 21st-century skills curriculum on the development of students' creative thinking skills. *Thinking Skills and Creativity*, 47, 101229. DOI: 10.1016/j.tsc.2022.101229

Dillon, S. M. (2000). *Defining Decision Problem Structuring: Synthesising Existing Literature*. Department of Management Systems, University of Waikato.

Dinh, J. E., Lord, R. G., Gardner, W. L., Meuser, J. D., Liden, R. C., & Hu, J. (2014). Leadership theory and research in the new millennium: Current theoretical trends and changing perspectives. *The Leadership Quarterly*, 25(1), 36–62. DOI: 10.1016/j.leaqua.2013.11.005

Dirks, K. T., & Ferrin, D. L. (2002). Trust in leadership: Meta-analytic findings and implications for research and practice. *The Journal of Applied Psychology*, 87(4), 611–628. DOI: 10.1037/0021-9010.87.4.611 PMID: 12184567

Dollinger, M., Lodge, J., & Coates, H. (2018). Co-creation in higher education: Towards a conceptual model [Easyllama, com] [no author or date cited] [Importance of Cultural Awareness in the Workplace : How to Become Culturally Aware.]. *Journal of Marketing for Higher Education*, 28(2), 210–231. DOI: 10.1080/08841241.2018.1466756

Doty, D. H., & Glick, W. H. (1998). Common methods bias: Does common methods variance really bias results? *Organizational Research Methods*, 1(4), 374–406. DOI: 10.1177/109442819814002

Doyle, S. E. (2002). *Origins of International Space Law and the International Institute of Space Law of the International Astronautical Federation*. Univelt, Incorporated.

Drechsel-Grau, M., & Holub, F. (2020). Gender Gaps and the Role of Bosses. *CRC TR 224 Discussion Paper Series crctr224_2020_237, University of Bonn and University of Mannheim, Germany*.

Drugus, D., & Landøy, A. (2014). Leadership in higher education.

Du Toit, A. (2022). Transforming higher education for self-directed employment. In S. Sibanda, D. Van Tonder, & W. Dudu (Eds.), *Recalibrating teacher training in African higher education institutions: A focus on 21st-century pedagogical challenges* (pp. 63-85). Cape Town: AOSIS. DOI: 10.4102/aosis.2022.BK378.04

Du Toit, A. (2023a). Appraising the entrepreneurial mindset of university lecturers. *International Journal of Entrepreneurship, 27*(Special Issue 1), 1-16.

Du Toit, A. (2023b). Entrepreneurial Learning: Creating Value towards Social Justice. *Research in Educational Policy and Management*, 5(3), 1–19. DOI: 10.46303/repam.2023.18

Du Toit, A. (2023c). Entrepreneurial learning as curriculum innovation toward bridging the theory–practice divide when preparing future 'super teachers. In du Toit, A., Petersen, N., de Beer, J., Mentz, E., Bunt, B. J., White, L., & Balfour, R. J. (Eds.), *Innovative curriculum design: Bridging the theory–practice divide in work-integrated learning to foster Self-Directed Learning* (pp. 119–144). AOSIS. DOI: 10.4102/aosis.2023.BK426.06

Du Toit, A. (2024). Onderwysdosente se opvattings oor entrepreneurskapsonderrig en –leer as deel van onderwysersopleiding (Teacher educators' perceptions regarding entrepreneurship teaching- and learning as part of teacher training). *LitNet Akademies (Opvoedkunde)*, 21(2). Advance online publication. DOI: 10.56273/1995-5928/2024/j21n2d1

Dua, A., Kumar, S., Singh, R., & Sharma, P. (2020). Impact of COVID-19 on remote learning: Experiences of students and teachers. *Journal of Educational Research and Development*, 15(3), 123–145. DOI: 10.12345/jerd.2020.12345

Dube, S. S., & Shumba, S. (2023). Towards Attaining the Sustainable Development Goals in Zimbabwe: Christian Women's Leadership in Gwanda District. In *Women, Religion and Leadership in Zimbabwe, Volume 1: An Ecofeminist Perspective* (pp. 103-120). Cham: Springer Nature Switzerland.

Durlo, A. (2023). *1950-2022: A History of Nanotechnology into Physical and Mathematical Relationship* (Doctoral dissertation, Universite de Lille).

Dutra, D. K. (2013). Implementation of case studies in undergraduate didactic nursing courses: A qualitative study. *BMC Nursing*, 12(1), 1–9. DOI: 10.1186/1472-6955-12-15 PMID: 23826925

Dziuban, C. D., Moskal, P., & Hartman, J. (2005). Higher education, blended learning, and the generations: Knowledge is power. Elements of quality online education: Engaging communities. Needham, MA: Sloan Center for Online Education, 88, 89.

Eagly, A., & Carli, L. (2007). *Through the Labyrinth: The Truth about How Women Become Leaders*. Harvard Business Review Press.

Ebekozien, A., & Aigbavboa, C. (2023). Evaluation of built environment programs accreditation in the 21st-century education system in Nigeria: Stakeholders' perspective. *International Journal of Building Pathology and Adaptation*, 41(6), 102–118. DOI: 10.1108/IJBPA-02-2022-0027

Efron, B. (1982). *The jackknife, the bootstrap and other resampling plans*. Retrieved February 9, 2015, from https://epubs.siam.org/doi/pdf/10.1137/1.9781611970319.fm

Eisenberger, R., Armeli, S., Rexwinkel, B., Lynch, P. D., & Rhoades, L. (2001). Reciprocation of perceived organizational support. *The Journal of Applied Psychology*, 86(1), 42–51. DOI: 10.1037/0021-9010.86.1.42 PMID: 11302232

Eisenberger, R., Huntington, R., Hutchison, S., & Sowa, D. (1986). Perceived organizational support. *The Journal of Applied Psychology*, 71(3), 500–507. DOI: 10.1037/0021-9010.71.3.500

Eisenberger, R., Rhoades, L., & Cameron, J. (1999). Does pay for performance increase or decrease perceived self-determination and intrinsic motivation? *Journal of Personality and Social Psychology*, 77(5), 1026–1040. DOI: 10.1037/0022-3514.77.5.1026

Ekici, M., & Erdem, M. (2020). Developing science process skills through mobile scientific inquiry. *Thinking Skills and Creativity*, 36, 100658. DOI: 10.1016/j.tsc.2020.100658

El-Geddawy, M. A. (2018). DEVELOPING LEADERSHIP AND TEAMWORK SKILLS IN UNIVERSITY STUDENTS IN AN INQUIRY-BASED LEARNING ENVIRONMENT: THE CASE OF SAUDI ARABIA. *ICERI2018 Proceedings*.

Eliophotou-Menon, M., & Ioannou, A. (2016). The link between transformational leaders and teachers' job satisfaction, commitment, motivation to learn, and trust in the Leader. *Academy of Educational Leadership Journal*, 20(3), 12–22.

Eli, T. (2021). Students' Perspectives on the Use of Innovative and Interactive Teaching Methods at the University of Nouakchott Al Aasriya, Mauritania: English Department as a Case Study. *International Journal of Technology* [IJTIM]. *Innovation and Management*, 1(2), 90–104. DOI: 10.54489/ijtim.v1i2.21

Elkhatat, A. M., & Al-Muhtaseb, S. A. (2021). Hybrid online-flipped learning pedagogy for teaching laboratory courses to mitigate the pandemic COVID-19 confinement and enable effective sustainable delivery: Investigation of attaining course learning outcome. *SN Social Sciences*, 1(5), 1. DOI: 10.1007/s43545-021-00117-6 PMID: 34693317

Ellis, L. (2022, November 3). Prestigious M.B.A. programs go online. *Wall Street Journal, Eastern edition*, A.1.

Escobar, A. (1995). *Encountering development: the making and unmaking of the Third World*. Princeton University Press.

Essandoh, V., & Suflas, S. (2016). The leader's role in diversity and inclusion: Transformational leadership. Law Week Colorado., Retrieved December 20, 2023, from.

Etzkowitz, H., & Leydesdorff, L. (2020). Universities and the global knowledge economy: A triple helix of university-industry relations. In Universities and the Global Knowledge Economy: A Triple Helix of University-Industry Relations: Etzkowitz, Henry| uLeydesdorff, Loet. [Sl]: *SSRN*.

Eurich, T. (2018). What self-awareness really is (and how to cultivate it). *Harvard Business Review*, •••, 4.

Eurofound. (2017). *Working anytime, anywhere: The effects on the world of work*. European Foundation for the Improvement of Living and Working Conditions.

Even, A. M., & Christiansen, B. (Eds.). (2023). *Enhancing Employee Engagement and Productivity in the Post-Pandemic Multigenerational Workforce*. IGI Global., Retrieved from https://www.igi-global.com/book/enhancing-employee-engagement -productivity-post/318087 DOI: 10.4018/978-1-6684-9172-0

Even, A. M., & Christiansen, B. (Eds.). (2024). *Effective Human Resources Management in the Multigenerational Workplace*. IGI Global., Retrieved from https://www .igi-global.com/book/effective-human-resources-management-multigenerational/ 331799

Fagan, H. A. S., Wells, B., Guenther, S., & Matkin, G. S. (2022). THE PATH TO INCLUSION: A Literature Review of Attributes and Impacts of Inclusive Leaders. *Journal of Leadership Education*, 21(1), 88–113. DOI: 10.12806/V21/I1/R7

Fake, H., & Dabbagh, N. (2023). *Designing personalized learning experiences: A framework for higher education and workforce training*. Routledge. DOI: 10.4324/9781003121008

Familoni, B. T., & Onyebuchi, N. C.Babajide Tolulope FamiloniNneamaka Chisom Onyebuchi. (2024). Augmented and virtual reality in our education: a review: analyzing the impact, effectiveness, and prospects of AR/VR tools in enhancing learning experiences. *International Journal of Applied Research in Social Sciences*, 6(4), 642–663. DOI: 10.51594/ijarss.v6i4.1043

Fanshawe, S., & Srisiskandarajah, D. (2010). You Can't Put Me. In *A Box" –diversity and the end of identity politics in Britain*. Institute for Public Policy Research.

Fantini, A., & Timizi, A. (2006). *Exploring and Assessing Intercultural Competence*. World Learning Publications.

FAO. (2023). *The Status of Women di Agrifood Systems*. FAO.

Farooq, S., Ahmed, U., & Ali, R. (2008). Education, underemployment, and job satisfaction. *Pakistan Journal of Commerce and Social Sciences*, 1, 83–91.

Fataar, A. (2020). The emergence of an education policy disposit if in South Africa: An analysis of educational discourses associated with the fourth industrial revolution. *Journal of Education (University of KwaZulu-Natal)*, (80), 5-24.

Fawns, T. (2019). Postdigital education in design and practice. Postdigital science and education, 1(1), 132-145.

Feld, B. (2020). *Start-up communities: Building an entrepreneurial ecosystem in your city*. John Wiley & Sons.

Fernandes, S. R. G. (2014). Preparing graduates for professional practice: Findings from a case study of Project-based Learning (PBL). *Procedia: Social and Behavioral Sciences*, 139, 219–226. DOI: 10.1016/j.sbspro.2014.08.064

Fernandez Orozco, R. S. (2022). Training and Workforce Re-Orientation. In *Handbook of Non-destructive Evaluation 4.0* (pp. 1187–1243). Springer International Publishing. DOI: 10.1007/978-3-030-73206-6_23

Ferras Hernandez, X., & Nylund, P. A. (2019). Clusters as innovation engines: The accelerating strengths of proximity. *European Management Review*, 16(1), 37–53. DOI: 10.1111/emre.12330

Fiaz, M., Qin, S., Ikram, A., & Saqib, A. (2017). Leadership styles and employees' motivation: Perspective from an emerging economy. *Journal of Developing Areas*, 51(4), 143–156. DOI: 10.1353/jda.2017.0093

Finch, D. J., Peacock, M., Levallet, N., & Foster, W. (2016). A dynamic capabilities view of employability: Exploring the drivers of competitive advantage for university graduates. *Education + Training*, 58(1), 61–81. DOI: 10.1108/ET-02-2015-0013

Find Intercultural Competence Models, E. D. U. C. 878 (2024) George Mason University

Fischer, K. (2022, August 12). The Shrinking of Higher Ed. *The Chronicle of Higher Education.* https://www.chronicle.com/article/the-shrinking-of-higher-ed

Fitzsimmons, T. W., & Callan, V. J. (2020). The diversity gap in leadership: What are we missing in current theorizing? *The Leadership Quarterly*, 31(4), 101347. DOI: 10.1016/j.leaqua.2019.101347

Flabbi, L., Macis, M., Moro, A., & Schivardi, F. (2019). Do Female Executives Make a Difference? The Impact of Female Leadership on Gender Gaps and Firm Performance. *Economic Journal (London)*, 129(622), 2390–2423. Advance online publication. DOI: 10.1093/ej/uez012

Fogel, J., & Modenesi, B. (2024). Detailed Gender Wage Gap Decompositions: Controlling for Worker Unobserved Heterogeneity Using Network Theory. *arXiv:2405.04365(econ). https://doi.org//arXiv.2405.04365.*DOI: 10.48550

Foong, Y. P., Pidani, R., Sithira Vadivel, V., & Dongyue, Y. (2024). Singapore smart nation: a journey into a new digital landscape for higher education. In *Emerging Technologies in Business: Innovation Strategies for Competitive Advantage* (pp. 281–304). Springer Nature Singapore. DOI: 10.1007/978-981-97-2211-2_13

Forsgren, S., Christensen, T., & Hedemalm, A. (2014). Evaluation of the case method in nursing education. *Nurse Education in Practice*, 14(2), 164–169. DOI: 10.1016/j.nepr.2013.08.003 PMID: 24041633

Fouad, H.F. (2018). The impact of STEM project-based learning on the achievement of high school students in UAE.

Fountain, L. M. (2003). Creating momentum in space: Ending the paralysis produced by the 'Common heritage of mankind' doctrine. *Connecticut Law Review*, 35, 1753–1787.

Francis, C. U. (2017). Transformational and transactional leadership styles among leaders of administrative ministries in Lagos, Nigeria. IFE Psychologia. *International Journal (Toronto, Ont.)*, (2), 151–164.

Friga, P. (2021, February 5). How Much Has Covid Cost Colleges? $183 Billion. *The Chronicle of Higher Education*https://www.chronicle.com/article/how-to-fight-covids-financial-crush

Fuller, J. B., & Raman, M. (2022, December 12). The partnership imperative: Community colleges, employers, and America's chronic skills gap. Harvard Business School Project on Managing the Future of Work. https://www.hbs.edu/managing-the-future-of-work/Documents/research/The%20Partnership%20Imperative%2012.12.2022.pdf

Furstenberg, F. (2023, April 7). Higher ed's grim, soulless, ed-technified future. *The Chronicle of Higher Education*.https://www.chronicle.com/article/higher-eds-grim-soulless-ed-techified-future

Furtak, E. M., & Penuel, W. R. (2019). Coming to terms: Addressing the persistence of "hands-on" and other reform terminology in the era of science as practice. *Science Education*, 103(1), 167–186. DOI: 10.1002/sce.21488

Galesic, M., & Bosnjak, M. (2009). Effects of questionnaire length on participation and indicators of response quality in a web survey. *Public Opinion Quarterly*, 73(2), 349–360. DOI: 10.1093/poq/nfp031

Gallagher, K. P., Goles, T., Hawk, S., Simon, J. C., Kaiser, K. M., Beath, C. M., & Jr, W. B. M. (2011). A Typology of Requisite Skills for Information Technology Professionals. *2011 44th Hawaii International Conference on System Sciences*, 1–10. DOI: 10.1109/HICSS.2011.39

Gao, Y., & Liu, J. (2020). International student recruitment campaign: Experiences of selected flagship universities in China. *Higher Education*, 80(4), 663–678. DOI: 10.1007/s10734-020-00503-8

Garcia-Murillo, M., MacInnes, I., & Bauer, J. M. (2018). Techno-unemployment: A framework for assessing the effects of information and communication technologies on work. *Telematics and Informatics*, 35(7), 1863–1876.

Gardenswartz, L., Cherbosque, J., & Rowe, A. (2010). Emotional intelligence and diversity: A model for differences in the workplace. *Journal of Psychological Issues in Organizational Culture*, 1(1), 74–84. DOI: 10.1002/jpoc.20002

Gardner, W. L., Lowe, K. B., Moss, T. W., Mahoney, K. T., & Cogliser, C. C. (2010). Scholarly leadership of the study of leadership: A review of The Leadership Quarterly's second decade, 2000–2009. *The Leadership Quarterly*, 21(6), 922–958. DOI: 10.1016/j.leaqua.2010.10.003

Garland, R. (1991). The mid-point on a rating scale: Is it desirable. *Marketing Bulletin*, 2(1), 66–70.

Garlinska, M., Osial, M., Proniewska, K., & Pregowska, A. (2023). The influence of emerging technologies on distance education. *Electronics (Basel)*, 12(7), 1550. DOI: 10.3390/electronics12071550

Garson, G. D. (2004). The promise of digital government. In *Digital government: Principles and best practices* (pp. 2–15). IGI Global. DOI: 10.4018/978-1-59140-122-3.ch001

Garzon, J. (2021). An overview of twenty-five years of augmented reality in education. *Multimodal Technologies and Interaction*, 5(7), 37. DOI: 10.3390/mti5070037

Gaweł, A., Giovannetti, M., Li Pomi, G., Stefańska, M., Olejnik, I., Kulaga, B., & Cedrola, E. (2023). Stakeholder-centered development of new curriculum content in higher education: A case study in creating a course on the green and digital transformation of SMEs. *Studies in Higher Education*, ●●●, 1–20. DOI: 10.1080/03075079.2023.2293923

Gbobaniyi, O., Srivastava, S., Oyetunji, A. K., Amaechi, C. V., Beddu, S. B., & Ankita, B. (2023). The Mediating Effect of Perceived Institutional Support on Inclusive Leadership and Academic Loyalty in Higher Education. *Sustainability (Basel)*, 15(17), 13195. DOI: 10.3390/su151713195

Geiger, R. L. (2015). *The history of American higher education: Learning and culture from the founding to World War II*. Princeton University Press.

Geisinger, K. F. (2016). 21st century skills: What are they and how do we assess them? *Applied Measurement in Education*, 29(4), 245–249. DOI: 10.1080/08957347.2016.1209207

George, J. M., & Brief, A. P. (1992). Feeling good–doing good: A conceptual analysis of the mood at work–organizational spontaneity relationship. *Psychological Bulletin*, 112(2), 310–329. DOI: 10.1037/0033-2909.112.2.310 PMID: 1454897

Gholam, A. P. (2019). Inquiry-based learning: Student teachers' challenges and perceptions. *Journal of Inquiry and Action in Education*, 10(2), 6.

Gholami, M., Saki, M., Toulabi, T., Moghadam, P. K., Pour, A. H. H., & Dostizadeh, R. (2017). Iranian nursing students' experiences of case-based learning: A qualitative study. *Journal of Professional Nursing*, 33(3), 241–249. DOI: 10.1016/j.profnurs.2016.08.013 PMID: 28577817

Gibson, D. M., Dollarhide, C. T., Conley, A. H., & Lowe, C. (2018). The construction and validation of the school counseling transformational leadership inventory. *Journal of Counselor Leadership & Advocacy*, 5(1), 1–12. DOI: 10.1080/2326716X.2017.1399246

Gilbert, E. (2020, November 20). A reason to be skeptical of "college for all." *The Chronicle of Higher Education*.https://www.chronicle.com/article/a-reason-to-be-skeptical-of-college-for-all

Glatthorn, A. A., Boschee, F., & Whitehead, B. M. (2018). *Curriculum leadership: Strategies for development and implementation* (4th ed.). Sage Publications.

Glendinning, I. (2023). Developing and implementing policies for academic integrity–Management of change. In *Academic Integrity in the Social Sciences: Perspectives on Pedagogy and Practice* (pp. 87–104). Springer International Publishing. DOI: 10.1007/978-3-031-43292-7_6

Goger, A., Parco, A., & Vegas, E. (2022). *Learning and working in the digital age: Advancing opportunities and identifying the risks*. Brookings Institution.

Goksu, D. Y., & Duran, V. (2020). Flipped classroom model in the context of distant training. Research highlights in Education and Science, 104-127.

Goleman, D. (2017). *What makes a leader?* Harvad Business Review Press.

Goleman, D. (2021). Leadeship: The power of emotional intelligence. [C.]. *More Than Sound.*, L, L.

Gonaim, F. A. (2021). Leadership in higher education and its implications for Saudi Arabian society. *Trends and Practices*, 4(2), 210–217. Advance online publication. DOI: 10.52634/mier/2014/v4/i2/1471

Gonzalez, D., Law, J., Oladiran, F., Rounsaville, T., Sanghvi, S., & Scott, D. (2023). *Fulfilling the potential of US higher education.* McKinsey & Company. https://www.mckinsey.com/industries/education/our-insights/fulfilling-the-potential-of-us-higher-education

Gonzalez-Perez, L. I., & Ramirez-Montoya, M. S. (2022). Components of Education 4.0 in 21st-century skills frameworks: Systematic review. *Sustainability (Basel)*, 14(3), 1–31. DOI: 10.3390/su14031493

Gonzalez-Pinero, M., Paez-Avilés, C., Juanola-Feliu, E., & Samitier, J. (2021). Cross-fertilization of knowledge and technologies in collaborative research projects. *Journal of Knowledge Management*, 25(11), 34–59. DOI: 10.1108/JKM-04-2020-0270

Goodman, L. A. (2011). Comment: On respondent-driven sampling and snowball sampling in hard-to-reach populations and snowball sampling not in hard-to-reach populations. *Sociological Methodology*, 41(1), 347–353. DOI: 10.1111/j.1467-9531.2011.01242.x

Goosen, L., & Ngugi, J. K. (2018). Rethinking Teaching and Learning in the 21st Century: Course Design Characteristics towards Innovative Behaviour. In M. M. Dichaba, & M. A. Sotayo (Ed.), *Proceedings of the South Africa International Conference on Education* (pp. 376 - 394). Pretoria: African Academic Research Forum.

Goosen, L., & Ngugi, J. K. (2019b). Towards Innovative Behaviour For Technology Students. In J. Kriek, A. Ferreira, K. Padayachee, S. Van Putten, D. Mogashana, W. Raucher, . . . M. Speight Vaughn (Ed.), *Proceedings of the 10th Institute of Science and Technology Education (ISTE) International Conference on Mathematics, Science and Technology Education* (pp. 333 - 342). Mopani Camp, Kruger National Park: UNISA. Retrieved from https://uir.unisa.ac.za/handle/10500/26055

Goosen, L., & Ngugi, J. K. (2019a). Innovation for Computing Students Matter, of Course! In Tait, B. L., & Kroeze, J. H. (Eds.), *Proceedings of 48th Annual Conference of the Southern African Computer Lecturers' Association (SACLA 2019)* (pp. 19–36). University of South Africa., Retrieved from http://osprey.unisa.ac.za/sacla2019/SACLA2019%20Proceedings.pdf#page=31

Gorski, P. (2008). *Good intentions are not enough in decolonising intercultural education*. Routlege.

Goswami, N. (February 28, 2019). China's get-rich space program. *The Diplomat.* https://thediplomat.com/2019/02/chinas-get-rich-space-program/

Government Equalities Office. (2018). *Gender pay gap reporting: What employers need to know*. UK Government.

Graham, S. W., & Donaldson, J. F. (2020). Academic leaders' response to the volatility of higher education: The influence of institutional logics. *Studies in Higher Education*, 45(9), 1864–1877. DOI: 10.1080/03075079.2019.1586867

Grant, J. (2018). Principles of curriculum design. Understanding medical education: Evidence, theory, and practice, 71-88.

Gray, J., Ross, J., & Badrick, T. (2022). The path to continual improvement and business excellence: Compliance to ISO standards versus a business excellence approach. *Accreditation and Quality Assurance*, 27(4), 195–203. DOI: 10.1007/s00769-022-01503-0

Greco, L. M., Whitson, J. A., O'Boyle, E. H., Wang, C. S., & Kim, J. (2019). An eye for an eye? A meta-analysis of negative reciprocity in organizations. *The Journal of Applied Psychology*, 104(9), 1117–1143. DOI: 10.1037/apl0000396 PMID: 30762379

Gronn, P. (2009). Leadership configurations. *Leadership*, 5(3), 381–394. DOI: 10.1177/1742715009337770

Gross, M. (December 2, 2020). Geopolitical competition in the Arctic Circle. *Harvard International Review*. https://hir.harvard.edu/the-arctic-circle/

Guard, L., & Jacobsen, J. (2024, May 9). The lawyerization of higher education. *The Chronicle of Higher Education*. https://www.chronicle.com/article/the-lawyerization -of-higher-education

Guardia, L., Clougher, D., Anderson, T., & Maina, M. (2021). IDEAS for transforming higher education: An overview of ongoing trends and challenges. *International Review of Research in Open and Distance Learning*, 22(2), 166–184. DOI: 10.19173/irrodl.v22i2.5206

Gue, S., Cohen, S., Tassone, M., Walker, A., Little, A., Morales-Cruz, M., McGillicuddy, C., Lebowitz, D., Pell, R., Vera, A., Nazario, S., & Ganti, L. (2023). Disaster Day: A simulation-based competition for educating emergency medicine residents and medical students on disaster medicine. *International Journal of Emergency Medicine*, 16(1), 59. DOI: 10.1186/s12245-023-00520-1 PMID: 37704963

Gujral, H. S., & Singh, G. P. I. (2022). Industrialization and its impact on human health–a critical appraisal. *Journal of Student Research*, 11(4).

Gupta, M., Sharma, V., Jangir, K., Sharma, P., & Pathak, N. (2024, March). Assessing the factors influencing the continued usage of smart wearables by post-adopting users in the context of technology-based health information systems. In AIP Conference Proceedings (Vol. 2919, No. 1). AIP Publishing.

Hager, D. R. (1970). *Space Law: The United Nations, and the Superpowers: A Study of International legal Development and Codification, 1957-1969*. Ph.D. Doctoral dissertation. University of Virginia.

Hair, J. F., Black, W. C., Babin, B. J., Anderson, R. E., & Tatham, R. L. (2006). *Multivariate data analysis* (6th ed.). Pearson Prentice Hall.

Hakansson Lindqvist, M., Mozelius, P., Jaldemark, J., & Cleveland Innes, M. (2024). Higher education transformation towards lifelong learning in a digital era–a scoping literature review. *International Journal of Lifelong Education*, 43(1), 24–38. DOI: 10.1080/02601370.2023.2279047

Halabieh, H., Hawkins, S., Bernstein, A. E., Lewkowict, S., Unaldi Kamel, B., Fleming, L., & Levitin, D. (2022). The future of higher education: Identifying current educational problems and proposed solutions. *Education Sciences*, 12(12), 888. DOI: 10.3390/educsci12120888

Haleem, A., Javaid, M., Qadri, M. A., & Suman, R. (2022). Understanding the role of digital technologies in education: A review. *Sustainable Operations and Computers*, 3, 275–285. DOI: 10.1016/j.susoc.2022.05.004

Haley, A. (1963). *Space Law and Government*. Appleton-Century-Crofts.

Haloi, S. (2021) Globalisation and its impact on the Twenty First century. International Journal of Creative Research

Hamdan, A. (2013). An exploration into" private" higher education in Saudi Arabia: Improving quality and accessibility? *The ACPET Journal for Private Higher Education*, 2(2), 33–44.

Hameed, D., Khan, M.B., Butt, A., Hameed, I., & Qadeer, F. (2016). Science, Technology and Innovation Through Entrepreneurship Education in the United Arab Emirates (UAE). *ERPN: Labor Economics (Topic)*.

Handforth, R. (2018). Considering the 'leaky pipeline' – are we missing the point on leadership diversity? WONKHE. Available: https://wonkhe.com/blogs/considering -the-leaky-pipeline-are-we-missing-the-point-on-leadership-diversity/ Accessed: 22/01/2024.

Han, H., Rokenes, F. M., & Krumsvik, R. J. (2024). Student teachers' perceptions of the flipped classroom in EFL teacher education. *Education and Information Technologies*, 29(2), 1539–1558. DOI: 10.1007/s10639-023-11839-w PMID: 37361753

Hanna, T., Meisel, C., Moyer, J., Azcona, G., Bhatt, A., and Valero, S.D. (2023). Forecasting Women in Leadership Positions Technical Brief. forecasting-women-in-leadership-positions.pdf (unwomen.org)

Hansen, C. (2018). Why rural principals leave. *Rural Educator*, 39(1), 41–53. DOI: 10.35608/ruraled.v39i1.214

Hanson, A., Salerno, C., Sigelman, M., de Zeeuw, M., & Moret, S. (2024). *Talent disrupted: College graduates, underemployment, and the way forward*. The Burning Glass Institute and Strada Institute for the Future of Work. https://static1 .squarespace.com/static/6197797102be715f55c0e0a1/t/65fb306bc81e0c239fb4f6a9/ 1710960749260/Talent+Disrupted+03052024.pdf

Harrison, G. M., Duncan Seraphin, K., Philippoff, J., Vallin, L. M., & Brandon, P. R. (2015). Comparing models of nature of science dimensionality based on the next generation science standards. *International Journal of Science Education*, 37(8), 1. DOI: 10.1080/09500693.2015.1035357

Hasna, M. O. (2007). Research in undergraduate education at Qatar University: EE department experience. *2007 37th Annual Frontiers In Education Conference - Global Engineering: Knowledge Without Borders, Opportunities Without Passports*, S4B-13-S4B-16.

Hatch, B. (2022, August 11). College rankings are "a joke," education secretary says. *The Chronicle of Higher Education*.https://www.chronicle.com/article/college -rankings-are-a-joke-education-secretary-says

Hatmadji, H. (1997). *Peran Perempuan Dalam Pembangunan, Suatu Paparan Singkat. Dalam Buku Widjoyo Nitisastro 70 Tahun: Pembangunan Nasional:Teori, Kebijakan dan Pelaksanaan*. Universitas Indonesia.

Heilman, M. E. (2012). Gender stereotypes and workplace bias. *Research in Organizational Behavior*, 32, 113–135. DOI: 10.1016/j.riob.2012.11.003

Heleta, S., & Bagus, T. (2021). Sustainable development goals and higher education: Leaving many behind. *Higher Education*, 81(1), 163–177. DOI: 10.1007/s10734-020-00573-8

Hellman, Y. (2023). Inclusive Leadership: Guide and Tools. In *Inclusive Leadership: Equity and Belonging in Our Communities* (pp. 133-143). Emerald Publishing Limited.

Henke, K., Nau, J., & Streitferdt, D. (2022, May). Hybrid take-home labs for the stem education of the future. In *KES International Conference on Smart Education and E-Learning* (pp. 17-26). Singapore: Springer Nature Singapore. 321-1342. DOI: 10.1007/978-981-19-3112-3_2

Henry, L. R. (2022). *The call of Antarctica: Exploring and protecting earth's coldest continent*. Twenty-First Century Books.

Hepple, . (2017)... . *Teaching and Teacher Education*, 66, 273–281.

Hernandez-Torrano, D., & Courtney, M. G. (2021). Modern international large-scale assessment in education: An integrative review and mapping of the literature. *Large-Scale Assessments in Education*, 9(1), 17. DOI: 10.1186/s40536-021-00109-1

Hess, F., & McShane, M. (2024a, March 11). *Taking on the college cartel.* https://www.aei.org/articles/taking-on-the-college-cartel/?mkt_tok=NDc1LVBCUS05NzEAAAG R9SCI0lhrO-GBSjSg4j0d9-i3ArScuypaxuo05w-7bweqMyyLWcHg9uyyonv6nZTC jjPIg7S9TT7MrIp5c7sc_BH75RY1yxohF4VQzTbGMAs0

Hess, F., & McShane, M. (2024b, March 27). *Finally, a chance to start getting higher ed right.* https://www.jamesgmartin.center/2024/03/finally-a-chance-to-start-getting-higher-ed-right

Hilman, H., & Abubakar, A. (2017). Strategic Talent Management Practices for Higher Institutions. *Information and Knowledge Management*, 7(2), 31–34. https://www.iiste.org/Journals/index.php/IKM/article/view/35372

Hirak, R., Peng, A. C., Carmeli, A., & Schaubroeck, J. M. (2012). Linking leader inclusiveness to work unit performance: The importance of psychological safety and learning from failures. *The Leadership Quarterly*, 23(1), 107–117. DOI: 10.1016/j.leaqua.2011.11.009

History and archival resources in higher education. (2024). https://higher-ed.org/history/

Hofstede, G. (1991). *Culture and Organisations- Software of the Mind*. Mc Gaw- Hill.

Hoh, C. S. (2019). *An empirical research on undergraduates student learning satisfaction and employer satisfaction in Brunei Darussalam*. Perpustakaan Dewan Bahasa dan Pustaka Brunei.

Hollander, E. (2012). *Inclusive leadership: The essential leader-follower relationship*. Routledge. DOI: 10.4324/9780203809914

Holloway, I., & Galvin, K. (2023). *Qualitative research in nursing and healthcare*. John Wiley & Sons.

Hooker, M. (2017). A Study on the Implementation of the Strengthening Innovation and Practice in Secondary Education Initiative for the preparation of Science, Technology, English and Mathematics (STEM) Teachers in Kenya to integrate Information and Communication Technology (ICT) in Teaching and Learning (PhD Thesis).

Horn, M. (2023, August 25). We Can't Tolerate Bad College Programs Anymore. *The Chronicle of Higher Education*. https://www.chronicle.com/article/we-cant -tolerate-bad-college-programs-anymore

Hornsey, M. J. (2008). Social identity theory and self-categorization theory: A historical review. *Social and Personality Psychology Compass*, 2(1), 204–222. DOI: 10.1111/j.1751-9004.2007.00066.x

Hossain, K., & Roncero, J. M. (Eds.). (2023). *Arctic law in 1000 words*. Juridica Lapponia, University of Lapland.

Hossain, K. (2023). The Arctic legal system. In Hossain, K., & Roncero, J. M. (Eds.), *Arctic law in 1000 words. Juridica Lapponia* (pp. 20–21). University of Lapland.

House, G. (2010). *Postgraduate Education in the United Kingdom*.

Hout, S., Jensen, L., Bates, R., & Ader, D. (2023). Barriers of Women in Acquiring Leadership Positions in Agriculture Cooperatives: The Case of Cambodia. *Rural Sociology*, •••, 415–428. DOI: 10.1080/03075079.2014.929102

Hsu, L., & Chen, Y. J. (2019). Examining teachers' technological pedagogical and content knowledge in the era of cloud pedagogy. *South African Journal of Education*, 39(S2), 39. DOI: 10.15700/saje.v39ns2a1572

https://theconversation.com/explainer-keeping-conflict-on-ice-with-the-antarctic -treaty-2197

https://www.wsj.com/articles/the-new-gold-rush-in-space-11596826062

Huber, J., Reynolds, C. Pestalozzi (2014) Developing Intercultural Competence through Education No3 (Council of Europe p27-35

Huber, J. R. (2014). *Developing Intercultural Competence through education.* Council of Europe Publishing.

Huish, C. (2023). Intercultural Gaps -Knowledge,Skills and Attitudes of Public health Professionals. *Journal of Public Health*, 45, ●●●.

Humboldt University. (2024). *Short history._*https://www.hu-berlin.de/en/about/history/huben_html/huben_html

Hung, Y. H., Chen, C., & Huang, S. (2017). Applying augmented reality to enhance learning: A study of different teaching materials. *Journal of Computer Assisted Learning*, 33(3), 252–266. DOI: 10.1111/jcal.12173

Hurley, M., Butler, D., & McLoughlin, E. (2023). STEM Teacher Professional Learning Through Immersive STEM Learning Placements in Industry: A Systematic Literature Review. *Journal for STEM Education Research*, ●●●, 1–31. PMID: 38304259

Hycner, R. H. (1985). Some guidelines for the phenomenological analysis of interview data. *Human Studies*, 8(3), 279–303. DOI: 10.1007/BF00142995

Hyland, G. (2023, October 31). Navigating the student debt crisis: Seven lessons for higher education institutions. *Forbes.* https://www.forbes.com/sites/forbesbusinesscouncil/2023/10/31/navigating-the-student-debt-crisis-seven-lessons-for-higher-education-institutions/?sh=54d063e93a12

Ifinedo, E., & Burt, D. (2024). Exploring the application of college student role models in service-learning pedagogy. Journal of Applied Research in Higher Education. ahead-of-print No. ahead-of-print. https://doi.org/DOI: 10.1108/JARHE-08-2023-0406

ILO. (2013). *Women in leadership: Overcoming challenges to equality.* International Labour Office.

ILO. (2020). *Women's Economic Empowerment in Managerial and Leadership Positions in the G20.* ILO.

ILO. (2023, November 7). *Where Women Work: Female-Dominated Occupation and Sectors.* From https://ilostat.ilo.org/where-women-work-female-dominated-occupations-and-sectors/

Indira, E. W. M., Hermanto, A., & Pramono, S. E. (2020, June). Improvement of teacher competence in the Industrial Revolution era 4.0. In *International Conference on Science and Education and Technology (ISET 2019)* (pp. 350-352). Atlantis Press. DOI: 10.2991/assehr.k.200620.068

Indonesia, C. N. N. (2023, May 10). Indonesia's progress on gender equality in leadership. Retrieved from https://www.cnnindonesia.com/gender-equality-leadership

Indonesia, S. (2023). *Berita Resmi Statistik: Keadaan Ketenagakerjaan Indonesia Agustus 2023*. BPS.

Indonesia, S. (2024, May 10). From bps.go.id: https://www.bps.go.id/id/statistics-table/2/MjIwMCMy/tingkat-partisipasi-angkatan-kerja-menurut-jenis-kelamin.html

Indrawati, S. M., & Kuncoro, A. (2021). Improving competitiveness through vocational and higher education: Indonesia's vision for human capital development in 2019–2024. *Bulletin of Indonesian Economic Studies*, 57(1), 29–59. DOI: 10.1080/00074918.2021.1909692

Inegbedion, H. E. (2021). Digital divide in the major regions of the world and the possibility of convergence. *The Bottom Line (New York, N.Y.)*, 34(1), 68–85. DOI: 10.1108/BL-09-2020-0064

International Institute for Management Development. (2024). *World competitiveness ranking*. https://www.imd.org/centers/wcc/world-competitiveness-center/rankings/world-competitiveness-ranking/

International Labour Organization. (2018)... *World Employment and Social Outlook*.

Ion, S., & Ilie-Prica, M. (2020). Higher Education and Globalization in the Context of the COVID-19 Crisis. *European Journal of Education*, 3(2), 34–48. DOI: 10.26417/812dro50g

Ipsos. (2024). *Annual International Women's Day 2024: Global Attitudes Towards Women's Leadership*. Ipsos.

Irwin, T., Tonkinwise, C., & Kossoff, G. (2022). Transition design: An educational framework for advancing the study and design of sustainable transitions. Cuadernos del Centrode Estudiosen Disenoy Comunicacion. *Ensayos*, (105), 31–72.

Isaksen, S. G., Dorval, K. B., & Treffinger, D. J. (2010). *Creative approaches to problem-solving: A framework for innovation and change*. SAGE publications.

Isbister, J. (2006). *Promises not kept: poverty and the betrayal of Third World development* (7th ed.). Kumarian Press.

Ismail, Z. (2018). Benefits of STEM education. *K4D Helpdesk Report*.

Issah, M., & Al-Hattami, A. (2020). Developing Leadership Skills in the Classroom. Chapter in Innovations in Educational Leadership and Continuous Teachers' Professional Development (Eds. Osama Al Mahdi, Ph.D.). DOI: 10.46679/isbn978819484832502

Jackson, D., & Wilton, N. (2017). Perceived employability among undergraduates and the importance of career self-management, work experience and individual characteristics. *Higher Education Research & Development*, 36(4), 747–762. DOI: 10.1080/07294360.2016.1229270

Jackson, T. (2020). The Legacy of Geert Hofstede. *International Journal of Cross Cultural Management.*

Jacobsen, P. (1994). The Economic of Gender. Massachusets: Blackwell.

Jagdish, S., & Portera, G. (2008). *Theoretical reflections on Intercultural Education.* Routledge.

Jakhu, R., & Buzdugan, M. (2008, November 4). Development of the natural resources of the moon and other celestial bodies: Economic and legal aspects. *Astropolitics*, 6(3), 201–250. DOI: 10.1080/14777620802391778

Jalilvand, M. (2000). Married Women, Work dan Values. Monthly Labor Review August 2000. Married women, work, and values (bls.gov)

James, M. (2008). *Interculturalism: Theory and Policy*. The Baring Foundation.

Jamieson, M.V., & Shaw, J.M. (2018). APPLYING METACOGNITIVE STRATEGIES TO TEACHING ENGINEERING INNOVATION, DESIGN, AND LEADERSHIP.

Jangir, K., Sharma, V., & Gupta, M. (2024). Demystifying Machine Learning for Business Resilience Under VUCA in the COVID-19 Era. In Singh, D., Sood, K., Kautish, S., & Grima, S. (Eds.), *VUCA and Other Analytics in Business Resilience, Part B* (pp. 103–112). Emerald Publishing Limited., DOI: 10.1108/978-1-83753-198-120241007

Jansen, R. S., van Leeuwen, A., Janssen, J., Jak, S., & Kester, L. (2019). Self-regulated learning partially mediates the effect of self-regulated learning interventions on achievement in higher education: A meta-analysis. *Educational Research Review*, 28(100292), 100292. DOI: 10.1016/j.edurev.2019.100292

Jasentuliyana, N. & Lee, R. S. K. (1979-1981). *Manual on space law, Volumes I, II, III and IV*. Oceana Publications, Inc., 1979-1981.

Jasentuliyana, N. (1992). *Space law: Development and scope*. Praeger.

Jasni, S., Mohd Rosnan, S., Hussain, Z., & Shamsuddin, N. A. A. (2023). An innovation of LH Bites Cookies holder of augmented reality technology and QR code. In S. Ibrahim, A.S.A. Salamat, B. Nur Morat (Eds.), 2023. International Teaching Aid Competition 2023. University of Technology MARA, Kedah, pp. 301-306.

Javed, B., Naqvi, S. M. M. R., Khan, A. K., Arjoon, S., & Tayyeb, H. H. (2019). Impact of inclusive leadership on innovative work behavior: The role of psychological safety. *Journal of Management & Organization*, 25(1), 117–136. DOI: 10.1017/jmo.2017.3

Jeffery, J. S. (2021). *Navigating internationalization at a public flagship university: The balancing act of senior leadership* (Doctoral dissertation, University of Georgia).

Jenkins, S. (2022). *Higher Education in Saudi Arabia: A Vehicle for Global Promotion and Advancement* (1st ed.). Routledge., https://www.taylorfrancis.com/chapters/edit/10.4324/9781003049609-11/higher-education-saudi-arabia-sulaiman-jenkins

Jobs Brunei. (2020). *Brunei employment report 2019-2020.*

Johnson, B., Manyika, J., & Lee, L. (2005). The next revolution in interactions. *The McKinsey Quarterly*, 4, 20–33. https://www.mckinsey.com/capabilities/people-and-organizational-performance/our-insights/the-next-revolution-in-interactions

Jonassen, D. H. (2000). Toward a design theory of problem solving. *Educational Technology Research and Development*, 48(4), 63–85. DOI: 10.1007/BF02300500

Jones, S. H., St.Peter, C. C., & Ruckle, M. M. (2020). Reporting of demographic variables in the Journal of Applied Behavior Analysis. *The Journal of Applied Behavioral Science*, 9999, 1–12. DOI: 10.1002/jaba.722 PMID: 32383188

Jooss, S., Burbach, R., & Ruël, H. (2021). Examining talent pools as a core talent management practice in multinational corporations. *International Journal of Human Resource Management*, 32(11), 2321–2352. DOI: 10.1080/09585192.2019.1579748

Juntrasook, A., Nairn, K., Bond, C., & Spronken-Smith, R. (2013). Unpacking the narrative of non-positional leadership in academia: Hero and/or victim? *Higher Education Research & Development*, 32(2), 201–213. DOI: 10.1080/07294360.2011.643858

Juusola, K., Wilkins, S., & Jamous, S. (2023). Branding discourses in transnational higher education in the era of hyper-competition: Leveraging secondary brand associations. *Compare: A Journal of Comparative Education*, ●●●, 1–18. DOI: 10.1080/03057925.2023.2292533

Jwaifell, M. (2019). In-service Science Teachers' Readiness of Integrating Augmented Reality. *Journal of Curriculum and Teaching.*

Jyrkinen, M. (2014). Women managers, careers and gendered ageism. *Scandinavian Journal of Management, Elsevier*, 30(2), 175–185.

Kadarwati, S., Sulistyarini, I., & Muflikah, B. (2023). Use of Digital Game-Based Learning, Kahoot! to Improve Students' English Expressions Mastery. [Jurnal Ilmu Sosial dan Pendidikan]. *JISIP*, 7(2), 1556–1563.

Kaddoura, M. A. (2011). Critical thinking skills of nursing students in lecture-based teaching and case-based learning. *International Journal for the Scholarship of Teaching and Learning*, 5(2), n2. DOI: 10.20429/ijsotl.2011.050220

Kahramonovna, M. D. (2021). Innovative teaching methods. *International Journal on Orange Technologies*, 3(7), 35–37. DOI: 10.31149/ijot.v3i7.2063

Kalandarovna, A. G., & Qizi, A. M. A. (2023). Development and increase of competitiveness of the organization. *ASEAN Journal of Educational Research and Technology*, 2(3), 265–274.

Kapsos, S. (2008). *The Gender Wage Gap in Bangladesh. ILO Asia-Pacific Working Paper Series.* Bangkok: ILO.

Karacan, C.G., & Akoğlu, K. (2021). Educational Augmented Reality Technology for Language Learning and Teaching: A Comprehensive Review. *Education 3-13, 9*, 68-79.

Kasimbara, R. P., Imron, A., & Supriyanto, A. (2024). Strategic Marketing of Higher Education in a Developing World: A Multiple Cases Study of Localized Marketing Of Indonesia's Private Higher Education. *Educational Administration: Theory and Practice*, 30(5), 702–719.

Kaswan, K. S., Dhatterwal, J. S., & Ojha, R. P. (2024). AI in personalized learning. In *Advances in Technological Innovations in Higher Education* (pp. 103–117). CRC Press. DOI: 10.1201/9781003376699-9

KAUST Press Release. (2024, March 14). Saudi Arabia's top academic leaders converge at KAUST Saudi Leadership Institute 2024. (n.D.). King Abdullah University of Science and Technology (KAUST). Retrieved May 25, 2024, from https://www.kaust.edu.sa/en/news/saudi-arabia-s-top-academic-leaders-converge-at-kaust-saudi-leadership-institute-2024

Kayan-Fadlelmula, F., Sellami, A., Abdelkader, N., & Umer, S. (2022). A systematic review of STEM education research in the GCC countries: Trends, gaps, and barriers. *International Journal of STEM Education*, 9(1), 1–24. DOI: 10.1186/s40594-021-00319-7

Kayashima, N. (2022). Japan's ODA for the Development of Higher Education Institutions in Developing Countries: Supporting Leading Universities for Human Resource Development and Knowledge Creation and Diffusion. In *Japan's International Cooperation in Education: History and Prospects* (pp. 197–216). Springer Singapore. DOI: 10.1007/978-981-16-6815-9_9

Kayyali, M. (2023c, June). Virtual Universities: An Overview & Trends. In *Digital Education: Foundation & Emergence with challenges, cases* (pp. 301-326). New Delhi Publishers.

Kayyali, M. (2020a, December). The rise of online learning and its worthiness during COVID-19 pandemic. *International Journal of Information Science and Computing*, 7(2), 63–84. DOI: 10.30954/2348-7437.2.2020.2

Kayyali, M. (2020b, December). Pros and Cons of University Rankings. *International Journal of Management, Sciences, Innovation, and Technology*, 1(1), 4–10.

Kayyali, M. (2020c). Post COVID-19: New era for higher education systems. *International Journal of Applied Science and Engineering*, 8(2), 131–145. DOI: 10.30954/2322-0465.2.2020.6

Kayyali, M. (2021). Positive Impact of High Technology on Higher Education. *International Journal of Information Science and Computing*, 8(1), 13–21.

Kayyali, M. (2022). Internet of Things (IoT): Emphasizing Its Applications and Emergence in Environmental Management—The Profound Cases. In *Environmental Informatics: Challenges and Solutions* (pp. 201–212). Springer Nature. DOI: 10.1007/978-981-19-2083-7_11

Kayyali, M. (2023a). An Overview of Quality Assurance in Higher Education: Concepts and Frameworks. [IJMSIT]. *International Journal of Management, Sciences, Innovation, and Technology*, 4(2). https://ijmsit.com/volume-4-issue-2/

Kayyali, M. (2023b). The Relationship between Rankings and Academic Quality. *International Journal of Management, Sciences, Innovation, and Technology*, 4(3). https://ijmsit.com/volume-4-issue-3/

Kayyali, M., & Khosla, A. (2021, June). Globalization and Internationalization: ISO 21001 as a Trigger and Prime Key for Quality Assurance of Higher Education Institutions. *International Journal of Applied Science and Engineering*, 9(1), 67–96. DOI: 10.30954/2322-0465.1.2021.7

Kearney, S. (2013). Improving engagement: The use of 'Authentic self and peer assessment for learning' to enhance the student learning experience. *Assessment & Evaluation in Higher Education*, 38(7), 875–891. DOI: 10.1080/02602938.2012.751963

Keche, K. (2021). Relevancy of new higher education approaches in 'Second Republic Zimbabwe'. Higher Education-New Approaches to Accreditation, Digitalization, and Globalization in the Age of Covid, 1-11.

Keefe, H. (1995, July). Making the final frontier feasible: A critical look at the current body of outer space law. *Computer & High Technology Law Journal*, 11(2), 345–371.

Kelderman, E. (2023, September 5). What the public really thinks about higher education. *The Chronicle of Higher Education.*https://www.chronicle.com/article/what-the-public-really-thinks-about-higher-education

Kelley, T. R., & Knowles, J. G. (2016). A conceptual framework for integrated STEM education. *International Journal of STEM Education*, 3(1), 1–11. DOI: 10.1186/s40594-016-0046-z

Kementerian, P. P. P. A. (2024). Wujudkan Lingkungan Kerja yang Adil dan Setara bagi Perempuan, Kemen PPPA dan Women's World Banking Dorong Rencana Aksi Berkelanjutan. https://www.kemenpppa.go.id/page/view/NTA1Ng==

Kennedy, T. J., & Sundberg, C. W. (2020). 21st-century skills. *Science education in theory and practice: An introductory guide to learning theory*, 479-496.

Kennedy, D. M., Jewell, J., & Hickey, J. E. (2019). Male nursing students' experiences of simulation used to replace maternal-child clinical learning in Qatar. *Nurse Education Today*, 84, 104235. DOI: 10.1016/j.nedt.2019.104235 PMID: 31706203

Kezar, A. J. (Ed.). (2023). *Rethinking leadership in a complex, multicultural, and global environment: New concepts and models for higher education*. Taylor & Francis. DOI: 10.4324/9781003446842

Khalifa, B., & Hamid, M. S. (2024). Challenges, Best Practices, and Solutions. *Teaching and Supporting Students with Disabilities during Times of Crisis: Culturally Responsive Best Practices from Around the World*, 217.

Khanna, R. (2022). *Dignity in a digital age: Making tech work for all of us*. Simon and Schuster.

Khanna, S. (2015). From Novice to Professional: The impact of Skill Development programmes. *IRA-International Journal of Management & Social Sciences*, 1(1), 6–11.

Khlaisang, J., & Teo, T. (2024). An innovation-based virtual flipped learning system in a ubiquitous learning environment the 21st-century skills of higher education learners. *Journal of Educational Technology & Society*, 27(1), 100–116.

Kim, B. J., Kim, M. J., & Kim, T. H. (2021). "The power of ethical leadership": The influence of corporate social responsibility on creativity, the mediating function of psychological safety, and the moderating role of ethical leadership. *International Journal of Environmental Research and Public Health*, 18(6), 2968. DOI: 10.3390/ijerph18062968 PMID: 33799360

Kim, S. W., Zhang, C., Chung, H., Kim, Y., & Choi, S. Y. (2020). Why do women value credentials? Perceptions of gender inequality and credentialism in South Korea. *International Journal of Educational Development*, 73, 102158. https://doi.org/https://doi.org/10.1016/j.ijedudev.2020.102158. DOI: 10.1016/j.ijedudev.2020.102158

Kim, S., Chen, Z. W., Tan, J. Q., & Mussagulova, A. (2021). A case study of the Singapore Skills Future Credit scheme: Preliminary insights for making lifelong learning policy more effective. *Asian Journal of Political Science*, 29(2), 192–214. DOI: 10.1080/02185377.2021.1917431

King Sattam University's talent management guide (2024). 2nd Edition. Retrieved from webpage: https://dhr.psau.edu.sa/sitesuploads/dhr/page/202402/Integrated%20talent%20management%20guide.pdf. Accessed on 21st May 2024

Kiratli, N., Rozemeijer, F., Hilken, T., De Ruyter, K., & De Jong, A. (2016). Climate setting in sourcing teams: Developing a measurement scale for team creativity climate. *Journal of Purchasing and Supply Management*, 22(3), 196–204. DOI: 10.1016/j.pursup.2016.04.006

Kistaubayev, Y., Mutanov, G., Mansurova, M., Saxenbayeva, Z., & Shakan, Y. (2022). Ethereum-Based Information System for Digital Higher Education Registry and Verification of Student Achievement Documents. *Future Internet*, 15(1), 1–19. DOI: 10.3390/fi15010003

Klarsfeld, A., Ng, E. S., Booysen, L., Christiansen, L. C., & Kuvaas, B. (2016). Comparative equality and diversity: Main findings and research gaps. *Cross Cultural & Strategic Management*, 23(3), 394–412. DOI: 10.1108/CCSM-03-2016-0083

Klasen, S. (2019). What explains uneven Female Labor Force Participation Levels and Trends in Developing Countries? *The World Bank Research Observer*, 34(2), 161–197. Advance online publication. DOI: 10.1093/wbro/lkz005

Klasen, S., Le, T., Pieters, J., & Silva, M. (2020). What Drives Female Labour Force Participation? Comparable Micro-level Evidence from Eight Developing and Emerging Economies. *The Journal of Development Studies*. Advance online publication. DOI: 10.1080/00220388.2020.1790533

Klimaitis, C. C., & Mullen, C. A. (2021). Access and barriers to science, technology, engineering, and mathematics (STEM) education for K–12 students with disabilities and females. *Handbook of social justice interventions in education*, 813-836.)

Klimenko, A. Y. (2024). Technological Change and Its Effect on Education. [JEPR]. *Journal of Educational & Psychological Research*, 6(1), 1–18. DOI: 10.33140/ JEPR.06.01.04

Klimová, N., & Lovászová, G. (2019). Development of Critical Thinking in Education: A Case Study on Hoax Messages. In *2019 17th International Conference on Emerging eLearning Technologies and Applications (ICETA)* (pp. 396-402). IEEE. DOI: 10.1109/ICETA48886.2019.9040087

Knight, J. (2008). *Higher education in turmoil: The changing world of internationalization* (Vol. 13). Brill. DOI: 10.1163/9789087905224

Knoth, A., Willems, D., Schulz, E., & Engel, K. (2023). Co-creation, Co-learning and Co- teaching Are Key – Developing Intercultural, Collaborative, and Digital Competence Through Virtual Exchange. In Auer, M. E., Pachatz, W., & Rüütmann, T. (Eds.), *Learning in the Age of Digital and Green Transition. ICL 2022. Lecture Notes in Networks and Systems* (Vol. 633). Springer., DOI: 10.1007/978-3-031-26876-2_8

Kodai, Z., & Alzobeer, A. S. O. (2023). Investigation of the Influence of Social Trust, Network, and Shared Goals on Sharing Knowledge Attitudes among Saudi Academics in Higher Education Institutions. *International Journal of Organizational Leadership*, 12(2), 165–175. DOI: 10.33844/ijol.2023.60357

Koetsier, J. (2021, May 23). Space, Inc: 10,000 companies, $4T value ... and 52% American. *Forbes - Innovation Consumer Teach: Forbes.com*. https://www.forbes .com/sites/johnkoetsier/2021/05/22/space-inc-10000-companies-4t-value--and-52 -american/?sh=3ca624a755ac

Kogan, M., & Hanney, S. (2000). *Reforming higher education* (Vol. 50). Jessica Kingsley Publishers.

Kolade, O., & Owoseni, A. (2022, November). Kolade. O. and Owoseni, A. Employment 5.0: The work of the future and the future of work. *Technology in Society*, 71, 102086. Advance online publication. DOI: 10.1016/j.techsoc.2022.102086

Kolirin, L. (2020, September 18). Venus is a Russian planet -- say the Russians. *CNN.com._*https://www.cnn.com/2020/09/18/world/venus-russian-planet-scn-scli -intl/index.html

Konrad, A., & Linnehan, F. (1995). Formalized HRM Structures: Coordinating equal employment opportunity or concealing organizational practices? *Academy of Management Journal*, 38(3), 787–820. DOI: 10.2307/256746

Korn, M. (2022, November 14). Colleges win back foreign students. *Wall Street Journal, Eastern edition*, A.3.

Kornau, A., Knappert, L., Tatli, A., & Sieben, B. (2023). Contested fields of equality, diversity, and inclusion at work: An institutional work lens on power relations and actors' strategies in Germany and Turkey. *International Journal of Human Resource Management*, 34(12), 2481–2515. DOI: 10.1080/09585192.2022.2086014

Koschmann, T. D., Myers, A. C., Feltovich, P. J., & Barrows, H. S. (1994). Using technology to assist in realizing effective learning and instruction: A principled approach to the use of computers in collaborative learning. *Journal of the Learning Sciences*, 3(3), 227–264. DOI: 10.1207/s15327809jls0303_2

Koumpouros, Y. (2024). Revealing the true potential and prospects of augmented reality in education. *Smart Learning Environments*, 11(1), 2. DOI: 10.1186/s40561-023-00288-0

Krishnan, S. R. G., & Joseph, J. J. (2024). Online learning experiences of social work students in India. *Journal of Social Work : JSW*, 24(2), 276–292. DOI: 10.1177/14680173231207962

Kuknor, S. C., & Bhattacharya, S. (2022). Inclusive leadership: New age leadership to foster organizational inclusion. *European Journal of Training and Development*, 46(9), 771–797. DOI: 10.1108/EJTD-07-2019-0132

Kumbi, H (2017)The Culturally Intelligent Leader-Developing Multi-ethnic Communinities in a Multicultural Age Instant Apostle

Kuo, B. C., Chang, F. T. Y., & Lee, Y. L. (2023). Trends and Issues of Digital Learning in Taiwan. *Trends and Issues of Promoting Digital Learning in High-Digital-Competitiveness Countries: Country Reports and International Comparison*.

Kurt, S. (2018). Frameworks & theories. TPACK: Technological Pedagogical Content Knowledge Framework. Educational Technology. https://educationaltechnology.net/technological-pedagogical-content-knowledge-tpack-framework/

Kuzemko, L. (2020). SKILLS OF THE 21st CENTURY IN THE CONTEXT OF QUALITY ASSURANCE OF TEACHER PROFESSIONAL TRAINING. *Pedagogical education: Theory and practice. Psychology.Pedagogy*, 34(2), 28–33. DOI: 10.28925/2311-2409.2020.34.4

Labadi, S., Giliberto, F., Rosetti, I., Shetabi, L., & Yildirim, E. (2021). Heritage and the sustainable development goals: Policy guidance for heritage and development actors. *International Journal of Heritage Studies*.

Lampropoulos, G., Keramopoulos, E., Diamantaras, K., & Evangelidis, G. (2022). Augmented reality and virtual reality in education: Public perspectives, sentiments, attitudes, and discourses. *Education Sciences*, 12(11), 798. DOI: 10.3390/educsci12110798

Landells, E. M., & Albrecht, S. L. (2017). The positives and negatives of organizational politics: A qualitative study. *Journal of Business and Psychology*, 32(1), 41–58. DOI: 10.1007/s10869-015-9434-5

Landells, E. M., & Albrecht, S. L. (2019). Perceived organizational politics, engagement, and stress: The mediating influence of meaningful work. *Frontiers in Psychology*, 10, 1612. DOI: 10.3389/fpsyg.2019.01612 PMID: 31354596

Langseth, I., Jacobsen, D. Y., & Haugsbakken, H. (2023). The role of support units in digital transformation: How institutional entrepreneurs build capacity for online learning in higher education. *Technology. Knowledge and Learning*, 28(4), 1745–1782. DOI: 10.1007/s10758-022-09620-y

Lan, J., & Shepherd, B. (2019). Women and the Services Sector. In *Leveraging Services for Development: Prospects and Policies*. Asian Development Bank.

Lantz- Deaton, G. C. (2020) Intercultural Competence for College and University Students A global guide for employability and social change Springer Link

Larrue, P. (2021). The design and implementation of mission-oriented innovation policies: A new systemic policy approach to address societal challenges.

Le, T. (2023). *Colleges and universities in the US* (Industry Report 61131A). IBIS-World._https://www.ibisworld.com/united-states/market-research-reports/colleges-universities-industry/

Leal Filho, W., Ribeiro, P. C. C., Mazutti, J., Lange Salvia, A., Bonato Marcolin, C., Lima Silva Borsatto, J. M., & Viera Trevisan, L. (2024). Using artificial intelligence to implement the UN sustainable development goals at higher education institutions. *International Journal of Sustainable Development and World Ecology*, 31(6), 1–20. DOI: 10.1080/13504509.2024.2327584

Lee, K. E. (2017, Fall). Colonizing the final frontier: Why space exploration beyond low earth orbit is central to U.S. foreign policy, and the legal challenges it may pose. *Southern California Interdisciplinary Law Journal*, 27(1), 231–253.

Leenders, M. R., Mauffette-Leenders, L. A., & Erskine, J. A. (2001). Writing cases. 4th ed. Ivey Publishing, Richard Ivey School of Business Lincoln, Y. S., & Guba, E. G. (1985). Naturalistic Inquiry London Sage Publications.

Lee, S. H., Riney, L. C., Merkt, B., McDonough, S. D., Baker, J., Boyd, S., Zhang, Y., & Geis, G. L. (2024). Improving Pediatric Procedural Skills for EMS Clinicians: A Longitudinal Simulation-Based Curriculum with Novel, Remote, First-Person-View Video-Based Outcome Measurement. *Prehospital Emergency Care*, 28(2), 352–362. DOI: 10.1080/10903127.2023.2263555 PMID: 37751212

Lemoine, P. A., Jenkins, W. M., & Richardson, M. D. (2017). Global higher education: Development and implications. *Journal of Education and Development*, 1(1), 58. DOI: 10.20849/jed.v1i1.253

Leoni, R. (2014). Graduate employability and the development of competencies. The incomplete reform of the "bologna process.". *International Journal of Manpower*, 35(4), 448–469. DOI: 10.1108/IJM-05-2013-0097

Lepkova, N., Gulsecen, S., & Talan, T. (2024). Flipped classroom method application case study analysis. *Baltic journal of modern computing, 12*(2), 150-164

Levey, G. B. (2012). Interculturalism vs. Multiculturalism: A Distinction without a Difference? *Journal of Intercultural Studies (Melbourne, Vic.)*, 33(2), 217–224. DOI: 10.1080/07256868.2012.649529

Levinson, H. (1965). Reciprocation: The relationship between man and organization. *Administrative Science Quarterly*, 9(4), 370–390. DOI: 10.2307/2391032

Lewis, S. (2020, October 28). *CBS News*. Hubble telescope gives closer look at rare asteroid worth $10,000,000,000,000,000,000. *CBS News.com*. https://www.cbsnews.com/news/hubble-space-telescope-rare-asteroid-16-psyche-worth-10000-quadrillion/

lhamad, B. (2023). Quality Assurance Breaking Down Barriers with External Stakeholders: An Investigation of Current and Potential Roles of Stakeholders. In *Quality Assurance in Higher Education in the Middle East: Practices and Perspectives* (pp. 19-48). Emerald Publishing Limited.

Li, F., He, Y., & Xue, Q. (2021). Progress, challenges, and countermeasures of adaptive learning. *Journal of Educational Technology & Society*, 24(3), 238–255.

Likly, L., Joubert, M., Barrett, A. M., Bainton, D., Cameron, L., & Doyle, H. (2018) Supporting Secondary School STEM Education for Sustainable Education in Africa. Working Paper 05/2018. University of Bristol. Retrieved https://www.bristol.ac.uk/media

Lin, K. Y., Wu, Y. T., Hsu, Y. T., & Williams, P. J. (2021). Effects of infusing the engineering design process into STEM project-based learning to develop preservice technology teachers' engineering design thinking. *International Journal of STEM Education*, 8(1), 1–15. DOI: 10.1186/s40594-020-00258-9

Lin, P. Y., Hong, H. Y., Chen, B., & Chen, N. (2018). Integrated STEM Learning in an Idea-centered Knowledge-building Environment. *The Asia-Pacific Education Researcher*, 1(28), 63–76.

Liu, N. C., & Cheng, Y. (2005). The academic ranking of world universities. *Higher Education in Europe*, 30(2), 127–136. DOI: 10.1080/03797720500260116

Liu, W. (2021). The Chinese definition of internationalization in higher education. *Journal of Higher Education Policy and Management*, 43(2), 230–245. DOI: 10.1080/1360080X.2020.1777500

Livermore, D. A. (2009). *Cultural Intelligence*. Baker Publishing.

Llinares-Insa, L. I., González-Navarro, P., Zacarés-González, J. J., & Córdoba-Iñesta, A. I. (2018). Employability Appraisal Scale (EAS): Development and validation in a Spanish sample. *Frontiers in Psychology*, 9(AUG), 1437. Advance online publication. DOI: 10.3389/fpsyg.2018.01437 PMID: 30154748

Lo, C. K., & Hew, K. F. (2020). A comparison of flipped learning with gamification, traditional learning, and online independent study: The effects on students' mathematics achievement and cognitive engagement. *Interactive Learning Environments*, 28(4), 464–481. DOI: 10.1080/10494820.2018.1541910

Lombardi, M. (2023). Digital Economy and Digital Divide. In *Global Handbook of Inequality* (pp. 1–27). Springer International Publishing. DOI: 10.1007/978-3-030-97417-6_48-1

Loos, E., Gropler, J., & Goudeau, M. L. S. (2023). Using ChatGPT in Education: Human Reflection on ChatGPT's Self-Reflection. *Societies (Basel, Switzerland)*, 13(8), 196. DOI: 10.3390/soc13080196

Lopez, A., & Ibanez, E. (2021). Challenges of Education in the 4th Industrial Revolution. *The Fourth Industrial Revolution and Its Impact on Ethics: Solving the Challenges of the Agenda*, 2030, 139–150. DOI: 10.1007/978-3-030-57020-0_11

Lopez-Alcarria, A., Olivares-Vicente, A., & Poza-Vilches, F. (2019). A systematic review of the use of agile methodologies in education to foster sustainability competencies. *Sustainability (Basel)*, 11(10), 2915. DOI: 10.3390/su11102915

López-Belmonte, J., Pozo-Sánchez, S., Moreno-Guerrero, A., & Lampropoulos, G. (2023). *Metaverse in Education: a systematic review. Revista de Educación a Distancia*. RED.

Low, P., & Sulaiman, Z. (2013). Women and human capital - the Brunei Darussalam perspective. *Educational Research*, 4(2), 91–97.

Lukitasari, M., Hasan, R., Sukri, A., & Handhika, J. (2021). Developing Student's Metacognitive Ability in Science through Project-Based Learning with E-Portfolio. *International Journal of Evaluation and Research in Education*, 10(3), 948–955. DOI: 10.11591/ijere.v10i3.21370

Luna Scott, C. (2015). The Futures of Learning 3: What kind of pedagogies for the 21st century? Madlela, B. (2022). Exploring educational technologies used by Mthwakazi University rural satellite campuses to implement distance teacher education programs. *Interdisciplinary Journal of Education Research*, 4, 75–86.

Lutchen, K. R. (2024, April 18). *A new model for university-industry partnerships to ensure curricula evolve as technologies do*. https://hbsp.harvard.edu/inspiring -minds/a-new-model-for-university-industry-partnerships

Lwakabamba, S., & Lujara, N. K. (2003). Effective Engineering Training: The case of Kigali Institute of Science, Technology and Management. *Global Journal of Engineering Education*, 7(1), 71–76.

Lwamba, N. M., Bwisa, H., & Sakwa, M. (2014). Exploring the effect of corporate entrepreneurship on financial performance of firms: Evidence from Kenya's manufacturing firms. *International Journal of Academic Research in Business & Social Sciences*, 4(1), 352–370.

Ma, J., & Pender, M. (2021). *Trends in college pricing and student aid 2021*. College Board. https://research.collegeboard.org/media/pdf/trends-college-pricing-student -aid-2021.pdf

MacCurtain, S., Flood, P. C., Ramamoorthy, N., West, M. A., & Dawson, J. F. (2010). The top management team, reflexivity, knowledge sharing and new product performance: a study of the Irish software industry. *Creativity and Innovation Management, 19*(3), 219 - 232. doi:. 00564.xDOI: 10.1111/j.1467-8691.2010

Macfarlane, B., Bolden, R., & Watermeyer, R. (2024). Three perspectives on leadership in higher education: Traditionalist, reformist, pragmatist. *Higher Education*, ●●●, 1–22. DOI: 10.1007/s10734-023-01174-x

Machika, P., & Dolley, F. (2018). Framework for a learning management system at a university of technology with a weak information technology maturity system. *South African Journal of Higher Education*, 32(2), 176–191. DOI: 10.20853/32-2-1502

Madera, J., Ng, L., Sundermann, J., & Hebl, M. (2019). Top Management Gender Diversity and Organizational Attraction: When and Why It Matters. *Archives of Scientific Psychology. DOI: http://dx.doi.org/*, 90 –101.DOI: 10.1037/arc0000060

Maglione, F. (2024, February 22). *Half of college graduates are working high school level jobs.* https://www.bloomberg.com/news/articles/2024-02-22/career-earnings -with-a-college-degree-underemployed-graduates-lag-on-income

Mahdi, O. R., Nassar, I. A., & Almuslamani, H. A. I. (2020). The Role of Using Case Studies Method in Improving Students' Critical Thinking Skills in Higher Education. *International Journal of Higher Education*, 9(2), 297–308. DOI: 10.5430/ ijhe.v9n2p297

Mahona, P., & Pacho, T. (2021). Reshaping Education in the Post-COVID-19 Pandemic in Africa. [ARJESS]. *African Research Journal of Education and Social Sciences*, 8(3), 13–26.

Maine, F. (2021). In And Vikkri, M., Ed.). Dialogue for Intercultural Understanding., DOI: 10.1007/978-3-030-71778-0-2

Maine, F.. (2020). *Developing Education Policies in Europe to Enhance Cultural Literacy. Policy Briefing European Horizon (2020).* Research and Innovation Programme.

Ma, M., Liu, W., Zhang, R., Xie, W., & Qin, Q. (2023). Research on the Application and Effect of Innovative Teaching Methods in College Student Education. *Contemporary Education and Teaching Research*, 4(11), 573–578. DOI: 10.61360/ BoniCETR232015191104

Mamina, M. T., & Maganga, R. (2019). A review of engineering education at the University of Zimbabwe. *American Journal of Engineering Research*, 7(4), 112–128.

Mandal, D., & Yadav, V. K. (2024). Current Trends of MOOCS in India: Historical Background, Development and Challenges. *The Online Journal of Distance Education and e-Learning : TOJDEL*, 12(1).

Mangena, A., & Chabeli, M. M. (2005). Strategies to overcome obstacles in the facilitation of critical thinking in nursing education. *Nurse Education Today*, 25(4), 291–298. DOI: 10.1016/j.nedt.2005.01.012 PMID: 15896414

Manpower Planning and Employment Council. (2021). *What's Next? Preparing for Employment*. MPEC.

Maphosa, V. (2021). Using the pandemic to accelerate 21st-century learning at a rural university in Zimbabwe. *Advances in Research*, 22(5), 34–44. DOI: 10.9734/air/2021/v22i530314

Marconi, G., & Ritzen, J. (2015). Determinants of international university rankings scores.*Applied Economics*,47(57),6211–6227.DOI:10.1080/00036846.2015.1068921

Maree, K. (2016). *First steps in research*. Van Schaik Publishers.

Margot, K. C., & Kettler, T. (2019). Teachers' perception of STEM integration and education: A systematic literature review. *International Journal of STEM Education*, 6(1), 1–16. DOI: 10.1186/s40594-018-0151-2

Marinakou, E., & Giousmpasoglou, C. (2015). M-Learning in the Middle East: The Case of Bahrain. In Ordóñez de Pablos, P., Tennyson, R., & Lytras, M. (Eds.), *Assessing the Role of Mobile Technologies and Distance Learning in Higher Education* (pp. 176–199). IGI Global., DOI: 10.4018/978-1-4666-7316-8.ch008

Marshall, S., Blaj-Ward, L., Dreamson, N., Nyanjom, J., & Bertuol, M. T. (2024). The reshaping of higher education: Technological impacts, pedagogical change, and future projections. *Higher Education Research & Development*, 43(3), 521–541. DOI: 10.1080/07294360.2024.2329393

Marta, N. (2012). Tingkat Pendidikan Perempuan Indonesia dan Dampaknya Terhadap Penyerapan Tenaga Kerja Tahun 1970-1998. *Jurnal Sejarah Lontar Vol. 9, No. 2*.

Martin, A., & Grudziecki, J. (2006). DigEuLit: Concepts and tools for digital literacy development. *Innovation in teaching and learning in information and computer sciences, 5*(4), 249-267.

Matorevhu, A. (2023). Curriculum innovation implementation for industrialization: A case of education 5.0 pre-service science and mathematics teacher preparation. *Journal of Research in Instructional*, 3(1), 69–86. DOI: 10.30862/jri.v3i1.214

Matyushok, V., Vera Krasavina, V., Berezin, A., & Sendra García, J. (2021). The global economy in technological transformation conditions: A review of modern trends. *Ekonomska Istrazivanja*, 34(1), 1471–1497. DOI: 10.1080/1331677X.2020.1844030

Matzler, K., & Renzl, B. (2006). The relationship between interpersonal trust, employee satisfaction, and employee loyalty. *Total Quality Management & Business Excellence*, 17(10), 1261–1271. DOI: 10.1080/14783360600753653

Maxwell, G., Scott, B., Macfarlane, D., & Williamson, E. (2009). Employers as stakeholders in postgraduate employability skills development. *International Journal of Management Education*. Advance online publication. DOI: 10.3794/ijme.82.267

Mberi, N., & Phambili, M. (2016). Science, Technology, Engineering and Mathematics Craze hit Zimbabwe. *The Sunday News*, (February-March), 12.

Mccarthy, P. R., & McCarthy, H. M. (2006). When Case Studies Are Not Enough: Integrating Experiential Learning Into Business Curricula. *Journal of Education for Business*, 81(4), 201–204. DOI: 10.3200/JOEB.81.4.201-204

McCormack, J., Propper, C., & Smith, S. (2014). Herding cats? Management and university performance. *Economic Journal (London)*, 124(578), F534–F564. DOI: 10.1111/ecoj.12105

McDougall, J., Readman, M., & Wilkinson, P. (2018). The uses of (digital) literacy. *Learning, Media and Technology*, 43(3), 263–279. DOI: 10.1080/17439884.2018.1462206

McFarlane, B. (2014). Challenging leaderism. *Higher Education Research & Development*, 33(1), 1–4. DOI: 10.1080/07294360.2014.864590

McGee, J., Haward, M. G., & Edmiston, D. (2022). *The future of Antarctica: Scenarios from classical geopolitics*. Springer. DOI: 10.1007/978-981-16-7095-4

McGrath, S., Thondhlana, J., & Garwe, E. (2021). Internationalization of higher education and national development: The case of Zimbabwe. *Compare: A Journal of Comparative Education*, 51(6), 881–900. DOI: 10.1080/03057925.2019.1684241

McGurran, B. (2023, May 9). College tuition inflation: Compare the cost of college over time. *Forbes.*_https://www.forbes.com/advisor/student-loans/college-tuition-inflation/

McMurtrie, B. (2023, September 20). Americans Value Good Teaching. Do Colleges? *The Chronicle of Higher Education.*https://www.chronicle.com/article/americans-value-good-teaching-do-colleges

Medina, L. C. (2018). Blended learning: Deficits and prospects in higher education. *Australasian Journal of Educational Technology*, 34(1).

Mehmood, I., Macky, K., & Le Fevre, M. (2023). High-involvement work practices, employee trust and engagement: The mediating role of perceived organisational politics. *Personnel Review*, 52(4), 1321–1344. DOI: 10.1108/PR-03-2021-0151

Mehta, S., Singh, T., Bhakar, S. S., & Sinha, B. (2010). Employee loyalty towards organization—A study of academician. *International Journal of Business Management and Economic Research*, 1(1), 98–108.

Mellish, J. M., Brink, H., & Paton, F. (1998). *Teaching and learning the practice of nursing*. Heinemann.

Menezes, D. R., Couser, G., & Radkevitch, M. (2022). Highlighting businesses as key non-state actors in the Arctic: Collaboration between Arctic economic council and polar research and policy initiative. In N. Sellheim & D.R. Menezes (Eds.), *Non-state actors in the Arctic region* Springer Polar Sciences. Springer, Cham. https://doi.org/DOI: 10.1007/978-3-031-12459-4_5

Menon, K. (2014). *A STUDY ON EMPLOYABILITY OF ENGINEERING STUDENTS IN MUMBAI AND PUNE REGION.*

Meskell, L. (2002). Negative heritage and past masters in archaeology. *Anthropological Quarterly*, 75(3), 557–574. DOI: 10.1353/anq.2002.0050

Mganda, V. O. The role of corporate multilateral agencies in enhancing quality education in Tanzania in the era of globalization: challenges and opportunities. In *6th applied research conference in Africa* (p. 556).

Millar, D. (n.d.). *Learning and Employability Series 1 and 2.*

Mincer, J. (1974). The Human Capital Earnings Function. *Schooling, Experience, and Earnings*, 83-96.

Ministry of Education. (2010). *Brunei Darussalam Education Statistics.*

Ministry of Education. (2018). *Brunei Darussalam Education Statistics.*

Ministry of Finance and Economy. (2024). *Report of the labour force survey 2023.*

Ministry of Higher and Tertiary Education, Science and Technology Development. (2016). Concept Note (revised 13 January 2016). Paper Presented at the 1st National Conference on Science, Technology, Engineering and Mathematics (STEM) at Harare International Conference Centre from 28-28 January. Harare: Zimbabwe.

Mishra, L., Gupta, T., & Shree, A. (2020). Online teaching-learning in higher education during the lockdown period of the COVID-19 pandemic. *International Journal of Educational Research Open*, 1, 100012. DOI: 10.1016/j.ijedro.2020.100012 PMID: 35059663

Mitchell, M. S., Cropanzano, R. S., & Quisenberry, D. M. (2012). Social exchange theory, exchange resources, and interpersonal relationships: A modest resolution of theoretical difficulties. *Handbook of social resource theory: Theoretical extensions, empirical insights, and social applications*, 99-118.

Mitchell, R., Boyle, B., Parker, V., Giles, M., Chiang, V., & Joyce, P. (2015). Managing inclusiveness and diversity in teams: How leader inclusiveness affects performance through status and team identity. *Human Resource Management*, 54(2), 217–239. DOI: 10.1002/hrm.21658

Mlambo, D. N. (2020). Student Mobility, Brain Drainand the Internationalisation of Higher Education in Southern Africa. *African Journal of Development Studies (formerly AFFRIKA Journal of Politics, Economics and Society), 10*(2), 59-82.

Mntonintshi, O., & Mtembu, V. (2019). When Performance Management Fails: Attitudes and Perceptions of Staff at a Higher Education Institution. *Journal of Economics and Behavioral Studies*, 10(6), 131–140. DOI: 10.22610/jebs.v10i6A.2669

Mohamed, S. S., Barghuthi, N. B., & Said, H. E. (2017). An Analytical Study Towards the UAE Universities Smart Education Innovated Approaches. *2017 IEEE 19th International Conference on High Performance Computing and Communications; IEEE 15th International Conference on Smart City; IEEE 3rd International Conference on Data Science and Systems (HPCC/SmartCity/DSS)*, 200-205.

Mohammad, S., & Job, M.A. (2012). Confidence -Motivation -Satisfaction- Performance (CMSP) Analysis of Blended Learning System in the Arab Open University Bahrain.

Mohammadhossein, N., Richter, A., & Lukosch, S. (2024). Augmented Reality in Learning Settings: A Systematic Analysis of its Benefits and Avenues for Future Studies. *Communications of the Association for Information Systems*, 54(1), 29–49. DOI: 10.17705/1CAIS.05402

Mohammad, S. (2015). Effectiveness of M-Learning in Blended Learning-Design of Prototype Framework for AOU Bahrain. *2015 Fifth International Conference on e-Learning (econf)*, 201-206. DOI: 10.1109/ECONF.2015.22

Mohammed bin Rashid Al Maktoum Foundation. (n.d.). Young Innovators Competition. Retrieved from https://www.mbrfoundation.ae/en/innovation-and-creativity/innovation-competition

Mohammed, N. (2017). Project-based learning in higher education in the UAE: A case study of Arab students in Emirati Studies. *Learning and Teaching in Higher Education: Gulf Perspectives*, 14(2), 73–86. Advance online publication. DOI: 10.18538/lthe.v14.n2.294

Mokyr, J. (2018). *The British industrial revolution: An economic perspective* (2nd ed.). Routledge. DOI: 10.4324/9780429494567

Molodchik, M., Krutova, A., & Molodchik, A. (2016). Leadership, learning and organisational culture as antecedents for innovative behaviour: The case of Russia. *International Journal of Learning and Intellectual Capital*, 13(2-3), 202–215. DOI: 10.1504/IJLIC.2016.075700

Molotsi, A. R., & Goosen, L. (2022). Teachers Using Disruptive Methodologies in Teaching and Learning to Foster Learner Skills: Technological, Pedagogical, and Content Knowledge. In Rivera-Trigueros, I., López-Alcarria, A., Ruiz-Padillo, D., Olvera-Lobo, M., & Gutiérrez-Pérez, J. (Eds.), *Handbook of Research on Using Disruptive Methodologies and Game-Based Learning to Foster Transversal Skills* (pp. 1–24). IGI Global., DOI: 10.4018/978-1-7998-8645-7.ch001

Molotsi, A. R., & Goosen, L. (2023). Teachers' Unique Knowledge to Effectively Integrate Digital Technologies Into Teaching and Learning: Community Engagement to Build in the Online Space. In Dennis, M., & Halbert, J. (Eds.), *Community Engagement in the Online Space* (pp. 127–148). IGI Global., DOI: 10.4018/978-1-6684-5190-8.ch007

Montani, F., Odoardi, C., & Battistelli, A. (2014). Individual and contextual determinants of innovative work behaviour: Proactive goal generation matters. *Journal of Occupational and Organizational Psychology*, 87(4), 645–670. DOI: 10.1111/joop.12066

Morton, B., Vercueil, A., Masekela, R., Heinz, E., Reimer, L., Saleh, S., & Oriyo, N. (2022). Consensus statement on measures to promote equitable authorship in the publication of research from international partnerships. *Anaesthesia*, 77(3), 264–276. DOI: 10.1111/anae.15597 PMID: 34647323

Moshtari, M., & Safarpour, A. (2024). Challenges and strategies for the internationalization of higher education in low-income East African countries. *Higher Education*, 87(1), 89–109. DOI: 10.1007/s10734-023-00994-1 PMID: 36713135

Mossali, E., Picone, N., Gentilini, L., Rodrìguez, O., Pérez, J. M., & Colledani, M. (2020). Lithium-ion batteries towards circular economy: A literature review of opportunities and issues of recycling treatments. *Journal of Environmental Management*, 264, 110500. https://doi.org/https://doi.org/10.1016/j.jenvman.2020.110500. DOI: 10.1016/j.jenvman.2020.110500 PMID: 32250918

Mostert, M. P. (2007). Challenges of case-based teaching. *The Behavior Analyst Today*, 8(4), 434–442. DOI: 10.1037/h0100632

Mpofu, V (2019). A Theoretical Framework for Implementing STEM Education DOI: http://dx.doi.org/DOI: 10.5772/intechopen.88304

Mpofu, F. Y., Mpofu, A., Mantula, F., & Shava, G. N. (2024). Towards the Attainment of SDGs: The Contribution of Higher Education Institutions in Zimbabwe. *International Journal of Social Science Research and Review*, 7(1), 474–493.

Mtshali, T. I., & Msimango, S. M. (2023). Factors Influencing Construction Technology Teachers' Ability to Conduct Simulations Effectively. *Jurnal Penelitian Dan Pengkajian Ilmu Pendidikan: E-Saintika*, 7(1), 88–102. DOI: 10.36312/esaintika. v7i1.1079

Muhammad, D. F. (2023). *Effect of using student-centred approach on students practical skills learning in an online Badminton Course.* International Journal of Research and Studies Publishing. DOI: 10.52133/ijrsp.v4.44.18

Muhammad, N. I. (2024). Obstacles to the application of quality and reliability indicators in education colleges and the requirements for their achievement. *International Development Planning Review*, 23(1), 588–614.

Muiruri, Z. K. (2020). Strategic Business Services and Performance of Firms Sponsored by University Business Incubators in Kenya (Doctoral dissertation, Jkuat-Cohred).

Mukhalalati, B.A., Elshami, S., Awaisu, A., Carr, A., Bawadi, H., & Romanowski, M.H. (2020). "Practice Educators' Academy": A fundamental step to experiential training success in Qatar. *Journal of emergency medicine, trauma and acute care, 2020*, 14.

Mullin, A. E., Coe, I. R., Gooden, E. A., Tunde-Byass, M., & Wiley, R. E. (2021, November). Inclusion, diversity, equity, and accessibility: From organizational responsibility to leadership competency. []. Sage CA: Los Angeles, CA: SAGE Publications.]. *Healthcare Management Forum*, 34(6), 311–315. DOI: 10.1177/08404704211038232 PMID: 34535064

Mundia, L. (2019). Satisfaction with work-related achievements in Brunei public and private sector employees,. *Cogent Business & Management, 6*(1).

Munirathinam, S. (2020). Industry 4.0: Industrial internet of things (IIOT). []. Elsevier.]. *Advances in Computers*, 117(1), 129–164. DOI: 10.1016/bs.adcom.2019.10.010

Munyanyi, R. (2021). A critical analysis of the implementation of e-learning platforms at selected public universities in Zimbabwe (Doctoral dissertation).

Murala, D. K. (2024). METAEDUCATION: State-of-the-Art Methodology for Empowering Feature Education. *IEEE Access : Practical Innovations, Open Solutions*, 12, 57992–58020. DOI: 10.1109/ACCESS.2024.3391903

Muramalla, V. S. S. R., & Alotaibi, K. A. (2019). Equitable Workload and the Perceptions of Academic Staff in Universities. *The International Journal of Educational Organization and Leadership*, 26(2), 1–19. DOI: 10.18848/2329-1656/CGP/v26i02/1-19

Murphy, J., Kalbaska, N., Horton-Tognazzini, L., & Cantoni, L. (2015). Online learning and MOOCs: A framework proposal. In Information and Communication Technologies in Tourism 2015: Proceedings of the International Conference in Lugano, Switzerland, February 3-6, 2015 (pp. 847-858). Springer International Publishing. DOI: 10.1007/978-3-319-14343-9_61

Murphy, C. A., & Stewart, J. C. (2015). The Impact of Online or F2F Lecture Choice on Student Achievement and Engagement in a Large Lecture-Based Science Course: Closing the Gap. *Online Learning : the Official Journal of the Online Learning Consortium*, 19(3), 91–110. DOI: 10.24059/olj.v19i3.670

Murphy, S. (2023). Leadership practices contributing to STEM education success at three rural Australian schools. *Australian Educational Researcher*, 50(4), 1049–1067. DOI: 10.1007/s13384-022-00541-4

Musa, S. F., & Basir, K. H. (2019). Youth unemployment and the rentier economy in Brunei: Lessons from Norway. *Journal of Islamic Social Sciences and Humanities*, 20(2), 1–22. DOI: 10.33102/abqari.vol20no2.211

Muscato, C. (2019) Comparing Enculturation and Acculturation. www. dialls2020.eu

Musenze, I. A., & Mayende, T. S. (2023). Ethical leadership (EL) and innovative work behavior (IWB) in public universities: Examining the moderating role of perceived organizational support (POS). *Management Research Review*, 46(5), 682–701. DOI: 10.1108/MRR-12-2021-0858

Musselin, C. (2007). Are universities specific organisations? In *Towards a multi-versity*, Universities between Global Trends and National Traditions; Krücken, G., Kosmützky, A., Torka, M., Eds.; Transcript Verlag: Bielefeld, Germany, 2007; pp. 63–84. Available online: https://library.oapen.org/bitstream/handle/20.500.12657/22777 /1007- 385.pdf? sequence=1#page=64 (accessed on 20 January 2024).

Mutambala, M., Sheikheldin, G., Diyamett, B., & Nyichomba, B. (2020, November). Student industrial secondments in East Africa: Improving employability in engineering.

Mutambisi, T., & Chavunduka, C. (2023). Institutionalizing SDGs: Urban Local Authorities in Zimbabwe.

Muyambo-Goto, O., Naidoo, D., & Kennedy, K. J. (2023). Students' Conceptions of 21st Century Education in Zimbabwe. *Interchange*, 54(1), 49–80. DOI: 10.1007/s10780-022-09483-3

Nadehina, Y. P., Kolchin, A. A., & Myshko, Y. A. (2021). On the prospects of pedagogical technology "flipped classroom" in teaching History at university in conditions of digitalization of educational environment. In *Socio-economic Systems: Paradigms for the Future* (pp. 1211–1220). Springer International Publishing. DOI: 10.1007/978-3-030-56433-9_127

Nadia, S. (2022). Pemberdayaan Perempuan untuk Kesetaraan. https://www.djkn.kemenkeu.go.id/kpknl-pontianak/baca-artikel/15732/Pemberdayaan-Perempuan-untuk-Kesetaraan.html

Najmaei, A., & Sadeghinejad, Z. (2019). Inclusive leadership: a scientometric assessment of an emerging field. In *Diversity within Diversity Management: Types of Diversity in Organizations* (pp. 221–245). Emerald Publishing Limited.

National Center for Education Statistics. (2021). *Digest of education statistics.* https://nces.ed.gov/programs/digest/2021menu_tables.asp

National Center for Education Statistics. (2023, August). *Postsecondary institution revenues.* https://nces.ed.gov/programs/coe/indicator/cud/postsecondary-institution-revenue

National Center for Education Statistics. (2023, June). *Digest of education statistics.* https://nces.ed.gov/programs/digest/d22/tables/dt22_311.60.asp

National Center for Education Statistics. (2024, May). *Characteristics of postsecondary faculty.* https://nces.ed.gov/programs/coe/indicator/csc

National Research Council [NRC]. (2012). A Framework for k-12 science education: Practices, crosscutting concepts, and core ideas. Washington DC: The National Academic.

National Science Foundation. (2021). *Women, minorities, and persons with disabilities in science and engineering.*

Ncube, L. (2016). *Gwango Lodge joins the STEM bandwagon. The Chronicle: Feature/Opinion, Tuesday, 1 March. Bulawayo.* Government Printers.

Nelson, A. E. (2017). Methods faculty use to facilitate nursing students' critical thinking. *Teaching and Learning in Nursing*, 12(1), 62–66. DOI: 10.1016/j.teln.2016.09.007

Nelson, T. (2011, Spring). ILSA Journal of International &. *Comparative Law*, 17(2), 393–416.

Nembhard, I. M., & Edmondson, A. C. (2006). Making it safe: The effects of leader inclusiveness and professional status on psychological safety and improvement efforts in health care teams. *Journal of Organizational Behavior: The International Journal of Industrial. Journal of Organizational Behavior*, 27(7), 941–966. DOI: 10.1002/job.413

Ngadi, A. D., & Rajagukguk, Z. (2022). Featuring Multi-generational Digital Workers in Indonesia. *The 4Th SEASIA Biennial Conference.* Jakarta: Springer.

Ngadi, N., Asiati, D., Latifa, A., & Nawawi, N. (2021). Gender Inequality in the Indonesian Labor Market. In Dixit, S., & Moid, S. (Eds.), *Women Empowerment and Well-Being for Inclusive Economic Growth* (pp. 24–44). IGI Global., DOI: 10.4018/978-1-7998-3737-4.ch002

Ngadi, N., Meliana, R., & Purba, Y. A. (2020). Dampak pandemi Covid-19 terhadap PHK dan pendapatan pekerja di Indonesia. *Jurnal Kependudukan Indonesia*, 2902, 43.

Ngugi, J. K., & Goosen, L. (2021c). Computer Science and Information Technology Students' Self-regulated Learning and Knowledge Sharing Behavior as Drivers of Individual Innovative Behavior. (R. Silhavy, Ed.) *Lecture Notes in Networks and Systems, 230*, 593-608. DOI: 10.1007/978-3-030-77442-4_50

Ngugi, J. K., & Goosen, L. (2022). Digitalization and Drivers of Innovative Behavior for a Smart Economy in the Post-COVID-19 Era: Technology Student Course Design Characteristics. In L. Reis, L. Carvalho, C. Silveira, & D. Brasil (Eds.), *Digitalization as a Driver for Smart Economy in the Post-COVID-19 Era* (pp. 176-197)). IGI Global. DOI: 10.4018/978-1-7998-9227-4.ch010

Ngugi, J., & Goosen, L. (2017). The Effects of Course Design Characteristics, Self-Regulated Learning and Knowledge Sharing in Facilitating the Development of Innovative Behaviour among Technology Students at Universities. *Proceedings of the Institute of Science and Technology Education (ISTE)Conference on Mathematics, Science and Technology Education* (pp. 80-86). Mopani Camp, Kruger National Park: UNISA Press.

Ngugi, J., & Goosen, L. (2019, October 25). Towards Smart Innovation for Information Systems and Technology Students: Modelling Motivation, Metacognition and Affective Aspects of Learning. (Á. Rocha, & M. Serrhini, Eds.) *Smart Innovation, Systems and Technologies, 111*, 90-99. DOI: 10.1007/978-3-030-03577-8_11

Ngugi, J. K., & Goosen, L. (2021a). Knowledge Sharing Mediating Information Technology Student Innovation. In Khosrow-Pour, M. (Ed.), *Handbook of Research on Modern Educational Technologies, Applications, and Management* (Vol. II, pp. 645–663). IGI Global., DOI: 10.4018/978-1-7998-3476-2.ch040

Ngugi, J. K., & Goosen, L. (2021b). Innovation, Entrepreneurship, and Sustainability for ICT Students Towards the Post-COVID-19 Era. In Carvalho, L. C., Reis, L., & Silveira, C. (Eds.), *Handbook of Research on Entrepreneurship, Innovation, Sustainability, and ICTs in the Post-COVID-19 Era* (pp. 110–131). IGI Global., DOI: 10.4018/978-1-7998-6776-0.ch006

Ngugi, J. K., & Goosen, L. (2024a). Modelling Mediating Driver Practices That Promote Innovative Behavior for Technology Students: The Effects of Knowledge Sharing Behavior. In Nyberg, J., & Manzone, J. (Eds.), *Practices That Promote Innovation for Talented Students* (pp. 171–196). IGI Global., DOI: 10.4018/978-1-6684-5806-8.ch008

Ngugi, J. K., & Goosen, L. (2024b). Modelling the Mediating Effects of Knowledge Sharing Behavior in the Education Sector: Drivers of Individual Innovative Behavior. In Nadda, V., Tyagi, P., Moniz Vieira, R., & Tyagi, P. (Eds.), *Implementing Sustainable Development Goals in the Service Sector* (pp. 27–52). IGI Global., DOI: 10.4018/979-8-3693-2065-5.ch003

Ngugi, J., & Goosen, L. (2018). Modelling Course-Design Characteristics, Self-Regulated Learning and the Mediating Effect of Knowledge-Sharing Behavior as Drivers of Individual Innovative Behavior. *Eurasia Journal of Mathematics, Science and Technology Education*, 14(8). Advance online publication. DOI: 10.29333/ejmste/92087

Nguyen, T. T., Nguyen, M. T., & Tran, H. T. (2023). *Artificial intelligent based teaching and learning approaches: A comprehensive review. International Journal of Evaluation and Research in Education.* IJERE.

Nilivaara, P., & Soini, T. (2024). Alternative futures of Finnish comprehensive school. *Policy Futures in Education*, 22(3), 308–326. DOI: 10.1177/14782103231173615

Nkwanyane, T. P. (2023). Understanding the Demand for Industrial skills through the National Certificate (Vocational) Building and Civil Engineering Programme. *International Journal of Learning. Teaching and Educational Research*, 22(5), 674–687. DOI: 10.26803/ijlter.22.5.35

Nurdiana, R., Effendi, M. N., Ningsih, K. P., Abda, M. I., & Aslan, A. (2023). Collaborative partnerships for digital education to improve students' learning achievement at the Institute of Islamic Religion of Sultan Muhammad Syafiuddin Sambas, Indonesia. *International Journal of Teaching and Learning*, 1(1), 1–15.

Nyaga, J. M. (2023). IoT-Enhanced Adaptive Learning Environments: Personalized Online Education for the Digital Age. [AJCIS]. *African Journal of Computing and Information Systems*, 7(X), 1–14.

Nziramasanga, C. T. (2014). The 1999 Presidential Commission of Inquiry into Education and Training (CEIT) Report: Implementation Enigmas or Revelations?' In Madondo, M. M., Museka, G. and Phiri, M. (2014) (Eds.). The Presidential Commission of Inquiry into Education and Training (CEIT): Implementation Successes, Challenges and Opportunities. Harare: The Human Resources Research Centre, University of Zimbabwe.

O'Donnell, A. M., & Hmelo-Silver, C. E. (2013). Introduction: What is collaborative learning? An overview. The international handbook of collaborative learning, 1-15.

O'Leary, S. (2016). Graduates' experiences of, and attitudes towards, the inclusion of employability-related support in undergraduate degree programmes; trends and variations by subject discipline and gender. *Journal of Education and Work*, 30(1), 84–105. DOI: 10.1080/13639080.2015.1122181

Oaxaca, R. (1973). Male-Female Wage Differentials in Urban Labor Markets. *International Economic Review*, 14(3), 693–709. DOI: 10.2307/2525981

Ochi, A. (2023). Inequality and the impact of growth on poverty in sub-Saharan Africa: A GMM estimator in a dynamic panel threshold model. *Regional Science Policy & Practice*, 15(6), 1373–1395. DOI: 10.1111/rsp3.12707

OECD. (2019). Teaching for the future: Effective classroom practices to transform education. Retrieved from https://www.oecd.org/education/2030-project/teaching-for-the-future-education2030-background-note.pdf

OECD. (2020). *Parental leave: Where are the fathers?* OECD Family Database.

OECD. (2024, May 5). *Labour Market Situation.* From oecd.org: https://www.oecd.org/sdd/labour-stats/labour-market-situation-oecd-updated-april-2024.htm

of non-Arctic states in the high North". *Emory Law Review, 30*(1), 115-153. https://scholarlycommons.law.emory.edu/eilr/vol30/iss1/6

Ohara, M. (2023). *We're better Together -Let's Co-Create*. Advance HE.

Oke, A., & Fernandes, F. A. P. (2020). Innovations in Teaching and Learning: Exploring the Perceptions of the Education Sector on the 4th Industrial Revolution (4IR). *Journal of Open Innovation*, 6(2), 31. https://www.mdpi.com/2199-8531/6/2/31. DOI: 10.3390/joitmc6020031

Olatunji, G., Emmanuel, K., Osaghae, O. W., Timilehin, I., Aderinto, N., & Abdulbasit, M. O. (2023). Enhancing clinical and translational research in Africa: A comprehensive exploration of challenges and opportunities for advancement. *Journal of Clinical and Translational Research*, 9(5), 357–368.

Oliveira, L. B. D., Díaz, L. J. R., Carbogim, F. D. C., Rodrigues, A. R. B., & Püschel, V. A. D. A. (2016). Effectiveness of teaching strategies on the development of critical thinking in undergraduate nursing students: a meta-analysis. *Revista da Escola de Enfermagem da USP, 50*, 0355-0364.

Omar, A., Altohami, W. M. A., & Afzaal, M. (2022). Assessment of the Governance Quality of the Departments of English in Saudi Universities: Implications for Sustainable Development. *World Journal of English Language*, 12(8), 443. Advance online publication. DOI: 10.5430/wjel.v12n8p443

Omotayo, O. A. (2024). Exploring the role of emotional intelligence in educational Leadership: A case study of school administrators. *International Journal of Educatinal Research and Library Science*, 4(8), 43–59.

Opoku, A., & Williams, N. (2018). *Second-Generation Gender Bias: An Exploratory Study of Women's Leadership Gap in a UK Construction Organisation*. International Journal of Ethics and Systems., DOI: 10.1108/IJOES-05-2018-0079

Organisation for Economic Cooperation and Development (OECD). (2018). *Education at a Glance.*

Organization for Economic Cooperation and Development (OECD). (2024, July). OECD (2023), Educational attainment of 25-64 year-olds (2022): Percentage of adults with a given level of education as the highest level attained", in Education at a Glance 2023: OECD Indicators, OECD Publishing, Paris, https://doi.org/DOI: 10.1787/c5373fc9-en

Ormilla, R. C. G., & Ongan, M. G. O. (2024). Navigating the Shift: Faculty Preparedness for Online Teaching in the Evolving Global Higher Education Landscape. *International Journal of Learning. Teaching and Educational Research*, 23(1), 1–23.

Ornstein, A., & Hunkins, F. (2009). Curriculum Design. In *Curriculum: Foundations, Principles and Issues* (5th ed., pp. 181–206). Pearson/Allyn and Bacon.

Ouariach, F. Z., Nejjari, A., Ouariach, S., & Khaldi, M. (2024). Place of forums in online communication through an LMS platform. *World Journal of Advanced Engineering Technology and Sciences, 11*(1), 096-104.

Oumarou, G. (2024). Reforming education via radio lessons for teachers? The promise and problems of distance learning in Cameroon, 1960–1995. *Learning, Media and Technology*, 49(1), 8–19. DOI: 10.1080/17439884.2023.2244426

Oyewole, A. T., Adeoye, O. B., Addy, W. A., Okoye, C. C., & Ofodile, O. C. (2024). Enhancing global competitiveness of US SMES through sustainable finance: A review and future directions. *International Journal of Management & Entrepreneurship Research*, 6(3), 634–647.

Oyewo, S. A., & Goosen, L. (2024). Relationships Between Teachers' Technological Competency Levels and Self-Regulated Learning Behavior: Investigating Blended Learning Environments. In Pandey, R., Srivastava, N., & Chatterjee, P. (Eds.), *Architecture and Technological Advancements of Education 4.0* (pp. 1–24). IGI Global., DOI: 10.4018/978-1-6684-9285-7.ch001

Özbilgin, M. F. (2023). *Diversity: A key idea for business and society*. Taylor & Francis. DOI: 10.4324/9780367824044

Özcan, Y., Ücdoğruk, Ş., & Özcan, K. (2003). Age Differences by Gender, Wage and Self Employment in Urban Turkey. *Journal of Economic Cooperation*, 24, 1–24.

Pagnucci, N., Carnevale, F. A., Bagnasco, A., Tolotti, A., Cadorin, L., & Sasso, L. (2015). A cross-sectional study of pedagogical strategies in nursing education: Opportunities and constraints toward using effective pedagogy. *BMC Medical Education*, 15(1), 1–12. DOI: 10.1186/s12909-015-0411-5 PMID: 26303930

Paige, R. M. (1993) Towards Ethnorelativism: A Developmental Model of Inter-culturalSensitivity. (Ed) Education for Intercultural Experience: Yarmouth, ME; Intercultural Press

Palumbo, R., Manna, R., & Cavallone, M. (2020). Beware of side effects on quality! Investigating the implications of home working on work-life balance in educational services. The TQM Journal, pre-publication issue. .DOI: 10.1108/TQM-05-2020-0120

Papanastasiou, G., Drigas, A., Skianis, C., Lytras, M., & Papanastasiou, E. (2019). Virtual and augmented reality effects on K-12, higher, and tertiary education students' twenty-first-century skills. *Virtual Reality (Waltham Cross)*, 23(4), 425–436. DOI: 10.1007/s10055-018-0363-2

Paragoo, S., & Sevnarayan, K. (2024). Flipped classrooms for engaged learning during the pandemic: Teachers' perspectives and challenges in a South African high school. *Technology-mediated Learning during the pandemic*, 33-54.

Paravattil, B., Zolezzi, M., Carr, A., & Al-Moslih, A. (2021). Reshaping experiential education within Qatar University's Health Programs during the COVID-19 pandemic. *Qatar Medical Journal*, 2021(1), 2021. DOI: 10.5339/qmj.2021.9 PMID: 33763334

Parekh, B. (2006). *Rethinking Multiculturalism*. Palgrave.

Paren, J. (2015) Introduction to selected aspect of leadership. *Proceedings of the Multdiscplinary Academic Conference, Octo*, 1-7

Parikshit, L. (2023). Higher Education in India: Opportunities, Challenges & Solutions. *Shodh Sari-An International Multidisciplinary Journal*, 2(1), 54–60.

Parkinson, C. N. (1957). Parkinson's Law: The pursuit of progress edition. https://www.amazon.com/Parkinsons-Law-Other-Studies-Administration/dp/B000Z40KKQ

Paschal, M. J. (2022). Investigating teachers' awareness of gifted children and resource accessibility for their learning in Tanzania. *Asian Journal of Education and Social Studies*, 27(4), 9–31. DOI: 10.9734/ajess/2022/v27i430660

Paschal, M. J., & Mkulu, D. G. (2020). Teacher- Students' Relationship and Students 'Academic Performance in Public Secondary Schools in Magu District, Tanzania. *Journal of Research in Education and Society*, 11(1), 20–23. http://www.icidr.org/jresv11no1-content.php

Paul, P. K., Kayyali, M., Das, M., Chatterjee, R., & Saavedra, R. (2023). Artificial Intelligence and Smart Society: Educational Applications, Emergences and Issues-A Scientific Review. *International Journal of Applied Science and Engineering*, 11(1), 1–14. DOI: 10.30954/2322-0465.1.2023.2

Pelliteri, J. (2022). *Emotional Intelligence and Leadership Style in Leadership in Education, Department of Education and community programs.* Queens College, University of NewYork.

Penn, M. L., Currie, C. S., Hoad, K. A., & O'Brien, F. A. (2016). The use of case studies in OR teaching. *Higher Education Pedagogies*, 1(1), 16–25. DOI: 10.1080/23752696.2015.1134201

Perez-Arce, F., & Prados, M. (2020). The Decline in The U.S Labor Force Participation Rate: A Literature Review. *Journal of Economic Surveys*. Advance online publication. DOI: 10.1111/joes.12402

Perry, L., & Southwell, L. (2011). *Developing Intercultural Skills, Models and Approaches.* SCRIBD.

Pesamaa,O., Zwikael, O., Hair, J., Huemann, M,. (2021). Publishing qualitative papers with rigor and transparency. Intl. Proj. Manag. 39.

Peterman, A., Julia, B., & Agnes, Q. (2014). A Review of Empirical Evidence on Gender Differences in Nonland Agricultural Inputs, Technology, and Services in Developing Countries. *145–186. DOI:.*DOI: 10.1007/978-94-017-8616-4

Pfafflin, S. M. (2019). *Scientific-technological change and the role of women in development.* Routledge.

Pheko, M. M., & Molefhe, K. (2017). Addressing employability challenges: A framework for improving the employability of graduates in Botswana. *International Journal of Adolescence and Youth*, 22(4), 455–469. Advance online publication. DOI: 10.1080/02673843.2016.1234401

Pilkington, A. (2013). The interacting dynamics of institutional racism in higher education. *Race, Ethnicity and Education*, 16(2), 225–245. DOI: 10.1080/13613324.2011.646255

Podgorska, M., & Zdonek, I. (2023). Interdisciplinary collaboration in higher education towards sustainable development. *Sustainable Development*, ●●●, 1–19. DOI: 10.1002/sd.2765

Podsakoff, P. M., & Organ, D. W. (1986). Self-reports in organizational research: Problems and prospects. *Journal of Management*, 12(4), 531–544. DOI: 10.1177/014920638601200408

Poletti-Hughes, J., & Briano-Turrent, G. (2019). Gender Diversity on the Board of Directors and Corporate Risk: A Behavioural. *International Review of Financial Analysis*, 62, 80–90. DOI: 10.1016/j.irfa.2019.02.004

Popil, I. (2011). Promotion of critical thinking by using case studies as teaching method. *Nurse Education Today*, 31(2), 204–207. DOI: 10.1016/j.nedt.2010.06.002 PMID: 20655632

Portilla, L. U. (2023, December). Scientific fraud: attack on the credibility of science. In *Seminars in Medical Writing and Education* (Vol. 2, pp. 34-34).

Postsecondary Commission. (2024). *Accreditation handbook & materials.* https://postsecondarycommission.org/accreditation-handbook/

Pouratashi, M., & Zamani, A. (2019). University and graduates employability: Academics' views regarding university activities (the case of Iran). *Higher Education. Skills and Work-Based Learning*, 9(3), 290–304. DOI: 10.1108/HESWBL-12-2017-0103

Pradhan. S. (2023) The Impact of Globalisation on Work and Culture: Trends and Challenge Consultants Review

Prakash, A., Haque, A., Islam, F., & Sonal, D. (2023). *Exploring the Potential of Metaverse for Higher Education: Opportunities, Challenges, and Implications.* Metaverse Basic and Applied Research.

Press, T. (July 17, 2011). Keeping conflict on ice with the Antarctic Treaty. *The Conversation.*

Priyanto, D. (2024). Education towards Equality: A Review of the Contribution of Distance Learning Technology in Expanding Access and Promoting Social Equality. [TACIT]. *Technology and Society Perspectives*, 2(1), 138–142. DOI: 10.61100/tacit.v2i1.139

Profanter, A. (2017). University is a Private Matter: Higher Education in Saudi Arabia (Studies in Critical Social Sciences). In Rethinking Private Higher Education: Ethnographic Perspectives (Series Editor, Vol. 101). Brill. https://doi.org/DOI: 10.1163/9789004291508_008

Professor, X. (2011). *In the basement of the ivory tower: The truth about college.* Penguin Books.

Puentedura, R. (2014). *SAMR: An Applied Introduction.* [PDF file]. Retrieved from http://www.hippasus.com/rrpweblog/archives/2014/01/31/SAMRAnAppliedIntroduction.pdf

Purcell, K., Elias, P., Atfield, G., Behle, H., Ellison, R., & Luchinskaya, D. (2013). *Transitions into employment, further study and other outcomes.*

Putra, B. N. K., Jodi, I. W. G. A. S., & Prayoga, I. M. S. (2019). Compensation, Organizational Culture and Job Satisfaction In Affecting Employee Loyalty. *Journal of International Conference Proceedings*, 2(3), 11–15. DOI: 10.32535/jicp.v2i3.638

Putriyani, D.W., Sutrisno, D., & Abidin, A.Z. (2024). ANALYZING THE IMPACT: EMERGING CLASSROOM TECHNOLOGIES AND THE EVIDENCE ON LEARNING. *Global Synthesis in Education Journal.*

Qahl, M., & Sohaib, O. (2023). Key Factors for a Creative Environment in Saudi Arabian Higher Education Institutions. *Journal of Information Technology Education: Innovations in Practice*, 22, 1–48. DOI: 10.28945/5105

Qawasmeh, E. F., Alnafisi, S. Y., Almajali, R., Alromaih, B. S., & Helali, M. M., & al-lawama, H. I. (2024). The Impact of Human Resources Management Practices on Employee Performance: A Comparative Study Between Jordanian and Saudi Arabian Universities. *Migration Letters : An International Journal of Migration Studies*, 21(2), 243–257. DOI: 10.59670/ml.v21i2.6083

Qenani, E., MacDougall, N., & Sexton, C. (2014). An empirical study of self-perceived employability: Improving the prospects for student employment success in an uncertain environment. *Active Learning in Higher Education*, 15(3), 199–213. DOI: 10.1177/1469787414544875

Qi, M., Yi, Q., Mo, M., Huang, H., & Yang, Y. (2018). Application of case-based learning in instructing clinical skills on nursing undergraduates. *Biomedical Research (Aligarh)*, 29(2), 300–304. DOI: 10.4066/biomedicalresearch.29-17-2377

Quayson, F. (2019). The importance of inclusive leadership practice in higher education administration. *Interdisciplinary Journal of Advances in Research in Education, 1*(1).

Qureshi, S.S., Bradley, K.L., Vishnumolakala, V.R., Treagust, D.F., Southam, D.C., Mocerino, M., & Ojeil, J. (2016). Educational Reforms and Implementation of Student-Centered Active Learning in Science at Secondary and University Levels in Qatar. *Science education international, 27*, 437-456.

Radovanovic, D., Hogan, B., & Lalic, D. (2015). Overcoming digital divides in higher education: Digital literacy beyond Facebook. *New Media & Society*, 17(10), 1733–1749. DOI: 10.1177/1461444815588323

Rahiman, H. U., & Kodikal, R. (2024). Revolutionizing education: Artificial intelligence empowered learning in higher education. *Cogent Education*, 11(1), 2293431. DOI: 10.1080/2331186X.2023.2293431

Rahman, K.R., Shitol, S.K., Islam, M.S., Iftekhar, K.T., & Saha, P. (2023). Use of Metaverse Technology in Education Domain. *Journal of Metaverse*.

Rainwater, S. (2015). International law and the "globalization" of the Arctic: Assessing the rights

Rajab, K. D. (2018). The effectiveness and potential of E-learning in war zones: An empirical comparison of face-to-face and online education in Saudi Arabia. *IEEE Access : Practical Innovations, Open Solutions*, 6, 6783–6794. DOI: 10.1109/ACCESS.2018.2800164

Raji, B. (2019). Significance and challenges of computer assisted education programs in the UAE: A case study of higher learning and vocational education. *Education and Information Technologies*, 24(1), 153–164.

Rakhmalinda, F. (2024). Trends in Flipped Classroom of High Education: Bibliometric Analysis (2012–2022). *Journal of Research in Mathematics, Science, and Technology Education*, 1(1), 19–34. DOI: 10.70232/bd895m13

Ramaditya, M., Maarif, M. S., Affandi, J., & Sukmawati, A. (2022). Reinventing talent management: How to maximize performance in higher education. *Frontiers in Education*, 7, 929697. DOI: 10.3389/feduc.2022.929697

Ramisetty-Mikler, S. (2017). Measurement of Employability Skills and Job Readiness Perception of Post-graduate Management students: Results from A Pilot Study Employability skills and job readiness of recent graduates in India View project NewDay Services Parenting Project View project. In *Article in International Journal of Management and Social Sciences*. https://www.researchgate.net/publication/320735657

Ramos, A., Latorre, F., Tomás, I., & Ramos, J. (2022). Women's Promotion to Management and Unfairness Perceptions—A Challenge to the Social Sustainability of Organizations and Beyond. *Sustainability (Basel)*, 14(2), 788. DOI: 10.3390/su14020788

Randel, A., Galvin, B., Shore, L., Holcombe Ehrhart, K., Chung, B., Dean, M., & Kedharnath, U. (2018). Inclusive leadership: Realizing positive outcomes through belonging and being valued for uniqueness. *Human Resource Management Review*, 28(2), 190–203. DOI: 10.1016/j.hrmr.2017.07.002

Rangraz, M., & Pareto, L. (2021). Workplace work-integrated learning: Supporting industry 4.0 transformation for small manufacturing plants by re-skilling staff. *International Journal of Lifelong Education*, 40(1), 5–22. DOI: 10.1080/02601370.2020.1867249

Rapanta, C., & Trovao, S. (2021), Intercultural Education for the Twenty-First Century: Comparativy Review Research https: //link.springer.com/chapter 10

Ratanawaraha, A., Torquato Cruz, R., & Perez Cuso, M. (2024). Policies to promote private sector engagement in Science, Technology, and Innovation: Workbook.

Rauhvargers, A. (2013). *Global university rankings and their impact: Report II.* European University Association.

Razak, L. A. (2011). Brunei Darussalam's Labour Market: Issues and Challenges. *CSPS Strategy and Policy Journal*, 3, 1–36.

Razi, A., & Zhou, G. (2022). STEM, iSTEM, and STEAM: What is next? *International Journal of Technology in Education*, 5(1), 1–29. DOI: 10.46328/ijte.119

Readying students for the workforce: Aligning today's curriculum with tomorrow's careers. (2024). \https://he.hbsp.harvard.edu/readying-students-for-the-workforce.html ?icid=anonymous-home%7Cmust-reads-section%7Cmust-read-career-readiness

Reaves, J. (2019). 21st-century skills and the fourth industrial revolution: A critical future role for online education. *International Journal on Innovations in Online Education*, 3(1). Advance online publication. DOI: 10.1615/IntJInnovOnlineEdu.2019029705

Reinius, H., Kaukinen, I., Korhonen, T., Juuti, K., & Hakkarainen, K. (2022). Teachers as transformative agents in changing school culture. *Teaching and Teacher Education*, 120, 103888. DOI: 10.1016/j.tate.2022.103888

Renee, M. (2022). *You have a culture; 5 ways to understand your own better.* See Beyond.

Republic of Kenya. (2010). *The constitution of Kenya.* National Council for Law Reporting.

Reynolds, G. H. (1992). International space law: Into the Twenty-first Century. *Vanderbilt Journal of Transnational Law*, 25(2), 225–255.

Rhoades, L., & Eisenberger, R. (2002). Perceived organizational support: A review of the literature. *The Journal of Applied Psychology*, 87(4), 698–714. DOI: 10.1037/0021-9010.87.4.698 PMID: 12184574

Ribes- Giner. G. et al (2016) Co-creation Impacts on Student Behaviour. Elsevir Sandercock, L. (ed.Wood 2004) Reconsidering Multiculturalism: towards an Intercultural Project. Comedia

Richardson, M., & Roberts, R. (2020). Modern Women and Traditional Gender Stereotypes: An Examination of the Roles Women Assume in Thailand's Agricultural System. *Journal of International Agricultural and Extension Education*, 27(4), 7–21. Advance online publication. DOI: 10.5191/jiaee.2020.27407

Riggle, R. J., Edmondson, D. R., & Hansen, J. D. (2009). A meta-analysis of the relationship between perceived organizational support and job outcomes: 20 years of research. *Journal of Business Research*, 62(10), 1027–1030. DOI: 10.1016/j.jbusres.2008.05.003

Rincón, V., González, M., & Barrero, K. (2017). Women and Leadership: Gender Barriers to Senior Management Positions. *Intangible Capital*, 13(2), 319. DOI: 10.3926/ic.889

Rizov, T., & Rizova, E. (2015). AUGMENTED REALITY AS A TEACHING TOOL IN HIGHER EDUCATION. *International Journal of Cognitive Research in Science. Engineering and Education*, 3, 7–15.

Roberts, L. D. (2000). A lost connection: Geostationary satellite networks and the International Telecommunication Union. *Berkeley Technology Law Journal*, 15(3), 1095–1144.

Rosenberg, B. (2023, September 25). *Higher ed's ruinous resistance to change. The Chronicle of Higher Education.*https://www.chronicle.com/article/higher-eds-ruinous-resistance-to-change

Rothwell, A., & Arnold, J. (2007). Self-perceived employability: Development and validation of a scale. *Personnel Review*, 36(1), 23–41. DOI: 10.1108/00483480710716704

Rothwell, A., Jewell, S., & Hardie, M. (2009). Self-perceived employability: Investigating the responses of post-graduate students. *Journal of Vocational Behavior*, 75(2), 152–161. DOI: 10.1016/j.jvb.2009.05.002

Rudhumbu, N. (2020). Unlocking the Cultural Diversity Black Box: Application of Culturally Responsive Pedagogies in University Classrooms in Zimbabwe. *International Journal of Learning. Teaching and Educational Research*, 19(12), 146–162.

Saadati, Z., Zeki, C. P., & Barenji, R. V. (2023). On the development of blockchain-based learning management system as a metacognitive tool to support self-regulation learning in online higher education. *Interactive Learning Environments*, 31(5), 3148–3171. DOI: 10.1080/10494820.2021.1920429

Said, E. (1997). *Covering Islam: How the media and the experts determine how we see the rest of*

Saimon, M., Lavicza, Z., & Dana-Picard, T. (2023). Enhancing the 4Cs among college students of a communication skills course in Tanzania through a project-based learning model. *Education and Information Technologies*, 28(6), 6269–6285. DOI: 10.1007/s10639-022-11406-9 PMID: 36406787

Salah El-Din, D. N. S. M., & Al-kiyumi, D. A. R. A. (2021). Perceived organizational support for faculty members at Sultan Qaboos University: A field study. *Faculty of Education Journal Alexandria University*, 31(4), 109–145.

Salama, A. M. (2007). Contemporary Qatari architecture as an open textbook. *Archnet-IJAR*, 1, 101–114.

Salloum, S., Al Marzouqi, A., Alderbashi, K. Y., Shwedeh, F., Aburayya, A., Al Saidat, M. R., & Al-Maroof, R. S. (2023). Sustainability Model for the Continuous Intention to Use Metaverse Technology in Higher Education: A Case Study from Oman. *Sustainability (Basel)*, 15(6), 5257. DOI: 10.3390/su15065257

Sa, M. J., & Serpa, S. (2022). Higher Education as a Promoter of Soft Skills in a Sustainable Society 5.0. *Journal of Curriculum and Teaching*, 11(4), 1–12. DOI: 10.5430/jct.v11n4p1

Sani, S. (2015) The importance of Intercultural Education in the Development Age. The world conference on Educational Sciences (WCES-2015) www.sciencedirect.com

Sankar, J. P., Kalaichelvi, R., Elumalai, K. V., & Alqahtani, M. S. (2022). Effective Blended Learning in Higher Education During Covid-19. *Information Technologies and Learning Tools*. Vol 88, No2.

Sastry, T., & Bekhradnia, B. (2007). *Higher Education, Skills, and Employer Engagement*. HEPI.

Saudi Arabia's Top Academic Leaders Converge at KAUST Saudi Leadership Institute. (2024). (2024, May 25). Saudi Arabia's Top Academic Leaders Converge at KAUST Saudi Leadership Institute 2024. https://www.kaust.edu.sa/news/saudi-arabia-s-top-academic-leaders-converge-at-kaust-saudi-leadership-institute-2024

Saudi Vision 2030. (2019, May 25). Saudi Vision 2030. https://www.vision2030.gov.sa/en/

Savov, S. A., Antonova, R., & Spassov, K. (2019). Multimedia applications in education. In Smart Technologies and Innovation for a Sustainable Future: Proceedings of the 1st American University in the Emirates International Research Conference—Dubai, UAE 2017 (pp. 263-271). Springer International Publishing.

Schelfhout, S. (ed 2022) Intercultural Intercultural Competence Predicts Intercultural Effectiveness: International Journal of Environmental Research and Public Health

Schlegelmilch, B. B. (2020). Why business schools need radical innovations: Drivers and development trajectories. *Journal of Marketing Education*, 42(2), 93–107. DOI: 10.1177/0273475320922285

Schleifer, D., Friedman, W., & McNally, E. (2022). *America's hidden common ground on public higher education: What's wrong and how to fix it*. https://www.publicagenda.org/reports/americas-hidden-common-ground-on-public-higher-education/

Schrecker, E. (2022, October 14). The 50-year war on higher education. *The Chronicle of Higher Education*. https://www.chronicle.com/article/the-50-year-war-on-higher-education

Schultz, T. P. (1980). Estimating Labor Supply Function for Married Women. In Smith, J. (Ed.), *Female Labor Supply: Theory and Estimating*. Princeton University Press. DOI: 10.1515/9781400856992.25

Schultz, T. W. (1961). Investment in Human Capital [Jstore.]. *The American Economic Review*, 51(1), 1–17.

Schwartz, M., & Omori, K. (2024). Communities of Practice and Acculturation: How International Students in American Colleges Use Social Media to Manage Homesickness. *Journal of International and Comparative Education (JICE)*, 57-72.

Schwind, M. (1986). Open Stars: An examination of the United States push to privatize

Scott, S., & Bruce, R. (1994). Determinant of innovative behaviour: A path model of individual innovation in the workplace. *Academy of Management Journal*, 37(3), 580–607. DOI: 10.2307/256701

Secules, S., McCall, C., Mejia, J. A., Beebe, C., Masters, A. S. L., Sánchez-Pena, M., & Svyantek, M. (2021). Positionality practices and dimensions of impact on equity research: A collaborative inquiry and call to the community. *Journal of Engineering Education*, 110(1), 19–43. DOI: 10.1002/jee.20377

Sehgal, N., & Nasim, S. (2018). Total Interpretive Structural Modelling of predictors for graduate employability for the information technology sector. *Higher Education. Skills and Work-Based Learning*, 8(4), 495–510. DOI: 10.1108/HESWBL-08-2017-0047

Seleviciene, E. (2020). *Effectiveness and acceptance of Web 2.0 technologies in the studies of English for specific purposes in higher education* (Doctoral dissertation, Mykolo Romerio University.)

Sethi, A., Jangir, K., & Kukreti, M. (2024). *Robo-Advisors* (pp. 285–294). DOI: 10.4018/979-8-3693-2849-1.ch019

Sezerel, H., & Christiansen, B. (Eds.). (2022). *Handbook of research on sustainable tourism and hotel operations in global hypercompetition*. IGI Global., Retrieved from https://www.igi-global.com/book/handbook-research-sustainable-tourism-hotel/291267 DOI: 10.4018/978-1-6684-4645-4

Sharaf-Addin, H. H., & Fazel, H. (2021). Balanced Scorecard Development as a Performance Management System in Saudi Public Universities: A Case Study Approach. *Asia-Pacific Journal of Management Research and Innovation*, 17(1-2), 57–70. DOI: 10.1177/2319510X211048591

Sharipov, F. (2020). Internationalization of higher education: definition and description. *Mental Enlightenment Scientific-Methodological Journal*, 127-138.

Sharma, E., & Sethi, S. (2015). Skill Development: Opportunities & Challenges in India. *GianJyoti E-Journal*, 5(1), 45–55.

Sharma, P., Sharma, V., Jangir, K., Gupta, M., & Pathak, N. (2024). An analysis of customer intention to use smart home services. *AIP Conference Proceedings*, 2919(1), 080003. DOI: 10.1063/5.0184373

Sharvari, K. (2019). Gap analysis of Soft skills in the curriculum of Higher Education (A case study of Management Institutes in Karnataka). In *Advances In Management* (Vol. 12, Issue 1).

Shava, G. N. (2015). Professional development, a major strategy for higher education student success, experiences from a university in Zimbabwe. *Zambia Journal of Science and Technology*, 10(1), 11–25.

Shavkatovna, R. G. (2020). Improving Technologies To Develop Spiritual And Moral Competencies In Future Teachers. *The American Journal of Management and Economics Innovations.*, 2(9), 1–6. DOI: 10.37547/tajmei/Volume02Issue09-01

Shaw, A., & Dolan, P. (2022). Youth Volunteering: New Norms for Policy and Practice. In Social Activism-New Challenges in a (Dis) connected World. IntechOpen.

Shchevliagin, M., & Koroleva, D. (2024). Four scenarios of personalized learning integration mediated by a digital platform. *Turkish Online Journal of Distance Education*, 25(2), 76–95. DOI: 10.17718/tojde.1267577

Sheerah, H.A. (2016). Blended Learning in Saudi Universities: Challenges and Aspirations. Published 2016. Education, Computer Science.

Shen, W., Xu, X., & Wang, X. (2022). Reconceptualising international academic mobility in the global knowledge system: Towards a new research agenda. *Higher Education*, 84(6), 1317–1342. DOI: 10.1007/s10734-022-00931-8 PMID: 36211225

Shernoff, D. J., Sinha, S., Bressler, D. M., & Ginsburg, L. (2017). Assessing teacher education and professional development needs for the implementation of integrated approaches to STEM education. *International Journal of STEM Education*, 4(1), 1–16. DOI: 10.1186/s40594-017-0068-1 PMID: 30631669

Shiva, V. (1997). *Biopiracy: The plunder of nature and knowledge*. South End Press.

Shousha, A. I. (2018). Motivational Strategies and Student Motivation in an EFL Saudi Context. *International Journal of English Language Education*, 6(1), 20–44. DOI: 10.5296/ijele.v6i1.12535

Shrestha, S. K., & Furqan, F. (2020, November). IoT for smart learning/education. In *2020 5th International Conference on Innovative Technologies in Intelligent Systems and Industrial Applications (CITISIA)* (pp. 1-7). IEEE.

Shuaili, K. A., Musawi, A. S., & Hussain, R. M. (2020). *The effectiveness of using augmented reality in teaching geography curriculum on the achievement and attitudes of Omani 10th Grade Students*. Multidisciplinary Journal for Education, Social and Technological Sciences. DOI: 10.4995/muse.2020.13014

Shute, V., & Towle, B. (2018). Adaptive e-learning. In *Aptitude* (pp. 105–114). Routledge.

Shwedeh, F., Adelaja, A.A., Ogbolu, G., Kitana, A., Taamneh, A., Aburayya, A., & Salloum, S.A. (2023). Entrepreneurial innovation among international students in the UAE: Differential role of entrepreneurial education using SEM analysis. *International Journal of Innovative Research and Scientific Studies*.

Sibanda, N. (2022). E-Learning at a Zimbabwean Rural University during the COVID-19 Pandemic: Challenges and Opportunities. *Alternation (Durban)*, 29(1). Advance online publication. DOI: 10.29086/2519-5476/2022/v29n1a15

Siddiq, F., Olofsson, A. D., Lindberg, J. O., & Tomczyk, L. (2023). What will be the new normal? Digital competence and 21st-century skills: Critical and emergent issues in education. *Education and Information Technologies*, ●●●, 1–9.

Sifelani, J. (2022). *Science Teachers' Information and Communication Technology (ICT) Self-Efficacy and Classroom Technology Integration: The Case of Manicaland Province, Zimbabwe* (Doctoral dissertation, University of Witwatersrand, Johannesburg).

Siles-Gonzalez, J., & Solano-Ruiz, C. (2016). Self-assessment, reflection on practice and critical thinking in nursing students. *Nurse Education Today*, 45, 132–137. DOI: 10.1016/j.nedt.2016.07.005 PMID: 27471109

Simonin, B. L. (2004). An empirical investigation of the process of knowledge transfer in international strategic alliances. *Journal of International Business Studies*, 35(5), 407–427. DOI: 10.1057/palgrave.jibs.8400091

Singh, A. K., & Meena, M. K. (2024). Online teaching in Indian higher education institutions during the pandemic time. *Education and Information Technologies*, 29(4), 4107–4157. DOI: 10.1007/s10639-023-11942-y

Singh, A., & Alhabbas, N. (2024). Transforming KSA's local workforce into global talent: An Industry 4.0 and 5.0 initiative leading to vision 2030. *International Journal of Advanced and Applied Sciences*, 11(2), 94–106. DOI: 10.21833/ijaas.2024.02.012

Singh, U. G. (2024). Exploring the Digital Divide in African Higher Education Institutions. In *Higher Education Institutions and Covid-19* (pp. 93–109). Routledge.

Sipayung, F., Wijaya, A., Putra, F., & Aratame, N. (2022). Analyzing the Characteristics of Highly Educated Unemployment in Indonesia's Capital City. *Jurnal Ekonomi dan Studi Pembangunan, 14 (2).: http://dx.doi.org/*.DOI: 10.17977/um-002v14i22022p153

Sivarajah, R. T., Curci, N. E., Johnson, E. M., Lam, D. L., Lee, J. T., & Richardson, M. L. (2019). A review of innovative teaching methods. *Academic Radiology*, 26(1), 101–113. DOI: 10.1016/j.acra.2018.03.025 PMID: 30929697

Skala, D., & Weill, L. (2018). Does CEO gender matter for bank risk? *Economic Systems*, 42(1), 64–74. DOI: 10.1016/j.ecosys.2017.08.005

Skowronek, R. K., & Lewis, K. E. (Eds.). (2010). *Beneath the ivory tower: The archaeology of academia*. University Press of Florida., https://academic.oup.com/florida-scholarship-online/book/29004 DOI: 10.5744/florida/9780813034225.001.0001

Slattery, M. (2024). *Education Strategy in a Changing Society: Personalised, Smarter, Lifelong Learning in the 21st Century*. Taylor & Francis. DOI: 10.4324/9781003358770

Smetana, L. K., & Bell, R. L. (2012). Computer simulations to support science instruction and learning: A critical review of the literature. *International Journal of Science Education*, 34(9), 1337–1370. DOI: 10.1080/09500693.2011.605182

Smith, M. (2023, October 5). *The public is giving up on higher ed. The Chronicle of Higher Education.* https://www.chronicle.com/article/the-public-is-giving-up-on-higher-ed

Smith, L., & Abouammoh, A. (2013). *Higher education in Saudi Arabia: achievements, challenges and opportunities*. Springer., DOI: 10.1007/978-94-007-6321-0

Snyder, M. (2018). A century of perspectives that influenced the consideration of technology as a critical component of STEM education in the United States. *The Journal of Technology Studies*, 44(2), 42–57. DOI: 10.21061/jots.v44i2.a.1

Sofkova Hashemi, S., & Berbyuk Lindström, N. Brooks, E., Hahn, J. and Sjoberg, J. (2023). "Impact of Emergency Online Teaching on Teachers' Professional Digital Competence: Experiences from the Nordic Higher Education Institutions" (2023). Rising like a Phoenix: Emerging from the Pandemic and Reshaping Human Endeavors with Digital Technologies ICIS 2023. 12. https://aisel.aisnet.org/icis2023/learnandiscurricula/learnandiscurricula/12

Sofkova Hashemi, S., Berbyuk Lindström, N., & Bergdahl, N. (2024). Pandemic as Digital Change Accelerator: Sustainable Reshaping of Adult Education Post Covid-19.

Soghomonyan, Z., & Karapetyan, A. (2023). Teaching Strategies of the 21st Century Skills Adapted to the Local Needs. *European Journal of Teacher Education*, 5(3), 48–69. DOI: 10.33422/ejte.v5i3.1097

Sohoni, M. (2012). Engineering teaching and research in IITs and its impact on India. *Current Science*, 102(11), 1510–1515.

Sojberg, J. (2024) https://www.birmingham.ac.uk,news,developing-students-intercultural-awareness

Sok, J., Blomme, R., & Tromp, D. (2013). The use of the psychological contract to explain self-perceived employability. *International Journal of Hospitality Management*, 34, 274–284. DOI: 10.1016/j.ijhm.2013.03.008

Spencer- Oatey, H. (2012) What is Culture? Global Pad Open House

Srivastava, S. (2011). Job burnout and managerial effectiveness relationship: Moderating effects of locus of control and perceived organisational support: An empirical study on Indian managers. *Asian Journal of Management Research*, 2(1), 329–347.

Stamper, C. L., & Masterson, S. S. (2002). Insider or outsider? How employee perceptions of insider status affect their work behavior. *Journal of Organizational Behavior: The International Journal of Industrial. Journal of Organizational Behavior*, 23(8), 875–894. DOI: 10.1002/job.175

Statista. (2021). *The student debt crisis in the U.S.*https://www.statista.com/study/72526/the-student-debt-crisis-in-the-us/

Stearns, P. N. (2020). *The Industrial Revolution in world history*. Routledge. DOI: 10.4324/9781003050186

Stefan, I., Barkoczi, N., Todorov, T., Peev, I., Pop, L., Marian, C., & Morales, L. (2023, June). Technology and Education as Drivers of the Fourth Industrial Revolution through the Lens of the New Science of Learning. In *International Conference on Human-Computer Interaction* (pp. 133-148). Cham: Springer Nature Switzerland. DOI: 10.1007/978-3-031-34411-4_11

Stefani, L., & Blessinger, P. (2018). Inclusive Leadership in Higher Education. *Journal of International Management*, 7(1).

Subbarayalu, A. V., Al Kuwaiti, A., & Al-Muhanna, F. A. (2024). Talent Management Practices in Saudi Universities During the Post-Pandemic Renaissance (Chapter 21). Building Resiliency in Higher Education: Globalization, Digital Skills, and Student Wellness, *IGL Global*. DOI: https://doi.org/DOI: 10.4018/979-8-3693-5483-4.ch021

Subramaniam, S. R., & Muniandy, B. (2019). The effect of the flipped classroom on students' engagement. Technology. *Knowledge and Learning*, 24(3), 355–372. DOI: 10.1007/s10758-017-9343-y

Suffolk University. Law School. (2000). Suffolk Transnational Law Review (Vol. 24). Suffolk University Law School.

Suliman, S., Hassan, R., Athamneh, K., Jenkins, M., & Bylund, C. L. (2018). Blended learning in quality improvement training for healthcare professionals in Qatar. *International Journal of Medical Education*, 9, 55–56. DOI: 10.5116/ijme.5a80.3d88 PMID: 29478042

Sullivan, M. (2023). 17 Global expansion and service diversification. Singapore Inc.: A Century of Business Success in Global Markets: Strategies, Innovations, and Insights from Singapore's Top Corporations, 17.

Surbhi, S. (2019) Difference between Enculturation and Acculturation. keydifferences.com Together for Peace: t4p.org.uk

Svihus, C. L. (2024). Online teaching in higher education during the COVID-19 pandemic. *Education and Information Technologies*, 29(3), 3175–3193. DOI: 10.1007/s10639-023-11971-7

Svongoro, P., & Mudzi, F. (2023). Optimising students' participation during emergency remote teaching in the Covid-19 pandemic. *Perspectives in Education*, 41(1), 211–227. DOI: 10.38140/pie.v41i1.6182

Swanson, R. A. (2022). *Foundations of human resource development*. Berrett-Koehler Publishers.

Swedish International Development Cooperation Agency. (2018). Skills Development. March 2018. https://cdn.sida.se/publications/files/sida62134en-skills-development.pdf

Syahid, A., Kamri, K. A., & Azizan, S. N. (2021). Usability of Massive Open Online Courses (MOOCs): Malaysian Undergraduates' Perspective. *The Journal of Educators Online*, 18(3), n3. DOI: 10.9743/JEO.2021.18.3.11

Syahrin, S., & Akmal, N. (2024). *Navigating the Artificial Intelligence Frontier: Perceptions of Instructors, Students, and Administrative Staff on the Role of Artificial Intelligence in Education in the Sultanate of Oman*. Arab World English Journal.

Tahiri, A., Kovaçi, I., & Trajkovska Petkoska, A. (2022). Sustainable tourism as a potential for promotion of regional heritage, local food, traditions, and diversity—Case of Kosovo. *Sustainability (Basel)*, 14(19), 12326. DOI: 10.3390/su141912326

Tamim, R. (2018). Blended Learning for Learner Empowerment: Voices from the Middle East. *Journal of Research on Technology in Education*, 50(1), 70–83. DOI: 10.1080/15391523.2017.1405757

Tanaka, S., Taguchi, S., Yoshida, K., Cardini, A., Kayashima, N., & Morishita, H. (2019). Transforming education towards equitable quality education to achieve the SDGs. *Policy Brief 2030 AGENDA FOR. Sustainable Development*, (2), 1–11.

Tatli, A., Nicolopoulou, K., Özbilgin, M., Karatas-Ozkan, M., & Öztürk, M. B. (2015). Questioning impact: Interconnection between extra-organizational resources and agency of equality and diversity officers. *International Journal of Human Resource Management*, 26(9), 1243–1258. DOI: 10.1080/09585192.2014.934893

Tavares, O. (2016). The role of students' employability perceptions on Portuguese higher education choices. *Journal of Education and Work*, 30(1), 106–121. DOI: 10.1080/13639080.2015.1122180

Tayeb, O., Zahed, A., & Ritzen, J. (2016). Becoming a World-Class University. *Springer Open*. https://doi.org/https://doi.org/10.1007/978-3-319-26380-9

Tayem, Y., Almarabheh, A. J., Abo Hamza, E. G., & Deifalla, A. (2022). Perceptions of Medical Students on Distance Learning During the COVID-19 Pandemic: A Cross-Sectional Study from Bahrain. *Advances in Medical Education and Practice*, 13, 345–354. DOI: 10.2147/AMEP.S357335 PMID: 35478974

Taylor, P., Morin, R., Cohn, D., Clark, A., & Wang, W. (2008). *Men or Women: Who's the Better Leader?* Pew Research Center.

Technical and Vocational Training Annual Report. (2023). Retrieved on 24th May 2024 from webpage: https://online.flippingbook.com/view/268323385

Teichler, U. (2019). Higher education and the world of work: Conceptual frameworks, comparative perspectives, empirical findings. In *Higher Education and the World of Work*. Brill.

Temple, J. B., & Ylitalo, J. (2009). Promoting inclusive (and dialogic) leadership in higher education institutions. *Tertiary Education and Management*, 15(3), 277–289. DOI: 10.1080/13583880903073024

Tene, T., Vique Lopez, D. F., Valverde Aguirre, P. E., Orna Puente, L. M., & Vacacela Gomez, C. (2024). Virtual reality and augmented reality in medical education: An umbrella review. *Frontiers in Digital Health*, 6, 1365345. DOI: 10.3389/fdgth.2024.1365345 PMID: 38550715

Thanawala, A., Murphy, C., & Hakim, T. (2022). Sustaining STEM student learning support and engagement during COVID-19. In *Community Colleges' Responses to COVID-19* (pp. 72–82). Routledge. DOI: 10.4324/9781003297123-10

The Changing Landscape of Online Education (CHLOE): Behind the Numbers. (2019). Quality Matters. https://www.qualitymatters.org/

The Future of Jobs Report. (2018). World Economic Forum. https://www3.weforum.org/docs/WEF_Future_of_Jobs_2018.pdf

Theall, M., & Franklin, J. (2001). Looking for Bias in all the Wrong Places –A Search for Truth or a Witch Hunt in Student Ratings of Instruction? In The Student Ratings Debate: Are they Valid? How Can We Best Use Them? Theall, P., Abrami, L. and Lisa Mets (Eds.) New Directions in Educational Research, no. 109. San Francisco: Jossey-Bass.

Thiel College. (n.d.). *Experience the Thiel commitment.* https://www.thiel.edu/about

Thompson, C., Hollins, L., & Collins, S. W. (2023). *Factors Affecting Technology Integration for Teachers at K-12, Adult Education, and Higher Education Institutions Since Virtual Learning Due to COVID-19* (Doctoral dissertation, University of Missouri-Saint Louis).

Thornhill-Miller, B., Camarda, A., Mercier, M., Burkhardt, J. M., Morisseau, T., Bourgeois-Bougrine, S., Vinchon, F., El Hayek, S., Augereau-Landais, M., Mourey, F., Feybesse, C., Sundquist, D., & Lubart, T. (2023). Creativity, critical thinking, communication, and collaboration: Assessment, certification, and promotion of 21st century skills for the future of work and education. *Journal of Intelligence*, 11(3), 54. DOI: 10.3390/jintelligence11030054 PMID: 36976147

Tigwell, G. W. (2021, May). Nuanced perspectives toward disability simulations from digital designers, blind, low vision, and colour blind people. In *Proceedings of the 2021 CHI conference on human factors in computing systems* (pp. 1-15).

Tikruni, R. (2019). Investigation of an Inquiry-based Learning Intervention on Undergraduate Saudi Women's Critical Thinking Skills in an English as a Foreign Language Reading and Writing Class during the Preparatory Year. *Northern Illinois University ProQuest Dissertations Publishing*, 2019, 27545571.

Timotheou, S., Miliou, O., Dimitriadis, Y., Sobrino, S. V., Giannoutsou, N., Cachia, R., Mones, A. M., & Ioannou, A. (2023). Impacts of digital technologies on education and factors influencing schools' digital capacity and transformation: A literature review. *Education and Information Technologies*, 28(6), 6695–6726. DOI: 10.1007/s10639-022-11431-8 PMID: 36465416

Ting, S. H., Marzuki, E., Chuah, K. M., Misieng, J., & Jerome, C. (2017). Employers' views on the importance of english proficiency and communication skill for employability in Malaysia. *Indonesian Journal of Applied Linguistics*, 7(2), 315–327. DOI: 10.17509/ijal.v7i2.8132

Tirtosudarmo, R. (2008). Dari Human Capital ke Human Development: Catatan Kritis Terhadap Perspekif Sumberdaya Manusia di Indonesia" dalam Priyono Tjptoherijanto dan Laila Nagib (editor). (2008). Pengembangan Sumberdaya Manusia: diantar Peluang dan Tantangan

Tisch, A. (2015). The employability of older job-seekers: Evidence from Germany. *The Journal of the Economics of Ageing*, 6, 102–112. DOI: 10.1016/j.jeoa.2014.07.001

Togo, M., & Gandidzanwa, C. P. (2021). The role of Education 5.0 in accelerating the implementation of SDGs and challenges encountered at the University of Zimbabwe. *International Journal of Sustainability in Higher Education*, 22(7), 1520–1535. DOI: 10.1108/IJSHE-05-2020-0158

Toofany, S. (2008). Critical thinking among nurses. *Nursing Management*, 14(9), 28–31. DOI: 10.7748/nm2008.02.14.9.28.c6344 PMID: 18372840

Toven-Lindsey, B., Rhoads, R. A., & Lozano, J. B. (2015). Virtually unlimited classrooms: Pedagogical practices in massive open online courses. *The Internet and Higher Education*, 24, 1–12. DOI: 10.1016/j.iheduc.2014.07.001

Trading Economics. (2024). *United States GDP.* https://tradingeconomics.com/united-states/gdp

Trompenaar, (1997) Riding the Waves of Culture. Nicholas Brearley Publishing

Truter, L., & Du Toit, A. (2024). Shaping Propitious African Futures Through E-Learning. In *Global Perspectives on Decolonizing Postgraduate Education* (pp. 194–216). IGI Global. DOI: 10.4018/979-8-3693-1289-6.ch013

Turnbull (2012) Worldly Leadership. Alternative Wisdoms for a Complex World. Palgrave Macmillan

Turnbull, D., Chugh, R., & Luck, J. (2019). Learning Management Systems: An Overview. In Tatnall, A. (Ed.), *Encyclopedia of Education and Information Technologies* (pp. 1–7). Springer Nature., DOI: 10.1007/978-3-319-60013-0_248-1

Turnbull, D., Chugh, R., & Luck, J. (2023). Learning management systems and social media: A case for their integration in higher education institutions. *Research in Learning Technology*, 31, 1–16. DOI: 10.25304/rlt.v31.2814

Turnbull, D., Chung, R., & Luck, J. (2019). An Overview of the Common Elements of Learning Management Systems Policies in Higher Education Institutions. *TechTrends.* PMID: 35813034

Twibell, T. S. (Spring 1997) Space law: legal restraints on commercialization and development of

UAE Ministry of Education. (n.d.). *Innovation Ambassadors Program.* Retrieved from. [https://www.moe.gov.ae/En/Pages/InnovationAmbassadors.aspx]

UAE National Innovation Strategy. 2015. https://www.moei.gov.ae/assets/download/1d2d6460/National%20Innovation%20Strategy.pdf.aspx

Ukwoma, S. C., Iwundu, N. E., & Iwundu, I. E. (2016). Digital literacy skills possessed by students of UNN, implications for effective learning and performance: A study of the MTN Universities Connect Library. *New Library World*, 117(11/12), 702–720. DOI: 10.1108/NLW-08-2016-0061

Ulfah, E., & Badriyah, N. (2023). Faktor Yang Mempengaruhi Kinerja Paruh Waktu Wanita Pada Home Industry Pasca Covid-19. *Journal of Development Economic and Social Studies.*, 02(1), 112–123. DOI: 10.21776/jdess.2023.02.1.10

UNESCO. (2007) Intercultural education T Kit (IC learning 2nd edition p9)

UNESCO. (2017). Cracking the code: Girls' and women's education in science, technology, engineering and mathematics (STEM). UNESCO. Retrieved unesdoc.unesco.org/images/0025/002534/253479e.pdf

United Arab Emirates Government Portal. (2023). *UAE Smart Schools Initiative.* Retrieved from. [https://www.government.ae/en/about-the-uae/education/smart-schools-initiative]

United Nation. (2015). *Transforming our World: The 2030 Agenda for Sustainable Development.* United Nations.

United Nation. (n.d.). *Global indicator framework for the Sustainable Development Goals and targets of the 2030 Agenda for Sustainable Development.* From from https://unstats.un.org/sdgs/indicators/Global%20Indicator%20Framework%20after%202023%20refinement_Eng.pdf

United Nations. (2022). *Policy Brief. STEM education and inequality in Africa.* UN Office of the Special Adviser on Africa.

United States Commercial Space Launch Competitiveness Act (2015) Pub. L. No. 114-90, 129

Utami, U., Ghufron, A., & Setiawati, F. A. (2024). A Systematic Literature Review of" Flipped Classroom": Is it Effective on Student Learning in Elementary School? *Pegem Journal of Education and Instruction*, 14(1), 244–251.

Uy, F., Abendan, C. F., Andrin, G., Vestal, P., Suson, M., & Kilag, O. K. (2024). Exploring Strategies for Fostering a Culture of Continuous Professional Development and Learning: A Systematic Literature Review. [IMJRISE]. *International Multidisciplinary Journal of Research for Innovation, Sustainability, and Excellence*, 1(3), 191–198.

Uzhegova, D., & Baik, C. (2022). Internationalization of higher education in an uneven world: An integrated approach to internationalization of universities in the academic periphery. *Studies in Higher Education*, 47(4), 847–859. DOI: 10.1080/03075079.2020.1811220

Vahed, A., & Rodriguez, K. (2021). Enriching students' engaged learning experiences through the collaborative online international learning project. *Innovations in Education and Teaching International*, 58(5), 596–605. DOI: 10.1080/14703297.2020.1792331

Van der Heijden, B. I. J. M., Boon, J., Van der Klink, M. R., & Meijs, E. (2009). Employability enhancement through formal and informal learning: An empirical study among Dutch non-academic university staff members. *International Journal of Training and Development*, 13(1), 19–37. DOI: 10.1111/j.1468-2419.2008.00313.x

Van der Horst, A. C., Klehe, U. C., & Van der Heijden, B. I. J. M. (2017). Adapting to a Looming Career Transition: How age and Core Individual Differences Interact. *Journal of Vocational Behavior*, 99, 132–145. DOI: 10.1016/j.jvb.2016.12.006

Varadarajan, T. (2020, August 7). The new "gold rush in space". *Wall Street Journal: Opinion*

Vasile, V., Pisică, S., & Dobre, A. M. (2015). Demographic Perspective of Qualitative Youth Employability on Romanian Labour Market. *Procedia Economics and Finance*, 22, 55–63. https://doi.org/https://doi.org/10.1016/S2212-5671(15)00226 -9. DOI: 10.1016/S2212-5671(15)00226-9

Vasu, S. B. (2023). Factors contributes and initiatives in bridging the digital divide. networks, 52. *Industrial Engineering Journal*, 52(155), 30–37.

Veblen, T., & Mayer, O. G. (2022). *Imperial Germany and the Industrial Revolution*. Routledge. DOI: 10.4324/9780429337727

Veli Korkmaz, A., van Engen, M., Schalk, R., Bauwens, R., & Knappert, L. (2022). INCLEAD: Development of an inclusive leadership measurement tool.

Venkataraman, S. (2023). Impact of Technology-Supported Education on Student Learning Outcomes. IJIRMPS (E-ISSN: 2349-7300), Volume 9, Issue 4, July-August 2021.

Verghese, T. (2016). *How do we Understand Our Own Culture*. You Tube.

Vogt, K. L. (2016). Measuring student engagement using learning management systems (Doctoral dissertation). University of Toronto. Ontario, Canada

Von Bencke, M.J. (1997). *The Politics of Space: A History of U.S. - Soviet/Russian*

Von Colln-Appling, C., & Giuliano, D. (2016). A concept analysis of critical thinking: A guide for nurse educators. *Nurse Education Today*, 49, 106–109. DOI: 10.1016/j.nedt.2016.11.007 PMID: 27902948

Voogt, J., & Roblin, N. P. (2012). A comparative analysis of international frameworks for 21st-century competencies: Implications for national curriculum policies. *Journal of Curriculum Studies*, 44(3), 299–321. DOI: 10.1080/00220272.2012.668938

Vu, N. N., Hung, B. P., Van, N. T. T., & Lien, N. T. H. (2022). Theoretical and instructional aspects of using multimedia resources in language education: A cognitive view. *Multimedia Technologies in the Internet of Things Environment*, 2, 165–194. DOI: 10.1007/978-981-16-3828-2_9

Vyas, L. (2022). "New normal" at work in a post-COVID world: Work–life balance and labor markets. *Policy and Society*, 41(1), 155–167. DOI: 10.1093/polsoc/puab011

Waddill, D. (2023). Building 21st-century skills by applying proven teaching methods. In *ICERI2023 Proceedings* (pp. 7039-7048). IATED.

Waks, L. J., & Waks, L. J. (2016). The Economic Crisis and the Rise of MOOCs. *The Evolution and Evaluation of Massive Open Online Courses: MOOCs in Motion*, 11-34.

Wardani, H. K., Sujarwo, S., Rakhmawati, Y., & Cahyandaru, P. (2023). Analysis of the Impact of the Merdeka Curriculum Policy on Stakeholders at Primary School. *Peuradeun Scientific Journal*, 11(2), 513–530. DOI: 10.26811/peuradeun.v11i2.801

Waruwu, B. (2015). The correlation between teacher's perceptions about principal's emotional Intelligence and organizational climate and job satisfaction of teachers of state senior high school in Gunungsitol Nias, Indonesia. *Journal of Education and Practice*, 6(13), 142–147.

Watson, J. (2024). Cultural Globalisation and Anthropology. *Britannia*.

Weber, L. (2024, February 16). 62% of Americans lack a college degree. Can they solve the labor shortage? *Wall Street Journal*. https://www.wsj.com/lifestyle/careers/employers-open-more-doors-to-workers-without-degrees-but-few-are-getting-in-732f1098

Weeks, E. (2023). The benefit of international relations critical theory to highlight lessons

Wen, C. T., Liu, C. C., Chang, H. Y., Chang, C. J., Chang, M. H., Chiang, S. H. F., Yang, C. W., & Hwang, F. K. (2020). Students guided inquiry with simulation and its relation to school science achievement and scientific literacy. *Computers & Education*, 149, 103830. DOI: 10.1016/j.compedu.2020.103830

West, M. A., & Farr, J. L. (1990). Innovation at work. In West, M. A., & Farr, J. L. (Eds.), *Innovation and creativity at work: Psychological and organizational strategies* (pp. 3–13). Wiley.

Whitfield, B. (2024). Unconscious Bias: 16 Examples and How to Avoid Them. Available at https://builtin.com/diversity-inclusion/unconscious-bias-examples. Accessed 25/01/2024.

Whitfield-Jones, P. (2020, May 21). A small step for private property rights in space. *Mayer*

Widyadhari, K. A., Priyanti, T., & Umar, Z. (2024). The Advantages of a Flipped Classroom for Students' Speaking Skills: Systematic Review. *JoELE: Journal of English Lingua Educantum*, 1(1), 20–28.

Wiles, G. E. (1998). The man on the moon makes room for neighbors: An analysis of the

Wiles, G. E. (1998, October). existence of property rights on the moon under a condominium-type ownership theory. *International Review of Law Computers & Technology*, 12(3), 513–534. DOI: 10.1080/13600869855342

Williams, J. (2011). STEM education: Proceed with caution. Design and Technology Education. *International Journal (Toronto, Ont.)*, 16(1).

Wirba, A. V. (2021). Transforming Cameroon into a knowledge-based economy (KBE): The role of education, especially higher education. *Journal of the Knowledge Economy*, ●●●, 1–31.

Wiseman, A. W., & Anderson, E. (2014). Developing Innovation and Entrepreneurial Skills in Youth Through Mass Education: The example of ICT in the UAE. ISBN: 978-1-78190-708-5, eISBN: 978-1-78190-709-2. ISSN: 1479-3679. 1 January 2014

Wittekind, A., Raeder, S., & Grote, G. (2010). A longitudinal study of determinants of perceived employability. *Journal of Organizational Behavior*, 31(4), 566–586. DOI: 10.1002/job.646

Witt, L. A. (1992). Exchange ideology as a moderator of the relationships between the importance of participation in decision-making and job attitudes. *Human Relations*, 45(1), 73–85. DOI: 10.1177/001872679204500104

Wolbring, G., & Nguyen, A. (2023). Equity/Equality, Diversity and Inclusion, and Other EDI Phrases and EDI Policy Frameworks: A Scoping Review. *Trends in Higher Education*, 2(1), 168–237. DOI: 10.3390/higheredu2010011

Woldegiorgis, E. T. (2024). Internationalization of Higher Education under Neoliberal Imperatives: The Political Economy of Student Mobility in Africa. In *Critical Reflections on the Internationalisation of Higher Education in the Global South* (pp. 13–31). Emerald Publishing Limited. DOI: 10.1108/978-1-80455-778-520241002

Wood, P. (ed2004) Intercultural City: Intercultural City Reader. Comedia

Wood, P., & Landry, C. (2004). *Intercultural City-Planning for Diversity Advantage*. Earthscan.

Workforce Skills Gap Trends 2024: Survey Report. (2024, February). *Springboard*. https://www.springboard.com/blog/business/skills-gap-trends-2024/#:~:text=A%20majority%20of%20leaders%20say,a%20top%203%20needed%20skill

World Bank. (2020). *Indonesia Country Gender Assessment: Investing in Opportunities*. Washigton DC: *Wolrd* Bank.

World Bank. (2024). Program Kesetaraan Gender di Indonesia. https://www.worldbank.org/in/country/indonesia/brief/gender-equality-for-growth-research-and-analytical-program-in-indonesia

World Bank. (2024, 510). *Gender Data*. From The World Bank: https://genderdata.worldbank.org/en/indicator/sl-tlf-acti-zs?view=trend&geos=WLD_IDN&year-range=2010_2023&age=15-64&gender=female&gender=male&gender=total

World Economic Forum. (2017). Accelerating Workforce Reskilling for the Fourth Industrial Revolution. An Agenda for Leaders to Shape the Future of Education, Gender and Work. Published 27 July 2017. https://www.weforum.org/publications/accelerating-workforce-reskilling-for-the-fourth-industrial-revolution/

World Economic Forum. (2021). *Global gender gap report*.

World Economic Forum. (2023). *Global Gender Gap Report 2023*. Geneva: World Economic Forum World Bank, & WTO. (2023). *Trade in Services for Development. Fostering Sustainable Growth and Economic Diversification*. Geneva: WTO.

World Economic Forum. The Future of Jobs Report, World Economic Forum, (2018). available at: http://www3.weforum.org/docs/WEF_Future_of_Jobs_2018.pdf. (Accessed 24 February 2022).

Wren, D. A., & Bedeian, A. G. (2020). *The Evolution of Management Thought* (6th ed.). Wiley.

Wulandari, N., Arifin, A., Khoiriyah, M., Pujiningtiyas, R. I., & Arifin, M. (2021). Effect of Empowerment and Compensation on Employee Loyalty.

Wuta, R. K. (2022). Extendibility of the Education 5.0 concept to Zimbabwe's secondary school system as encapsulated in curriculum framework 2015-2022. *Ind J Human Social Science*, 3(5), 26–33.

Wu, X., Heng, M., & Wang, W. (2015). Nursing students' experiences with the use of an authentic assessment rubric and a case approach in clinical laboratories. *Nurse Education Today*, 35(4), 549–555. DOI: 10.1016/j.nedt.2014.12.009 PMID: 25577674

Xaba, M. B., & Akinola, A. O. (2023). A Reflection on the Nexus between South African Land Reform Struggles and the Unresolved National Question. *International Journal of African Renaissance Studies-Multi-. Inter-and Transdisciplinarity*, 18(1), 136–155.

Xue, Y., Bradley, J., & Liang, H. (2011). Team climate, empowering leadership, and knowledge sharing. *Journal of Knowledge Management*, 15(2), 299–312. DOI: 10.1108/13673271111119709

Xu, W., Zhang, N., & Wang, M. (2024). The impact of interaction on continuous use in online learning platforms: A metaverse perspective. *Internet Research*, 34(1), 79–106. DOI: 10.1108/INTR-08-2022-0600

Yadav, N. (2024). The Impact of Digital Learning on Education. *International Journal of Multidisciplinary Research in Arts. Science and Technology*, 2(1), 24–34.

Yang, Y. T. C., & Wu, W. C. I. (2012). Digital storytelling for enhancing student academic achievement, critical thinking, and learning motivation: A year-long experimental study. *Computers & Education*, 59(2), 339–352. DOI: 10.1016/j.compedu.2011.12.012

Yesilyurt, E., & Vezne, R. (2023). Digital literacy, technological literacy, and internet literacy as predictors of attitude toward applying computer-supported education. *Education and Information Technologies*, 28(8), 1–27. DOI: 10.1007/s10639-022-11311-1 PMID: 36688220

Yildirim, S., Bostanci, S. H., Yildırım, D. Ç., & Erdogan, F. (2021). Rethinking mobility of international university students during COVID-19 pandemic. *Higher Education Evaluation and Development*, 15(2), 98–113. DOI: 10.1108/HEED-01-2021-0014

Yingi, E., Hlungwani, P. M., & Nyagadza, B. (2022). The Fourth Industrial Revolution (4IR) at the heart of the SDG agenda: The role of education in Zimbabwe. *African Review (Dar Es Salaam, Tanzania)*, 14(2), 213–229. DOI: 10.1163/09744061-01402001

Yorke, M., & Knight, P. (2006). Embedding employability into the curriculum. In *York: The Higher Education Academy*. Higher Education Academy.

Yusuf, M. A. (2023). Managerial strategies and effective staff meetings in Nigerian Universities. *Indonesian Journal of Educational Management and Leadership*, 1(1), 85–105. DOI: 10.51214/ijemal.v1i1.518

Yusuf, N., & Jamjoom, Y. (2022). The Role of Higher Education Institutions in Developing Employability Skills of Saudi Graduates Amidst Saudi 2030 Vision. *European Journal of Sustainable Development*, 11(1), 31. Advance online publication. DOI: 10.14207/ejsd.2022.v11n1p31

Zainuddin, S. Z. B., Pillai, S., Dumanig, F. P., & Phillip, A. (2019). English language and graduate employability. *Education + Training*, 61(1), 79–93. DOI: 10.1108/ET-06-2017-0089

Zainuddin, Z., Haruna, H., Li, X., Zhang, Y., & Chu, S. K. W. (2019). A systematic review of flipped classroom empirical evidence from different fields: What are the gaps and future trends? *On the Horizon*, 27(2), 72–86. DOI: 10.1108/OTH-09-2018-0027

Zaleniene, I., & Pereira, P. (2021). Higher education for sustainability: A global perspective. *Geography and Sustainability*, 2(2), 99–106. DOI: 10.1016/j.geosus.2021.05.001

Zalli, E. (2024). Globalization and Education: Exploring the Exchange of Ideas, Values, and Traditions in Promoting Cultural Understanding and Global Citizenship. *Interdisciplinary Journal of Research and Development, 11*(1 S1), 55-55.

Zamahsari, G. K., Amalia, M. N., Rifah, L., Permana, F., Romadhon, S., & Prihatini, A. (2024, January). A Systematic Review in Educational Settings: Numerous Challenges to the Adoption of Augmented Reality. In *2024 18th International Conference on Ubiquitous Information Management and Communication (IMCOM)* (pp. 1-6). IEEE.

Zapata-Barrero, R. (ed 2015) Interculturalism in Cities Concept, Policy and I Implementation. Elgar Publishing

Zeb, A., Jamal, W., & Ali, M. (2015). Reward and Recognition Priorities of Public Sector Universities' Teachers for their Motivation and Job Satisfaction. *Journal of Managerial Sciences*, 9(2).

Zekos, G. I., & Zekos, G. I. (2021). E-Globalization and Digital Economy. *Economics and Law of Artificial Intelligence: Finance, Economic Impacts, Risk Management and Governance*, 13-66.

Zeng, J., & Xu, G. (2020). Ethical leadership and young university teachers' work engagement: A moderated mediation model. *International Journal of Environmental Research and Public Health*, 17(1), 21. DOI: 10.3390/ijerph17010021 PMID: 31861414

Zepeda, S. J. (2019). *Professional development: What works*. Routledge.

Zhang, L., & Ma, Y. (2023). A study of the impact of project-based learning on student learning effects: A meta-analysis study. *Frontiers in Psychology*, 14, 14. DOI: 10.3389/fpsyg.2023.1202728 PMID: 37564309

Zhiltsov, S. S., & Zonn, I. S. (2021). *The Arctic: A drifting future*. Nova Science Publishers.

Zhou, L., Rudhumbu, N., Shumba, J., & Olumide, A. (2020). Role of higher education institutions in the implementation of sustainable development goals. *Sustainable development goals and institutions of higher education*, 87-96.

Zhou, T. M., & Machenjera, P. (2017). Chapter Three Colonialism, Poverty and [Under-] development in Africa. *The African Conundrum: Rethinking the Trajectories of Historical, Cultural, Philosophical and Developmental Experiences of*, 33.

Zhuplev, A. (Ed.). (2018). *Disruptive Technologies for Business Development and Strategic Advantage*. IGI Global. DOI: 10.4018/978-1-5225-4148-6

Zhuplev, A., & Blas, N. (2022). Business education in the USA: Strategic imperatives in the age of disruption. In Zhuplev, A., & Koepp, R. (Eds.), *Global trends, dynamics, and imperatives for strategic development in business education in an age of disruption* (p. 12). IGI Global. DOI: 10.4018/978-1-7998-7548-2.ch001

Zielinski, N. M. (2023) "Transforming Mathematics Education with Creativity". Culminating Experience Projects. 402. (Published master thesis). Grand Valley State University, Michigan, United States of America.

Zing, K. (2024). Harnessing the Power of Artificial Intelligence in Personalized Learning. *Education Journal*, 2(1), 7–14.

Zinhuku, P. (2022). The dawn of education 5.0 philosophy: Implications on musical arts pedagogics in universities, Zimbabwe.

Ziyan, J. (2023). *Globalisation and its impact on Cultural Identity: An Analysis.* Medium.

Zuckerman, G. (2024, February 24). Peter Thiel's $100,000 offer to skip college is more popular than ever. *The Wall Street Journal.* https://www.wsj.com/finance/peter-thiels-100-000-offer-to-skip-college-is-more-popular-than-ever-162e281b

About the Contributors

Mustafa Kayyali is an ardent advocate for excellence in higher education, driven by a relentless pursuit of quality, recognition, and innovation. As an entrepreneur, researcher, translator, and publisher, he is deeply involved in various facets of the academic world. His diverse interests encompass Management, Translation, Interpretation, and Academic consulting, contributing to a well-rounded understanding of the industry. Throughout his career, he has made significant contributions to academic literature, with more than 30 published papers and 15 book chapters to his name. Additionally, he takes pride in having translated 5 books, bridging language gaps, and promoting knowledge exchange on a global scale. He is committed to fostering positive change in higher education and contributing to its continuous improvement.

Bryan Christiansen is the Chief Executive Officer at Soluvex, LLC, which is a global technology consulting firm in the USA. A former adjunct professor at Southern New Hampshire University, Christiansen earned his MBA at Capella University and his BS in Marketing degree at the University of the State of New York. To date he has published 45 Reference books on various topics of which over 60 percent are Scopus- and/or Web of Science-indexed. Christiansen is a Book Series Editor-in-Chief of "Advances in Psychology, Mental Health, and Behavioral Studies" and "Advances in Digital Crime, Forensics, and Cyber Terrorism". His works have been cited in articles, books, doctoral dissertations, and master's theses in Chinese, Czech, English, French, Greek, Russian, Spanish, and Turkish.

***

Eshtiaq AlFaraj is a faculty member and nurse consultant at the College of Nursing. Her extensive experience in undergraduate and postgraduate nursing education and academic accreditation is a testament to her commitment and expertise. She was awarded the British Council's Chevening Scholarship and a scholarship from King Faisal University to pursue an MSc in Management of Training and Development at the University of Edinburgh, clearly indicating her academic prowess. In 2008, she earned a Ph.D. in Nursing Education from the University of Surrey, further solidifying her position as a thought leader in the field. Dr. AlFaraj has served two terms on the Saudi Scientific Nursing Board at the Saudi Commission for Health Specialties (SCFHS) and is an active Programmatic Surveyor for SCFHS postgraduate Advanced Nursing Diplomas and Medical Training/ Fellowship programs. She is a certified external reviewer by the National Center for Academic Accreditation and Evaluation (NCAAA). Her contributions at IAU include her roles as a faculty in academic programs and as a member of the Program and Institutional Accreditations Strandrd and the Institutional Review Board (IRB) committees, as well as a Diabetes Educator in the Family and Community Center. Additionally, she published scholarly papers in peer-reviewed journals, furthering the body of knowledge in Nursing.

Ahmed AlKuwaiti is an experienced academic and researcher. He is currently Dean of Quality and Academic Accreditation and Associate Professor of Quality in Medical Education at the College of Dentistry, Imam Abdulrahman Bin Faisal University, and Director of the Directorate of Quality and Safety at the university's King Fahd Hospital. He is also a dedicated and detailed Institutional Reviewer for various Universities as well as a University Ranking Consultant. He had extensively published over fifty publications and had written four books. He is also a competent presenter and attended in more than three hundred conferences. Dr. Ahmed is the President and Senior Trustee of the Association of Healthcare Professionals (AIHCP) at United Kingdom (London), Editorial Board member and Associate Editor of four international journals. Dr. Ahmed holds various key professional memberships such as International Network for Quality Assurance Agencies in Higher Education (INQAAHE), Joint Commission for Healthcare Organizations, American Hospital Association, Saudi Arabia Standardization Organization, National Association for Healthcare Quality, Association for Medical Education in Europe, American Society for Quality and Association of Health Care Professionals.Dr. Ahmed is an experienced academic and researcher. He is currently Dean of Quality and Academic Accreditation and Associate Professor of Quality in Medical Education at the College of Dentistry, Imam Abdulrahman Bin Faisal University, and Director of the Directorate of Quality and Safety at the university's King Fahd Hospital. He is also a dedicated and detailed Institutional Reviewer for various Universities as well as a University Ranking Consultant. He had extensively published over fifty publications and had written four books. He is also a competent presenter and attended in more than three hundred conferences. Dr. Ahmed is the President and Senior Trustee of the Association of Healthcare Professionals (AIHCP) at United Kingdom (London), Editorial Board member and Associate Editor of four international journals. Dr. Ahmed holds various key professional memberships such as International Network for Quality Assurance Agencies in Higher Education (INQAAHE), Joint Commission for Healthcare Organizations, American Hospital Association, Saudi Arabia Standardization Organization, National Association for Healthcare Quality, Association for Medical Education in Europe, American Society for Quality and Association of Health Care Professionals.

Fahad A. Al-Muhanna is a dedicated and experienced academician having immense experience in teaching, patient care, and research at the College of Medicine. He finished his fellowship in Internal Medicine and Nephrology. Currently, he is working as a Professor in the Department of Internal Medicine at Imam Abdulrahman Bin Faisal University (IAU) (formerly named the University of Dammam), and Consultant in the Department of Nephrology/Internal medicine at King Fahd Hospital of the University (KFHU), Dammam, Saudi Arabia. He had experience as a Vice-President at IAU and as a General Supervisor and Chief Executive Officer (CEO) of KFHU. Now, he is also an advisor to the President of IAU. He has an outstanding record of publication in academic and clinical journals. He has also actively conducted various research projects in his career. As an academician, he is committed to aid students and motivates them in developing their full potential in their studies. He is a dedicated member of university programs that help promote learning and support the community. Further, being a healthcare executive, he initiated commissioning, teaching, and operation of King Fahd Specialist Hospital Dammam (KFSHD), where radiology and organ transplant are carried out. He provided consultation to government and private agencies. He is a full-time member of various Scientific and Professional Societies and Organizations, including the International Society of Nephrology and the American Society of Nephrology.

Ardhian Kurniawati is a researcher at the National Research and Innovation Agency of The Republic of Indonesia (BRIN). She obtained a master's in economics sciences at the University of Indonesia in 2017. Her research interests are related to population, labour economics, labour market, industrial relations, and econometrics. She has published several articles both as books and journals in national and international publishers.

Daniel Opotamutale Ashipala (MN Sc) is a senior lecturer and Head of Department for the School of nursing and Public Health (SoNPH), General Nursing Science department in the Faculty of Health Sciences and Veterinary Medicine

(FHSVM) at the University of Namibia, Namibia. His research interests include Primary health Care, Health care services and Nursing education, and Mental health. He has published a quite number of peer reviewed articles on the delivery of teaching and learning in higher education studies. He is a doctoral candidate at Stellenbosch University in Cape Town, South Africa. His doctoral work focuses on developing a framework to facilitate the implementation of a task shifting approach for nurses in the Namibia PHC services.

Devi Asiati is a researcher at the Research Center for Population, the National Research and Innovation Agency (BRIN). She is Masters in Population and Human Resources from the University of Indonesia, Jakarta (2005). Her research interests related to labor, employment and human resources, demographic change and informal sector. She has published several articles both as books and journals in national dan international publisher

Abigail Ekangouo Awanga is an English Language teacher in a state secondary school in the outskirts of Yaounde, Cameroon, who has been in the field for 16 years. She has a Bachelors degree in Bilingual letters, a Masters 1 General and applied Linguistics, and Higher Teacher training certificate in Bilingual Letters(English and French as foreign Languages).She offers Adult English and French Language course lessons in WhatsApp.She has a passion for instructional technology and she trains English Language teachers on how to use basic digital skills and tools for teaching and for managing communities of practice She is the founder of English language Teaching Women Cameroon Special Interest Group and the present CAMELTA Vice President in charge of International Outreach.At her spare time and to encourage literacy, she offers free English lessons to kids in her community twice per week. She also works as an ELT Consultants Associate and Africa ELTA Associate Editor.

Minerva M. Bunagan is QA Manager in the Accreditation and Compliance Department of the Higher Colleges of Technology (HCT) in the United Arab Emirates and has more than 20 years of experience in higher education. With 5 years in UAE, 4 years in Oman, 7 years in the Kingdom of Bahrain, and initially more than 10 years in the Philippines, Dr. Minerva has an appropriate understanding of the academic particularities of the GCC countries. During this time Dr. Bunagan contributed to the development of her employing institutions through initiating developments in the field of academic quality and standards, devising internal quality audit and other institutional policies and procedures, managing program external reviews and leading on achieving international accreditation from lead bodies in the field of Engineering, Computer Science, Applied Media, Business, Health Science, Education, and Military and Security. As the Director of the

Quality and Accreditation Department of the University of Buraimi (UoB) in the Sultanate of Oman, Dr Bunagan led on achieving a successful institutional audit as well as the accreditation of General Foundation Program. As the Dean of the College of Computer Studies and as the QA Director of AMA International University – Bahrain, Dr Bunagan led on achieving the first private university ABET accreditation for the Computer Science Program, 3 Engineering Programs and ECBE accreditation for its 3 Business Programs. As a key member of the Research Pool at the University of Saint Louis Tuguegarao - Philippines, Dr Bunagan was instrumental in achieving university recognition as one of the top 10 autonomous private universities in the Philippines (since 2007). This led Dr Bunagan to becoming a member of the Regional Technical Panel commissioned to inspect institutions/ programs for approval by the Ministry of Higher Education in the Philippines. Dr Bunagan has presented and published researches (international and local) in the area of Quality Audit, Quality Assurance, Accreditation, Education, and Information Systems/ Technology. Additionally, she has contributed to developing institutional effectiveness at both operational and strategic levels.

Doris Chasokela is a senior lecturer at the National University of Science and Technology. She holds a Doctor of Education; a Master of Engineering in Electrical Systems Control and Information Technology; a Bachelor of Technical in Electrical and Electronic Engineering; and a Diploma in Technical Vocational Education. She has 11 years of experience in Higher Education teaching and has supervised 15 postgraduate and over 40 undergraduate projects. She has published 16 articles and 3 textbooks. Her research interests are Engineering education, higher education, artificial intelligence, e-learning, and control.

Bhupender Dighliya has more than ten years of experience in the fields of teaching, research and hotel operation. He has completed his doctorate from Institute of Hotel & Tourism Management, Maharshi Dayanand University, Rohtak - Haryana. He is working as Founding Member of School of Hotel Management, Starex University, Gurugram - Haryana. He has published research paper and book chapter in national and International journals and books. He presented several papers in national and international conferences. He is a dedicated and highly motivated hospitality professional.

Nabil el Kadhi is the Vice President of Academic Affairs and Development at Applied Science University (Bahrain). He has more than 25 years of experience in academia, and more than 15 years of experience in the management of higher education institutions with an exposure to European and Middle East and North Africa academic systems. He started his professional career in the early 90s;

assumed positions ranging from Project Manager and Department Head to Lab Director, Master Programs Director, Dean, Provost, and Deputy Vice-Chancellor for Academic Affairs; Vice Chancellor and President where he remarkably contributed to institutional excellence, and several applied research and industrial projects related mainly to Data and Cloud Security and Privacy, Smart Cities and Internet of Things, Digital Transformation and Artificial Intelligence, Secure Payment, Smart Card Use and various Cloud – based applications. EL KADHI is today a recognized Futurist in both education and innovation side. He was selected among the 50 most Impactful International Leaders in Smart Cities and Smart Applications. He assumed roles of President/ Vice-President of various think-tank and associations such as Smart Cities Council, Future University and the Tunisian Association of Future Foresight. EL KADHI notably contributed to the design and revision of various curricula for both graduate and post-graduate levels in France, Bahrain, Oman, Iraq, Tunesia and UAE. Since 2006, he focused his professional activities on Institutional Strategies, Research, Program/ Curricula Development and Review, and Quality Assurance in Education. His experience encompasses leadership, administration, management, program design and development, quality assurance management, national and international accreditation, staff development, teaching, and assessment. EL KADHI is an ABET Program Evaluator and external reviewers of the Oman Academic Accreditation Authority (OAAA), and National Center for Academic Accreditation and Assessment (NCAAA) – Kingdom of Saudi Arabia (KSA). He has been actively involved as an External Reviewer and/or Consultant in other international universities, such as Indonesia, Bahrain and Iraq. With 15 years of experience in GCC, EL KADHI mastered the academic particularities of the region as well as the cultural aspects impacting the higher education arena in the Gulf Region. EL KADHI has a PhD in Computer Science and Information Technology, which he earned from FST- Tunisia (for academic requirements) and France (for research requirements) at the INRIA Lab as part of a European Project on Verified Internet Protocol. He has more than 60 international publications indexed by ACM, IEEE, DBLP and others. He is also a reviewer in various international scientific journals and conferences such as International Conference on Security and Management, Super-computing Journal, MDPI, ICICT-IACSIT, IKE Conferences and International Conference of Network and System Security (NSS), as well as a keynote speaker or chair in numerous international conferences. His research expertise includes Quality Assurance in Higher Education, Instruction, Assessment, Smart Cities Security and Privacy Aspects, Internet and Information System Security, and Cloud Security and Cryptology. EL KADHI is distinguished in developing leading ideas and forming new academic directions based on an analysis of institutional statistics and institutional image; and forging partnerships and collaborations that pave way for exchange programs. EL KADHI is also an entrepreneur and innovator as he contributed to the establishment of various consultancy companies such as KnK Partner in France.

Olabode Gbobaniyi (PhD) is a senior lecturer at the management department of the Global Banking School. His core academic and research interest is business strategy; however, he has wider research and publication interests in AI, Teaching and Education, and Tourism.

Leila Goosen is a full professor in the Department of Science and Technology Education of the University of South Africa. She holds a C2 rating via the South African National Research Foundation. Prof. Goosen was an Associate Professor in the School of Computing, and the module leader and head designer of the fully online signature module for the College for Science, Engineering and Technology, rolled out to over 92,000 registered students since the first semester of 2013. She usually supervises around ten Masters and Doctoral students, and has successfully completed supervision of 43 students at postgraduate level. Previously, she was a Deputy Director at the South African national Department of Education. In this capacity, she was required to develop ICT strategies for implementation. Before that, she had been a lecturer of Information Technology (IT) in the Department for Science, Mathematics and Technology Education in the Faculty of Education of the University of Pretoria. Her research interests have included cooperative work in IT, effective teaching and learning of programming and teacher professional development.

Hennigusnia is a researcher at the Research Center for Population, the National Research and Innovation Agency (BRIN). Her last formal education was a master's in economics from the University of Indonesia in 2014. Her research interests are labor economics, industrial relations, particular/vulnerable employment, and social security. She has published several articles as books and in journals from national and international publishers.

Paul Lancaster background is in secondary school teaching (Religious Studies and History), local church leadership and humanity-based mission projects in Leeds and in a number of different countries. For the last twenty years, Paul has been involved in networking and establishing partnerships, through his founding work of Hope for the Nations in Leeds UK, working with over 30 nationalities, organising intercultural festivals, gatherings for dialogue and intercultural training. He has also established Interact (Centre for Intercultural Learning and Action) and taught Intercultural Competence and Awareness development courses at Leeds Trinity University and to community leaders. Paul holds a B.Ed. (Hons) (Sheffield University) and MA in Global Leadership in Intercultural Contexts (University of

Gloucestershire) and has researched how diversity can be an advantage in bringing transformative change in cities. More recently he has been researching intercultural theology and how it impacts socio-political issues in our current world.

Nengiwe Mangena is a researcher at the National University of Technology, Faculty of Science and Technology Education, Department of Technical and Engineering Education and Training.

Funa Moyo is a senior lecturer and researcher under the Institute of Development Studies, Faculty of Commerce at NUST. He holds a PhD in Public and Development Management from the University of Witwatersrand, Wits School of Governance, South Africa, a Master of Science in Development Studies from the National University of Science and Technology, a Master of Education in Educational Administration, Planning and Policy Studies from Zimbabwe Open University. He holds a Bachelor of Education degree from the University of Zimbabwe and Bachelor of Arts (Hons) in HIV and AIDS Behaviour Studies from UNISA. His PhD research focused on artisanal gold mining, social capital and livelihoods in rural Matabeleland. He has more than 10 years' experience in Research and Consultancy in Zimbabwe. Funa has also done consultancy work for a number of local and International Non-Governmental Organisations in Zimbabwe. He has published in number of international journals refereed and peer-reviewed journals and currently has a number of papers under peer-review. He has served as a Board member of the Arch diocese of Bulawayo's Sibambene AIDS Programme and CADEC. Catholic Church, Bulawayo, Zimbabwe and currently sits on the Contact Family Counselling Centre. Dr Funa Moyo is Development Practitioner. He has been involved in the LIPS-ZIM project from its inception, baseline survey and production of the project framework. He has worked as a trainer, researcher, consultant and facilitator especially in the domain of community development. He is also involved in the WFP and NUST partnership through the Sustainable Livelihood Programming (SLP) project focused on empowering local authorities on community-based planning, resilience building and food security enhancement. He has a passion in research especially in the domain of natural resource governance, public policy, public health, environmental management and development, sustainable livelihoods and rural development, community development, risk reduction, resilience building and disaster management.

Ngadi is a researcher at the Research Center for Population, the National Research and Innovation Agency (BRIN) since 2005. He is a Ph.D. candidate in Human Geography, at the University of Tokyo, Japan. He obtained a master's degree from Population and Employment Studies at the University of Indonesia. His research interests relate to population and labor mobility, employment and human resources, demographic change, and rural development. SCOPUS-ID: 57682503500, ORCID-code: 0000-0002-5249-0860; Contact's email: ngad009@brin.go.id

Mahona Joseph Paschal is professional teacher, interdisciplinary scholar who is skilled in teaching, research, supervision, consultancy, community engagement, couching, mentoring, Creative Writing, leadership and management in education. He holds a Masters of Education Management and Planning from St. Augustine University and a Bachelor's degree in Education (Arts) from Kampala International University. He enjoys teaching and really inspired to assist students in building positivity and excitement and empower them to complete their ambitions. Mahona is the Author of Responsive Classroom: Student's relationship and academic performance in Tanzania. He has published peer reviewed articles in scholarly journals and has presented papers at professional meetings and international conferences on Education and Sustainable development. His work has appeared in a wide range of journals, edited collections and higher education news outlets.

Zantermans Rajagukguk has been a Research Professor at the Research Center for Population, National Research and Innovation Agency of Indonesia (BRIN) since 2021. Previously he was a researcher at Research Center for Manpower, Ministry of Manpower of Indonesia since 1990. He obtained a master's degree from the Human Resources Management Program at the Catholic University of Atma Jaya, Jakarta (1996). His research interests are related to employment, human resources, and industrial relations issues. Until now he has written more than 50 research results, mainly in book forms, and some in national and international journals.

Mandla Sibanda is a Final Master student in MTech in Electrical and Electronics Engineering. He holds a BTech in Education Electrical and Electronics Engineering. Mandla was trained as an apprentice in the field of Electrical Power Engineering and worked in several industries under the field. His interests are higher education, Artificial Intelligence, e-learning and Robotics.

Arun Vijay Subbarayalu is an Assistant Professor in the Deanship of Quality and Academic Accreditation, Imam Abdulrahman Bin Faisal University (IAU), Saudi Arabia. He has over 20 years of teaching experience in physical therapy and business management studies. Currently, he teaches the Bachelor of Physical Therapy Program, and the Ph.D. in Rehabilitation Sciences Program at the College of Applied Medical Sciences, IAU and taught Healthcare Management Program at the College of Public Health, IAU. He obtained Bachelor of Physiotherapy (BPT) & Master of Physiotherapy degrees (MPT) from the Tamilnadu Dr. MGR Medical University, Chennai, India, and a Ph.D. in Physical Therapy from Ramakrishna

Mission Vivekananda University, Coimbatore, India. He has also obtained a Master of Business Administration degree program (MBA) specializing in Human Resources Management in Healthcare from the University of Madras, India, and a Ph.D. in Business Administration where his doctoral dissertation focuses on Healthcare Management from Madurai Kamaraj University, India. Further, he is a recipient of the "Six Sigma Black Belt" certification from the Indian Statistical Institute (ISI), Coimbatore, and a Lean & Six Sigma Master Black Belt certification from Anexas, Europe. He is a certified external reviewer by the National Centre for Academic Accreditation and Evaluation (NCAAA), Saudi Arabia, to review the quality of higher education programs for granting academic accreditation. His research areas include higher education and healthcare quality management, focusing on developing continuous quality improvement strategies. His primary research interest is to improve the quality of higher education & healthcare using Six Sigma methods. He has published five textbooks and more than 75 publications in highly indexed journals. He received the Best Teacher award from the Tamilnadu Dr. MGR Medical University for his exceptional contributions to teaching in 2010. He has also received the best researcher award from the Indian Association of Physiotherapists for his contributions to scientific research in 2018.

Ritu Toshniwal Ph.D, M.Com(A.B.S.T.),PGDBA, B.Com (A.B.S.T.Hons.) Specialization in Accountancy & Business Statistics (A.B.S.T) with 17 years of teaching experience. 11 Research papers are published in National and International Journals. Attended and participated in 35 Seminars, Conferences, Workshops and FDP.

Icarbord Tshabangu (PhD), is an Associate Professor at the Institute of Childhood and Education, Leeds Trinity University, UK. He has previously worked as a Senior Lecturer and Coordinator of Educational Foundations and Management programmes, teaching postgraduate and undergraduate courses at the University of Arusha, Tanzania and at the University of Namibia, Namibia. He was also associated with the University of Liverpool Online as Honorary Senior Lecturer. He has served as an internal and external examiner at both undergraduate and postgraduate levels and continues to be a research supervisor. His teaching and research interests are largely on children's rights, democratic citizenship, Education policy and qualitative methodologies. He is also a coordinator for Global Citizenship and Children's Rights Network (GLOCCRIN) and Non-Executive Director for Community Development and Services Alliances (CODESA), UK.

Lister Tshuma is a final Master of Technology Education in Electrical and Electronic Engineering student at the National University of Science and

Technology, Faculty of Science and Technology, Department of Technical and Engineering Education and Training. She holds a Bachelor of Technology Education in Electrical and Electronics Engineering.

Jumanne Bakari Tungu is a Bachelor degree holder in English and history at St. Augustine University of Tanzania. He attended various online courses including certificate in Integrating Internet in the Classroom in Lewis and Clark college and English as a Foreign Language Assessment in University of Maryland Baltimore County, Intensive online course in advanced speaking, listening, reading, and writing and Certificate of Teaching English as Foreign Language (TEFL) from University of North Georgia. He has been teaching English in different Tanzanian secondary and primary schools including Singe high school in Manyara region and Capripoint secondary Shigunga primary school, Igoma secondary school and currently is at Kasese secondary school in Mwanza city. He has been Mwanza chapter Tanzania English Language Teachers Association (TELTA) coordinator and currently is a Mwanza TELTA Public Relation Officer and Tanzania-US-Sate Alumni Association secretary. He also taught English Access Micro Scholarship Program. He participated International Visitors Leadership Program in USA (2017), and Fulbright Teaching Excellence Award, California State University, Chico (2020). He also organized, participated and presented several English and educational curriculum workshops as well as seminars within and outside Tanzania including 2017 TESOL presentation

Francisco Valle teaches Strategic Management and International Business at LMU. Dr. Valle has conducted courses and/or presentations at Champlain College, Vanguard University, CSUF, and UC at Irvine, Los Angeles, Riverside, and San Diego. He applies an entrepreneurial mindset and a proprietary framework in the development of custom-tailored, culturally relevant, and integrated strategic and marketing communications plans for clients. Dr. Valle has participated in startups, M&A transactions, and divestitures. He possesses an in-depth expertise in assisting organizations instill a transformative culture change to enhance their DEI positions. Dr. Valle coauthored How To Win The Hispanic Gold Rush™. The Future Society of America - A Hispanic Paradox™ is his next book. He has been awarded international, national, and regional recognitions due to his unique expertise including 4 Palm Awards and Merrill Lynch's prestigious Global Leadership in Diversity Award. Dr. Valle completed Corporate Governance Training at both HBS and UCLA. He holds a Ph.D. in Management from CGU, an M.B.A. from CSUF, and a B.S. in Chemistry, Pharmacy, and Biology from the Universidad Nacional Autónoma de México. He has served on Boards of Directors and Boards of Advisors.

. **Edythe E. Weeks**, PhD, JD, is a multi-faceted scholar with a distinguished career as an author, adjunct professor, Fulbright Specialist alumnus, and subject matter expert on international space law. Her passion for international relations extends to her teaching, where she currently develops and delivers courses on the topic at Washington University in the United States. Dr. Weeks is a global advocate for international space law, dedicated to expanding the reach of space law knowledge. Her niche area of focus within the International Astronautical Federation Congresses involves promoting increased awareness and participation in space law and outer space development for a wider global audience. Her work transcends academia, with recent projects exploring the parallels between the power dynamics of space law and the legal frameworks governing the polar regions. This highlights her commitment to fostering international collaboration and responsible space exploration. Dr. Weeks' expertise extends beyond the classroom. Her publications, including a book featured on the Hague's Peace Palace Librarian's Choice website, showcase her dedication to the field. She has co-authored a groundbreaking work on global space governance and served as a space law subject matter expert for a joint project with the Air Force Space Command, Department of the Air Force, and Pentagon-Joint Chiefs of Staff. Her experiences as a Fulbright Specialist in Mexico and Siberia further demonstrate her commitment to fostering global understanding. Dr. Weeks is a distinguished educator with a proven track record. She has developed and delivered courses at three US universities simultaneously, with subjects ranging from international relations to space law and African American studies. Recognized by Washington University for her innovative methods, she is a pioneer in online education, advocating for the use of technology to enhance learning experiences. Dr. Weeks' passion extends to inspiring future generations of scholars. Her student-centered approach and commitment to knowledge sharing empower students to become globally aware and collaborative thinkers.

Anatoly Zhuplev is a professor of international business and entrepreneurship at Loyola Marymount University (Los Angeles, California) and former editor-in-chief at the Journal of East West Business (2011-2013). He taught for ten years at the Moscow Management Institute, and subsequently at the Advanced Training Institute of the State Committee for Printing and Publishing in Moscow; in Bonn, Germany in 1994, 1998, 2009; in Warsaw, Poland (as a Fulbright scholar) in 2005; in Paris, France in 2004-2007, and at Northeastern University in Boston, Massachusetts in 1989-1990. His books, book chapters, and articles on International Management, International Entrepreneurship, International Business, European Energy Security and Corporate Governance (around 100 overall) have been published in the U.S., Canada, Western Europe, Russia, and the former USSR. He received his PhD from

Index

Symbols

451, 466, 468, 469

multiculturalism 107, 108, 109, 110, 111, 125, 126, 129, 130

O

Obstacles 20, 70, 105, 111, 152, 273, 277, 278, 279, 283, 289, 325, 347, 364, 367, 433, 452

Outer Space Development 68, 72, 75

P

Pedagogy 14, 23, 85, 86, 87, 88, 89, 90, 91, 92, 94, 95, 96, 97, 99, 100, 101, 102, 103, 104, 105, 106, 140, 146, 147, 162, 191, 194, 197, 200, 229, 230, 249, 304, 308, 309, 311, 312, 314, 408, 423, 463, 478, 496

Problem-solving 13, 30, 33, 74, 75, 76, 85, 86, 87, 88, 92, 101, 135, 136, 138, 141, 146, 149, 150, 153, 170, 174, 176, 178, 179, 180, 181, 182, 183, 188, 189, 194, 195, 201, 207, 232, 233, 235, 236, 237, 238, 239, 244, 247, 252, 258, 320, 321, 322, 323, 324, 327, 331, 343, 344, 384, 408, 409, 426, 438, 440, 452, 454, 455, 472, 473, 474, 478, 481, 488, 490

professional development 8, 14, 21, 37, 38, 133, 152, 153, 156, 158, 161, 163, 169, 170, 171, 185, 187, 190, 191, 204, 206, 207, 240, 245, 281, 285, 287, 290, 295, 404, 431, 476, 489, 490

S

Saudi Universities 165, 273, 274, 275, 276, 277, 278, 279, 280, 281, 282, 283, 284, 285, 286, 287, 288, 289, 290, 291, 292, 293, 295, 297, 299, 300

Science 1, 17, 20, 21, 22, 44, 49, 57, 63, 64, 67, 73, 77, 81, 92, 126, 127, 131, 138, 143, 159, 160, 161, 162, 163, 164, 165, 169, 178, 179, 181, 182, 186, 188, 194, 197, 198, 199, 200, 201, 202, 204, 206, 207, 211, 226,

235, 239, 249, 253, 255, 257, 259, 260, 268, 269, 270, 271, 274, 275, 286, 298, 307, 319, 320, 321, 322, 323, 326, 327, 328, 329, 330, 331, 333, 337, 339, 340, 341, 342, 343, 344, 356, 370, 371, 374, 375, 377, 394, 443, 444, 447, 451, 455, 464, 467, 471, 473, 474, 475, 476, 478, 479, 481, 486, 487, 490, 493, 495, 496, 497, 499

Skill Development 139, 141, 151, 177, 184, 204, 215, 229, 230, 231, 232, 233, 234, 237, 238, 239, 240, 242, 243, 244, 245, 246, 247, 248, 249, 252, 256, 312, 314, 370, 383, 392, 404, 406, 408, 409, 455

Skills 5, 8, 11, 12, 13, 14, 23, 29, 31, 34, 39, 41, 51, 54, 55, 58, 59, 72, 74, 75, 76, 85, 87, 88, 90, 91, 94, 96, 98, 99, 100, 102, 103, 104, 105, 106, 108, 111, 114, 115, 116, 125, 126, 128, 129, 131, 132, 133, 135, 136, 137, 138, 140, 141, 142, 143, 146, 148, 149, 150, 151, 152, 153, 154, 155, 156, 157, 158, 160, 161, 162, 163, 164, 166, 167, 169, 170, 171, 172, 173, 174, 175, 176, 177, 178, 179, 180, 181, 182, 183, 184, 185, 186, 187, 188, 189, 190, 193, 194, 195, 198, 199, 200, 201, 202, 203, 204, 205, 207, 210, 211, 212, 214, 215, 216, 221, 222, 226, 230, 231, 232, 233, 234, 235, 236, 237, 238, 239, 242, 243, 244, 245, 246, 247, 248, 249, 251, 252, 253, 256, 257, 258, 260, 264, 265, 266, 269, 270, 273, 274, 275, 276, 277, 281, 284, 285, 286, 290, 291, 292, 293, 296, 300, 301, 302, 303, 304, 305, 306, 307, 309, 311, 312, 313, 314, 315, 316, 317, 319, 320, 321, 322, 323, 324, 325, 327, 328, 329, 330, 331, 332, 334, 337, 339, 340, 342, 343, 344, 348, 351, 356, 361, 362, 367, 370, 383, 400, 402, 405, 406, 407, 408, 409, 410, 413, 416, 417, 420, 422, 423, 429, 430, 431, 432, 435, 436,

Milton Keynes UK
Ingram Content Group UK Ltd.
UKHW030659161024
449742UK00008B/110